THE BICENTENNIAL EDITION
OF THE
WORKS OF JOHN WESLEY

General Editor RICHARD P. HEITZENRATER

Textual Editor FRANK BAKER

THE WORKS OF
JOHN WESLEY

VOLUME 21

JOURNAL AND DIARIES
IV

(1755–65)

EDITED BY

W. REGINALD WARD

(JOURNAL)

AND

RICHARD P. HEITZENRATER

(DIARIES)

ABINGDON PRESS

NASHVILLE

1992

The Works of John Wesley, Volume 21
JOURNAL AND DIARIES, IV, 1755–65

Library of Congress Cataloging in Publication Data
(Revised for vol. 21)

Wesley, John, 1755–65.
The works of John Wesley.

Includes bibliographical references and indexes.
Contents: v. 1. Sermons I, 1–33—v. 2. Sermons II, 34–70—[etc.]—v. 21. Journal and diaries IV 1755–65 / edited by W. Reginald Ward and Richard P. Heitzenrater.
1. Methodist Church—Collected works. 2. Theology—Collected words—18th century. I. Outler, Albert Cook, 1908–1989. II. Ward, W. Reginald. III. Heitzenrater, Richard P. IV. Davies, Rupert. V. Title.

BX8217.W5 1984 2301.7 83-22434

ISBN 0-687-46225-8 (v. 21)
ISBN 0-687-46223-1 (v. 20)
ISBN 0-687-46222-3 (v. 19)
ISBN 0-687-46214-2 (v. 9)
ISBN 0-687-46221-5 (v. 18)
ISBN 0-687-46213-4 (v. 4)
ISBN 0-687-46212-6 (v. 3)
ISBN 0-687-46211-8 (v. 2)
ISBN 0-687-46210-X (v. 1)

THE MONOGRAM USED ON THE CASE AND HALF-TITLE IS ADAPTED BY RICHARD P. HEITZENRATER FROM ONE OF JOHN WESLEY'S PERSONAL SEALS

MANUFACTURED IN THE UNITED STATES OF AMERICA

THE BICENTENNIAL EDITION OF THE WORKS OF JOHN WESLEY

THIS edition of the works of John Wesley reflects the quickened interest in the heritage of Christian thought that has become evident during the last half-century. A fully critical presentation of Wesley's writings had long been a desideratum in order to furnish documentary sources illustrating his contribution to both catholic and evangelical Christianity.

Several scholars, notably Professor Albert C. Outler, Professor Franz Hildebrandt, Dean Merrimon Cuninggim, and Dean Robert E. Cushman, discussed the possibility of such an edition. Under the leadership of Dean Cushman, a Board of Directors was formed in 1960 comprising the deans of four sponsoring theological schools of Methodist-related universities in the United States: Drew, Duke, Emory, and Southern Methodist. They appointed an Editorial Committee to formulate plans, and enlisted an international and interdenominational team of scholars for the Wesley Works Editorial Project.

The works were divided into units of cognate material, with a separate editor (or joint editors) responsible for each unit. Dr. Frank Baker was appointed textual editor for the whole project, with responsibility for supplying each unit editor with a critically developed, accurate Wesley text. The text seeks to represent Wesley's thought in its fullest and most deliberate expression, in so far as this can be determined from the available evidence. Substantive variant readings in any British edition published during Wesley's lifetime are shown in appendices to the units, preceded by a summary of the problems faced and the solutions reached in the complex task of securing and presenting Wesley's text. The aim throughout is to enable Wesley to be read with maximum ease and understanding, and with minimal intrusion by the editors.

This edition includes all Wesley's original or mainly original prose works, together with one volume devoted to his *Collection of Hymns* (1780) and another to his extensive work as editor and publisher of extracts from the writings of others. An essential feature of the project is a Bibliography outlining the historical settings of the works published by Wesley and his brother Charles, sometimes jointly, sometimes separately. The Bibliography also offers full analytical data for identifying each of the two thousand editions of these 450 items that were published during the lifetime of John Wesley, and notes the location of copies. An index is supplied for each unit, and a General Index for the whole edition.

The Delegates of the Oxford University Press agreed to undertake publication, but announced in June 1982 that because of severe economic problems they would regretfully be compelled to withdraw from the enterprise with the completion in 1983 of Vol. 7, the *Collection of Hymns*. Abingdon Press offered its services, beginning with the publication of the first volume of the *Sermons* in 1984, the bicentennial year of the formation of American Methodism as an autonomous church. The new title now assumed, however, refers in general to the bicentennial of Wesley's total activities as author, editor, and publisher, from 1733 to 1791, especially as summarized in the first edition of his collected works in thirty-two volumes, 1771-74.

Dean Robert E. Cushman of Duke University undertook general administration and promotion of the project until 1971, when he was succeeded as President by Dean Joseph D. Quillian, Jr., of Southern Methodist University, these two universities having furnished the major support and guidance for the enterprise. During the decade 1961-70, the Editorial Committee supervised the task of setting editorial principles and procedures, and general editorship was shared by Dr. Eric W. Baker, Dean William R. Cannon, and Dean Cushman. In 1969 the Directors appointed Dr. Frank Baker, early attached to the project as bibliographer and textual editor for Wesley's text, as Editor-in-Chief also. Upon Dean Quillian's retirement in 1981, he was succeeded as President of the project by Dean James E. Kirby, Jr., also of Southern Methodist University. In 1986, the Directors appointed Richard P. Heitzenrater as General Editor to begin the chief editorship of the project with the *Journal and Diaries* unit. Dean Dennis M. Campbell of Duke University, was elected President of the project in 1990.

Other sponsoring bodies have been successively added to the original four: Boston University School of Theology, the Conference of the Methodist Church of Great Britain, The General Commission on Archives and History of The United

Methodist Church, The United Methodist Board of Higher Education and Ministry, and the World Methodist Council. For the continuing support of the sponsoring institutions the Directors express their profound thanks. They gratefully acknowledge also the encouragement and financial support that have come from the Historical Societies and Commissions on Archives and History of many Annual Conferences, as well as the donations of private individuals and foundations.

On June 9, 1976, The Wesley Works Editorial Project was incorporated in the State of North Carolina as a nonprofit corporation. In 1977, by-laws were approved governing the appointment and duties of the Directors, their Officers, and their Executive Committee.

The Board of Directors

CONTENTS

ILLUSTRATIONS

N.B. This volume of Wesley's *Journal* covers a period for which no corresponding diary material has survived.

SIGNS, SPECIAL USAGES, ABBREVIATIONS

[ ]	Indicate editorial insertions or substitutions in the original text, or (with a query) doubtful readings.
	Indicate conjectural readings in manuscripts where the original text is defective.
. . .	Indicate a passage omitted by the writer from the original and so noted by Wesley, usually by a dash.
[. . .]	Indicate a passage omitted silently by Wesley from a text he was quoting, to which the present editor is drawing attention; the brackets are not used in editorial annotations and introductions.
(( ))	Enclose passages within a manuscript struck through for erasure.
[[ ]]	Enclose passages supplied by the present editors from cipher or shorthand, from an abstract or similar document in the third person, or reconstructed from secondary evidence.
a,b,c	Small superscript letters indicate footnotes supplied by Wesley.
1,2,3	Small superscript figures indicate footnotes supplied by the editor.
Cf.	Before a scriptural or other citation by Wesley, indicates that he was quoting with more than minimal inexactness, yet nevertheless displaying the passage as a quotation.
See	Before a scriptural citation indicates an undoubted allusion, or a quotation which was not displayed as such by Wesley, and which is more than minimally inexact.

Wesley's publications. Where a work by Wesley was first published separately, its title is italicized; where it first appeared within a different work such as a collected volume, the title appears within quotation marks. References such as '*Bibliography*, No. 3' are to the forthcoming Bibliography in this edition (Vols. 33-34), which has a different numbering system from Richard Green's *Wesley Bibliography.*

Book-titles in Wesley's text are italicized if accurate, and given in roman type with capitals if inaccurate. If a title consists of only one generic word which forms a major part of the original title, it is italicized; but if it is inaccurate (such as 'Sermons' for a volume entitled *Discourses*), it is printed in lower case roman.

Abbreviations. Works and institutions frequently cited are abbreviated thus:

BCP	The Book of Common Prayer, London, 1662.

Bibliography	Frank Baker, *A Descriptive and Analytical Bibliography of the Publications of John and Charles Wesley* (in preparation), vols. 33-34 in this edn.
Curnock	Nehemiah Curnock, ed., *The Journal of the Rev. John Wesley, A.M.*, 8 vols., London, Epworth Press, 1938.
CWJ	Thomas Jackson, ed., *The Journal of the Rev. Charles Wesley, M.A.*, 2 vols., London, Wesleyan Methodist Bookroom, 1849.
Jackson	Thomas Jackson, ed., *The Works of the Rev. John Wesley*, 4th edn., 14 vols., London, Mason, 1840-42.
JW	John Wesley (1703–91).
JWJ	John Wesley's *Journal.*
OED	Sir James A. H. Murray, et al., *A New English Dictionary on Historical Principles,* 11 vols., Oxford, Clarendon Press, 1884–1933.
SPCK	Society for Promoting Christian Knowledge.
SPG	Society for the Propagation of the Gospel.
Telford	John Telford, ed., *The Letters of the Rev. John Wesley,* 8 vols., London, Sharp, 1931.
Works (1771–74)	John Wesley, *The Works of the Rev. John Wesley, M.A.*, 32 vols., Bristol, Pine, 1771–74.
WHS	*The Proceedings of the Wesley Historical Society,* 1898– .

AN

EXTRACT

OF THE

Rev. Mr. JOHN WESLEY'S

JOURNAL,

FROM

FEBRUARY 16, 1755, to JUNE 16, 1758.

BRISTOL:
Printed by WILLIAM PINE, in *Wine-Street.*
MDCCLXI.

Journal

From February 16, 1755, to June 16, 1758

February 16, 1755. Having heard a confused account from a place near Camelford, in Cornwall, I wrote to a friend near it and received the following answer:

According to your desire, I have inquired into the particulars of the late affair at Delabole[1] Quarry. The rock is about thirty yards thick, but the most valuable part of the stone lies undermost.

There were nine partners who shared the advantage of this part of the quarry. Being greedy of gain, they brought out as much of the under part as possible; and the rather, because the time for which they had hired it was within a month of expiring.

On Monday, Dec. 2, William Lane, John Lane, William Kellow, and five more of the partners met in the morning and sent one of their number for Theophilus Kellow to come to work. He came but was so uneasy, he could not stay but quickly returned home. William Kellow was sent for in haste and went to look after his mare, which had cast her foal. The other seven continued labouring till twelve. All the workmen usually dine together. But these wrought on when the rest withdrew, till in a moment they were covered with rocks of all sizes, falling about ten yards, some of which were thought to be three ton weight. William Lane had some years since known the love of God. He was sitting, cleaving stones, when the rock calved in[2] upon him, with a concave surface which just made room for his body. Only one edge of it lit upon him and broke one of his thigh bones. When they dug away the stones, he was earnestly praying to God and confessing his unfaithfulness. As

[1] Orig., 'Dineboul'. Pearce notes that high quality slate has been produced from this mine from ancient times and that the quarry is now 400 feet deep and a mile in circumference; John Pearce, ed., *The Wesleys in Cornwall* (Truro, Barton, 1964), p. 118, n. 87. The parish register records the death of the victims of the disaster. In 1662, Delabole was reputed the 'best quarry of slate in the country', and it retained a national reputation for quality as long as slate was in demand. J. Whetter, *Cornwall in the 17th Century* (Padstow, 1974), p. 120. It was at this time that output began to expand rapidly. *The Victoria County History of the County of Cornwall*, William Page, ed. (Folkestone, Dawson, 1975), 1:519-20.

[2] A dialect form of 'caved in'. This passage of JW is quoted by *OED* as an example of Midlands usage. Sir James A. H. Murray, et al., *A New English Dictionary on Historical Principles*, 11 vols. (Oxford, Clarendon Press, 1884–1933).

soon as he looked up, he began exhorting all around instantly to make their peace with God. His bone being set, he soon recovered both his bodily strength and the peace and love which he had lost. Another who sat close by his side was covered over and killed at once. Close to him John Lane (son of William) was standing; he was thrown upon his face, he knew not how, and a sharp-edged stone pitched between his thighs, on which a huge rock fell and was suspended by it, so as to shadow him all over. The other five were entirely dashed in pieces.

Doth not God save those that trust in him?

Tuesday, April 1. I rode from Bristol to a village named Kingswood, near Wotton-under-Edge.[3] The church was exceeding full, and the congregation was serious and well-behaved. And I had since the satisfaction of being informed that many of them are much changed, at least in their outward behaviour.

Wed. 2. With some difficulty we reached Stanley;[4] there has been lately a great awakening in this country. I never saw such a congregation here before, notwithstanding the wind and rain. And all present seemed to receive the word with gladness and readiness of mind.[5] There is a solid, serious people in these parts, who stand their ground against all opposition. The warmest opposers are the Jacobites, who do not love us because we love King George. But they profit nothing, for more and more people 'fear God and honour the king'.[6]

We rode on Thursday in the afternoon through heavy rain and almost impassable roads to Evesham, and on Friday 4 to Birmingham, a barren, dry, uncomfortable place. Most of the seed which has been sown for so many years the 'wild boars' have 'rooted up'[7]—the fierce, unclean, brutish, blasphemous *antinomians*[8]

[3] Kingswood was a parish 5¼ miles south-west of Dursley, and about 2 miles from Wotton-under-Edge.

[4] This could be either or both of two textile villages, King's Stanley or Leonard Stanley, 3¼ and 4¼ miles, respectively, from Stroud.

[5] See Acts 17:11. [6] 1 Pet. 2:17. [7] See Ps. 80:13 (BCP).

[8] Among the earliest forces in Birmingham Methodism was James Relly (1722–78) at that time one of Whitefield's preachers, who broke with him on grounds of antinomianism, an enduring influence in Birmingham. JW encountered him in Ireland (see below, July 25, 1756) and was continuously hostile to him. Relly ended up as a universalist; W. C. Sheldon, *Early Methodism in Birmingham* (Birmingham, 1903), p. 14. It is a curious commentary on the 'mystic foxes' that a few years later JW took John Hilton (or Helton) to Birmingham. Hilton later withdrew from the connexion to become a Quaker; Thomas Jackson, ed., *Lives of Early Methodist Preachers*, 6 vols. (4th edn., London, Wesleyan Conference Office, 1871), 5:181-82; hereafter, Jackson, *Early Methodist Preachers*. An entertaining account of Relly is given in A. C. H. Seymour, *The Life and Times of Selina, Countess of Huntingdon*, 2 vols. (London, Painter, 1840), 2:371n. Hereafter, Seymour, *Huntingdon*.

have utterly destroyed it. And the *mystic* 'foxes' have taken true pains to 'spoil'[9] what remained with their New Gospel. Yet it seems God has a blessing for this place still, so many still attend the preaching, and he is eminently present with the small number that is left in the society.

Sat. 5. I preached at Wednesbury and at eight on Sunday morning. But the great congregation assembled in the afternoon as soon as the service of the church was over, with which we take care never to interfere. A solemn awe seemed to run all through the company in the evening when I met the society. We have indeed preached the gospel here 'with much contention'.[10] But the success overpays the labour.

Mon. 7. I was advised to take the Derbyshire road to Manchester. We baited at an house six miles beyond Lichfield.[11] Observing a woman sitting in the kitchen I asked, 'Are you not well?' And found she had just been taken ill (being on her journey) with all the symptoms of an approaching pleurisy. She was glad to hear of an easy, cheap, and (almost) infallible remedy, an handful of nettles, boiled a few minutes, and applied warm to the side.[12] While I was speaking to her an elderly man, pretty well dressed, came in. Upon inquiry he told us he was travelling as he could towards his home, near Hounslow, in hopes of agreeing with his creditors, to whom he had surrendered his all. But how to get on he knew not, as he had no money and had caught a tertian ague.[13] I hope a wise Providence directed this wanderer also, that he might have a remedy for both his maladies.[14]

Soon after we took horse, we overtook a poor man, creeping forward on two crutches. I asked whither he was going. He said, toward Nottingham where his wife lived. But both his legs had been broke while he was on shipboard. And he had now spent all his money. This man likewise appeared exceeding thankful and ready to acknowledge the hand of God.

[9] Cf. S. of S. 2:15.

[10] 1 Thess. 2:2.

[11] Probably Alrewas, a village 5 miles north-east of Lichfield; see Nehemiah Curnock, ed., *The Journal of the Rev. John Wesley, A.M.*, 8 vols. (London, Epworth Press, 1938), 4:109 n. Hereafter, Curnock.

[12] Wesley's *Primitive Physick* (1747; see vol. 17 in this edn.) offered nine remedies for pleurisy. Remedy no. 477 (to which he appended the letter 'I' for 'infallible') read: 'Or, of decoction of nettles; and apply the herb hot, as a poultice.' He specialized in the use of simple ingredients, readily available.

[13] Wesley's *Primitive Physick* listed four basic remedies for the tertian ague.

[14] Wesley frequently implied very much more than he stated, as here. It seems clear that he both supplied a remedy for the man's illness, and gave him money to take him on his journey, as he also did to the cripple in the following paragraph.

In the afternoon we came to Barton Forge,[15] where a gentleman of Birmingham has set up a large iron-work and fixed five or six families with a serious man over them, who lost near all he had in the great riot at Wednesbury. Most of them are seeking to save their souls. I preached in the evening, not to them only but to many gathered from all parts, and exhorted them to love and help one another.

Tue. 8. I had designed to go straight on to Hayfield. But one from Ashbourne[16] pressed me much to call there, which accordingly I did at seven in the morning and preached to a deeply serious congregation. Seventeen or eighteen then desired to join in a society, to whom I spoke severally and was well pleased to find that near half of them knew the pardoning love of God. One of the first I spoke to was Miss [Judith] Beresford[17]—a sweet but short-lived flower!

Through much hail, rain, and wind, we got to Mr. B[addeley]'s at Hayfield,[18] about five in the afternoon. His favourite daughter died some hours before we came—such a child as is scarce heard of in a century. All the family informed me of many remarkable circumstances, which else would have seemed incredible. She spake exceeding plain, yet very seldom, and then only a few words. She was scarce ever seen to laugh, or heard to utter a light

[15] Probably at Barton-under-Needwood, a parochial chapelry 5 miles south-west of Burton upon Trent.

[16] Orig., 'Ashbourn'.

[17] The first Methodist mission in Ashbourne had taken place only in the previous year when Thomas Hanby came in (as JW did now) from Barton Forge. At his first meeting in the house of Thomas Thompson, who kept the toll-gate half a mile from the town, Judith Beresford was dramatically converted and 'continued to stand fast, growing in grace, till the Lord took her in glorious triumph to Himself' in 1756, aged 24; see Jackson, *Early Methodist Preachers*, 2:140-41, and below, May 5, 1757. It is not clear whether she was related to the William Berrisford (1736–1801), who was converted in this precise neighbourhood (Snelstone) eleven years later and who became a notable local preacher, whose 'diligence in religious service was truly apostolical', *Methodist Magazine* 27 (1805):97-101.

[18] John Baddeley, rector of Hayfield, Derbys., a chapelry in the parish of Glossop, 4½ miles north-west of Chapel-en-le-Frith, had been converted in 1748. JW compared him with Grimshaw of Haworth: 'both one and the other formed irregular Societies and took in laymen to assist them'; John Telford, ed., *The Letters of the Rev. John Wesley*, 8 vols. (London, Sharp, 1931), 3:151 (hereafter, Telford). Baddeley, however, though most warmly appreciative of JW and his present visit, counselled against separation from the Church and the ordination of the preachers, partly because it would encourage itinerants (in American parlance) to locate, 'the general and great bane of true scriptural Christianity. Has it not eaten out the life of religion, and caused the power of godliness to dwindle in Dissenters of every denomination among us?' *Arminian Magazine* 2 (1779):319; *Letters*, 26:559 in this edn. For his personal and family disasters, see below, Mar. 23, 1765. A John Baddeley matriculated from Magdalen Hall, 1732, age 21.

or trifling word. She could not bear any that did, nor anyone who behaved in a light or unserious manner. If any such offered to kiss or touch her she would turn away and say, 'I don't like you.' If her brother or sisters spoke angrily to each other or behaved triflingly, she either sharply reproved (when that seemed needful) or tenderly entreated them to give over. If she had spoke too sharply to any, she would humble herself to them and not rest till they had forgiven her. After her health declined, she was particularly pleased with hearing that hymn sung, 'Abba, Father',[19] and would be frequently singing that line herself,

'Abba, Father, hear my cry.'

On Monday, April 7, without any struggle, she fell asleep, having lived two years and six months.[20]

Wed. 9. In the evening I preached at Manchester. The mob was tolerably quiet as long as I was speaking, but immediately after, raged horribly. This I find has been their manner for some time. No wonder—since the good justice encourages[21] them.

Thur. 10. I rode to Hayfield again, to bury Mr. B[addeley]'s child. Abundance of people were gathered together, and I found uncommon liberty in preaching. Who would have looked for such a congregation as this in the Peak of Derbyshire?

I returned to Manchester the next day and had a quiet congregation both that evening and the following.

19 Apparently the first part of stanza 7 of 'The Backslider's Confession', from the Wesleys' *Hymns and Sacred Poems* (1740), pp. 147-49, which began,

When I was a little child,
  O what sweetness did I prove,

and of which the closing stanza was:

Abba, Father! hear my cry,
  Look upon thy weeping child;
Weeping at thy feet I lie;
  Kiss me, and be reconciled:
Take me up into thine arms,
  Let me hang upon thy breast,
Hide me there secure from harms,
  Lull my sorrowing soul to rest.

20 This paragraph is omitted from the editions of 1768 and 1788, clearly by error, so that they both open the following paragraph: 'On Monday, April 7, in the evening I preached at Manchester.'

21 *Works* (1774): 'since the good justices encourage'. The reference is doubtless to Robert Dukinfield; see May 7, 1747, n. 28 (20:173 in this edn.).

Sun. 13. I met the society at five and showed them wherein I feared they had grieved the Spirit of God and provoked him to deliver them to be thus outraged by 'the beasts of the people'.[22] I then rode to Hayfield once more, where Mr. B[addeley] read prayers and preached a solemn and affecting sermon relative to the late providence. In the afternoon I again found great liberty of spirit in applying those awful words, 'What is a man profited, if he shall gain the whole world, and lose his own soul?'[23]

Mon. 14. I rode by Manchester (where I preached about twelve) to Warrington.[24] At six in the morning, Tuesday 15, I preached to a large and serious congregation, and then went on to Liverpool, one of the neatest, best-built towns I have seen in England. I think it is full twice as large as Chester. Most of the streets are quite straight.[25] Two-thirds of the town, we were informed, have been added within these forty years. If it continues to increase in the same proportion, in forty years more it will nearly equal Bristol. The people in general are the most mild and courteous I ever saw in a seaport town—as indeed appears by their friendly behaviour, not only to the Jews and Papists who live among them but even to the *Methodists* (so called). The preaching-house[26] is a little larger than that at Newcastle. It was thoroughly filled at seven in the evening. And the hearts of the whole congregation seemed to be moved before the Lord and before the presence of his power.

Every morning, as well as evening, abundance of people gladly attended the preaching. Many of them, I learned, were dear lovers of controversy. But I had better work. I pressed upon them all, 'repentance toward God, and faith in our Lord Jesus Christ'.[27]

Sun. 20. I explained after the evening preaching the Rules of the Society and strongly exhorted the members to adorn their profession by all holiness of conversation.

Mon. 21. I rode to Bolton. Being now among those who were no 'strangers to the covenant of promise',[28] I had no need to lay

[22] Ps. 68:30 (BCP).

[23] Matt. 16:26.

[24] Warrington was a market town and parish on the Lancashire side of the Mersey; its rapid economic development was commencing. In this year, an act of parliament was obtained to create the Sankey Canal from the Mersey, 1 mile west of the town, to the St. Helen's collieries.

[25] Orig., 'strait'.

[26] For the vicissitudes of the Pitt Street Chapel, and its evolution from conservatism to radicalism, see D. Gowland, *Methodist Secessions: The Origins of Free Methodism in Three Lancashire Towns*, Chetham Society, 3d. ser., 26 (Manchester, 1979), pp. 20-21, 27, 30.

[27] Acts 20:21 (*Notes*).

[28] Eph. 2:12 (*Notes*).

the foundation again but exhorted them to 'rejoice evermore'.[29] Their number is a little reduced since I was here before. And no wonder, while the sons of strife are on every side, some for Mr. Bennet, some for Mr. Wh[itford]. The little flock notwithstanding hold on their way, looking straight to the prize of their high calling.[30]

Thur. 24. We rode in less than four hours the eight miles (so called) to New Hall Hey.[31] Just as I began to preach the sun broke out and shone exceeding hot on the side of my head. I found, if it continued, I should not be able to speak long, and lifted up my heart to God. In a minute or two it was covered with clouds, which continued till the service was over. Let any who please call this *chance*—I call it an answer to prayer.

Fri. 25. About ten, I preached near Todmorden. The people stood, row above row, on the side of the mountain. They were rough enough in outward appearance. But their hearts were as melting wax.[32]

One can hardly conceive anything more delightful than the vale through which we rode from hence. The river ran through the green meadows on the right. The fruitful hills and woods rose on either hand. Yet here and there a rock hung over, the little holes in which put me in mind of those beautiful lines:

Te, domine, intonsi montes, te saxa loquentur
Summa Deum, dum montis amat juga pendulus hircus,
Saxorumque colit latebrosa cuniculus antra! [33]

At three in the afternoon I preached at Heptonstall, on the brow of the mountain. The rain began almost as soon as I began to speak. I prayed that if God saw best it might be stayed till I had

[29] 1 Thess. 5:16.

[30] See Phil. 3:14. For Bennet's part in breaking up the Bolton society, see Mar. 31, 1752 (20:414 in this edn.).

[31] Orig., 'Newell-hay'. New Hall Hey Bridge is in the southern part of Rawtenstall.

[32] See Ps. 22:14.

[33] 'Thee, O Lord, the leafy mountains shall proclaim as God, while the poised he-goat loves the mountain ridges, and the coney haunts the rock caverns, full of hiding places.' JW printed these lines again in the *Journal* for Apr. 3, 1786, where he attributed them to a paraphrase by Dr. Burton of Ps. 104. This was John Burton (1696–1771), a whiggish politician who wrote *Sacrae Scripturae locorum quorundam Versio Metrica* (1736), a scholar of Corpus Christi College, Oxford, from 1733 fellow of Eton, rector of Maple Durham (the best of the Eton livings) till 1766, and a Georgia Trustee. For his correspondence with JW, see *Letters*, 25:434-37, 439-42, 461-63, 508 in this edn.

delivered his word. It was so, and then began again. But we had only a short stage to Ewood.[34]

Sat. 26. I preached at seven to a large and serious congregation, and again at four in the afternoon. When I began, in a meadow near the house, the wind was so high, I could hardly speak. But the winds too are in God's hand. In a few minutes that inconvenience ceased. And we found the Spirit of God breathing in the midst of us, so that great was our rejoicing in the Lord.

Sun. 27. A little before I took horse I looked into a room as I walked by and saw a good old man bleeding almost to death. I desired him immediately to snuff vinegar up his nose and apply it to his neck, face, and temples. It was done—and the blood entirely stopped in less than two minutes.[35]

The rain began about five and did not intermit till we came to Haworth,[36] notwithstanding which a multitude of people were gathered together at ten. In the afternoon I was obliged to go out of the church, abundance of people not being able to get in. The rain ceased from the moment I came out till I had finished my discourse. How many proofs must we have that there is no petition too little, any more than too great, for God to grant?

Mon. 28. I preached at Keighley; on Tuesday at Bradford, which is now as quiet as Birstall. Such a change has God wrought in the hearts of the people since John Nelson was in the dungeon here. My brother met me at Birstall in the afternoon.[37]

Wed. 30. We began reading together 'A Gentleman's Reasons for his Dissent from the Church of England'.[38] It is an elaborate

[34] Ewood Hall, the house of William Grimshaw's first wife, Sarah née Lockwood, was located ½ mile north-east of Mytholmroyd, West Yorkshire. Grimshaw made it an evangelistic centre, kept up a religious society there, and maintained open house to Methodist preachers, including JW. It passed to Grimshaw's son, John. Frank Baker, *William Grimshaw, 1708-63* (London, Epworth Press, 1963), pp. 35-36, 106, 108, 111, 146, 162-65.

[35] To several remedies for 'Bleeding at the Nose' in his *Primitive Physick*, Wesley added in the 1755 edn.: 'Or, wash the temples, nose, and neck with vinegar.'

[36] Orig., 'Howarth', as frequently; the 1788 edn. reads, 'Harworth'.

[37] Charles Wesley anticipated this encounter in a letter to his wife: 'This evening I expect to find my brother at Birstal. I pity his poor wife, if now upon the road. There she is likely to stick till the warm weather comes. The roads are almost impassable for wheels.' Thomas Jackson, ed., *The Journal of the Rev. Charles Wesley, M.A.*, 2 vols. (London, Wesleyan Methodist Bookroom, 1849), 2:201 (hereafter, *CWJ*). For John Nelson's problems at Birstall, see May 15, 1744 (19:29-30 in this edn.).

[38] *The Dissenting Gentleman's Answer to the Rev. Mr. White's three Letters: in which a Separation from the Establishment is fully justified, the Charge of Schism is refuted and retorted, and the Church of England and the Church of Jesus Christ are impartially compared, and found to be constitutions of a quite different nature.* This was published anonymously in London in 1746 by the Rev. Micaiah Towgood (1700–92). He wrote three letters and a postscript

and lively tract and contains the strength of the cause. But it did not yield us one proof that it is lawful for us (much less our duty) to separate from it.

Thursday, May 1. I finished the 'Gentleman's Reasons' (who is a Dissenting minister at Exeter). In how different a spirit does this man write from honest Richard Baxter! The one dipping, as it were, his pen in tears, the other in vinegar and gall. Surely one page of that loving, serious Christian weighs more than volumes of this bitter, sarcastic jester.

Sun. 4. I preached at one, and again at five, to some thousands at the foot of the hill. I believe this hollow would contain sixty thousand people, standing one above another. And a clear, strong voice might command them all, although if they stood upon a plain I doubt whether any human voice could be distinctly heard by half that number.

Tue. 6. Our Conference began at Leeds. The point on which we desired all the preachers to speak their minds at large was, whether we ought to separate from the Church. Whatever was advanced on one side or the other was seriously and calmly considered. And on the third day we were all fully agreed in that general conclusion, that (whether it was *lawful* or not) it was no ways *expedient*.[39]

(1746–50) in reply to John White, perpetual curate of Nayland, which were collected under the title of *A Dissent from the Church of England fully Justified* (London, 1753; very frequently reprinted) and described by JW (see below Jan. 9, 1758) as 'the most saucy and virulent satire on the Church of England that ever my eyes beheld'. The Presbyterian grandson of one of the clergy ejected in 1662, Towgood had been minister at Moretonhampstead (1722–36) and Crediton (1737–49), and was now one of the ministers of the James's Meeting in Exeter, a congregation which moved to George's Meeting in 1760. Notwithstanding JW's criticisms, Towgood was a charitable man (of Arian tendencies) well fitted to hold together congregations moving from orthodoxy to Unitarianism, and was a leading figure in the establishment of the second Exeter Academy. He retired from the ministry in 1782. A. Brockett, *Nonconformity in Exeter, 1650–1875* (Manchester, 1962) pp. 105-9, 139-41.

39 JW's minutes of the Leeds Conference are even more terse than this laconic account: 'Sixty three preachers being present, it was considered at large, Ought we to separate from the Established Church? After a free and full debate, continued for several days, it was agreed by all that we ought not'; *The Proceedings of the Wesley Historical Society* 4 (1904):67 (hereafter, *WHS*). The issue was the more painful, not merely because of the conflict it generated between the stiff churchmanship of Charles Wesley and the desire of experienced preachers like Cownley and Walsh to administer the sacraments, but because of the almost desperate indecision in JW himself. As he subsequently explained to Samuel Walker, the question '"Is it lawful to separate?" . . . was debated first . . . in seven or eight long conversations. And it was then only when we could not agree concerning this, that we proceeded to weigh the expediency of it.' The arguments for separation were a curious mixture of rationalism, Protestantism, and pietism in that order, with JW admitting 'I will freely acknowledge that I cannot answer these arguments to my own

Mon. 12. We drove (my wife and I) to Northallerton.

Tue. 13. I rode on to Newcastle. I did not find things here in the order I expected. Many were on the point of leaving the Church, which some had done already—and, as they supposed, on my authority! O how much discord is caused by one jarring string! How much trouble by one man who does not walk by the same rule, and agree in the same judgment, with his brethren!

May 18. Being Whitsunday, I preached about eight at Gateshead Fell and returned before the service at St. Andrew's began. At the Sacrament many found an uncommon blessing and felt God has not yet left the Church.

In the following week I spake to the members of the society severally and found far fewer than I expected prejudiced against the Church—I think, not above forty in all. And I trust the plague is now stayed.[40]

Wed. 21. I preached at Nafferton,[41] near Horsley, about thirteen miles from Newcastle. We rode chiefly on the new western road, which lies on the old Roman wall.[42] Some part of this is still to be seen, as are the remains of most of the towers, which were built a mile distant from each other, quite from sea to sea. But where are the men of renown who built them and who once made all the land tremble? Crumbled into dust! Gone hence, to be no more seen,[43] till the earth shall give up her dead!

Thur. 22. Mr. Wardrobe,[44] minister of Bathgate in Scotland,

satisfaction. So that my conclusion (which I cannot yet give up) that it is lawful to continue in the Church, stands, I know not how, almost without any premises that are able to bear its weight' (*Letters*, 26:594). This was perhaps the nadir of JW's confidence in the Church; mob violence died rapidly away; the inability of the Church to generate policy facilitated an accommodation with Methodism; JW became a popular institution; and notwithstanding nineteenth-century allegations about Methodists being rebuffed from the Lord's Table of the parish church, it seems to have been the stricter discipline of Dissent which provided the practical barrier; cf. Mar. 28, 1743 (19:320-21 in this edn.), and W. W. Stamp, *The Orphan House of John Wesley* (London, Mason, 1863), pp. 6-7. For information about the Leeds discussions generally, see Luke Tyerman, *The Life and Times of John Wesley*, 3 vols. (London, Hodder and Stoughton, 1870–71), 2:200-11. Hereafter, Tyerman, *John Wesley*.

[40] See Num. 16:48, 50.

[41] Nafferton was a tiny township in the parish of Ovingham, 9 miles east of Hexham, and (as JW estimated) about 13 miles west of Newcastle.

[42] The present A69.

[43] See Ps. 39:15 (BCP).

[44] Thomas Wardrobe (d. 1756), minister at Hallbank Hexham Presbyterian Church, in touch with the 'praying Societies' which linked the Scottish revival with older Cameronian traditions. He had invited JW to preach in 1746 and was spoken of by him in the same breath as Doddridge and Watts; *Arminian Magazine* 1 (1778):375; letter of Apr. 24, 1765, Telford, 4:294. His death is noted below, under May 30, 1756. For an account of him, see John Whitehead, *The Life of the Rev. John Wesley, M.A.*, 2 vols. (London, Couchman, 1793–96), 1:306n. He was minister at Bathgate, 1750–56.

preached at the Orphan House in the evening, to the no small amazement and displeasure of some of his zealous countrymen.

Sat. 24. I preached at Sheep Hill. The cold drove us into the house, which being much crowded was as hot as an oven. Riding afterwards in the keen north wind, it seized upon my breast immediately. However, I made a shift to preach at Chester,[45] and then went on to Sunderland.

Sun. 25. I preached at eight, though not without pain, not having recovered my voice. We had an useful sermon at church. As soon as the Sacrament was over, I preached in the High Street (it being Trinity Sunday) upon 'There are three that bear record in heaven.'[46] And my voice was so restored that I could command the whole congregation, though it was exceeding large.

Mon. 26. I rode to Morpeth and preached in the market-place to a small but quiet congregation. In the evening I preached in the new room at Alnwick. But I could scarce be heard, my voice being very weak. In the morning it was stronger. So I preached with more ease at five. And then returned to Newcastle.

Thur. 29. I had the pleasure of seeing Mr. Gillies from Glasgow.[47] He preached for me in the evening, to the still greater astonishment of the warm men who 'could never have thought it of him'! Shall we not have more and more cause to say:

> Names and sects and parties fall;
> Thou, O Christ, art all in all.[48]

Fri. 30. I walked to the infirmary. It is finely situated on the top of the hill and is the best ordered of any place of the kind I have seen in England. Nor did I ever see so much seriousness in an hospital before: none were laughing or talking lightly; many were reading the Bible. And when I talked to and prayed with one the whole ward listened with deep attention.

Monday, June 2.[49] I left Newcastle and came to Durham just as

[45] I.e., Chester-le-Street.

[46] 1 John 5:7.

[47] See above, Apr. 17, 1753, n. 15 (20:453 in this edn.).

[48] John and Charles Wesley, *Hymns and Sacred Poems* (1740), p. 195, the closing couplet of Part IV of 'The Communion of Saints', beginning 'Christ, from whom all blessings flow'; see *Collection of Hymns* (1780), No. 504 (7:693 in this edn.), and George Osborn, ed., *The Poetical Works of John and Charles Wesley*, 13 vols. (London, Wesleyan Conference Office, 1868–72), 1:362; hereafter, *Poetical Works*.

[49] Orig., '1'.

Jacob Rowell[50] had done preaching, or rather, attempting to preach, for the mob was so noisy that he was constrained to break off. I reached Osmotherley in the evening and found a large congregation waiting. I preached immediately, God renewing my strength and comforting my heart.

Here I inquired of eye- and ear-witnesses concerning what lately occurred in the neighborhood.[51]

> On Tuesday,[52] March 25 last, being the week before Easter, many persons observed a great noise near a ridge of mountains in Yorkshire called Black Hambleton.[53] It was observed chiefly in the south-west side of the mountain, about a mile from the course where the Hamilton Races are run, near a ridge of rocks commonly called Whiston Cliffs or Whiston White Mare,[54] two miles from Sutton, about five from Thirsk.
>
> The same noise was heard on Wednesday by all who went that way. On Thursday, about seven in the morning, Edward Abbot, weaver, and Adam Bosomworth, bleacher, both of Sutton, riding under Whiston Cliffs, heard a *roaring* (so they termed it) like many cannons or loud and rolling thunder. It seemed to come from the cliffs, looking up to which they saw a large body of stone, four or five yards broad, split and fly off from the very top of the rocks.

[50] Jacob Rowell (1722–84), who began to preach as an exhorter in Allendale in 1749, spent almost all his recorded ministry in the north-east, forming a great circuit in the Dales. Known to all there as a preacher of apostolic labours and sufferings, he has left remarkably little trace in the records. JW reckoned him one of the best preachers in the connexion, and though he had to restrain the enthusiasm of Rowell's Weardale societies for separation from the Church, and thought him somewhat light on the article of Christian perfection, described him generously in the Conference Minutes of 1784 as 'a faithful old soldier, fairly worn out in his Master's service'. Telford, 5:155; 4:142, 321; *Wesleyan Methodist Magazine* 66 (1843):906. For Rowell's Notebooks see *Methodist Recorder* (Winter, 1905), pp. 47-49.

[51] This account was first published in *Felix Farley's Bristol Journal* for Sept. 27–Oct. 4, 1755, p. 4 (see *Letters*, 26:597-600 in this edn.) and was copied by the *London Magazine*, the *Gentleman's Magazine*, and other journals, and included also in JW's *Serious Thoughts occasioned by the late Earthquake at Lisbon* (1755) with the comment that 'were it not for the unparalleled stupidity of the English, all England would have rang [with it] long ago, from one sea to another'; see Thomas Jackson, ed., *The Works of the Rev. John Wesley*, 14 vols. (4th edn., London, Mason, 1872), 11:2-5; see vol. 15 in this edn. Hereafter, Jackson. This latter version formed the basis of the present account. The report in the *Gentleman's Magazine* was denounced as a fabrication by a contributor, but JW's testimony was upheld by John Langhorne, later assistant preacher at Lincoln's Inn and translator of Plutarch's *Lives*. *Wesleyan Methodist Magazine* 66 (1843):206-8; *Gentleman's Magazine* 25 (1755):514; 26 (1756):56, 103, 159.

[52] Orig. (*JWJ*), 'Thursday'—an error.

[53] Orig. (in letter and *JWJ*), 'Hamilton'.

[54] Orig. (*JWJ*), 'Whitson-Cliffs', 'Whitson-White-Mare', corrected in the errata and Wesley's own copy of his *Works* (1774). The original printed letter was correct.

They thought it strange but rode on. Between ten and eleven a larger piece of the rock, about fifteen yards thick, thirty high, and between sixty and seventy broad, was torn off and thrown into the valley.

About seven in the evening one who was riding by observed the ground to shake exceedingly, and soon after, several large stones or rocks of some ton weight each rose out of the ground. Others were thrown on one side, others turned upside down, and many rolled over and over. Being a little surprised and not very curious, he hasted on his way.

On Friday and Saturday the ground continued to shake, and the rocks to roll over one another. The earth also clave asunder in very many places and continued so to do till Sunday morning.

Being at Osmotherley, seven miles from the cliffs, on Monday, June 1 [i.e., 2], and finding Edward Abbot there, I desired him the next morning to show me the way thither. I walked, crept, and climbed round and over great part of the ruins. I could not perceive by any sign that there was ever any cavity in the rock at all, but one part of the solid stone is cleft from the rest in a perpendicular line, and smooth as if cut with instruments. Nor is it barely thrown down but split into many hundred pieces, some of which lie four or five hundred yards from the main rock.

The ground nearest the cliff is not raised but sunk considerably beneath the level. But at some distance it is raised in a ridge of eight or ten yards high, twelve or fifteen broad, and near an hundred long. Adjoining to this lies an oval piece of ground thirty or forty yards in diameter, which has been removed whole as it is from beneath the cliff, without the least fissure, with all its load of rocks, some of which were as large as the hull of a small ship. At a little distance is a second piece of ground, forty or fifty yards across, which has been also transplanted entire, with rocks of various sizes upon it and a tree growing out of one of them. By the removal of one or both of these I suppose the *hollow* near the cliff was made.

All round them lay stones and rocks, great and small, some on the surface of the earth, some half sunk into it, some almost covered, in variety of positions. Between these the ground was cleft asunder in a thousand places. Some of the apertures were nearly closed again, some gaping as at first. Between thirty and forty acres of land, as is commonly supposed (though some reckon above sixty), are in this condition.

On the skirts of these I observed in abundance of places the green turf (for it was pasture land) as it were pared off, two or three inches thick, and wrapped round like sheets of lead. A little farther it was not cleft or broken at all but raised in ridges five or six foot long, exactly resembling graves in a churchyard. Of these there is a vast number.

That part of the cliff from which the rest is torn lies so high and is now of so bright a colour, that it is plainly visible to all the country round, even at the distance of several miles. We saw it distinctly, not only from the street in Thirsk but for five or six miles as we rode toward York. So we did likewise in the great North Road between Sandhutton and Northallerton.

But how may we account for this phenomenon? Was it effected by a merely natural cause? If so, that cause must either have been fire, water, or air. It could not be fire, for then some mark of it must have appeared, either at the time or after it. But no such mark does appear, nor ever did—not so much as the least smoke, either when the first or second rock was removed, or in the whole space between Tuesday and Sunday.

It could not be water, for no water issued out when the one or the other rock was torn off. Nor had there been any rains some time before. It was in that part of the country a remarkably[55] dry season. Neither was there any cavity in that part of the rock wherein a sufficient quantity of water might have lodged. On the contrary, it was one single, solid mass, which was evenly and smoothly cleft in sunder.

There remains no other natural cause assignable but imprisoned air. I say, *imprisoned*, for as to the fashionable opinion that the exterior air is the grand agent in earthquakes, it is so senseless, unmechanical, unphilosophical a dream as deserves not to be named but to be exploded.[56] But it is hard to conceive how even imprisoned air could produce such an effect. It might indeed *shake*, tear, raise, or sink the earth, but how could it cleave a solid rock? Here was not room for a quantity of it sufficient to do anything of this nature, at least unless it had been suddenly and violently expanded by fire, which was not the case. Could a small quantity of air, without that violent expansion, have torn so large a body of rock from the rest to which it adhered in one solid mass? Could it have shivered this into pieces and scattered several of those pieces some

[55] Orig., 'remarkable', altered in the errata and Wesley's own copy of his *Works* (1774). The letter and the *Serious Thoughts* have 'remarkable'.

[56] Letter, 'explored'.

hundred yards round? Could it have transported those promontories of earth with their incumbent load and set them down, unbroken, unchanged at a distance? Truly I am not so great a volunteer in faith as to be able to believe this.[57] He that supposes this must suppose air to be not only a very strong (which we allow) but a very wise agent, while it bore its charge with so great caution as not to hurt or dislocate any part of it.

What then could be the cause? What, indeed, but God, who arose to shake terribly the earth; who purposely chose such a place, where there is so great a concourse of nobility and gentry every year, and wrought in such a manner that many might see it and fear, that all who travel one of the most frequented roads in England might see it, almost whether they would or no, for many miles together? It must likewise for many years, maugre all the art of man, be a visible monument of his power. All that ground being now so encumbered with rocks and stones that it cannot be either ploughed or grazed. Nor can it well serve any use but to tell all that see it, Who can stand before this great God?

Hence we rode to Thirsk, where I met the little society, and then went on to York. The people had been waiting for some time. So I began preaching without delay and felt no want of strength, though the room[58] was like an oven through the multitude of people.

Fri. 6. I read Dr. Sharp's elaborate tracts on the *Rubrics* and *Canons*.[59] He justly observes with regard to all these: (1) that our governors have power to dispense with our observance of them; (2) that a *tacit* dispensation is of the same force with an *explicit*

[57] This sentence is not present in the printed letter, but was added in Wesley's *Serious Thoughts*, para. 17; for the phrase, 'volunteer in faith', see vol. 11, p. 49.

[58] The room in Pump Yard, Newgate. It held 120 people and was registered for public worship. J. Lyth, *Glimpses of Early Methodism in York and the Surrounding District* (York, Sessions, 1885), pp. 80-81. Hereafter, Lyth, *York Methodism*.

[59] In this work, Sharp spoke strongly against preaching by unlicensed persons. Thomas Sharp, *The Rubric in the Book of Common Prayer, and Canons of the Church of England, as far as they relate to Parochial Clergy, considered in a course of Visitation Charges* (London, 1753), pp. 176-77. In his *Remarks on a Book entitled, An Earnest Appeal to men of Reason and Religion* (Newcastle, 1743), p. 4, he confessed his disappointment that JW, 'an honest and well-meaning man, [was] . . . fallen into error or carried away with a warm spirit of enthusiasm'. Thomas Sharp, D.D. (1693–1758), younger son of John Sharp, Archbishop of York, became a fellow of Trinity College, Cambridge, 1716, and chaplain to Archbishop Dawes. After a number of cathedral appointments, he was appointed rector of Rothbury and archdeacon of Northumberland in 1725. A prebendary of Durham in 1732, he became a prolific writer on theological subjects. His ninth son, Granville Sharp, was the anti-slavery agitator.

dispensation; (3) that their continued connivance at what they cannot but know is a tacit dispensation. I think this is true. But if it be, he has himself answered his own charge against the Methodists (so called). For suppose the canons did forbid field preaching as expressly as playing at cards and frequenting taverns, yet we have the very same plea for the former as any clergyman has for the latter. All our governors, the king, the archbishop and bishops, connive at the one as well as the other.

Sat. 7. One of the residentiaries sent for Mr. Williamson,[60] who had invited me to preach in his church, and told him, 'Sir, I abhor persecution, but if you let Mr. Wesley preach it will be the worse for you.' He desired it nevertheless, but I declined. Perhaps there is a providence in this also. God will not suffer my little remaining strength to be spent on those who will not hear me but in an honourable way.

Sun. 8. We were at the Minster in the morning and at our parish church in the afternoon. The same gentleman preached at both,[61] but though I saw him at the church I did not know I had ever seen him before. In the morning he was all life and motion; in the afternoon he was as quiet as a post. At five in the evening the rain constrained me to preach in the oven again. The patience of the congregation surprised me. They seemed not to feel the extreme heat nor to be offended at the close application of those words, 'Thou art not far from the Kingdom of God.'[62]

Mon. 9. I took my leave of the richest society, number for number, which we have in England. I hope this place will not prove (as Cork has some time done) the Capua[63] of our preachers.

60 Probably William Williamson, B.A., vicar of St. Mary Bishophill Junior, York, 1748 till his death in 1758.

61 The appointed preacher at York Minster for the day was Richard Thompson (*c.* 1699–1795) who matriculated from Merton College, Oxford, 1737, graduated B.A. in 1740, and M.A. in 1743. He was prebendary of Langtoft and rector of Kirk Deighton near Wetherby from 1748. The passage as a whole, however, suggests that Thompson had made a private arrangement for a substitute to preach his turns at the Minster.

62 Mark 12:34.

63 Wesley undoubtedly alludes to Cicero, *Orationes De Lege Agraria* (*Speeches on the Agrarian Law*), I.20: 'Quidenim cavendum est in coloniis deducendis? Si luxuries, Hannibalem ipsum Capua corrupit'—'For what is to be guarded against in establishing colonies? If it is luxury, Capua corrupted Hannibal himself' (Loeb). This was supposedly when Hannibal and his troops wintered comfortably in Capua, which was contended for by both him and the Romans, 216–11 B.C. The allusion is repeated below, July 18, 1759.

When I came to Epworth the congregation was waiting. So I went immediately to the cross, and great was our 'glorying in the Lord'.[64]

Tue. 10. I met the stewards of the Lincolnshire societies, who gave us an agreeable account of the work of God in every place.

Wed. 11. I preached in a meadow at Misterton to a larger congregation than ever met there before.

Thur. 12. At eight I preached at Clayworth, and at Rotherham in the evening. Here likewise was such a number of people assembled as was never before seen in that town. Is not this one clear proof of the hand of God, that although the novelty of this preaching is over, yet the people flock to hear it in every place far more than when it was a new thing?

Fri. 13. In the evening I preached at Sheffield. In the morning I examined the members of the society and was agreeably surprised to find that though none had visited them since I did it myself two years ago, yet they were rather increased than diminished in number, and many of them growing in grace.

Mon. 16. I preached in the evening at Nottingham, and on Thursday afternoon reached London. From a deep sense of the amazing work which God has of late years wrought in England, I preached in the evening on those words, 'He hath not dealt so with any nation.'[a] No, not even with Scotland or New England.[65] In both these God has indeed made bare his arm, yet not in so astonishing a manner as among us. This must appear to all who

[a] Ps. 147:20.

---

[64] Cf. 2 Cor. 7:4.

[65] JW's comments may have been occasioned by his reading of John Gillies, *Historical Collections Relating to Remarkable Periods of the Success of the Gospel*, 4 vols. (1754–96); cf. below, June 24, 1755. Hereafter, Gillies, *Historical Collections*.

To the modern eye it is JW's last point which most strikingly hits off the difference between the revival in England and the (in various ways more spectacular) awakenings in Scotland and New England. It took much greater effort to shift the social rigidities impeding religious change in England than in Scotland or New England, but, the difference being applied, the results came steadily until about the time of JW's death when the dikes burst on both sides of the Atlantic. It is also difficult not to believe that the success of the establishments of New England and Scotland in generating revival from the normal parochial action of their ministry, and in containing the excitements generated by Whitefield, itself set bounds to the continuation of revival, from which JW's campaign, not church-based, was free; certainly when, at the end of the eighteenth century, the forces of conservatism were everywhere shaken, Methodism proved capable of rapid expansion on both sides of the Atlantic as New England Congregationalism did not. On the reason for Methodism's less happy experience in Scotland, see W. R. Ward, 'Scottish Methodism in the Age of Jabez Bunting', *Scottish Church History Society, Records* 20 (1978):47-63.

impartially consider: (1) the *numbers* of persons on whom God has wrought; (2) the *swiftness* of his work in many, both convinced and truly converted in a few days; (3) the *depth* of it in most of these, changing the heart as well as the whole conversation; (4) the *clearness* of it, enabling them boldly to say, 'Thou hast loved *me*, thou hast given thyself for *me*';[66] (5) the *continuance* of it. God has wrought in Scotland and New England at several times for some weeks or months together. But among us he has wrought for near eighteen years together without any observable intermission. Above all let it be remarked that a considerable number of the regular clergy were engaged in that great work in Scotland, and in New England above an hundred, perhaps as eminent as any in the whole province, not only for piety but also for abilities both natural and acquired. Whereas in England there were only two or three inconsiderable clergymen with a few, young, raw, unlettered men, and these opposed by well-nigh all the clergy, as well as laity, in the nation. He that remarks this must needs own, both that this is a work of God—and that 'he hath not' wrought so 'in any' other 'nation'.

Mon. 23. I was considering, What could be the reasons why the hand of the Lord (who does nothing without a cause) is almost entirely stayed in Scotland and in great measure in New England? It does not become us to judge peremptorily, but perhaps some of them may be these: (1) Many of them became 'wise in their own eyes';[67] they seemed to think they were the men, and there were none like them.[68] And hence they refused God the liberty of sending by whom he would send, and required him to work by men of learning or not at all. (2) Many of them were *bigots*, immoderately attached either to their own opinions or mode of worship. Mr. Edwards[69] himself was not clear of this. But the Scotch bigots were beyond all others, placing Arminianism (so called) on a level with Deism, and the Church of England with that of Rome. Hence they not only suffered in themselves and their brethren a *bitter zeal* but applauded themselves therein, in showing the same spirit against all who differed from them as the Papists did against our forefathers. (3) With pride, bitterness, and bigotry, *self-indulgence* was joined; self-denial was little taught and practised. 'Tis well if some of them did not despise, or even condemn, all self-denial in things indifferent, as in apparel or

[66] Cf. Gal. 2:20. [67] Isa. 5:21. [68] See Zeph. 2:15.
[69] Jonathan Edwards (1703–58), the eminent theologian of the New England revival.

food, as nearly allied to popery. No marvel then that the Spirit of God was grieved. Let *us* profit by their example.[70]

Tue. 24. Observing in that valuable book, Mr. Gillies's *Historical Collections*,[71] the custom of Christian congregations in all ages to set apart seasons of solemn thanksgivings, I was amazed and ashamed that we had never done this, after all the blessings we had received. And many to whom I mentioned it gladly agreed to set apart a day for that purpose.

Mon. 30. I set out for Norwich and came thither the next evening. As a large congregation was waiting, I could not but preach,[72] though weary enough. The two following days I spoke to each member of the society, and on Friday, July 4, took horse again, though how I should ride five miles I knew not. But God so strengthened both man and beast that I reached Bury [St. Edmunds] the same night and London the next, far less tired than when I set out from Norwich.

Monday 7 was our first day of solemn thanksgiving for the numberless spiritual blessings we have received. And I believe it was a day which will not soon be forgotten.[73]

Thur. 17. One spent the evening with us who is accounted both a sensible and a religious man. What a proof of the Fall! Even with all the advantages of a liberal education this person, I will be bold to say, knows just as much of heart-religion, of scriptural Christianity, the religion of love, as a child three years old of algebra. How much then may we suppose a Turk or heathen to know? Hardly more; perhaps just as much.

Tue. 22. To oblige a friendly gentlewoman I was a witness to her will, wherein she bequeathed part of her estate to charitable uses, and part, during his[74] natural life, to her dog Toby. I suppose, though she should die within the year, her legacy to

[70] What underlies JW's moralizing and is obscured by it, is that religious revival in a Reformed context acutely raised the question of the defences of the 'pure' church in a way that his own creation of a disciplined religious society open to those of various theological and denominational allegiances did not. Hence in New England many of the awakened became Separates, and the bulk of the Separates became Baptists; while in Scotland there was a strong Cameronian element in the prehistory of revival. How close the (basically different) movements of secession and evangelism might come was clearly shown in 1741 when the Associate Presbytery invited Whitefield to Scotland, turned against him when he arrived, and thus left him free to show the potentialities for revival in the establishment.

[71] See above, n. 65; and Apr. 17, 1753, n. 15 (20:453 in this edn.).

[72] At a place called the Foundery, near Orford Hill.

[73] For the day of thanksgiving, see *Arminian Magazine* 5 (1782):578, and above, June 24.

[74] Altered in JW's MS note and in his errata to his *Works* (1774) to 'her', but clearly in error, referring as it must to Toby rather than to his mistress.

Toby may stand good. But that to the poor is null and void, by the Statute of Mortmain![75]

Sun. 27. I buried the body of Ephraim B[edder],[76] once a pattern to all that believed. But from the time he left off fasting and universal self-denial, in which none was more exemplary for some years, he sunk lower and lower, till he had neither the power nor the form of religion left. In the beginning of his illness he was in black despair. But much prayer was made for him. Toward the close of it, it pleased God to restore to him the light of his countenance. So, I trust, his backsliding only cost him his life—and he may yet live with God for ever.

I was much affected about this time by a letter sent from a gentleman in Virginia.[77] Part of it runs thus:

> The poor Negro slaves here never heard of Jesus or his religion till they arrived at the land of their slavery in America, whom their masters generally neglect, as though immortality was not the privilege of *their* souls in common with their own. These poor Africans are the principal objects of my compassion, and I think the most proper subject of your charity.
>
> The inhabitants of Virginia are computed to be about 300,000, and the one-half of them are supposed to be Negroes. The number of these who attend on my ministry at particular times is uncertain. But I think there are about three hundred who give a stated attendance. And never have I been so much struck with the appearance of an assembly as when I have glanced my eye on one

[75] Statutes of Mortmain limiting the power of the Church to acquire land had begun with Magna Charta. The Act of 9 Geo. II.c.36 prohibited grants of real property to bodies corporate or to trusts for charitable uses except by deed sealed and witnessed twelve months before the death of the donor, and enrolled in chancery within six months.

[76] See Jan. 2, 1753, n. 67 (20:443 in this edn.).

[77] Samuel Davies (1723–61), president of Princeton, 1759–61. At the time this letter was written, Davies was an active New Light Presbyterian evangelist, building upon a nondenominational revival in Hanover County, east Virginia, among people untouched by the Anglican establishment and ignorant of Whitefield's first visit to Virginia (Sidney Ahlstrom, *Religious History of American People* [New Haven, Yale, 1972], p. 316). His success in securing licences for numerous meeting-houses led the Virginia clergy to appeal to the Bishop of London for a strict construction of the Toleration Act; this they obtained, though Davies was supported by Doddridge and Avery (H. J. Eckenrode, *Separation of Church and State in Virginia* [Richmond, Va., 1910; repr. New York, 1971], pp. 32-33). He also used his English connections to raise funds for the building of Nassau Hall, College of New Jersey; having failed to bring Jonathan Edwards to Virginia, he succeeded him as president of Princeton, disapproving of the inoculation of students—an operation which had cost his predecessor's life (J. McLachlan, *Princetonians, 1748–68* [Princeton, 1976], pp. xviii, 46, 71; G. W. Pilcher, *Samuel Davies, Apostle of Dissent in Colonial Virginia* [Knoxville TN 1971]; hereafter, Pilcher, *Samuel Davies*). For other letters to JW, see below, Mar. 1, 1756; Jan. 28, 1757.

part of the house, adorned (so it has appeared to me) with so many black countenances, eagerly attentive to every word they heard, and some of them covered with tears. A considerable number of them, about an hundred, have been baptized after they had been fully instructed in the great truths of religion and had evidenced their sense of them by a life of the strictest virtue. As they are not sufficiently polished to dissemble with a good grace, they express the sensations of their hearts so much in the language of simple nature and with such genuine indications of artless[78] sincerity that it is impossible to suspect their professions, especially when attended with a suitable behaviour.

Mr. Todd,[79] minister of the next congregation, has near the same number under his care. And several of them also, he informs me, discover the same seriousness. Indeed there are multitudes of them in various parts who are eagerly desirous of instruction. They have generally very little help to read; and yet, to my agreeable surprise, sundry of them, by dint of application, in their very few leisure hours, have made such a progress that they are able to read their Bible, or a plain author, very intelligibly. But few of their masters will be at the expense of furnishing them with books. I have supplied them to the utmost of my ability. They are exceedingly delighted with Watts's *Songs*. And I cannot but observe that the Negroes, above all of the human species I ever knew, have the nicest ear for music. They have a kind of ecstatic delight in psalmody, nor are there any books they so soon learn or take so much pleasure in as those used in that heavenly part of divine worship.

Sunday, August 3. I dined with one who lived for many years with one of the most celebrated beauties in Europe. She was also proud, vain, and nice to a very uncommon degree. But see the end! After a painful and nauseous disease, she rotted away above ground and was so offensive for many days before she died that scarce any could bear to stay in the room.

[78] Orig., 'earthless', altered to the edited text only in *Works* (1774).

[79] John Todd (1719–93) was born in County Armagh where there may have been some connection between his family and the Tennents. Certainly after the Todd family had migrated to Pennsylvania, John chose education at the College of New Jersey, and then licensing by the Tennents' Presbytery of New Brunswick, which in 1751 despatched him to Virginia to assist Samuel Davies. Todd established himself near the present Richmond and became the Presbyterian leader in Virginia when Davies assumed the presidency of Princeton. Todd succeeded not only as a preacher, but as a politician (helping to disestablish the Anglican Church in Virginia) and as a business man, doing well out of the War of Independence, ending up with several houses and farms, a mill, government stocks, 20,000 acres in Kentucky (besides his Virginia property), 14 slaves, and considerable personalty. McLachlan, *Princetonians*, pp. 21-22.

Mon. 4. Hearing my old friend, Mr. H——s, was now a beggar and forsaken of all, I called (after a separation of sixteen years) at his lodgings, to offer him any service in my power. I was pleasingly surprised to find him reading the Bible! But still, I am afraid, all is not right. For the hand of God seems to be upon him still, and his mind is so hurried he can settle to nothing. O what a pattern of holiness and stability of mind was this very man, till he was stolen away by the men 'whose words are smoother than oil'.[80] But were they not to him 'very swords'?[81]

Wed. 6. I mentioned to the congregation another means of increasing serious religion, which had been frequently practised by our forefathers and attended with eminent blessing: namely, the joining in a covenant to serve God[82] with all our heart and with all our soul.[83] I explained this for several mornings following, and on Friday many of us kept a fast unto the Lord, beseeching him to give us wisdom and strength to 'promise unto the Lord our God and keep it'.[84]

Mon. 11. I explained once more the nature of such an engagement and the manner of doing it acceptable to God. At six in the evening, we met for that purpose at the French Church in Spitalfields. After I had recited the tenor of the covenant proposed, in the words of that blessed man, Richard Alleine, all the people stood up in testimony of assent, to the number of about eighteen hundred persons. Such a night I scarce ever saw before. Surely the fruit of it shall remain for ever.

Sat. 16. I buried the remains of a rough, honest, friendly man,

[80] Cf. Ps. 55:22 (BCP).

[81] Ibid.

[82] At one level this comment arises from JW's recent reading of Gillies, *Historical Collections* (see above, June 24, 1755, n. 71). These included an account of a solemn renewing of covenant in Massachusetts in 1680, which led to a revival among a company who had bound themselves by a church covenant before leaving England fifty years before. But the Covenant Service which JW came to use was largely derived from Richard Alleine (1611–81) and his son-in-law Joseph (1634–68), the latter of whom had been much influenced by JW's own paternal grandfather, and whose covenant had been in use in JW's family. JW was also influenced by *The Life and Death of Thomas Haliburton* (2nd edn., 1715), of which he published an *Abstract* early in 1739. Haliburton made his covenant with God and was converted shortly afterwards; JW had the same experience of covenanting and conversion shortly after publishing the book. What he was now moving towards was neither a church nor an individual covenant, but the apostolic act of a society, and it proved so successful as to be frequently used, especially on New Year's Day or the first Sunday in the New Year, and other important occasions. *WHS* 22 (1940):126-31.

[83] 1768, 1788, omit 'with all our heart and', surely in error.

[84] Cf. Ps. 76:11 (BCP).

Capt. Edward Stotesbury.[85] But the lion was become a lamb before God took him to himself.

Sun. 17. I took my leave of the congregation in Moorfields by applying those awful words, 'It is appointed for men once to die,'[86] and early in the morning set out for Cornwall. In the evening I preached to a sleepy congregation at Reading on 'It is a fearful thing to fall into the hands of the living God.'[87] And to much such another on Tuesday evening at Salisbury on 'Harden not your hearts.'[88]

On Wednesday 20, at noon, I preached at Shaftesbury to a much more lively people. In the afternoon both my fellow-traveller and I were fairly worn out. We betook ourselves to prayer and received strength. Nor did we faint any more till on Friday 22 we reached Plymouth Dock. And I found myself far less weary then than on Monday when I came to Colebrook.

Having spent two days comfortably (and I hope usefully), on Monday 25 I rode over the mountains close by the sea to Looe,[89] a town near half as large as Islington, which sends *four* members to the Parliament! And each county in North Wales sends *one*! At Fowey a little company met us and conducted us to Luxulyan.[90] Between six and seven I preached in what was once the courtyard of a rich and honourable man. But he and all his family are in the dust, and his very memory is almost perished.[91] The congregation was large and deeply serious. But it was still larger on Tuesday evening, and several seemed to be cut to the heart. On Wednesday they flocked from all parts. And with what eagerness did they receive the Word! Surely many of these last will be first!

Thur. 28. I preached at St. Mewan.[92] I do not remember ever to have seen the yard in which I stood quite full before. But it would not now contain the congregation. Many were obliged to stand without the gate. At five in the morning I preached at St. Austell[93]

[85] It may have been the Stotesburys who provided JW with quiet for literary work at Newington Green; Charles Wesley was much attached to his wife, Mary Stotesbury, and celebrated her death on Mar. 17, 1759, with a poem. *CWJ*, 2:72, 352-53.

[86] Cf. Heb. 9:27.

[87] Heb. 10:31.

[88] Heb. 3:8. These three successive sermons from Hebrews almost certainly reflect Wesley's reading of the Scriptures according to the Church of England calendar, which presented Heb. 4–13 for the Second Lessons at Evening Prayer for the first ten days in August.

[89] Orig., 'Loo'.

[90] Orig., 'Luxillian'.

[91] Methrose, a Tudor farm-house, was built by Nicholas Kendall whose family, in fact, still flourished elsewhere. The tenant in JW's time was a Mr. Meager. It is located a mile south of the village of Luxulyan. See below, Sept. 26, 1757; and Sept. 1, 1762.

[92] Orig., 'St. Mewan's'.

[93] Orig., 'St. Awstle's'; 1788, 'St. Austle's'.

to more than our room could contain. In the evening I was at St. Ewe. One or two felt the edge of God's sword and sunk to the ground. And indeed it seemed as if God would suffer none to escape him, as if he both heard and answered our prayer,

> Dart into all the melting flame
> Of love, and make the mountains flow.[94]

Sat. 30. As I was riding through Truro, one stopped my horse and insisted on my alighting. Presently two or three more of Mr. Walker's society[95] came in, and we seemed to have been acquainted with each other many years. But I was constrained to break from them. About five I found the congregation waiting, in a broad, convenient part of the street in Redruth. I was extremely weary. And our friends were so glad to see me that none once thought of asking me to eat or drink. But my weariness vanished when I began to speak. Surely God is in this place.[96]

Sun. 31. Understanding there were many present who did once run well, I preached at eight (the rain ceasing just in time) on, 'How shall I give thee up, Ephraim?'[97] Many endeavoured, but in vain, to hide their tears. I was agreeably surprised at church to hear the prayers read, not only with deliberation but with uncommon propriety. At one, the congregation was nearly double to what it was in the morning. And all were still as night. Surely these are *patient* hearers. God grant they may be *fruitful* ones!

At five, I preached in Gwennap[98] to several thousands—but not one of them light or inattentive. After I had done, the storm arose, and the rain poured down till about four in the morning. Then the

[94] From a long paraphrase on Isa. 64, beginning, 'O that thou wouldst the heavens rend!' John and Charles Wesley, *Hymns and Sacred Poems* (1740), p. 200; *Poetical Works*, 1:366.

[95] Samuel Walker (1714–61), vicar of Truro, 1746 till his death. Educated at Exeter College, Oxford, whence he graduated B.A., Walker was curate of Doddiscombesleigh (6 miles south-west of Exeter), 1737–38; tutor in the family of Lord Rolle, 1738–40; and vicar of Lanlivery, 1740–46. Under the influence of George Conon, the master of Truro Grammar School, he turned to seriousness of religious life, devoted himself exclusively to pastoral work, and in 1752 resigned the vicarage of Tolland which he held in plurality. In 1754 he formed a religious society in his parish, and in 1755 a clerical association. In subsequent years, he did his best to persuade JW of the unlawfulness of separating from the Church of England, and in 1758 got him to suppress much of a pamphlet he had written against separation, believing that it might have the opposite effect to that intended. See especially G. C. B. Davies, *The Early Cornish Evangelicals 1735–60* (London, SPCK, 1951).

[96] Gen. 28:11.

[97] Hos. 11:8.

[98] Orig., 'Gwenap'.

sky cleared, and many of them that feared God gladly assembled before him.

Monday, Sept. 1. I preached at Penryn, to abundantly more than the house could contain.

Tue. 2. We went to Falmouth. The town is not now what it was ten years since. All is quiet from one end to the other. I had thoughts of preaching on the hill near the church. But the violent wind made it impracticable, so I was obliged to stay in our own room. The people could hear in the yard likewise and the adjoining houses, and all were deeply attentive.

Wed. 3. At four Mrs. M.[99] came into my room all in tears and told me she had seen, as it were, our Lord standing by her, calling her by her name, and had 'ever since been filled with joy unspeakable'. Soon after, came her sister, in almost the same condition, and afterward her niece, who likewise quickly melted into tears and refused to be comforted.[1] Which of these will endure to the end? Now at least God is among them.

After preaching again to a congregation who now appeared ready to devour every word, I walked up to Pendennis Castle, finely situated on the high point of land which runs out between the bay and the harbour, and commanding both. It[2] might easily be made exceeding strong. But our wooden castles are sufficient.[3]

In the afternoon we rode to Helston, once turbulent enough but now quiet as Penryn. I preached at six, on a rising ground about a musket shot from the town. Two drunken men strove to interrupt, but one soon walked away. The other leaned on his horse's neck and fell fast asleep.

What has done much good here is the example of W—— T——. He was utterly without God in the world when his father died and left him a little estate encumbered with huge debt. Seven or eight years ago he found peace with God. He afterward sold his estate, paid all his debts, and with what he had left furnished a little shop. Herein God has blessed him in an

[99] Probably Mrs. Maddern; see July 4, 1745 (20:76 in this edn.).

[1] See Jer. 31:15.

[2] Orig., 'But', altered to 'It' in Wesley's *Works* (1774).

[3] Wesley may have come across the speech of Thomas Coventry, Baron Coventry, on June 17, 1635: 'The wooden walls are the best walls of this kingdom'; John Rushworth, *Historical Collections*, 8 vols. (London, 1659–1701), II.297. It seems more likely, however, that this image for England's navy is a direct reminiscence of Themistocles' interpretation in 480 B.C. of the second oracle at Delphi: 'Safe shall the wooden wall continue for thee and thy children,' interpreted, 'The wooden wall is your ships' (see Herodotus, vii.141-43).

uncommon manner. Meantime all his behaviour is of a piece. So that more and more of his neighbours say, 'Well, this is a work of God!'

Thur. 4. In the evening heavy rain began just as I began to give out the hymn. But it ceased before I named my text. I spoke very plain, and it seemed to sink into many hearts. As they showed by attending at five in the morning, when we had another happy and solemn hour.

About noon, Friday 5, I called on W. Row[e], in Breage,[4] in my way to Newlyn.[5] 'Twelve years ago', he said, 'I was going over Gulval Downs, and I saw many people together. And I asked what was the matter. And they told me, "A man going to preach." And I said, "To be sure it is some *mazed* man." But when I saw you, I said, "Nay, this is no mazed man." And you preached on God's raising the dry bones. And from that time I could never rest till God was pleased to breathe on *me* and raise my dead soul!'

I had given no notice of preaching here. But seeing the poor people flock from every side, I could not send them empty away. So I preached at a small distance from the house and besought them to consider our 'great high priest, who is passed through into the heavens'.[6] And none opened his mouth, for the lions of Breage, too, are now changed into lambs. That they were so fierce ten years ago is no wonder. Since their wretched minister told them from the pulpit (seven years before I resigned my fellowship) that John Wesley was expelled the college for a base child and had been quite mazed ever since; that all the Methodists at their private societies put out the lights, etc., with abundance more of the same kind. But a year or two since it was observed, he grew thoughtful and melancholy. And about nine months ago, he went into his own necessary house and hanged himself![7]

When we came to Newlyn we were informed that a strong, healthy man was the morning before found dead in his bed. Many were startled. So I endeavoured to deepen the impression by preaching on those words, 'There is no work, nor device, nor knowledge, nor wisdom, in the grave whither thou goest.'[8]

[4] Orig., 'Breag'.

[5] Orig., 'Newlin'.

[6] Cf. Heb. 4:14.

[7] Rev. Henry Lanyon (1711–54), son of Tobias Lanyon of Gwinear, gent., educated at Pembroke College, Cambridge, 1728–33; buried at Germoe, Aug. 23, 1754.

[8] Eccles. 9:10.

Sat. 6. In the evening I preached at St. Just. Except at Gwennap, I have seen no such congregation in Cornwall. The *sun* (nor could we contrive it otherwise) shone full in my face when I began the hymn. But just as I ended it a cloud arose, which covered it till I had done preaching. Is anything too small for the providence of him by whom our 'very hairs are numbered'?[9]

Sun. 7. Last year a strange letter, written at Penzance, was inserted in the public papers.[10] Today I spoke to the two persons who occasioned that letter. They are of St. Just's parish, sensible men, and no Methodists. The name of one is James Tregear, of the other Thomas Sackerly. I received the account from James two or three hours before Thomas came. But there was no material difference. In July was twelvemonth, they both said, as they were walking from St. Just church town toward Sancreed,[11] Thomas, happening to look up, cried out, 'James, look, look! What is that in the sky?' The first appearance, as James expressed it, was three large columns of horsemen, swiftly pressing on, as in a fight, from south-west to north-east, a broad streak of sky being between each column. Sometimes they seemed to run thick together, then to thin their ranks. Afterward they saw a large fleet of three-mast ships, in full sail toward the Lizard Point. This continued above a quarter of an hour. Then, all disappearing, they went on their way. The meaning of this, if it was real (which I do not affirm), time only can show.

I preached at eight in the morning and five in the afternoon,[12] and then hastened to St. Ives. But we did not reach it till between nine and ten. So I delayed visiting Mr. K.[13] till the morning. He is

[9] Cf. Matt. 10:30.

[10] The story appeared in the Historical Chronicle (Oct. 31) of the *Gentleman's Magazine*, relating that 'About three weeks since, two persons of St. Just, six miles westward of Penzance in Cornwall, about 10 at night, saw in the sky, a large fleet of ships, and soon after a cloud came before it, and the scene was changed to an army or armies, seeming to be smartly engaged in battle. It lasted fifteen minutes, and divers others saw this phenomenon.' *Gentleman's Magazine* 24 (1754):482.

[11] Orig., 'Sanchrist', altered in the *Works* (1774) to 'Sancreet', and again altered in the *Works* errata and JW's own copy to 'Sancreed', its present name.

[12] At Penzance.

[13] John Knill (1733–1811), who was articled with Robert Hichens (or Kitchen) of Penzance, solicitor, and also served with a London firm. He was collector of customs at St. Ives, 1762–82, and mayor in 1767. He became private secretary to the Earl of Buckinghamshire (who became Lord-lieutenant of Ireland in 1777), and his agent in St. Ives. He built the famous steeple at St. Ives, and in 1797 established a trust to endow the quinquennial dancing ceremony still performed around it. A few days later JW related to Ebenezer Blackwell how this incident 'opened me a way in to the mayor's family'. *Letters*, 26:587 in this edn.

a young attorney, who for some time past has frequently attended the preaching. On Saturday morning he fell raving mad. I never saw him till this morning. He sung, and swore, and screamed, and cursed, and blasphemed, as if possessed by Legion.[14] But as soon as I came in he called me by my name and began to speak. I sat down on the bed, and he was still. Soon after, he fell into tears and prayer. We prayed with him and left him calm for the present.

Tue. 9. I desired as many of our brethren as could to observe Wednesday the tenth as a day of fasting and prayer. Just as we were praying for him (we were afterwards informed), he left off raving and broke out, 'Lord! How long? Wilt thou hide thy face for ever? All my bones are broken. Thy wrath lieth heavy upon me. I am in the lowest darkness and in the deep. But the Lord *will* hear; he *will* rebuke thee, thou unclean spirit. He *will* deliver me out of thy hands.' Many such expressions he uttered for about half an hour and then raved again.

Thur. 11. He was more outrageous than ever. But while we were praying for him in the evening, he sunk down into a sound sleep, which continued for ten hours. Nor was he furious any more, although the time of deliverance was not come.

Sat. 13. I preached once more at St. Just, on the first stone of their new society house.[15] In the evening, as we rode to Camborne, John Pearce[16] of Redruth was mentioning a remarkable incident. While he lived at Helston, as their class was meeting one evening, one of them cried with an uncommon tone, 'We will not stay here; we will go to such an house'—which was in a quite different part of the town. They all rose immediately and went, though neither they nor she knew why. Presently after they were gone, a spark fell into a barrel of gunpowder which was in the next room and blew up the house. So did God preserve those who trusted in him and prevent the blasphemy of the multitude.

Sun. 14. I preached about eight at Brea,[17] to a very numerous congregation. And I believe God spoke to the hearts of many—of backsliders in particular. Soon after ten, we went to Redruth

[14] See Mark 5:9.

[15] The second chapel at St. Just, almost twice the size of the building it replaced.

[16] Orig., 'Pearse'. John Pearce, joiner, of Penhallicks Estate, Redruth. His mother-in-law had long been acquainted with JW, having before her marriage worked in the house of Richard Andrew, draper, one of JW's first hosts. John Pearce, ed., *Wesleys in Cornwall* (Truro, Barton, 1964), p. 124 (hereafter, Pearce, *Wesleys in Cornwall*).

[17] Orig., 'Bray'.

church. A young gentlewoman in the next pew, who had been laughing and talking just before, while the Confession was reading seemed very uneasy, then screamed out several times, dropped down, and was carried out of church. Mr. Collins[18] read prayers admirably well and preached an excellent sermon on 'Christ also suffered, leaving us an example, that we should tread in his steps.'[19]

At one I preached on faith, hope, and love. I was surprised at the behaviour of the whole multitude. At length God seems to be moving on all their hearts. About five I preached at St. Agnes, where all received the truth in love, except two or three, who soon walked away. Thence I rode on to Cubert.[20] At noon I was much tired. But I was now as fresh as in the morning.

Mon. 15. We walked an hour near the sea-shore, among those amazing caverns, which are full as surprising as Poole's Hole or any other in the Peak of Derbyshire. Some part of the rock in these natural vaults glitters as bright and ruddy as gold. Part is a fine sky-blue, part green, part enamelled, exactly like mother-of-pearl; and a great part, especially near the Holywell[21] (which bubbles up on the top of a rock and is famous for curing either scorbutic or scrofulous disorders), is crusted wherever the water runs with an hard white coat like alabaster.

At six in the evening I preached at Port Isaac. The next day I rode to Camelford and preached in the market-place about six, on 'Ye must be born again.'[22] Some were much afraid there would be disturbance. But the whole congregation was quiet and attentive.

Thur. 18. Just as we came in at Launceston[23] the heavy rain

18 Rev. John Collins; see July 4, 1745, n. 12 (20:77 in this edn.).

19 Cf. 1 Pet. 2:21.

20 1761 (followed by 1768, 1788), 'St. Cubert'; *Works* (1774), 'St. Cuthbert', followed by some later edns.

21 Orig., 'Holy Well'; 1½ miles north-west of Cubert parish church. 'In this parish is that famous and well-known spring of water called Holy-well (so named, the inhabitants say, for that the virtues of this water was [*sic*] first discovered on All-hallows-day). The same stands in a dark cavern of the sea-cliff rocks . . . from the top of which . . . distils continually drops of water, from the white, blue, red and green veins of those rocks. . . in the place where those drops of water fall, it swells to a lump of considerable bigness, and there petrifies. . . [in] the several colours. . . and is of a hard brittle nature, apt to break like glass. The virtues of this water are very great. It is incredible what numbers in summer season frequent this place and waters from counties far distant.' William Hals, et al., *A Complete Parochial History of the County of Cornwall*, 4 vols. (Truro, 1867–73), 1:273.

22 John 3:7.

23 Orig., 'Lanceston'.

began. Between five and six I preached in a gentleman's dining-room capable of containing some hundreds of people. At five in the morning I preached in the town hall and soon after took my leave of Cornwall.

Fri. 19. In the evening I reached North Molton.[24] But being wet and tired, and the people not having notice, I did not preach till the morning. A few, I found, stand steadfast here also, though a neighbouring gentleman[25] has threatened them much unless they will leave this way, has turned many out of their work or farms, and headed the mob in person.

On Saturday evening I preached at Tiverton to a well established people.

Sun. 21. I rode to Cullompton, where the minister preached an excellent, practical sermon. At one I preached on the parable of the sower, and about five in the market-house at Tiverton. The congregation was larger than for some years. Yet all behaved as though they really desired to save their souls.

Mon. 22. It rained the greater part of the day, which lessened the congregation at Charlton.

Tue. 23. We walked up to Glastonbury Tower, which a gentleman is now repairing.[26] It is the steeple of a church, the foundation of which is still discernible. On the west side of the tower there are niches for images, one of which, as big as the life, is still entire. The hill on which it stands is extremely steep and of an uncommon height, so that it commands the country on all sides, as well as the Bristol Channel. I was weary enough when we came to Bristol. But I preached till all my complaints were gone. And I had now a little leisure to sit still and finish the *Notes on the New Testament*.[27]

[24] Orig., 'North Moulton', as also on Oct. 4, 1757.

[25] Charles Wesley notes (*CWJ*, 2:221): 'Mr Robarts was the first that planted the Gospel in this place. The Squire and Minister, as usual, were the chief persecutors. Both people and Preacher were cruelly treated; but conquered all by love and patience. The captain of the mob cut his own throat, but lived long enough to repent, and ask pardon of the poor injured people.' The preacher is probably John Roberts, who served intermittently in the west before his first (and last) full appointment at Norwich in 1787. The squire and holder of the impropriate rectory of North Molton was John Parker, whose son of the same name became first Baron Boringdon.

[26] The tower, which has lost its top storey, is all that is left of St. Michael's, Glastonbury Tor; N. Pevsner, *South and West Somerset* (London, 1958), p. 180. The vicar of Collumpton 1733–56 was John Reynolds.

[27] 'New' was added only in the errata and JW's MS notes in his copy of the *Works* (1774). JW dated the preface to this work, Jan. 4, 1754 (cf. 20:483 in this edn.), and it was published as a large quarto volume in 1756.

Friday, October 3. I rode over to Pill, a place famous from generation to generation, even as Kingswood itself, for stupid, brutal, abandoned wickedness. But what is all the power of the world and the devil when the day of God's power is come? Many of the inhabitants now seem desirous of turning from the power of Satan to God.[28]

Sun. 5. I preached on the south-west side of Bristol. I suppose a considerable part of the congregation had hardly ever heard a sermon in the open air before. But they were all, rich and poor, serious and attentive. No rudeness is now at Bristol.

Thur. 9. I preached on the Green, near Pill, to a large and serious congregation. It rained most of the time, but none went away, although there were many genteel hearers.

Mon. 13. I preached about noon at Shepton Mallet and in the evening at Coleford, where the congregation is so increased that they must enlarge the house.

Tue. 14. About one I preached near Bradford, and again in the evening.[29]

Wed. 15. I preached at Bath. Even here a few are joined together and hope they shall be scattered no more.

I dined with some serious persons, in a large, stately house, standing on the brow of a delightful hill.[30] In this paradise they live, in ease, in honour, and in elegant abundance. And this they *call* 'retiring from the world'! What would Gregory Lopez have called it?

In the evening the society met at Bristol. I had desired again and again that no person would come who had not calmly and deliberately resolved to give himself up to God. But I believe not ten of them were wanting. And we now solemnly and of set purpose, by our own free act and deed, jointly agreed to take the Lord for our God. I think it will not soon be forgotten; I hope, not to all eternity.

Sun. 19. I preached once more in Stokes Croft, to a deeply serious congregation.[31]

[28] See Acts 26:18.

[29] *Works* (1774) omits the entries for Oct. 13 and 14.

[30] Said by Curnock to be Prior Park, the residence of Ralph Allen, whose favourite niece, Gertrude Tucker, William Warburton married in 1746. After his marriage, Warburton himself resided chiefly at Prior Park. Richard Hurd, *A Discourse by Way of a General Preface to the Quarto Edition of Bishop Warburton's Works* (London, 1794), pp. 49-50.

[31] *Works* (1774) omits this entry.

Mon. 20. I left Bristol, and taking several societies[32] in the way, on Thursday 23 preached at Reading. Several soldiers were there, and many more the next night, when I set before them 'the terrors of the Lord'.[33] And I scarce ever saw so much impression made on this dull, senseless people.

Sat. 25. I reached London, notwithstanding all the forebodings of my friends, in at least as good health as I left it.

Sun. 26. I entered upon my London duty, reading prayers, preaching, and giving the Sacrament at Snowsfields in the morning; preaching and giving the Sacrament at noon in West Street Chapel; meeting the leaders at three, burying a corpse at four, and preaching at five in the afternoon. Afterwards I met the society and concluded the day with a general love-feast.

Mon. 27. We set out for Leigh in Essex. But being hindered a little in the morning, the night came on without either moon or stars when we were about two miles short of Rayleigh.[34] The ruts were so deep and uneven that the horse could scarce stand, and the chaise was continually in danger of overturning, so that my companions thought it best to walk to the town, though the road was both wet and dirty. Leaving them at Rayleigh, I took horse again. It was so thoroughly dark that we could not see our horses' heads. However, by the help of him to whom the night shineth as the day,[35] we hit every turning, and without going a quarter of a mile out of our way, before nine came to Leigh.

Wed. 29. I returned to London. In my scraps of time on this and two or three other days I read over (what I had often heard much commended) Lord Anson's *Voyage*.[36] What pity he had not a better historian! One who had eyes to see, and courage to own, the hand of God.

Thursday, November 5 [i.e., 6]. Mr. Whitefield called upon me. Disputings are now no more. We love one another and join hand in hand to promote the cause of our common Master.

In the afternoon I buried the remains of Samuel Larwood,[37] who died of a fever on Sunday morning, deeply convinced of his

[32] On the 21st he preached at Bray, and on the 22nd at Salisbury and Westcombe.
[33] Cf. Job 6:4; 2 Cor. 5:11.
[34] Orig., 'Raleigh'.
[35] See Ps. 139:12.
[36] Lord George Anson, *A Voyage Round the World in the Years 1740, 1741, 1742, 1743 and 1744 by George Anson, Esq*. Compiled from the papers of Lord Anson. Richard Waller and Benjamin Robins, eds. (London, 1748; frequently reprinted).
[37] See Feb. 23, 1747, n. 44 (20:158 in this edn.).

unfaithfulness and yet hoping to find mercy. He had lately taken and repaired a building in Southwark, called by the venerable men[38] who built it, Zoar. His executor offering it to me, on the evening of Friday 6 [i.e., 7], that solemn day, which we observed with fasting and prayer for our king and country, I preached there to a large and quiet congregation. But most of them appeared wild enough. And such were we till grace made the difference.

Mon. 10. I preached at the Wells.[39] And I did not wonder that God gave an uncommon blessing to those who then assembled in his name, considering the difficulties they had broke through. The frost was very severe, accompanied with such a fog as perhaps the oldest man there never saw before. The lamps could not be seen across the street, and hardly the ground by those who had lights in their hands. Many lost their way when they were just at their own doors. And it was almost as hard to breathe as to see. How easy it is for God to punish a sinful nation, even without employing an arm of flesh![40]

Mon. 17. As we were walking towards Wapping,[41] the rain poured down with such violence that we were obliged to take shelter till it abated. We then held on to Gravel Lane, in many parts of which the waters were like a river. However, we got on pretty well till the rain put out the candle in our lantern. We then were obliged to wade through all till we came to the chapel-yard. Just as we entered it a little streak of lightning appeared in the south-west. There was likewise a small clap of thunder and a vehement burst of rain, which rushed so plentifully through our shattered tiles that the vestry was all in a float.[42] Soon after I began reading prayers, the lightning flamed all round it, and the thunder rolled just over our heads. When it grew louder and louder, perceiving many of the strangers to be much affrighted, I broke off the prayers after the Collect, 'Lighten our darkness, we beseech thee, O Lord,'[43] and began applying 'The Lord sitteth above the water-flood; the Lord remaineth a king for ever.'[44] Presently the lightning, thunder, and rain ceased, and we had a remarkably calm evening.

It was observed that exactly at this hour they were acting

[38] 1768, 1788, 'venerable man'.
[39] Sadler's Wells; cf. above, Apr. 19, 1754, n. 63 (20:485 in this edn.).
[40] See 2 Chr. 32:8.
[41] Wapping was a parish adjoining the eastern part of the City of London.
[42] *OED* notes no example of this usage.
[43] BCP, Evening Prayer, Collect 3.
[44] Ps. 29:9 (BCP).

Macbeth in Drury Lane, and just as the mock thunder began the Lord began to thunder out of heaven. For a while it put them to a stand. But they soon took courage and went on. Otherwise it might have been suspected that the fear of God had crept into the very theatre!

Tue. 18. We had a solemn watch-night at Zoar.

Wed. 26. Being much importuned thereto, I wrote *Serious Thoughts on the Earthquake at Lisbon*,[45] directed, not as I designed at first, to the small vulgar, but the great—to the learned, rich, and honourable heathens, commonly called Christians.

Tuesday, December 2. I received a remarkable letter,[46] part of which I have here subjoined:

> It may seem strange, sir, that I whom you have no personal knowledge of should write with the freedom I am now going to take. But I trust you desire as much to instruct as I to be instructed. I have long laboured under a disease which comes the nearest to that which is named scepticism. I rejoice at one time in the belief that the religion of my country is true. But how transient my joy! While my busy imagination ranges through nature, books, and men, I often drop into that horrible pit of Deism, and in vain bemoan my fall. The two main springs which alternately move my soul to these opposite opinions are, first, 'Can it be that the great God of the boundless universe, containing many thousand better worlds than this, should become incarnate here and die on a piece of wood?' There I lose my belief of Christianity.
>
> But on the other hand I think, Well, let me examine the fitness of things which Deism boasts of. And certain it is, I discern nothing but beauty and wisdom in the inanimate parts of the creation. But how is the animate side of nature? It shocks me with powerful cruelty and bleeding innocence. I cannot call the earth (as Fontenelle does), 'a great rolling globe, covered over with fools', but rather, a great rolling globe, covered over with slaughter-houses—where few beings can escape but those of the butcher kind, the lion, wolf, or tiger. And as to man himself, he is undoubtedly the supreme lord, nay, the uncontrollable tyrant of this globe. Yet survey him in a state of Deism, and I must pronounce him a very poor creature. He is then a kind of Jack

[45] See Frank Baker, *A Descriptive and Analytical Bibliography of the Publications of John and Charles Wesley* (in preparation), vols. 33-34 in this edn., No. 212; and vol. 14 in this edn. See also above, June 2, 1755, n. 51.

[46] From John Walsh, a deist, who probably also contributed the letter printed below, July 29, 1759. For other letters from him to JW, see *Arminian Magazine* 2 (1779):376, 432; 3 (1780):103-5; see also *Letters*, 2:616-18 in this edn.

Ketch,[47] an executioner-general. He may, nay, he must destroy, for his own subsistence, multitudes of beings that have done him no wrong. He has none of that heavenly power to restore life. And can he be fond of the permission to take it away? One who like me is subject to the tender passions will never be proud of this:

No dying brute I view in anguish here,
But from my melting eye descends a tear.

The very beasts are entitled to my compassion, but who can express the anxieties I feel for the afflictions sustained by virtuous men, and my abhorrence of the cruel! Yet in Deism I can discern no reward for the one or punishment for the other. On this view of things, the Castilian king might well say, he 'could have directed God to amend his creation'.

I think upon the whole, the God of wisdom would not have made a world so much in want of a Redeemer as this, and not give it one; therefore at present I am again a Christian. O that the Son of God would confirm me his! As yet my soul is like a weather-beaten bird that hovers over the great ocean, tired and afraid of dropping; death and eternity are ready to receive it, the pleasant land is out of sight, hid by fogs and mists, and the way unknown to gain the happy groves.

I was formerly apt to mention my scepticism both to clergymen and laymen with a view of lessening the evil. But they rather increased it. Few clergymen cared to discourse on the subject, and if they did, they generally expected that a few weak reasons should eradicate at once strong and deep-rooted prejudices. And most laymen discovered an utter ignorance of the religion they pretended to believe and looked upon me as if I had the plague for owning I did not believe it. What method could I take? I long avoided speaking of religion to any but its great Author, who, I hope, has at last led me to one that is capable of removing my spiritual darkness. May the Giver of all goodness reward you in that day, when (according to the prophet Daniel) 'The wise shall shine as the brightness of the firmament, and they that turn many to righteousness, as the stars for ever!'[48]

Fri. 12. As I was returning from Zoar I came as well as usual to Moorfields, but there my strength entirely failed, and such a faintness and weariness seized me that it was with difficulty I got home. I could not but think how happy it would be (suppose we

[47] Orig., 'Jack-catch'.
[48] Cf. Dan. 12:3.

were ready for the Bridegroom) to sink down and steal away at once without any of the hurry and pomp of dying! Yet it is happier still to glorify God in our death as well as our life.

About this time I received a serious, sensible letter, the substance of which was as follows:

Scarce any nation passes a century without some remarkable fluctuation. How should it be otherwise? For how can that be perpetually stable wherein man, full of instability, is principally concerned? It is certain, therefore, that all the quiet in a nation is ordered by divine wisdom, as all the confusions and convulsions are permitted by divine justice. Let us view the present state of Great Britain in this light, resting assured that all which befalls us is intended to promote our good, in this world and that which is to come.

This land is ripe for judgments. How few are there herein who even *intend* to please God in *all* they do! And all besides are subjects of divine wrath. For all who live without any regard to God are wilful sinners against God, and every hour liable to the stroke of his offended justice.

And what shall these do when visited by the sword, the plague, the famine, or the furious elements?[49] O that they would turn to God, through the Saviour of sinners! Surely then they would find mercy! Yea, and probably see the salvation of God, even in the land of the living.

But what shall the Christians do in the time of public calamities? Be still, look up, and follow Providence. 'Be still', O my soul, in the midst of tumults and the distress of nations. Take no comfort in anything but in the consciousness of divine love. Listen to his voice and quietly wait to see the hand of God over all. If you are uncertain what to do, 'look up', and expect wisdom from above. If you fear, look up for courage and faith to act well on all occasions. If the sword is at your throat, look up for submission to the wise and gracious will of God. Look up for power to pray without ceasing, and in everything to give thanks. 'Follow Providence.' Do not run *before* but *after* the hand that leads the simple-hearted, with a steady attention and a determinate purpose to do what is pleasing to him.

But what shall the Christians do if the storm come, if our country be actually *invaded*? The general answer must be the same: Be still, look up, follow Providence. A particular answer is hard to give yet. Only so far one may say:

[49] This passage recalls the opening (espec. para. 3) of Wesley's *Serious Thoughts occasioned by the late Earthquake at Lisbon*, and the letter (by an unknown writer) was probably a response to this publication.

(1) We must take great care of our spirits. If we sink into the world's fears or joys, we shall lose our hold on God. The spirit of the Christians and the spirit of the world are entirely different. They can never agree in what appertains to the work of God, either in his dispensations of grace or justice. (2) Everyone should deeply consider what he is called to. Some may think it would be a sin to defend themselves. Happy are they if they can refrain from judging or condemning those that are of a different persuasion. Certain it is, some have fought and died in a just cause with a conscience void of offence. To some therefore it may be matter of duty to repel the common enemy. (3) They who believe they are called to this should proceed in all things in a Christian spirit. They should if possible join in one body. They should endeavour to avoid trifling company and conversation. They should learn the exercise with prayers and hymns. But who of us is sufficient for these things?

Sun. 14. The minds of many people being deeply affected with a prospect of public calamities, I explained those comfortable words in the First Lesson, Isa. 26:20: 'Come, my people, enter thou into thy chambers and shut thy doors about thee; hide thyself as it were for a little moment, until the indignation be overpast.'

Tue. 16. I set out for Lewisham, appointing one to meet me with my horse at the Stone's End.[50] But he mistook his way and so left me to walk on, in my boots and great coat. When I came within a quarter of a mile of Lewisham Bridge a coach drove swiftly by me. I wondered why the coachman stopped, till he called and desired me to come up to him. The reason then appeared: the low grounds were quite covered with water, so that I could not have attempted to reach the bridge without hazarding my life.

Tue. 23. I was in the robe-chamber, adjoining to the House of Lords, when the King put on his robes. His brow was much furrowed with age[51] and quite clouded with care. And is this all the world can give even to a king? All the grandeur it can afford? A blanket of ermine round his shoulders, so heavy and cumbersome he can scarce move under it! An huge heap of borrowed hair with a few plates of gold and glittering stones upon his head! Alas, what bauble is human greatness! And even this will not endure! Cover the head with ever so much hair and gold, yet

[50] Between Southwark and Newington near the Marshalsea at the intersection of Borough Road, Borough High Street, and Newington Causeway, from which on Paterson's Road Map the miles are measured on the Portsmouth Road. *WHS* 7 (1909):71.

[51] George II was already 72, had outlived his son, and had himself less than five years before him.

Scit te Proserpina canum;
Personam capiti detrahet illa tuo.[52]

January 1, 1756. We had a large congregation at four in the morning. How much are men divided in their expectations concerning the ensuing year! Will it bring a large harvest of temporal calamities? Or of spiritual blessings? Perhaps of both—of temporal afflictions preparatory to spiritual blessings.

Mon. 5. This week I wrote *An Address to the Clergy*,[53] which, considering the situation of public affairs, I judged would be more serviceable[54] and more easily borne at this time than at any other.

Wed. 14. Mr. Walsh[55] wrote to me as follows:

Rev. and very dear Sir,

In Mr. Booker's[56] letter are many palpable falsehoods. But what exasperated him so he does not tell. It was my opposing his Arian principles—my telling him, I had the same arguments to prove the divinity of Christ, as to prove the Godhead of the Father.

(1) The Father is called God אל; so is the Son, Isa. 9:6. (2) The Father is called אלהים; so is the Son, Hos. 1:7. (3) The Father is called יהוה; so is the Son, Jer. 23:6. (4) The Father is said to be 'from everlasting'; so the Son is called אבי עד, Isa. 9:6. Not the 'everlasting Father', but 'the Father' or 'Author of eternity'. (5) The Father is said to create all things; so is the Son, John 1[:1] and Col. 1[:16]. (6) The Father is said to be almighty; so is the Son. (7) The Father is omnipresent; so is the Son, Matt. 20:18. (8) The Father is omniscient; so is the Son, Rev. 2:7.[57] (9) The Father forgives sins; so does the Son, Mark 2[:5]. (10)[58] The Father is Judge of all; so is the Son.

[52] 'Proserpine knows you to be whiteheaded; she will strip off the mask from your head.' Martial, *Epigrammata*, iii.143. In the appendix to his *Works* (1774), JW paraphrased: 'Death will deprive thee of thy borrowed hair.'

[53] See *Bibliography*,; No. 214; and vol. 14 in this edn. In this tract, dated Feb. 6, 1756 (Jackson, 10:480-500), JW set forth the gifts and acquirements, natural and spiritual, which he thought desirable in ministers of the church. He came close to saying that the Christian ministry required omniscience reinforced by intense spiritual and pastoral devotion.

[54] Orig., and *Works* (1774), 'seasonable', altered in 1768, 1788.

[55] Thomas Walsh; see Sept. 2, 1752, n. 47 (20:439-40 in this edn.).

[56] The Rev. Moore Booker of Delvin (see Aug. 2, 1752, n. 30; 20:435 in this edn.), who wrote *Two Letters concerning the Methodists* (1751, Dublin; repr. in 1752 and later); cf. Aug. 7, 1752. Other editions read 'Mr. B——', altered in *Works* (1774) to 'Booker'.

[57] This citation appears to be an error, but it is difficult to be certain whether Walsh intended Rev. 2:19 or some other text.

[58] There is some confusion in the numbering: in the original Nos. 3, 4 are unnumbered; Nos. 5-10 are numbered respectively 4, 5, 6, 7, 7, and 8.

But still he disputed whether any man should pray to Christ. I gave these reasons for it. (1) All men are bound to *honour* the Son, 'as they honour the Father'.[59] But we are to honour the Father by praying to him. Therefore we should so honour the Son. (2) God commands, 'Let all the angels of God worship him.'[60] This is done, Rev. 5[:11-12]. And it is certain praise and thanksgiving are superior rather than inferior to prayer. (3) St. Paul prayed to him, 2 Cor. 12:8-9. (4) St. Stephen prayed to him, Acts 7:59. (The word 'God' is not in the original.) (5) All believers in the apostolic age prayed to him, 1 Cor. 1:2. For what is to 'call upon his name' but to pray to him?

When he could not answer these reasons, he called them *cant* and said, 'Much learning has made thee mad.' What he calls 'contempt' was confronting him with Scripture and reason in defence of the Godhead of Christ. I acknowledge, I have been an opposer of Arianism ever since I knew what it was, but especially since my late illness, during which I had such glorious evidence of the eternal power and Godhead of my great Redeemer. I bless God, I love Mr. B[ooker] as well as all mankind. But it grieves me to see the people led in the high road to hell, instead of heaven—especially at a time which calls upon all to awake and 'prepare to meet' their God.

Saturday 17 and in the spare hours of the following days, I read over Mr. Pike's *Philosophia Sacra*,[61] a treatise admirably well wrote by an ingenious man who says all that can be said for Mr. Hutchinson's hypothesis.[62] But it is only an hypothesis still—much *supposition* and little *proof.*

Mon. 26. I rode to Canterbury and preached in the evening to such a congregation as I never saw there before. In which were abundance of the soldiers and not a few of their officers.

Wed. 28. I preached about noon at Dover, to a very serious but small congregation. We afterwards walked up to the castle on the top of a mountain. It is an amazingly fine situation. And from hence we had a clear view of that vast piece of the cliff which a few days ago divided from the rest and fell down upon the beach.

Fri. 30. In returning to London I read the life of the late Czar, Peter the Great.[63] Undoubtedly he was a soldier, a general, and a

[59] John 5:23.

[60] Heb. 1:6.

[61] Samuel Pike, *Philosophia Sacra: or, The Principles of Natural Philosophy Extracted from Divine Revelation* (London, 1753). Pike (1717?–1773) was a Sandemanian.

[62] For John Hutchinson, see Dec. 20, 1746, n. 11 (20:151 in this edn.).

[63] The most recent biography at the time was by Alexander Gordon, *The History of Peter the Great, Emperor of Russia,* 2 vols. (Aberdeen, 1755).

statesman, scarce inferior to any. But why was he called a Christian? What has Christianity to do either with deep dissimulation or savage cruelty?

Friday, February 6. The Fast Day was a glorious day,[64] such as London has scarce seen since the Restoration. Every church in the city was more than full, and a solemn seriousness sat on every face. Surely God heareth the prayer,[65] and there will yet be 'a lengthening of our tranquility'.[66]

Even the Jews observed this day with a peculiar solemnity. The form of prayer which was used in their synagogue began, 'Come, and let us return unto the Lord, for he hath torn and he will heal us,'[67] and concluded with those remarkable words, 'Incline the heart of our Sovereign Lord King George, as well as the hearts of his lords and counsellors, to use us kindly, and all our brethren, the Children of Israel; that in his days and in our days we may see the restoration of Judah, and that Israel may dwell in safety, and the Redeemer may come to Zion. May it be thy will! And we all say, *Amen*.'[68]

Mon. 23. I paid another visit to Canterbury but came in too late to preach.

Tue. 24. Abundance of soldiers and many officers came to the preaching. And surely the fear and the love of God will prepare them either for death or victory.

Wed. 25. I dined with Col. ——,[69] who said, 'No men fight like those who fear God. I had rather command five hundred such than any regiment in his Majesty's army.'

Thur. 22 [i.e., 26]. I had so severe a cold that I could hardly speak to be heard. However, I preached morning and evening as I could, and the next day returned to London.

Monday, March 1. I set out for Bristol. Some time after, I

[64] The fast was ordered by proclamation on Dec. 20, 1755, and took place on Feb. 6, 1756.

[65] See Prov. 15:29.

[66] Cf. Dan. 4:27.

[67] Hos. 6:1.

[68] Curnock (4:148-49) here introduced one of the set-pieces JW excluded from the journal, describing it as 'a fragment of another version of the Journal'. On JW's practice in this matter see above, vol. 18, Introduction, pp. 90-91.

[69] Probably not Col. Gallatin (see Apr. 24, 1751, n. 89; 20:386 in this edn.), who had been promoted major, but one of his superiors in the same regiment, the First (or Royal) Regiment of Dragoons, which was stationed in Canterbury; perhaps Col. Henry Hawley or Lt. Col. John Toovey.

received the copy of another letter, dated March 2, from the Rev. Mr. Davies in Virginia,[70] part of which I have subjoined:

When the books arrived, I gave public notice after sermon and desired such Negroes as could read and such white people as would make good use of them, and were not able to buy, to come to my house. For some time after, the poor slaves, whenever they could get an hour's leisure, hurried away to me and received them with all the genuine indications of passionate gratitude. All the books were very acceptable, but none more so than the psalms and hymns, which enabled them to gratify their peculiar taste for psalmody. Sundry of them lodged all night in my kitchen. And sometimes when I have awaked at two or three in the morning, a torrent of sacred psalmody has poured into my chamber. In this exercise some of them spend the whole night.

The good effects of this charity are already apparent. It convinces the heathen that however careless about religion the generality of the white people are, yet there are some who think it a matter of importance. It has excited some of their masters to emulation, and they are ashamed that strangers on the other side the Atlantic Ocean should be at such pains to teach their domestics, while themselves are negligent about it. Such of the Negroes as can read already are evidently improving in knowledge. It has excited others to learn to read, for as I give books to none but such as can read, they consider them as a reward for their industry. And I am told that in almost every house in my congregation, and in many other places, they spend every leisure hour in endeavouring to learn. Many do this from a sincere desire to know the will of God. And if some should do it from the meaner principle of vanity or curiosity, yet I cannot but rejoice that it renders them the more capable of receiving instruction. To all this I may add that the very distributing these books gives me an opportunity of speaking seriously, and with particular application, to many who would not otherwise come in my way.

There are thousands of Negroes in this colony who still continue in the grossest ignorance and are as rank pagans now as they were in the wilds of Africa. Not a few of these are within the bounds of my congregation. But all are not of this character. Upon some my ministry of late has been successful. Two Sundays ago I had the pleasure of seeing forty of their black faces at the Lord's Table,

[70] Samuel Davies (see above, July 27, 1755, n. 77) was at this time writing generally to thank his English benefactors of whom JW may have been one. See Samuel Davies, *Letters from the Rev. Samuel Davies, etc. showing the State of Religion in Virginia, particularly among the Negroes* (London, 1757); and [S. Davies,] 'Old Documents', *Virginia Evangelical and Literary Magazine* 4 (1821):538-52, both quoted in Pilcher, *Samuel Davies*, p. 115.

several of whom give unusual evidence of their sincerity in religion. Last Sunday I baptized seven or eight who had been catechized for some time. Indeed, many of them appear determined to press into the kingdom, and I am persuaded will find an abundant entrance when many of the children of the kingdom are shut out.

I have distributed some of the books among the poor white people, with a charge to circulate them among such of their neighbours as would seriously read them, that they might be as extensively serviceable as possible. And some of them have since discovered to me what solemn impressions they received in reading them.

I sent a few of each sort to my friend, Mr. Wright,[71] minister of Cumberland, about ninety miles hence, where there are not a few Negroes thoughtful about Christianity, and sundry real converts. And he informs me they have met with a very agreeable and promising reception. He takes much pains in instructing them and has set up two or three schools among them, where they attend on Sundays, before and after sermon, for they have no other leisure time.

Wed. 3. I found Bristol all in a flame, voters and non-voters being ready to tear each other in pieces.[72] I had not recovered my

[71] John Wright, Presbyterian minister of Farmville, Cumberland County, Va., July 1755–63. John Wright was a pupil of Samuel Davies, subsequently going on to the College of New Jersey and approving himself both to President Aaron Burr and Jonathan Edwards. He was licensed by the Presbytery of New Castle in 1752, and supplied Samuel Davies's pulpits while the latter was fund-raising in England. He thought that Braddock's military reverses in 1755 helped to produce revival in Virginia. From late in 1757, Wright was frequently in difficulties of both health and conduct, and a series of charges, 'the horrid crime of sodomy', 'drunkenness, Popery and Racing', though not all sustained, led finally to his suspension by the Hanover Presbytery in 1763. He died before 1789. McLachlan, *Princetonians*, pp. 63-65. Pilcher, *Samuel Davies*, pp. 115, 168-69.

[72] Two crises coincided. The invasion threat which had led to the institution of the Fast Day on Feb. 6 was not yet passed, and, on March 1, to the amusement of his brother, JW had sent a written offer to the Secretary of the Treasury to raise a corps of self-financing volunteers for a year's service in defence (Telford, 3:164-65). At the same time Howell Harris got the Gentlemen of the Breconshire Agricultural Society to offer to the King to 'form themselves into a troop of light horse' (Morgan Hugh Jones, *The Trevecka Letters* [Caenarvon, 1932], p. 191, n. 15). JW also anxiously intervened in the Bristol election in favour of John Spencer and against Jarrit Smith, whom he described as a Jacobite (Telford, 3:166). The truth was that political organization in Bristol (the third largest urban constituency) was provided by a Tory Steadfast Society and a Whig Union Club. On the retirement of two Tory members in 1754, the two clubs failed to arrange a compromise and shared the representation between Nugent (Whig) and Beckford (Tory). On the death of the latter, which created the present vacancy, the dissenting interest in the borough refused a compromise and pressed the claims of Spencer, whose candidacy was supported by a substantial grant from Secret Service Funds. Smith, however, was elected in a contest so expensive as to compel a compromise between the parties for nearly twenty years. Sir Lewis Namier and John Brooke, *The House of Commons 1754–1790*, 3 vols. (London, 1964), 1:283-84. Cf. *A Word to those Freemen of the Established Church who make the Scriptures the one Rule of their Faith and Practice* (*Bibliography,* No. 219).

voice so as either to preach or speak to the whole society, but I desired those members who were freemen to meet me by themselves, whom I mildly and lovingly informed how they ought to act in this hour of temptation. And I believe the far greater part of them received and profited by the advice.

Thur. 11. I rode to Pill and preached to a large and attentive congregation. A great part of them were seafaring men. In the middle of my discourse a press-gang landed from a man of war and came up to the place. But after they had listened a while, they went quietly by and molested nobody.

Mon. 15. I rode to the Old Passage. But on[73] finding we could not pass, we went to Purton,[74] which we reached about four in the afternoon. But we were no nearer still, for the boatmen lived on[75] the other side, and the wind was so high we could not possibly make them hear. However, we determined to wait a while, and in a quarter of an hour they came of their own accord. We reached Coleford before seven and found a plain, loving people, who received the word of God with all gladness.

Tue. 16. Examining the little society, I found them grievously harassed by disputatious Baptists on one side[76] and Quakers on the other. And hereby five or six persons have been confused. But the rest cleave so much the closer together. Nor does it appear that there is now one trifler, much less a disorderly walker among them.

Wed. 17. I learned the particulars of that surprising storm which was here the year before last. It began near Cheltenham, on June 14, 1754, and passed on over Coleford in a line about three miles broad. It was rain mixed with hail. The hail broke all the windows it had access to, stripped all the trees both of fruit and leaves, and destroyed every green thing. Many of the stones were as large as hen-eggs; some were fourteen or fifteen inches round. The rain occasioned such a torrent of water in the street as bore away man and beast. A mile or two farther it joined with the waters of a mill-dam, which it broke down, and carried away

[73] 'on' added in the errata and Wesley's MS notes in his *Works* (1774).

[74] Purton is a hamlet on the south side of the Severn Estuary about 15 miles south-west of Gloucester.

[75] 'on' was similarly added only in the corrections in 1774.

[76] *Works* (1774) and 1788 read 'by disputations. Baptists on one side', probably in error, which in the errata and in his own copy of the *Works* Wesley 'improved' by making the passage read: 'by disputations. Anabaptists were on one side.'

several houses. How frequent would *accidents* of this kind be if chance, not God, governed the world!

Thur. 18. We rode through hard rain to Brecon and came just at the hour appointed for preaching. The town hall, in which I was desired to preach, is a large and commodious place, and the whole congregation (one poor gentleman excepted) behaved with seriousness and decency.

Fri. 19. I rode over to Howell Harris at Trevecca, though not knowing how to get any further. But he helped us out of our difficulties, offering to send one with us who would show us the way and bring our horses back. So I then determined to go on to Holyhead, after spending a day or two at Brecon.

Sat. 20. It being the day appointed for the justices and commissioners to meet, the town was extremely full. And curiosity (if no better motive) brought most of the gentlemen to the preaching. Such another opportunity could not have been of speaking to all the rich and great of the county. And they all appeared to be serious and attentive. Perhaps one or two may lay it to heart.

Sun. 21. I delayed preaching till nine for the sake of the tender and delicate ones. At two we had near the whole town, and God reserved the great blessing for the last. Afterward we rode to Trevecca. But our guide was ill. So in the morning we set out without him.

Before I talked with him myself, I wondered H. Harris did not go out and preach as usual. But he now informed me, he preached till he could preach no longer, his constitution being entirely broken. While he was thus confined, he was pressed in spirit to build a large house, though he knew not why or for whom. But as soon as it was built, men, women, and children, without his seeking, came to it from all parts of Wales. And except in the case of the orphan-house at Halle, I never heard of so many signal interpositions of divine providence.[77]

[77] After his disruption with David Rowland in 1751, Howell Harris had failed in his attempt to organize a rival Methodist organization, his health suffered severely, he ceased to itinerate, and even his letter-writing almost dried up. But, like all the evangelicals, he had long been fascinated by Francke's institutions at Halle. His enthusiasm for founding a community was sustained by his affection for the Moravians (he visited their settlement at Fulneck in 1756), and a community (like the County Club for Gentlemen, which he turned into the Breconshire Agricultural Society) might be a vehicle for his schemes of economic development. The great building periods at Trevecca were 1752–59 and 1769–72. In November 1755, he reckoned to have at Trevecca 'above 100 souls and about 50 in farms belonging here' employed in more than seventy different trades. By 1756, the

Mon. 22. It continued fair till we came to Builth, where I preached to the usual congregation. Mr. Phillips[78] then guided us to Rhaeadr,[79] about fourteen English miles. It snowed hard behind us and on both sides but not at all where we were.

Tue. 23. When we took horse, there was nothing to be seen but a waste of white, the snow covering both hills and vales. As we could see no path, it was not without much difficulty, as well as danger, that we went on. But between seven and eight the sun broke out, and the snow began to melt. So we thought all our difficulty was over, till about nine the snow fell faster than ever. In an hour it changed into hail, which as we rode over the mountains, drove violently in our face. About twelve this turned into hard rain, followed by an impetuous wind. However, we pushed on through all, and before sunset came to Dolgellau.[80]

Here we found everything we wanted except sleep, of which we were deprived by a company of drunken, roaring sea-captains, who kept possession of the room beneath us till between two and three in the morning. So that we did not take horse till after six, and then we could make no great speed, the frost being exceeding sharp and much ice in the road. Hence we were not able to reach Tan-y-bwlch[81] till between eleven and twelve. An honest Welshman here gave us to know (though he spoke no English) that he was just going over the sands. So we hastened on with him and by that means came in good time to Caernarvon.

Here we passed a quiet and comfortable night and took horse about six in the morning. Supposing, after we had rode near an hour, that a little house on the other side was the ferry-house, we went down to the water and called amain, but we could not procure any answer. In the meantime it began to rain hard, though the wind was extremely high. Finding none would come over, we went to a little church[82] which stood near for shelter. We had waited about an hour when a woman and girl came into the churchyard, whom I did not mind, supposing they could speak no English. They were following a sheep, which ran close to us. I then asked, 'Is not this Bol-y-don[83] Ferry?' The girl answered, 'Bol-y-don Ferry! No. The ferry is two miles further.' So we

Trevecca community was attracting attention—besides JW, Edward Perronet, Marmaduke Gwynne, Sir Edward Williams, and Joseph Harris visited it—and this brought Harris out of his isolation and led him to start preaching again.

78 Edward Phillips, rector of Maesmynis; see May 3, 1743, n. 95 (19:324 in this edn.).

79 Orig., 'Royader'.

80 Orig., 'Dollygelle'.

81 Orig., 'Tannabull'.

82 Llanfair-is-gaer Church.

83 Orig., 'Baldon'.

might have called long enough. When we came to Bol-y-don, the wind fell, the sky cleared up, the boat came over without delay and soon landed us in Anglesey. On our way to Holyhead one met and informed us, the packet sailed the night before. I said, 'Perhaps it may carry me, for all that.' So we pushed on and came thither in the afternoon. The packet did sail the night before and got more than half-seas-over.[84] But the wind turning against them and blowing hard, they were glad to get back this afternoon.

I scarce ever remember so violent a storm as blew all the night long. The wind continued contrary the next day.

Sun. 27 [i.e., 28]. About nine in the morning I spent some time with a few serious people and gave notice of preaching at four in the afternoon, as soon as the evening service was ended. It began soon after three. Ten minutes before four, Mr. E[llis][85] began catechizing the children in Welsh. I stayed till after five. As there was no sign of his concluding, I then went home and found the people waiting, to whom I expounded those solemn words, 'Watch and pray always, that ye may be counted worthy to escape all those things which are coming upon the earth.'[86]

Mon. 29. We left the harbour about twelve, having six or seven officers and abundance of passengers on board. The wind was full west, and there was great probability of a stormy night. So it was judged best to put back, but one gentleman making a motion to try a little longer, in a short time brought all over to his opinion. So they agreed to go out and 'look for a wind'.

The wind continued westerly all the night. Nevertheless, in the morning we were within two leagues of Ireland! Between nine and ten I landed at Howth[87] and walked on for Dublin. The congregation in the evening was such as I never saw here before. I hope this also is a token for good.

Wed. 31. In conversing with many I was surprised to find that all Ireland is in perfect safety![88] None here has any more

[84] 1768, 1788, 'half the seas over'; 1774, 'half sea over'.

[85] Thomas Ellis, vicar of Holyhead; see Feb. 26, 1748, n. 82 (20:209-10 in this edn.).

[86] Cf. Luke 21:36.

[87] Orig., 'Hoath'.

[88] Ireland was indeed nearing the end of a generation of political torpor. Lord Dorset, the viceroy, had come into conflict with the Irish Parliament and the great Irish families about the disposal of budget surpluses, and was dismissed from office in February 1755. JW was, however, hardly warranted in his state of alarm; what set fire to the tinder in Ireland was not the threat to empire created by the Seven Years War, but the reorganization necessitated by overwhelming success in the war. W. E. Lecky, *History of Ireland in the 18th Century*, 5 vols. (London, 1882; repr. 1902), 1:463-68. Hereafter, Lecky, *Ireland.*

apprehension of an invasion than of being swallowed up in the sea, everyone being absolutely assured that the French *dare not* attempt any such thing!

Thursday, April 1. I bought one or two books at Mr. Smith's on the Blind Quay.[89] I wanted change for a guinea, but he could not give it, so I borrowed some silver of my companion. The next evening a young gentleman came from Mr. Smith's to tell me, I had left a guinea on his counter. Such an instance of honesty I have rarely met with, either in Bristol or London.

Sat. [i.e., Sun.] 4. I went to the College Chapel, at which about forty persons were present. Dr. K.[90] preached a plain, practical sermon, after which the Sacrament was administered. I never saw so much decency at any chapel in Oxford, no, not even at Lincoln College. Scarce any person stirred or coughed or spit from the beginning to the end of the service.

In the evening our house was crowded above and below, yet many were obliged to stand without. The whole congregation appeared stayed and solid. Do even the people of Dublin know the day of their visitation?

Mon. 5. Inquiring for one whom I saw three or four days ago in the height of a violent pleurisy, I found he was perfectly recovered and returned into the country. A brimstone plaster in a few minutes took away both the pain and the fever. O why will physicians play with the lives of their patients! Do not others (as well as old Dr. Cockburn)[91] know that 'no end is answered by *bleeding* in a pleurisy which may not be *much better* answered without it'?[92]

Tonight the sleepers here began to open their eyes, it being rumoured that an express was come to the Lord-lieutenant, to inform him, 'The French were hastening their preparation, being determined to land in Ireland.'[93] And so they will—if God gives them leave. But he has the reins in his own hand.

[89] According to Curnock, L. Smith, bookseller, who in 1728 resided at the 'Philosophers' Heads', Blind Quay.

[90] James Knight had graduated B.A. from Trinity College, Dublin, in 1733, became a Fellow in 1738, and D.D. in 1748. *Catalogue of Graduates in the University of Dublin* (Dublin, 1869), p. 326.

[91] An old school friend of Charles Wesley, now frequently his host in his home at York. He gave generously to the building of the York chapel (Lyth, *York Methodism*, pp. 83-90). He died in Jamaica in August 1768.

[92] Cf. below, Feb. 16, 1757.

[93] The management of the Irish political system now reached one of its recurrent crises which coincided with economic difficulties and fresh fears of confessional conflict in Europe, springing from the reversal of alliances. This led to fears that the French might try

Tue. 6. One was informing me of an eminent instance of the power of faith. 'Many years ago', said she, 'I fell and sprained my ankle, so that I never expected it would be quite well. Seven years since, last September, I was coming home from the preaching in a very dark night and, stumbling over a piece of wood, fell with the whole weight of my body upon my lame foot. I thought, O Lord, I shall not be able to hear thy word again for many weeks. Immediately a voice went through my heart, Name the name of Christ and thou shalt stand. I leaped up and stretched out my foot and said, "Lord, Jesus Christ, I name thy name; let me stand." And my pain ceased. And I stood up. And my foot was as strong as ever.'

Fri. 9. I spent an hour with Dr. F——,[94] a sensible, agreeable man. He said, 'Six weeks ago, the —— informed the Lord-l[ieutenant][95] that he had express orders from his Majesty to put this kingdom into a posture of defence against the intended invasion. And he was empowered to raise what men he pleased. And nothing has ever been done since. So that we conclude the whole to be a grimace, a mere trick of state.'

Sun. 11. I met about an hundred children, who are catechized publicly twice a week. Thomas Walsh began this some months ago, and the fruit of it appears already. What a pity that all our preachers, in every place, have not the zeal and wisdom to follow his example!

Tue. 13. I breakfasted with one of the most lovely old men I ever saw, John Garret,[96] a Dutchman by birth and a speaker among the Quakers.

Thence we went to a poor, dying backslider. When we came in he was crying to God out of the deep.[97] But before we left him his

to land in Ireland. These fears reached a fresh crescendo in the winter of 1759–60, when a French fleet left Dunkirk to cruise in Irish waters, while a powerful fleet was collected at Brest with a view, it was believed, to landing an army in Munster.

[94] 'F' is added in *Works* (1774) only.

[95] Only *Works* (1774) fills the blank by 'Lord L.' The Lord-lieutenant of Ireland, 1755–57, was the Marquis of Hartington, later Duke of Devonshire.

[96] Gharret van Hassen (*c.* 1695–1765), born in Holland, who came to England on his way to Philadelphia, but settled at Colchester as a woolcomber and, convinced after years of 'unregenercy and sin', joined the Friends in 1735. He received the gift of ministry. In 1737 he settled permanently in Dublin, though paying religious visits in England and Scotland (*WHS* 5 [1906]:339). Charles Wesley describes him as 'an old Dutch Quaker who seemed to have deep experience of the things of God'(*CWJ,* 2:37). He is apparently not to be identified with the Thomas Garret noted by C. H. Crookshank in his *History of Methodism in Ireland*, 3 vols. (Belfast, Allen, 1885), 1:123 (hereafter, Crookshank, *Ireland*). He was a zealous worker, with a special concern for young people, whose public service was restricted by ill-health.

[97] See Ps. 130:1 (BCP).

heaviness was gone, and he desired nothing but to be with Christ.[98]

Wed. 14. I looked over a celebrated book, *The Fable of the Bees*.[99] Till now I imagined, there had never appeared in the world such a book as the works of Machiavel[li]. But Dr. Mandeville goes far beyond it. The Italian only recommends *a few* vices as useful to *some* particular *men* and on *some* particular *occasions*. But the Englishman loves and cordially recommends vice of every kind. Not only as useful now and then but as absolutely *necessary* at *all* times for *all* communities! Surely Voltaire would hardly have said so much! And even Mr. Sandeman[1] could not have said more!

April 16, being Good Friday, near four hundred of the society met to follow the example of their brethren in England and renew their covenant with God. It was a solemn hour. Many mourned before God, and many were comforted.

In the following week all our preachers met. I never before found such unanimity among them. They appeared now to be not only of one heart but likewise of one mind and judgment.

Sun. 25. One of the Germans stumbled in while I was expounding, 'Is Christ the minister of sin?'[2] For a time she seemed greatly diverted. But the application spoiled her mirth. She soon hung down her head and *felt* the difference between the chaff and the wheat.

Mon. 26. I set out for Cork, purposing to see as many societies as I could in my way. In the afternoon I came to Edenderry, where the little society have built a commodious preaching-house. I had designed to preach abroad, but the keen north wind drove us into the house. The congregation (though they had no previous notice) filled it from end to end. But some of them found it too hot and hurried out, while I applied, 'Ye must be born again.'[3]

About this time I received the following letter:

98 See Phil. 1:23.

99 Bernard de Mandeville, *The Fable of the Bees, or Private Vices Public Benefits; with an Essay on Charity and Charity-Schools, and a Search into the Nature of Society* (London, 1714).

1 Robert Sandeman (1718–71), early apprenticed as a linen-weaver at his native Perth, came under the religious influence of the Scottish seceder John Glas (see Oct. 29, 1745, n. 74 (20:97 in this edn.) and married his daughter in 1737. Becoming an elder in the Glasite communion, he exercised a ministry so powerful as to give his own name to the branches of that body in England and America. In 1757, he was to become well known for his criticisms of Hervey's *Theron and Aspasio* (1755). Why JW thought he could sustain this charge against a man principally noted for standard Glasite opposition to Erastianism and for biblical literalism in ritual matters is not clear.

2 Cf. Gal. 2:17.

3 John 3:7.

Reverend Sir,

I once through the influence of those about me was ready to join the common cry against you, not knowing what I did. But since, by hearing your discourses, with some of Mr. Walsh's, and by reading your *Sermons* and *Appeals*, I have learned a better lesson. I have learned that true Christianity consists, not in a set of opinions or of forms and ceremonies, but in holiness of heart and life, in a thorough imitation of our divine Master. And this I take to be the doctrine of the Church of England, nor do I apprehend you differ from her at all in doctrine. And I am grieved to know, you have too much cause to differ from many of her present clergy. Why then should I cavil at you for feeding those sheep that are starved by their own shepherds? For endeavouring to recover them from that stupid lethargy and open wickedness which involve the generality of mankind? This is your happiness; would to God it could be mine! I have often had a strong desire for it and would now gladly dedicate my life to it, if my poor abilities and mean education, together with the Twenty-third Article of our Church, did not crush the thought. However, as I do not see you vary from the doctrine of the Church, I should not scruple to join with you. My chief motives (beside that strong desire) are: First, I reflect, there is scarce a station in life, at least in the trading world, without its attendant frauds or vices, which are now scarce separable from it. Secondly, I am at present of no use in society, so that on account of any advantage which now accrues from me to the public I need not scruple giving myself to my darling employment. Thirdly, I am convinced, a man may instruct and reform himself by instructing and reforming others. But may I attempt this otherwise than by the *ordinary* method of admitting labourers into the Lord's vineyard? Your thoughts on this subject would be received as a singular favour. For which I shall impatiently wait, who am, reverend sir,

Your affectionate and ready servant

Wed. 28. I rode to Tullamore, where one of the society, Edward Wallis, gave me a very surprising account of himself. He said:

When I was about twenty years old I went to Waterford for business. After a few weeks, I resolved to leave it, and packed up my things in order to set out the next morning. This was Sunday, but my landlord pressed me much not to go till the next day. In the afternoon we walked out together and went into the river. After a while, leaving him near the shore, I struck out into the deep. I soon heard a cry and, turning, saw him rising and sinking in the channel of the river. I swam back with all speed and, seeing him sink again, dived down after him. When I was near the bottom he clasped his arm round my neck and held me so fast that I could not rise. Seeing death before me, all my sins came into my mind, and I faintly called for mercy. In a while my senses went away, and I thought I was in a place full of light and glory with abundance of people. While I was thus, he who held me died, and I floated up to the top of the water. I then immediately came to myself and swam to the shore, where several stood who had seen us sink, and said they 'never knew such a deliverance before'—for I had been under the water full twenty minutes. It made me more serious for two or three months. Then I returned to all my sins.

But in the midst of all, I had a voice following me everywhere: 'When an able minister of the gospel comes, it will be well with thee.' Some years after, I entered into the army. Our troop lay at Phillipstown, when Mr. W.[4] came. I was much affected by his preaching but not so as to leave my sins. The voice followed me still. And when Mr. J. W. came, before I saw him I had an unspeakable conviction that he was the man I looked for. And soon after, I found peace with God, and it was well with me indeed.

Thur. 29. I preached on one side the market-place, to a numerous congregation. I was afterward invited by some of the officers to spend an hour with them at the barracks. It at least freed them from prejudice against the present work of God, if it answered no further end.

Fri. 30. I was pressed to turn aside to Athlone, a gentlewoman of Barbados,[5] who was obliged to return thither shortly, having a great desire to see me. So I went to Athlone and spent one or two hours in close conversation with her and her husband. We had a comfortable meeting in the evening, and most of the gentry in the town were present—but who can warn them to flee from the wrath to come?[6] They are 'increased in goods and need nothing'![7]

Saturday, May 1. I rode to Birr through rain, hail, and snow, such as is usual on the first of January. I had designed to preach abroad, but the wind was too sharp to be borne either by me or the people.

Sun. 2. We rode to Mountmellick. About five I preached in the

[4] Perhaps Thomas Williams; see 19:228, n. 18, in this edn.; see also A. H. Williams, ed., *John Wesley in Wales, 1739–90* (Cardiff, University of Wales Press, 1971), pp. xxv and 8, n. 2. Hereafter, Williams, *Wesley in Wales*.

[5] Cf. below, Nov. 26, 1758.

[6] See Matt. 3:7.

[7] Cf. Rev. 3:17.

market-place. I was on the point of concluding when a violent storm came. Till then 'the bottles of heaven were stayed.'[8]

Tue. 4. We rode to Portarlington, where on Wednesday 5, at the desire of several who could not attend the early preaching, I preached in the Assembly-Room at ten, on 'Ye must be born again.'[9] Many of the *best in the town* (so called) were present and seemed not a little amazed. Many more came in the evening, among whom I found an unusual liberty of spirit. For the present most of them seemed much affected. But how soon will the thorns grow up?

Thur. 6. I rode to Kilkenny. One of the dragoons who were quartered here soon found us out. A few both of the army and of the town are joined[10] and constantly meet together. I preached in the barracks in one of the officers' rooms. Still, in Ireland, the first call is to the soldiery.

Fri. 7. We rode to Waterford, where after preaching I earnestly exhorted the society to 'love as brethren'.[11] On the same subject I preached in the morning and spent great part of the day in striving to remove misunderstandings and offences. It was not lost labour. Six and twenty were left in the morning; before night seven and fifty were joined together.

T. Walsh preached at five, but the room being too small, they were obliged to go into the yard. In the evening we had high and low, rich and poor, both in the yard and adjoining gardens. There seemed now to be a general call to this city. So I thought it best the next morning, Monday 10, to leave Mr. Walsh there, while I went forward to Clonmel, the pleasantest town beyond all comparison which I have yet seen in Ireland. It has four broad, strait streets of well-built houses, which cross each other in the centre of the town. Close to the walls, on the south side, runs a broad, clear river. Beyond this rises a green and fruitful mountain and hangs over the town. The vale runs many miles both east and west and is well cultivated throughout.

I preached at five in a large loft capable of containing five or six hundred people. But it was not full, many being afraid of its falling, as another did some years before, by which several of the hearers were much hurt, and one so bruised that she died in a few days.

Tue. 11. I was at a loss where to preach, the person who owned

[8] Cf. Job 38:37.

[9] John 3:7.

[10] I.e., in society membership.

[11] 1 Pet. 3:8.

the loft refusing to let me preach there or even in the yard below. And the commanding officer, being asked for the use of the barrack yard, answered, it was not 'a proper place'. 'Not', said he, 'that I have any objection to Mr. Wesley. I will hear him if he preaches under the gallows.' It remained to preach in the street, and by this means the congregation was more than doubled. Both the officers and soldiers gave great attention, till a poor man, special[12] drunk, came marching down the street, attended by a popish mob, with a club in one hand and a large cleaver in the other, grievously cursing and blaspheming, and swearing he would 'cut off the preacher's head'. It was with difficulty that I restrained the troopers, especially them that were not of the society. When he came nearer, the mayor stepped out of the congregation and strove by good words to make him quiet. But he could not prevail, on which he went into his house and returned with his white wand.

At the same time he sent for two constables, who presently came with their staves. He charged them not to strike the man, unless he struck first. But this he did immediately, as soon as they came within his reach, and wounded one of them in the wrist. On this the other knocked him down, which he did three times before he would submit. The mayor then walked before, the constables on either hand, and conducted him to the jail.

Wed. 12. In the evening I preached in the new house at Cork, very near as large as that in Dublin and far better finished in every respect, though at four hundred pounds less expense.

Mon. 17. Walking up the Redhouse Walk (which runs between two rows of meadows with the river winding through them and a chain of fruitful hills on the right hand and on the left), I saw the plain reason why strangers usually complain of the unwholesomeness of the water in Cork. Many women were filling vessels with the river water (which is that commonly used in the city for tea and most other purposes), when the tide was at the height. Now although this is not salt, yet it cannot but affect both the stomach and bowels of tender persons.

Wed. 19. I preached in the evening on 'Christ crucified, to the Jews a stumbling-block, and to the Greeks foolishness'.[13] While I was speaking a gentleman in the gallery cried out with a loud voice and swore to it: 'I am of the Church. I stand up for the Church.

[12] The adverbial use was uncommon even in Wesley's day.
[13] 1 Cor. 1:23.

I will shed my blood for the Church.' But finding none to contradict him, he sat down, and I finished my discourse.

Thur. 20. One came in a great consternation to inform us, Capt. F. (the gentleman who spoke) was raising a mob against the evening. This report spread up and down, and greatly increased the evening congregation. But no mob appeared, nor was there any disturbance, but such a blessing as we have seldom found—I suppose, in answer to the prayers of many who had been earnestly crying unto God.

On Sunday last I was desired by one to call on her dying father, though she said he was speechless and senseless. But as soon as I spoke he appeared sensible; while we prayed he recovered his speech. The next day he was able to walk abroad but continued deeply serious. On Friday 21 his illness returned, and he lay down and died in peace.

Mon. 24. I preached in the market-place at Kinsale.

Tue. 25. I walked to the Fort. It commands the entrance of the harbour and has three tier of guns, one over the other. It is built upon the firm rock, is of a large extent, and the upper part of a great height from the water. But all is out of repair: many of the cannon are dismounted, most of them unfit for service, so that many think a second rate man-of-war might take it in a few hours' time.

At one I preached in the Exchange. Abundance of soldiers, and the colonel, with several officers, were present. So that I conceived some hopes that the seed sown, even at Kinsale, will not all be lost.

At five I preached in the market-house at Inishannon[14] to a very large and well-behaved congregation, and then went on to Bandon.

Fri. 28. I rode out with Mrs. Jones,[15] as I did every day, to save her life, if possible. From the hill we had a fair view of Castle Bernard,[16] with the park adjoining, in which, a few years ago, Judge Bernard[17] used to take such delight. Indeed it is a beautiful place in every respect. The house is one of the most elegant I have

[14] Inishannon was a small township and substantial parish 12 miles south-west of Cork on the river Bandon and the main road from Cork to Bantry.

[15] The wife of Thomas Jones, merchant; see July 20, 1749, n. 34 (20:285 in this edn.); for her death, aged 71, see below, July 31, 1760.

[16] Orig., 'Barnard'.

[17] Orig., 'Barnard'. He died in 1721, great-grandfather of Francis, 1st Earl of Bandon. Cf. May 10, 1787.

seen in the kingdom, both as to the structure and the situation, standing on the side of a fruitful hill and having a full command of the vale, the river, and the opposite mountain. The ground near the house is laid out with the finest taste, in gardens of every kind, with a wilderness, canals, fishponds, waterworks, and rows of trees in various forms. The park includes part of each hill, with the river between, running through the meadow and lawns, which are tufted over with trees of every kind, and every now and then a thicket or grove. The judge finished his plan, *called the land after his name*, and dropped into the dust.

Sun. 30. I returned to Cork. About that time I received a letter from Mr. Gillies, part of which follows:

> The Lord hath been pleased to inflict a heavy stroke upon us, by calling home his faithful servant Mr. Wardrobe.[18] Concerning his death a Christian friend writes thus:
>
> 'May 7, Four in the morning. I am just come from witnessing the last sighs of one dear to you, to me, and to all that knew him. Mr. Wardrobe died last night. He was seized on sabbath last, just as he was going to the kirk, with a most violent cholic, which terminated in a mortification of his bowels. The circumstances of his death are worthy to be recorded. With what pleasure he received the message and went off in all the triumph of a conqueror! Crying out, "My warfare is accomplished." "I have fought the good fight." "My victory is completed. Crowns of grace shall adorn this head" (taking off his cap), "and palms be put into these hands. Yet a little while, and I shall sing for ever, 'I know that my Redeemer liveth.'" When he was within a few moments of his last he gave me his hand and a little after said, "Now lettest thou thy servant depart in peace; for mine eyes have seen thy salvation." Were I to repeat half what he spoke I should write you three hours. It shall suffice at this time to say, that as he lived the life, so he died the death of a Christian. We weep not for him; we weep for ourselves. I wish we may know how to improve this awful judgment, so as to be also ready, not knowing when our Lord cometh.'

Mr. Adams,[19] minister of Falkirk, writes thus:

> On Friday night, about ten, I witnessed Mr. Wardrobe of Bathgate's entrance into the joy of his Lord. But ah! Who can help

[18] See above, May 22, 1755, n. 44.

[19] John Adams (*c.* 1703–57) minister of Falkirk from 1744, when he was also Moderator of the General Assembly; he was a leader on the popular side. He wrote *An Inquiry into the Powers Committed to the General Assemblies of this Church* (Glasgow, 1754).

mourning the loss to the Church of Christ? His amiable character gave him a distinguished weight and influence, which his Lord had given him to value, only for its subserviency to his honour and glory. He was suddenly taken ill on the last Lord's Day, and from the first moment believed it was for death. I went to see him on Thursday evening and heard some of the liveliest expressions of triumphant faith, zeal for the glory of Christ and the salvation of souls, mixed with the most amiable humility and modesty. 'Yet a little while', said he, 'and this mortal shall put on immortality. Mortality shall be swallowed up of life, this vile body fashioned like to his glorious body! O for the victory! I shall get the victory. I know in whom I have believed.' Then with a remarkable audible voice, lifting up his hands he cried out, 'O for a draught of the well of the water of life, that I may begin the song before I go off to the Church Triumphant! I go forth in thy name, making mention of thy righteousness, even thine only. I die at the feet of mercy.' Then, stretching out his arms, he put his hand upon his head, and with the most serene and steady, majestic eye I ever saw, looking upward, he said, 'Crowns of grace, crowns of grace, and palms in their hands! O Lord God of truth, into thy hands I commend my spirit!' After an unexpected revival, he said, 'Oh, I fear his tarrying, lest the prospect become more dark. I sometimes fear he may spare me to live, and be less faithful than he has helped me to be hitherto.' He says to me, 'You that are ministers, bear a proper testimony against the professors of this age, who have a form of godliness without the power.' Observing some of his people about his bed, he said, 'May I have some seals among you! O where will the ungodly and sinners of Bathgate appear? Labour all to be in Christ.' Then he stretched out his hand to several and said, 'Farewell, farewell, farewell! And now, O Lord, what wait I for? My hope is in thee!' Once or twice he said, 'Let me be laid across the bed to expire, where I have sometimes prayed and sometimes meditated with pleasure.' He expressed his grateful sense of the assiduous care which Mr. Wardrobe of Cult had taken of him, and on his replying, 'Too much could not be done for so valuable a life,' said, 'O speak not so, or you will provoke God. Glory be to God that I have ever had any regard paid me, for Christ's sake.' I am greatly sunk under the event. O help me by your prayers to get the proper submission and improvement.

Thursday, June 3, I received a remarkable letter from a clergyman with whom I had been a day or two before. Part of it ran thus:

I had the following account from the gentlewoman herself, a person of piety and veracity. She is now the wife of Mr. J—— B——, silversmith in Cork.

'About thirty years ago I was addressed by way of marriage by Mr. Richard Mercier, then a volunteer in the army. The young gentleman was quartered at that time in Charleville, where my father lived, who approved of his addresses and directed me to look upon him as my future husband. When the regiment left the town, he promised to return in two months and marry me. From Charleville he went to Dublin, thence to his father's, and from thence to England, where, his father having bought him a cornetcy of horse, he purchased many ornaments for the wedding, and returning to Ireland let us know that he would be at our house in Charleville in a few days. On this the family was busied to prepare for his reception and the ensuing marriage, when one night, my sister Molly and I being asleep in our bed, I was awakened by the sudden opening of the side-curtain and starting up saw Mr. Mercier standing by the bedside. He was wrapped up in a loose sheet and had a napkin folded like a night-cap on his head. He looked at me very earnestly and lifting up the napkin, which much shaded his face, showed me the left side of his head, all bloody and covered with his brains. The room meantime was quite light. My terror was excessive, which was still increased by his stooping over the bed and embracing me in his arms. My cries alarmed the whole family, who came crowding into the room. Upon their entrance, he gently withdrew his arms and ascended as it were through the ceiling. I continued for some time in strong fits. When I could speak I told them what I had seen. One of them a day or two after, going to the postmaster for letters, found him reading the newspapers, in which was an account that Cornet Mercier, going into Christ Church belfry in Dublin, just after the bells had been ringing, and standing under the bells, one of them which was turned bottom upwards suddenly turning again, struck one side of his head and killed him on the spot. On further inquiry we found he was struck on the left side of his head.'

Sun. 6. I gave my last exhortation to the society in Cork, and setting out early on Monday 7, in the evening came to Limerick.

Sat. 13 [i.e., 12]. The account which one of our sisters gave of Ann Beauchamp was as follows:

August 18, 1753. I went to see S[ister] Beauchamp, who had been ill for about a week. I asked her in what state she found her soul. She answered, I am quite happy. I know that my Redeemer liveth and has taken away all my sins. And my heart is comforted with the presence of God: I long to die, that I may be with him. I asked, But are you resigned either to live or die, as he shall see fit? She answered, I cannot say I am willing to live—it would go hard with me to live now. Pray that the Lord may perfect his work of sanctification in my soul.

Being asked if she could freely part with all her friends, she said, Yes; and as to my children, I have cast them upon the Lord. I know he will take care of them, and I give them freely up to him without one anxious thought. She then prayed for her friends and acquaintance, one by one, and afterward fervently and with tears for each person in her band; then for Mr. John Wesley, desiring she might be found at his feet in the day of the Lord.

Soon after, she called her mother, desired forgiveness for anything wherein she had ignorantly offended her, and exhorted her not to grieve, adding, God will comfort you and give you strength to bear your trial. It is your loss, but it is my everlasting gain, and I am going but a little before you. She then prayed over her and, kissing her, took her leave. In the same manner she took leave of all about her, exhorting, praying for, and kissing them one by one. Afterward she called for and took her leave of her servants.

Seeing one of her neighbours in the room, she called her and said, O Mary, you are old in years and old in sin. The Lord has borne long with you, and you know not the day or the hour when he will call you. I am young, and he is calling me away; and what should I do without an interest in Christ? Was my work now to do, it would never be done; but blessed be God, it is not. I know the Lord hath washed me from my sins in his own blood and is preparing me for himself. O fly from the wrath to come and never rest till you rest in the wounds of Jesus! I am almost spent, but had I strength I could exhort you all till morning.

To another she said, Martha, Martha! Thou art careful and troubled about many things. But one thing is needful. And this one thing you have neglected. O seek God, and he will supply all your wants. It is time for you to begin: your glass is almost run, and what will all your toil profit when you come to be as I am now? Find time for this, whatever goes undone. My neighbours used to wonder how I could find time, and think me foolish for spending it so. But now I know it was not foolishness. Soon I shall receive an exceeding great reward.

Perhaps some of you will say, you was never called. Then remember, I call you now. I exhort every one of you to seek the Lord while he may be found. Think not to make excuses in that day: God will have his witnesses. And I shall appear as a witness against you. If you repent not, these my dying words will rise up in judgment against you.

To her ——— she said, I forgive you all that you have done against me. And I have prayed the Lord to forgive you. Return to him now, and he will receive you, for he desires not the death of a sinner. I am a witness of this, for he has forgiven all my sins. Oh! I want strength to sing his praise! But I am going where I shall sing his praise for ever.

Then calling for her husband she said, My dear, God has given you many calls, even in dreams. And when we will not hear his call, it is often his way to make us feel his rod by removing our darling from us. I was *your* darling. And seeing you refused the many calls of God, he is now taking me away from you, if by any means he may bring you to himself. She then prayed for and took her leave of him.

The next day when I came in and asked, How do you find yourself now? she answered, Blessed be God, very well. I know that my Redeemer lives. He is dear to me, and I am dear to him. I know he is preparing me for himself, and I shall soon be with him.

She then prayed earnestly for entire sanctification, till, a friend coming in, she said, The Lord has brought you and all my dear friends to my remembrance. I have not forgotten you in my prayers. You must come and pray my last prayer. When you see me near my deliverance, go all to prayer and continue therein till my spirit is gone. Let there be no crying over *me*, but all of you sing praises and rejoice over me.

She never once complained of her pain but behaved from the beginning with that patience, sweetness, and love to all, that bespoke a soul which knew herself just entering into the joy of her Lord. This she did[20] the next morning, August the 20th, after crying out as in an ecstasy:

> Bold I approach the eternal throne,
> And claim the crown through Christ my own.

Wed. 16. I rode over to Newmarket and preached to an earnest congregation of poor people. In the morning, at the request of some of the neighbouring gentry, I deferred preaching till ten o'clock. Many of them were then present and seemed not a little astonished. Perhaps they may remember it—a week.

In the afternoon I rode to Ballingarrane,[21] a town of Palatines,[22]

[20] *Works* (1774), 'Thus she died', apparently a hasty correction of a supposed printing error, made without realizing that 'Thus she did' referred to 'entering into the joy of her Lord'.

[21] Orig., 'Ballygarrane'.

[22] In 1709 during the ravages of Louis XIV in the Palatinate, many poor Protestant

which came over in Queen Anne's time. They retain much of the temper and manner of their own country, having no resemblance of those among whom they live. I found much life among this plain, artless, serious people. The whole town came together in the evening and praised God for the consolation. Many of those who are not outwardly joined with us walk in the light of God's countenance;[23] yea, and have divided themselves into classes in imitation of our brethren, with whom they live in perfect harmony.

Fri. 18. In examining the society I was obliged to pause several times. The words of the plain, honest people came with so much weight as frequently to stop me for a while and raise a general cry among the hearers. I rode back through Adare, once a strong and flourishing town, well-walled and full of people, now without walls and almost without inhabitants: only a few poor huts remain. At a small distance from these are the ample ruins of three or four convents, delightfully situated by the river, which runs through a most fruitful vale.

Mon. 21. I talked with one who was in deep distress. She had been represented to me as in despair. But I soon found her disorder (natural or preternatural) had nothing to do with religion. She was greatly troubled but knew not why—not for her sins; they scarce came into her mind. I know not that prayer will avail for her till she is troubled in quite another manner, till she cries out from her inmost soul, 'God be merciful to me a sinner!'[24]

Tue. 22. I called on Mrs. F——, whom I saw some years since in despair of quite another kind. Between nine and ten years ago her daughter married without her consent. This was followed by other distressing circumstances, in the midst of which she cried out, 'God has forsaken me.' She was immediately seized with violent pain. She could not see the sun or the light, only a dim twilight. She could not taste her meat or drink, any more than the white of an egg. She had a constant impulse to kill herself, which she believed she must do, and attempted several times. After

refugees were brought off by the Royal Navy, and some 800 families of them were settled in Limerick and Kerry where they distinguished themselves by sober industry though (in Lecky's view) not beyond the advantages conferred by their leases (Lecky, *Ireland*, 1:351-52). Methodist penetration of this community began with preaching by Thomas Williams in 1749 and took deep root, proving compatible with their German traditions and continued affection for the Luther Bible (cf. May 12, 1749, n. 75, 20:272 in this edn.). For population of Limerick, see 'New Geography of Ireland', which gives the population of Limerick in 1760 as 25,480 in 3,640 houses; quoted in D. Macpherson, *Annals of Commerce* (London, 1805; repr. New York, 1972), 3:325.

[23] See Ps. 89:15.

[24] Luke 18:13.

having continued thus three years and an half, she resolved to endure it no longer. Accordingly she procured a knife to cut her throat, and did cut through the skin but could get no further. It seemed to her as if the flesh were iron. She threw down the knife, burst into tears, fell upon her knees, and began (what she had not done all the time) to pour out her soul before God. Fear and sorrow fled away. She rejoiced in God. She saw the light of the sun. Her natural taste returned. And she has been ever since in health of body and peace of mind.

Wed. 23. I took my leave of Limerick and rode to Sixmilebridge.[25] There I left T. Walsh to preach in Irish, and went on to Rathlaheen.[26]

Thur. 24. I went on to Ennis, a town consisting almost wholly of Papists, except a few Protestant gentlemen. One of these (the chief person in the town) had invited me to his house and walked with me to the court-house, where I preached to an huge, wild, unawakened multitude, Protestants and Papists, many of whom would have been rude enough, if they durst.

Fri. 25. Mr. Walsh preached at six, first in Irish and then in English. The papist[27] priest had contrived to have his service just at the same hour. And his man came again and again with his bell, but not one in ten of his people would stir. At eight I preached to a far more serious congregation. And the word seemed to sink into their hearts.

We took horse about ten and rode through the fruitful and pleasant country[28] of Galway. After having heard so much of the barrenness of this county, I was surprised to observe in riding almost the whole length of it, from south-east to north-west, to find only four or five miles of rocky ground like the west of Cornwall; all the rest exceeded most that I have seen in Ireland. We came to Galway pretty well tired and would willingly have rested at the inn where we alighted from our horses, but the landlord informed us he had no room: both his house and stables were full. Two regiments of soldiers passing through the town had taken up all the inns. However, we procured a private lodging which was full as agreeable.

[25] Orig., 'Six Mile Bridge'.

[26] Orig., 'Rathlahine'. This is presumably the modern seat, Rathlaheen, 3 miles south-east of Newmarket.

[27] Used both as an adjective (similar to 'popish') and a noun, instead of 'Papist', now only in dialect (see *OED*).

[28] 1774, 'county'.

The town is old, and[29] not ill built, most of the houses being of stone and several stories high. It is encompassed with an old, bad wall and is in no posture of defence, either toward the land or toward the sea. Such is the supine negligence of both English and Irish!

Five or six persons, who seemed to fear God, came to us at our lodgings. We spent a little time with them in prayer, and early in the morning set out for Castlebar.

This day likewise I was agreeably surprised at the pleasantness and fruitfulness of the country. About noon, two or three friends met us and begged us to turn aside to Hollymount, a town twelve miles from Castlebar, where the minister[30] readily consented to my preaching in the church. Many Papists as well as Protestants were there, and my heart was much enlarged toward them. Through a delightful mixture of vales and gently-rising[31] hills we then rode on to Castlebar.

Sun. 27. The rector[32] having left word that I should have the use of the church, I preached there morning and afternoon to such a congregation as (they said) was never there before. And surely the Word of God had free course: I saw not one light or inattentive hearer. Mr. Walsh afterward preached in the sessions-house to another large and serious congregation. And Tuesday 29, being St. Peter's Day, I read prayers and preached to as large a congregation as on Sunday. In the afternoon I rode over to Newport, eleven miles from Castlebar. About thirty years ago a little company of Protestants settled here by a riverside, on the very extremity of the land, and built a small town. It has a fruitful hill on each side and a large bay to the west, full of small fertile islands, containing from one to several thousand acres. Of these they compute above three hundred, and near an hundred are inhabited, but by Papists alone, there not being so much as a

29 1774 only adds 'old, and'.

30 James Clark, now acting for the rector of Hollymount, who published a huge anti-Methodist tract based on a sermon preached at Hollymount in 1756, entitled *Montanus Redivivus; or Montanism Revived, in the Principles and Discipline of the Methodists (commonly called the Swadlers)* (Dublin, 1760). JW heard of the sermon and replied to it with a copy of his sermon on 'Catholic Spirit', a gesture which led to correspondence. JW's letters are printed in Telford, 3:181, 199. Many of Mrs. Delany's letters were written from Hollymount, not (as she said) 'Holy Mount . . . a *hired place* the Dean [of Down, her husband] has taken till a Deanery-house is built.' Lady Llanover, ed., *The Autobiography and Correspondence of Mary Grenville, Mrs Delany*, 6 vols. (London, 1861–62), 2:370.

31 Orig., 'gentle-rising', altered in 1774.

32 Thomas Ellison (1698–1761), vicar of Castlebar, 1731–61, having been curate from 1721. He entered Trinity College, Dublin, 1718; B.A., 1720; M.A., 1730.

single Protestant among them! I went directly to the rector's,[33] who had before given me an invitation. Between seven and eight, I preached to (I suppose) more than all the Protestants in the town. Deep attention sat on every face. Perhaps God touched some hearts.

Wed. 30. At eleven Mr. H[ern] read prayers, and I preached on Gal. 6:14. The church stands at a distance from the town, and it rained hard, but that could not stop the congregation. In the afternoon I returned to Castlebar.

Thursday, July 1. There is just such a work here as was some years since at Athlone. The whole town is *pleased*, but few are *convinced*. The stream runs very wide but very shallow.

Sun. 4. I read prayers and preached at Ballyhean, Mr. E[llison]'s[34] other church. The congregation at Castlebar in the afternoon was larger than ever before. In the morning, Monday 5, the greater half of them were present, and we had a solemn parting. In the afternoon we came to Hollymount, some years since one of the pleasantest places in Ireland. Dr. Vesey,[35] then Archbishop of Tuam, fixed on this spot, nine miles from his see, built a neat commodious house on a little eminence, laid out fruit- and flower-gardens round it, brought a river to run through them, and encompassed the whole with walks and groves of stately trees. When he had finished his plan, round a stone pillar which stands in a basin surrounded by a small green plat of ground he placed the following inscription:

Linquenda tellus, et domus, et placens
Uxor, cum numerosa et speciosa prole,
Chara charae matris sobole:
  Neque harum, quas colis, arborum
  Te praeter invisam cupressum
  Ulla brevem dominum sequetur![36]

[33] Rev. James Hern, rector of Newport, Galway. James Hern was scholar of Trinity College, Dublin, 1737; B.A., 1739. He was rector of Bamshoole, 1743–78.

[34] See note 32 above.

[35] John Vesey (1638–1716), Bishop of Limerick, 1673–79; Archbishop of Tuam, 1679 till his death, 1691. The son of a Presbyterian minister turned Episcopalian, he was educated at Trinity College, Dublin, taking his M.A. in 1667, and D.D. in 1672. After minor preferments, he was created dean of Cork in 1667, and then raised to the bench. Unpopular as an archbishop from having annexed a quarter of the tithes of the parishes of his see, he also suffered greatly at the hands of the native Irish, who did not take to his architectural improvements at the time of the Revolution. He died in the residence here described.

[36] Horace, *Odes*, II.xiv.21-24, with an interpolation in lines two and three by the author of the inscription or by JW himself (who gives the correct reading below, Oct. 13, 1779,

I was just going to preach in the churchyard, when Mr. C[lark] sent his son with the key of the church. Almost half the congregation were Papists, whom all the threats of their priest could not keep away. Not expecting to see any of them again, I spake very plain once for all.

In the morning we rode through Tuam,[37] a neat little town, scarce half so large as Islington; nor is the cathedral half so large as Islington church. The old church at Kilconnell, two miles from Aughrim, is abundantly larger. If one may judge by the vast ruins that remain (over all which we walked in the afternoon), it was a far more stately pile of building than any that is now standing in Ireland. Adjoining to it are the ruins of a large monastery; many of the cells and apartments are pretty entire. At the west end of the church lie abundance of skulls, piled one upon another, with innumerable bones round about, scattered as dung upon the earth. O sin, what hast thou done?

Wed. 7. I preached at Aughrim morning and evening, and then rode over to Castlegar.[38] Mr. M—— has now lost both his brother and his two daughters, two of the most agreeable women in the kingdom, caught away in the full bloom of youth and beauty—if they can be termed 'lost' who all committed their souls unto him they loved, in the full triumph of faith.

Thur. 8. A coachful of us, with several horsemen and others on foot, went to Ahascragh in the morning. The rest of the congregation were mostly Papists. But all heard with earnest attention. I preached in the evening at Athlone, where on Friday 9 we had a solemn watch-night.

Sun. 11. We had a blessed opportunity in the evening on the Connaught side of the river. Almost all the Protestants in the town were present, with abundance of Papists. And many of them

and in Sermon 28, 'Sermon on the Mount, VIII', 1:624 in this edn.). Thomas Jackson, in his third edition of Wesley's *Works*, translated the lines: 'You must leave behind you these grounds, this house, and your charming wife [with your numerous and handsome progeny, the endearing offspring of their beloved mother!]. And of all those trees which you are planting, none, except the loathed cypress, will follow you, their short-lived owner, to the tomb.'

37 Tuam, a substantial market town 16 miles north-west of Galway, was also the head of the largest diocese in Ireland, and the seat of an archbishop (down to the unions which commenced in 1834). The cathedral, which includes some of the finest Romanesque work in Ireland, was repaired in 1688, extensively damaged by fire in the 1780's, and largely rebuilt before 1878.

38 Orig., 'rode on to Castlegarr'. *Works* (1774) alters 'on' to the more accurate 'over', and alters the place to the much better known Castlebar, as do the editions of 1768 and 1788. It seems clear that Castlegar is intended, 2½ miles north-east of Galway.

acknowledged the doctrine of Christ *crucified* to be the power of God and the wisdom of God.[39]

Mon. 12. After preaching at Abbeyderg,[40] about noon I went on to Longford. Many supposed the mob would be too violent there to allow me a peaceable hearing. I began at five in the yard of the Old Barrack. An huge crowd soon flocked in, but most of the Papists stood at the gate or just without the wall. They were all still as night, nor did I hear an uncivil word while we afterwards walked from one end of the town to the other.

Tue. 13. A large congregation was present at five and stood unmoved, notwithstanding some heavy showers. At noon I preached at Cleggill,[41] at five in the Barrack Yard again, where the concourse of people was greater than before. Mr. P[iers],[42] the minister of a neighbouring parish, and another clergyman who came with him, received the truth in love; Mrs. P[iers] (his wife) found rest to her soul.

But how is it that almost in every place, even where there is no lasting fruit, there is so great an impression made at first upon a considerable number of people? The fact is this. Everywhere the work of God rises higher and higher till it comes to a point. Here it seems for a short time to be at a stay. And then it gradually sinks again.

All this may easily be accounted for. At first curiosity brings many hearers. At the same time God draws many by his preventing grace to hear his Word and comforts them in hearing. One then tells another. By this means, on the one hand, curiosity spreads and increases, and on the other, drawings of God's Spirit touch more hearts, and many of them more powerfully than before. He now offers grace to all that hear, most of whom are in some measure affected and, more or less moved with approbation of what they hear, desire to please God and [extend] goodwill to his messenger. These principles, variously combined and increasing, raise the general work to its highest point. But it cannot stand here. For in the nature of things curiosity must soon decline. Again, the drawings of God are not followed, and thereby the Spirit of God is grieved. The consequence is, he strives with

39 See 1 Cor. 1:23-24.

40 Orig., 'Abidarrig'; a village about 7 miles south of Longford railway station.

41 Orig., 'Cleg-hill'.

42 Fletcher Piers, (*c.* 1713–67), rector of Killashee from 1749 till his death. He graduated B.A. from Trinity College, Dublin, in 1733. Walter Shirley preached in his church in 1760. *Arminian Magazine* 20 (1797):407-8.

this and this man no more, and so his drawings end. Thus both the natural and supernatural power declining, most of the hearers will be less and less affected. Add to this that in the process of the work 'it must be that offences will come.'[43] Some of the hearers, if not preachers also, will act contrary to their profession. Either their follies or faults will be told from one to another and lose nothing in the telling. Men once curious to hear will now draw back; men once drawn, having stifled their good desires, will disapprove what they approved before and feel dislike instead of goodwill to the preacher. Others who were more or less convinced will be afraid or ashamed to acknowledge that conviction. And all these will catch at ill stories (true or false) in order to justify their change.[44] When by this means all who do not savingly believe have quenched the Spirit of God, the little flock goes on from faith to faith, the rest sleep on and take their rest.[45] And thus the number of hearers in every place may be expected first to increase and then decrease.

Wed. 14. At noon I preached at Coolalough, where the preachers and stewards met.

Thur. 15. In the evening, I preached at Tullamore in Barrack Street. And many who never had so much curiosity as to walk an hundred yards to hear the preaching vouchsafed to hear it at their own doors. In the middle of the sermon came a quarter-master, very drunk, and rushed in among the people. In a short time he slipped off his hat and gave all the attention of which he was capable. So did many of the soldiers and many officers. O let some lay it to heart!

Fri. 16. We walked down to Lord Tullamore's[46] (that was his title then), an old mile from the town. His gardens are extremely pleasant. They contain groves, little meadows, kitchen gardens, plats of flowers, and little orchards intermixed with fine canals and pieces of water. And will not all these make their owner happy? Not if he has one unholy temper! Not unless he has in himself a fountain of water, springing up into everlasting life.[47]

About this time I received a letter without a name, part of which I have subjoined:

[43] Cf.Matt. 18:7.

[44] 1768, 1788, 'to do justice to their charge'.

[45] See Matt. 26:45.

[46] Charles Moore (1712–64), 2nd Baron Moore of Tullamore, who in 1758 was created Earl of Charleville. He was twice Grand Master of the Freemasons, an Irish privy councillor, and governor of King's County.

[47] See John 4:14.

Sir,

Having observed your Christian condescension in those labours of love so truly calculated for the use of *common people*, I presume to beg your pen in behalf of the *next class* of God's creatures. And I would ask if nature, reason, and revelation do not all plead in favour even of the brute creation? Is it not *unnatural* and inhuman to put them to more pain than is necessary for the service of man? Can *reason* consent to the making sport with the life or misery of any creature? May not the great law of equity, doing as we would be done to, be extended even to them? May we not suppose ourselves in *their* place and thence determine what they may fairly expect from us? Hath not the Supreme Being given injunctions against cruelty toward them and commanded that they should enjoy the rest of his day? Did he not rebuke the prophet for smiting his beast without cause? And mention the 'much cattle' as one motive to the divine compassion in sparing the 'great city'? The Scripture saith, 'A good man is merciful to his beast.' And can he be a good man that is not so, if goodness consists in imitating him whose 'mercy is over all his works'? For 'he openeth his hand and satisfieth the desire of every living thing.'

If tenderness, mercy, and compassion to the brute creatures were impressed on the infant breast and conducted into action according to its little power, would it not be confirmed in the human heart? And might not this early prepossession be for ever established there and, through an happy bias, extend its benevolence to the whole creation?

Does not experience show the sad effects of a contrary education? While children, instead of being taught benevolence to irrationals, are suffered to torment first poor, little insects, and then every helpless creature that comes in their way; can it be expected that, being thus inured to cruelty and oppression even in their tender years, they should relent when they come to age, and be susceptible of compassion, even to rationals? It cannot. For is pity shown to man only because he has reason? If so, those would lose their claim to our compassion who stand in the greatest need of it, namely, children, idiots, and lunatics. But if pity is shown to all that are capable of pain, then may it justly be expected that we should sympathize with everything that has life.

I am persuaded, you are not insensible of the pain given to every Christian, every humane[48] heart, by those savage diversions, bull-baiting, cock-fighting, horse-racing, and hunting. Can any of these irrational and unnatural sports appear otherwise than cruel, unless through early prejudice or entire want of consideration and reflection? And if man is void of these, does he deserve the name of

[48] 1768, 1788, 'human'.

man? Or is he fit for society? And besides, how dreadful are the concomitant and the consequent vices of these savage routs! Yet such cowards are we grown, that scarce any man has courage to draw his pen against them!

Sat. 17. I preached in Tyrrellspass at five, and T. Walsh at eight. Hence we rode to Ballybeg,[49] near Drumcree, where we found a little company of earnest people, most of them rejoicing in the love of God. To these were added a few from the County of Cavan. Joseph Charles[50] going thither some time since, on temporal business, occasionally spoke of the things of God. Many believed his report, and some found his words 'the power of God unto salvation'.[51]

Sun. 18. A little before twelve (the usual hour in Ireland) the morning service began at Rosmead[52] church, where Mr. Booker[53] preached an useful sermon. I preached at five to abundance of plain country people and two coachfuls of gentry. O how hard is it for these to enter into the kingdom of heaven![54]

Mon. 19. No sooner did we enter Ulster than we observed the difference. The ground was cultivated just as in England, and the cottages not only neat, but with doors, chimneys, and windows. Newry, the first town we came to (allowing for the size) is built much after the manner of Liverpool. I preached soon after seven to a large congregation, and to great part of them at five in the morning. Afterwards I spoke to the members of the society, consisting of churchmen, Dissenters, and Papists (that were). But there is no striving among them, unless to 'enter in at the strait gate'.[55]

Wed. 21. In the morning there was such violent lightning, thunder, and rain, that the very beasts ran out of the fields, and the birds flew from their usual coverts to take shelter in the houses. But before we took horse the sky cleared up, and we had a pleasant ride to Terryhoogan,[56] near Scarva. The road lay on the edge of a smooth canal, with fruitful, gently-rising hills on either side. We were at a lone house, but the people found their way thither in the evening from all quarters. I preached in a meadow

[49] Ballybeg is 6¼ miles north-west of Navan, Co. Meath, and Drumcree 4 miles north-west of Delvin, Co. Westmeath.

[50] See May 7, 1749, n. 65 (20:271 in this edn.).

[51] Rom. 1:16.

[52] Rosmead is in Co. Westmeath, 1½ miles north-east of Delvin.

[53] See Aug. 2, 1752, n. 30 (20:435 in this edn.).

[54] See Mark 10:24.

[55] Luke 13:24.

[56] Orig., 'Terryhugan'. Scarva is a small village in Co. Down, 11 miles west of Newry.

near the house, the congregation sitting on the grass. And surely they had ears to hear. God give them hearts to understand!

Thur. 22. We rode through heavy rain to Lisburn. I preached in the market-house at seven. One man only gainsaid, but the bystanders used him so roughly that he was soon glad to hold his peace.

Fri. 23. The rector[57] with his curate called upon me, candidly proposed their objections, and spent about two hours in free, serious, friendly conversation. How much evil might be prevented or removed would other clergymen follow their example!

I rode in the afternoon to Belfast,[58] the largest town in Ulster. Some think it contains near as many people as Limerick; it is far cleaner and pleasanter. At seven I preached in the market-house to as large a congregation as at Lisburn, and to near the same number in the morning. But some of them did not stay till I concluded. They went away in haste when I showed how 'Christ crucified' is 'to the Greeks foolishness'.[59]

Hence we rode along the shore to Carrickfergus, said to be the most ancient town in Ulster. The walls are still, as it were, standing, and the castle built upon a rock. But it is little more than a heap of ruins, with eight or nine old, dismounted, rusty cannon. What it was in the reign of its founder, King Fergus, does not much concern us to know.

I preached in the sessions-house at seven to most of the inhabitants of the town. But Satan had prepared one of his instruments when I had done to catch the seed out of their hearts. A poor enthusiast[60] began a dull, pointless harangue, about hirelings and false prophets. But the doorkeeper crying out, 'I am going to lock the doors,' cut his discourse short.

Sun. 25. I preached at nine in the upper court-house, which was considerably larger than the other. James Relly[61] began his

[57] Richard Dobbs (1694–1775) was rector of Lisburn from 1743 till his death. He entered Trinity College, Dublin, in 1720, graduating B.A. in 1723, M.A. in 1726, B.D. and D.D. in 1750, and fellow in 1724. He was rector of Tullyhogue, 1731–45, and of Cloghenry, 1745–75. His monument in Lisburn churchyard states that 'he was a man of extensive learning, great piety and strict honesty; he lived respected and esteemed and died lamented in charity with all men.'

[58] In 1757, when the first regular census was made, Belfast contained 1779 houses and 8549 inhabitants, of whom only 556 were Catholics. About the same time Limerick was reckoned to contain some 3959 houses and over 25,000 inhabitants. Lecky, *Ireland*, 1:339, 343.

[59] 1 Cor. 1:23.

[60] Perhaps James Relly; see entry for July 25.

[61] See above, Apr. 3, 1755, n. 8.

bad work again, as soon as I had done speaking. But I walked quietly away, as did also the congregation.

At eleven I went to church, to the surprise of many, and heard a lively, useful sermon. After dinner one of our brethren asked if I was 'ready to go to the meeting'. I told him, 'I never go to a meeting.'[62] He seemed as much astonished as the old Scot at Newcastle, who left us 'because we were mere Church of England men'. We are so, although we condemn none *who have been brought up* in another way.

About five, even the larger court-house being too small to contain the congregation, I the more readily complied with the desire of the prisoners to preach in the street near the prison door. I spoke as plain and home as ever in my life, on 'Ye must be born again.'[63] Poor James was now resolved to speak and got on a little eminence on purpose. And what could hinder him? Why—

Vox faucibus haesit![64]

He cawed and cawed but could utter nothing, hardly three words together. This also hath God wrought.[65] He hath stopped the mouth of the gainsayer and preserved the weak from being offended.

Mon. 26. Mr. Walsh met me at Belfast and informed me that the day before he was at Newtown[ards] intending to preach. But while he was at prayer Mr. M[ortime]r came with a drunken mob, seized him by the throat, and dragged him along, till a stout man[66] seized him and constrained him to quit his hold. Mr. W[alsh], having refreshed himself at a friend's house, began a second time. But in a quarter of an hour Mr. M[ortimer], having rallied his mob, came again, on which Mr. W[alsh] gave him the ground and walked away over the fields.

In the evening I spoke very plain at Lisburn, both to the great vulgar and the small. But between Seceders, old self-conceited Presbyterians, New Light men, Moravians, Cameronians,[67] and

62 1768, 1788, 'I never go to meeting'—the more technical term for attending a Dissenting service.

63 John 3:7.

64 Virgil, *Aeneid*, ii.774: 'His voice stuck in his throat.'

65 See Num. 23:23, a favourite text of JW, frequently used thus.

66 Mr. Beers. Crookshank, *Ireland*, 1:116.

67 Many of these divisions arose from suspicions that 'old self-conceited Presbyterians' were no longer true to the Westminster Confession. The Seceders were those who began to apply to the Associate Presbytery in Scotland in the early 1740's for 'a supply of ordinances'; they increased rapidly but in 1747 divided into Burghers and Antiburghers,

formal churchmen, it is a miracle of miracles if any here bring forth fruit to perfection.[68]

The country between Lisburn and Moira is much like Berkshire, having fruitful vales on each side of the road and well-wooded hills running even with them at a small distance. At seven, I preached in the market-house at Lurgan. Many of the gentry were met in the room over it, it being the time of the assembly. The violins were just tuning. But they ceased till I had done, and the novelty (at least) drew and fixed the attention of the whole company.

Wed. 28. I read Mr. Barton's ingenious lectures on Lough Neagh near Lurgan,[69] which turns wood into stone and cures the King's Evil and most cutaneous distempers. Under part of this lake there is first a stratum of firm clay and under that a stratum of trees four foot thick, all compacted into one mass, doubtless by the pressure of the incumbent earth (perhaps water, too), which it has probably sustained ever since the general deluge.

In the evening we had the largest congregation which I have seen since we left Cork. It was almost as large at five in the morning. Why should we despair of doing good at Lurgan also?

Thur. 29. I preached at Newry, and the three following days; on Monday, August 2, I returned to Rosmead.[70]

Tue. 3. We rode to Tullamore through heavy rain, which a strong wind drove full in our face. The only *wild Irish* whom I have seen yet, a knot of officers, were present at preaching in the evening and behaved tolerably well.

Wed. 4. I preached at Portarlington in the evening, and was going to take horse in the morning, when a gentleman came and said he was just setting out for Dublin and would be glad of my

although the Scottish Burghers' oath did not concern the Irish at all. The Irish 'New Lights' had their origin among those at Belfast in 1720 who wished to avoid the divisions which had come among the English Dissenters by resisting doctrinal subscriptions as tests of orthodoxy. Attempts in the Ulster Synod to check the progress of Enlightenment were denounced by the Seceders in 1747 as the very essence of New Light doctrine. The Cameronians were those who sympathized with Scots of that description who had resisted the Scottish establishment of 1690; many of these now supported the Associate Presbytery, but some were caught up in the revival. J. S. Reid, *History of the Presbyterian Church in Ireland*, 3 vols. (London, 1835-53).

68 See Luke 8:14.

69 Richard Barton, *Lectures in Natural Philosophy, designed to be a foundation for reasoning pertinently upon the Petrifactions, Gems, Chrystals, and Sanative Quality of Lough Neagh in Ireland; and intended to be an Introduction to the Natural History of several Counties contiguous to that Lake* (Dublin, 1751). Barton also wrote poetry and theology.

70 Orig., 'August 1, . . . Rosmide', corrected only in *Works* (1774).

company in his chariot. I accompanied him to Johnstown, where we dined and then took horse and rode on to Dublin.

Fri. 6. On this and the next day, I finished my business in Ireland so as to be ready to sail at an hour's warning.

Sun. 8. We were to sail, the wind being fair. But as we were going aboard, it turned full east. I find it of great use to be in suspense. It is an excellent means of breaking our will. May we be [as] ready either to stay longer on this shore as to launch into eternity.[71]

On Tuesday evening I preached my farewell sermon. Mr. Walsh did the same in the morning. We then walked to the quay.[72] But it was still a doubt whether we were to sail or no, Sir T—— P——[73] having sent word to the captain of the packet[74] that if the wind was fair he would go over and, it being his custom (*hominis magnificentiam*!),[75] to keep the whole ship to himself. But the wind coming to the east he would not go; so about noon we went on board. In two or three hours we reached the *mouth* of the *harbour*. It then fell calm. We had five cabin passengers, beside Mr. Walsh, Haughton,[76] Morgan,[77] and me. They were all civil and tolerably serious; the sailors likewise behaved uncommonly well.

Thur. 12. About eight we begun singing on the quarter-deck, which soon drew all our fellow-passengers, as well as the captain, with the greatest part of his men. I afterwards gave an exhortation.

[71] 1768, 1788, altered the original to 'shore or to launch into eternity', probably a revision caused by the printer's omission of the first 'as'. The original used the earlier spelling 'lanch', altered in *Works* (1774) to 'launch'.

[72] Orig., 'the Key'.

[73] Probably Sir Thomas Parker (1695–1784), Lord Chief Baron of the Exchequer, 1742–72; knighted 1742.

[74] Orig., 'pacquet', as usual; in this edition, normally modernized to 'packet' without notice.

[75] 'The ostentation of the man!' Possibly an imitation of Plautus, *Menaechmi*, IV.iv.16 (615): *'Homini impudentem audaciam.'*

[76] John Haughton had been an itinerant since the 1740s; most of his service was spent in Ireland. After a successful spell of preaching in Dublin (1761) he obtained episcopal ordination. He became rector of Kilrea *c.* 1776, entertained JW there in 1778, and died soon afterwards. Crookshank, *Ireland,* 1:150, 306, 320.

[77] James Morgan (1736–74), after a religious quest of some years, began to preach in 1755 and became one of JW's helpers. He published three sermons on *The Crucified Jesus* (1772) and *The Life and Death of Mr. Thomas Walsh* (London, 1762), his fellow Irishman. Ill health led him to settle in Dublin, and in 1771 he gently rebuffed JW's suggestion that he was well enough to itinerate. A letter on his state of health was printed in *Arminian Magazine* 7 (1784):446-48. It is said that 'he afterwards sunk into deep *mysticism*, and that he buried his most excellent talent in the earth.' Charles Atmore, *The Methodist Memorial; being an Impartial Sketch of the Lives and Characters of the Preachers* (Bristol, Edwards, 1801), p. 286. Hereafter, Atmore *Memorial.*

We then spent some time in prayer. They all kneeled down with us. Nor did their seriousness wear off all the day. About nine, we landed at Holyhead after a pleasant passage of twenty-three hours.

Fri. 13. Having hired horses for Chester, we set out about seven. Before one we reached Bangor, the situation of which is delightful beyond expression. Here we saw a large and handsome cathedral but no trace of the good, old monks of Bangor, so many hundreds of whom fell a sacrifice at once to cruelty and revenge.[78] The country from hence to Penmaenmawr[79] is far pleasanter than any garden. Mountains of every shape and size, vales clothed with grass or corn, woods and smaller tufts of trees, were continually varying on the one hand, as was the sea prospect on the other. Penmaenmawr itself rises almost perpendicular to an enormous height from the sea. The road runs along the side of it so far above the beach that one could not venture to look down, but that there is a wall built all along about four foot high. Meantime, the ragged cliff hangs over one's head as if it would fall every moment.[80] An hour after we had left this awful place, we came to the ancient town of Conwy. It is walled round. And the walls are in tolerably good repair. The castle is the noblest ruin I ever saw. It is four-square and has four large round towers, one at each corner,[81] the inside of which have been stately apartments. One side of the castle is a large church, the windows and arches of which have been curiously wrought.[82] An arm of the sea runs round two sides of the hill on which the castle stands—once the delight of kings, now overgrown with thorns and inhabited by doleful birds only.

78 JW had clearly reached the cathedral town of Bangor on the south side of the Menai Straits. The monks whom he recalled belonged, however, to Bangor-is-y-coed in the Dee valley, 5 miles south-east of Wrexham. Their monastery was founded by Durawd, a northern chief, and Cyngen, Prince of Powis; and it refused to accept the customs of Rome from Augustine, who handed them over to public vengeance. When Ethelfrith, king of Northumbria, came against Wales, they were the first victims at the battle of Chester, 613. *WHS* 2 (1900):217.

79 Orig., 'Penmenmaur'; on the north Wales coast, 4 miles north of Conwy.

80 JW echoes the conventional travellers' view: 'The lines of the narrow road cut in the cliff, and rendered only less appalling with each generation are the burden of a score of writers. Dr. Johnson tells us how frightened he was at the prospect, and how relieved when he got safely to Bangor.' N. G. Bradley, *Highways and Byways in North Wales* (London, 1898), pp. 267-68. A new road over Penmaenmawr was constructed in 1772 with financial assistance from private citizens in Dublin and the Irish Parliament.

81 Orig., 'on each side', revised only in the errata and JW's own copy of his *Works* (1774).

82 JW here seems to have mistaken the Great Hall for the chapel, which was in the Chapel Tower. Williams, *Wesley in Wales*, p. 54.

About eight we reached Plas Bach,[83] where as soon as I named my name, William Roberts[84] received us with all gladness. But neither he nor any of his family could speak one sentence of English. Yet our guide helped us out pretty well. After supper we sung and went to prayers. Though they could not speak it, most of them understood English. And God spoke to their hearts.

Sat. 14. Several of the neighbours came early in the morning and gladly received a few words of exhortation. We then rode on through one of the pleasantest countries in the world, by Holywell to Chester. Here we had a comfortable meeting in the evening, as well as the next day, both in the room[85] and in the square.

Mon. 16. The rain was suspended while I preached to a large and quiet congregation.

Tue. 17. I rode to Bolton. Though I came unexpected, the house was well filled. After resting a day, on Thursday 19, I went on to Manchester and preached in the evening to a large congregation without the least disturbance. The tumults here are now at an end, chiefly through the courage and activity of a single constable.

Fri. 20. I rode to Chelmorton in the Peak. Although the poor people had no previous notice, they supplied the want of it by sending quickly to the neighbouring villages. Between seven and eight the house was pretty well filled. And many of them were extremely thankful.

Sat. 21. We set out early and, after spending an hour at Ashbourne, hastened on to Lichfield.[86] But it was not without difficulty, the waters being out, to a very uncommon degree in many places. About eight we reached Wednesbury, tired enough. There we stayed the next day.

Mon. 23. We rode forward to Redditch. It had rained all the way, so that Mr. Walsh was obliged to go to bed as soon as we

[83] Orig., 'Place-bagh'.

[84] William Roberts of Plas Bach, Llansanffraid Glan Conwy (d. 1760), was a Calvinistic Methodist. Converted by Peter Williams in 1748, he supported Howell Harris in the disruption of 1750, and in 1759, he moved with his wife and children to Y Geuffordd near Talgarth in Breconshire. His son Thomas joined his mother on his father's death and, in 1773, moved to Trevecca to join Howell Harris's family and to become later one of its trustees. It appears that JW had intended to pay this visit, probably on Howell Harris's suggestion, on his outward journey to Ireland. *WHS* 24 (1944):89; Williams, *Wesley in Wales,* p. 55.

[85] This was a barn rented in 1752, and re-erected in the same year, after it had been destroyed by a mob. F. F. Bretherton, *Early Methodism in and around Chester, 1749–1812* (Chester, 1903), pp. 29-35.

[86] Orig., 'Ashbourn', 'Litchfield'.

came in. Having dried some of our clothes, Mr. Bruce[87] and I took horse again about two, having one with us who knew the by-roads, the common road being unpassable through the floods. About five we came to a broad water,[88] which our guide did not care to pass. Mr. Bruce, seeing a foot-bridge, walked over it, leading his horse by a long rein through the water. But in an instant the horse disappeared. However, he soon emerged and gained the bank. I rode through at a small distance very safely, and in the evening preached at Evesham.

Tue. 24. Finding we could not ride the usual way, we procured another guide and rode by Andoversford[89] to Stroud. Mr. Jones[90] and my brother met us here.

Wed. 25. We rode on to Bristol.

Thur. 26. About fifty of us being met,[91] the Rules of the Society were read over and carefully considered one by one. But we did not find any that could be spared. So we all agreed to abide by them all and to recommend them with our might.

We then largely considered the necessity of keeping in the Church and using the clergy with tenderness. And there was no dissenting voice. God gave us all to be of one mind and one judgment.

Fri. 27. The Rules of the bands were read over and considered one by one; which, after some verbal alterations, we all agreed to observe and enforce.

Sat. 28. The rules of Kingswood School[92] were read and considered one by one. And we were all convinced, they were agreeable to Scripture and reason. In consequence of which it was agreed:

87 This Bruce has already appeared as a travelling companion of JW (see Jan. 19, 1754, n. 49; 20:484 in this edn.) and was to appear again as a companion into Scotland (see Apr. 9, 1772). The general context makes it unlikely that he was either the Welsh-speaking guide a week earlier (see above, Aug. 13, 1756) or the York doctor conjectured by Curnock (5:452, n. 3).

88 The general context suggests that this great flood was close to Evesham itself, a town surrounded on three sides by the river Avon and connected by a seven-arch bridge with the parish of Bengeworth which was within the borough. Samuel Lewis, *A Topographical Dictionary of England*, 4 vols. (4th edn., London, 1840), 2:172; hereafter, Lewis, *England.*

89 Orig., 'Andover Ford'.

90 Dr. John Jones; see Dec. 30, 1746, n. 3 (20:150 in this edn.).

91 JW's annual conference with the preachers lasted for three days.

92 These rules were summarized by JW in *A Plain Account of Kingswood School* (1781), a tract that he seems to have had by him in draft for a dozen years or more and that, among other things, answered the need recognized in the first of these resolutions; see Jackson, 13:294. A. G. Ives, *Kingswood School in Wesley's Day and Since* (London, Epworth Press, 1970), p. 89.

(1) That a short account of the design and present state of the school be read by every Assistant in every society; and

(2) That a subscription for it be begun in every place and (if need be) a collection made every year.

My brother and I closed the conference by a solemn declaration of our purpose, never to separate from the Church. And all our brethren concurred therein.[93]

For a few days I was laid up with a flux. But on Sunday, September 5, I crept out again and preached at Kingswood in the morning, and Stokes Croft in the afternoon. Mon. 6. I set out in the machine, and on Tuesday evening came to London.

Wednesday and Thursday I settled my temporal business. It is now about eighteen years since I began writing and printing books.[94] And how much in that time have I gained by printing? Why, on summing up my accounts, I found that on March 1, 1756 (the day I left London[95] last), I had gained by printing and preaching together a debt of twelve hundred and thirty-six pounds.

Fri. 10. I preached at a famous place commonly called 'The Bull and Mouth Meeting',[96] which had belonged, I suppose, near an hundred years to the people called Quakers. As much of real religion as was ever preached there, I trust, will be preached there still—and perhaps in a more rational, scriptural, and intelligible manner.

[93] An agreement never to separate from the Church, in the same terms as that of Mar. 16, 1752, was signed by fifteen preachers. *Wesleyan Methodist Magazine* 70 (1847):869.

[94] Wesley's literary labours in fact began in 1733, with his *Collection of Forms of Prayer for Every Day in the Week*, and by the end of 1739, he had published over a dozen items in several different categories, including two sermons, three collections of hymns, and several edited works; see *Bibliography*, Nos. 1-15, in this edn. Perhaps he is thinking of his peculiarly *evangelical* publications, which began in 1738, eighteen years earlier, with his sermon on *Salvation by Faith* and *The Doctrine of Salvation, Faith, and Good Works*, and had been preceded by eight other works. The Extracts from his *Journal*, however, did not begin until 1740. He may mean printing at his own expense, i.e., *publishing*.

[95] The connection between this entry and the next is that JW returned to London intending to print a new edition of his *Explanatory Notes Upon the New Testament* (1755). Charles Wesley to Samuel Walker, Sept. 6, 1756, printed in E. Sidney, *Life and Ministry of Samuel Walker* (2nd edn., London, 1838), pp. 228-29.

[96] This meeting-house in Bull and Mouth Street, leading from St. Martin's-le-Grand to Butcher Hall Lane, was built for the Quakers in the reign of Charles II and retained by them till 1760, when the Sandemanians took it over. They attracted the support of several Independent ministers. For the last occasion when JW preached there, see below, Dec. 21, 1763. W. Wilson, *History and Antiquities of Dissenting Churches and Meeting-houses in London*, 4 vols. (London, 1808–14), 3:364-65.

Sat. 11. I read over Mr. Fry's *Case of Marriage between near Relations considered*.[97] It is the best tract I ever read upon the subject—I suppose the best that is extant.[98] And two points, I think he has fully proved: (1) That many marriages commonly supposed to be unlawful are neither contrary to the law of nature nor the revealed law of God nor the law of the land. (2) That ecclesiastical courts have no right to meddle with any case of this kind.[99]

Thur. 16. I walked over to Bishop Bonner's,[1] and preached to a large and serious congregation. I found some faintness, the sun being extremely hot, but more in walking from thence to Westminster, where I preached at seven. In the night my old disorder returned and gradually increased in spite of all medicines. However, on Sunday and Monday it was so far suspended that I abated nothing of my usual employment.

Wed. 22. I was considering I had not yet asked help of the Great Physician, and I resolved to delay no longer. In that hour I felt a change. I slept sound that night and was well the next day.

Sunday, October 3. My disorder returned as violent as ever. But I regarded it not while I was performing the service at Snowsfields in the morning or afterward at Spitalfields,[2] till I went to the Lord's Table in order to administer. A thought then came into my mind. 'Why do I not apply to God in the beginning, rather than the end of an illness?' I did so and found immediate relief, so that I needed no farther medicines.

Tue. 5. I wrote a second letter to the authors of the *Monthly Review*—ingenious men, but no friends to the Godhead of Christ. Yet upon farther consideration I judged it best to drop the

[97] John Fry, *The Case of Marriages between near Kindred particularly considered* (London, 1756). The author was probably the Quaker, John Fry (1701–75). Born at Sutton Benger, Wilts., the son of a cloth merchant, he was apprenticed in London before 1717, and became a member of the Bull and Mouth Meeting. After moving to Yorkshire late in 1723, he returned to Sutton Benger in 1725, remaining for the rest of his life as a general dealer. He received a gift of ministry *c.* 1724. He was the father of Joseph Fry who founded the Bristol chocolate firm.

[98] The preceding sentence was added only in 1774.

[99] Cf. Wesley's re-reading of this work, Nov. 14, 1785, commenting: 'I think he has proved to a demonstration that no marriages are forbidden, either by the law of God or of England, but those of brothers and sisters, and those of the ascending and descending line. . . .'

[1] For Bishop Bonner's Hall, see Sept. 4, 1754, n. 1 (20:493 in this edn.).

[2] Orig., 'Spittle-fields', 'Spittalfields' in 1768, 'Spittlefields' in *Works* (1774).

controversy.[3] It is enough that I have delivered my own soul: 'if they scorn, they alone shall bear it.'[4]

Sun. 10. I preached to an huge multitude in Moorfields, on 'Why will ye die, O house of Israel?'[5] It is field preaching which does the execution still. For usefulness there is none comparable to it.

Mon. 11. I went to Leigh. Where we dined a poor woman came to the door with two little children. They seemed to be half starved, as well as their mother, who was also shivering with an ague. She was extremely thankful for a little food, and still more so for a few pills which seldom fail to cure that disorder.

In this little journey I read over a curiosity indeed, a French heroic poem—Voltaire's *Henriade*.[6] He is a very lively writer, of a fine imagination, and allowed, I suppose by all competent judges, to be a perfect master of the French language. And by him I was more than ever convinced that the French is the poorest, meanest language in Europe; that it is no more comparable to the German or Spanish than a bagpipe is to an organ; and that with regard to poetry in particular, considering the incorrigible uncouthness of their measure and their always writing in rhyme (to say nothing of their vile double rhymes, nay, and frequent false rhymes), it is as impossible to write a fine poem in French as to make fine music upon a Jew's harp.

Sat. 16. I baptized Hannah C——, late a Quaker. God, as usual, bore witness to his ordinance. A solemn awe spread over the whole congregation, and many could not refrain from tears.

Wed. 20. I received the following letter:

Rev. Sir,

The glory of God and the good of mankind are the motives that induce me to write the following. . . .

As it is our duty to do all we can to make all around us happy, I think there is one thing which may be done to promote so blessed an end, which will at the same time be very advantageous to them that practise it, namely, to efface all the obscene words which are written on houses, doors, or walls by evil-minded men. This which

[3] Neither of these letters protesting against 'the coupling the hymns of the Moravians and Methodists together', dated Sept. 9 and Oct. 5, 1756, actually appeared in the pages of the *Monthly Review*, but Wesley later published them himself in his *Arminian Magazine* (see vol. 27 in this edn.).

[4] Cf. Prov. 9:12.

[5] Ezek. 18:31; 33:11.

[6] The first English edition of Voltaire's *Henriade* (in French) was published at London, 1728.

I recommend to others, I constantly practise myself, and if ever I omit doing it I am severely checked unless I can produce some good reason for that omission. I do it with a sponge which for that purpose I carry in my pocket. The advantages I reap from hence are: (1) Peace of conscience in doing my duty. (2) It helps me to conquer the fear of man, which is one of my greatest trials. (3) It is matter of joy that I can do any, the least, service to anyone. And as all persons, especially the young, are liable to temptations to impurity, I can't do too much to remove such temptations, either from myself or others. Perhaps too, when the unhappy writers pass by and see their bad labours soon effaced, they may be discouraged from pursuing so shameful a work, yea, and brought to a better mind.

Perhaps in some places it might not be amiss in the room of what is effaced to write some serious sentence or short text of Scripture. And wherever we do this, would it not be well to lift up our heart to God in behalf of those sinners, in this or the like manner, 'Lord, lay not this sin to their charge'; 'Father, forgive them; for they know not what they do'?

Mon. 25. I began reading that excellent book, *The Gospel Glass*,[7] to the morning congregation—a method which I find more profitable for 'instruction in righteousness'[8] than any other manner of preaching.

Tue. 26. I began reading over with the preachers that were in town Mr. Pike's *Philosophia Sacra*.[9] It contains the marrow of Mr. Hutchinson's philosophy clearly and modestly proposed. But upon a close examination, I found the proofs were grievously defective. I shall never receive Mr. Hu[tchinson]'s creed, unless *ipse dixit*[10] pass for evidence.

Sat. 30. I yielded to importunity and spent an hour with poor Mr. V——, who was awakened and found peace in attending our preaching and soon after turned Quaker. I did wonder at it once,

[7] Lewis Stuckley (d. 1687), *A Gospel Glasse, Representing the Miscarriages of English Professors, &c.* (London, 1667). Stuckley was amongst the clergy ejected in 1662. JW read this work again just before his death. Diary, Jan. 19, 1791 (Curnock, 8:122). He probably read now from the abridgment he had published in vol. 33 of his *Christian Library* (1753).

[8] 2 Tim. 3:16.

[9] Little as JW cared for this work (see above, Jan. 17, 1756), he had mildly defended it against the *Monthly Reviewers* (see Telford, 3:205). Samuel Pike, at this time an Independent minister, resigned his charge and took over the Bull and Mouth Meeting, where JW had just preached, for the Sandemanians in 1766 (see above, Sept. 10, 1756, n. 96).

[10] 'He himself said it'.

but I do not now. One so full of himself might turn Papist or Mahometan.

Monday, November 1. Was a day of triumphant joy, as All Saints' Day generally is.[11] How superstitious are they who scruple giving God solemn thanks for the lives and deaths of his saints!

Tue. 9. Having procured an apparatus on purpose, I ordered several persons to be electrified,[12] who were ill of various disorders, some of whom found an immediate, some, a gradual cure. From this time I appointed, first some hours in every week and afterward some hours[13] in every day, wherein any that desired it might try the virtue of this surprising medicine. Two or three years after, our patients were so numerous that we were obliged to divide them; so part were electrified in Southwark, part at the Foundery, others near St. Paul's, and the rest near the Seven Dials. The same method we have taken ever since. And to this day, while hundreds, perhaps thousands, have received unspeakable good, I have not known one man, woman, or child, who has received any hurt thereby. So that when I hear any talk of the danger of being electrified (especially if they are medical men who talk so), I cannot but impute it to great want either of sense or honesty.

Fri. 12. I read over Leusden's dissertation in defence of the Hebrew points, and was fully convinced there is at least as much to be said on this as on the other side of the question.[14] But how is it that men are so *positive* on both sides, while demonstration is to be had on neither? Certainly to be peremptory and *dogmatical* can never be so inexcusable as in a point so doubtful as this!

Mon. 22. I read with the preachers this week the Glasgow abridgement of Mr. Hutchinson's *Works,* wherein the abridgers have expressed with surprising exactness not only his sense but his very spirit. But in truth I cannot admire either. Nay, I admire

[11] And was regularly kept as such by JW.

[12] On JW's interest in this subject see Oct. 9, 1747, n. 36 (20:195 in this edn.).

[13] *Works* (1774), 'an hour'.

[14] Leusden (1624–99) was a Dutch orientalist. It is not clear which of the works of Jan Leusden is here referred to, but it was probably a collection of dissertations over which he presided, published as *Philologus Hebraus-Graecus* (Utrecht, 1683). An English version of Leusden's *Hebrew and Caldick Grammar* was published at Utrecht, 1686. See also Wesley's reference to Peter Whitfield's dissertation on the same topic below, Apr. 25, 1757. Leusden's edition of the Greek NT had asterisked verses, which together included all the words used by the scripture writers; it was recommended by Francke and much used in the Holy Club as a means of getting up New Testament Greek quickly. Richard P. Heitzenrater, ed., *Diary of an Oxford Methodist; Benjamin Ingham, 1733–1734* (Durham, Duke University Press, 1985), pp. 15, 22, 232.

his hypothesis less and less, as I see the whole is unsupported by Scripture—very ingenious but quite precarious.[15]

Wednesday, December 1. One or two remarkable letters were put into my hands. Part of the first ran thus:

> Blessed be God, who desireth not the death of a sinner! It pleased him not to cut off my son in his sins. He gave him time to repent, and not only so, but a heart to repent. He showed him his lost estate by nature, and that unless he was reconciled to God by his Son and washed in his blood from all his sins, he could never be saved. After he was condemned at York for a robbery on the highway, I attended him in the condemned room. And blessed be God, he enabled me to preach the everlasting gospel to him. It was on Saturday he was condemned. It was on the Saturday following the Lord touched his heart. He then began to wrestle with God in prayer and left not off till Sunday in the afternoon, when God, who is rich in mercy, applied the blood of his Son and convinced him he had forgiven him all his sins. He felt his soul at peace with God and longed to depart and to be with Christ. The following week his peace increased daily, till on Saturday, the day he was to die, he came out of the condemned room clothed in his shroud and went into the cart. As he went on, the cheerfulness and composure of his countenance were amazing to all the spectators. At the place of execution, after he had spent some time in prayer, he rose up, took a cheerful leave of his friends, and said, 'Glory be to God for free grace.' His last words were, 'Lord Jesus, receive my soul.'

Part of the other letter, wrote by himself to his wife, was as follows:

> Righteous is the Lord, and just are his judgments! His hand of justice cuts my life short, but his hand of mercy saves my soul. You

[15] There is a mistake here. JW or his printer may have been led into error by recollection of recent polemical entries against the theories of John Hutchinson, and may have intended to refer to Francis Hutcheson (1694–1746), an Ulster Presbyterian, who in 1729 became Professor of Moral Philosophy at Glasgow and exercised a powerful influence on the Scottish common-sense school. The work then referred to would be: Francis Hutcheson, *A System of Moral Philosophy to Which is Prefixed Some Account of the Life, Writings and Character of the Author*, by Dr. William Leachman, 2 vols. (Glasgow, 1755). The short title used by JW, however, more closely resembles that of *An Abstract from the Works of John Hutchinson, Esq.; being a Summary of his Discoveries in Philosophy and Divinity*, of which there were Edinburgh and London, but not Glasgow, editions in 1753 and 1755. JW again refers erroneously to the Glasgow abridgment of Hutchinson's works below (see July 31, 1758). That JW actually refers to Hutchinson here, is suggested by a summary of his views in the *Survey of the Wisdom of God in Creation*, introduced by the phrase 'Mr. Hutchinson (not the professor of Glasgow, but a private English gentleman) supposes . . .' (2nd edn., Bristol, 1770), 3:276 (see also vol. 17 in this edn.).

for one are a witness of the course of life I led. Were it in my power I would gladly make amends to you and everyone else that I have wronged. But seeing it is not, I hope that God, and you, and everyone else, will accept of my willing mind. In a few hours now I shall be delivered out of this miserable world. But glory be to God, he has given repentance and remission of sins to me, the worst of sinners. He has taken away the sting of death, and I am prepared to meet my God. Let my example encourage every sinner to forsake sin and come unto God through Jesus Christ. As a dying man I give you this advice, Give yourself wholly up to God. Pray to him and never rest till you have secured an interest in the blood of Christ. Live in his fear, and you (as well as I) shall die in his favour. So no more from,

Your dying husband,
Richard Varley.[16]

York Castle,
August 20

Mon. 6. I began reading to our preachers the late Bishop of Cork's excellent treatise on *Human Understanding*[17]—in most points far clearer and more judicious than Mr. Locke's, as well as designed to advance a better cause.

Fri. 10. A person, who was dying of a cancer in her breast and deeply convinced of sin, sent a post-chaise in which I went to her at Epsom. I left her on Saturday morning in strong hope she should not go hence till her eyes had seen his salvation.[18]

In my fragments of time in the following week I read Mr. Hanway's accurate history of Shah Nadir, commonly called Kouli Khan—a scourge of God indeed![19] A prodigy of valour and conduct, but an unparalleled monster of rapine and cruelty. Alexander the Great, yea Nero or Domitian, was an innocent in comparison of him.

[16] Richard Varley was executed at the Tyburn outside Micklegate Bar, York, on Aug. 28, 1765, for highway robbery. W. Knipe, *Criminal Chronology of York Castle* (York, 1867), pp. 64-65.

[17] Peter Browne, *The Procedure (or Progress), Extent, and Limits of Human Understanding* (London, 1729), a work long highly esteemed by JW. Browne (*c.* 1665–1735), became a fellow of Trinity College, Dublin, 1692; provost, 1699; and Bishop of Cork and Ross in 1710. Cf. A. R. Winnet, *Peter Browne, Provost, Bishop, Metaphysician* (London, 1974).

[18] See Luke 2:30.

[19] Jonas Hanway, *An Historical Account of the British Trade over the Caspian Sea: with a journal of Travels from London through Russia, into Persia, and back again through Russia, Germany and Holland. To which is added the Revolutions during the present Century, with the Particular History of the great Usurper, Nadir Kouli*, 4 vols. (London, 1753; repr., 2 vols., 1754).

Sun. 26. I buried the remains of Joseph Yarner, an Israelite indeed.[20] The peace which filled his heart during his last hours gave such a bloom to his very countenance as remained after death, to the surprise of all who remembered the cloud that used to hang upon it.

Monday, January 3, 1757. I visited a poor dying backslider, full of good resolutions. But who can tell when these imply a real change of heart? And when they do not, when they spring from fear only, what will they avail before God?

Mon. 10. I walked to Bishop Bonner's, with Mr. D——,[21] lately entered at Cambridge, full of good resolutions. May God continue him humble and simple of heart! Then his sense and learning will do him good. But how great are the odds against him!

Sat. 22. I called upon one who did run well for several years. But for a considerable time he had cast off the very form of religion. Yet his heart was not utterly hardened. He determined to set out once more. And since that time he has been more confirmed in walking suitably to the gospel.

Fri. 28. Mr. Meier, chaplain to one of the Hanoverian regiments, called and spent an hour with me. I am surprised at the seriousness of all the German ministers with whom I have had occasion to converse—entirely different from that pertness and affectation of wit which is too common in our own country.[22]

The following letter (which I received two or three months after) was dated on this day:

> Though you and I may differ in some little things, I have long loved you and your brother, and wished and prayed for your success as zealous revivers of experimental Christianity. If I differ from you in temper and design, or in the essentials of religion, I am sure the error must lie on my side. Blessed be God for hearts to love one another!
>
> As I knew your correspondence must be very extensive and your labours various and incessant, I intended to have kept my peculiar love for you a secret till we arrived where seas shall no more roll

[20] John 1:47.

[21] Of the tiny handful of alumni whose listings in Venn in any way correspond to this description, all had outstandingly successful careers. The one most likely to be referred to here is Robert Dowbiggin (1737–94), who was admitted sizar at St. John's on Jan. 10, 1755, and matriculated in Michaelmas 1757. He graduated 10th wrangler in 1760, and ended up prebendary and sub-dean of Lincoln in 1769, and chaplain to the bishop.

[22] For a similar comment on the seriousness of the German clergy, cf. Jan. 6, 1778.

between us. But your late pious charity[23] constrains me to give you the trouble of a letter. I am confident God will attend it with his blessing and render you useful at the distance of near four thousand miles.

How great is the honour God has conferred upon you in making you a restorer of declining religion! And after struggling through so much opposition and standing almost single, with what pleasure must you behold so many raised up, zealous in the same cause, though perhaps not ranked under the same name nor openly connected with you!

I am endeavouring in my poor manner to promote the same cause in this part of our guilty globe. My success is not equal to my wishes, but it vastly surpasses both my deserts and my expectation. I have baptized near an hundred and fifty adult Negroes, of whom about sixty are communicants. Unpolished as they are, I find some of them have the art to dissemble. But, blessed be God, the generality of them, as far as I can learn, are real Christians. And I have no doubt but sundry of them are genuine children of Abraham. Among them, in the first place, and then among the poor white people, I have distributed the books you sent me.

I desire you to communicate this to your brother as equally intended for him. And let me and my congregation, particularly my poor Negro converts, be favoured with your prayers. In return for which I hope neither you nor your cause will be forgotten by

Reverend sir,
Your affectionate fellow-labourer,
and obliged servant,
Samuel Davies.[24]

Hanover (in Virginia)
Jan. 28, 1757

Sun. 30. Knowing God was able to strengthen me for his own work, I officiated at Snowsfields as usual before I went to West Street, where the service took me up between four and five hours. I preached in the evening and met the society, and my strength was as my day. I felt no more weariness at night than at eight in the morning.

Sunday, February 6. The number of communicants at Spitalfields made this Lord's day a little more laborious than the former. But God added proportionably to my strength. So I felt no difference.

[23] JW had sent a present of books.
[24] Orig., 'Davis'. For Davies, see above, July 27, 1755, and n. 77.

Thur. 10. At the request of the author I took some pains in correcting an ingenious book, shortly to be published.[25] But the more I consider them, the more I doubt of all systems of astronomy. I doubt whether we can certainly know either the distance or magnitude of any star in the firmament. Else why do astronomers so immensely differ, even with regard to the distance of the sun from the earth? Some affirming it to be only three,[26] others ninety, millions of miles!

About this time the following note was given into my hand at Wapping:

> John White, master at arms, aboard his Majesty's ship *Tartar*, now at Plymouth, desires to return Almighty God thanks for himself and all the ship's company, for their preservation in four different engagements they have had with four privateers which they have taken, particularly the last, wherein the enemy first boarded them. They cleared the deck, boarded in their turn, and took the ship, thirty of the enemy being killed and fifty more wounded. Only two of our crew were wounded, who, it is hoped, will recover.

Wed. 16. Calling on a friend, I found him just seized with all the symptoms of a pleurisy. I advised him to apply a brimstone plaster, and in a few hours he was perfectly well. Now, to what end should this patient have taken a heap of drugs and lost twenty ounces of blood? 'To what end? Why, to oblige the doctor and apothecary.' Enough! Reason good!

Tue. 22. I preached at Deptford. Even this wilderness does at length 'blossom and bud as the rose'.[27] Never was there such life in this little flock before nor such an increase in the number of hearers.

The following letter was wrote on Saturday 28:

> Reverend and dear Sir,
>
> When I was at Freshford, on January 30, in the morning, I scrupled singing those words,

[25] Nicholas Robinson, M.D. (1697?–1775), *The Christian Philosopher: or, A Divine Essay on the Principle of Man's Universal Redemption*, 2 vols. (London, 1757); cf. Wesley, Sermon 57, 'On the Fall of Man', I.1 (2:401 in this edn.); James Everett, *Adam Clarke Portrayed*, 3 vols. (London, 1843–49), 1:243-44; Thomas Jackson, *Recollections of my Life and Times* (London, 1873), p. 245; and Christopher Walton, *William Law* (London, 1854), p. 579n.

[26] Orig., 'twelve' in all contemporary editions, but corrected to 'three' in the errata to Wesley's *Works* and in his personal copy.

[27] Cf. Isa. 27:6; 35:1, conflated.

Ye now afflicted are,
  And hated for his name,
And in your bodies bear
  The tokens of the Lamb.

I thought I was not afflicted or hated for the name of Christ. But this scruple was soon removed. For at Bradford,[28] in the evening, I was pressed for a soldier and carried to an inn, where the gentlemen were. Mr. Pearce,[29] hearing of it, came and offered bail for my appearance the next day. They said they would 'take his word for ten thousand pound'; but not for me—I 'must go to the round-house', the little stone room on the side of the bridge. So thither I was conveyed by five soldiers. There I found nothing to sit on but a stone and nothing to lie on but a little straw. But soon after, a friend sent me a chair on which I sat all night. I had a double guard, twelve soldiers in all—two without, one in the door, and the rest within. I passed the night without sleep but not without rest, for, blessed be God, my peace was not broken for a moment. My body was in prison, but I was Christ's freeman—my soul was at liberty. And, even there I found some work to do for God—I had fair opportunity of speaking to them who durst not leave me. And I hope it was not in vain.

In the morning, I had leave to go to a private house with only one soldier to guard me. About three in the afternoon, I was carried before the commissioners, and part of the act read which empowered them to take 'such able-bodied men as followed no business and had no lawful or sufficient maintenance'. Then I said, 'If these are the men you are to take, I am not a proper person. For I do follow a lawful calling, in partnership with my brother, and have also an estate.' The Justice said, 'If you will make oath of that, I think we must let you go.' But the commissioners said, no man could swear for himself. I said, 'Gentlemen, give me time and you shall have full proof.' After a long debate, they took a fifty-pound bond for my appearance on that day three weeks. All the time I could bless God that he counted me worthy to suffer for his name's sake.

The next day I set out for Cornwall. I tarried at home four days, and then, setting out with my brother James, came to Bradford last Saturday. On Monday in the afternoon I appeared before the commissioners with the writings of my estate. When the justice had perused them, and my brother had taken his oath, I was set at liberty. So the fierceness of man turns to God's praise, and all this

[28] I.e., Bradford-on-Avon.

[29] On Richard Pearce, landlord of the Cross Keys, see July 8, 1751, n. 14 (20:394 in this edn.).

is for the furtherance of the gospel. I hope you will return God thanks for my deliverance out of the hands of unreasonable and wicked men.

William Hitchens[30]

Sun. 27. After the service at Snowsfields, I found myself much weaker than usual and feared I should not be able to go through the work of the day, which is equal to preaching eight times. I therefore prayed that God would send me help, and, as soon as I had done preaching at West Street, a clergyman who was come to town for a few days came and offered me his service. So when I asked for strength, God gave me strength, when for help, he gave this also.

I had been long desired to see the little flock at Norwich. But this I could not decently do till I was able to rebuild part of the Foundery there, to which I was engaged by my lease. A sum sufficient for that end was now unexpectedly given me by one of whom I had no personal knowledge. So I set out Monday 28 and preached in Norwich on Tuesday evening, March 1.[31] Mr. Walsh had been there twelve or fourteen days, and not without a blessing. After preaching I entered into contract with a builder and gave him part of the money in hand. On Wednesday and Thursday I settled all our spiritual and temporal business, and on Friday and Saturday returned with Mr. Walsh to London.

Sun. 6. I had no help, and I wanted none, for God renewed my strength. But on Sunday 13, finding myself weak at Snowsfields, I prayed (if he saw good) that God would send me help at the chapel.[32] And I had it. A clergyman whom I never saw before came and offered me his assistance. And as soon as I had done preaching, Mr. Fletcher came, who had just then been ordained priest, and hastened to the chapel on purpose to assist, as he supposed me to be alone.[33]

[30] See Apr. 4, 1751, n. 68 (20:382 in this edn.).

[31] 'March 1' was added by JW only in the errata to his *Works* (1774) and in his personal copy of that volume.

[32] Cf. above, Feb. 27, 1757.

[33] John Fletcher (1729–85) was born in Nyon, Switzerland, Jean Guillaume de la Fléchère. Like his father, he undertook military service abroad and, by a series of accidents, landed in England, where in 1752 he became tutor to the family of Thomas Hill of Tern Hall in Shropshire. Impressed by Methodist preaching, he was converted in 1755, ordained deacon and priest on successive Sundays, and came straight to assist JW at West Street. He made Tern Hall his home, assisting the vicar of Madeley, ten miles away, and was presented by Thomas Hill to the living in 1760. His zeal as a pastor was second only to his personal sanctity, which made a deep impression everywhere, not least on the

Mon. 14. I went with T. Walsh to Canterbury, where I preached in the evening with great enlargement of spirit, but with greater in the morning, being much refreshed at the sight of so large a number of soldiers. And is not God able to kindle the same fire in the fleet which he has already begun to kindle in the army?

Wed. 16. I had the satisfaction to find an old stout-hearted sinner, who had been defying God for near fourscore years, now become as a little child and complaining of his own ignorance and ingratitude to God.

Fri. 18. I returned to London.

Sun. 20. Mr. Fletcher helped me again. How wonderful are the ways of God! When my bodily strength failed, and none in England were able and willing to assist me, he sent me help from the mountains of Switzerland! And an help meet for me in every respect; where could I have found such another?

Fri. 25. After I had read to a serious clergyman the conclusion of *The Doctrine of Original Sin*,[34] he moved that 'we might spend some time in prayer.' And I found great liberty of spirit in praying for Dr. Taylor, and a strong hope that God would show him 'the truth as it is in Jesus'.[35]

About this time many of the children of God rested from their labours.

On Sunday 13 I buried Elizabeth Langdon, who after severe inward trials was for several days in great pain but in great peace.

On Sunday 20[36] I buried Hannah Lee, a pattern of industry, meekness, and patience.

ministerial students at Trevecca, of which the Countess of Huntingdon made him absentee superintendent in 1768. He resigned this post in 1771, when he came out strongly on the Arminian side in the Calvinist controversy. JW hoped to have him as his successor in the Methodist work but, instead, preached his funeral sermon on the text Ps. 37:37, 'Mark the perfect man, and behold the upright, for the end of that man is peace'; Sermon 114, 3:610-29 in this edn. See also Patrick P. Streiff, *Jean Guillaume de la Fléchère; Ein Beitrag zur Geschichte des Methodismus* (Bern, 1984).

[34] Wesley may have been referring to his own work with that title, for on March 24 he had come to the end of his Part VI, even though he later decided to add still another part (see *Bibliography*, No. 222; and vol. 12 in this edn.). It is perhaps more likely, however, that he was referring to the closing pages of Dr. John Taylor's 3rd edn. of 1750—the one which Wesley himself used—which contained his *Supplement to the Scripture Doctrine of Original Sin*. In the last paragraph preceding his postscript, Taylor summarized: 'But whatever qualities parents propagate to children, or Adam to his posterity, I think I have demonstrated that these qualities as they are infused into our nature at the formation of it, cannot be *sinful* in *us*, or render us the objects of God's wrath' (p. 225).

[35] Cf. Eph. 4:21. For John Taylor, see Aug. 28, 1748, n. 47 (20:245-46 in this edn.).

[36] Orig., '25'; corrected in 1788.

And on Sunday 27 I buried Mary Naylor,[37] who for several years was a most eminent pattern of truly Christian courage, plainness of speech, and plainness of apparel. A week before I had an opportunity of telling her all that was in my heart concerning her change (not for the better) in all these particulars. In the beginning of her illness, she was in great darkness and distress of soul. But while prayer was made for her, her bodily pain ceased, and her soul received comfort.

And on Monday 21, just at midnight, she quietly fell asleep.

Wed. 30. I rode to a gentleman's near Beaconsfield[38] and preached at six in the evening in a large convenient place filled with serious hearers, several of whom had come five or six miles.

Thur. 31.[39] I was earnestly importuned to go over to High Wycombe. I went and preached there at noon on the parable of the sower.[40] Perhaps some of the seed which has been sown here for many years will at length bring forth fruit.

At six it seemed as if the whole town of Beaconsfield was assembled together. And I bear them witness, they gave earnest heed, high and low, to the things which were spoken. A large number of them were present in the morning[41] on Friday, April 1. Fair beginnings these! But 'he that endureth to the end, the same shall be saved.'[42]

In returning to London, I read a tract on the law of nature wrote by a counsellor of Geneva.[43] I am sorry to find Dr. Taylor's poison spread to the Alps also! And even printed and published at Geneva[44] without any hindrance or animadversion!

Sun. 3. I paid one more visit to Thomas Singleton, an amiable young man, called away at five and twenty in the dawn of a flourishing business. The next day his spirit returned to God.

On Good Friday in the evening at the meeting of the society,

[37] On Mary Naylor, a great favourite of Charles Wesley, see Jan. 24, 1743, n. 43 (19:313 in this edn.).

[38] Orig., 'Beconsfield'. Beaconsfield was a market town and parish 23¼ miles north-west of London.

[39] Orig., 'Saturday 31'.

[40] Mark 4:3-20 (the Sermon Register lists Mark 4:18).

[41] Orig. has period here, followed by a new paragraph, corrected by *Works* (1774).

[42] Cf. Matt. 10:22 (*Notes*).

[43] Cf. Sermon 120, 'The Unity of the Divine Being', §18: 'Thus Monsieur Burlomachi (of Geneva), in his curious treatise on the law of nature, does not make any more use of the Bible than if he had never seen it' (4:68 in this edn.). This refers to Jean Jacques Burlamaquie (1694–1750), who published *Principes du Droit Naturel* in Geneva, where he was a state counsellor, in 1748. It was translated into English by Thomas Nugent in the same year, as *The Principles of Natural Law*, and went through many editions.

[44] Orig., 'Genoa', clearly a misprint, but corrected only in *Works* (1774).

God was eminently present with us. I read over and enlarged upon Joseph Alleine's directions for a thorough conversion to God,[45] and desired all who were able would meet me on Monday, that we might 'perform our vows unto the Lord'.[46]

Mon. 11. At five in the evening about twelve hundred of the society met me at Spitalfields.[47] I expected two to help me, but none came. I held out till between seven and eight. I was then scarce able to walk or speak, but I looked up and received strength. At half hour after nine God broke in mightily upon the congregation. 'Great' indeed 'was our glorying' in him; we were 'filled with consolation'.[48] And when I returned home between ten and eleven, I was no more tired than at ten in the morning.

Tue.[49] 12. I set out at five for Bedford. About seven the rain began. It did not intermit till noon and was driven upon us by a most furious wind. In the afternoon we had some intervals of fair weather, and before five we reached Bedford.

Mr. Parker, now mayor,[50] received us gladly. He hath not borne the sword in vain.[51] There is no cursing or swearing heard in these streets, no work done on the Lord's Day. Indeed there is no open wickedness of any kind now to be seen in Bedford. O what may not one magistrate do who has a single eye and a confidence in God!

Both in the evening and the following morning, I preached the law as well as the gospel. The next evening, I preached on 'All things are ready; come ye to the marriage.'[52] And God eminently confirmed his word. It seemed as if not one would be left behind.

Wed. 14. We rode to Leicester, where John Brandon[53] has

[45] Apparently from the *Christian Library*, vol. 23. Joseph Alleine, *An Alarme to Unconverted Sinners in a Serious Treatise: showing 1. What Conversion is not. . . 2. What it is. . . Whereunto are annexed divers practical Cases of Conscience judiciously resolved (with Epistles to the unconverted Reader)* (London, R. Baxter and R. Alleine [uncle and father in law of Joseph Alleine], 1672). The tract was kept constantly in print, and the title was altered to *A Sure Guide to Heaven*.

[46] Cf. Num. 15:8.

[47] This was surely another example of a Covenant Service, with Communion, in the former Huguenot chapel where he had held the first such gathering, Aug. 11, 1755. David Tripp believes there was 'a steady association of the Covenant Service with the Eucharist' which is 'why the Covenant was so often renewed in Spitalfields'. *The Renewal of the Covenant in the Methodist Tradition* (London, 1969), p. 26.

[48] Cf. 2 Cor. 7:4.

[49] Orig., 'Monday', corrected in 1788.

[50] On William Parker, see Oct. 8, 1753, n. 23 (20:476 in this edn.).

[51] See Rom. 13:4.

[52] Cf. Matt. 22:4.

[53] John Brandon, a dragoon, who is said to have been the first Methodist in Leicester; he preached a good deal in the district and was an itinerant 1765–66. *Wesleyan Methodist Magazine* 57 (1834):102-3; Telford, 3:243.

gathered a small society. I preached at seven. The house[54] (supposed to contain a thousand people) was thoroughly filled. I believe there were forty or fifty soldiers, and all heard as for life.

Thur. 15. Being informed the straight[55] road to Birmingham was scarce passable, we went round by Coventry. Before six we reached Birmingham.

Sat. 16. I spoke to each member of the society. What havoc have the two opposite extremes, mysticism and antinomianism, made among this once earnest and simple people! Had it not been good for those men not to have been born, by whom these little ones have been offended?[56]

In the afternoon I rode to Dudley where the work of God increases greatly, notwithstanding the immense scandal which has been given by those who once rejoiced in the love of God. One of these has lately killed his own child by a blow upon the head. After preaching I talked with M. B., who has been long 'a mother in Israel'.[57] 'I was under strong convictions', said she, 'when twelve or thirteen years old, and soon after found peace with God. But I lost it by degrees, and then contented myself with living a quiet, harmless life, till Mr. Charles Wesley came to Wednesbury in the year 1742. Soon after this, my convictions returned, though not with terror as before, but with strong hope, and in a little time I recovered peace and joy in believing. This I never lost since, but for forty-eight hours (by speaking angrily to my child). Not long after, Mr. Jones[58] talked particularly with me about the wickedness of my heart. I went home in great trouble, which did not cease till one day, sitting in my house, I heard a voice say in my inmost soul, "Be ye holy, for I am holy." From that hour for a year and a quarter (though I never lost my peace), I did nothing but long and weep and pray for inward holiness. I was then sitting one day, Aug. 23, 1744, about eight in the morning,

[54] The first Methodist place of worship in Leicester was a licensed room in the house of hosier, William Lewis, and his wife, who were never Methodists, but members of the Presbyterian Great Meeting; the 'house' accommodating a thousand was doubtless the Presbyterian Meeting House, built in 1708. In 1753, however, the Lewises purchased for Methodist use the 'Old Barn' in Millstone Lane, a former tithe-barn, playhouse, cool-house, and riding school. When this building was vested in Methodist trustees in 1768, it was re-christened 'the Tabernacle'. James Thompson, *History of Leicester in the Eighteenth Century* (Leicester, 1871), pp. 264-65.

[55] Orig., 'strait'.

[56] See Matt. 18:6; 26:24 conflated.

[57] Judg. 5:7. Probably Mary Bird, who with her father John, sought to have justice executed at the time of the Wednesbury riots.

[58] James Jones; see Feb. 18, 1744, n. 44 (20:10 in this edn.).

musing and praying as usual, when I seemed to hear a loud voice saying at once to my heart and to my outward ears, "This day shall salvation come to this house." I ran upstairs, and presently the power of God came upon me, so that I shook all over like a leaf. Then a voice said, "This day is salvation come to this house." At the instant I felt an entire change. I was full of love and full of God. I had the witness in myself that he had made an end of sin and taken my whole heart for ever. And from that moment I have never lost the witness nor felt anything in my heart but pure love.'

Sun. 17. The rain constrained me to preach within at eight, though the house would ill contain the congregation. But we prayed that God, if he saw good, would 'stay the bottles of heaven'[59] for the sake of those at Wednesbury. And before we came thither the rain stayed, so that I proclaimed Christ crucified[60] in the open air to such a congregation as no house could have contained. At five, I preached to a still larger congregation on 'He that believeth shall be saved.'[61] As soon as I had done, the rain returned and continued great part of the night.

Mon. 18. In the evening, I preached at Bilbrook to an earnest congregation and joined twenty of them in a society, one of whom had Christ clearly revealed in him thirty years ago. But he could find none who understood what he said till the 'Methodists' (so called) came. He clave to them immediately, rejoicing with them and over them, who were partakers of like precious faith.[62]

Tue. 19. Between Nantwich and Poole a thick black cloud came across us, out of which issued such a violent wind as was ready to bear us off our horses. But in five minutes time the wind fell, and the cloud bore clear away.

Wed. 20. The congregation at Chester in the evening was as quiet and serious as that at the Foundery, and the society was near a third part larger than when I was here in autumn.

Thur. 21. I rode to Liverpool, where I found about half of those I left in the society. James S[cholefie]ld[63] had swept away the rest,

[59] Job 38:37.

[60] See 1 Cor. 1:23.

[61] Cf. Mark 16:16.

[62] 2 Pet. 1:1.

[63] James Scholefield had been an itinerant in the north-west since at least 1752, but his connexion was ended at the next Conference. In a letter to his wife JW relates: '. . . this place . . . is at present the seat of war. For poor James Scholfield sets me at open defiance. But I am not afraid of that: I fear only fair words. And that weapon he is not at present inclined to use. I suppose that he has carried off about half the Society, by telling them how cruelly I have treated him'; *WHS* 27 (1949):61. It was doubtless these troubles which caused JW to pay so long a visit to Liverpool.

in order to which he had told lies innumerable. But none who make lies their refuge will prosper. A little while and his building will moulder away.

Sun. 24. We had two very useful sermons at St. Thomas's Church:[64] the one on 'counting the cost' before we 'begin to build';[65] the other on 'Be ye angry, and sin not.'[66] And both of them were exactly suitable to the present case of many in the congregation.

The upper part of the high spire of the church was blown down in the late storm. The stones, being bound together by strong iron cramps, hung waving in the air for some time. Then they broke through roof, gallery, pews, and pavement, and made a deep dint in the ground.

Mon. 25. I walked to the infirmary standing on an hill at the north end of the town. The seamen's hospital is joined to it on each side by semicircular piazzas. All is extremely clean and neat, at least equal to anything in London. The old seamen have smaller or larger allowance, according to their families. So that nothing is wanting to make their lives easy and comfortable—but the love of God.

I afterward spent an hour with Mr. Peter Whitfield, a man of strong understanding and various learning. His *Dissertation* in defence of the Hebrew points (which he sent me the next morning) is far more satisfactory than anything which I ever heard or read upon the subject.[67]

Thur. 28. I talked with one who by the advice of his pastor had very calmly and deliberately beat his wife with a large stick till she was black and blue, almost from head to foot. And he insisted it

[64] St. Thomas's, Park Lane, Liverpool, was consecrated in 1750. It had a tower and a slender spire 216 feet in height, and was locally esteemed one of the finest in Europe. In 1757 a hurricane removed 42 feet of the spire, and it was rebuilt to a height lower by 18 feet. In 1783 it was struck by lightning and much battered by storms, and it could be seen from a great distance vibrating in high winds. The spire was finally dismantled to the level of the tower in 1822. Richard Brooke, *Liverpool During the Last Quarter of the Eighteenth Century* (Liverpool, 1853), pp. 53-54.

[65] Cf. Luke 14:28.

[66] Eph. 4:26.

[67] Peter Whitfield, *A Dissertation on the Hebrew Vowel-Points* (Liverpool, 1748). He was a sugar-boiler, who is said to 'have dropped the Liverpool Dissenters . . . because they . . . dropped the deity of our Lord Jesus Christ'; *WHS* 2 (1900):151. Francis Okeley, the Moravian, described him a few months later as 'not only a profound scholar, and well acquainted with the learned languages, but an honest and sincere searcher after truth, and not ashamed to countenance it'; *Wesleyan Methodist Magazine* 86 (1863):1102. JW was reading Whitfield again Aug. 21, 1787 (see Diary).

was his 'duty so to do, because she was surly and ill-natured'. And that he was full of faith all the time he was doing it and had been so ever since!

Sat. 30. I took a view of the Free School, a truly noble benefaction. Here seventy boys and thirty girls are entirely provided for. The building forms three sides of a square and is rather elegant than magnificent. The children are taught to work in their several ways, as well as to read and write. The school, the dining-rooms, and the lodgings are all plain and clean. The whole was the gift of one man, Mr. Blundell, a merchant of Liverpool.[68]

Monday, May 2. I preached at Warrington about noon to a wild, staring people (very few excepted) who seemed just ripe for mischief. But the 'bridle' was 'in their jaws'.[69] In the evening I preached at Manchester.

Wed. 4. I rode over to Hayfield and preached at one in the church to a congregation gathered from all parts.

Thur. 5. I inquired of John Johnson[70] concerning Miss Beresford.[71] The sum of his account was this:

> She was always an innocent, sober young woman, having the form of godliness,[72] till she was convinced of sin and soon after justified. She was a pattern both of piety and industry. Notwithstanding her fortune and her sickliness, she was never unemployed; when she had no other work, working for the poor. And the whole tenor of her conversation was such that it is still a common saying, 'If Miss Beresford is not gone to heaven, nobody ever will.'

[68] One of the first charitable institutions in Liverpool was the 'Bluecoat School, founded in 1708 by Bryan Blundell. A ship's captain and owner, Blundell made his fortune first by transporting the poor to the New World, and later by the slave trade. Struck by the plight of homeless children wandering in the streets of the town, he bought a small building in School Lane, hired a master at £20 a year, and undertook to feed, clothe, and educate fifty children. Thanks to his efforts at raising money by private subscription (he contributed one-tenth of his own annual income for support of the school), a larger building was constructed on a piece of ground donated by the corporation. By 1756, one hundred children were being cared for, and his charity was well endowed, "commanding the interest and support of all that was respectable in Liverpool".' François Vigier, *Change and Apathy; Liverpool and Manchester during the Industrial Revolution* (Cambridge, MA, 1970), p. 58.

[69] Cf. Isa. 30:28.

[70] John Johnson (1725–1803), a Somerset man, who spent much of his service as an itinerant, 1755–81, in Ireland. Here he was employed for a time as a sort of general superintendent by JW, and married first Miss Hoar, and secondly Mrs. King. When ill-health ended his notable itinerant ministry, he settled at Lisburn. *Methodist Magazine* 27 (1804):474; *Crookshank,* Ireland, 1:127, 387.

[71] On Judith Beresford see above, Apr. 8, 1755, n. 17.

[72] 2 Tim. 3:5.

She had a vehement love to the Word of God and spared no pains in order to hear it. Frequently she would not go to bed all night, lest she should miss the morning preaching. She lost no opportunity of meeting with her brethren, to whom her heart was closely united; nor was she afraid or ashamed to own the poorest of them, wherever she met them and whatever company she was in. The very sight of them occasioned a joy in her soul which she neither could nor desired to hide.

When her sickness confined her to her room, she rejoiced with joy unspeakable, more especially when she was delivered from all her doubts concerning Christian perfection. Never was anyone more athirst for this, for the whole mind that was in Christ. And she earnestly exhorted all her brethren, vehemently to press after it.

The more her bodily strength decayed, the more she was strengthened in spirit. She called upon all that were with her, 'Help me to rejoice; help me to praise God,' having no fear, but a jealousy over herself lest she should exceed in her desire to be with Christ.

As soon as I came to Ashbourne, she sent for me and broke out: 'I am just at my journey's end. What a mercy that I who have done so little for God should be so soon taken up to him! Oh, I am full of the love of God. I dare not exercise my faith fully upon God; the glory of the Lord is so great that I cannot bear it. I am overwhelmed. My natural life is almost gone, with the brightness of his presence. Sometimes I am even forced to cry out, 'Lord, stay thy hand, till I come into glory.' I asked, 'Have you lately felt any remains of sin in you?' She said, 'I felt pride some weeks ago.' And it seems this was the last time. She added, 'I have now no will, the will of God is mine. I can bring my dearest friends before the Lord. And while I am praying for them, the glory of the Lord so overpowers me that I am lost and adore in silence the God of heaven.' She cried out: 'Tell all from me that perfection is attainable, and exhort all to press after it. What a blessing is it that I have no weary hours! Though I am confined to my bed night and day and can take scarce anything but water to refresh me, yet I am like a giant refreshed with wine.'

Afterward she broke out: 'If I had lived in what the world calls pleasure, what a miserable creature should I have been now! What should I be if I had no God on my side? When the fire has made me bright, then I shall go to my God.'

She prayed largely for all states of mankind, but particularly for the prosperity of the Church and for the society at Ashbourne, that God would continue and increase his work among them.

When she altered for death, she called for her mother and brothers, to each of whom she gave an earnest exhortation. Then she said: 'Now I have no more to do here. I am ready to die. Send to

Mr. W[esley] and tell him I am sorry I did not sooner believe the doctrine of perfect holiness. Blessed be God, I now *know* it to be the truth!' After greatly rejoicing in God for two days more, she said one morning: 'I dreamed last night I heard a voice, "Christ will come today for his bride." It is for *me*. He will come for me today.' And a few hours after, without one struggle or sigh or groan, she sweetly fell asleep.

One who was intimately acquainted with her writes thus:

Glory be to God for the blessed privilege I enjoyed of being with her, night and day, for a month before she died. When I went to her first she had kept her bed some days and was extremely weak. And yet she spoke considerably plainer than ever I heard her in my life. She called as soon as I entered the room: 'My dear friend, give me your hand. Let us rejoice that my time is so near approaching. Do not mourn, you know it is what we expected.' I was soon brought to wish her safe on the happy shore. She said: 'This is true friendship. But how is it that I do not feel greater transports of love, now I am so near the time of seeing my Lord face to face? Indeed I am ashamed to approach him before whom the angels veil their faces!' She often said, 'I take it as a fresh token of his love that he sent *you* to me at this time.' Her pains were great, but she bore all with invincible patience and resignation, and often said, 'I find it good for me to be afflicted; in his time I shall come out thoroughly purified.' Afterward she said: 'I experience more upon this bed of my own nothingness and the free grace of God in Christ than ever I did in all my life. The best of my performances would be damnable without Christ.'

Several days before her death, her love was so great that she cried, 'I am overcome, I am overcome, I am overcome.' And when she had scarce strength to speak, she praised God in a wonderful manner. Even when she was light-headed her talk was wholly concerning the things of God. She called to Mr. Wesley, as if he had been by her, and said: 'O sir, how hard it is for the rich to enter into the kingdom of heaven! I am saved. But I am but just saved.' When her fever abated she told me she had dreamed that she was with him. And sometimes I could scarce persuade her but he had been there.

She after asked if I saw no more appearance of death in her face yet. When I told her there was, she begged I would indulge her with a looking-glass. And looking earnestly into it she said with transport, 'I never saw myself with so much pleasure in my life.'

On Saturday morning at six she said, 'My Saviour will come today and fetch his bride.' Yet about eight she said: 'If *you* had felt what I have done this morning, it would have killed you. I had lost sight of God.' (Perhaps in the last conflict 'with principalities and powers'.)[73] From this time she was filled with joy but spoke little. Her eyes were still lifted up to heaven till her soul was released with so much ease that I did not know when she drew her last breath.

So died Judith Beresford, as it were an hundred years old, at the age of four and twenty. A little more of her life and of her spirit may be learned from one or two of her letters:

How can you love me, since there is still such a mixture of evil in all I say and do? But why should I ask this question? The Lord himself loves me, and in the late dispensation of his providence he has mercifully discovered to me some sins of a refined nature, which before I was almost ignorant of, and now wait and pray to be delivered from. And I can joyfully add, the Lord is nigh to all that call upon him. He will fulfil my desire, though not *as* I desired. . . . His way and his will are best. But how long shall I acknowledge this without implicitly submitting to it? My own will I am apt to think good in such cases and to grieve when it is crossed. So that I easily discern how needful it is for me to be tried and made to sacrifice to the Lord of that which costs me something. I need not say—for the above, alas! will tell you—that I cannot answer all your questions in the affirmative. For did I continually find God present with me and always walk in the light of his countenance, most surely there could be no part dark in me. Yet this I can say, that I see his hand stretched out to save and to deliver. And my trust is that before I go hence I shall behold all his salvation. And if it can serve any good purpose, he will open my lips to declare his praise and let a poor creature glorify him in her death. For this I pray and rejoice in hope, knowing the God whom I serve is able to fulfil in me all the good pleasure of his will and the work of faith with power.

As to the shadows of this world, I think I may truly say, they are nothing to me. The evil (for certainly it must be *some*) that at times interposes between God and my soul is, I believe, of a more spiritual nature. The stirrings of pride I sometimes feel, and I trust shall bewail as long as one spark remains.

My dear friend, adieu! I trust we shall have an happy meeting at last. In the meantime, I am persuaded, a few lines from you would add greatly to my peace and comfort. I am,

Your very loving and (I hope)
Obedient child

Sept. 7, 1756 J. B.

[73] Cf. Eph. 6:12.

In answer to a letter wherein I desired some account of her experience, she wrote as follows:

How does it add to the glory of the almighty Saviour that from my very infancy this rebel heart has felt the drawings of his love! Therefore, since you desire to know how I was first convinced that I was a poor, guilty sinner, I must begin with saying that goodness and mercy have followed me all my days. But I know not how to proceed; the workings of sin and grace that I have felt are beyond description. Yet out of the mouth of babes and sucklings the Lord can perfect praise.

My childhood was spent in much simplicity and peace. The Lord drew me to himself with the cords of love, and I found great joy in pouring out my soul before him. Original sin I was quite ignorant of, but actual sins I felt and bewailed, and after some time spent in weeping for them, I felt peace and renewed my resolutions. But they could not last long, for pride, envy, and all manner of evil now sprung up in my heart. Yet at times I had strong convictions and often resolved to be very serious when I was older.

So I went on from eight or ten years old till seventeen. Then I was indeed as bad as bad could be, desired nothing but to be admired and was filled with all that foolish vanity which poor young women are most prone to. Christmas 1750, I was advised to partake of the Lord's Supper. I knew it was right but was conscious of my ignorance and unfitness for it. However, I endeavoured to prepare myself and was pretty well satisfied after I had made a formal confession of my sins and shed some tears for them.

About this time there was a great talk of *Methodism*, and a cousin of mine was brought to seek the Lord. I went to visit her in January 1751, and told her before I came away, I knew I was 'not what I ought to be' and should 'be glad to be instructed'. From this time we carried on a correspondence, and by degrees light broke in upon my heart. But alas! though I well knew that in me was no good thing and seemed to disclaim my own righteousness, yet the idol lurked within, and I really trusted in my own prayers and other duties. In this manner I went on that whole year, toward the end of which my corruptions were more violent. Sin took occasion by the commandment, and I was often ready to be carried away by the torrent.

February 1752, it pleased God to take my dear friend. This appeared to me a heavy judgment. Yet I afterwards saw how it was tempered with mercy, as it taught me to trust in none but the everlasting arm. Her death happily proved the occasion of her elder sister's conversion. The blessing of a Christian friend was restored to me, and we received each other as from the Lord.

In ’53 and ’54 I had great outward afflictions and at times strong inward conflicts, though, blessed be God, I generally found comfort in pouring out my complaints before him. But towards the end of 1754, I began to feel my hope decline, and for several nights in secret prayer I was in strong agony of spirit. The Lord then, while I was upon my knees, stripped off all my fig-leaves. At the same time he showed me the all-sufficiency of Jesus Christ to save sinners, to save me, the chief, and I was enabled to cry out, ‘My Lord and my God! I have redemption in thy blood.’ From this happy time I went on my way rejoicing, though I was at times grievously assaulted, both by the stirrings of my old corruptions and temptations from the devil, blasphemous thoughts in particular. I always experienced something of this before the Sacrament—but the Lord made a way for me to escape.

In the beginning of the year 1755, we had preaching near Ashbourne. This I had wished for long. And now I was honoured with suffering a little for the name of Christ. At first I was rather ashamed, but the Lord strengthened me. And so great a blessing did I find by conversing with these dear people, that I feared none of those things which I did or might suffer. My acquaintance were now less fond of my company, and they that looked upon me shaked their heads. This proved an unspeakable blessing, for often had I cause to fear the love of men.

From the time of my becoming serious, or rather beginning to aim at it, my health visibly declined. This at first occasioned me some trouble, because all cried out, it was ‘being too religious’. But afterwards I saw great mercy in this chastisement and the consequences of it, one of which was that I had a *just excuse*, even in the judgment of others, for refraining from many things which in my circumstances could not otherwise have been avoided without great opposition from those who were near and dear unto me. Not that I ever fasted—God knows I have been deficient in this as well as every other duty. But I had an happy liberty of using some little self-denial, for which the Lord be praised.

O how has he led me and carried me in his bosom! Is it not wonderful? And yet I have not told you a tenth part. But the time fails. And my strength fails. Praise God with me, and let us magnify his name together.

Oct. 1, 1756

I believe this was one of the last letters she wrote. Shortly after, she was called hence.

So unaffected, so composed a mind,
So firm, yet soft, so strong, yet so refined,
Heaven, as its purest gold, with torture tried;
The saint sustained it, but the woman died.[74]

An account of a widely different nature I received about this time from Ireland:

> Thomas B——, about three miles from Tyrrellspass, was at the point of death by a violent rupture. While they were praying for him in the society he was at once restored to perfect health. He continued in health for several years and in the knowledge and love of God. But no sooner did he return to folly than his disorder returned. And in some months it put an end to his life. He died as stupid as an ox.

Mon. 9. I rode over the mountains to Huddersfield.[75] A wilder people I never saw in England. The men, women, and children filled the street as we rode along and appeared just ready to devour us. They were, however, tolerably quiet while I preached; only, a few pieces of dirt were thrown, and the bellman came in the middle of the sermon but was stopped by a gentleman of the town. I had almost done when they began to ring the bells, so that it did us small disservice. How intolerable a thing is the gospel of Christ to them who are resolved to serve the devil!

Wed. 11. I preached about one at Wakefield in a small meadow near the town. When I began the sun shone exceeding hot, but in a few minutes it was covered with clouds. The congregation was more quiet and serious than ever I saw there before. Almost as soon as I had done speaking the sun broke out again.

Thur. 12. I finished Dr. Rogers's essay on the learning of the ancients.[76] I think he has clearly proved that they had microscopes

[74] Alexander Pope, 'Epitaph on Mrs. Corbet, who died of a Cancer in the Breast', lines 7-10; see also Feb. 28, 1776; and July 1, 1781.

[75] Huddersfield, 11 miles south of Bradford, was a market town and parish, the rapid development of which was about to commence. It was in 1765 that Sir John Ramsden, the proprietor of most of the town, erected a circular cloth hall 'for the accommodation of the manufacturers'. Lewis, *England*, 2:478.

[76] J. Rogers, *Dissertation on the Knowledge of the Ancients in Astronomy and Optical Instruments, on the Earth's Diurnal and Annual Motions* (London, 1755). Wesley also refers approvingly to Rogers and his work on comets in his *Survey of the Wisdom of God in the Creation* and in Sermon 69, 'The Imperfection of Human Knowledge', I.5 (2:572, and n. 22, in this edn.). Rogers was a doctor of medicine who held that 'the moon cannot be supposed to be kept in her orbit by gravitation, nor can that be supposed the cause of double tides in twenty-four hours . . . the true cause of both [being] . . . electricity.' *Dissertation*, pp. 132-33.

and telescopes, and knew all that is valuable in the modern astronomy. But indeed he has fully shown the whole frame of this to be quite uncertain, if not self-contradictory.

The latter end of the week I spent at Bradford.

Sun. 15. At five the house contained the congregation, but at eight they covered the plain adjoining to it. The sun was hot till the clouds interposed. It was a solemn and comfortable season. As soon as the service of the Church was ended I began at the end of the house[77] again and exhorted a willing multitude to 'follow after charity'.[78] A shower of rain and hail fell as I drew to a conclusion, but it did not disturb the congregation.

Soon after, I took horse for Birstall. The congregation here was treble to that at Bradford. But as they stood one above another on the circular slope of the hill, my voice commanded them all. Though I spoke longer than I usually do, I found no weariness or weakness. Shall not 'they that trust in the Lord renew their strength'?[79] Yea, as long as the sun and moon endureth.

On Monday and Tuesday I preached in the neighbouring towns.

Wed. 18. I rode in the afternoon from Halifax over the huge, but extremely pleasant and fruitful, mountains to Heptonstall. A large congregation was waiting for us, not only on the ground, but on the side and tops of the neighbouring houses. But no scoffer or trifler was seen among them. It rained in the adjoining valley all or most of the time that I was preaching. But it was fair with us on the top of the mountain. What an emblem of God's taking up his people into a place of safety while the storm falls on all below!

Here I was informed of the earthquake the day before. On Tuesday, May 17, many persons in several parts within five or six miles heard a strange noise under the ground, which some compared to thunder, others to the rumbling of carts. Quickly after, they felt the earth rock under them and wave to and fro. Many who[80] were within doors heard their pewter and glass clatter; many in the fields felt the ground shake under their feet; and all agreed as to the time, though they knew nothing of each others' account.

Thur. 19. I preached at Ewood about seven, not intending to preach again till the evening. But Mr. Grimshaw begged I would

[77] An old cock-pit taken by the society in 1756.

[78] 1 Cor. 14:1.

[79] Cf. Isa. 40:31.

[80] Orig., 'which', altered in Wesley's *Works* (1774).

give them one sermon at Gaulksholme,[81] after which we climbed up the enormous mountain, I think equal to any I saw in Germany, on the brow of which we were saluted by a severe shower, which an high wind drove full in our faces almost till we came to Haslingden.[82] Here I learned that the earthquake observed near Heptonstall had been sensibly felt by very many persons from Bingley, three miles eastward of Keighley, to the neighbourhood of Preston. It was everywhere preceded by an hoarse rumbling about three o'clock, so that in a few minutes it had run from east to west between fifty and sixty miles.

Fri. 20. I preached near Padiham[83] at eight, to a large, wild congregation;[84] about noon at Roughlee, where those who stood firm in the storm had melted away in the calm. At Keighley I had neither voice nor strength left. But while I was preaching my strength returned.

Sat. 21. I had a little conference with our preachers. In the afternoon I preached at Bingley. I have not lately seen so genteel a congregation, yet the word of God fell heavy upon them.

Sun. 22. After preaching at five I took horse for Haworth. A December storm met us upon the mountain. But this did not hinder such a congregation as the church could not contain. I suppose we had near a thousand communicants, and scarce a trifler among them. In the afternoon, the church not containing more than a third of the people, I was constrained to be in the churchyard. The rain began as soon as I began to speak. But they regarded it not. For God sent into their hearts

> The former and the latter rain,
> The love of God, and love of man.[85]

Mon. 23. I took horse at four. It rained till noon without any

[81] Orig., 'Gawksham'. Described below as a 'lone house in the side of an enormous mountain'; see July 21, 1759.

[82] Orig., 'Haslenden'. Haslingden was a market town and chapelry in the parish of Whalley, 17 miles north of Manchester, where William Darney had formed a society as early as 1744.

[83] Orig., 'Paddiham'. Padiham was a chapelry in the parish of Whalley, 3½ miles north-west of Burnley.

[84] One of the 'wild' hearers was Robert Worsick, whose grandmother ran after JW brandishing an axe and threatening to kill him. Tyerman, *John Wesley*; see also new edn. (London, 1890), 2:275.

[85] John and Charles Wesley, *Hymns and Sacred Poems* (1742), p. 175, the closing couplet of st. 9 is a paraphrase of Ps. 133 (*Poetical Works,* 8:251).

intermission. And we had heavy showers in the afternoon. However, we reached Ambleside in the evening.

Tue. 24. We rode by Keswick to Whitehaven. Within a few miles of the town I was so tired that I could scarce either ride or walk. But all weariness was gone before I had preached a quarter of an hour.

Wed. 25. I was surprised to see not only hedges and shrubs without a green leaf upon them but abundance of trees likewise naked as in the depth of winter. Upon inquiring I found that on the 23rd of October [1756][86] a violent wind had gone through all these parts, which not only threw down chimneys, walls, and barns, and tore up trees by the roots, but scorched every green thing that it touched as with fire, so that all the leaves immediately fell off, and not only bushes and fruit-trees but elms, oaks, and firs, withered away to the very roots.

Fri. 27. I preached at Branthwaite[87] about noon. Many of the congregation came from far. The rain was suspended from ten till evening, so that they had opportunity both of coming and returning. This also was an answer to prayer. And is any such too little to be remembered?

Whit Sunday, May 29. After preaching at eight and at two I hastened to Cockermouth. I began without delay and cried to a listening multitude, 'If any man thirst, let him come unto me and drink.'[88] The word had free course. Even the gentry desired[89] to drink of the 'living water'.[90]

Mon. 30. I rode to Wigton,[91] a neat, well-built town, on the edge of Cumberland. I preached in the market-place at twelve. The congregation was large and heavily attentive. Between four and five we crossed Solway Firth,[92] and before seven reached an ill-looking house called The Brow, which we came to by mistake, having passed the house we were directed to. I believe God directed us better than man. Two young women, we found, kept the house, who had lost both their parents, their mother very lately. I had great liberty in praying with them and for them. Who

[86] *Works* (1774), 'that some time before'.

[87] Branthwaite was a tiny township 6 miles south-west of Cockermouth.

[88] John 7:37.

[89] *Works* (1774), 'seemed desirous'.

[90] John 7:38.

[91] Wigton was a substantial market town and parish 11 miles south-west of Carlisle. On early Wigton Methodism, see *Methodist Recorder* (Nov. 12, 1903), p. 9.

[92] Orig., 'Solway Frith', the normal spelling in Wesley's lifetime.

knows but God will fasten something upon them which they will not easily shake off?

Tue. 31. I breakfasted at Dumfries and spent an hour with a poor backslider of London, who had been for some years settled there. We then rode through an uncommonly pleasant country (so widely distant is common report from truth) to Thornhill,[93] two or three miles from the Duke of Queensborough's seat,[94] an ancient and noble pile of building, delightfully situated on the side of a pleasant and fruitful hill. But it gives no pleasure to its owner, for he does not even behold it with his eyes. Surely this is a sore evil under the sun:[95] a man *has* all things and *enjoys* nothing.

We rode afterward partly over and partly between some of the finest mountains, I believe, in Europe—higher than most, if not than any, in England and clothed with grass to the very top. Soon after four, we came to Leadhills,[96] a little town at the foot of the mountains, wholly inhabited by miners.

Wednesday, June 1. We rode on to Glasgow, a mile short of which we met Mr. Gillies[97] riding out to meet us.

In the evening the tent (so they call a covered pulpit) was placed in the yard of the poorhouse, a very large and commodious place. Fronting the pulpit was the infirmary, with most of the patients at or near the windows. Adjoining to this was the hospital for lunatics—several of them gave deep attention. And cannot God give them also the spirit of a sound mind?[98] After sermon they brought four children to baptize. I was at the kirk in the morning while the minister baptized several immediately after sermon. So I was not at a loss as to their *manner* of baptizing. I believe this removed much prejudice.

Fri. 3. At seven the congregation was increased, and earnest attention sat on every face. In the afternoon, we walked to the college and saw the new library[99] with the collection of pictures. Many of them are by Raphael, Rubens, Van Dyck,[1] and other

[93] Orig., 'Thorny-hill'.

[94] Charles Douglas, 3rd Duke of Queensberry, resided not here at Drumlanrig Castle, but at Amesbury, Wilts.

[95] See Eccles. 5:13, etc.

[96] Orig., 'Lead-hill'.

[97] On Dr. John Gillies, see Apr. 17, 1753, n. 15 (20:453 in this edn.).

[98] See 2 Tim. 1:7.

[99] The University of Glasgow, long straitened for library resources and more inclined to spend its funds on professors' houses, was provided with new library buildings 1732–44, about half the cost being defrayed by the Duke of Chandos.

[1] Orig., 'Vandyke'.

eminent hands. But they have not room to place them to advantage, their whole building being very small.

Sat. 4. I walked through all parts of the old cathedral, a very large and once beautiful structure, I think, more lofty than that at Canterbury and of nearly the same length and breadth.[2] We then went up the main steeple, which gave us a fine prospect both of the city and the adjacent country. A more fruitful and better cultivated plain is scarce to be seen in England. Indeed nothing is wanting but more trade (which would naturally bring more people) to make a great part of Scotland no way inferior to the best counties in England.

I was much pleased with the seriousness of the people in the evening. But still I prefer the English congregation. I cannot be reconciled to men sitting at prayer or covering their heads while they are singing praise to God.

Sun. 5. At seven the congregation was just as large as my voice could reach. And I did not spare them at all. So if any *will* deceive himself, I am clear of his blood. In the afternoon it was judged two thousand, at least, went away, not being able to hear. But several thousands heard very distinctly, the evening being calm and still. After preaching I met as many as desired it of the members of the praying societies.[3] I earnestly advised them to meet Mr. Gillies every week, and at their other meetings not to talk loosely and in general (as their manner had been) on some head of religion, but to examine each others' hearts and lives.

Mon. 6. We took horse early and in three hours reached the Kirk of Shotts, where the landlord seemed to be unusually affected by a few minutes' conversation. As did also the woman of the house where we dined. We came to Musselburgh at five. I went to an inn and sent for Mr. Bailiff Lindsey,[4] whom I had seen several years ago. He came immediately and desired me to make his house my home. At seven I preached in the poorhouse to a large and deeply attentive congregation. But the number of

[2] N. Pevsner gives the dimensions of Canterbury as: 515 ft. long, east transept 155 ft., west transept 125 ft., choir vault 69 ft. high, nave vault 60 ft. high; *North East and East Kent* (London, 1969), p. 166. From the plan given by J. G. Dunbar, Glasgow Cathedral appears to be about 250 ft. long; *The Historic Architecture of Scotland* (London, 1966), p. 151.

[3] Societies for prayer, formalized by increasing institutionalization in the early eighteenth century and then reinvigorated by the Concert of Prayer, launched by the leaders of revival in Reformed New England, were one of the links binding revivalist Scotland with its Cameronian past.

[4] Probably either Richard Lindsey or Francis Lindsey (1703–91). James Paterson, *History of the Regality of Musselburgh* (Musselburgh, 1857), pp. 125, 212.

people making the room extremely hot, I preached in the morning before the door. Speaking afterwards to the members of the society, I was agreeably surprised to find more than two-thirds knew in whom they had believed, and the tree was known by its fruits. The national shyness and stubbornness were gone, and they were as open and teachable as little children. At seven, five or six and forty of the fifty dragoons and multitudes of the townspeople attended. Is the time come that even these wise Scots should become fools for Christ's sake?

Wed. 8. I rode to Dunbar.[5] Here also I found a little society, most of them rejoicing in God their Saviour. At eleven I went out into the main street and began speaking to a congregation of two men and two women. These were soon joined by above twenty little children, and not long after by a large number of young and old. On a sudden the sun broke out and shone full in my face, but in a few moments I felt it not. In the afternoon I rode to Berwick-upon-Tweed. They did not expect me till the next day. However, a congregation quickly assembled, and one as large, if not larger, at five in the morning.

Thur. 9. Today *Douglas*, the play which has made so much noise, was put into my hands.[6] I was astonished to find, it is one

[5] Dunbar was a substantial burgh, market town, and parish 28 miles north-east of Edinburgh. The first Methodist preaching in Dunbar had been provided by Newcastle preachers and by William Darney. Jackson, *Early Methodist Preachers,* 5:141.

[6] JW here records a sensation without explaining that it represented an important conjuction of eighteenth century culture and politics. John Home (1722–1808), the author of *Douglas, A Tragedy* (1757), was a minister of the Kirk who had made an unusually early impression in the General Assembly, an ally of William Robertson and Alexander Carlyle, and a member of a group of Moderates who decided to challenge the power of what they held to be a censorious minority in control of the Church. In 1747 he wrote a tragedy, *Agis*, which was rejected by Garrick. Home, however, obtained the favour of Argyll and Bute, and wrote a second tragedy, *Douglas*, which was also rejected by Garrick (Johnson 'defied Mr. Sheridan to show ten good lines in it'. James Boswell, *Journal of a Tour to the Hebrides*, ed. F. A. Pottle and G. H. Bennett [London, 1963], p. 358). Production in Edinburgh was now the only resort, and the play was rehearsed privately in the house of an actress with an eminent cast of scholars and ministers. The Edinburgh Presbytery took action against the play as written by a minister, as containing profane passages, and as attended by ministers. Calling on other presbyteries for assistance, they received from the Presbytery of Duns in which the Moderates were in control, a reply described as 'one of the unremembered curiosities of insolent literature' (L. Drummond and James Bullock, *The Scottish Church 1688–1743* [Edinburgh, 1973], p. 77; N. Morren, *Annals of the General Assembly of the Church of Scotland* [Edinburgh, 1838–40], 2:112-32). Carlyle claimed to have broken the power of the ruling party, for although an act was passed forbidding the attendance of the clergy at the theatre, when 'Mrs Siddons 1st appeared in Edinr, during the sitting of the Genl Assembly [of 1784] That Court was oblig'd to fix all important business for the Alternate Days when she did not act, as all the younger members, clergy as well as layity took their station in the theatre on those days' (A. Carlyle, *Anecdotes and*

of the finest tragedies I ever read. What pity that a few lines were not left out! And that it was ever acted at Edinburgh!

Fri. 10. I found myself much out of order, till the flux stopped at once, without any medicine. But being still weak, and the sun shining extremely hot, I was afraid I should not be able to go round by Kelso. Vain fear! God took care for this also. The wind which had been full east for several days turned this morning full west and blew just in our face. And about ten the clouds rose and kept us cool till we came to Kelso.[7]

At six William Coward[8] and I went to the market-house. We stayed some time, and neither man, woman, nor child came near us. At length I began singing a Scotch psalm, and fifteen or twenty people came within hearing, but with great circumspection, keeping their distance as though they knew not what might follow. But while I prayed their number increased, so that in a few minutes there was a pretty large congregation. I suppose the chief men of the town were there, and I spared neither rich nor poor. I almost wondered at myself, it not being usual with me to use so keen and cutting expressions. And I believe, many felt that for all their form they were but heathens still.

Sat. 11. Near as many were present at five, to whom I spoke full as plain as before. Many looked as if they would look us through, but the shyness peculiar to this nation prevented their saying anything to me, good or bad, while I walked through them to our inn.

Characters of the Times, ed. J. Kinsley [London, 1973], p. 163). Home was now able to put on triumphant performances of *Douglas* and *Agis* in London (1757–58); he was rewarded by the Prince of Wales and was believed by Horace Walpole to have been given a pension by the Princess of Wales, which enabled him to frustrate the proceedings of his presbytery by resigning his living (R. R. Sedgwick, ed., *Letters from George III to Lord Bute 1756–66* [London, 1939], p. 8; Horace Walpole, *Horace Walpole's Correspondence*, ed. W. S. Lewis, 48 vols. [New Haven, Yale University Press, 1937–83], 9:207). He became private secretary to Lord Bute and then to the Prince of Wales, later George III. A royal pension and a Scottish sinecure followed, Home taking full advantage of the right conferred by the latter, *ex officio* to attend the General Assembly of the Kirk in the Moderate interest. Many other tragedies followed, which reappeared in a collected edition in 1822.

7 Kelso was a substantial burgh and market town 41 miles south-east of Edinburgh.

8 William Coward (d. 1770) was described by JW (who preached his memorial sermon) as 'that wise and good man' (see May 19, 1770). 'A man of some respectability in the world, a strict Churchman, and eminently correct in his morals', Coward was converted under Methodist preaching, 'opened his house to receive the Methodist Ministers, and very soon himself became an eminently zealous and useful Local Preacher. The venerable Messrs. John and Charles Wesley, George Whitefield and Charles Perronet, made his house their home in their visits to those parts; and from their society he received much profit, whilst they beheld in him the grace of God, and were glad' (*Wesleyan Methodist Magazine* 49 [1826]:799). He was also a class leader and overseer of the poor. *WHS* 7 (1909):90.

About noon I preached at Wooler,[9] a pretty large town, eighteen miles from Kelso. I stood on one side of the main street near the middle of the town. And I *might* stand. For no creature came near me till I had sung part of a psalm.[10] Then a row of children stood before me, and in some time about an hundred men and women. I spoke full as plain as I did at Kelso. And Pharisees themselves are not out of God's reach.

In the afternoon we came to Alnwick, and at six I preached in the court-house to a congregation of another spirit.

Sun. 12. At seven they were gathered from all parts, and I was greatly refreshed among them. At five, the court-house being too small, I was obliged to go out into the market-place. O what a difference is there between these living stones[11] and the dead, unfeeling multitudes in Scotland!

Mon. 13. I proclaimed the love of Christ to sinners, in the market-place at Morpeth. Thence, we rode to Plessey. The society of colliers here may be a pattern to all the societies in England. No person ever misses his band or class; they have no jar of any kind among them, but with one heart and one mind provoke one another to love and to good works.[12] After preaching I met the society in a room as warm as any in Georgia. This, with the scorching heat of the sun when we rode on, quite exhausted my strength. But after we came to Newcastle, I soon recovered and preached with as much ease as in the morning.

Thur. 16. In the evening, I preached at Sunderland. I then met the society and told them plain, none could stay with us unless he would part with all sin—particularly robbing the king, selling or buying run goods, which I could no more suffer than robbing on the highway.[13] This I enforced on every member the next day. A few would not promise to refrain. So these I was forced to cut off. About two hundred and fifty were of a better mind.

Sat. 18. The desk was placed in the evening just opposite to the sun, which when I begun was covered with a cloud. But it broke out in a few minutes and shone full in my face for three-quarters of an hour. But it was no inconvenience at all, nor were my eyes any more dazzled than if it had been under the earth.

9 Orig., 'Woller'. Wooler was a respectable market town and parish 46 miles north-west of Newcastle.

10 1788, 'a part of the psalm'.

11 See 1 Pet. 2:4-5.

12 See Heb. 10:24.

13 See John Wesley, *A Word to a Smuggler* (1767), II.1: '. . . open smuggling . . . is robbing on the highway.'

Sun. 19. I preached at eight to the usual congregation, and hastened to Shields,[14] lest I should be too late for the church. Between twelve and one I preached in a kind of square. But here we had a new kind of inconvenience. Every four or five minutes a strong wind covered us over with a shower of dust, so that it was not easy to look up or to keep one's eyes open. The rain constrained[15] me to preach within at Newcastle. I took the opportunity of making a collection for the poor, many of whom can very hardly support life in the present scarcity.

Wed. 22. In the evening and the following morning I preached at Chester-le-Street.[16] Observing some very fine but not very modest pictures in the parlour where we supped, I desired my companion, when the company was gone, to put them where they could do no hurt. He piled them on an heap in a corner of the room, and they have not appeared since.

Thur. 23. I preached at South Biddick about noon on 'I will heal thy backsliding.'[17] God was with us at Sunderland in the evening in an uncommon manner. And the next day I left the people there more in earnest than they have been for some years.

Sat. 25. We walked to Swalwell about noon. The sun was scorching hot, and there was no wind or cloud. But it did us no hurt; the congregation was such as I never saw there before. And I believe God blessed his word to them that were nigh and them that had been far from him.

Sun. 26. I preached at Gateshead at eight, at Sheep Hill about noon, and at five in the evening at Newcastle near Pandon Gate. The rain only threatened till I had done, but soon after poured down. How well does God *time* great and small events for the furtherance of his kingdom!

Mon. 27. I preached at Horsley and found some life even there. Thence, we rode across the Tyne to Prudhoe,[18] a little town on the top of an high hill. I preached at the side of Mr. H——'s[19] house, and I suppose all the town who could get out were present, and most of them at five in the morning. At both times it pleased God to make bare his arm,[20] not only to wound but to heal.

14 The rapid transition to Newcastle suggests that JW had already crossed the Tyne to North Shields, a seaport and market town at the Tyne mouth.

15 *Works* (1774): 'But not long after the rain began, which constrained'.

16 Orig., 'Chester on the Strate'.

17 Hos. 14:4.

18 Prudhoe was a small township in the parish of Ovingham, 12½ miles south-west of Newcastle.

19 Anthony Humble. *WHS* 11 (1917):22; 26 (1948):148.

20 See Isa. 52:10.

Tue. 28. I returned to Newcastle hoarse and weak. But who can be spent in a better cause?

Thur. 30. I read Mr. Baxter's account of his own life and times.[21] It seems to be the most impartial account of those times which has yet ever appeared. And none that I have seen so accurately points out the real springs of those public calamities.

Sunday, July 3. The high wind obliged me to stand on the western side of Gateshead. By this means the sun was just in my face. But it was not long before the clouds covered it. As I began speaking in the afternoon near Pandon Gate, the rain began, scattered the careless hearers, and ceased. An earnest, attentive multitude remained, to whom I explained part of the Second Lesson for the day, concerning the 'joy' which is 'in heaven over one sinner that repenteth'.[22]

Mon. 4. I took my leave of Newcastle, and about noon preached at Durham in a pleasant meadow near the river's side. The congregation was large and wild enough. Yet in a short time they were deeply attentive. Only three or four gentlemen put me in mind of the honest man at London who was so gay and unconcerned while Dr. Sherlock[23] was preaching concerning the day of judgment. One asked, 'Do you not hear what the doctor says?' He answered, 'Yes, but I am not of this parish!' Toward the close I was constrained to mention the gross ignorance I had observed in the rich and genteel people throughout the nation. On this they drew near and showed as serious an attention as if they had been poor colliers.

We took horse at two. The clouds and wind in our face kept us cool till we came to Hartlepool.[24] Mr. Romaine[25] has been an instrument of awakening several here, but for want of help they

21 Richard Baxter, *Reliquiae Baxterianae: or his own narrative of his life and times* (London, 1696). See also 'Introduction', 18:3-4 in this edn

22 Luke 15:7; the Calendar appointed Luke 15 as the Second Lesson at Morning Prayer for June 3.

23 Thomas Sherlock (1678–1761) became extraordinarily popular as a preacher from the time he was elected Master of Temple (1704–53). A supporter of Walpole, he became Bishop of Salisbury (1734), declined York and Canterbury (1743, 1747), but became Bishop of London in 1748.

24 Hartlepool was a seaport, market town, and parish 19 miles south-east of Durham.

25 William Romaine (1714–95), the son of a French Protestant who died at Hartlepool in 1757, and himself born in the town, graduated B.A. from Christ Church, Oxford, in 1734. He engaged in controversy with William Warburton. In the 1750s, he abandoned his original Arminian views and became the strongest defender of high Calvinism and an ardent follower of Whitefield. For many years Romaine was the only evangelical clergyman in London, and he subsisted on various lectureships until he stood for the living

soon slept again. I preached in the main street to near all the town. And they behaved with seriousness.

Tue. 5. At seven in the evening, I preached in the main street at Stockton. None but two or three gentlemen seemed unconcerned. I went thence to meet the society. But many others begged to stay with them, and so earnestly that I could not refuse. And indeed it was a day of God's power. I scarce know when we have found the like.

Wed. 6. At eleven I preached near the market-place in Yarm. Many gentry were there, and all serious. I find in all these parts a solid, serious people, quite simple of heart, strangers to various opinions, and seeking only the faith that worketh by love.[26] And most of the believers are waiting and longing for the fullness of the promises.

One young woman, late a Papist, I talked with at large, who last night took leave of her priest. Instead of staying to be sent for, she sent for him and after asking him several questions, frankly told him she had 'now found the true religion and by the grace of God would continue therein'. She has been concerned for her soul from thirteen years of age. Soon after, she found the peace of God and has never lost it since.

About seven I preached at Osmotherley.

Thur. 7. I rode through one of the pleasantest parts of England to Hawnby.[27] Here the zealous landlord turned all the Methodists out of their houses. This proved a singular kindness, for they built some little houses at the end of the town in which forty or fifty of them live together. Hence, with much ado, I found my way to Robin Hood's Bay and preached on the quay to the greatest part of the town. All (except one or two, who[28] were very wise in their own eyes)[29] seemed to receive 'the truth in love'.[30]

This day, between Helmsley and Kirkbymoorside,[31] we rode

of St. Anne's, Blackfriars, with St. Andrew of the Wardrobe in 1764, his election being confirmed by chancery in 1766. A learned preacher, his theological and spiritual views were also embodied in a number of published works.

26 See Gal. 5:6.

27 Orig., 'Hornby'. The circumstances make it clear that this was not Hornby but Hawnby, a parish 6¼ miles north-west of Helmsley.

28 Orig., 'which', altered to 'who' in *Works* (1774).

29 See Isa. 5:21.

30 Eph. 4:15.

31 Helmsley is a market town and parish 23 miles north of York; Kirkbymoorside another market town and parish 29 miles north-east of York.

over a little river which suddenly disappears and after running a mile under ground rises again and pursues its course.[32]

Sun. 10. I preached at seven, on 'Repent and believe the gospel.'[33] At the church, which stands on the hill, a mile from the town, we had a sound, useful sermon. Afterwards, I preached at a little village called Normanby, and about five on the quay. In the evening, talking with the society, I saw more than ever the care of God over them that fear him. What was it which stopped their growing in grace? Why, they had a well-meaning preacher among them who was inflaming them more and more against the clergy. Nor could he advise them to attend the public ordinances. For he never went either to church or Sacrament himself. This I knew not, but God did, and by his wise providence prevented the consequences which would naturally have ensued. William Manuel[34] was pressed for a soldier, so the people go to church and Sacrament as before.

Mon. 11. We set out early. This and the three next days were the hottest I ever knew in England. A gentleman who formerly traded to Guinea assured me that the spirits in his thermometer (the same he had when abroad) rose as high as they did within a few degrees of the Line.[35] About nine we should have been glad to bait; but there being no inn to be found, we lay down for a quarter of an hour under some trees, and then rode on to Slingsby. The minister, an old acquaintance of my father's,[36] having desired to

[32] At the Hodge Beck, Kirkbymoorside, which at this point is dry every July, but reemerges lower down at Howkeld Head; *WHS* 5 (1906):129-30.

[33] Mark 1:15.

[34] Manuel, it is known, was conscripted with William Thompson at the end of 1756 (see *WHS* 7 [1909]:70). Atmore's memoir of the latter graphically indicates the conflict in the parish to which JW alludes: 'One time, while Mr. Thompson was preaching, an unruly mob arose (instigated by the minister of the parish) and cruelly assaulted him, and several of the principal Methodists, carrying them off in triumph, and taking the people without, without any kind of *trial*, on board a transport, which then lay ready to sail with a fleet of men of war. Mr. Thompson was confined in prison, expecting every hour to be sent on board the transport also. . . . This outrage, committed against all law and order, coming to the ears of the late Countess of Huntingdon . . . she, with some others of considerable respectability, made application to Government; by which means Mr. Thompson and the people were soon set at liberty. An action was also brought against the worthy clergyman, who had like to have paid dear for his zeal: for had not Mr. Thompson himself used his utmost efforts to stop the process, it would probably have proved the ruin of him and his family' (see Atmore, *Methodist Memorial*, pp. 418-19). The fate of Manuel, concealed in this confused account of a dispute involving the Impressment Acts, does not transpire. The vicar of Normanby, 1745 till his death in 1762, was Thomas Langstaffe B.A., sizar of Trinity College, Cambridge, 1735.

[35] I.e., the Equator.

[36] The rector of Slingsby from 1740 till his death *c.* 1772 was James Gordon M.A.

see me, I called at his house before I preached. And I could gladly have stayed longer with him, but I knew the congregation waited. One poor drunkard made a little disturbance, but after he was silenced all were still and steadily attentive.

It continued intensely hot. But having the wind in our faces (as we generally had all along from Newcastle and that which way so ever we rode), we received no hurt till we came to York. But the difficulty was, how to preach there in a room which in winter used to be as hot as an oven. I cut the knot[37] by preaching in Blake's Square, where (the mob not being aware of us) I began and ended my discourse to a numerous congregation without the least disturbance.

Tue. 12. I set a subscription on foot for building a more commodious room.[38] In the evening I preached at Acomb[39] to a calm, solid congregation. The next evening I preached at Poppleton,[40] where the poor gladly received the gospel. The rich *heard* it and even seemed to *approve*.[41] God give them to *understand* and *practise* it.

Thur. 14. I resolved to preach in the square once more, knowing God has the hearts of all men in his hands. One egg was thrown and some bits of dirt. But this did not hinder a large congregation from taking earnest heed to what was spoken of 'Christ the wisdom of God, and the power of God'.[42]

Fri. 15. At three in the morning[43] there were all the probable signs of a violently hot day. But about four God sent a cooling rain. It ceased about seven. But the clouds continued and shaded us to Pocklington. Yet it was too hot to bear the house. So I stood in the main street and cried, 'If any man thirst, let him come unto me and drink.'[44] A large mob soon gathered on the other side. And for fear they should not make noise enough, the good churchwarden hired men to ring the bells. But it was lost labour. For still the bulk of the congregation heard, till I quietly finished my discourse.

Before seven I reached Epworth and preached in the market-place to a listening multitude.

Sat. 16. I rode on to Laceby, about thirty measured miles. After

[37] Clearly an allusion to the proverbial phrase to 'cut the Gordian knot', used in Edmund Waller's 'To the King'; cf. Shakespeare, *Henry V*, I.i.46.

[38] At Peasholme Green.

[39] Orig., 'Acombe'.

[40] Orig., 'Popleton'.

[41] Two of JW's rich hearers, Thomas Prince of Poppleton and William Horseman of Water Poppleton, became trustees of Peasholme Green. Lyth, *York Methodism*, p. 294.

[42] Cf. 1 Cor. 1:24.

[43] 1774 only adds 'in the morning'.

[44] John 7:37.

so many long journeys which I hardly felt, this short one quite exhausted my strength. However, I quickly recovered, so as to preach at three in a meadow to a large congregation. They all kneeled when I prayed, and showed such a genuine simplicity as greatly revived my spirit. At seven I preached in the new room[45] which they have just finished at Grimsby.

Sun. 17. At seven in the morning the house just contained the people. I designed to preach abroad in the afternoon, but the rain drove us into the house again—as many as could crowd in.[46] The rest stood without, though many, I fear, were wet to the skin.

Tue. 19. Before I left Newcastle, I heard a strange relation, which I knew not what to think of. I then desired T. Lee,[47] who was going to the place, to inquire particularly concerning it. He did so, and in consequence of that inquiry wrote me the following account:

> R—— J—— lived about twelve miles from Newcastle. His son some time since married without his consent. At this he was so enraged that he wished his 'right arm might burn off if ever' he 'gave or left him sixpence'.
>
> However, in March last, being taken ill, he made his will and left him all his estate. The same evening he died. On Thursday 10 his widow, laying her hand on his back, found it warm. In the evening those who were with him went into the next room to take a little refreshment. As they were eating they observed a disagreeable smell but could find nothing in the room to cause it. Returning into the room where the corpse lay, they found it full of smoke. Removing the sheet which covered the corpse, they saw (to their no small amazement) the body so burned that the entrails were bare and might be seen through the ribs. His right arm was nearly burned off, his head so burned that the brains appeared. And a smoke came out of the crown of his head, like the steam of boiling water. When they cast water upon his body it hissed, just as if cast on red-hot iron. Yet the sheet which was upon him was not singed,

[45] This was built by the efforts of Thomas Capiter and William Blow (see Oct. 24, 1743, n. 40, 19:350 in this edn.) in a yard behind, and belonging to, the latter's house, and registered as a Dissenting place of worship in 1759. G. Lester, *Grimsby Methodism, 1743–1889* (London, 1890), pp. 42, 132.

[46] *Works* (1774), 'again; as many as could crowded in'.

[47] Thomas Lee (1717–86), born at Keighley, was first impressed by, and then converted under, the preaching of Grimshaw and Methodists. He was employed by Grimshaw as a preacher, encountering much persecution. JW took him into his work about 1755, and he continued till his death. John Nelson described him as 'a right old Methodist preacher, and the power of God attends his word.' For his life, see Jackson, *Early Methodist Preachers*, 4:152-69.

but that under him, with the pillow-bier[48] and pillow and the plank on which he lay, were all burned and looked as black as charcoal.

They hasted to put what was left of him into the coffin, leaving some to watch by it. But after it was nailed up, a noise of burning and crackling was heard therein. None was permitted to look into it till it was carried to Ebchester[49] churchyard. It was buried near the steeple. As soon as it was brought to the grave, the steeple was observed to shake. The people hastened away; and it was well they did, for presently part of the steeple fell. So that had they stayed two minutes longer they must have been crushed in pieces. All these circumstances were related to me and my wife by those who were eye- and ear-witnesses.[50]

I preached in a ground adjoining to the house. Toward the conclusion of my sermon, the person with whom I lodged was much offended at one who sunk down and cried aloud for mercy. Herself dropped down next and cried as loud as her; so did several others quickly after. When prayer was made for them, one was presently filled with peace and joy in believing.[51] In the morning I left the rest refusing to be comforted till Christ should be revealed in their hearts.

Wed. 20. I preached at Ferry in my way, and in Epworth market-place about seven. The rain began just as I began speaking. But God heard the prayer, and it was stayed.

Sat. 23. I preached at Westwoodside,[52] where the breach of fifteen years is now healed,[53] all the wanderers being returned to the fold with him who led them astray.

Sun. 24. As we rode over Haxey Carr[54] towards Misterton, one was relating a surprising thing that happened lately. A woman of Stockwith told her sister who lived with her, 'I do not think to go to market today, for I dreamed that I was drowned in riding across one of the drains on Haxey Carr.' But she was soon laughed out of it and went. She rode over the carr with many other market-folks, and in crossing one of the drains where the water was scarce a

[48] Orig., 'pillow-beers', corrected to 'pillow-bier' in *Works* (1774); i.e., pillow-case.

[49] Orig,. 'Abahester'; *Works* (1774), 'Abchester'. Ebchester was a small chapelry in the parish of Lanchester, 14 miles north-west of Durham.

[50] This narrative was criticized in *The London Chronicle* (July 25, 1776).

[51] See Rom. 15:13.

[52] Westwoodside is a village 1 mile west of Haxey.

[53] See June 6, 1742 (19:274 in this edn.).

[54] Orig., 'Car'. A carr or car is a fen (wet boggy ground) or a meadow rescued from a bog or fen.

yard deep, slipped off[55] her horse. Several looked on, but none once thought of pulling her out till she was past recovery.

At one I preached to the largest congregation I have seen since I left Newcastle. All behaved with deep seriousness but one man, whom I afterwards learned to be a Baptist preacher. Just as I was taking horse, he came again and laboured hard to begin a dispute. But having neither time nor strength to spare, I gave him the ground and rode away.

The congregation at Epworth was full as large, if not larger, than that at Misterton. Among them was a poor gray-headed sinner, a mocker at all religion. But his mocking is past. He was in tears most of the time and is now 'feeling after'[56] God.

Mon. 25. I left Epworth with great satisfaction, and about one preached at Clayworth. I think none was unmoved but Michael Fenwick,[57] who fell fast asleep under an adjoining haystack.[58] From thence we rode to Rotherham. When I came in I had no strength and no voice left. However, in an hour I was able to preach to the largest congregation that, I suppose, was ever seen there.

Tue. 26. I was not able to sit up above two or three hours together. However, I preached in the morning and evening, and spoke severally to the members of the society.[59]

Wed. 27. I preached about noon at Barley Hall, and in the evening at Sheffield. After spending a short time with the society, I lay down as soon as possible. But I could not sleep before twelve o'clock, and not long together after. Yet I felt no faintness in the morning, but rose lively and well, and had my voice more clear and strong in preaching than it had been for several days.

55 Orig., 1761 only, the dialect form, 'off of'.

56 Cf. Acts 17:27.

57 Orig., 'Fennick', clearly a phonetic spelling, altered in 1774 to the normal spelling, 'Fenwick'. Michael Fenwick (d. 1797) 'was a very eccentric character; he had a weak head, but his most intimate friends generally supposed him to possess a good heart. He travelled some time with Mr. Wesley, but his eccentricities were so great that he was dismissed from that post. He almost idolized Mr. Wesley, and imitated him, as far as he was able, in his manner of speaking, praying, preaching and writing' (Atmore, *Memorial*, p. 123). He was excluded from Conference and not stationed for some years before he was killed by lightning. His immediate offence was to complain that he had not been named in the *Journal*, to which JW made this humorous riposte. His goodness of heart was sufficiently evidenced in old age by his visiting prisoners in York Castle and by giving the poor most of his £12 pension. *WHS* 5 (1906):185.

58 Altered only in *Works* (1774) to the synonym 'hayrick'.

59 1788 omits this paragraph, probably in error.

Thur. 28. I received a strange account from Edward Bennet's[60] eldest daughter:

> On Tuesday, the 12th[61] of this month, I told my husband in the morning, I desire you will not go into the water today; at least not into the deep water on the far side of the town. For I dreamed I saw you there out of your depth, and only your head came up just above the water. He promised me he would not, and went to work. Soon after four in the afternoon, being at John Hanson's, his partner's house, she was on a sudden extremely sick, so that for some minutes she seemed just ready to expire. Then she was well in a moment. Just at that time John Hanson, who was an excellent swimmer, persuaded her husband to go into the water on the far side of the town. He objected, the water was deep and he could not swim; and being much importuned to go in, stood some time after he was undressed, and then, kneeling down, prayed with an earnest and loud voice. When he rose from his knees, John, who was swimming, called him again, and treading the water said, 'See, it is only breast high.' He stepped in and sunk. A man who was near cutting fern and [who] had observed him for some time, ran to the bank and saw his head come up just above the water. The second or third time he rose, he clasped his hands and cried aloud, 'Lord Jesus, receive my spirit.' Immediately he sunk and rose no more.
>
> One might naturally inquire, What became of John Hanson? As soon as he saw his partner sink, he swam from him to the other side, put on his clothes, and went straight home.

About noon I preached at Woodseats, in the evening at Sheffield. I do indeed *live* by preaching!

How quiet is this country now, since the chief persecutors are no more seen! How many of them have been snatched away in an hour when they looked not for it! Some time since, a woman of Thorpe often swore she would wash her hands in the heart's blood of the next preacher that came. But before the next preacher came she was carried to her long home.[62] A little before John Johnson settled at Wentworth, a stout healthy man who lived there told his neighbours, 'After May Day, we shall have nothing but praying and preaching. But I will make noise enough to stop

60 Edward Bennet, a sugar baker, was usually JW's host in Sheffield. The building of the first Methodist chapel in Sheffield in 1741 owed much to his generosity. He later joined the Calvinists. James Everett, *Historical Sketches of Wesleyan Methodism in Sheffield and its Vicinity*, 2 vols. (Sheffield, Montgomery, 1823), pp. 34, 43.

61 1768, 1788, '19th'.

62 See Eccles. 12:5.

it.' But before May Day he was silent in his grave. A servant of Lord R[ockingham][63] was as bitter as him and told many lies purposely to make mischief. But before this was done his mouth was stopped. He was drowned in one of the fishponds.

Fri. 29. I preached at Nottingham. We want nothing here but a larger house.[64]

Sat. 30. I preached in the evening at Leicester to a large congregation.

Sun. 31. I rode over to Markfield. The church contained us tolerably well in the morning, but in the afternoon, though many stayed without, it was much crowded and sultry hot. I was quite faint and weary while I read prayers, but in preaching my strength was restored. At six I preached once more at Leicester and delivered my own soul.

Monday, August 1. I had much conversation with Mr. [Simpson][65] (whom against a thousand appearances I *will* believe to be an honest, though irresolute, man).

> While I was very uneasy (said he) in the year 1741, my brother brought me to Mr. Spangenberg and then to others of the German Brethren, to whom I was more and more attached, till in the year 1743 I went over to Marienborn. There I saw many things which I could not approve, and was more and more uneasy till I returned to England. I was afterward much employed by the Brethren. I was ordained deacon. But still I had a sore and burdened conscience and gained no ground in my spiritual warfare. Rather, having laid aside prayer and searching the Scripture, I was more and more dead to God. But in 1750, I awoke again and was under great agonies of mind. And from this time I wrote to the Count again and again, and to most of the labourers, but to no purpose. Andrew Frey's account[66] is true. The spirit of levity and frolicsomeness,

[63] Charles Watson-Wentworth, 2nd Marquis of Rockingham (1730–82), succeeded to the marquisate in 1750, and was Lord-lieutenant of the North and East Ridings in 1752. After falling from royal favour in 1762, he was briefly premier 1765–66, and again in 1782; but in central politics he was principally celebrated as leader of a Whig faction between those dates. In local politics, with his seat at Wentworth Woodhouse, near Sheffield, he was the great magnate of the West Riding.

[64] The temporary accommodation in Bottle Lane was replaced by an octagon chapel in 1764. R. C. Swift, *Lively People—Methodism in Nottingham, 1740–1929* (Nottingham, 1982), p. 10.

[65] On John Simpson, who here makes his last appearance in the *Journal*, see Apr. 19, 1740, n. 37 (19:146 in this edn.). JW's present judgment of him as 'honest though irresolute' differed little from his earlier assessment of Simpson as upright but misguided. See June 22, 1742 (19:279 in this edn.).

[66] On this account, see Nov. 3, 1753, n. 36 (20:480 in this edn.).

which he justly describes, broke in about 1746 and is not purged out yet. In May last I wrote and delivered a declaration to the Brethren met in conference at Lindsey House,[67] that I did not dare to remain in their connection any longer. The same declaration I made to them here, a few days ago. What farther I am to do I know not. But I trust God will direct me.

Tue. 2. On his expressing a desire to be present at our Conference, I invited him to it, and on Wednesday 3, in the evening, he came to the Foundery. Our Conference began the next morning and continued till the Thursday following. From the first hour to the last there was no jarring string, but all was harmony and love.[68]

Mon. 8. I took a walk in the Charterhouse. I wondered that all the squares and buildings, and especially the schoolboys, looked so little. But this is easily accounted for. I was little myself when I was at school, and measured all about me by myself. Accordingly the upper boys, being then bigger than myself, seemed to me very big and tall—quite contrary to what they appear now, when I am taller and bigger than them. I question if this is not the real ground of the common imagination that our forefathers, and in general men in past ages, were much larger than now—an imagination current in the world eighteen hundred years ago. So Virgil supposes his warrior to throw a stone that could scarce be wielded by twelve men.

Qualia nunc hominum producit corpora tellus.[69]

So Homer long before: Οἷοι νῦν βροτοί εἰσι.[70] Whereas in reality men have been, at least ever since the Deluge, very nearly the same as we find them now, both for stature and understanding.

Mon. 22. I set out in the machine and the next evening reached Bristol.

67 A property in Chelsea on the banks of the Thames, formerly belonging to the Duke of Ancaster, and leased by Zinzendorf in 1750. Daniel Benham, *Memoirs of James Hutton* (London, Hamilton, Adams, 1856), pp. 256-57. Hereafter, Benham, *Hutton*.

68 Notwithstanding that, as JW's correspondence makes clear, the question of separation from the Church was again discussed. Telford, 3:221-28; Tyerman, *John Wesley*, 2:281.

69 Virgil, *Aeneid*, xii.900: 'men of such stature as the earth now produces'.

70 Homer, *Iliad*, v.304: 'such as men are now'. Cf. Sermon 102, 'Of Former Times', §4, where Wesley deals with the same theme, and introduces the same two quotations from Virgil and Homer (3:443 in this edn.).

Fri. 26. I preached at nine to a small congregation of earnest people at Clutton, and in the evening at Middlezoy. On Saturday 27, we rode on to Tiverton.

Sun. 28. I preached in the market-house to as large a congregation as ever I saw here. And all were quiet. So can God make, when it is best, all our enemies to be at peace with us.

Mon. 29. We rode through vehement wind and many hard showers to Launceston. This gave me a violent fit of the toothache, which however did not hinder my preaching. Such a night I never remember to have passed before, but all is good which lies in the way to glory.

Tue. 30. We rode to Camelford, where my toothache was cured by rubbing treacle upon my cheek. At six I preached in the market-place. How are the lions in this town also become lambs!

Wed. 31. I preached about noon at Trewalder, and in the evening at Port Isaac. This was long a barren soil but is at length likely to bring forth much fruit.

Friday, September 2. I rode to St. Agnes. We found the great man, Mr. Donnithorne,[71] was dead. His mother and sister sent to invite me to their house. After preaching, I went thither and was received into a comfortable lodging with the most free and cordial affection. So in this place the knowledge of God has already travelled, 'from the least unto the greatest'.[72]

Sat. 3. Some who live here gave me an account of the earthquake on July 15.[73] There was first a rumbling noise under the ground, hoarser and deeper than common thunder. Then followed a trembling of the earth, which afterward waved once or twice to and fro, so violently that one said he was obliged to take a back step or he should have fallen down, and another that the wall against which he was leaning seemed to be shrinking from him.

This morning I talked at large with old Mrs. Donnithorne, who has her understanding entire, reads without spectacles, walks without a staff, and has scarce a wrinkle at ninety years of age. But what is more than all this, she is teachable as a child and groaning for salvation. In the afternoon, I spent an hour with Mr.

[71] Orig., 'Donythorne'. Joseph Donnithorne (d. 1757), eldest son of Nicholas Donnithorne, sheriff of Cornwall in 1731; he is said to have cleared £40,000 from Trevellas mine.

[72] Acts 8:10.

[73] This is described by Wm. Borlase in his *Natural History of Cornwall* (Oxford, 1758), pp. 55-58, and ascribed to July 15.

Vowler,[74] curate of the parish, who rejoices in the love of God and both preaches and lives the gospel.

Sun. 4. I—— T——[75] preached at five. I could scarce have believed if I had not heard it, that few men of learning *write* so correctly as an unlearned tinner speaks *extempore*. Mr. V[owler] preached two such thundering sermons at church as I have scarce heard these twenty years. O how gracious is God to the poor sinners of St. Agnes! In the church and out of the church, they hear the same great truths of the wrath of God against sin and his love to those that are in Christ Jesus.

Mon. 5. I rode on to Illogan,[76] but not to the house where I used to preach. Indeed his wife promised Mr. P—— before he died that she would always receive the preachers. But she soon changed her mind. God had just taken her only son, suddenly killed by a pit falling upon him. And on Tuesday last a young, strong man, riding to his burial, dropped off his horse, stone dead. The concurrence of these awful providences added considerably to our congregation.

Tue. 6. I went on to Camborne and rejoiced to hear that the gentleman who pressed Mr. Maxfield[77] no longer persecutes the Methodists nor will suffer anyone else to do it. And in the late dearth, he relieved great numbers of the poor and saved many families from perishing. I preached at six on 'I will heal their backsliding',[78] and God applied his word. Several who had left the

[74] James Vowler (*c.* 1728–58), matriculated from Exeter College, Oxford, 1747, B.A., 1750; curate of Perranzabuloe, 1750–58; curate of St. Agnes, 1757; and a friend of Samuel Walker, the brother of James, his vicar at Perranzabuloe. He is described by a correspondent of Gillies as 'greatly blessed, and the people flock to him every night in the week, but one, which he reserves for making his plain practical sermons. His house is full, and more than it can hold, every night, and by day (taking a bit of bread in his pocket) he walks round his large parish . . . and inquires into the state of their souls . . . and by what we hear, a greater reformation among the common sinners was never known in any parish or neighbourhood.' Gillies, *Historical Collections* (1845 edn.), p. 532.

[75] Probably John Turnough (or Turner), who was an itinerant preacher 1755–*c.* 1763. There is independent evidence of a simple and pellucid style developing among the Methodist poor of Cornwall. Cf. Richard Rodda's autobiographical letter to JW in Jackson, *Early Methodist Preachers*, 2:295-319, reprinted from *Arminian Magazine* 7 (1784):298 seq. The report of the revival at St. Just in 1781 is also characteristically Cornish, viz., that 'the travelling Preachers had very little share [in it]. They were the Leaders whom it pleased God chiefly (indeed almost wholly) to use!' *Arminian Magazine* 7 (1784):268.

[76] Orig., 'Illuggan'.

[77] For this episode, see June 20, 1745 (20:69-70 in this edn.). The reformed culprit may have been Henry Tompkins, mentioned in the narrative.

[78] Hos. 14:4. This may have been at Crowan, since the Sermon Register lists his preaching there from this text.

society for some years came after sermon and desired to be readmitted. O how should our bowels yearn over all who did once run well![79] This is the very thing we want—or how many souls might we yet pluck out of the jaws of the lion!

Wed. 7. I observed more and more the effects of that burning wind which was in these parts on Sunday the 28th of last month. It not only scorched all the leaves of the trees, so as to bring midwinter upon them in two hours, but burned up all the leaves of potatoes and cabbage and every green thing which it touched. What a mercy that it did not come a month sooner! Then it would have left little work for the reapers.

Thur. 8. As we rode through Gwithian parish,[80] Mr. Harris[81] pointed out the place where his father and many of his ancestors lived. It is now only a mountain of sand. Within a few years this so increased as to bury both the church and the whole town.

I preached at six to a numerous congregation in Ludgvan. Some years since, when there was a flourishing society in Gulval (the parish adjoining), there was none at all here. But how is the scene changed! In Gulval not one class, not one member, remains; in Ludgvan there is a lively society!

Fri. 9. I preached in the new house at St. Just, the largest and most commodious in the county.

Sat. 10. We rode to the Land's End. I know no natural curiosity like this. The vast, ragged stones rise on every side when you are near the point of land, with green turf between as level and smooth as if it were the effect of art. And the rocks which terminate the land are so torn by the sea that they appear like great heaps of ruins.

Sun. 11. I preached at St. Just at nine. At one the congregation in Morvah stood on a sloping ground, rank above rank, as in a theatre. Many of them bewailed their want of God. And many tasted how gracious he is.[82]

At five I preached in Newlyn to an huge multitude. And one only seemed to be offended—a very 'good sort of woman' who took great pains to get away, crying aloud, 'Nay, if going to church and Sacrament will not *put us to heaven*, I know not what will.'

Mon. 12. I preached in Lelant at one. Many from St. Ives were present, from whom I learned that Mr. Swindells[83] would have

[79] See Gal. 5:7. [80] Gwithian was a small parish 7½ miles west of Redruth.
[81] See Sept. 16, 1744, n. 95 (20:40 in this edn.). [82] See Ps. 34:8 (BCP).
[83] On Robert Swindells, see June 21, 1747, n. 53 (20:178 in this edn.).

preached abroad the day before but was hindered. 'Tis well he was, for this occasioned the offer of a meadow near the town, far more convenient than the street. At six I stood at the bottom of it, the people rising higher and higher before me. I believe, not many were left in the town, and all behaved as in the presence of God. The next evening the congregation was enlarged by the addition of many from the country. And Wednesday 14, their number was larger still. We did not open the door of the room till just half [an] hour past eight, by which means the heat was not intolerable till I had done preaching. I then retired and left the other preachers to perform the rest of the service.

Thur. 15. As we rode toward Helston, I think the sun was near as hot as it was at midsummer. Yet all along the trees looked as in the depth of winter, that scorching wind having destroyed all it touched.

Fri. 16. I looked over Mr. Borlase's *Antiquities of Cornwall*.[84] He is a fine writer and quite master of his subject, who has distinguished with amazing accuracy the ancient Saxon monuments from the more ancient Roman and from those of the Druids, the most ancient of all.

Sat. 17. I preached at Porkellis at one, and at Redruth in the evening.

Sun. 18. At eight, many of the French prisoners were mixed with the usual congregation. This was doubled at one, but still came nothing near to that which assembled at Gwennap in the evening. It rained all the time I preached, but none went away. A shower of rain will not fright experienced soldiers.

Here I learned a remarkable occurrence. A few days ago some hundred English, who had been prisoners in France, were landed at Penzance by a cartel ship.[85] Many of these passed through Redruth going home, but in a most forlorn condition. None showed more compassion to them than the French. They gave them food, clothes, or money, and told them, 'We wish we could do more. But we have little for ourselves here.' Several who had

[84] William Borlase, *Observations on the Antiquities, Historical and Monumental, of the County of Cornwall* (Oxford, 1754). Borlase (1695–1772) was educated at Exeter College, Oxford, proceeding M.A., 1719. He became rector of Ludgvan in 1722, and vicar of St. Just in 1732, holding both livings till his death. He complained of the offences of his St. Just parishioners against temperance and the Sabbath, and was in his way an effective pastor as well as antiquarian. These later interests did not impress his brother Walter, the persecutor of Methodists; see Apr. 10, 1744, n. 6 (20:22-23 in this edn.).

[85] I.e., a ship used for the exchange of prisoners of war. JW's use of this term is a dozen years earlier than the first usage recorded in *OED*.

only two shirts gave a naked Englishman one. A French boy, meeting an English boy who was half naked, took hold of him and stopped him, cried over him a while, and then pulled off his own coat and put it upon him!

Mon. 19. In the evening both the house and court at Penryn were more than filled. So that I willingly embraced the offer of Mr. H—— and preached before his door at twelve on Tuesday. It was an extremely pleasant place, on the side of an hill, commanding a fruitful vale, the opposite hills, and Falmouth harbour. Tall trees hung over me and surrounded a bowling-green which was behind me. A wide door is now open at Penryn also. O that none may shut it!

At six in the evening, I reached Besore and began preaching immediately. It was a season of uncommon refreshment, particularly to some of Truro. Afterwards I met the society in the house. A young man was cut to the heart and cried aloud, then another and another, till my voice was quite lost. But I continued crying to God, and he heard and gave an answer of peace.[86] Many were filled with consolation, and four, who had wandered for some years, resolved to set out anew.

Yet I was not quite reconciled to my lodging. Not but the Grotto itself was very venerable, but I did not like the circumstance of having a man and his wife in the same room. I therefore willingly accepted an invitation from Mr. Painter[87] and walked over with him to Truro.

Wed. 21. I walked to Besore and preached at five. Afterwards, I spoke to each member of the society. They surprised me much. So lively and tender-hearted a people I have not lately seen! After spending an hour with a few friends in Truro, I rode forward to Grampound[88]—a mean, inconsiderable, dirty village. However, it is a borough town! Between twelve and one, I began preaching in a meadow to a numerous congregation. While we were singing, I observed a person in black on the far side of the meadow, who said, 'Come down; you have no business there.' Some boys who were on a wall, taking it for granted that he spoke to them, got down in all haste. I went on, and he walked away. I afterwards understood that he was the minister and the mayor of

[86] See Gen. 41:16.

[87] Painter was a grocer and maltster of Truro, whose will was proved in 1789.

[88] Orig., 'Grampond'. Most of Grampound was in the parish of Creed, the rector of which, 1751–74, was Walter Harte; the rest was in the parish of Probus, the vicar of which, 1730–58, was John Reynolds.

Grampound. Soon after, two constables came and said, 'Sir, the mayor says, you shall not preach within his[89] borough.' I answered, 'The mayor has no authority to hinder me. But it is a point not worth contesting.' So I went about a musket shot farther and left the borough to Mr. Mayor's disposal.

A large congregation was at St. Ewe's[90] in the evening, many of whom were in Mr. Walker's societies.[91] Some of them came from St. Columb's,[92] twelve miles off. And they did not come in vain. The flame of love ran from heart to heart, and scarce any remained unmoved.

Thur. 22. I rode to Mevagissey,[93] which lies on the south sea, just opposite to Port Isaac on the north. When I was here last we had no place in the town, I could only preach about half a mile from it. But things are altered now. I preached just over the town to almost all the inhabitants. And all were still as night. The next evening a drunken man made some noise behind me. But after a few words were spoken to him, he quietly listened to the rest of the discourse.

On the south side of the town there is an extremely fine walk, broad and smooth, over the top of high rocks, from whence is a view of the main sea at a vast distance below and all the coast, east and west.

Sat. 24. At half hour after twelve I preached once more and took my leave of them. All the time I stayed the wind blew from the sea, so that no boat could stir out. By this means all the fishermen (who are the chief part of the town) had opportunity of hearing.

At six I preached at St. Austell,[94] a neat little town, on the side of a fruitful hill.

Sun. 25. The whole church service was performed by a clergyman above ninety years of age. His name is Stephen Hewgoe.[95] He has been vicar of St. Austell between sixty and

[89] 1768, 1788, 'this'.

[90] In the *Index Villaris* of 1751, this village still appears as 'St. Tue', which was being transformed into 'St. Ewe'—still the name of the parish itself. Wesley was thinking of the 'St. Ewe's Church', however, and in this context the plural continued to be used, so that this came to be 'The Church of All Saints of St. Ewes'—in the parish of St. Ewe.

[91] See above, Aug. 30, 1755.

[92] Here again the parish was and is known as St. Columb, but Wesley uses the possessive case, thinking primarily of St. Columba's (or St. Columb's) Church.

[93] Orig., 'Mevagizzy'.

[94] Orig., 'St. Awstle', and in 1788, 'St. Austle'.

[95] Orig., 'Hugo'. Rev. Stephen Hewgoe was buried on Jan. 7, 1758. He had been admitted as sizar to Queens' College, Cambridge, in 1689, and graduated B.A. in 1692/3.

seventy years. O what might a man full of faith and zeal have done for God in such a course of time!

At two, I preached in St. Stephen's[96] near a lone house on the side of a barren mountain. But neither the house nor the court could contain the people. So we went into a meadow, where all might kneel (which they generally do in Cornwall) as well as stand and hear. And they did hear and sing and pray as for life. I saw none careless or inattentive among them.

About five, I preached at St. Austell to an exceeding civil people. But when will they be wounded, that they may be healed?

Mon. 26. I rode to Methrose in Luxulyan parish.[97]

I have not seen so stately a room in Cornwall as either this hall or the chamber over it. The place likewise where the gardens were, the remains of the terrace walk, the stately trees still left, with many other tokens, show that grand men lived here once. But they are vanished like smoke, their estates torn in pieces, and well-nigh their memory perished.

Tue. 27. We rode to Liskeard,[98] I think one of the largest and pleasantest towns in Cornwall. I preached about the middle of the town, in a broad, convenient place. No person made any noise at all. At six in the morning I had nearly the same congregation. Afterwards I examined the society and was agreeably surprised to hear that every one of them had found peace with God—and (what was still more remarkable) that none of them has left their first love, that at this day not one is in darkness!

Wed. 28. We rode on to the Dock, which gave us a very different prospect. Of those whom I joined several years ago, hardly one-half remained. Such is the fruit of disputing! And yet the congregations are more numerous than ever. And as deeply attentive as any in the kingdom. So there is hope God will yet revive his work.

Saturday, October 1. I preached at Launceston.

Sun. 2. I rode to Week St. Mary.[99] A large congregation was gathered there, many of whom came seven or eight miles. The house stands in the midst of orchards and meadows, surrounded

[96] A village 4 miles west of St. Austell. Pearce notes that the spot where JW preached is still pointed out and that the house in which he was entertained still stands. Pearce, *Wesleys in Cornwall*, p. 131, n. 108.

[97] All editions except *Works* (1774) read, 'I rode to Luxilian', which he alters in 1774 to 'I rode to Medros in Luxillian parish.' For Methrose, see above, Aug. 25, 1755, n. 91; see also Sept. 1, 1762.

[98] Orig., 'Lescard', but 1768, 1788, 'Leskeard'.

[99] Orig., 'Mary-Week'.

by gently rising hills. I preached on the side of a meadow newly mown to a deeply attentive people.

Mon. 3. I rode to Bideford[1] but did not reach it till after five, the hour appointed for my preaching. So I began without delay in an open part of the street where we alighted. One man made a little noise at first, but he was easily silenced. All the rest (a large number) quietly attended, though the wind was piercing cold, while I opened and applied, 'God forbid that I should glory, save in the cross of our Lord Jesus Christ.'[2]

Tue. 4. Between twelve and one, I reached North Molton and finding the congregation ready began immediately. There have been great tumults here since I saw them before. But God has now rebuked the storm. When the gentry would neither head nor pay the mob any more, the poor rabble were quiet as lambs. We rode on to Tiverton in the afternoon. On the three following days I saw as many of the societies as I could.

Sat. 8. We had heavy rain for some miles. Then it cleared up, and we had a pleasant ride to Bristol.

Mon. 10. I rose at my usual hour. But the soreness and swelling of my face, occasioned by my taking cold on Saturday, made it impracticable for me to preach. In the evening I applied boiled nettles. They took away the pain in a moment and the swelling in a few hours.

Sun. 16. I began visiting the classes at Kingswood, steady but not zealous. It is impossible they should stand here long—they must go on, or go back.

Mon. 17. About two I preached at Paulton, but no house could contain us. So that I was forced to stand in the open air, though the wind was very high and very cold. Thence we rode to the honest colliers at Coleford. These have the zeal which their brethren at Kingswood want, in consequence of which they are the most numerous, as well as the most lively society in Somersetshire.

Tue. 18. I preached to a very different congregation at Bradford, well-dressed and well-bred, and yet of the very same spirit, hungering and thirsting after righteousness.[3]

Wed. 19. After preaching at Freshford, I rode on to Kingswood.

Fri. 21. Being at dinner, in a moment I felt as if a small bone

[1] Bideford was a seaport, market town, and parish 39 miles north-west of Exeter.

[2] Gal. 6:14.

[3] See Matt. 5:6.

had stuck in the palate of my mouth. Nothing was to be seen, but the swelling and inflammation increased till toward evening (notwithstanding all means that could be used) and then spread to both the tonsils. In the morning, I was rather worse than better till about half an hour after eight. Then, as the disorder came in a moment, it went in a moment, and I was as well as ever.

Mon. 24. I preached about noon at Bath, and in the evening at Eastcott[4] near Lavington.

Tue. 25. In my return a man met me near Hanham and told me the school-house in Kingswood[5] was burned down. I felt not one moment's pain, knowing that God does all things well. When I came thither I received a fuller account. About eight on Monday evening, two or three boys went into the gallery up two pair of stairs. One of them heard a strange crackling in the room above. Opening the staircase door, he was beat back by smoke, on which he cried out, 'Fire, murder, fire!' Mr. Baynes[6] hearing this, ran immediately down and brought up a pail of water. But when he went into the room and saw the blaze, he had not presence of mind to go up to it but threw the water upon the floor. Meantime one of the boys rung the bell; another called John Maddern[7] from the next house, who ran up, as did James Burges[8] quickly after, and found the room all in a flame. The deal partitions took fire immediately, which spread to the roof of the house. Plenty of water was now brought, but they could not come nigh the place where it was wanted, the room being so filled with flame and

[4] Orig., 'Escott'. Eastcott, Wilts., was a tything in the parish of Urchfont, 1½ miles north-east of East Lavington.

[5] I.e., the school opened in 1748, not the original school for colliers' children.

[6] William Baynes had been a master at Kingswood 'for some time'. He obtained ordination from the Bishop of Bath and Wells in 1760, and subsequently assisted JW as a curate in his London chapels. Atmore reports that 'his ministerial talents were not great, but he was generally esteemed a very sensible and pious man. In the time of the American War, he suffered his mind to be too much occupied with the politics of the day,' which may mean that he took a different line from JW. He died of a violent fever on Dec. 27, 1777. Atmore, *Memorial*, p. 43.

[7] John Maddern, a Cornishman, was an itinerant in 1747, but in the early 1750s was assistant to James Rouquet (who was appointed to re-establish Kingswood School *c.* 1751) and English master. He married Molly Francis, the mistress in charge of the parallel girls' school, of whom JW thought highly. The Madderns are thought to have left the school in the reorganization which followed the fire. Nothing is known of his later circumstances and death. Another John Maddern, perhaps his son, was among the boys converted in a revival at Kingswood in 1768. See May 5, 1768.

[8] Burges was one of JW's hosts during his early ministry at Bristol in 1739, and seems even then to have been connected with Whitefield's colliers' school at Kingswood; see 19:391, 397, 414 in this edn. He reappears only in 1759, in one of JW's statements of grievances against his wife, she having told Burges that JW beat her. Telford, 4:76.

smoke that none could go into it. At last a long ladder which lay in the garden was reared up against the wall of the house. But it was then observed that one of the sides of it was broke in two, and the other quite rotten. However John How[9] (a young man who lived next door) ran up it with an axe in his hand. But he then found the ladder was so short that as he stood on the top of it he could but just lay one hand over the battlements. How he got over to the leads none can tell, but he did so and quickly broke through the roof, on which a vent being made, the smoke and flame issued out as from a furnace. Those who were at the foot of the stairs with water, being able to go no further, then went through the smoke to the door of the leads and poured it down through the tiling. By this means the fire was quickly quenched, having only consumed a part of the partition, with a box of clothes, and a little damaged the roof and the floor beneath.

It is amazing that so little hurt was done. For the fire, which began in the middle of the long room (none can imagine how, for no person had been there for several hours before) was so violent that it broke every pane of glass but two in the window both at the east and west end. What was more amazing still was that it did not hurt either the beds (which when James Burges came in seemed all covered with flame) nor the deal partitions on the other side of the room, though it beat against them for a considerable time. What can we say to these things but that God had fixed the bounds which it could not pass?[10]

We observed Friday the 28th as a solemn fast. And from this time the work of God revived in Bristol. We were[11] indeed brought very low. A society of nine hundred members was shrunk to little more than half the number. But God now began to turn our captivity and put a new song in our mouth.[12]

Thursday, November 3. I preached in the new preaching-house at Pill. How is the face of things changed here! Such a sink of sin was scarce to be found! And now how many are rejoicing in God their Saviour![13]

Mon. 7. Leaving the flame just kindling in Bristol, I rode to

[9] Thought to be the son of the John How; see Oct. 16, 1751, n. 47 (20:404 in this edn.).

[10] See Job 14:5.

[11] 1788, 'are'.

[12] See Ps. 40:3.

[13] See Luke 1:47.

Newbury, and on Tuesday[14] to London. I found the same fire kindled here also, and increasing more and more.

Mon. 14. I rode to Bedford and talked largely with Mr. ——, whom God had well-nigh set at liberty. But his feet are again in the net. He did not indeed deny, nor much extenuate, any of the things he had often related. But at length he told me in terms: 'There are such things among the Brethren that I can never join them more. Yet I dare not speak against them and join any other people for fear of grieving the Saviour!' O Lord, when shall this witchcraft come to an end! When wilt thou maintain thine own cause!

Wed. 16. We rode to Newmarket, and the next day to Norwich, where I now found a prospect of doing good. The congregation daily increased and grew more and more serious. I spoke to many who were deeply convinced of sin and some who were rejoicing in God and walking in the light of his countenance.[15]

Wed. 23. I was shown Dr. Taylor's new meeting-house, perhaps the most elegant one in Europe.[16] It is eight-square, built of the finest brick, with sixteen sash-windows below, as many above, and eight skylights in the dome, which indeed are purely ornamental. The inside is finished in the highest taste and is as clean as any nobleman's saloon.[17] The Communion Table is fine mahogany, the very latches of the pew doors are polished brass. How can it be thought that the old, coarse gospel should find admission here?

Thur. 24. A man had spoken to me the last week, as I was going through Thetford,[18] and desired me to preach at Lakenheath[19] near Mildenhall in Suffolk. I now purposed so to do and rode thither from Thetford. One Mr. Evans[20] had lately built a large and convenient preaching-house there at his own expense. It was more than filled at six o'clock, many standing at the door. At five

[14] 1761, 1768, and 1788 read 'Thursday', but the alteration in the *Works* (1774) of 'Tuesday', is to be preferred, for his Sermon Register shows that on Wednesday, Nov. 9, he preached in West Street Chapel, London.

[15] See Ps. 89:15.

[16] On Dr. John Taylor, see Aug. 28, 1748, n. 47 (20:245-46 in this edn.). Paradoxically, Taylor's lavish octagon encouraged JW to build octagonal chapels on grounds of economy.

[17] In Wesley's day, a lofty and spacious reception room in a palace or mansion, now obsolete and remembered mainly in its French form 'salon', or in its secondary usage as a large hall for various kinds of entertainments, or as spacious accommodation during travel.

[18] Thetford was a substantial borough and market town 30 miles south-west of Norwich.

[19] Lakenheath was a parish 5¾ miles north of Mildenhall.

[20] Orig., 'Mr. E.', the full name supplied in *Works* (1774).

in the morning (as uncommon a thing as this was in those parts), the house was nearly filled again with earnest, loving, simple people. Several of them came into Mr. E.'s house afterward, stood awhile, and then burst into tears. I promised to call upon them again and left them much comforted.

Sat. 26. I returned to London. Much confusion had been in my absence, occasioned by some imprudent words spoken by one who seemed to be strong in the faith.

Mon. 28. I heard all who were concerned face to face, but was utterly unable to judge whether there was wilful sin, lying, on either side, or only human infirmity. For the present I leave it to the searcher of hearts, who will bring all things to light in due season.

Wed. 30. I had another long hearing of the same intricate cause. But with no more success: one side flatly affirmed, the other flatly denied. This is strange! But it is more strange that those who *seem* so strong in faith should have no union of spirit with each other.

Friday, December 5 [i.e., 2 or 9?]. I baptized Henriquez Judah Seniore, a Portugese Jew, more than sixty years of age. He seemed to have no confidence in himself, but to be waiting for 'the consolation of Israel'.[21]

Sun. 11. In the evening I retired to Lewisham and spent the following days in finishing *A Preservative against unsettled Notions in Religion*, designed for the use of all those who are under my care, but chiefly of the young preachers.[22]

Sun. 17 [i.e., 18]. I had an opportunity (which I had long desired) of spending an hour or two with the Rev. Mr. ——. I would have appointed a time for our meeting weekly. But he declined it. Why? I cannot tell.

Fri. 23. John Nelson wrote me a letter, part of which I have subjoined:

> We have had four triumphant deaths lately of three men and one woman. The woman was Hannah Richardson of Briestfield.[23]

[21] Luke 2:25.

[22] J. Wesley, *A Preservative against Unsettled Notions in Religion* (Bristol, 1758). This work consisted of thirteen pieces, eleven of them extracted from the works of JW himself, with the 'design . . . not to reclaim but to preserve; not to convince those who are already perverted, but to prevent the perversion of others.' The appended booklist of 153 items was doubtless especially for the service of the 'young preachers'.

[23] Orig., 'Brestfield'.

When Enoch Williams[24] preached there she was the bitterest persecutor in the town and vowed if ever he preached there again she would help to stone him to death. But he never went to try. The only one 'of this way'[25] in the town was Ruth Blacker. Against her she was violently enraged, till Ruth went to her house, reasoned the case, and at length persuaded her to go to Dewsbury to hear Mr. Charles Wesley. That day God begot her by his Word, so that she could never rest till she found Christ in her own heart. And for two years she has been a steady follower of him. By her zeal and circumspect walking many have been since stirred up to seek the Lord. As soon as she was taken ill, she began to praise God more than ever for the work he had wrought in her soul. She said: 'At first I thought, I had no will, and that God's love was all that was in my heart. But when my little child gave a sudden shriek, I found my heart was not free. And it damped the love of God in my soul for two hours. But the Lord is come again, and now I am fully assured, he does take up all the room in my heart. He has sanctified me throughout, body, soul, and spirit. I am a witness for Jesus Christ that he is a greater Saviour than Adam was a sinner. O watch and pray, and ye shall not be overcome in the hour of temptation. Keep close to your meetings, and the Lord will meet you. If you neglect these or private prayer you will become barren in your own souls, and the God of this world will get an advantage over you. But if you keep close to God and one another, you will find Jesus a Saviour to the uttermost, as I, the most unworthy of mankind, do.' For some time before she died her prayer was turned into praise. All her prayer then was, 'Thy will be done.' We have one by us that we think will hardly live till tomorrow, who is above seventy and is as a shock of corn full ripe, crying out, 'Come Lord Jesus!'

In the Christmas week I rode down to Bristol, where, Sunday, January 1, 1758, we began the year with the great congregation at four, rejoicing and praising God.

Tue. 3. At the request of several of my friends I wrote *A Letter to a Gentleman at Bristol*[26] in order to guard them from seeking salvation by works on one hand and antinomianism on the other. From those who lean to either extreme I shall have no thanks. But 'wisdom is justified of her children.'[27]

[24] Enoch Williams was one of the earliest itinerant preachers, 'but the hardships he was called on to endure proved too much for his constitution, and soon . . . he left the world in great peace, at Birstall, in Yorkshire.' Atmore, *Memorial,* p. 505.

[25] Acts 9:2.

[26] Orig., 1761, and even *Works* (1774), 'of Bristol'. See *Bibliography,* No. 223; and vol. 13 in this edn.

[27] Matt. 11:19.

Wed. 4. I rode to Kingswood and rejoiced over the school, which is at length what I have so long wished it to be, a blessing to all that are therein and an honour to the whole body of Methodists.

Mon. 9. I began a letter to Mr. Towgood, author of *The Dissenting Gentleman's Reasons*[28]—I think, the most saucy and virulent satire on the Church of England that ever my eyes beheld. How much rather would I write practically than controversially! But even this talent I dare not bury in the earth.

Fri. 13. Having ended my business at Bristol, I rode to Newbury and the next day to London. Now, if it be the will of God, I should be glad of a little rest. If not, let me rejoice to be without it.

Tue. 17. I preached at Wandsworth. A gentleman come from America has again opened a door in this desolate place. In the morning I preached in Mr. Gilbert's[29] house. Two Negro servants of his and a Mulatto[30] appear to be much awakened. Shall not his saving health be made known to all nations?[31]

Sat. 28. I was inquiring of William Hurd,[32] Who discharged him from the army? And he might fairly say, God discharged him—his officers being determined not to do it. Nevertheless he stood among the men whom they had picked out for that purpose. And when he came in his turn, his discharge was written, and no man gainsaid.

Sun. 29. We had an uncommon blessing at West Street and a still greater at Spitalfields. Some could not refrain from crying aloud to God. And he did not cast out their prayers. Many thanksgivings have since been offered to God for the blessings of that hour.

Wednesday, February 1. I talked with a gentlewoman who had been a mighty good Christian for near seventy years. But she now

28 Orig., 'Toogood'. On Towgood and his work, see above, Apr. 30, 1755, n. 38.

29 Nathaniel Gilbert (d. 1774) claimed descent from Sir Humphrey Gilbert. A man of property, he was for some time Speaker of the House of Assembly in Antigua. His brother Francis, taking refuge in England in disgrace, came under the influence of Perronet and JW, and began the conversion of Nathaniel by sending him JW's *An Earnest Appeal to Men of Reason and Religion* (1743). When Francis returned to Antigua two years later in 1759, the pair became evangelists and pioneered Methodist work in the West Indies. *Wesleyan Methodist Magazine* 77 (1854):58-61; *Arminian Magazine* 3 (1780):387-89; 6 (1783):329, 330.

30 Orig., 'Malatto', changed to 'Mulatto' in 1788.

31 See Ps. 67:2.

32 For his death, see below, Feb. 1, 1764.

found herself out and began to cry with many tears to the friend of sinners for pardoning mercy.

Fri. 3. Mr. Parker[33] (last year mayor of Bedford) preached at the Foundery. A more artless preacher I never heard, but not destitute of pathos. I doubt not, he may be of much use among honest, simple-hearted people.

Sun. 12. At the request of the vicar, Mr. J——,[34] I rode over to Uxbridge. I preached for him both morning and afternoon, to a large and serious congregation. How uncommon a providence is this! The gospel was preached in the church at Hayes. Several of the parishioners ran from it and took pews at Hillingdon. It followed them into Hillingdon church, where I preached twice in one day. Some of them went to Uxbridge. And now it is come to torment them at Uxbridge also!

Wed. 15. I read over the *Memoirs of the House of Brandenburg*.[35] *Quanta de spe decidi!*[36] 'Tis hard to determine from his writing whether the author be a Mahometan or a Christian. I suppose he is as near one as the other![37]

On Friday 17, the Public Fast,[38] I preached at West Street in the morning, at Spitalfields in the afternoon, and Bull and Mouth in the evening, everywhere to a crowded audience. Indeed every place of worship throughout the city was extremely crowded all the day long. Surely all the prayers which have been offered up this day will not fall to the ground!

Mon. 20. I rode, through much rain, to Maldon[39] in Essex. Their new preaching-house is large,[40] but it would in no wise

33 On William Parker, see Oct. 8, 1753, n. 23 (20:476 in this edn.).

34 According to Curnock, Richard Mills was vicar of Uxbridge in 1758, and Edward Jennings church warden.

35 An English translation of this work by Frederick the Great, originally published in Berlin as *Memoires pour servir à l'histoire de Brandebourg* (Berlin, 1750) appeared in London, 1751.

36 'How my hopes fell!' See Terence, *Heauton Timorumenos* (The Self Tormentor), II.iii.9.

37 The closing sentence was added only in JW's *Works* (1774).

38 Curnock notes that none of these sermons is recorded in the Sermon Register, presumably because they were special to the fast-day and needed no repetition. The register seems to have been kept solely to guard against the unconscious selection of sermons and/or texts already used in places visited.

39 Maldon was a borough, port, and market town 10 miles east of Chelmsford.

40 If JW's sermons were not for the opening services, they came very soon afterwards, for the foundation stone of the new chapel was laid in 1757, and the building opened early in 1758. The chapel, which was adjacent to the house of Mr. Davis, one of the prominent early Methodists in Maldon, replaced 'The Cats' Castle', so-called from being formerly occupied by an old lady who was bent on having a retinue of twenty-one cats (but could never raise more than twenty). *WHS* 10 (1915):15.

contain the congregation which flocked together in the evening. For a time there was much persecution here, but all is now calm and quiet. And probably good will be done, if those who now run well do not draw back to perdition.[41] We had a large congregation at five in the morning and more than we had room for in the evening. Fair blossoms! But which of these will bring forth fruit? O Lord, thou knowest![42]

Wed. 22. It rained without ceasing till we came to a small inn nineteen miles from Maldon. Here we dried our clothes. Soon after, the rain ceased, and we had a pleasant ride to London.[43]

Mon. 27. Having a sermon to write against the assizes at Bedford,[44] I retired for a few days to Lewisham.

Friday, March 3. I returned to London.

Mon. 6. I took horse about seven o'clock. The wind being east, I was pleasing myself that we should have it on our back. But in a quarter of an hour it shifted to the north-west and blew the rain full in our face. And both increased, so that when we came to Finchley Common it was hard work to sit our horses. The rain continued all the way to Dunstable, where we exchanged the main road for the fields, which having been just ploughed were deep enough. However, before three we came to Sundon.

Hence on Thursday 9, I rode to Bedford and found the sermon was not to be preached till Friday. Had I known this in time, I should never have thought of preaching it, having engaged to be at Epworth on Saturday.

Mr. [Francis Okeley][45] came to me in the evening and said he

[41] See Heb. 10:39.

[42] Ps. 40:9, etc.

[43] A full version of events of Feb. 23 and 25 was given in a MS journal letter by JW, printed in Curnock, 4:250-53.

[44] Sermon 15, *The Great Assize* (1:355-75 in this edn.; and *Bibliography*, No. 224).

[45] Francis Okeley (1719–94), whose father was mayor of Bedford (1719–20) and later died in a debtors' prison, was converted in 1736. He was one of the members of the Fetter Lane Society who joined the Moravians and was instrumental in the spread of evangelical preaching in Bedford along with Jacob Rogers. He was a candidate for the Moravian seminary at Ysenburg in 1744. He created a religious society in Bedford before going up to Cambridge to found the (very High-Church) Cambridge Methodist group. On his return to Bedford, he became pastor to a Baptist congregation, but turned to Moravianism. He was involved in the Moravian negotiations for a special relationship with the Church of England, but could not obtain ordination from Thomas Sherlock, Bishop of London (see *WHS* 3 [1901]:134-35; 16 [1928]:146; Seymour, *Huntingdon,* 1:244; and Benham, *Hutton,* p. 240). Becoming dissatisfied with his ministry among the Moravians, he joined JW on his Irish tour in 1758, but nettled him by not throwing in his lot with Methodism (Telford, 4:34-36). Okeley returned to live quietly in Bedford, moving steadily into mysticism. Having failed to obtain Anglican [re]ordination in 1763, and a place in Trevecca college in 1765, he continued to minister to a small Moravian congregation in Northampton, enjoying the respect rather than the fellowship of the Brethren (see

could not remain as he was any longer, that he had no rest in his spirit while he was thus halting between two, and therefore desired to go with me without delay. I answered, if he was so resolved, he was welcome to set out with me for Epworth the next day. He said he would. We spent some time in prayer and parted for the present.

Fri. 10. The congregation at St. Paul's was very large and very attentive. The judge,[46] immediately after sermon, sent me an invitation to dine with him. But having no time, I was obliged to send my excuse, and set out between one and two. The north-east wind was piercing cold and, blowing exactly in our face, soon brought an heavy shower of snow, then of sleet, and afterward of hail. However, we reached Stilton at seven, about thirty miles from Bedford.

Rest was now the more sweet, because both our horses were lame. However, resolving to reach Epworth at the time appointed, I set out in a post-chaise between four and five in the morning, but the frost made it so bad driving that my companion came with the lame horses into Stamford as soon as me. The next stage I went on horseback, but I was then obliged to leave my mare and take another post-chaise. I came to Bawtry about six. Some from Epworth had come to meet me but were gone half an hour before I came. I knew no chaise could go the rest of the road. So it remained only to hire horses and a guide. We set out about seven, but I soon found my guide knew no more of the way than myself. However, we got pretty well to Idle Stop,[47] about four miles from Bawtry, where we had just light to discern the river at our side and the country covered with water. I had heard that one Richard Wright lived thereabouts, who knew the road over the moor perfectly well. Hearing one speak (for we could not see him) I called, 'Who is there?' He answered, 'Richard Wright.' I soon

A. Reincke, *Members of the Moravian Church . . . 1727–54* [Bethlehem, Pa., 1873], p. 42). On all this see J. Walsh, 'The Cambridge Methodists', in *Christian Spirituality: Essays in Honour of Gordon Rupp*, ed. Peter Brooks [London, 1975], pp. 251-83; Benham, *Hutton*, p. 547). John and William Okeley, doubtless his brothers, were in the Moravian party which went to Philadelphia in 1742.

[46] Sir Edward Clive (1704–71), justice of common pleas, 1753–70. Wesley's sermon, *The Great Assize* (Rom. 14:10), was published at the request of the High Sheriff and included in the fourth volume of *Sermons on Several Occasions* (1760; Sermon 15, 1:355-75 in this edn.).

[47] Orig., 'Idle-Stop'; about 3 miles south-west of Haxey, where the River Idle was diverted toward the Trent when Cornelius Vermuyden drained Hatfield Chase in the seventeenth century. See W. B. Stonehouse, *History and Topography of the Isle of Axholme* (1839), pp. 315-17.

agreed with him, and he quickly mounted his horse and rode boldly forward. The north-east wind blew full in our face, and I heard them say it was 'very cold!' But neither my face nor hands nor feet were cold, till between nine and ten we came to Epworth. After travelling more than ninety miles, I was little more tired than when I rose in the morning.

Sun. 12. I was much comforted at church, both morning and afternoon, by the serious behaviour of the whole congregation, so different from what it was formerly. After evening service, I took my stand in the market-place with a multitude of people from all parts. Toward the end of the sermon the rain was heavy, but it neither lessened nor disturbed the congregation.

Mon. 13. I preached in the shell of the new house, and then set out for York. The banks over which we crept along were ready to swallow up man and beast. However, we came safe to York in the afternoon. After settling the little affairs, on Wednesday 15 I rode to Leeds, where in the evening a multitude of people were present. I never before saw things in so good order here and took knowledge the Assistant had not been idle.

I was apprehensive, having been at an uncommon expense, of being a little straitened for money. But after preaching, one with whom I had never exchanged a word put a letter into my hand in which was a bill for ten pounds. Is not 'the earth the Lord's, and the fullness thereof'?[48]

Thur. 16. I rode through heavy rain to Manchester. I was scarce set down when Mr. [Okeley][49] came from Bedford. If he comes sincerely (as I believe) God will bless him, but if not, *Ego in portu navigo*.[50] He can *find out* nothing with regard to *me*—I have no secrets.

Fri. 17. In riding from Manchester to Bolton I read the life of Theodore, King of Corsica; a great man, both as a general and as a prince, and one who, if he had not been sacrificed to the French, might have made a shining figure in history.[51]

[48] Cf. Ps. 24:1.

[49] Okeley's own description of JW's preaching in Liverpool is given in *Wesleyan Methodist Magazine* 86 (1863):1101.

[50] Terence, *Andria*, III.i.22: 'I ride safe in the harbour', i.e., have fulfilled my responsibility. Cf. Nov. 28. 1747 (20:198 in this edn.).

[51] Anon., *The History of Theodore I, King of Corsica* (London, Roberts, 1743). Théodore-Étienne, Baron de Neuhof (*c.* 1690–1755), adventurer, was the son of a Westphalian baron who embroiled himself with the local nobility by a *mésalliance*, and made a career in France under the protection of the Duchess of Orleans. Théodore, raised by the duchess, became involved in Swedish plots to restore the Stuarts. He was

Sat. 18. We rode to Liverpool.

Thur. 23. I walked over to Mr. E.'s, a gentleman who had little thought of God till his favourite child lay at the point of death. It then came into his mind to pray for his life. He did so, and the child recovered. This struck him to the heart, and he rested no more till his own soul was healed.

I never saw the house so crowded as it was on Easter Day, March 26, especially with rich and genteel people—whom I did not at all spare. They are now warned to flee from the wrath to come.[52] God grant they may remember the warning!

Tue. 28. We went on board and set sail for Dublin. The wind was fair, and the day extremely fine. Seven or eight miles from the town a small boat overtook us, which brought me letters from London. Some of these earnestly pressed me to return to London, or, however, 'not to go to Ireland'. I consulted my friends, and just as we began our little debate the wind, which till then was fair and small, turned from east to west and blew harder and harder. But the point was soon decided. For upon inquiry we found the boat was gone back, and no other was to be had. Presently after, the wind returned to the east, and we saw the hand of God.

The Liverpool boat went away in such haste that it left a young man, James Glasbrook,[53] behind; so we were five in all. We had seven more cabin passengers and many common ones. So good-natured a company I never met with in a ship before. The sea was as smooth as glass, the sun shone without a cloud, and the wind was quite fair, so we glided on, till about nine I went to prayers with them and then quietly lay down.

Wed. 29. We were even with the great Welsh mountain, Penmaenmawr, at five in the morning. But it then fell calm, so that we were scarce abreast of Holyhead in the evening. This gave us time to speak to all our fellow-passengers. And some fruit

taken up by Alberoni and Ripperda, and had relations with Law. When the Corsicans rebelled against the Genoese, he presented himself as their only hope, scoured Europe on their behalf, and was elected their king. He could not defeat the Genoese and, after eight months, was confronted with much Corsican opposition and left the country. By 1742, he was a British agent, and Horace Walpole raised a subscription which kept him in comfort till his death.

[52] See Matt. 3:7.

[53] One of Wesley's itinerant preachers from 1758 until he 'desisted' in 1774. He later became a Presbyterian minister in New York. His name is variously spelled, sometimes 'Glazebrook', sometimes 'Glassbrook', but in 1771 he signed himself 'Glasbrook', the spelling which most frequently appears in Wesley's annual Minutes.

quickly appeared. For no oath, no immodest or passionate word, was any more heard in the ship while we were on board.[54]

Thur. 30. Having no wind still, I desired our brethren to come on the quarter-deck, where we no sooner began singing an hymn than both passengers and sailors gladly assembled. The wind sprung up almost as soon as I began, and about nine the next day we entered Dublin Bay, after so smooth and pleasant a passage as the captain declared he had not had at that time of year for forty years.

Considering the shortness of the warning, we had a large congregation in the evening, but a very small one in the morning, April 1. At this I did not wonder when I was informed that the preaching at five had been discontinued for near a year and an half. At eight likewise, Sunday 2, the congregation was small. I took knowledge that the people of Dublin had neither seen nor heard much of self-denial since T. Walsh left the kingdom.

All the evenings of the following week we had numerous congregations. Nothing is wanting here but rigorous discipline—which is more needful in this than in any other nation, the people in general being so soft and delicate that the least slackness utterly destroys them.

Thur. 6. We walked round the college[55] and saw what was accounted most worthy of observation. The new front is exceeding grand, and the whole square (about as large as Peckwater[56] in Christ Church) would be beautiful, were not the windows too small, as everyone will see when the present fashion is out of date.

Fri. 7. I preached in the evening on Reuben's character, 'unstable as water',[57] so applicable to most of this nation. Some were deeply convinced and resolved not to rest till they were stablished in grace.

Sun. 9. I exhorted the society to follow the example of their English brethren by jointly renewing their covenant with God. On Tuesday evening I read the letters, by one of which a poor backslider, who had been wandering near eleven years, was cut to

[54] For Okeley's description of this journey, see *Wesleyan Methodist Magazine* 86 (1863):1103.

[55] The west façade of Trinity College, then nearing completion, was finished in 1759, built on parliamentary funds. The palladian facade, 300 feet long, designed by the London architects Keene and Sanderson, was a source of pride to the college, and was splendidly illuminated on the occasion of the marriage of George III in September 1761. C. Maxwell, *A History of Trinity College, Dublin 1591–1892* (Dublin, 1946), p. 172.

[56] I.e., Peckwater quadrangle in Oxford.

[57] Gen. 49:4.

the heart and determined to return to him from whom he had so deeply revolted.

Thur. 13. I explained at large the nature and manner of entering into covenant with God and desired all who were purposed so to do to set Friday apart for solemn fasting and prayer. Many did so and met both at five in the morning, at noon, and in the evening.

Sun. 16. I was much grieved at St. Peter's Church at such a sight as I never saw in England, communicants as well as others behaving in a manner that shocked common sense as well as religion. O who has the courage to speak plain to these rich and honourable sinners? If they perish in their iniquity,[58] will not their blood be on the watchman's head?[59]

Mon. 17. We met in the evening to renew our covenant with God. It was a glorious season. I believe all that were present found that God was there.

Tue. 18. Among the letters I read in public last week was one from Mr. Gillies,[60] giving an account of a society lately formed at Glasgow for promoting Christian knowledge among the poor, chiefly by distributing Bibles among them, and other religious books. I could not then help expressing my amazement that nothing of this kind had been attempted in Ireland and inquiring if it was not high time that such a society should be formed in Dublin. This morning Dr. Tisdale[61] showed me a paper which the archbishop[62] had just sent to each of his clergy, exhorting them to 'erect a society for the distribution of books among the poor'. Thanks be to God for this! Whether we or they, it is all one, so God be known, loved, and obeyed.

Thur. 20. In the evening I met all the married men and women of the society. I believe it was high time. For many of them seemed to know very little of relative duties. So that I brought strange things to their ears when I enlarged on the duties of husbands and wives and parents.[63]

[58] See Ezek. 33:8.

[59] See Ezek. 33:6.

[60] On John Gillies see Apr. 17, 1753, n. 15 (20:453 in this edn.).

[61] Orig., 'Dr. T.' the name given in full in *Works* (1774). Anthony Tisdall of Dublin. J. B. Leslie and G. B. Swanzy, *Biographical Succession Lists of the Clergy of the Diocese of Down* (Enniskillen, 1936), p. 58.

[62] Charles Cobbe; see Aug. 10, 1747, n. 4 (20:188 in this edn.).

[63] In 1760, at the end of the fourth volume of his *Sermons on Several Occasions*, Wesley added some of the material which probably concerned him on this occasion, an extract from William Whateley's *A Bride-Bush*, which Wesley abridged for his *Christian Library* in 1753, and reduced still further for 'The Duties of Husbands and Wives' in 1760.

Fri. 21. I dined at Lady ——'s.[64] We need great grace to converse with great people! From which therefore (unless in some rare instances) I am glad to be excused. *Horae fugiunt et imputantur*![65] Of these two hours I can give no good account.

Sun. 23. I was much concerned to see two gentlemen, who were close to me at St. Patrick's Church, fall a-talking together in the most trifling manner immediately after they had received the Lord's Supper. Indeed, one who sat by could not but reprove them, whom I seconded in strong terms. And so far (at least) we gained: they talked no more till the service was ended.

Mon. 24. I left Dublin. But our chaise-horse tired before we had drove eight miles. So I went into another chaise and reached Kilcock between eleven and twelve. We were agreeably surprised to hear the maid of the inn singing one of our hymns and to find that her mistress had the evening before been at the preaching in Dublin. This accounted for the profound civility with which all the servants behaved. About one, I took horse and rode on with Robert Swindells to Edenderry.

On the road I read Mr. Walker's account of the siege of Londonderry,[66] and the relation of that of Drogheda, by Dr. Bernard, a vain, childish, affected writer.[67] Sir Henry Tichburn's[68] account of that siege is wrote in a strong and masculine manner and is worthy to be joined with Mr. Walker's plain and clear account of that other amazing scene of providence.

Tue. 15 [i.e., 25]. I read an account of the Irish Rebellion wrote by Dr. Curry,[69] a Papist of Dublin, who labours to wash the Ethiop

[64] It has been surmised that this was Lady Arabella Denny (1707–92), a wealthy widow who devoted herself to charitable works. *WHS* 5 (1905):73-74.

[65] 'The hours are flying, and are being put to our account.' This proverb was based on Martial, *Epigrammata*, v.20.13.

[66] George Walker, *A True Account of the Siege of Londonderry* (London, 1689). Walker (1618–90), the Protestant incumbent of Lissan, Co. Derry, 1669, and Donaghmore, Co. Tyrone, 1674, raised a regiment at Dungannon in 1688, and was joint governor of Derry during the siege in 1689. His *True Account* was cast in the form of a diary. Bishop-designate of Derry in 1690, he was killed at the Battle of the Boyne.

[67] Nicholas Bernard, *The Whole Proceedings of the Siege of Drogheda, &c.* (London, 1642; repr. Dublin, 1736). Bernard, who died in 1661, was dean of Ardagh, 1632–61, and chaplain to Oliver Cromwell.

[68] Orig., 'Titchburn'. Sir Henry Tichborne, *History of the Siege of Drogheda with Sir John Temple's History of the Irish Rebellion* (Dublin, 1724). Tichborne (*c.* 1581–1667) was made governor of Drogheda at the outbreak of the rebellion in 1641, and successfully defended it for four months.

[69] John Curry, *Historical Memoirs of the Irish Rebellion in 1641* (London, 1758). John Curry, whose family had lost 'a considerable landed property' in the seventeenth-century confiscations, and who built up a good medical practice in Dublin, is now regarded as a

white[70] by numberless falsehoods and prevarications. But he is treated according to his merit by Mr. Harris,[71] in a tract entitled, *Fiction Unmasked.*

In the evening, I preached under the castle-wall to a very numerous congregation, though some of the Quakers (so called) had laboured much to dissuade their people from coming. And one poor man lately reclaimed, by hearing our preachers, from a course of open, scandalous sin, they did persuade to stay at home. When he turns back to his vomit,[72] who shall answer for *his* blood?

Wed. 26. I walked round the poor remains of the castle. The situation is extremely fine. It stands on the top of a gently rising hill, commanding the prospect all four ways and having rows of tall trees reaching down to the vale on three sides, with a grove covering it on the north-east. But the house, as well as the gardens round about it, are now utterly run to ruin. I wonder none has rebuilt it—unless there is a curse on the place for the sins of its former inhabitants!

Thur. 26 [i.e., 27]. I finished Mr. Spearman's *Inquiry*, an ingenious, sensible book.[73] But I cannot at all agree with his scheme. I still think Mr. Hutchinson's whole system is not only quite unsupported by Scripture but loaded with insuperable difficulties.[74] I cannot yet see the possibility of any motion without so much as a *vacuum disseminatum*.[75] Is it not flatly impossible, if all be full and all matter be impenetrable? Much less can I conceive how the streams of light and air can move continually in opposite

skilful propagandist in an age in which propaganda was the only Catholic weapon. 'Honest, with some analytical skill, he was essentially a forensic historian, striving to correct what he considered to be misrepresentations of past events which put the Irish Catholics in an unfavourable light' (R. B. McDowell, *Ireland in the Age of Imperialism and Revolution* [Oxford, 1979], p. 185). He died in 1781.

70 Cf. Jer. 13:23.

71 Walter Harris, *Fiction Unmasked, or an Answer to a Dialogue lately Published by a Popish Physician* (Dublin, 1752). Harris (1686–1761), the most noted Irish historiographer of his generation, devoted great effort to producing an improved edition and translation of Ware's 'Works Concerning Ireland'; he also wrote a good deal in the field of recent Irish history, including this reply to Curry. He became vicar-general to the Protestant Bishop of Meath in 1753.

72 See Prov. 26:11.

73 Robert Spearman, *An Enquiry after Philosophy and Theology* (Edinburgh, 1755). Spearman (1703–61) employed a life of leisure in Co. Durham in 'rambling speculations in theology'. He was a pupil of John Hutchinson, editied his works, and wrote an account of his life.

74 On Hutchinson, see Dec. 20, 1746, n. 11 (20:151 in this edn.), and above, Nov. 22, 1756, n. 15.

75 This phrase was unilluminatingly translated by Jackson (3:441) as 'a vacuum diffused through different parts of the universe', the impulse to fill which made motion possible.

directions, and that in space absolutely full, without jostling[76] with each other!

In the evening, I preached at Portarlington. Both this day and the next I was much concerned for my rich, gay hearers, and God gave me such a word for them as I scarce ever had before.

Hence, at his earnest request, I rode over to Mr. L——[77] who said he 'could not die in peace till he had seen' me. For some time he had been quite distracted, but he spoke quite sensibly yesterday while Mr. Swindells was there, saying with many tears, he had 'never prospered in anything since he used Mr. W. so ill'. That night he had sound and refreshing sleep, which he had not had for many weeks before, and when we called, most of what he said was reasonable and connected. Perhaps God may put an end to the troubles which have lately encompassed him on every side.

Sat. 29. I preached in the market-place at Mountmellick in the evening and at eight in the morning. At eleven I went to church. Soon after, seven or eight troopers came into the same pew. Several were in the next pew, and others scattered up and down the church. In the middle of the service a person came in and whispered to one of them in our pew. Soon after, another person came in and whispered to the corporal. Several of them then whispered together, after which four went out but quickly returned with many swords and pistols. After whispering together again, they all rose up from all parts and went out of the church in a body. This put the whole congregation in an uproar, and many ran out in all haste. Afterwards the secret appeared to be this. Three weeks ago a man of the town grossly abused a trooper, whose patience at length being worn out, he gave him a cut across the head. A report now came that the man was dead. On this the mob gathered to seize the trooper. But the others resolved not to give him up to a mob but to the peace-officer.

I suppose most of the Protestants in the town were present at the evening sermon. Many Papists also stood in the skirts of the congregation, though liable to heavy penance for it. I preached much longer than I am accustomed, finding it an acceptable time. Well might Kempis say, 'He rides easily whom the grace of God carries.'[78]

[76] Orig., 'justling'.

[77] *Works* (1774): 'L——y', although other evidence points to John Laborde of Closeland, who died soon afterwards. He had entertained JW in 1749.

[78] Thomas à Kempis, *The Christian's Pattern* (1753), II.ix.1, 'He rideth easily enough whom the grace of God carrieth.'

Monday, May 1. I strove to put an end to the bitter contentions which had well-nigh torn the society in pieces. I heard the contending parties face to face and desired them to speak at large. God gave his blessing therewith: the snare was broken,[79] and they were cordially reconciled. Only one person was out of all patience and formally renounced us all. But within an hour God broke her heart also, and she asked pardon with many tears. So there is reason to hope, they will for the time to come 'bear one another's burdens'.[80]

In the evening I preached at Tullamore, not only to a large number of Protestants, but to many Papists and almost all the troopers in town.

Tue. 2. I wrote a short Answer to Dr. Free's weak, bitter, scurrilous invective against the people called Methodists.[81] But I doubt whether I shall meddle with *him* any more. He is too *dirty* a writer for *me* to touch.

Wed. 3. I preached at four in the afternoon at Coolalough and at eight in the morning, after which I rode on to Tyrrellspass. The letters which I read here were seasonable as rain in the time of drought. I had before found much weariness, but God thereby gave a check to my faintness of spirit and enabled me to 'gird up the loins of my mind'.[82]

In the evening, the weather being calm and mild, I preached on the side of a meadow, the people standing before me, one above another, on the side of a gently-rising hill. And many did indeed at that hour 'taste and see that the Lord is gracious'.[83]

Fri. 5. In the evening I preached at Drumcree, in the new room, built in the taste of the country. The roof is thatch, the walls mud, on which a ladder was suspended by ropes of straw. Hence we rode to Rosmead. The congregation here was not large but deeply serious.

Sun. 7. I preached at eight and at five. Afterward I was desired

[79] See Ps. 124:7.

[80] Gal. 6:2.

[81] On Apr. 5, 1758, the Rev. Dr. John Free (*c.* 1712–91), a prolific controversialist, had published *Certain Articles Proposed to the Serious Considerations of the Court of Assistants of the Worshipful Company of Salters in London* (London, Owen, 1758), attacking the Methodists. Wesley replied on May 2, with *A Letter to the Rev. Dr. Free.* On June 14, Free published a sermon directed at Wesley entitled, *Rules for the Discovery of False Prophets.* This called forth a reply from Wesley, *A Second Letter to the Rev. Dr. Free.* See *Bibliography,* Nos. 227-28; and 9:315-30 in this edn.

[82] 1 Pet. 1:13.

[83] Cf. Ps. 34:8 (a conflation of AV and BCP).

to make a collection for a distressed family. Mr. Booker,[84] the minister of the parish, willingly stood at the door to receive it and encouraged all that went by to be 'merciful after their power'.[85]

Mon. 8. I rode to Newry and preached at seven to a large and serious congregation.

Tue. 9. We rode by the side of the canal, through a pleasant vale, to Terryhoogan.[86] The room built on purpose for us here is three yards long, two-and-a-quarter broad, and six foot high. The walls, floor, and ceiling are mud, and we had a clean, chaff bed. At seven, I preached in a neighbouring ground, having a rock behind me and a large congregation sitting on the grass before me. Thence, we retired to our hut and found it true,

Licet sub paupere tecto
Reges et regum vita praecurrere amicos.[87]

Wed. 10. I suppose all the inhabitants of the village, with many others, were present at five in the morning. Among these was a poor woman, brought to bed ten days before, who had walked four Irish miles (seven English) with her child in her arms, to have it baptized by *me*. Another, who lived at Terryhoogan, had earnestly desired the same thing, if she was delivered before I left the country. She was delivered two or three hours before the preaching. So God gave her what she asked of him.

In riding to Lisburn I read Mr. Rollin's *Ancient History*.[88] Could so masterly a writer make so palpable blunders? Or are they owing to the translator? I have observed many as gross as that in the fourth volume. 'A revered old age was the fruit of Gelon's wisdom. . . . He was succeeded by Hiero, his eldest brother. This young prince . . . .'[89] How? If Gelon enjoyed revered *old age*, could his *eldest brother* be *young* after his death?

84 See Aug. 2, 1752, n. 30 (20:435 in this edn.).

85 Cf. John Wesley, *The Nature, Design, and General Rules of the United Societies in London, Bristol, Kingswood, and Newcastle upon Tyne* (1743), §5: '*Secondly*, by doing good, by being in every kind merciful after their power . . .'.

86 Orig., 'Terry-hugan'.

87 Horace, *Epistles*, I.x.32-34: 'though humble be your home, yet in life's race you may outstrip kings and the friends of kings' (Loeb).

88 Charles Rollin, *The Ancient History of the Egyptians, Carthaginians, Assyrians, Babylonians, Medes and Persians, Macedonians and Grecians*, 10 vols. (2nd edn., London, 1738–40; first published in 13 vols. in Paris, 1731–38).

89 JW offers a compacted version; ibid., 3:299-300. *The Oxford Classical Dictionary* offers no opinion whether Hieron was a younger or older brother of Gelon; but as the latter died in 478 B.C., aged *c.* 62, and Hieron lived till 467/6 B.C., he may well have been the younger.

Abundance of people attended the preaching in the evening, as well as in the morning.

Fri. 12. I preached about noon at Comber and then rode on to Newtownards.[90] This seems to have been a place of strength, large fragments of walls still remaining. I preached at seven on the green to the largest congregation I have seen since I came into the kingdom. All were quietly attentive, and when I had done, went away in deep silence.

Sat. 13. We went into the church, the burial-place of Mr. Colvin's[91] father and ancestors. The choir, turned into a chapel many years ago, is grand and finely finished. But as no man cares for it since the estate was sold, it is swiftly running to ruin.

In the evening we had a larger congregation than before. I was afraid my voice would not reach them all. But God gave me strength, so that I believe every one present might hear distinctly.

Sun. 14. I preached in the market-house at Belfast about one, and in the court-house at Carrickfergus in the evening.

Mon. 15. I rode over the mountains to Larne,[92] a small seaport ten miles north of Carrickfergus. The sun shone bright and exceeding hot, and the wind was pretty high. They fixed the table just fronting the midday sun, and where an eddy of wind poured in continually. And it was well they did. For the sun tempered the wind, so that I could bear both better than either. I suppose most of the town were present, rich and poor, and I believe the word of God did not return empty.

In the evening I preached at Carrick[fergus] again. The old Earl of Donegal,[93] one of the richest peers in Ireland, took much pleasure here in his stately house, surrounded by large and elegant gardens. But his only son proved an idiot. And the present heir regards them not. So the roof of the house is fallen in, and the horses and sheep which feed in the gardens make wild work with

[90] Orig., 'Newtown' in all contemporary editions. Comber was a parish 14 miles north-west of Downpatrick.

[91] This is an error for Robert Colville (d. 1749). JW returned to this strange case in the entry for June 11, 1778, where the whole matter is elucidated in the notes.

[92] Orig., 'Larn'.

[93] The reference here is to Arthur Chichester, 3rd Earl of Donegal (1666–1706), who lost his life on military service in Spain in the War of the Spanish Succession. His son and heir by his second marriage died without issue in 1757, and was succeeded in the earldom by his nephew Arthur Chichester (1739–99), of the Surrey branch of the family. The 5th earl's second and third marriages were to ladies with Irish connections, but he resided at St. James's Square, London.

the parterres and curious trees which the old lord so carefully planted.

Tue. 16. We rode to Lurgan. In the morning I walked to Lough Neagh, the most beautiful lake I ever saw. On the south-east shore stands a small mount, supposed to be raised by the Danes, on the top of which is a kind of arbour, benched round with turf, which might contain twenty or thirty people.

This was the hottest day I ever felt in Ireland—near as hot as any I remember in Georgia. The next morning I was desired to see the house of an eminent scholar near the town. The door into the yard we found *nailed* up, but we got in at a gap which was stopped with thorns. I took the house at first for a very old barn, but was assured he had built it within five years—not indeed by any old, vulgar model but purely to his own taste. The walls were part mud, part brick, part stone, and part bones and wood. There were four windows but no glass in any, lest the pure air should be kept out. The house had two stories but no staircase and no door. Into the upper floor we went by a ladder through one of the windows, through one of the lower windows into the lower floor, which was about four foot high. This floor had three rooms, one three-square,[94] the second had five sides, the third, I know not how many. I give a particular description of this wonderful edifice to illustrate that great truth—there is no folly too great, even for a man of sense, if he resolve to follow his own imagination!

I spent Friday and Saturday at Newry, a town risen out of its ashes within these twenty years.

Sun. 21. I was much pleased with the seriousness and decency of the congregation at church. But they were a little hurried in the middle of the service. A young man dropped down as dead. In a little time, however, he came to himself and was led out of church.

Mon. 22. I rode through a barren, dreary country, and by a miserable road to Castleblayney.[95] The morning was extremely hot, but we had a cooler ride in the afternoon to Cootehill.[96] I preached at seven in an open place near the street to a tolerably serious congregation. At six in the morning there were more

[94] Having three equal sides—now dialect.

[95] Orig., 'Castle Blaney'. Castleblayney was a fortified post maintained by the descendants of Sir Edward Blayney in return for the grant of land they received in the reign of James I. It developed into a town only with the establishment of the linen market towards the end of the eighteenth century.

[96] Orig., 'Coot-hill'. Cootehill was a market town in the parish of Drumgoon, 12 miles north-east of Cavan.

rather than fewer, who then seemed to *feel* as well as *hear*. I walked afterward to the German house,[97] about as large as the chapel in Snowsfields. They have pitched upon a delightful situation, laid out a garden by it, planted trees round the ground, and every way approved themselves 'wise in their generation'.[98] They often put me in mind of the monks of old, who had picked out the pleasantest spots in our nation. But when their time was come, God swept them away, in an hour they looked not for it.

In the evening I preached at Dingins, in the county of Cavan, on the very edge of Ulster. Many came from far, a few of whom have tasted that the Lord is gracious.

Wed. 24. I preached in the morning at Granard in the barrack-yard. I have rarely seen a congregation in a new place so much affected. About one, I preached at Edgeworthstown[99] to a very genteel congregation, extremely different from that which gathered at Longford in the yard of the great inn—the rudest, surliest, wildest people that I have found since I came into the kingdom. However, they stood pretty quiet, till some pieces of turf were thrown among them over the houses. And when they had recovered from the hurry it put them into, they behaved decently till I concluded.

Thur. 25. I preached at Cleggill[1] about one, and then rode on to Drumsna.[2] Wood, water, fruitful land, and gently-rising hills contribute to make this place a little paradise. Mr. Campbell, the proprietor of the whole, resolved to make it such. So he planted groves, laid out walks, formed the plan of a new town, with a barrack at one end and his own seat at the other. But alas! death stepped in between, and all his plan fell to the ground.

I lodged at the only gentleman's house in the town, whose wife adorns the gospel.

Sat. 27. I rode through Jamestown,[3] once a strong place, now an heap of ruins, and through Carrick[on Shannon] and Boyle, both enclosed by a pleasant and fruitful country. Soon after, we entered the county of Sligo,[4] the best peopled that I have seen in

[97] There was a Moravian chapel in Cootehill.

[98] Cf. Luke 16:8.

[99] Orig., 'Edgeworthtown'. Edgworthstown (or Mostrim) was a small town and large parish 6¾ miles south-east of Longford.

[1] Orig., 'Cleg-hill'.

[2] Orig., 'Drumersnave'.

[3] Orig., 'James's Town'. Jamestown was a tiny parliamentary borough situated on the Shannon in the parish of Kiltoyhart, Co. Leitrim.

[4] Orig., 'Sligoe'. Sligo was an important seaport, borough, and county town 103¾ miles north-west of Dublin.

the kingdom. Eight villages we counted within seven miles; the town itself, I think, is little less than Limerick. The country round it is fertile and well-improved, even the mountains, to the very top. It lies two miles from the sea, having a large harbour, covered by mountains on each side.

The mob had been in motion all the day. But their business was only with the forestallers of the market, who had bought up all the corn far and near, to starve the poor and load a Dutch ship, which lay at the quay.[5] But the mob brought it all out into the market and sold it for the owners at the common price. And this they did with all the calmness and composure imaginable and without striking or hurting anyone.

I preached in the evening near the main street to a small, quiet, serious company; at nine, Sunday 28, in the market-house to a numerous congregation. But they were doubled at five in the afternoon, and God made his word quick and powerful. Even the rich and genteel part of the audience appeared to be deeply affected. O for labourers! for a few γνησία τέκνα,[6] desirous only to spend and be spent[7] for their brethren.

Mon. 29. I rode to Castlebar.

Thursday, June 1. I went to Newport. I believe all the Protestants in the town gladly attended the evening preaching, and few of them were wanting at five in the morning. How white are these fields to the harvest![8]

Friday, June 2. I rode to Hollymount and preached in the churchyard. I then visited my antagonist, Mr. Clark,[9] who was lying extremely ill.

Sat. 3. I preached at Manulla,[10] a village four miles from Castlebar. I was surprised to find how little the Irish Papists are changed in an hundred years. Most of them retain the same bitterness, yea, and thirst for blood, as ever and would as freely now cut the throats of all the Protestants as they did in the last century.

Sun. 4. As they have the Lord's Supper here but four times a year, I administered it in the evening to about sixty persons.

5 Orig., 'Kay'.
6 'true sons'; cf. 1 Tim. 1:2; Titus 1:4.
7 2 Cor. 12:15.
8 See John 4:35.
9 Rev. James Clark, rector of Hollymount; see above, June 27, 1756, n. 30.
10 Orig., 'Minulla'.

Scarce one of them went empty away.[11] Many were filled with consolation.[12]

Tue. 6. I set out at four (the hour I had appointed) on foot, the horse brought for me having neither bridle nor saddle. After a time one galloped after me full speed, till just as he overtook me, horse and man came down together. The horse's knee spouted out blood, as if an artery had been cut. But on a sudden the blood stopped, nor did he bleed any more all the way to Aughrim.[13]

I found a few here, and left more 'striving to enter in at the strait gate'.[14]

Fri. 9. About eight I preached at Ahascragh, to a congregation of whom four-fifths were Papists. Would to God the government would ensure to all the Papists in the land so much liberty of conscience that none might 'hinder them from hearing' the true Word of God! Then, as they hear, so let them judge. In the evening I preached at Athlone.

Sun. 11. We had an excellent sermon at church on the intercession of Christ. In the afternoon abundance of Papists, as well as Protestants, were present on the Connaught side of the river, while I explained the 'joy' that is 'in heaven over one sinner that repenteth'.[15] Toward the close, two or three eggs were thrown, and not long after, two stones. One of them fell on a gentleman's servant, the other on a drummer, which so enraged the dragoons (many of whom were in the congregation) that as soon as I concluded they run all ways to find the man that threw.

[11] See Luke 1:53.

[12] None was more in need of consolation at this moment than JW himself. As his letters to Ebenezer Blackwell show (June 5, July 12, 1758), his relations with his wife had reached a new pitch of bitterness, in no way helped by his desire that his brother should take charge of the English work for a year, thus freeing him to evangelize every dark corner in Ireland. Telford, 4:21-23.

[13] Orig., 'Aghrin'.

[14] Cf. Luke 13:24. Methodist commentators endeavoured from an early date to fill the silence of the journal at this point. Walter Shirley (1752–1786), brother of the 4th Earl Ferrers, and first cousin of the Countess of Huntingdon, had been rector of the nearby parish of Loughrea since 1746, and is represented as the legendary type of hunting parson. About 1758 he was converted, principally (in the belief of Henry Moore) by JW's agency, and certainly wrote to him in the most glowing terms a year later (Henry Moore, *The Life of the Rev. John Wesley*, 2 vols [London, Kershaw, 1824–25], 2:236-38). If it was indeed the case that Shirley's transformation was due to JW rather than to the influence of the devout circles surrounding the Countess of Huntingdon, this visit to Aughrim must have been the occasion for the decisive step, and Shirley must have been among the 'few . . . more "striving to enter in at the strait gate"'. He turned violently against JW in the Calvinist controversy of 1770. *Arminian Magazine* 13 (1790):106-7, 168-69, 332-35, 560.

[15] Luke 15:7.

The spirit they showed did much good by striking a terror into the rabble. But I was glad they did not discover the offender. I believe his fright was punishment enough.

Tue. 14 [i.e., 13]. I met the preachers and stewards at Coolalough. The congregation at noon was the largest I ever saw there. In the afternoon the perplexed case of I. C. and I. A. was referred to Mr. S. and Mr. H.,[16] who after a long hearing judged (as did all present): 'That I. C. had acted wrong in seizing and selling I. A.'s goods for rent, when no rent was due.'

After preaching in the evening I talked with Kath. Shea of Athlone concerning a strange account which I had heard. There are many now living who attest on their personal knowledge most of the particulars of it. She said:

> When I was ten years old the preaching began at Athlone. I liked, and often heard it, though my parents were zealous Papists, till they removed into the country. I then grew as zealous as them and was diligent in reading the papish[17] prayers till I was about thirteen, when taking the Mass-book one day to read my prayers, I could not see one word. I continued blind, just able to discern light from darkness but not to read or do any work. Till after three months, casting my eye on a New Testament, I could read clearly. I said to myself, 'I won't read this Protestant book. I will read my own book.' Accordingly I opened the Mass-book but could not see one word—it appeared all dark and black. I made the trial thrice over, holding the Mass-book in one hand and the Testament in the other. I could not see anything in the Mass-book but could read the Testament as well as ever. On this I threw away the Mass-book, fully resolved to meddle with it no more.
>
> Afterwards my parents returned to Athlone. Then I heard the preaching at all opportunities. For this they beat me many times and at last turned me out of doors. Yet after this my father brought me to the priest, who disputed with me very warmly. At length my father said, 'I think the girl is in the right.' And he opposed me no more to the day of his death.

Wed. 14. I preached at Tullamore about eleven, and at Birr in the evening.

Fri. 16. I set out for Limerick. I was wet through from head to foot before I came thither but received no hurt. Here I had a

[16] Probably Samuel Simpson (see May 8, 1748, n. 47; 20:225 in this edn.) and Samuel Handy (see Apr. 5, 1748, n. 16; 20:217 in this edn.)

[17] 1768, 1788, 'papist'; *Works* (1774), 'popish'. 'Papish' was regularly in use, however, as a hostile epithet—see *OED*. Cf. above, June 25, 1756.

particular account of the melancholy affair which was in the mouths of all men. On Sunday evening last, two officers were playing at dice when they quarrelled about a lewd woman. This occasioned a challenge from Mr. I., which the other would fain have declined. But he would not be denied and was so bent upon it, that he would not go to bed. About three in the morning they went out, with their seconds, to the island. Mr. B. proposed firing at twelve yards' distance. But Mr. I. said, 'No, no, six is enough.' So they kissed one another (poor farce!), and before they were five paces asunder, both fired at the same instant. The ball went into Mr. I.'s breast, who turned round twice or thrice and fell. He was carried home, made his will, and about three in the afternoon died like a man of honour!

How are 'the judgments of the Lord abroad in the earth'![18] About Easter last, Mr. Beauchamp was at a gentleman's house in the county of Clare, when a gentleman who was occasionally there, finding they were going to family prayers, ran away in all haste, swearing he 'would have none of their swaddling prayers'. Two or three weeks after, he imagined himself to be not very well. A physician was called, who for three or four days successively affirmed, there was no danger at all. On the fifth day a second physician was called, who feeling his pulse said, 'Why do you send for *me*? I can do nothing. He is a dead man.' Hearing this he cried out, 'Doctor, you have deceived me. I leave money enough. But my soul is lost.' He catched hold of one and another, crying, 'Save me, save me.' He endeavoured to throw himself into the fire. Being hindered from doing this, he seized upon his own arm and tore it with his teeth. And after a short time, in all the agony of rage, despair, and horror, expired.

[18] Cf. 1 Chr. 16:14.

A N

EXTRACT

OF THE

Rev. Mr. *JOHN WESLEY's*

JOURNAL,

FROM

JUNE 17, 1758, to MAY 5, 1760.

BRISTOL:
Printed by WILLIAM PINE, in *Narrow-Wine-Street.*
MDCCLXIV.

Journal

From June 17, 1758, to May 5, 1760

Saturday, June 17, 1758,[1] I met Thomas Walsh once more, in Limerick, alive, and but just alive.[2] Three of the best physicians in these parts have attended him, and all agree that it is a lost case; that by violent straining of his voice, added to frequent colds, he has contracted a pulmonary consumption which is now in the last stage and consequently beyond the reach of any human help. O what a man, to be snatched away in the strength of his years! Surely thy judgments are a great deep![3]

Wed. 21. Our little Conference began,[4] at which fourteen preachers were present. We settled all things here which we judged would be of use to the preachers or the societies, and consulted how to remove whatever might be an hindrance to the work of God.

Fri. 23. I rode over to Courtmatrix,[5] a colony of Germans, whose parents came out of the Palatinate about fifty years ago.[6] Twenty families of them settled here, twenty more at Killeheen,[7] a mile off; fifty at Ballingarrane,[8] about two miles eastward; and twenty at Pallas, four miles farther. Each family had a few acres of

[1] This opens 'Number XI' of the *Extracts*, published in 1764. The year was added in 1791.

[2] Thomas Walsh had returned to Cork from Bristol in mid-April, already very ill, the best doctors judging 'that his case was now past all remedy'; see Sept. 2, 1752, n. 47 (20:438-39 in this edn.). From Limerick, where JW met him for the last time, he was sent into the country for fresh air and nursing, but, making no progress, he moved to Dublin, where he died on Apr. 8, 1759. Jackson, *Early Methodist Preachers*, 3:265.

[3] Ps. 36:6.

[4] On this Limerick Conference, see Crookshank, *Ireland*, 1:131; and the Irish *Methodist Magazine* 27 (1804):517.

[5] Orig., 'Court-Mattress'. Courtmatrix is a hamlet near Rathkeale.

[6] On the Palatines generally, see above, June 16, 1756, n. 22. The meeting-house at Courtmatrix was built through the efforts, and partly through the labours, of Philip Embury (1728–73 or –75), a carpenter, converted through JW's preaching in 1752. He became a local preacher, and at the Conference mentioned in the previous paragraph, was proposed for the itinerancy. Being only placed on the reserve list, however, he married and in 1760 emigrated to America, the first Methodist local preacher so to do, and helped to create the first Methodist society there.

[7] Orig., 'Killiheen'.

[8] Orig., 'Balligarane'.

ground, on which they built as many little houses. They are since considerably increased in number of souls, though decreased in number of families. Having no minister, they were become eminent for drunkenness, cursing, swearing, and an utter neglect of religion. But they are washed, since they heard and received the truth which is able to save their souls.[9] An oath is now rarely heard among them, or a drunkard seen in their borders. Courtmatrix is built in the form of a square, in the middle of which they have placed a pretty large preaching-house. But it would not contain one half of the congregation—so I stood in a large yard. The wind kept off the rain while I was preaching. As soon as I ended it began.

Sun. 25. About six I preached in the island in a square, green enclosure, which was formerly Oliver Cromwell's camp. I have not seen such a congregation since we left London. To how much better purpose is this ground employed than it was in the last century!

Thur. 29. I rode to Clare, and at six preached in the street to many poor Papists and rich Protestants, almost all the gentry in the country being assembled together. Thence I went on to Ennis, and at ten the next morning had another genteel congregation in the court-house. In Ennis, many suppose, there are not less than fifty Papists to one Protestant. They would have been very ready to show their goodwill. But the sight of Mr. B——[10] kept them in awe. A report, however, was spread of some terrible things they were to do in the evening, and many were surprised to observe that more than nine in ten of the congregation were Papists. But none spoke an unkind or uncivil word, either while I preached or after I had done.

How unspeakable is the advantage, in point of common sense, which middling people have over the rich! There is so much paint and affectation, so many unmeaning words and senseless customs among people of rank, as fully justify the remark made seventeen hundred years ago:

Sensus communis in illa Fortuna rarus.[11]

[9] See Jas. 1:21.

[10] Perhaps Mr. Bindon (of Ennis), opposite whose house JW preached on May 27, 1762.

[11] Cf. Juvenal, *Satires*, viii.73-74, 'For in those high places regard for others is rarely to be found.' Whether the meaning of this quotation really supports JW's (frequently expressed) view that the middling orders suffered less from stiffness than their social betters is a question; cf. Feb. 7, 1772.

Sunday, July 2. I preached in the island near Limerick both morning and evening, standing on the side of a large hollow adjoining to the old camp. The ground on the sides of it sloped upward, so that the people sat on the grass row above row. Such an amphitheatre I never saw before, in which thousands of hearers were so commodiously placed. And they seemed earnestly to attend to our Lord's invitation, 'Come, for all things are now ready!'[12]

I did not then observe that I strained myself. But in the morning I was extremely hoarse. This increased all day, together with a load and stoppage in my breast. On Tuesday morning I began spitting blood, found a pain in my left side, a sensible decay of strength, and a deep wheezing cough—just the symptoms which I had some years since. I immediately applied a brimstone plaster to my side and used a linctus of roasted lemon and honey. Wednesday 5, my side was quite easy, and my hoarseness much abated. So in the evening I made shift to preach again, though not without difficulty. I had purposed preaching the next day at Shronell, about twenty-four English miles from Limerick, and at Clonmel, about the same distance from Shronell, but perceiving my strength would not suffice and yielding to the advice of my friends, rested another day.

Thur. 6. The news of Prince Ferdinand's victory[13] had half turned the heads of most of the Protestants, till they were brought to themselves by news of another kind, which ran through the city as in an instant. One who was well known therein, a great curser and blasphemer, and eminently 'without God in the world',[14] went a-fishing a little way from his own door and stood with his angling-rod on the edge of the water. Many were looking on when, his foot slipping, he fell forward and sunk. As help was at hand, he was soon drawn out. But it was too late. There was no remains of life. His soul was gone to give its account.

Fri. 7. I rode in a chaise to Charleville,[15] and thence on an easy

[12] Luke 14:17.

[13] The tide had turned in the Seven Years' War with Frederick the Great's victory over the French at Rossbach in November 1757. Pitt then had Prince Ferdinand of Brunswick (1721–92) seconded to the command of an army to protect Frederick's flank and reinforced it with British troops. Ferdinand was immediately successful and, in June 1758, defeated the French at Rheinberg and Crefeld.

[14] Eph. 2:12.

[15] Orig., 'Charlevill'. Charleville was a market town in the parish of Rathgoggan (and, until the union, a parliamentary borough) 29 miles north-west of Cork.

horse to Cork. James Massiot[16] died in peace the morning before; so I was just in time to perform the last office for him.

Sat. 8. The congregation was large, but my voice was so weak that many could not hear. Sun. 9. After the burial of James Massiot I preached to a multitude of people on 'Blessed are the dead which die in the Lord.'[17] And the longer I spoke, the more my voice was strengthened.

Tue. 11. I rode with James Morgan[18] to Bandon and preached in the market-house to a listening multitude. Wed. 12. I read over the *Analysis* of Lord Bolingbroke's Works.[19] Surely never did any man so flatly contradict, and so fully answer himself. Thur. 13. About noon I preached in the Exchange at Kinsale. The townsfolk 'care for none of these things'.[20] But we had a large congregation of soldiers, many of whom are good soldiers of Jesus Christ.[21]

In the evening I preached in the main street at Bandon. Having now need of all my voice, it was given me again, only with a little pain in my side, which ceased while I was speaking.

Sat. 15. I preached about noon at Inishannon and returned to Bandon. A fortnight since they laid the foundation of their preaching-house.[22] This evening I preached in the shell of it. But it would not contain the congregation. Truly these are 'swift to hear', though not 'slow to speak'.[23]

[16] James Massiot of Cork, the first of the Irish preachers to end his earthly course. After some years service in England, Massiot had been appointed to Ireland in 1756. His daughter married Joseph Cownley, whose relations with Massiot's niece figured in the charges made against Methodist preachers at the time of the Cork riots in 1750. Telford, 3:283.

[17] Rev. 14:13.

[18] See above, Aug. 11, 1756, n. 77.

[19] Thomas Church, *An Analysis of the Philosophical Works of the late Lord Viscount Bolingbroke* (London, 1755). This entry is of double interest. Thomas Church (1707–56), who prepared the *Analysis*, vicar of Battersea from 1740, and prebendary of St. Paul's from 1744, was a critic not only of Deism but of Methodism, with whom JW had maintained a lengthy and courteous exchange in the 1740s. See Wesley, *The Principles of a Methodist Farther Explained* (1746; 9:160-237 in this edn.). If Church's work is here (so-to-speak) received, it is noteworthy that it was through Bolingbroke (now so vehemently repudiated as a philosopher) that the young JW had sought church preferment. See Mar. 28, 1739, n. 69 (19:38 in this edn.).

[20] Cf. Acts 18:17.

[21] See 2 Tim. 2:3.

[22] Like similar erections in England, the Bandon preaching-house had to accommodate the preachers as well as the flock. It finally contained a gallery with a room for the preachers created by movable partitions which could be opened to accommodate the congregation. Crookshank, *Ireland*, 1:278.

[23] Jas. 1:19.

Sun. 16. I preached again in the shell of the house at eight, and in the main street at six in the evening. Observing many of the French officers there, I could not but pray for them in particular. Some of them were deeply attentive. Perhaps it was not for nothing that God brought them into a strange land.

Mon. 17. I returned to Cork. Wed. 18 [i.e., 19]. I began speaking severally to the members of the society. Many of them, I found, were truly alive to God. Old misunderstandings were removed. And I had the satisfaction of seeing them so united together as they had not been for many years.

Fri. 21. I met with a tract which utterly confounded all my philosophy. I had long believed that microscopic animals were generated, like all other animals, by parents of the same species. But Mr. Needham[24] makes it highly probably that they constitute a peculiar class of animals, differing from all others in this, that they neither are generated, or generate, nor subsist by food in the ordinary way.

Tue. 25. In the evening, I assisted the society in renewing their covenant with God. It was to many a season of great refreshment, and the fear of God was upon all.

Sun. 30. I began meeting the children in the afternoon, though with little hopes of doing them good. But I had not spoke long on our natural state before many of them were in tears, and five or six so affected that they could not refrain from crying aloud to God. When I began to pray, their cries increased, so that my voice was soon lost. I have seen no such work among children for eighteen or nineteen years.

Mon. 31. I finished the Glasgow *Abridgement* of Mr. Hutchinson's Works.[25] He was doubtless a man of uncommon understanding and indefatigable application. Yet the more I consider it, the less can I subscribe to his system either of divinity or philosophy, as I am more and more convinced that they have no foundation in Scripture or sound reason.

Tuesday, August 1. The captain with whom we were to sail was in great haste to have our things on board. But I would not send them while the wind was against us. On Wednesday he sent message after message. So in the evening we went down to the

[24] Walter Needham (1631?–91?) a physician and anatomist of note, who published many scientific papers and also the *Disquisitio Anatomica de Formato Foetu* (London, 1667), probably the work here referred to.

[25] See above, Nov. 22, 1756, n. 15.

ship near Passage [West]. But there was nothing ready, or near ready, for sailing. Hence I learned two or three rules, very needful for those who sail between England and Ireland: (1) Never pay till you set sail. (2) Go not on board till the captain goes on board. (3) Send not your baggage on board till you go yourself.

Thur. 3. I returned to Cork. On Saturday 5, we were called on board in all haste. But the captain being in no haste to sail, I preached at Cork again on Sunday at five, and then returned to Passage. He now said he would fall down to Cobh[26] directly; so we took boat and went down thither. But no captain appeared either this day or the next. So, that I might not lie idle, I went down to the beach and began preaching to as wild, unpromising a congregation as ever I saw in this kingdom. However, they performed more than they promised. For they grew more and more quiet and attentive. And some of them appeared to be deeply affected.

Mon. 7. Hearing nothing of our captain yet, in the afternoon I went to the middle of the town. Abundance of people ran together. But they were far too wild and noisy to admit of my giving out a psalm or naming a text in the usual way. So I fell abruptly upon as many as could hear, in a free and familiar manner. In a few minutes the whole body were quiet and tolerably attentive. They were more and more serious till I concluded with an hymn and a short prayer.

Immediately after preaching I was sent for to a gentleman who was struck with the palsy. I found the house full of his friends and relations, to whom I spoke freely and largely. They seemed to be more than ordinarily affected. Perhaps for this also we were detained at Cobh.

Tue. 8. I preached not far from the beach to a very decent and serious congregation. Presently after, a vessel sailed by bound for Wales. We went on board without delay, got out of the harbour by eleven, and by Wednesday noon were abreast of the Isle of Lundy. But we had not yet done our work; so the wind fell, and we did not get into the river till near sunset. Observing three or four sailors standing[27] together, I began explaining to them the nature of religion. In a few minutes all within the ship came together,

[26] Orig., 'Cove'; now Cobh or Queenstown. See Oct. 2, 1752, n. 53 (20:440 in this edn.).

[27] 1764, 1791, '. . . four of the sailors then standing'; *Works* (1774), 'four sailors there standing', altered by the errata and in Wesley's personal copy to the edited text.

and without the ceremony of naming a text I enlarged on 'The kingdom of heaven is not meats and drinks, but righteousness and peace and joy in the Holy Ghost.'[28] About eleven we landed at Pen-clawdd,[29] and in the morning rode to Swansea.[30]

Thur. 10. We rode through a pleasant country to Pyle.[31] We were setting out from thence, when a violent shower drove us into the house again and constrained us to talk with two or three travellers. I believe our labour was not lost, for they appeared to be greatly affected. I preached at Cardiff in the evening and the next morning. We reached the New Passage[32] about noon. But they did not tell us till half-hour after five that the boat would not pass that night. With much difficulty I procured a small boat to carry us over, leaving our horses behind. Landing soon after six, we walked on, and between nine and ten came to Bristol.

Here I met with a trial of another kind.[33] But this also shall be for good. On the following days was our yearly Conference,[34] begun and ended in perfect harmony. Thursday 17, I went to the cathedral to hear Mr. Handel's *Messiah*.[35] I doubt if that congregation was ever so serious at a sermon as they were during this performance. In many parts, especially several of the choruses, it exceeded my expectation.

Having promised to take a little journey into Wales, on Monday 21, I set out with Joseph Jones.[36] We were in the boat before nine, but did not land our horses till a quarter before three. However, I reached Cardiff in time enough to preach in the room, though not in the castle.

Tue. 22. I gathered up, as well as I could, the fragments of the society. At six in the evening, I preached in the castle. Wednesday

[28] Cf. Rom. 14:17.

[29] Orig., 'Penklawr'. Pen-clawdd is a village in the Gower peninsula, 3 miles west of Gowerton.

[30] Orig., 'Swansey'. Swansea was a large parish, borough, market town, and seaport 44 miles north-west of Cardiff, with a share in the election of a parliamentary burgess.

[31] Orig., 'Pile'. Pyle was a small parish united with Kenvig, 11½ miles south-east of Neath on the main road from Swansea to Cardiff.

[32] 1764, 1791, 'the Passage'.

[33] This probably refers to JW's deteriorating relations with his wife.

[34] For the MS Minutes of this Conference, see the supplement to Part V of *WHS* 4 (1904):69-73. Besides the usual administrative and disciplinary matters, there was a conversation upon Christian perfection.

[35] Despite the political controversy which Handel attracted, it is plain that JW thought highly of his music, though he wearily told Charles in 1768 that 'I have no time for *Handel or Avison* now.' Telford, 5:118; see below Aug. 29, 1762; and Mar. 29, 1774.

[36] See June 2, 1753, n. 51 (20:460 in this edn.).

23, we rode to Fonmon. The behaviour of Mr. Jones surprised me; it seemed as if he inherited the spirit of his father.[37] I preached at seven to a deeply serious congregation, and to a good part of them at five in the morning. Thursday 22, I wrote a *Second Letter* to Dr. Free,[38] the warmest opponent I have had for many years. I leave him now to laugh and scold and witticize and call names just as he pleases, for I have done. Friday 25, I rode to Cowbridge and preached at three in the afternoon in the new Assembly-Room. I observed no trifler there, though there were several of the better rank. About six, I preached in a green court at Llanmaes to a company of right,[39] old, simple Christians.[40] I could not get from them so soon as I designed, so that we did not reach Fonmon till near nine.

Sat. 26. One undertook to guide me the nearest way into the main[41] road. But in five or six miles he lost his way, so that for some time we wandered upon the mountains.[42] About noon, however, we got into the road, and an hour and half after, to Pyle. Before we left it, I spoke a few words to the woman of the house. She seemed quite struck. How few words suffice when God applies them to the heart!

I knew not where to go at Neath, but as we entered the town, a man fixed his eyes upon me (though he had never seen me before) and said, 'Sir, that is the house where the preachers put up their horses.' I had been there only a few minutes when another came in and said, 'Sir, Mrs. Morgan expects you. I will show you the

[37] JW's surprise at the good behaviour of Robert Jones III, the only surviving son of the Methodist squire of Fonmon, was due to the fact that he had disgraced himself at Kingswood School in 1749 and run away, Charles Wesley reporting to his mother that 'if Robin will not be led he must be driven; I mean whipt through Westminster or some other great school,' and that for her 'poor, wild boy', ruin was inevitable: 'his temporal ruin I mean; for as to his soul, there is not the smallest chance for that . . . in the modern way of education.' Ives, *Kingswood*, pp. 35-38; see Sept. 21, 1741, n. 9 (19:227 in this edn.). JW soon realized, however, that his present pleasing impressions were a mistake, and in 1784 was advising Robert that if he must flee the country to avoid his creditors he should go to Holland, not France: 'that is no place to save expense; but it is the only place to make your sons coxcombs and your daughters coquettes.' Telford, 7:232; see below, Aug. 29, 1763.

[38] See above, May 2, 1758.

[39] Almost certainly intended as an adjective signifying upright, righteous (now a rare usage), rather than as an adverb qualifying 'old'.

[40] The warm tone of this commendation recalls days when JW had seen primitive Christianity to be embodied in the religious societies; Philip Thomas's society at Llanmaes had been taken into the Methodist plan in 1748. Minutes of Conference 1748, *WHS*, Publication 1 (London, 1896), p. 59.

[41] 1764, 1791, 'mean'.

[42] There are in fact no mountains between Fonmon and Pyle.

way.' To Mrs. Morgan's we went and were as cordially received as if she had known us twenty years. It was market-day, so I preached about five in the room, a large, commodious place. I believe most that were present (several of whom were backsliders) felt that God was there.

Sun. 27. We reached Swansea at seven and were met by one who conducted us to his house, and thence to a kind of castle, in which was a green court surrounded by high, old walls. A large congregation assembled soon and behaved with the utmost decency. A very uncommon blessing was among them, as uses to be among them that are simple of heart.

The congregation was considerably more than doubled at five in the afternoon. Many gay and well dressed persons were among them—but they were as serious as the poorest. Peter Jaco,[43] who was driven to us by contrary winds, was agreeably surprised at them.

Mon. 28. I scarce ever saw such a rain in Europe as we had for a considerable part of this morning. In one of the main streets the water ran with a stream capable of turning a mill. However, having appointed to preach at noon, in Newton, about six miles from Swansea, I was determined not to break my word, though I supposed but few would attend. But I was mistaken. Such a number of people came together as no house in the town could contain. A barn was soon prepared. And it pleased God to send a gracious rain upon their hearts.

After preaching at Swansea in the evening, I met those who desired to join in a society and explained to them the nature and design of it,[44] with which they were quite unacquainted. Tuesday 29, I rode back to Neath in order to put the society there (an unlicked mass)[45] into some form. This on Saturday they had

[43] Peter Jaco (1729–81) was born at Newlyn and received a devout upbringing. In adolescence the attractions of pleasure and ambition induced in him acute feelings of guilt and depression, from which he was delivered by conversion under Methodist preaching in 1746. He began to preach, and in 1751 JW gave him charge of a number of local societies, appointing him as an itinerant in 1754. He was a useful preacher and 'had the inward state of his mind been answerable to his ministerial talents, he would have been . . . more extensively useful.' Ill-health, which in 1760 occasioned him to take bathing cures in Ireland, finally put an end to his itinerancy, and he was stationed in London from 1774, and from 1780 as a supernumerary; *WHS* 16 (1927):16. Atmore, *Memorial*, pp. 215-17; Jackson, *Early Methodist Preachers*, 1:260-68.

[44] Cf. JW's published description prefixed to his *General Rules* (*Bibliography*, No. 73; 9:69-73 in this edn.).

[45] See *OED*: 'Not reduced to form or order; unfinished, unpolished, rude or crude'; *s.v.*, 1.b.

begged me to do, but they seemed now to have quite forgotten it. Mr. Evans, the Presbyterian minister,[46] had turned them upside down. They looked as if they had never seen me before, all but five or six, who were much ashamed of their brethren.

Wednesday 30, I rode on to Margam. There used to be preaching here, till Lord Mansel, dying without children, left the estate to Mr. Talbot. He forbade all his tenants to receive the preachers, and so effectually put a stop to it. But he did not glory in it long. A few months after, God called him home.[47]

At noon, I preached again in the Assembly-Room at Cowbridge; in the castle at Cardiff in the evening. Thursday 31, I talked with several of the people and found the old spirit swiftly reviving. In the evening I preached in the town hall. Several eminent sinners were present. And God was present in an uncommon manner, as also at the meeting of the society.

Friday, September 1. After a busy and comfortable day, I preached once more in the castle. The word seemed to sink deep into the hearers, though many of them were of the genteeler sort. In the society we were much refreshed. Many followed me to Thomas Gl[ascott]'s[48] house, where two or three were cut to the heart, particularly both his daughters, and cried to God with strong cries and tears.

Sat. 2. We rode to the New Passage, crossed over in half an hour, and about five came to Bristol.

Sat. 9. I wrote the account of an extraordinary monument of divine mercy, Nathanael Othen, who was shot for desertion at Dover Castle in October 1757.[49] In the following week I met Mr.

[46] This may be William Evans (1716–70), who was in fact an Independent minister at Cwm Mawr and Rhyd-y-Maerdy in the Gower, 1754–70, a moderate Calvinist of evangelistic bent. He was, however, a well known defender of his theological tenets and took in at least one preacher from Howell Harris's Methodism.

[47] JW's moralizing has here played havoc with his history, and that on a matter which at the time of publication (1764) was in the recent recollection of his Welsh readers. It was Christopher, 3rd Baron Mansel, who died within a few months of succeeding to the title in 1744. His nephew, Rev. Thomas Talbot (*c.* 1720–58), the absentee rector of Collingbourne in Wiltshire, succeeded Bussy Mansel, 4th Baron, in 1750 and was buried at Margam, four and a half months before JW's visit. Williams, *Wesley in Wales*, p. 59, n. 5.

[48] Thomas Glascott, possibly a glazier by trade, an overseer of the poor, and a prominent member of the Cardiff society (Williams, *Wesley in Wales*, p. 3, n. 4; cf. Aug. 28, 1771; May 10, 1781; and Diary for Oct. 18, 1739; 19:412 in this edn.). He is said to have been present at the Conference of 1746 (see Curnock, 3:241, n. 1).

[49] *A Short Account of the Life and Death of Nathanael Othen*, published anonymously (Bristol, 1758; 3rd edn., Dublin, 1759); see ***Bibliography***, No. 229; and vol. 14 in this edn. Othen, a Hampshire postilion, who suffered endless trouble in a course of drunkenness,

Fletcher and the other preachers that were in the house and spent a considerable time in close conversation on the head of Christian perfection.[50] I afterwards wrote down the general propositions wherein we all agreed.

Thur. 14. I rode to Coleford and was much refreshed among the simple zealous colliers. Saturday 16, in the evening I preached at Bradford, as also at five and eight on Sunday morning. At two, as soon as we were in the house at Freshford, it poured down with rain; so that after as many as could had crowded in, the rest were constrained to go away. But the rain ceased as soon as we took horse, and we had a pleasant ride to Bristol.

Wed. 20. I rode over to Bath, but the room would ill contain the congregation. So I encouraged them in their design of taking a piece of ground and building without delay. In the evening I preached at Shepton, and several of the rich and honourable took it into their mind to come. But they came too late. For the house was already thoroughly filled with the poor. Thursday 21, as we rode homeward, we saw a sight indeed—a woman in the extremity of pain, rotting away piecemeal by the king's evil, full of sores from head to foot, with several of her bones appearing through the skin—and continually praising God with tears of joy for 'dealing so mercifully' with her.[51]

Sun. 24. The famous Roger Ball[52] had planted himself in Stokes Croft before I came. However, as there was a large congregation, I did not think it right to leave them to him, but began as usual and preached till near six o'clock without paying any regard to him.

Sunday, October 1. I took my leave of the congregation and of the children in Kingswood. And God gave us a parting blessing. Monday 2, I preached at Bradford (noon and night) and met the stewards of the Wiltshire and Somersetshire societies. In the

lewdness, and coining, was finally shot for deserting from the armed forces, and converted shortly before the end.

[50] This conversation, following upon that held at Conference and preceding that at the Conference of 1759, was one of the stages by which JW arrived at his 'Thoughts on Christian Perfection', which was reprinted in various tracts, most notably *A Plain Account of Christian Perfection as believed and taught by the Rev. Mr. John Wesley from . . . 1725 to . . . 1765* (Bristol, 1766; and subsequent revs. to 1777). See above, Aug. 11, 1758, n. 34; and vol. 12 in this edn.

[51] This appears to be the same case as that reported Sept. 2, 1754 (20:490 in this edn.).

[52] On Roger Ball (orig. 'Balls'), see Mar. 22, 1746, n. 40 (20:118 in this edn.).

evening, I baptized a young woman deeply convinced of sin. We all found the power of God was present to heal, and she herself felt what she had not words to express.

Tue. 3. One of Warminster,[53] who was at Bristol last week, had desired me to call at his house. I did so this morning and preached in his yard to a numerous congregation of saints and sinners, rich and poor, churchmen, Quakers, and Presbyterians, both of the old and new way. Some disturbance was expected, but there was none. The whole assembly behaved well. And instead of curses or stones we had many blessings as we rode through the town for Salisbury. Wednesday 4, I rested there. Thursday 5, I rode by Redbridge[54] and Fareham to Portsmouth, where at seven I preached in Mr. Whitefield's Tabernacle[55] to a small, serious congregation.

Fri. 6. I designed to go in a wherry to the Isle of Wight. But the watermen were so extravagant in their demands that I changed my mind and went in the hoy. And it was well I did; for the sea was so high, it would not have been easy for a small boat to keep above water. We landed at two and walked on, five little miles, to Newport. The neighbouring camp had filled the town with soldiers, the most abandoned wretches whom I ever yet saw. Their whole glorying was in cursing, swearing, drunkenness, and lewdness. How gracious is God that he does not yet send these monsters to their 'own place'![56]

At five I preached in the corn-market, and at six in the morning. A few even of the soldiers attended. One of these, Benjamin Lawrence, walked with us to Wootton Bridge,[57] where we intended to take boat. He was in St. Philip's Fort during the

[53] This was the only time JW preached at Warminster. The disturbances he expected began subsequently when regular preaching was introduced into the town, and continued till 1774. In that year the rioters were bound over by the assizes for good behaviour and required to make a public apology, and the preaching was suspended till 1780. *Wesleyan Methodist Magazine* 58 (1835):810, n. 11; S. Tuck, *History of Methodism in Frome* (Frome, 1837), p. 41.

[54] Redbridge was a hamlet in the parish of Millbrook 3½ miles west of Southampton.

[55] The Portsmouth Society is already listed in 'An account of the societies in connexion together under the care of Reverend Mr Whitefield' (Nov. 1747). E. Welch, ed., *Two Calvinistic Methodist Chapels 1743–1811* (London Record Society, 1975), p. 16.

[56] Acts 1:25.

[57] Orig., 'Wotton-Bridge'. Wootton was a tiny parish 4 miles north-east of Newport, 'bounded on the north by the Motherbank and on the east by an inlet of the sea, across which there is a narrow causeway, called Wootton Bridge, upwards of 900 feet in length, and on the high road from Ryde to Newport'. Lewis, *England*, 4:597.

whole siege,[58] concerning which I asked him many questions. He said:

> (1) Abundance of *cattle* was left in the fields till the French (long expected) came and took them. (2) Abundance of *wine* was left in the town, even more than the French could use. And there was not enough in the castle, even for the sick men. (3) A large, strong *stone house* was left standing, within a small distance of the fort. Behind this the French formed themselves, particularly before the last assault. (4) This might easily be accounted for. We had few officers of any experience, and the governor never came out of his house. (5) The French made two general assaults and were repulsed, and many blown up by our mines. But the mines having never been looked after till just when we wanted them, most of them were utterly useless, so that only two out of threescore did any execution. (6) In their third assault (which they were very hardly persuaded to make) Captain ——, who commanded the guard of an hundred men, at the sallyport, ran away before he was attacked, and his men, having none to command them, went after. I was left alone till I retired also. And the French, having none to oppose them, came in. (7) In the morning our men were mad to drive them out, and would have done it in an hour but that they were told the fort was given up, and ordered to cease firing. (8) We had at the approach of the enemy three thousand eight hundred and thirty-three effective men. And we had very near as many when we surrendered, with plenty of provision and ammunition.

O human justice! One great man is shot! And another is made a lord! We hired a small fisher-boat at Wootton Bridge, there being scarce any wind. But it increased more and more when we were on the sea, which was seven miles over. Our cock-boat danced on the waves and must have sunk if one large wave had come over her. But God suffered it not. We landed in two hours and walked away to Gosport.

[58] This story echoes the sense of national humiliation engendered by the early disasters of the Seven Years' War. In February 1756, Newcastle had been warned of French intentions to attack Minorca, but not till April was a fleet despatched under Byng to relieve it. He took a month to reach Gibraltar and then, finding Minorca already under siege, made excuses for not undertaking decisive action or allowing the governor of Gibraltar to reinforce the troops holding Fort St. Philip at Port Mahon under General Blakeney, a veteran of 84. The latter held out for seventy days before surrendering; Byng was court-martialled and shot in March 1757 (despite a recommendation to mercy from the court); Blakeney, after giving his own evidence as to the state of Minorca in Byng's trial, was lionized by George II and made a baron in the Irish peerage.

Sun. 8. The wind and rain drove us into the Tabernacle.[59] In the afternoon I preached in the main street at Fareham. A wild multitude was present. Yet a few only mocked; the greater part were soon deeply attentive.

Mon. 9. I set out for Sussex, and in the evening reached Rottingdean,[60] a village four miles east of Brighton.[61] The next day we rode over the Downs to Rye, lying on the top of a round, fruitful hill. I preached at seven to a crowded audience, with great enlargement of spirit.

Wed. 11. I rode to Rolvenden, about ten miles from Rye,[62] and preached at five to a large, serious congregation. A few drunkards stood in the road at some distance and took some pains to divert their attention. But it was labour lost. Thursday 12, it was a rainy morning, so that the house contained the congregation. Many of them were in tears, being deeply convinced that they were as yet 'without God in the world'.[63] About one I preached at Northiam.[64] The house was stowed as full as possible, but still many were constrained to stand without, though it rained much. About five in the evening I preached again at Rye.

Fri. 13. In the evening we had a solemn season. After I had concluded my sermon, I read over the Rules of the Society in the open congregation. The number of those who came at five in the morning showed that God had touched many hearts. On Saturday evening many were obliged to stand without, though the wind was high and extremely cold.

Sun. 15. After preaching at eight, I rode again to Northiam and preached in Mr. Stonestreet's orchard to far the largest congregation I have seen in Sussex. One of Rye, in our return

[59] See above, Oct. 5, 1758, n. 55.

[60] Rottingdean was a parish on the coastal road to Newhaven.

[61] Orig., 'Brighthelmstone'; this town was already flourishing on the strength of the writings of a local physician, Dr. Russell, 'who recommended the sea-water here as containing a greater proportion of salt than that of other places and therefore more efficacious in the cure of scrofulous and glandular complaints'. This appeal was strengthened in 1760 by the discovery of a chalybeate spring, found beneficial for debilitated constitutions. Lewis, *England.* 1:321-22.

[62] Rye was a cinque-port, borough, market town, and parish 63 miles south-east of London. Rolvenden was a substantial parish 2½ miles south-west of Tenterden.

[63] Eph. 2:12.

[64] Orig., 'Northjam'. The suggestion is that JW was diverted to Northiam, a parish 7¾ miles north-west of Rye, by his medical interests. Certainly his host on this occasion, John Stonestreet (1700–1788), was the village doctor, as well as a member of the Methodist society. Another doctor in the village, Thomas Frewen (son of a rector of the parish), had a considerable practice in smallpox inoculation and published an essay on *The Practice and Theory of Inoculation* (London, 1749). *WHS* 15 (1926):169-73.

thither, gave us a remarkable account: 'Mr. ——, one most eminent for profaneness, drunkenness, and all manner of wickedness, when you met the society on Thursday evening at your lodgings, was curious to listen at the window. The next day he surprised his company by crying out, "I am the greatest sinner on the whole earth." On Friday evening he was wounded more deeply still and was at the preaching at five in the morning.' Surely thus far God has helped him. But a thousand to one he will 'return as a dog to his vomit'.[65]

Mon. 16. I rode to Canterbury. As we came into the city a stone flew out of the pavement and struck my mare upon the leg with such violence that she dropped down at once. I kept my seat, till in struggling to arise she fell again and rolled over me. When she rose, I endeavoured to rise too, but found I had no use of my right leg or thigh. But an honest barber came out, lifted me up, and helped me into his shop. Feeling myself very sick, I desired a glass of cold water, which instantly gave me ease.

Tue. 17. I found reason to rejoice over this little flock, now free from all divisions and offences. And on Saturday, I cheerfully returned to London, after an absence of near eight months.

Here I rested four days,[66] and on Wednesday 25, went partly by coach, partly on horseback, to Maldon.[67] Friday 27, I rode on, through an extremely pleasant and fruitful country, to Colchester.[68] I have seen very few such towns in England. It lies on the ridge of an hill, with other hills on each side which run parallel with it at a small distance. The two main streets, one running east and west, the other north and south, are quite straight, the whole length of the town, and full as broad as Cheapside.

I preached at four on St. John's Green, at the side of an high old wall (a place that seemed to be made on purpose),[69] to an extremely attentive audience, and again at eight in the morning on Saturday 28, and at four in the afternoon. In the hours between, I took the opportunity of speaking to the members of the society. In

65 Cf. Prov. 26:11. The Journal entry for Nov. 3, 1767, indicates that this was indeed the case.

66 But according to the sermon register he preached thirteen times.

67 Orig., 'Maiden'.

68 Colchester was a large borough and market town, with a famous main street, 51 miles north-east of London.

69 This is one of innumerable examples of the evangelical preacher's instinct for theatre (in both senses). In a letter to the Countess of Huntingdon, JW described how 'the people stood on a smooth sloping ground, sheltered by the walls of an old castle, and behaved as men who felt that God was there.' Seymour, *Huntingdon*, 1:399.

three months here are joined together an hundred and twenty persons. A few of these know in whom they have believed, and many are sensible of their wants.

Sun. 29. At eight the congregation was very large. And I believe God made his word 'quick and powerful'.[70] At four in the afternoon, we had a Moorfields congregation. Many of the baser sort stood at a distance. But they made no disturbance, knowing the magistrates are determined to suffer no riot at Colchester.

Mon. 30. Though I was not quite recovered from the lameness occasioned by the fall of my horse, I made shift to ride to Norwich; where on the following days I had the satisfaction to observe that the society was not lessened (as I had feared) but rather increased since I left them. And there is a probability they will increase still, as they are far more established in grace.[71]

Friday, November 3. James Wheatley called upon me and offered me the Tabernacle.[72] But whether to accept the offer or not I cannot tell. This must be maturely considered.

I found all this week great liberty of spirit, and the congregations were large and attentive. It seems the time is come when our labour even at Norwich will not be in vain.

Sun. 5. We went to St. Peter's Church, the Lord's Supper being administered there. I scarce ever remember to have seen a more beautiful parish church,[73] the more so because its beauty results, not from foreign ornaments, but from the very form and structure of it. It is very large and of an uncommon height, and the sides are almost all window, so that it has an awful and venerable look, and at the same time surprisingly cheerful.

Mon. 6. A large congregation attended between four and five in the morning. I set out at six with much comfort, leaving a settled and well-united society. I preached at Kenninghall[74] about ten, and at Lakenheath in the evening. After resting a day, on Wednesday 8, I went on, an hard day's journey, to Bedford.[75]

70 Heb. 4:12.

71 See Heb. 13:9.

72 On James Wheatley and the Norwich Tabernacle, see Apr. 12, 1744, n. 15 (20:23-24 in this edn.).

73 Of several churches dedicated to St. Peter in Norwich this is doubtless St. Peter Morcroft in the Market Place, described by Pevsner as 'the Norfolk Parish church *par excellence*', notwithstanding his conviction that the prodigal decoration of the tower 'is more rich than aesthetically successful'. N. Pevsner, *North-east Norfolk and Norwich* (Harmondsworth, Penguin, 1962), pp. 249-50.

74 Kenninghall was a parish 3 miles south-east of East Harling.

75 At midsummer JW had received an account of Bedford Methodism and also of John Berridge from John Walsh, the former deist. *Arminian Magazine* 3 (1780):103-5.

I had designed to spend two evenings here. But Mr. Parker[76] informing me that Mr. Berridge[77] desired I would come to him as soon as possible, I set out for Everton on Thursday 9. I found Mr. B[erridge][78] taking horse, with whom I rode on, and in the evening preached at Wrestlingworth in a large church, well filled with serious hearers.

We lodged at Mr. Hicks's,[79] the vicar, a witness of the faith which once he persecuted. The next morning I preached in his church again. In the middle of the sermon a woman before me dropped down as dead, as one had done the night before. In a short time she came to herself and remained deeply sensible of her want of Christ.

Hence we rode to Mr. B[erridge]'s at Everton. For many years he was seeking to be justified by his works. But a few months ago he was thoroughly convinced that 'by grace we are saved through faith.'[80] Immediately he began to proclaim aloud the redemption that is in Jesus. And God confirmed his own word, exactly as he did at Bristol in the beginning, by working repentance and faith in the hearers, and with the same violent outward symptoms.

76 On William Parker, see Oct. 8, 1753, n. 23 (20:476 in this edn.).

77 This was the beginning of a notable friendship. John Berridge (1716–93) was the son of a wealthy Nottinghamshire farmer, educated at Cambridge, graduating B.A. in 1738. A diligent student, he became a fellow of Clare, and for the last years of his residence (1749–55), he served a curacy at Stapleford, securing some personal following with his preaching. According to Berridge's own account (written for his tombstone), he 'remained ignorant of my fallen state till 1730. Lived proudly on faith and works for salvation till 1754. Admitted to Everton vicarage, 1755. Fled to Jesus above for refuge, 1756' (Tyerman, *John Wesley*, 2:309-10). In 1758, he made the acquaintance of Wesley and Whitefield and enjoyed much exchange of pulpits with them. He first preached out of doors in 1759, but then organized an itinerant circuit for himself in Bedfordshire, Cambridgeshire, Essex, Hertfordshire, and Huntingdonshire, allowing himself three months annually to preach in London, especially in Whitefield's pulpits. Cases of abnormal psychic phenomena, which had disappeared from JW's preaching (as from the revivals abroad), became common again under Berridge. A character himself, Berridge produced many characters among his converts. Everton was a tiny Bedfordshire parish 4¾ miles north-east of Biggleswade; the advowson was held by the master and fellows of Clare Hall, Cambridge.

78 The identification of 'B' as 'Berridge' seems almost certain. Berridge had begun an itinerant ministry and, in spite of Wesley's sudden arrival, would feel unable to disappoint his colleague at Wrestlingworth. Indeed it seems just possible that on hearing of Wesley's presence in the area he wished in any case to secure his services as guest preacher at Wrestlingworth.

79 William Hicks, rector of Wrestlingworth, an early convert of Berridge 'who told me he was first convinced of sin Aug. 1, 1758, and, finding peace in about six weeks, first preached the gospel on September 17', became a constant companion of Berridge (see below, July 29, 1759). Wesley here, as sometimes elsewhere, spells the name 'Hickes'.

80 Cf. Eph. 2:8.

I preached at six in the evening and five in the morning, and some were struck just as at Wrestlingworth. One of these was brought into the house, with whom we spent a considerable time in prayer. I then hastened forward, and a little before it was dark, reached the Foundery.

Sun. 26. I was well-pleased to have some conversation with Mrs. A——t, lately come from Barbadoes. She gave me an account of her poor husband (first a red-hot predestinarian, talking of God's 'blowing whole worlds to hell', then a Quaker, now a deist), as also of the narrow escape which Mr. H. lately had: 'Ten negroes broke into his house, one of whom was upon the point of cutting his throat, when E. R.[81] knocked him down with a pewter pot, which put the rest into such confusion that she had time to secure herself and her children, and Mr. H. to leap out of a balcony.'

Wed. 29. I rode to Wandsworth and baptized two Negroes belonging to Mr. Gilbert, a gentleman lately come from Antigua.[82] One of these is deeply convinced of sin; the other rejoices in God her Saviour and is the first African Christian I have known. But shall not our Lord in due time have these heathens also 'for his inheritance'?[83]

Monday, December 4. I was desired to step into the little church behind the Mansion House, commonly called St. Stephen's, Walbrook.[84] It is nothing grand, but neat and elegant beyond expression. So that I do not wonder at the speech of the famous Italian architect who met Lord Burlington in Italy: 'My lord, go back and see St. Stephen's in London. We have not so fine a piece of architecture in Rome.'[85]

Fri. 8. Poor Mr. Goudicheau called upon me, formerly a Romish priest, now ready to perish for want of bread, though of

[81] Mr. H. and E. R. were Westley Hall and the mistress (clearly an Amazon) he had taken to the West Indies; see May 10, 1738, n. 9 (18:238 in this edn.). The identification is made implicitly by Henry Moore, JW's literary executor and biographer. Moore, *Wesley*, 1:89.

[82] On Nathaniel Gilbert, see above, Jan. 17, 1758, n. 29.

[83] Cf. Ps. 33:12.

[84] Orig., 'Wall-brook'.

[85] Richard Boyle, 3rd Earl of Burlington and 4th Earl of Cork (1695–1753), became enamoured of the architectural talents of Palladio during several years' residence in Italy in his youth, and soon after his return began (*c.* 1716) to alter and partly to reconstruct Burlington House, Piccadilly. St. Stephen's, Walbrook (1672–79), replacing a church destroyed in the Great Fire, was one of the earlier and most celebrated of Wren's city churches, the interior being a particularly successful transformation of a plain rectangle by Corinthian columns and a heavy dome, which was the prototype of St. Paul's Cathedral. Mervyn Blatch, *A Guide to London's Churches* (London, 1978), p. 162.

an unblemished character. Can anyone wonder that we have not many converts from the Church of Rome?

Mon. 11. Most of this week I spent in preparing materials for *A Survey of the Wisdom of God in the Creation*, or a full, plain, and correct system of natural philosophy.[86]

Mon. 18. I rode to Everton. The church was well filled soon after six in the evening. God gave me great liberty of speech and applied his word to the hearts of the hearers, many of whom were not able to contain themselves, but cried aloud for mercy.

Tue. 19. I rode on to Lakenheath. How surprising a providence has been over this little village! Forty years ago a poor man lived here who walked with God and was the means of awakening a few others. When these were nearly extinct, Charles Skelton came, awakened a few more, and forsook them.[87] A year ago, one of Lakenheath, seeing me passing through Thetford, desired me to come and preach there. I did so and occasionally mentioned to them Mr. Madan,[88] then at Thetford. They went over and invited him to Lakenheath, where soon after, he preached in the church. The rector desired he would help him to a curate—so now they have one that both preaches and lives the gospel.

Wed. 20. I rode to Norwich. James Wheatley now repeated his offer of the Tabernacle. But I was in no haste. I wanted to consult my friends and consider the thing thoroughly. One glaring objection to it was, 'The congregation there *will* not hear me.' He replied, 'Sir, you cannot tell that unless you will make the trial.' I consented so to do, on Thursday 21. But many declared, 'No! He shall never come into that pulpit'—and planted themselves in the way to prevent it. Hitherto only could they go. I went up and

[86] This work was published with a slightly more modest subtitle than this descriptive phrase; *A Survey of the Wisdom of God in the Creation; or a Compendium of Natural Philosophy*, 2 vols. (Bristol 1763), corrected in 3 vols. (Bristol, 1770), and enlarged in 5 vols. (London, 1777); see vol. 17 in this edn.

[87] On these events, see Apr. 21, 1754 (20:485 in this edn.); on Skelton, May 30, 1749, n. 96 (20:278 in this edn.).

[88] Martin Madan (1726–90), brother of Spencer Madan, Bishop of Peterborough (1794–1813), after a brief Oxford education, was called to the bar in 1748 and became a member of a convivial club (see July 17, 1774). Commissioned by the club to attend one of JW's sermons with a view to mimicking it, he was converted and confirmed in his new ways by the influence of David Jones and William Romaine. Obtaining ordination by the influence of the Countess of Huntingdon, he exercised a notable ministry at the Lock Hospital in London and itinerated in many other places, as well as standing in for Berridge at Everton. In 1780, he published *Thelypthora,* a Christian defence of polygamy which excited such a storm that he returned to private life, simply maintaining his literary work.

preached to a large congregation, without any let or hindrance. I preached there again on Saturday evening, and again God stopped the mouths of the lions.[89] Sunday 24, I preached in the Tabernacle at eight to a very serious congregation, and at the Foundery between four and five. About six, the Tabernacle was thoroughly filled, and mostly with quiet hearers. I saw none who behaved amiss but two soldiers, who struck some that desired them to be silent. But they were seized and carried to the commanding officer, who ordered them to be soundly whipped.

Mon. 25. Our service began in the Foundery at four, in the Tabernacle at eight. God was now especially pleased to make bare his arm.[90] There was a great cry among the people. Stony hearts were broke, many mourners comforted, many believers strengthened. Prejudice vanished away; a few only kept their fierceness till the afternoon. One of these, still vehemently angry, planted himself just over against me. But before I concluded he cried out, 'I am overcome, I am overcome.'

Having now weighed the matter thoroughly, I yielded to the importunity of our brethren. So in the evening the copy of the lease was perfected, which was executed the next morning—a whole train of providences so plainly concurring thereto that all might clearly see the hand of God.

Tue. 26. I took my leave of Norwich for the present, about noon preached at Kenninghall, and in the evening came to Lakenheath. Being informed some of the gentry in the town were very desirous to hear me preach if I would preach in the church, I sent them word: I had designed to be at Colchester the next day, but as they desired it, I would delay my journey and preach at ten the next morning.

Wed. 27. I was so much out of order that I knew not how I should get to church. Between nine and ten, I was informed that some hot men in the parish would not consent to my preaching there. I saw the hand of God and was thankful, having now a little more time to rest. In the afternoon the sun broke out through the fog, and we had a pleasant ride to Bury. But I was so extremely sick soon after I came in, that I knew not how I should be able to preach. An hour's sleep, however, refreshed me much, so that I found no want of strength in preaching. Indeed my disorder increased during the night. But while I was preaching in the

[89] Heb. 11:33.
[90] See Isa. 52:10.

morning, I felt myself well. And I found no more sickness or complaint of any kind. In the evening I reached Colchester.

Fri. 29. I found the society had decreased since L[awrence] C[oughlan][91] went away. And yet they had had full as good preachers. But that is not sufficient. By repeated experiments we learn that though a man preach like an angel, he will neither collect, nor preserve a society which is collected, without visiting them from house to house.

Today I walked all over the famous castle, perhaps the most ancient building in England. A considerable part of it is without question fourteen or fifteen hundred years old. It was mostly built with Roman bricks, each of which is about two inches thick, seven broad, and thirteen or fourteen long. Seat of ancient kings! British and Roman! Once dreaded far and near. But what are they now? Is not 'a living dog better than a dead lion'?[92] And what is it wherein they prided themselves? As do the present great ones of the earth:

> A little pomp, a little sway,
> A sunbeam in a winter's day,
> Is all the great and mighty have
> Between the cradle and the grave![93]

[91] Laurence Coughlan (d. 1785), an Irish itinerant of obscure origin but adventurous record (see *WHS* 27 [1949]:30-32). Said to have been converted from Catholicism, Coughlan laboured with effect in both England and Ireland, though (in JW's phrase) 'a person who had no learning at all' (Letter to the *St. James's Chronicle*, Feb. 10, 1765; Telford, 4:290). In 1764, he was ordained by the Greek bishop Erasmus 'on which account he was put away from the Methodist connexion' (Atmore, *Memorial*, p. 81). Though he seems to have sought ordination without JW's knowledge, this penalty seems improbable, though no more so than his (re)ordination by the Bishop of London, *c.* 1765, at the behest of JW and the Countess of Huntingdon. This ordination was for service with the S.P.G. in Newfoundland, 1766–73, during which time he had difficulty in securing his stipend from his parishioners; this may have been why he lost his wife's money (see Telford, 5:109; see also Aug. 27, 1768). His letters are calendared in *Calendar of Letters Preserved at USPG*, List & Index Society, Special Series 5 (London, Swift, 1972), B6, nos. 170, 175, 179, 184, 187, 194. Returning after seven years of 'servitude as a missionary', he secured employment in the Countess of Huntingdon's connexion and became minister of the Holywell Mount Chapel in London (Atmore, *Memorial*, p. 81; Seymour, *Huntingdon*, 2:296, 350, 403; Edwin Welch, ed., *Calendar and Index of Cheshunt College Archives* [London, 1981], pp. 79, 82, 83, 84, 113). When JW last reported seeing him in 1785, 'he was ill in body, but in a blessed state of mind . . . utterly broken in pieces, full of tears and contrition for his past unfaithfulness' and negotiating his return to the connexion. 'A short time after, while he was engaged in conversation with Mr Wesley in his study, he was seized with a paralytic stroke and was thus suddenly taken to the paradise of God' (Atmore, *Memorial*, p. 83; letter to John Stretton, Feb. 25, 1785, see Telford, 7:260).

[92] Eccles. 9:4.

[93] Cf. John Dyer, *Grongar Hill* (London, 1748), lines 89-92; and John Wesley, *A Collection of Moral and Sacred Poems*, 3 vols. (1744), 2:173, where Wesley prints the original

Sat. 30. I returned to London and received a pressing letter from Bristol,[94] in consequence of which I took horse on Monday morning, January the first, 1759, and came thither the next evening. After resting two days (only preaching morning and evening), I examined severally the members of the society. This was one great end of my coming down. Another was to provide for the poor. Accordingly on Sunday 7, I preached a sermon for them, to which God was pleased to give his blessing, so that the collection was a great deal more than double of what it used to be.

Wed. 10. Having finished my work at Bristol, I rode to Salisbury and advised our brethren concerning the preaching-house which they are about to build. On Friday 12, I went on to Whitchurch and preached at one to a large and serious congregation. In the afternoon, we rode to Basingstoke, where the people put me in mind of the 'wild beasts at Ephesus'.[95] Yet they were unusually attentive in the evening, although many of them could not hear. Saturday 13, after preaching to a small, serious company, I went on to London.

Sat. 27. I began reading, with huge expectation, a tract wrote by a son-in-law of the great Bengelius, Mr. Oetinger, *De Sensu Communi et Ratione*.[96] But how was I disappointed! So obscure a

version, with 'A little rule' in line 89 and 'the proud and mighty' in line 91. See also below, Aug. 19, 1760.

[94] This may very well have been from the Countess of Huntingdon, who met JW in Bristol on the 4th January and took him back to preach to an aristocratic gathering in her house. 'Her Ladyship felt "a particular call in Providence" to wrestle mightily with God in behalf of our nation, and for the important work of intercession prayer meetings were established at her house.' Into this work the Wesleys were drawn, as JW reports below, Feb. 27, 1759; Seymour, *Huntingdon*, 1:395-97.

[95] 1 Cor. 15:32 (*Notes*).

[96] Johann Albrecht Bengel (1687–1752) was the leading intellectual figure in Württemberger pietism of the first half of the eighteenth century, whose *Gnomon* had been much used by JW in the preparation of his *Explanatory Notes Upon the New Testament*. On the mutual relations of Bengel, Oetinger, and Zinzendorf, see Aug. 11-14, 1738, n. 63 (18:294 in this edn.). After Bengel's death the leadership of Württemberger pietism became split among three parties, each headed by Bengel's sons-in-law: that of P. D. Burk and C. G. Williardt, who set out to maintain Bengel's family contacts and estate; that of Bengel's younger pupils converted at the Tübingen Stift in 1748–49, led by E. F. Hellwaag; and that of his oldest pupils, associated with rather than organized by Friedrich Christoph Oetinger (1702–82), many of whom had flirted with Zinzendorf in their youth. Oetinger's special contribution was to attempt (in opposition to Leibniz and Newton) to delineate a Christian map of knowledge, embodying elements of Boehme, Paracelsus, and cabbalistic ideas acquired from the ghetto at Frankfurt, a construction of baffling complexity. The work now in JW's hand, *Die Wahrheit des Sensus Communis oder des allegemeinen Sinns in dem nach dem Grundtext erklärten Sprüchen und Prediger Salomo* (Tübingen, n.d.), arose from Oetinger's Waldorf period, 1746–52, and attempted to establish the limits of mere reason. The general feeling of life, light, and truth was what the

writer I scarce ever saw before: I think he goes beyond Persius[97] himself. When I had with huge labour read fifty or sixty pages, finding the sense did by no means make amends for the time and pains bestowed in searching it out, I took my leave of him for ever.

Saturday, February 3. I spent an hour with one who by the loss of his sight, his fortune, and his liberty (for he has been a prisoner some time), is likely to gain more than all the world can give.

Tue. 6. I took much pains to convince Mr. S——n[98] that he was not the wisest man in the world. But I could not 'change the Ethopian's skin'.[99] Yet even this is not too hard for God.

Fri. 9. I felt suddenly as if a needle had been run into the side of my face. I supposed it would be well by the morning, but found it abundantly worse, the tonsil being come down (as they term it), and the side of my face much swelled. It grew worse all day, so that it was with great difficulty I preached at Snowsfields in the evening. But on Sunday 11, it went away as unaccountably as it came. In the afternoon I called on E[lisabeth] H[arland] in St. George's Hospital. Many there had been greatly prejudiced against me. But it was now vanished away. Her behaviour had reconciled them quite. And all in the ward (sixty or seventy persons) seemed hardly to breathe all the time I was speaking and praying by her bedside.

Tue. 13. I preached at Deptford and Welling, and in the morning rode to Wandsworth. I preached Wednesday and Thursday evening in the town, in the mornings at Mr. Gilbert's.[1] Will this barren tree bear fruit at last? How long has God had patience with it?

Fri. 16. Being the Public Fast,[2] I preached at five in Wandsworth, at nine and three in the church at Spitalfields, and at half-hour past eight in the Foundery. Every place of public

Scripture called the heart, or the conscience, and constituted the *sensus communis*, 'the moral feeling of eternity' which was present in everyone. Heinrich Hermelink, *Geschichte der evangelischen Kirche in Württemberg von der Reformation bis zum Gegenwart* (Stuttgart, 1949), p. 227. Cf. Sigrid Grossmann, *Friedrich Christoph Oetingers Gottesvorstellung* (Göttingen, 1979).

97 Persius Flaccus (34-62), a stoic satirist who was a rich Etruscan knight. He was among the Latin poets translated by Dryden.

98 John Simpson; see Apr. 19, 1740, n. 37. His ineradicable indecisiveness had been recently noted, see above, Aug. 1, 1757.

99 Cf. Jer. 13:23; and cf. 'wash the Ethiop white' (Sermon 63, 'The General Spread of the Gospel', 2:487 in this edn.).

1 See above, Jan. 17, 1758, n. 29.

2 A French invasion was threatened; see Curnock, 4:299, n. 4. Wesley had noted Fast Days on Feb.6, 1756, and Feb. 17, 1758.

worship was crowded on this, as on the two preceding fast days. And it is plain, even *outward* humiliation has been a means of *outward* blessings.

Fri. 23. I saw a surprising spectacle: one who by a blow first lost her nose, then one eye, and then the other, with most of the roof of her mouth—and yet instead of murmuring, acknowledges the love of God in all and praises him continually.

Tue. 27. I walked with my brother and Mr. Maxfield to L[ady] H[untingdon]'s. After breakfast came in Mr. Whitefield, Madan, Romaine, Jones,[3] Downing,[4] and Venn[5] with some persons of quality and a few others. Mr. Whitefield, I found, was to have administered the Sacrament. But he insisted upon my doing it. After which, at the request of L[ady] H[untingdon], I preached on 1 Cor. 13:13. O what are the greatest of men to the great God? As the small dust of the balance.[6]

Thursday, March 1. I reached Everton about four in the afternoon. But Mr. Berridge did not expect me till the next day. So he thought it best I should preach in his house. The next evening the church was well filled. And my mouth was filled with arguments, which I trust God applied, for the conviction of some and the consolation of others.

Sat. 3. We had a mild, delightful day, and a pleasant ride to Colchester. In the evening and on Sunday morning, the house contained the congregation tolerably well. But in the afternoon, I was obliged to go out, and I suppose we had on St. John's Green five or six times as many as the room would contain. Such is the advantage of field preaching!

Mon. 5. On examining the society, I found that out of the hundred and twenty-six members I had left in October, we had lost only twelve; in the place of whom we have gained forty. And

[3] Probably John Jones; see Nov. 30, 1746, n. 3 (20:150 in this edn.).

[4] George Downing (*c.* 1729–1803?) matriculated at Wadham College, Oxford, 1745; M.A., 1751. He was a longstanding acquaintance of the Countess of Huntingdon, rector of Ovington, Essex, 1764–1803, and chaplain to the Earl of Dartmouth at Cheltenham.

[5] Henry Venn (1725–97), evangelical clergyman; educated at Jesus College, Cambridge, graduating B.A., 1746; M.A., 1749; fellow of Queens' College, Cambridge, 1749–57; lecturer of St. Swithun's, London Stone, 1753. After holding various curacies, he accepted that of Clapham in 1754, where he began a lifelong friendship with John Thornton and his family. Worn out by his powerful ministry as vicar of Huddersfield, 1759–71, he accepted the small living of Yelling, Hunts. till his death.

[6] Isa. 40:15. The following evening, many of the same group took part in a lively prayer meeting at the Countess of Huntingdon's house, vividly described by Charles Wesley (Seymour, *Huntingdon*, 1:396; and *CWJ* 2:219).

many of these whom we left in sorrow and heaviness are now rejoicing in God their Saviour.[7]

Tue. 6. I rode to Norwich. Wednesday 7, I inquired into the state of affairs at the Tabernacle[8] and found the society, once consisting of many hundred members, was mouldered into nothing. Of the fifteen or sixteen hundred subscribers, not twenty, not one, was left; but everyone that pleased went into the galleries, without any questions asked. So that everything was to be wrought out of the ore, or rather out of the cinders! Surely whatever help is done here, God must do it himself.

In the evening, I desired that those who were willing to join in a society would speak with me the next evening. About twenty did so, but the greater part of these appeared like frightened sheep. And no marvel, when they had been so long accustomed to hear all manner of evil of me.

Fri. 9. I preached morning and evening at the Foundery.[9] How pleasing would it be to flesh and blood to remain in this little, quiet place, where we have at length weathered the storm! Nay, I am not to consult my own ease, but the advancing the kingdom of God.

On Saturday and Sunday about forty more gave in their names. On Sunday in the afternoon, I met the society after ordering the doors to be shut, which they had not been for two years before. Thirty or forty more spoke to me on Monday. I think two-thirds of those I have yet seen have had a clear sense of God's pardoning love. Doth he not 'send by whom he will send'?[10]

Sun. 18. I administered the Lord's Supper to near two hundred communicants. So solemn a season I never remember to have known in the city of Norwich. As a considerable part of them were Dissenters, I desired everyone to use what posture he judged best. Had I *required* them to kneel, probably half would have sat. Now, all but one kneeled down.

Finding it was needful to see them once more at Colchester, I took horse between four and five in the morning. The frost was extremely sharp for some hours. It was then a fair, mild day. About two in the afternoon it began to rain, but we reached Colchester before we were wet through.

[7] See Luke 1:47.

[8] See above, Nov. 3, 1758. In Feb. 1775, Wheatley leased the Tabernacle to Lady Huntingdon.

[9] I.e., the Foundery in Norwich (see above, Feb. 27, 1757).

[10] Cf. Exod. 4:13.

The room was more than filled in the evening, so that many were obliged to go away. Wednesday 21, I baptized seven adults, two of them by immersion. And in the evening (their own ministers having cast them out 'for going to hear the Methodists'), I administered the Lord's Supper to them and many others whom their several teachers had repelled for the same reason.

Thur. 22. Before we set out the rough north wind fell, and we had a calm, sunshiny day. I preached in the Tabernacle at Norwich in the evening.

Sun. 25. I rode to Forncett,[11] twelve miles from Norwich, where also was a building of James Wheatley's, which without my desire he had included in the lease. We found William Cudworth[12] had preached there in the morning. It was exceeding good for my sense of honour to come just after him. The people looked as direful upon me as if it had been Satan in person. However, they flocked from all parts, so that the Tabernacle would not near contain them. I preached about two; God bare witness to his truth, and many were cut to the heart. After preaching I found Mr. Cudworth sitting in the pulpit behind me, whom I quietly and silently passed by. About six, I preached at the Tabernacle in Norwich, crowded with attentive hearers. Perhaps

[11] Orig., 'Forncet'. Forncett St. Mary, a small parish 7½ miles south-east of Wymondham, beside the road from Norwich to Kenninghall.

[12] William Cudworth (*c.* 1717–63) was by the mid-1740s a leading figure in a small Calvinistic Methodist connexion called 'The hearers and followers of the Apostles'. He gathered three of the former French churches in London together with others, which included the one in Petticoat Lane of which Joseph Hussey, the hyper-Calvinist (1660–1726), had formerly been minister. For a time he assisted Whitefield with the school at the Tabernacle. In the 1750s he preached often in the tabernacles at Norwich and Forncett, and at Bury St. Edmunds, and erected himself a London house and chapel on the site of what is now All Saints', Margaret Street. Cudworth, who was regarded by the Countess of Huntingdon as 'eminent [in] holiness and integrity', hurt Whitefield, and was viewed with unrelenting hostility by JW (Seymour, *Huntingdon*, 2:336; and A. Dallimore, *George Whitefield*, 2 vols. [London, 1970-80], 2:231, 233). In 1745–46, Cudworth and JW twice exchanged polemical tracts on the antinomian question, and in the later 1750s Cudworth twice replied to JW's *Preservative against unsettled Notions* (1758) and especially his remarks on *Theron and Aspasio* (See Richard Green, *Anti-Methodist Publications issued during the Eighteenth Century* [London, Kelly, 1902; repr. New York, 1973], nos. 189, 201; and *WHS* 11 [1917]:71). The publication of this latter tract had brought JW into close contact with the author, James Hervey. Before Hervey died he replied to JW in *Eleven Letters*, which were published posthumously by Hervey's brother; JW believed that Cudworth had persuaded Hervey to write this reply, that he had obtained 'full power to put out and *put in*' what he pleased, and had greatly increased the personal venom of the tract, a belief which, so far as the alteration of Hervey's MSS. is concerned, was unfounded. See letter to Hervey, Nov. 29, 1758 (Telford, 4:46-47); see also John Wesley, *Preface to a Treatise on Justification* (1765) and *Some Remarks on Mr Hill's Review* (1772); Jackson, 10:346, 380; and *WHS* 12 (1919):35n.

these too will be brought into order by and by. Hitherto there has been 'no king in Israel'.[13]

Monday and Tuesday, I spoke to as many of both societies, now united together, as had leisure and inclination to come. The whole number is about four hundred and twenty—of whom I do not think it improbable, two hundred may continue together.

Tue. 27. I had an interview with Mr. Cudworth. I observed upon the whole: (1) that his opinions are *all his own*, quite new, and his phrases as new as his opinions; (2) that all these opinions, yea, and phrases too, he affirms to be *necessary to salvation*, maintaining that all who do not receive them worship another God; and (3) that he is as incapable as a brute beast of being convinced even in the smallest point.

Wed. 28. I rode over to Forncett again and preached to a large congregation. Great part of them were now exceedingly softened, but some were still bitter as wormwood.[14] In the evening, we had another kind of congregation at the Foundery, by whom I was much comforted, but much more in meeting the bands, when all our hearts were melted down by the power of God.

Thur. 29. I divided the Norwich society into classes, without any distinction between them who had belonged to the Foundery or the Tabernacle. Sunday, April 1, I met them all at six, requiring everyone to show his ticket when he came in, a thing they had never heard of before. I likewise insisted on another strange regulation, that the men and women should sit apart. A third was made the same day. It had been a custom ever since the Tabernacle was built to have the galleries full of spectators while the Lord's Supper was administered. This I judged highly improper and therefore ordered none to be admitted but those who desired to communicate. And I found far less difficulty than I expected in bringing them to submit to this also.

The society now contained above five hundred and seventy members—an hundred and three of whom were in no society before, although many of them had found peace with God. I believe they would have increased to a thousand if I could have stayed a fortnight longer. Which of these will hold fast their profession? The fowls of the air will devour some. The sun will scorch more, and others will be choked by the thorns springing up. I wonder we should ever expect that half of those who 'hear the word with joy' will bring forth 'fruit unto perfection'.[15]

[13] Judg. 17:6, etc.

[14] Prov. 5:4.

[15] Luke 8:13-14.

Mon. 2. I left Norwich, and about seven o'clock came to Cross Keys Wash.[16] They would fain have persuaded us we could not pass. But finding we were resolved to try, our guide put forward and brought us over in half an hour, so that about eight we reached Sutton[17] and found a quiet, civil house, with everything we wanted.

Tue. 3. We came to Fosdyke Wash,[18] just time enough to pass. At three in the afternoon, we preached at Boston. A rude multitude quickly ran together, to a paddock adjoining to the town. A more unawakened congregation I have not seen for some years. However, the far greater part were attentive; nor did any interrupt, or offer the least rudeness.

At seven, I met the little society in the house. But they were the least part of the company. People crowded in from all sides, and I believe God touched most of their hearts.

Wed. 4. At six, finding the house would not contain one-fourth of the congregation, I was constrained to stand in the street. Abundance of people assembled together, whom I exhorted to 'repent and believe the gospel'.[19] The word of God fell heavy upon them, and I trust broke some of the stony hearts.

Hence we rode over the Fens, fifteen miles broad and near thirty long, to Coningsby, where we found a numerous congregation of a far different spirit. Scarce one of these but had 'tasted', more or less, 'of the powers of the world to come'.[20] After a comfortable opportunity here, we rode on to Horncastle.[21] We were but roughly saluted at our entrance. And the mob increased more and more till six. I then began to preach in a yard near the market-place to a large concourse of people. But their behaviour quite disappointed us, for there was no tumult, no noise, but an earnest attention through the whole congregation.

Thur. 5. I preached again at seven to nearly the same congregation, and was again refreshed by the remarkable decency

16 JW was following the route of the modern A17 road round the south end of The Wash. Cross Keys is a village 3 miles east of Sutton Bridge.

17 Long Sutton, a large parish 4¾ miles east of Holbeach.

18 Orig., 'Fossdyke'. Fosdyke was a small parish on Fosdyke Wash at the mouth of the river Welland, 7½ miles south of Boston.

19 Cf. Mark 1:15.

20 Cf. Heb. 6:5.

21 In 1762, a new convert in Horncastle (a substantial market town and parish 21 miles east of Lincoln) was still writing to JW lamenting the lack of experience and guidance there, 'for we are young and ignorant in this dark corner, and holiness and sanctification is a language little understood among us.' *Arminian Magazine* 4 (1781):339.

and seriousness of their behaviour. At four in the afternoon I preached at Mareham on the Hill,[22] two miles from Horncastle. The number of people constrained me to preach without, and the rain, to shorten my sermon—though none went away. Indeed I believe none were present who had not known some work of grace in their hearts.

Fri. 6. We rode over the Wolds (a chain of hills) to North Elkington, three miles from Louth.[23] The congregation was large, notwithstanding the rain, which drove full in our face till we came to Grimsby.

Sun. 8. The house was pretty well filled at eight. At two, I was obliged to go into the old churchyard, where was such a concourse of people as had hardly ever, they said, been seen at Grimsby before. As many as the room would well contain were present at the watch-night and at seven in the morning. I then commended them to the grace of God.

Mon. 9. I preached in the evening at Laceby, the next afternoon at Ferry (after riding through much water and continued rain), and in the evening in the new house at Epworth.

Fri. 13. Having appointed to preach at Alkborough[24] at one, I set out between seven and eight. I was in hopes of coming thither before church began, but I did not consider the Lincolnshire roads. With some difficulty we reached it before noon and found there was no service at the church. I preached in the churchyard at one to a listening multitude—most of whom, I suppose, had never heard this kind of preaching before. Many of them were in tears and pressed after me into the house where we met the society. I could not but hope that some of these will press into the kingdom of heaven.

Returning thence, I called on Mr. Romley[25] of Burton, one of my former parishioners, a lively, sensible man of eighty-three years old, by whom I was much comforted. An hour or two after, we took boat but could not cross over. The violence of the stream, swollen by the late rains, bore us down in spite of all we could do. Having striven against it a considerable time, we were obliged to

22 Orig., 'Marum in the Hill'. Mareham on the Hill was a tiny parish 2 miles south-east of Horncastle.

23 North Elkington was a tiny parish 3 miles north-west of Louth.

24 Orig., 'Awkborough'.

25 William Romley (born *c.* 1676), the father of John Romley (see June 7, 1742, n. 93; 19:273 in this edn.), the curate of Epworth who had refused JW the Sacrament on Jan. 2, 1743.

cast anchor. After waiting some time, we got near the shore and were towed up to the place of landing. A toilsome day was followed by a comfortable night. At half-hour after eight, the house at Epworth was well filled. And most of the congregation stayed till the whole service was concluded.

It was on this day that, after the battle of Bergen in Germany,[26]

Among the many wounded who were brought into Frankfort upon the Main there was the Right Honourable George Charles Dyhern,[27] Baron Lieutenant-General of the Saxon troops, in the service of the King of France. He was born of an ancient and noble family in Silesia on April 10th, 1710, so that it was just on his birthday, he received his wound. He was of equal abilities as a minister in the closet and a general in the field. In his younger years he had gone through a regular course of study in the university and made great proficiency in philosophy, especially in mathematics. Afterwards he studied polemic divinity, till he reasoned himself into an infidel. During his illness he showed not the least desire of pious company or serious discourse, till the surgeon let his valet de chambre know that he could not live long. The man then asked his master whether he did not choose to be visited by a clergyman. He answered with warmth, 'I shall not trouble those gentlemen. I know well myself what to believe and do.' His man, not discouraged, continued thus: 'My lord, have you ever found me wanting in my duty, all the time I have been in your service?' He answered, 'No.' 'Then', replied he, 'I will not be wanting now. The surgeons count you past hope of recovery, but everyone is afraid to tell you so. You stand upon the brink of eternity. Pray, sir, order a clergyman to be called.' He paused a little, but soon gave his hand to his servant, thanked him for his honesty, and ordered to send for me.[a] When I came the man told me plainly, the general was a professed infidel. I went in and, after a short compliment, said, 'I am told, my

[a] Dr. Fresenius, senior of the clergy at Frankfort.

---

[26] This account was written by Johann Philipp Fresenius; see Dec. 8, 1746, n. 7 (20:151 in this edn.).

[27] The Dyherns, now divided into several lines and under a variety of spellings, were among the most respected noble families of Silesia, Bohemia, and Lusatia, and now possessed both Bohemian and Prussian dignities (J. C. von Hellbach, *Adels Lexicon* [Ilmenan, 1825; repr. Graz, 1976], p. 304). A sprightly account of this action as it appeared to the residents of Frankfurt is given by Goethe in his autobiography (*Dichtung und Wahrheit*, Eng. trans. John Oxenford; *Autobiography of Johann Wolfgang von Goethe*, ed. K. J. Weintraub [Chicago, 1974], 1:98-101). To the chagrin of Goethe's father, Prince Ferdinand was defeated at the Battle of Bergen (Hesse) and had to yield the fortresses of Minden and Münster.

lord, your life is near an end. Therefore I presume, without any ceremony, to ask you one plain question: Is the state of your soul such that you can entertain a solid hope of salvation.' He answered, 'Yes.' 'On what do you ground this hope?' He replied, 'I never committed any wilful sin. I have been liable to frailties, but I trust in God's mercy and the merits of his Son, that he will have mercy upon me.' These words he uttered very slowly, especially, 'the merits of his Son'. I made the following reply: 'I am apt to believe, you are not tainted with the grossest vices. But I fear you a little too presumptuously boast of never having committed wilful sin. If you would be saved you must acknowledge your being utterly corrupted by sin and consequently deserving the curse of God and eternal damnation. As to your hoping for God's mercy 'through the merits of his Son', I beg leave to ask, Do you believe God has a Son? That his Son assumed our nature in order to be our Saviour; that in the execution of his office he was humbled unto death, even the death upon the cross, and that hereby he has given an ample satisfaction for us and recovered our title to heaven?' He answered, 'I cannot now avoid a more minute description of the true state of my soul. Let me tell you, doctor, I have some knowledge of philosophy, by which I have chose for myself a way of salvation. I have always endeavoured to live a sober life, to the uttermost of my power; not doubting but the Being of all beings would then graciously accept me. In this way I stood in no need of Christ and therefore did not believe on him. But if I take the Scriptures to be a divine revelation, this way of mine I perceive is not the right one. I must believe in Christ and through him come to God.' I replied, 'You say, *if* you take the Scriptures to be a divine revelation!' He fetched a deep sigh and said, 'O God, thou wilt make me say, *because* I take the Scriptures to be thy word.' I said, 'There are grounds and reasons enough to demonstrate the divine origin of Christianity, as I could show from its most essential principles, were not the period of your life so short. But we need not now that diffusive method. Faith being the gift of God, a poor sinner tottering on the brink of eternity has not time to inquire about grounds and reasons. Rather betake yourself to earnest prayer for faith; which if you do, I doubt not but God will give it you.' I had no sooner spoken these words but, pulling off his cap and lifting up his eyes and hands, he cried out, 'O Almighty God, I am a poor, cursed sinner, worthy of damnation. But Lord Jesus, eternal Son of God, thou diedst for my sins also. It is through thee alone I can be saved. O give me faith and strengthen that faith.' Being extremely weak, he was obliged to stop here. A little after he asked, 'Is faith enough for salvation?' 'Yes, sir,' said I, 'if it be living faith.' 'Methinks', said he, 'it is so already, and it will be more so by and by. Let us pray for it.' Perceiving he was very weak, to give him some rest I retired into the next room. But he soon sent to call me. I found him praying, and Jesus was all he prayed for. I reminded him of some Scriptures treating of faith in Christ, and he was much delighted with them. Indeed he was quite swallowed up by the grace of Jesus and would hear of nothing but Jesus Christ and him crucified. He cried out, 'I do not know how it is with me. I never in my life felt such a change. I have power to love Jesus and to believe in him, whom I so long rejected. O my Jesus, how merciful art thou to me.'

About noon I stepped home, but he sent for me directly, so that I could scarce eat my dinner. We were both filled with joy, as partakers of the same grace which is in Jesus Christ; and that in such a manner as if we had been acquainted together for many years. Many officers of the army came to see him continually, to all of whom he talked freely of Jesus, of the grace of the Father in him, and of the power of the Holy Ghost through him, wondering without ceasing at his having found Jesus and at the happy change by which all things on this side eternity were become indifferent to him.

In the afternoon he desired to partake of the Lord's Supper, which he received with a melting, praising, rejoicing heart. All the rest of the day he continued in the same state of soul. Toward evening he desired that if his end should approach, I would come to him, which I promised. But he did not send for me till the next morning. I was told by his valet that he slept well for some hours, and then awaking, prayed for a considerable time, continually mentioning the name of our Lord and his precious blood, and that he had desired several of the officers to make his conversation known to his Court (that of the King of Poland). After some discourse I asked, 'Has your view of Christ and his redemption been neither altered nor obscured since yesterday?' He answered, 'Neither altered nor obscured. I have no doubt, not even a remote one. It is just the same with me as if I had always thus believed and never doubted. So gracious is the Lord Jesus to me a sinner.'

This second day he was unwearied in prayer and exercises of faith. Toward evening he sent for me in haste. When I came, I found him dying and in a kind of delirium; so I could do no more than give him now and then a word of comfort. I prayed afterwards for him and those that were present, some of whom were of high birth and rank. I then, by imposition of hands, as usual, gave him a blessing, which being done, he expired immediately. A royal prince who was there (Prince Xavier of Saxony)[28] could not forbear

[28] Prince Franz Xavier of Saxony, known in France as Comte de Luçace (1730–1806), and son of Frederick August II, Elector of Saxony and King of Poland. He saw military service during the Seven Years' War (his father concluding a subsidy treaty with the

weeping. The rest of the officers bewailed the loss of their general, yet praised God for having shown such mercy toward him.

I wrote an account of it without delay to his mother, and had an immediate answer—she was a lady of seventy-two, of exemplary piety. She praised God for his mercy, adding that he had now answered the prayers which she had never ceased to offer on his behalf for eleven years.[29]

Sunday 15 (Easter Day), I preached at Epworth at eight, and then rode to Haxey church, where I was much refreshed by the decency and seriousness of the congregation. Between one and two, I began preaching; so large a congregation was never seen here before. About five, I preached at the market-place in Epworth. I was drawing to a conclusion when the rain began. But it drove away only a few careless hearers; the bulk of the people did not stir till I concluded.

Wed. 18. I set out for Selby.[30] We were in hopes the roads would now be passable. And they were tolerable till we came near the town, but here the late flood had carried away the bank over which we were to ride and left a great hole in its place. However, we made shift to lead our horses over a narrow path where the water was fordable. The congregation at Selby obliged me to stand in the garden, though the north wind was exceeding high. At seven in the evening, I preached at York.

Thur. 19. I visited two prisoners in the castle, which is, I suppose, the most commodious prison in Europe. Both of them seemed to be much convinced and not far from the kingdom of God.[31] At six, I preached in the shell of the new house[32] to a numerous and serious audience.

Fri. 20. The master of the inn at Tadcaster[33] offering us the use

French) and received a command of his own with the rank of General Lieutenant, but he spent the winters, not training his troops, but at Versailles. He served at Bergen with one of the evangelical counts of Solms as his deputy, but lost his luggage and war-chest at Minden. In 1760–62, he served again in Germany under the Duc de Broglie, and in 1763, his father having died and been succeeded by his ailing elder brother, he acted as administrator of the electorate for his nephew who was under age.

29 JW's source for this document by Dr. Frenesius is not known.

30 Selby was a large market town and parish 13 miles south of York.

31 See Mark 12:34.

32 On the beginnings of the work at Peaseholme Green, see above, July 12, 1757, n. 38.

33 Tadcaster was a market town and parish 9 miles south-west of York.

of his garden, I preached to a well-behaved congregation,[34] and about five found Mr. Grimshaw and many of our brethren at Leeds. Saturday 21, at half-hour past ten, we reached Stainland Chapel, near Elland.[35] It is an handsome building near the top of a mountain and surrounded with mountains on all sides. It was filled from end to end. Mr. Grimshaw read prayers, and I preached on part of the Second Lesson. In the room where I dressed myself were a young man and his sister, both ill of a fever. I know not that ever they heard the preaching; however, I desired we might go to prayers. They presently melted into tears. O may God preach his gospel to their hearts!

I preached at Manchester in the evening, where we had at length a quiet audience. Wretched magistrates, who, by refusing to suppress, encouraged the rioters, had long occasioned continual tumults here, but some are now of a better spirit.[36] And wherever magistrates desire to preserve the peace, they have sufficient power to do it.

Tue. 24. I rode over to Macclesfield.[37] Abundance of people ran together, but wild as colts untamed.[38] Their noise quite drowned my voice at first, but in a while they were tolerably quiet.

[34] The point of this observation is that in the decade since Methodism had been introduced into Tadcaster it had occasioned a good deal of disorder. One of William Shent's converts in the town, Thomas Ellis (1726–1803; converted 1753), had confronted a mob summoned by post-horn whenever he went out. *Methodist Magazine* 28 (1805):220-25.

[35] Orig., 'Eland'. The chequered history of this chapel, a monument to the undenominational evangelicalism of the north, is implicit even in the episode here described. 'The want of a suitable place of worship having long been experienced in the vicinage . . . a general subscription was entered into, and in the year 1755 the chapel . . . was erected, with the probable intention of being a chapel of ease under the Establishment. It is vested in trustees, and the deeds require the performance of the Church of England service. A dispute, however, arose among the trustees soon after its erection, when those who strenuously opposed its becoming a chapel of ease gained the ascendancy. Since that time it has been occupied, according to the temporary pre-eminence of each party, both by the ministers of the Wesleyan Methodist body and by those of the Independent persuasion.' The first remembered pastor was John Floyde (d. 1798), a Methodist itinerant from 1770 to 1782, when he settled at Halifax as a surgeon and apothecary. J. W. Walker, *A History of Wesleyan Methodism in Halifax and its Vicinity* (Halifax, Hartley and Walker, 1836), pp. 102-4; Atmore, *Memorial*, p. 143.

[36] On this matter, see May 7, 1747, and n. 28 (20:172-73 in this edn.).

[37] Orig., 'Maxfield'. Macclesfield had been transferred to the Manchester round from that of York in 1754, hence doubtless JW's arrival from that place. There was disorder on the occasion of the visit, but JW must have hoped to pick up some of the followers of John Bennet, who died a month later, on May 24, 1759. *WHS* 7 (1910):117.

[38] See Daniel Defoe, *Col. Jack* (1722; quoted in *OED*): 'She was a wild, untamed colt.' Cf. below, May 3, 1759; and June 18, 1788.

And before I had done, all but four or five lubberly men seemed almost persuaded to be Christians.[39]

Sun. 29. I rode to Stockport, designing to preach at one o'clock. But we were at a loss for a place. We fixed at length on a green near the town's end, and we had a quiet and solemn opportunity.

In my return, I called to see a girl about thirteen years of age. She had been in violent pain all over, with little intermission for near twenty months. After I had spoke a few words, she said, 'When I saw you before, I did not know the Lord, but now I know him and am known of him. I am his, and he is mine.' I asked, 'Do you never repine at your pain?' She said, 'No. I have not a murmuring thought. I am happy, always happy. I would not change this bed of affliction for the palace of King George.' I asked, 'Are you not proud of this? Is pride taken out of your heart?' She answered, 'I do not know. But I *feel* no pride. I feel that God is all.' 'But do you feel no fretfulness or peevishness?' 'I cannot tell that I do. Pain sometimes makes me cry out when they stir me. But I do not fret at anything.' 'Do you find no self-will?' 'Not that I know. I desire nothing but that the will of God be done.' 'Do not you desire life or death?' 'No, I leave all to him. But if it was his will, I should be glad to die. The world is full of danger. I should be glad to leave it and to be with Christ.'—O why was she then not taken to paradise? I fear, she has now no religion at all![40]

Mon. 30. We had a numerous congregation at Acton Bridge,[41] two or three miles from Northwich. Some large trees screened us both from the sun and wind. In the afternoon, I rode on to Chester. It was well the wind was pretty high, for the sun shone as hot as it uses to do in the dog-days. Wednesday, May 2, I rode over to Mold[42] in Flintshire, about twelve miles from Chester. The sun was very hot and the wind very cold. But as the place they had chose for me was exposed both to the sun and the wind, the one balanced the other. And notwithstanding the Chester Races, which had drawn the rich away, and the market-day, which had detained many of the poor, we had a multitude of people, the

[39] See Acts 26:28.

[40] The last two sentences were added in Wesley's *Works*, 1774.

[41] Acton, or Acton Bridge, was a small township in the parish of Weaverham, 4 miles west of Northwich.

[42] Orig., 'Mould'. Mold was a substantial parish, borough, and market town 6 miles south of Flint.

serious part of whom soon influenced the rest, so that all but two or three remained uncovered and kneeled down as soon as I began to pray.

Thur. 3. We crossed over from Chester to Liverpool. The congregations here were exceeding large, but many of them seemed to be like wild asses' colts.[43] Yet God is able to make them wise unto salvation.

Sun. 3 [i.e., 6]. I received much comfort at the *old* church in the morning,[44] and at St. Thomas's in the afternoon. It was as if both the sermons had been made for *me*. I pity those who can find no good at church! But how should they, if prejudice come between, an effectual bar to the grace of God?

Wed. 9. I rode to Downall Green[45] near Wigan, a town wicked to a proverb. We had a specimen of the manners of its inhabitants in the behaviour of a man that met us and accosted us with such language as would have become an inhabitant of the bottomless pit. One would have thought from their looks that a good part of the congregation was of the same spirit. But in a short time the word of God prevailed, and all their fierceness melted away.

In the evening, I preached at Bolton, and on Friday 11, about nine, at Lower Darwen,[46] a small village near Blackburn. At Lancaster we were informed, it was too late to cross the sands. However, we resolved to make the trial. We passed the seven-mile sand without difficulty and reached Flookburgh[47] about sunset.

Sat. 12. Setting out early, we came to Bootle, about twenty-four measured miles from Flookburgh, soon after eight, having crossed the Millom Sands[48] without either guide or

[43] See Job 11:12; cf. above, Apr. 24, 1759.

[44] St. Nicholas's, Liverpool. For JW's affection for St. Thomas's, see above, Apr. 24, 1757.

[45] Orig., 'Downam-Green'. Downall Green is a hamlet 5 miles south-west of Wigan.

[46] Orig., 'Darwent'. Lower Darwen was a township in the parish of Blackburn, 2 miles south of that town. It became a perpetual curacy only in 1829.

[47] Orig., 'Fluckborough'. Flookburgh was a chapelry in the parish of Cartmel, 5¼ miles east of Ulverstone in Morecambe Bay. Formerly a market town north of the sands, it is now a small village. Present ordnance survey maps of the area mark the public footpath with a red warning sign: 'Public rights of way across Marcombe Bay can be dangerous. Seek local guidance.'

[48] Orig., 'Millam-Sand'. Millom was a parish and former market town, bounded on the east by the Duddon estuary, which JW had just crossed. Like Morecambe Bay upon which he had ventured from Lancaster, it exposes a vast area of sand at low tide, still frequented by skilled fishermen for renowned cockles and mussels, but, with its rapid tidal movements, quicksand, and river water, hazardous to the unwary. The belief (here

difficulty. Here we were informed that we could not pass at Ravenglass before one or two o'clock, whereas had we gone on (as we afterward found), we might have passed immediately. About eleven we were directed to a ford near Muncaster Hall,[49] which they said we might cross at noon. When we came thither they told us we could not cross. So we sat still till about one. We then found, we could have crossed at noon. However, we reached Whitehaven before night. But I have taken my leave of the sand-road. I believe, it is ten measured miles shorter than the other—but there are four sands to pass, so far from each other that 'tis scarce possible to pass them all in one day, especially as you have all the way to do with a generation of liars, who detain all strangers as long as they can, either for their own gain or their neighbours. I can advise no stranger to go this way. He may go round by Kendal and Keswick, often in less time, always with less expense and far less trial of his patience.

Reflecting today on the case of a poor woman who had a continual pain in her stomach, I could not but remark the inexcusable negligence of most physicians in cases of this nature. They prescribe[50] drug upon drug, without knowing a jot of the matter concerning the root of the disorder. And without knowing this they cannot cure, though they can murder the patient. Whence came this woman's pain? (Which she would never have told, had she never been questioned about it.) From fretting for the death of her son. And what availed medicines while that fretting continued? Why then do not all physicians consider how far bodily disorders are caused or influenced by the mind? And in those cases which are utterly out of their sphere, call in the assistance of a minister—as ministers, when they find the mind disordered by the body, call in the assistance of a physician? But why are these cases out of their sphere? Because they know not God. It follows, no man can be a thorough physician without being an experienced Christian.

Tue. 15. I rode over to Lorton, a little village at the foot of a high mountain. Many came from a considerable distance and, I believe, did not repent of their labour. For they found God to be a

recorded by JW) that the experts on the crossings of the sands delayed travellers for profit is reported also of the inhabitants of Lindisfarne. Bootle was a market town and parish 5½ miles south of Ravenglass.

49 Probably the crossing at Hall Waberthwaite, still mapped as a public footpath, a mile south of Muncaster Castle, then and now the seat of the Pennington family.

50 Orig., 'prescribed', corrected in *Works*, 1774.

God both of the hills and valleys, and nowhere more present than in the mountains of Cumberland.

Thur. 17. I inquired into a signal instance of providence.[51] When a coal-pit runs far under the ground, it is customary here to build a partition wall from the bottom to the top of it, nearly from the shaft to within three or four yards of the end, in order to make the air circulate, which then moves down one side of the wall, turns at the end, and then[52] moves briskly up on the other side. In a pit two miles from the town, which ran full four hundred yards under the ground and had been long neglected, several parts of this wall were fallen down. Four men were sent down to repair it. They were about three hundred yards from the shaft when the foul air took fire. In a moment, it tore down the wall from end to end, and burning on till it came to the shaft, it then burst and went off like a large cannon. The men instantly fell on their faces, or they would have been burned to death in a few moments. One of them who once knew the love of God (Andrew English) began crying aloud for mercy. But in a very short time his breath was stopped. The other three crept on their hands and knees till two got to the shaft and were drawn up; but one of them died in a few minutes. John M'Combe was drawn up next, burned from head to foot, but rejoicing and praising God. They then went down for Andrew, whom they found senseless, the very circumstance which saved his life. For losing his senses, he lay flat on the ground, and the greatest part of the fire went over him; whereas had he gone forward on his hands and knees, he would undoubtedly have been burned to death. But life or death was welcome. For God had restored the light of his countenance.

Sat. 19. One was showing us the improvements begun by Sir William Lowther.[53] He had marked out places for new walks and for tufts of trees, laid out a new plan for his gardens, begun to alter the house, and was preparing to make a little paradise round about it. But death came between. And how little loss was this, if it removed him to the paradise of God!

[51] The sermon register indicates that JW was in Whitehaven, and presumably the incident took place there.

[52] 'then' added in *Works*, 1774.

[53] Sir Wm. Lowther, 3rd Bart., died in 1756, leaving the bulk of the property he had inherited from old Sir James, 4th Bart., in 1755 to young Sir James, later created Earl of Lonsdale (R. S. Ferguson, *Cumberland and Westmorland M.P.s* [London, 1871], p. 406; *Horace Walpole's Correspondence*, 3:413, 415, 417-18). The sermon register shows JW still at Whitehaven.

Sun. 20. I preached at eight in an open place at the Ginns,[54] a village on one side of the town. Many were there who never did, and never would, come to the room. O what a victory would Satan gain if he could put an end to field preaching! But that, I trust, he never will—at least not till my head is laid.

After preaching again at two, I took my leave of Whitehaven and rode to Cockermouth. At six, I preached at the end of the market-house. High and low, rich and poor, attended. And by far the greater part of the audience seemed to be conscious that God was there.

Mon. 21. I preached at ten in the market-place at Wigton, and came to Solway Firth just as the water was fordable. At some times it is so three hours in twelve; at other times, barely one. After making a short bait at Ruthwell,[55] we came to Dumfries before six o'clock. Having time to spare, we took a walk in the churchyard, one of the pleasantest places I ever saw. A single tomb I observed there, which was about an hundred and thirty years old. But the inscription was very hardly legible:

Quandoquidem remanent ipsis quoq[ue] fata sepulchris![56]

So soon do even our sepulchres die! Strange that men should be so careful about them! But are not many self-condemned therein? They *see* the folly, while they run into it. So poor Mr. Prior, speaking of his own tomb, has those melancholy words: 'For this last *piece of human vanity*, I bequeath five hundred pounds.'[57]

Tue. 22. We rode through a pleasant country to Thornhill,[58] near which is the grand seat of the Duke of Queensborough. How

[54] Orig., 'The Gins'.

[55] Orig., 'Ruthwell'. Ruthwell was a parish and village on the north side of Solway Firth, 6 miles west of Annan.

[56] Juvenal, *Satires*, x.146, inaccurately remembered. Dryden translated thus:

> For sepulchres themselves must crumbling fall,
> In time's abyss, the common grave of all.

[57] Matthew Prior (1664–1721), poet and diplomat, was buried at his own request 'at the feet of Spencer' in the Poets' Corner in Westminster Abbey, having left £500 for the erection of a monument. Prior's 'last piece of human vanity' was later quoted by Samuel Johnson in his *Lives of the English Poets*, 3 vols. (1779). Matthew Prior, *Some Memoirs of the Life and Publick Employments of Matthew Prior . . . With a copy of his last will and testament* (London, 1722), pp. v-vi.

[58] Orig., 'Thorny-hill'. Cf. the sentiments expressed above, May 31, 1757.

little did the late duke imagine that his son would plough up his park and let his house run to ruin! But let it go! In a little time the earth itself and all the works of it shall be burned up.

Hence we rode through and over huge mountains, green to the very top, to Leadhills, a village containing five hundred families, who have had no minister for these four years. So in Scotland, 'the poor have' *not* 'the gospel preached'![59] Who shall answer for the blood of these men?

Early in the evening we came to Lesmahagow, a village not so large as Leadhills. It has, however, two ministers. Here also we walked down to the churchyard, by the side of which a little, clear river runs, near the foot of an high and steep mountain. The wood which covers this makes the walks that run on its sides pleasant beyond imagination. But what taste have the good people of the town for this? As much as the animals that graze on the river-bank.

Wed. 23. We took horse soon after four and did not stop before we came to Glasgow—having hardly seen a cloud in the sky since we set out from Whitehaven.

I preached at seven in the Poor House, and at seven in the morning, Thursday 24. But in the evening, we were obliged to be abroad, and I used great plainness of speech. All suffered the word of exhortation; some seemed to be a little affected.

Sat. 26. I found the little society which I had joined here two years since had soon split in pieces. In the afternoon, I met several of the members of the praying societies[60] and showed them what Christian fellowship was and what need they had of it! About forty of them met me on Sunday 27, in Mr. Gillies's kirk[61] immediately after evening service. I left them determined to meet Mr. Gillies weekly at the same time and place. If this be done, I shall try to see Glasgow again. If not, I can employ my time better. At seven in the morning, we had a numerous congregation, though small compared to that in the evening. Yet my voice was so strengthened that I believe all could hear. I spoke very plain on, 'Ye must be born again.'[62] Now I am clear of the blood of this people. I have delivered my own soul.

Mon. 28. I rode through Edinburgh to Musselburgh and

[59] Cf. Matt. 11:5.

[60] See above, June 5, 1757, n. 3.

[61] The college church, Glasgow. On Gillies, see Apr. 17, 1753, n. 15 (20:453 in this edn.).

[62] John 3:7.

preached in the evening to a deeply attentive congregation. Wednesday 30, I rode on to Dunbar and, at six in the evening, preached in a large, open place (as also the next day). Both poor and rich quietly attended, though most of them shivering with cold—for the weather was so changed within a few days that it seemed more like December than May.

Lodging with a sensible man, I inquired particularly into the present discipline of the Scotch parishes. In one parish, it seems, there are twelve ruling elders, in another there are fourteen. And what are these? Men of great sense and deep experience? Neither one nor the other. But they are the *richest* men in the parish. And are the *richest* of course the *best* and the *wisest* men? Does the Bible teach this? I fear not. What manner of governors then will these be? Why, they are generally just as capable of governing a parish as of commanding an army.

About this time the work of God exceedingly increased under the Rev. Mr. Berridge[63] near Everton. I cannot give a clearer view of this than by transcribing part of the journal of an eye-witness.[64]

> Sunday, May 20. Being with Mr. B[lackwe]ll at Everton, I was much fatigued and did not rise. But Mr. B. did, and observed several fainting and crying out while Mr. B[erridg]e was preaching. Afterward at church I heard many cry out, especially children, whose agonies were amazing. One of the eldest, a girl ten or twelve years old, was full in my view, in violent contortions of body and weeping aloud—I think incessantly during the whole service. And several much younger children were in Mr. B[lackwe]ll's view, agonizing as this did. The church was equally crowded in the afternoon, the windows being filled within and without, and even the outside of the pulpit to the very top, so that Mr. B[erridg]e seemed almost stifled by their breath. Yet feeble and sickly as he is, he was continually strengthened, and his voice for the most part distinguishable in the midst of all the outcries. I believe there were present three times more men than women, a great part of whom came from far, thirty of them having set out at two in the morning from a place thirteen miles off. The text was, 'Having a form of godliness, but denying the power thereof'. When the power of religion began to be spoke of, the presence of God really filled the place. And while poor sinners felt the sentence of death in their

[63] 1764, 1791, 'Mr. B.'

[64] The writer of this report appears to have been Mrs. Elizabeth Blackwell, whose husband combatted her propensity to sleep in, by an elaborate policy of premiums and alarm clocks (*WHS* 4 [1903]:23). The account concludes with a letter from Berridge.

souls, what sounds of distress did I hear! The greatest number of them who cried or fell were men, but some women, and several children, felt the power of the same almighty Spirit and seemed just sinking into hell. This occasioned a mixture of various sounds, some shrieking, some roaring aloud. The most general was a loud breathing, like that of people half strangled and gasping for life. And indeed almost all the cries were like those of human creatures, dying in bitter anguish. Great numbers wept without any noise; others fell down as dead, some sinking in silence, some with extreme noise and violent agitation. I stood on the pew seat, as did a young man in the opposite pew, an able-bodied, fresh, healthy countryman. But in a moment, while he seemed to think of nothing less, down he dropped with a violence inconceivable. The adjoining pews seemed shook with his fall; I heard afterward the stamping of his feet, ready to break the boards, as he lay in strong convulsions at the bottom of the pew. Among several that were struck down in the next pew was a girl who was as violently seized as him. When he fell, Mr. B[lackwe]ll and I felt our souls thrilled with a momentary dread, as when one man is killed by a cannon-ball, another often feels the wind of it.

Among the children who felt the arrows of the Almighty, I saw a sturdy boy about eight years old, who roared above his fellows and seemed in his agony to struggle with the strength of a grown man. His face was red as scarlet. And almost all on whom God laid his hand turned either very red or almost black. When I returned, after a little walk, to Mr. B[erridg]e's house, I found it full of people. He was fatigued, but said he would nevertheless give them a word of exhortation. I stayed in the next room and saw the girl whom I had observed so peculiarly distressed in the church, lying on the floor as one dead, but without any ghastliness in her face. In a few minutes we were informed of a woman filled with peace and joy, who was crying out just before. She had come thirteen miles and is the same person who dreamed Mr. B[erridge] would come to her village on that very day whereon he did come, though without either knowing the place or the way to it. She was convinced at that time. Just as we heard of her deliverance, the girl on the floor began to stir. She was then set in a chair and, after sighing a while, suddenly rose up, rejoicing in God. Her face was covered with the most beautiful smile I ever saw. She frequently fell on her knees, but was generally running to and fro, speaking these and the like words: 'Oh, what can Jesus do for lost sinners! He has forgiven all my sins! I am in heaven! I am in heaven! Oh, how he loves *me*! And how I love him!' Meantime I saw a thin, pale girl, weeping with sorrow for herself and joy for her companion. Quickly the smiles of heaven came likewise on her, and her praises joined with those of the other. I also then laughed with extreme joy; so did Mr. B[lackwe]ll (who said it was more than he could well bear). So did all who knew the Lord and some of those who were waiting for salvation, till the cries of them who were struck with the arrows of conviction were almost lost in the sounds of joy.

Two or three well-dressed young women, who seemed careless before, now felt the power of God and cried out with a loud and bitter cry. Mr. B[erridge] about this time retired, and the Duke of M[anchester], with Mr. A[ste]ll,[65] came in. They seemed inclined to make a disturbance, but were restrained and, in a short time, quietly retired. We continued, praising God with all our might, and his work went on as when Mr. B[erridge] was exhorting. I had for some time observed a young woman all in tears, but now her countenance changed. The unspeakable joy appeared in her face, which quick as lightning was filled with smiles and became of a crimson colour. About the same time John Keeling of Potton fell into an agony. But he grew calm in about a quarter of an hour, though without a clear sense of pardon.

Immediately after, a stranger, well dressed, who stood facing me, fell backward to the wall, then forward on his knees, wringing his hands and roaring like a bull. His face at first turned quite red, then almost black. He rose and ran against the wall, till Mr. Keeling and another held him. He screamed out, 'O what shall I do, what shall I do? O for one drop of the blood of Christ!'[66] As he spoke, God set his soul at liberty; he knew his sins were blotted out, and the rapture he was in seemed too great for human nature to bear. He had come forty miles to hear Mr. B[erridge] and was to leave him the next morning, which he did, with a glad heart, telling all who came in his way what God had done for his soul.

I observed about the time that Mr. Coe (that was his name) began to rejoice, a girl eleven or twelve years old, exceeding poorly dressed, who appeared to be as deeply wounded and as desirous of salvation as any. But I lost sight of her till I heard the joyful sound of another born in Zion, and found upon inquiry it was her, the poor, disconsolate, gypsy-looking child. And now did I see such a sight as I don't expect again on this side eternity. The faces of the three justified children, and I think of all the believers present, did really shine; and such a beauty, such a look of extreme happiness and at the same time of divine love and simplicity, did I never see in human faces till now. The newly justified eagerly embraced one

[65] Robert Montagu, 3rd Duke of Manchester (*c.* 1710–62). He was MP for Hants. 1734–39, and Lord-lieutenant of the county from 1739 till his death. His seat was Kimbolton Castle, 10 miles south-west of Huntingdon. Astell was the local squire.

[66] An allusion to a line in Charles Wesley's *Hymns and Sacred Poems* (1749); see *Poetical Works*, 4:419.

another, weeping on each others' necks for joy. Then they saluted all of their own sex and besought both men and women to help them in praising God.

I have mentioned only one man, two women, and three children at this time justified in the house, but have perhaps omitted some. And it is probable there was more than one justified at the church, though but one came to speak of it; for all are not equally free to glorify God in the midst of his people. I wish all who find the same salvation with Mr. Coe were as ready to proclaim redeeming love!

Thursday, 24. Mr. B[lackwe]ll and I went to hear Mr. H[ick]s at Wrestlingworth, four miles from Everton. We discoursed with him first and were glad to hear he had wholly given himself up to the glorious work of God and that the power of the Highest fell upon his hearers, as upon Mr. B[erridg]e's. While he was preaching, fifteen or sixteen persons felt the arrows of the Lord and dropped down. A few of these cried out with the utmost violence and little intermission for some hours, while the rest made no great noise but continued struggling, as in the pangs of death. I observed besides these one little girl deeply convinced, and a boy, nine or ten years old. Both these, and several others, when carried into the parsonage house, either lay as dead, or struggled with all their might. But in a short time their cries increased beyond measure, so that the loudest singing could scarce be heard. Some at last called on me to pray, which I did, and for a time all were calm. But the storm soon began again. Mr. H[ick]s then prayed, and afterward Mr. B[erridge].[67] But still, though some received consolation, others remained in deep sorrow of heart.

Upon the whole I remark that few ancient people experience anything of this work of God, and scarce any of the rich. These generally show either an utter contempt of, or enmity to, it. Indeed, so did Mr. H[ick]s himself some time since, having so deep an aversion to it that he denied the Sacrament to those of his parish who went to hear Mr. B[erridg]e. Neither of these gentlemen have much eloquence, but seem rather weak in speech—the Lord hereby more clearly showing that this is his own work. It extends into Cambridgeshire, to within a mile of the university, and about as far into Huntingdonshire, but flourishes most of all in the eastern and northern parts of Bedfordshire.

There were three farmers, in three several villages, who violently set themselves to oppose it. And for a time they kept many from going to hear. But all three died in about a month. One of them owned the hand of the Lord was upon him and besought him in

[67] 1764, 1791, 'B—ll', altered in *Works* (1774) to 'B—'.

the bitterness of his soul to prolong his life, vowing to hear Mr. B[erridge] himself. But the Lord would not be entreated.

The violent struggling of many in the above-mentioned churches has broke several pews and benches. Yet it is common for people to remain unaffected there and afterward drop down in their way home. Some have been found lying as dead in the road, others in Mr. B[erridg]e's garden, not being able to walk from the church to his house, though it is not two hundred yards.

I have since received a letter from Mr. B[erridge], an extract of which I send you:

On Sunday sennight, a man of Wyboston,[68] a Nathanael indeed,[69] was so filled with the love of God during morning prayer that he dropped down and lay as one dead for two hours. He had been so filled with love all the week before that he was often for a time unable to work.

On Sunday night last, as I was speaking in my house, there was a violent outcry. One soul was set at liberty. We sung near an hour, and the Lord released three more out of captivity.

On Monday sennight, Mr. H[ic]ks accompanied me to Meldreth.[70] On the way we called at a farmer's house. After dinner I went into his yard, and seeing near an hundred and fifty people, I called for a table and preached, for the first time, in the open air. Two persons were seized with strong convictions, fell down, and cried out most bitterly. We then went to Meldreth, where I preached in a field, to about four thousand people. In the morning at five Mr. H[ic]ks preached in the same field to about a thousand. And now the presence of the Lord was wonderfully among us. There was abundance of weeping and strong crying. And I trust, beside many that were slightly wounded, near thirty received true heartfelt conviction.

At ten, we returned and called again at the farmer's house. Seeing about a dozen people in the brewhouse, I spoke a few words. Immediately the farmer's daughter dropped down in strong convictions. Another also was miserably torn by Satan, but set at liberty before I had done prayer. At four, I preached in my own house, and God gave the spirit of adoption to another mourner.

On Monday last, I went to Shelford,[71] four miles from Cambridge, near twenty from Everton. The journey made me quite ill, being so weary with riding that I was obliged to walk part of the way. When I came thither a table was set for me on the

68 Orig., 'Wybersley'. Wyboston is a hamlet in Beds., 3 miles south-west of St. Neots.
69 The reference is to John 2:47.
70 Orig., 'Meldred'. Meldreth was a small parish 4 miles north-east of Royston.
71 Great Shelford was a parish 4 miles south of Cambridge.

common, and to my great surprise I found near ten thousand people round it, among whom were many gownsmen from Cambridge. I was hardly able to stand on my feet and extremely hoarse with a cold. When I lifted up my foot to get on the table, an horrible dread overwhelmed me. But the moment I was fixed thereon I seemed as unconcerned as a statue. I gave out my text (Gal. 3:10-11) and made a pause to think of something pretty to set off with, but the Lord so confounded me (as indeed it was meet, for I was seeking not his glory but my own) that I was in a perfect labyrinth and found if I did not begin immediately I must go down without speaking. So I broke out with the first word that occurred, not knowing whether I should be able to add any more. Then the Lord opened my mouth, enabling me to speak near an hour, without any kind of perplexity and so loud that everyone might hear. The audience behaved with great decency. When sermon was over I found myself so cool and easy, so cheerful in spirit, and wonderfully strengthened in body, I went into an house and spoke again near an hour to about two hundred people. In the morning I preached again to about a thousand; Mr. H[ick]s engaged to preach in Orwell field[72] on Tuesday evening. I gave notice that I designed to preach on Monday sennight at Grantchester,[73] a mile from Cambridge.

Mr. H[ick]s and I have agreed to go into Hertfordshire; afterwards to separate and go round the neighbourhood, preaching in the fields wherever a door is opened, three or four days in every week. . . .

Believe me,
Your affectionate servant,
J. B.

Friday, June 1. The rain began when we took horse, and attended us all the way to Berwick. When I was tolerably dry I sent to the mayor, who readily granted the use of the town hall. Here I preached about seven to a drowsy congregation on 'Why will ye die, O house of Israel?'[74] And again a little after seven in the morning, on 'I would thou wert either hot or cold.'[75] In the evening, I preached in the court-house at Alnwick to a people of quite another spirit, 'having' the power as well as 'the form of godliness',[76] and panting after the whole image of God.[77]

[72] Orwell was a small parish 6 miles north of Royston. The reference suggests the parish was not yet enclosed.

[73] Orig., 'Grandchester'; Grantchester was a small parish 2 miles south-west of Cambridge.

[74] Ezek. 18:31.

[75] Cf. Rev. 3:15.

[76] Cf. 2 Tim. 3:5.

[77] See Ps. 42:1.

Whit Sunday, 3. I preached at eight in the court-house, but it was much crowded and exceeding hot. So in the afternoon, I went to the cross and cried aloud in the name of my Master, 'If any man thirst, let him come unto me and drink.'[78]

Mon. 4. I preached in Plessey square at one, to an earnest, loving congregation and inquired of one of them, James Gillies, concerning a report I had heard the day before. He informed me that when he was a little child, he had just learned his Christ-cross row.[79] But this he soon forgot. Between twenty and thirty, he was deeply convinced of sin; at which time, feeling a strong persuasion he could read, he went into a neighbour's house, took up a Bible, and read distinctly, which he has done ever since.

After preaching, I rode on to Newcastle. Certainly, if I did not believe there was another world, I should spend all my summers here, as I know no place in Great Britain comparable to it for pleasantness. But I seek another country,[80] and therefore am content to be a wanderer upon earth.

Wed. 6. I preached at Gateshead Fell, to a numerous congregation. In earnestness the colliers of Gateshead utterly shame the colliers of Kingswood, scarce thirty of whom think it worth while to hear the word of God on a week-day! Not even when I preach. And here the house will scarce contain the week-day congregation of a local preacher!

Sat. 9. I rode to Sunderland and preached in the shell of their house.[81] The people of this town likewise are hungry for the word and receive it with all gladness. Sunday 10, the house contained us at eight, but at one I was obliged to stand in the great street and declare to an attentive multitude, 'Ye must be born again.'[82] In the evening I preached to some thousands at Newcastle, near the Keelmen's Hospital; if haply God might bring back some of them who ran well many years ago.

Wed. 13. After preaching at the Fell I rode to Chester[-le-Street]. The congregation was deeply serious, both in the evening and at five in the morning. Thence we crossed the country to

[78] John 7:37.

[79] The alphabet, so called from the figure of a cross prefixed to it in horn-books. *OED*.

[80] See Heb. 11:16.

[81] The new chapel in Numbers Garth was the fourth meeting-house and the first chapel of the Methodists in Sunderland. It served until 1793, when the Sans Street Chapel was built, and was then sold for a grain warehouse. *Wesleyan Methodist Magazine* 133 (1910):169.

[82] John 3:7.

Newlands, where I was met by poor John Brown,[83] who has refrained from preaching till he is fallen into deep despair. I preached on 'I will heal their backsliding.'[84] But the word did not reach his heart.

I never saw near so large a congregation at Sheep Hill as we had at six in the evening. What is wanting in this whole country? Only more labourers.

Sat. 16. I rode to Widdrington and preached at one to a congregation gathered from all parts. The court-house at Alnwick was pretty well filled in the evening, and in the morning, Sunday 17. We had a sound useful sermon at church and a serious, well-behaved congregation. I preached in the market-place about five. And I trust God applied the word, 'Ye must be born again.'

Mon. 18. Having an uneasy horse, I was tired enough when we came into Morpeth. But after resting a while, I was strengthened to preach 'Christ crucified'[85] in the market-place to such a congregation as was never seen there before. And a solemn awe seemed to sit on every face, officers and gentlemen, as well as common people. After preaching at Plessey in the evening, I rode back to Newcastle.

Wed. 20. I endeavoured to compose the little differences which had much hurt the poor people at Gateshead Fell. O what zeal, what prudence and patience are requisite, to 'bear the manners'[86] of an untoward people and to train them up in Christian discipline, 'till they come to the full stature of Christ'![87]

Thur. 21. I preached at Nafferton at one.[88] As I was riding thence, one stopped me on the road and said, 'Sir, do not you remember when you was at Prudhoe[89] two years since, you breakfasted at Thomas Newton's? I am his sister. You looked upon me as you was going out and said, "Be in earnest." I knew not then what earnestness meant, nor had any thought about it. But the words sunk into my heart, so that I could never rest any more till I sought and found Christ.'

[83] See Nov. 28, 1742, n. 3 (19:303-4 in this edn.).
[84] Hos. 14:4.
[85] 1 Cor. 1:23.
[86] Cf. Acts 13:18.
[87] Cf. Eph. 4:13.
[88] On this day, he also wrote the preface to *A Short Exposition of the Ten Commandments. Extracted from Bishop Hopkins* and preached a second time.
[89] Orig., 'Pruddoe'.

Fri. 22. I rode to S[outh Biddic]k[90] and preached to my old congregation of colliers, on 'Why will ye die, O house of Israel?'[91] After preaching, a servant of Mr.——— came and said, 'Sir, my master discharges you from preaching any more on his ground; not out of any disrespect to *you*, but he will *stand by the Church.*' 'Simple Master Shallow!' as Shakespeare has it.[92] Wise master rector, his counsellor!

Sat. 23. I spoke to each of the society in Sunderland. Most of the robbers commonly called 'smugglers' have left us. But more than twice the number of honest people are already come in their place. And if none had come, yet should I not dare to keep those who *steal* either from the king or subject.

Sun. 24. I preached in the street at eight, about one at South Shields, and at five in North Shields. The greatest part of them seemed to hear as for their lives. So are these lions also become lambs. O for zealous, active, faithful labourers! How 'white are the fields unto the harvest'![93]

On Monday and Tuesday[94] evening, I preached abroad near the Keelmen's Hospital to twice the people we should have had at the house. What marvel the devil does not love field preaching? Neither do I—I love a commodious room, a soft cushion, an handsome pulpit. But where is my zeal if I do not trample all these under foot, in order to save one more soul?

Thur. 28. We had the general meeting of the stewards, by whom I found the societies in this circuit still contain about eighteen hundred members. I hope not many of these will be choked by the thorns![95]

Fri. 29. About eleven, I set out for Swalwell in a fair, mild morning. But in half an hour the rain poured down, so that in a few minutes I was wet from head to foot. And when I came thither, where to preach I knew not, for the house would not contain a third of the people. Just then the Dissenting minister sent, to offer me the use of his meeting-house.[96] I went thither

[90] Orig., 'S———k'; South Biddick was a village of colliers visited often by Wesley, 7 miles south-east of Newcastle.

[91] Ezek. 18:31, etc.

[92] Shakespeare appears not to have it in precisely this form, but affords ample material for the sentiment. Cf. Shakespeare, *Merry Wives of Windsor*, III.iv.50-51.

[93] Cf. John 4:35.

[94] All three contemporary editions read 'Wednesday', but this was revised in the errata to JW's *Works* (1774) and in manuscript in his personal copy, to 'Tuesday'.

[95] See Matt. 13:7, etc.

[96] Edward Arthur (d. 1780), minister of the Ebenezer Presbyterian chapel (built 1750)

without delay. There was a large congregation and a blessing in the midst of them.

Sat. 30. I preached in Winlaton[97] at noon. The sun was very hot and shone full upon my head. But the wind was very high and very cold, so that the one tempered the other while I was declaring the grace of God to a well-meaning multitude, who know little as yet, but are willing to know 'the truth as it is in Jesus'.[98] I preached at Sheep Hill in the evening, and returned to Newcastle as fresh as I was in the morning.

Sunday, July 1. Between eight and nine, I preached to a quiet multitude in Gateshead. At two, I preached in the Fell to the largest congregation which had ever been seen there, and in the evening near the Keelmen's Hospital to full as many as my voice would reach. It was a season of love, and God caused the mountains to flow down at his presence.[99]

While the society was gathering, I went to a young woman who was some days since suddenly struck with what they called 'madness'. And so it was, but a diabolical madness, as plainly appeared from numerous circumstances. However, after we had been at prayer, she fell asleep and never raged or blasphemed after.

Mon. 2. I rode to Durham and went at one to the meadow by the riverside where I preached two years ago.[1] The congregation was now larger by one half, but the sun was so scorching hot upon my head that I was scarce able to speak. I paused a little and desired God would provide us a covering, if it was for his glory. In a moment it was done—a cloud covered the sun, which troubled us no more. Ought *voluntary humility* to conceal these palpable proofs that God still 'heareth the prayer'?[2]

Between two and three we took horse. The sun now shone again and with so intense an heat that I know not how we could have endured it but that the wind came in our face, by the help of which we got pretty well to Hartlepool. I suppose we had all the town with us in the evening, either in the street or the adjoining

1753–60. Hew Scott, *Fasti Ecclesiae Scoticanae*, 7 vols. (Edinburgh, Oliver and Boyd, 1915–28), 7:483.

[97] Orig., 'Winlington'. Though commonly known (even in the *Journal*) as Winlaton Mill from the dominating presence of the Crawley iron-works, Winlaton was the proper name for this parochial district 1 mile north-west of the mill.

[98] Cf. Eph. 4:21.

[99] See Isa. 64:1.

[1] See above, July 4, 1757.

[2] Prov. 15:29.

houses. And God was pleased to touch the hearts of many, even among this dull, heavy, sleepy people.

Tue. 3. I wrote to Dr. Taylor as follows:[3]

Hartlepool, July 3, 1759

Rev. Sir,

I esteem you as a person of uncommon sense and learning, but your doctrine I cannot esteem. And some time since I believed it my duty to speak my sentiments at large concerning your doctrine of *Original Sin*. When Mr. Newton[4] of Liverpool mentioned this and asked whether you designed to answer, you said, you thought not; for it would only be 'a *personal controversy* between Jo[hn] W[esle]y and Jo[hn] T[aylo]r.' How gladly, if I durst, would I accept of this discharge from so unequal a contest! For I am thoroughly sensible, humanly speaking, it is 'formica contra leonem'.[5] How gladly, were it indeed no other than a *personal* controversy! But certainly, it is not; it is a controversy *de re*,[6] if ever there was one in the world. Indeed, concerning a thing of the highest importance; nay, all the things that concern our eternal peace. It is, *Christianity* or *heathenism*? For take away the scriptural doctrine of redemption or justification, and that of the new birth, the beginning of sanctification, or which amounts to the same, explain them as you do, suitably to your doctrine of original sin, and what is Christianity better than heathenism? Wherein (save in rectifying some of our *notions*) has the religion of St. Paul any pre-eminence over that of Socrates or Epictetus?

This is, therefore, to my apprehension, the least a *personal controversy* of any in the whole world. Your person and mine are out of the question. *The point* is, Are *those things* that have been believed for many ages, throughout the Christian world, real, solid *truths*, or *monkish dreams* and vain imaginations?

[3] Dr. John Taylor, see Aug. 28, 1748, n. 47 (20:245 in this edn.).

[4] John Newton (1725–1807), later the famous curate of Olney, 1764–80. After his adventurous early career as a seaman and slaver, Newton had married in 1750, and had been forced by ill-health to abandon the sea in 1754. From 1755 to 1760, he was a tide surveyor at Liverpool and became an enthusiastic follower of Whitefield. Newton entertained JW when the latter was preaching at Liverpool the previous year, and sometimes attended Methodist preaching (*Wesleyan Methodist Magazine* 86 [1863]:1101). In 1758, he was refused ordination by the Archbishop of York, and in 1760, he briefly took charge of an Independent congregation at Warwick. In 1764, he was ordained through the influence of the Earl of Dartmouth and appointed to Olney, of which the earl was patron. Here much of his best literary work was done, and his friendship with Cowper cemented. But after various discouragements, he accepted John Thornton's offer of the living of St. Mary Woolnoth with St. Mary Woolchurch, Lombard Street, in 1780. Here he sustained a notable evangelical ministry and spiritual correspondence and forged his links with Wilberforce and the anti-slavery crusade.

[5] 'An ant opposed to a lion' (Thomas Jackson).

[6] 'On a serious matter'.

But farther, it is certain, between you and me there need be no *personal* controversy at all. For we may agree to leave each other's person and character absolutely untouched, while we sum up and answer the several arguments advanced as plainly and closely as we can.

Either I or you mistake the whole of Christianity from the beginning to the end! Either my scheme or yours is as contrary to the scriptural as the Koran is. Is it mine or yours? Yours has gone through all England and made numerous converts. I attack it from end to end. Let all England judge whether it can be defended or not!

Earnestly praying that God may give you and me a right understanding in all things,

I am, Rev. sir,
Your servant for Christ's sake,
J. W.

Wed. 4. Mr. [Joseph] Jones[7] preached at five, I at eight. Toward the close of the sermon, a queer, dirty, clumsy man, I suppose a country wit, took a great deal of pains to disturb the congregation. When I had done, fearing he might hurt those who[8] were gathered about him, I desired two or three of our brethren to go to him, one after the other, and not say much themselves, but let him talk till he was weary. They did so, but without effect, as his fund of ribaldry seemed inexhaustible. W[illiam] A[lwood][9] then tried another way. He got into the circle close to him and, listening a while, said, 'That is pretty. Pray say it over again.' 'What, are you deaf?' 'No, but for the entertainment of the people. Come; we are all attention.' After repeating this twice or thrice, the wag could not stand it, but with two or three curses walked clear off.

In the evening, I began near Stockton market-place, as usual. I had hardly finished the hymn, when I observed the people in great confusion, which was occasioned by a lieutenant of a man-of-war, who had chosen that time to bring his press-gang and ordered them to take Joseph Jones and William Alwood. Joseph Jones telling him, 'Sir, I belong to Mr. Wesley,' after a few words he let

[7] Joseph Jones, see June 2, 1753, n. 51 (20:460 in this edn.).

[8] 1764, 1791, 'which'.

[9] William Alwood was an itinerant, 1756–64, and an attempt seems to have been made to get him back into the itinerancy in 1775, at which time he was a local preacher in the Chester circuit. *WHS* 3 (1902):182; Bretherton, *Methodism in Chester,* p. 280; Everett, *Sheffield,* pp. 107, 120-21.

him go; as he did likewise William Alwood after a few hours, understanding he was a licensed preacher. He likewise seized upon a young man of the town. But the women rescued him by main strength. They also broke the lieutenant's head and so stoned both him and his men that they ran away with all speed.

Fri. 6.[10] I rode on to Yarm. The heat of the day was hardly to be borne. But in the evening it was extremely pleasant. And the whole congregation were deeply serious.

Sat. 7. At one I was at Hutton Rudby,[11] six miles south of Yarm, where they have just built a preaching-house. But it would not contain a fourth of the congregation, and what place to choose I could not tell, no shade being at hand, and the sun shining near as hot as it used to do in Georgia. Finding no other way, I stood in the street, near an house which sheltered some of the people. The rest seemed not to know whether it was hot or cold, God so plenteously refreshed their souls. Much the same congregation was at Potto[12] in the evening, and with the same blessing.

Having preached considerably longer both at noon and night than I am accustomed to do, I was so hoarse in the morning, Sunday 8, that I knew not what I should do to go through the work of the day. However, I began it by preaching on the Green at Stokesley to a multitude of people. Thence I rode to Guisborough[13] at the foot of the mountains. The sun would have been unsupportable but that we had a strong wind full in our face for the greatest part of the day. At twelve, we had a lovely congregation in a meadow near the town, who drank in every word that was spoken as the thirsty earth the showers. The sixteen miles, so called, from hence to Robin Hood's Bay, took us

[10] This bald entry conceals the fact the JW was to take advantage of the bottomless hospitality of George Merryweather, a leading merchant in Yarm, with whom he had been in correspondence for at least eighteen months and over whose stables the Methodist society then met. Though never mentioned by name in the *Journal*, Merryweather enjoyed a unique local position, providing accommodation for all the preachers, sustaining a correspondence with the leading evangelical luminaries of the day, Methodist and otherwise, and securing for Yarm a very high input of effort by the itinerant preachers, which made it the head of a huge circuit of some forty places including all the main centres of south Durham and north Yorkshire. Merryweather had also a name for dealing faithfully, if sternly, as a class-leader. *WHS* 2 (1899):76.

[11] Hutton Rudby is a parish and village 4 miles west of Stokesley. There was a group emigration from Hutton Rudby to Nova Scotia in 1771, which included a number of Wesley's early converts. *Methodist Magazine* 38 (1815):359.

[12] Potto was a small township in the parish of Whorlton, 5¼ miles south-west of Stokesley.

[13] Orig., 'Gisborough'. Guisborough was a thriving market town and parish 49 miles north of York.

between five and six hours riding; so that when I came thither, I was quite exhausted. However, I went to the quay, where a large congregation was waiting. And all behaved well but an honest tar who was much disturbed at my saying, 'No man is delivered from the fear of death but he that fears God.'

Tue. 10. We took horse at half-hour past three and rode over the huge mountains to Scarborough.[14] I began to preach near the main street at seven. The congregation was large, and some of them wild enough. But in a short time all were quiet and still. Nor did I hear one unkind word when I had done.

In the afternoon, I rode to York, where I thought to rest a few days, being almost worn out. But it was judged quite necessary, I should go to Hull, lest the little flock should be discouraged. So on Friday 13, I set out early and reached Pocklington between eight and nine. The last time I was here, they rung the bells in order to drown my voice. But he who then paid the ringers is run away. So I had a quiet and serious audience. I had a far *finer* congregation at Hull. So for once 'the *rich* have the gospel preached'![15]

At night Charles Delamotte[16] called upon me and seemed to be the same loving, simple man still. I should not repent my journey to Hull were it only for this short interview.

Sat. 14. I preached at eight in Mr. Hilton's[17] yard near the great street in Beverley and was surprised to see so quiet and civil a congregation, where we expected nothing less. All the men were uncovered, and the whole audience was attentive from beginning to end; nor did one person give us a rude word while we rode from

[14] The visit to Scarborough was to give an impetus to a Methodist society recently formed by Thomas Brown, a Sunderland local preacher, who had moved to the town in 1756. The society had to suffer a good deal of violence (which JW himself clearly half-suspected) and, as in other Yorkshire coastal places, the attentions of the press-gangs. *Wesleyan Methodist Magazine* 49 (1826):594-96.

[15] Cf. Matt. 11:5.

[16] Charles Delamotte, settled at Barton-upon-Humber on his return from Georgia in 1738, and was buried at Aylesby, 4 miles west of Grimsby; see Oct. 14, 1735, n. 2 (18:136 in this edn.). This meeting with JW probably took place at the house of Mrs. Sarah Snowden (1736–1835), to which Wesley now paid the first of fifteen visits. Mrs. Snowden, the niece of Mrs. Mary Thompson, the first to provide regular hospitality for Methodist preachers in Hull and the wife of Thomas Snowden, a leader and local preacher, provided a residential base for the preachers in east Yorkshire, like that created by Merryweather in the North Riding. *Wesleyan Methodist Magazine* 60 (1837):885-99.

[17] Orig., 'Helton's', corrected to 'Hilton's' in 1774. Francis Hilton, shoemaker of Beverley, first offered his own home for preaching, then fitted up a large room in Turner's yard.

one end of the town to the other. This, with the large and earnest congregation at York in the evening, made me forget all my labour.

Sun. 15. I began reading to the society an account of the late work of God at Everton.[18] But I could not get through. At first there were only silent tears on every side. But it was not long before several were unable to refrain from weeping aloud. And quickly a stout young man dropped down and roared as in the agonies of death. I did not attempt to read any farther, but began wrestling with God in prayer. We continued herein till near nine o'clock. What a day of jubilee was this!

Tue. 17. I left York, and about noon preached at Tadcaster. Distant thunder did not lessen the number, but increased the seriousness of the congregation, who appeared entirely different from those I saw here two years ago.

At seven in the evening, I preached to an immense congregation at the foot of an high mountain near Otley. Wednesday 18, I rode on to Mr. Marshal's at Guiseley,[19] the Capua[20] of Yorkshire:

Hic nemus, hic gelidi fontes, hic mollia prata.[21]

'Tis well God is here—or who could bear it?

Hence we rode to Keighley, where is a loving, earnest, well-established people. Here many of our preachers met me and many of our brethren, and God was with us in all our assemblies.

Fri. 20. We went on to Colne (formerly, I suppose, a Roman colony)[22] situate on the top of an high, round hill, at the edge of

[18] No doubt the account given above, May 30, 1759.

[19] Mr. Marshal of Park Gate near Guiseley, who took services at home, night and morning, and was esteemed by Richard Burdsall 'a man of grace, a friend to society, and a monument to religion'. Richard Burdsall, *Memoirs of the life of Richard Burdsall* (new edn., London, 1838), pp. 115-17.

[20] An allusion to the aphorism '*Capua Hannibalem corrupit*'. Cf. the reference to the seductions of Cork, above, June 9, 1755.

[21] 'Here a grove, here cool springs, here smooth lawns'. Adapted from Virgil, *Eclogues*, x.42, 43.

[22] Colne was a market town and chapelry in the parish of Whalley, 35 miles south-east of Lancaster. It had indeed been a Roman station, though eighteenth-century historians were divided whether the name was derived from *Colunio*, the supposed name of the Roman station, or the Saxon *Culme*, 'coal'. Ekwall holds that Colne is a British river name identical with Calne (Wilts.) and reports the suggestion that 'it belongs to the root of Lat[in] *calare* "to call", Welsh *ceiliog* "cock" &c., and means "roaring river".' Eilert Ekwall, *Concise Oxford Dictionary of English Place-names* (4th edn., Oxford, 1960) p. 118.

Pendle Forest. I preached at eleven in an open space not far from the main street. And I have seldom seen a more attentive or decently behaved congregation. How is the scene changed since the drunken mob of this town used to be a terror to all the country!

We rode to Broad Clough[23] in the afternoon, a lone house in the midst of the Lancashire mountains. The people came in from all quarters, and it was a season of great refreshment. Among the rest was Mr. M[ilne]r,[24] who gave us an account of his late trials. I wonder the butcher (*doctor*, so called) to whom he was committed did not murder him. He took true pains so to do. But his chain did not reach so far.

Sat. 21. Mr. Grimshaw led us to Gaulksholme, another lone house on the side of an enormous mountain. The congregation stood and sat, row above row, in the sylvan theatre. I believe nothing on the post-diluvian earth can be more pleasant than the road from hence, between huge, steep mountains, clothed with wood to the top and washed at the bottom by a clear, winding stream. At four, I preached to a very large congregation at Heptonstall, and thence rode on to Haworth.

Sun. 22. At ten Mr. Milner read prayers. But the church would not near contain the congregation. So after prayers I stood on a scaffold close to the church, and the congregation in the churchyard. The communicants alone filled the church. In the afternoon the congregation was nearly doubled. And yet most of these were not curious hearers, but men fearing God.

Mon. 23. I preached near Huddersfield to the wildest congregation I have seen in Yorkshire; yet they were restrained by an unseen hand, and I believe some felt the sharpness of his word. I preached at Halifax in the evening, but the preaching-house was like an oven. Tuesday 24, the house was well filled at five. About seven in the evening, I preached at Bradford at the door of the house, as it could not contain one half of the congregation. Wednesday 25, I talked with most of those whom Edward Hales[25] had torn from their brethren. Just as he was coming to widen the

[23] Broad Clough Hall is a mile north of Bacup.

[24] On John Milner, vicar of Chipping, see Apr. 11, 1751, n. 73 (20:383 in this edn.).

[25] A young man from Wakefield who preached among members of the society who had seceded on Calvinistic grounds and was invited to become their pastor. His views changed, however, and, thus disappointed, the Calvinists postponed for many years their plan of chapel-building. W. W. Stamp, *Historical Notices of Wesleyan Methodism in Bradford and its vicinity* (London, 1841), pp. 39-40.

breach, it pleased God to take him to himself. The wanderers were now willing to return, and I received them again, I trust for ever.

Thur. 26. I preached in Gildersome at noon, and at Morley in the evening. A flame is suddenly broke out here where it was least of all expected. And it spreads wider and wider. When God *will* work, who is able to stay his hand?

Sun. 29. I preached about eight at Birstall. The congregation covered a large part of the field, and my voice was exceedingly strengthened, so that I believe all could hear. At one, I enforced those solemn words on an immense multitude: 'This is life eternal, to know thee the only true God, and Jesus Christ whom thou hast sent.'[26]

I shall easily be excused for adding here a farther account of the work of God in and near Everton.[27]

On Monday, July 9, I set out, and on Wednesday noon reached Potton, where I rejoiced at the account given by John Keeling of himself and others.[28] He *was* justified, it seems, on that memorable sabbath, but had not a clear witness of it till ten days after. About which time his sister (who was on that day in great distress) was also set at liberty. I discoursed also with Ann Thorn, who told me of much heaviness following the visions with which she had been favoured, but said she was at intervals visited still with such overpowering love and joy, especially at the Lord's Supper, that she often lay in a trance for many hours. She is twenty-one years old. We were soon after called into the garden, where Patty Jenkins (one of the same age) was so overwhelmed with the love of God that she sunk down and appeared as one in a pleasant sleep, only with her eyes open. Yet she had often just strength to utter, with a low voice, ejaculations of joy and praise; but no words coming up to what she felt, she frequently laughed while she saw his glory. This is quite unintelligible to many, for a stranger intermeddleth not with our joy. So it was to Mr. M[adan], who doubted whether God or the devil had filled her with love and praise. O the depth of human wisdom! Mr. R[omaine] the meantime was filled with a solemn awe. I no sooner sat down by her than the spirit of God

[26] John 17:3 (*Notes*).

[27] The convincing grounds which led H. J. Foster to ascribe this letter to John Walsh, the converted London deist, are set out in *WHS* 4 (1903):23-24 (on Walsh see above, Dec. 2, 1755, n. 46). Were he to be identical with the Lieutenant John Walsh mentioned in the *Arminian Magazine*, the statement of his experience given here under July 23 would be especially poignant; cf. *Arminian Magazine* 11 (1788):538.

[28] For this event, see above, May 30, 1759.

poured the same blessedness into my soul. Hers continued till the time we were to set out for Cockayne Hatley.[29] Then her strength was restored in a moment, and we walked together, sixteen in number, singing to the Lord as we went along.

Mr. Hicks preached an excellent sermon on the 'Strait Gate'. The next morning, Thursday 12, he gave me leave to take an extract from his journal. But I had only time to write the occurrences of one morning as follows:

'June 6, 1759. I spoke this morning at Orwell, on Isaiah 55:1. One who had been before convinced of sin fell down in a kind of fit and broke out in great anguish of soul, calling on the Lord Jesus for salvation. He wrought as in the agonies of death and was quite bathed in sweat. He beat the chair against which he kneeled, as one whose soul drew nigh unto hell. His countenance then cleared up at once, and we hoped he would be presently set at liberty. But on a sudden he was more distressed than ever, being in the sharpest conflict. Every muscle of his body was in strong agitation, as if nature was just dissolving. I never saw any convulsion fit so violent, but in a moment God dispelled the cloud. His face was again covered with smiles, and he spake as seeing the Lord near him. He cried unto him, and the Lord, hearing, pronounced him freely forgiven. At that instant he clapped his hands and cried aloud, "Jesus is mine! He is *my* Saviour!" His soul was in peace; neither did he find the least bodily pain or soreness. I asked, "For what would you undergo this again?" He said, "Not for all the world. But I would suffer more rather than be without Christ. Yea, for his sake, I would suffer all things." "An unwise man doth not consider this; a fool doth not understand it."

'This morning Ann Simpson, aged sixteen or seventeen, lay near an hour in the utmost distress, shrieking out, "Christ! Christ!" and no other word; her face all the time being violently distorted. I left her awhile, but could scarce sit down before I heard the voice of praise. I went and found her heaviness turned into joy, even the joyful assurance that *her* sins were pardoned. She sprang by me to a young woman who lay in a kind of trance, and clasped her in her arms, breathing forth praise to God. I retired again, but had not been long seated e'er she came in, running to me in a transport of praise. I asked her why she cried out continually, "Christ, Christ!" She answered: "I thought myself at that time on a little island and saw Satan in a hideous form, just ready to devour me, hell all round open to receive me, and myself ready to drop in, while no help appeared, nor any way to escape. But just as I was dropping in, the

[29] Orig., 'Cockin Hatley'. Cockayne Hatley was a tiny parish 6 miles north-east of Biggleswade.

Lord appeared between me and the great gulf, and would not let me fall into it. As soon as I saw him, all my trouble was gone and all the pain I felt before. And ever since I have been light and joyful and filled with the love of God.'"

So far Mr. Hicks, who told me he was first convinced of sin August 1, 1758, and, finding peace in about six weeks, first preached the gospel on September 17. From that time he was accounted a fool and a madman! About two thousand[30] souls seem to have been awakened by Mr. B[erridge] and him within this twelve months.

Fri. 13. Mr. R[omaine], as well as Mr. M[adan], was in doubt concerning the work of God here. But this morning they were both fully convinced, while Alice Miller, the little pale girl justified May 20 (who is in the sixteenth) and Molly Raymund, who is in the twelfth year of her age, related their experience, their artless confidence confirming all their words. We walked this forenoon to Tadlow in Cambridgeshire to hear Mr. B[erridge], but came too late for the sermon. However, the account we received of the wonderful works of God in this and the neighbouring places were matter of great rejoicing to *me*, as are all manifestations of the world to come.

Sat. 14. Mr. B[erridge], being ill, desired *me* to exhort a few people in his house, which the Lord enabled me to do with such ease and power that I was quite amazed. The next morning at seven his servant, Caleb Price, spoke to about two hundred people. The Lord was wonderfully present, more than twenty persons feeling the arrows of conviction. Several fell to the ground, some of whom seemed dead, others in the agonies of death, the violence of their convulsions exceeding all description. There was also great crying and agonizing in prayer, mixed with deep and deadly groans on every side.

When sermon was ended one brought good tidings to Mr. B[erridge] from Grantchester, that God had there *broken down* seventeen persons last week by the singing of hymns only, and that a child seven years old sees many visions and astonishes the neighbours with her innocent, awful manner of declaring them.

While Mr. B[erridge] preached in the church, I stood with many in the churchyard to make room for those who came from far. Therefore I *saw* little, but *heard* the agonizing of many, panting and gasping after eternal life. In the afternoon Mr. B[erridge] was constrained by the multitude of people to come out of the church and preach in his own close. Some of those who were here pricked

30 1764, 1791, 'four thousand', altered in *Works* (1774), to the edited text.

to the heart were affected in an astonishing manner. The first man I saw wounded would have dropped, but others catching him in their arms did indeed prop him up, but were so far from keeping him still that he caused all of them to totter and tremble. His own shaking exceeded that of a cloth in the wind. It seemed as if the Lord came upon him like a giant, taking him by the neck and shaking all his bones in pieces. One woman tore up the ground with her hands, filling them with dust and with the hard-trodden grass, on which I saw her lie with her hands clinched, as one dead, when the multitude dispersed. Another roared and screamed in a more dreadful agony than ever I heard before. I omitted the rejoicing of believers because of their number and the frequency thereof; though the manner was strange, some of them being quite overpowered with divine love and only showing enough of natural life to let us know they were overwhelmed with joy and life eternal. Some continued long as if they were dead, but with a calm sweetness in their looks. I saw one who lay two or three hours in the open air, and being then carried into the house, continued insensible another hour, as if actually dead. The first sign of life she showed was a rapture of praise, intermixed with a small joyous laughter.

Mon. 16. Mr. B[erridge] this evening preached in his house, where I observed Molly Raymund leaning all the while as if asleep. But an hour or two after, she desired to speak with him. I wondered she was not gone home, and was concerned that so little a girl should have so far to go in the dark without company. But Mr. B[erridge] told me, neither she nor the other justified children were afraid of anything.

Tue. 17. We walked toward Harston,[31] near which Mr. B[erridge] overtook us. He was greatly fatigued and dejected, and said, 'I am now so weak, I must leave off field preaching.' Nevertheless he cast himself on the Lord and stood up to preach, having near three thousand hearers. He was very weak at first and scarce able to speak, but God soon performed his promise, imparting new strength to him and causing him to speak with mighty power. A great shaking was among the dry bones. Incessant were the cries, groans, wringing of hands, and prayers of sinners, now first convinced of their deplorable state. After preaching he was lively and strong, so that the closeness of a crowded room neither affected his breath nor hindered his rejoicing over two children, one about eight, the other about six years old, who were crying aloud to God for mercy.

[31] Orig., 'Harlston'; Harston, a parish 6 miles south-west of Cambridge and some 4 miles south of Grantchester.

Not only Harston, but Stapleford[32] and Triplow,[33] to which Mr. B[erridge] was now going, were places in which he had never preached the gospel and probably never would have done had it not been for the thundering sermons made against him from their several pulpits. So does Satan frequently overshoot himself and occasion the downfall of his own kingdom.

I had been very ill the preceding week. Wherefore last night I had recourse to God in prayer, and this morning, instead of rising with difficulty at eight or nine as I had usually done, I rose with ease at five; and instead of losing my strength in a mile or two, I walked eighteen without any weakness or weariness.

Wed. 18. We called at the house where Mr. B[erridge] had been preaching in the morning, and found several there rejoicing in God, and several mourning after him. While I prayed with them many crowded into the house, some of whom burst into a strange, involuntary laughter, so that my voice could scarce be heard, and when I strove to speak louder a sudden hoarseness seized me. Then the laughter increased. I perceived it was from Satan and resolved to pray on. Immediately the Lord rebuked him; that laughter was at an end, and so was my hoarseness. A vehement wrestling with God ran through the whole company, whether sorrowful or rejoicing; till beside the three young women of the house, one young man and a girl about eleven years old, who had been counted one of the wickedest in Harston, were exceedingly blessed with the consolations of God.

Among those under conviction was an elderly woman, who had been a scoffer at the gospel and a keen ridiculer of all that cried out, but she now cried louder than any present. Another I observed who had known the Lord about five and twenty years. When Mr. B[erridge] first brought the gospel to her ears she was filled with gladness, knowing, this was the same salvation which God had long ago brought to her heart.

We walked hence to the middle of Shelford Moor, and seeing no person but a young woman who kept sheep, the solitude invited us to stop and sing an hymn, the sound whereof reaching her, she came up slowly, weeping as she came, and then stood by a brook of water over against us with the tears running down her cheeks apace. We sung another hymn for this mourner in Zion and wrestled for her with God in prayer. But he did not yet comfort her. And indeed I have observed of the people in general who hear Mr. B[erridge], their convictions are not only deep and violent, but last a long time. Wherefore those that are offended at them who rejoice

[32] Stapleford was a parish 4 miles south of Cambridge.

[33] Triplow, a parish 6 miles north-east of Royston.

should consider how terrible a cup they received first. Now they are all light, but they well remember the darkness and misery, the wormwood and the gall.

We met Mr. B[erridge] at Stapleford, five miles from Cambridge. His heart was particularly set on this people, because he was curate here five or six years, but never preached a gospel sermon among them till this evening. About 1500 persons met in a close to hear him, great part of whom were laughers and mockers. The work of God, however, quickly began among them that were serious, while not a few endeavoured to make sport by mimicking the gestures of them that were wounded. Both these and those who rejoiced in God gave great offence to some stern-looking men, who vehemently demanded to have those wretches horse-whipped out of the close. Need we wonder at this, when several of his own people are unwilling to let God work in his own way? And well may Satan be enraged at the cries of the people and the prayers they make in the bitterness of their souls, seeing we know these are the chief times at which Satan is cast out.

However, in a while many of the scoffers were weary and went away. The rest continued as insensible as before. I had long been walking round the multitude, feeling a jealousy for my God and praying him to make the place of his feet glorious. My patience at last began to fail, and I prayed, 'O king of glory, break some of them in pieces, but let it be to the saving of their souls.' I had but just spoke, when I heard a dreadful noise on the farther side of the congregation, and turning thither saw one Thomas Skinner coming forward, the most horrible human figure I ever saw. His large wig and hair were coal-black, his face distorted beyond all description. He roared incessantly, throwing and clapping his hands together with his whole force. Several were terrified and hasted out of the way. I was glad to hear him, after a while, pray aloud. Not a few of the triflers grew serious, while his kindred and acquaintance were very unwilling to believe even their own eyes and ears. They would fain have got him away, but he fell to the earth, crying, 'My burden! My burden! I cannot bear it!' Some of his brother scoffers were calling for horse-whips, till they saw him extended on his back at full length. They then said, he was dead. And indeed the only sign of life was the working of his breast and the distortions of his face, while the veins of his neck were swelled, as if ready to burst. He was just before the chief captain of Satan's forces. None was by nature more fitted for mockery. None could swear more heroically, to whip out of the close all who were affected by the preaching. His agonies lasted some hours. Then his body and soul were eased.

When Mr. B[erridge] had refreshed himself a little, he returned to the close and bid the multitude take warning by Skinner, who still lay roaring and tormented on the ground. All the people were now deeply serious, and several hundreds, instead of going when Mr. B[erridge] dismissed them, stayed in Mr. Jennings's yard. Many of these, especially men, were truly broken in heart. Mr. B[erridge] talked with as many as could come into the house, and, seeing what numbers stood hungering without, sent me word to pray with them. This was a grievous cross. I knew it was the Lord's will, but felt such weakness of body and sinking of spirit, and was withal so hoarse, that I supposed few could hear out of some hundreds who stood before me. However, I attempted, and in a moment the Lord poured upon me such a spirit of supplication and gave me so clear, strong an utterance that it seemed I was another man—a farther instance that the servants of God are not sent a warfare on *their own* charge.

No sooner had I finished than we were called to see John Dennis, aged twenty years, who lay on a table. His body was stiff and motionless as a statue, his very neck seemed as if made of iron. He was looking steadfastly up to heaven and praying aloud with a melodious voice. His words surprised Mr. B[erridge] as well as me, who said to the assembly, 'You need no better preacher; none can tell you the truths of the gospel more clearly.' And indeed his prayer unfolded the whole Christian system with the greatest accuracy. When he came out of the fit he was in perfect health, but declared he knew not a word of all he had spoken. His mother then informed us he had had these fits for two years, at least once a day, but he never spoke in any fit till three weeks ago; 'Ever since he prays in them, as tonight, but is himself as ignorant of the matter as if he had been dead all the time.'

It was late when I went to lodge about half a mile off, where I found a young woman reading hymns and the power of the Lord falling on the hearers, especially one young man, who cried aloud in such bitter anguish that I soon desired we might join in prayer. This was the seventh time of my praying in public that day, and had I been faithful I should probably have prayed seven more.

Thur. 19. I returned to Mr. J[ennin]gs's, who had set out at four in the morning to hear Mr. B[erridge] at Grantchester. He came soon after me, but was scarce able to speak. I never saw a man sweat in such manner, the large drops seeming fixed all over his face, just like beads of glass. The congregation at Grantchester this morning consisted of about one thousand persons, among whom the Lord was wonderfully present, convincing a far greater number now than even last night. Mr. J[ennin]gs was a mild, good-natured Pharisee, who never had been awakened. But he was now thoroughly convinced of his lost estate and stood for a time in utter despair, with his mouth wide open, his eyes staring and full of huge dismay. When he found power to speak he cried out: 'I thought I had led a good life! I thought I was not so bad as others! But I am the vilest creature upon earth! I am dropping into hell! Now, now—this very moment!' He then saw hell open to receive him, and Satan ready to cast him in. But it was not long before he saw the Lord Jesus and knew he had accepted him. He then cried aloud, in an unspeakable rapture, 'I have got Christ! I have got Christ!' For two hours he was in the visions of God. Then the joy, though not the peace, abated.

I had left Mr. J[ennin]gs but a little while when I heard John Dennis loudly praising God. I no sooner kneeled by him than the consolations of God came upon *me*, so that I trembled and wept much. Nor was the Spirit poured out upon *us* alone; all in the house were partakers of it. J[ohn] D[ennis] was kneeling when his fit came. We laid him on the ground, where he soon became stiff as last night and prayed in like manner. Afterwards his body grew flexible by degrees, but was convulsed from head to foot. When he was quite recovered he said he was quite resigned to the will of God, who gave him such strength in the inner man that he did not find any of these things grievous, neither could ask to be delivered from them.

I walked from Stapleford with twenty persons to hear Mr. B[erridge] at Triplow, and saw many other companies, some before, some behind, some on either hand, going the same way. This brought to my mind the words of Zechariah: 'And the inhabitants of one city should go to another, saying, Let us go speedily to pray before the Lord and to seek the Lord of Hosts. I will go also.'

Fifteen hundred or two thousand were assembled in the close at Triplow. The only unpolished part of the audience were a few gentlemen on horseback. They were much offended at the cries of those in conviction, but much more at the rejoicing of others, even to laughter. But they were not able to look them in the face for half a minute together. I looked after service at every ring which the people made about those that fell under the word. Here and there was a place with only one, but there were generally two or three together, and on one spot no less than seven, who lay on the ground as if slain in battle. I soon followed Mr. B[erridge] to the house and found both it and the orchard filled with serious people, to whom he spake till his strength failed and then, seeing them unwilling to depart, desired *me* to dismiss them with a prayer. I felt great reluctance, but so mightily, when I began, came the Spirit upon me, that I found no want of utterance while I was praying with about two hundred persons. I thought they had then gone away, but perceived an hour after, most of them were still in the house or orchard, sighs and groans, prayers, tears, and joyful praise being intermixed on every side.

Fri. 20. I was wakeful before five, but conferring with flesh and blood, I slept again. Mr. B[erridge] sent for me at seven. But I was then so weak I could not go till the people were dispersed. Three times more persons were struck with convictions this morning than had been last night. Mr. B[erridge] had prayed with them till near fainting, who then sent for me to come. And who knows what God might have done even by me, if I had not been indulging my vile body? I was glad to see a woman, supposed the chief sinner in the town, now rolling on the earth, screaming and roaring in strong convictions. The man of the house informed us of her having had nine or ten children by whoredom, and that being at last married, her husband was more angry with her for hearing the word than he would probably have been for committing adultery. Nor was her minister displeased that she never came to church, but mightily strove to prevent both her and all the sinners of his parish from going to hear the gospel. I observed also a beggar girl, seven or eight years old, who had scarce any clothes but a ragged piece of old rug. She too had felt the word of God as a two-edged sword and mourned to be covered with Christ's righteousness.

From Triplow I walked to Orwell, and thence to Everton, in weakness of body and heaviness of spirit. Mr. B[erridge] was preaching when I came in. Here God again refreshed my soul. I shook from head to foot, while tears of joy ran down my face, and my distress was at an end.

Sat. 21. I was troubled for some of our brethren, who began to doubt whether this was a work of God or of the devil. John Keeling in particular, who instead of his frank lively zeal and happiness in God, was now filled with gloomy discontent and grown dark, sullen, and reserved. As we were walking together he told me, it was his resolution to 'keep himself to himself, to let them who struggled so, struggle as they would, and leave all those to themselves whom Satan cast into visions or trances, till Satan brought them out again'. 'But' (he added) 'I am so uneasy, I don't know what to do, and most of our people begin to shun one another.' The snare was now broken. He saw the delusion he had been in, and I trust will hereafter shun the troublers of Israel.

Sun. 22. The church was quite filled, and hundreds were without. And now the arrows of God flew abroad. The inexpressible groans, the lamenting, praying, roaring, were so loud, almost without intermission, that we who stood without could scarce help thinking, all in the church were cut to the heart. But upon inquiry we found about two hundred persons, chiefly men, cried aloud for mercy; but many more were affected, perhaps as deeply, though in a calmer way.

I rejoiced to see many from Cambridgeshire, particularly John Dennis, Thomas Skinner, and the sorrowful young woman with whom we had prayed on Shelford Moor. Now too came good news from several parts, especially Grantchester, where ten more persons were cut to the heart in singing hymns among themselves. And the little child before mentioned continues to astonish all the neighbourhood. A noted physician came some time ago and closely examined her. The result was, he confessed it was 'no distemper of mind, but the hand of God'.

I sought for Thomas Skinner after morning service and found him with many more singing hymns under a tree. When they stopped I asked, 'How do you find your mind now?' Instead of speaking, he looked upon me with great steadiness, fetched a deep sigh, burst out into tears and prayers, and throwing himself along on the ground, fell into more and more agony, till he roared aloud. I told him how great a sinner I had been, but the more I spoke, the more was he distressed. Wherefore John Dennis and I went to prayer for him, but his deliverance was not yet. Make him, O Lord, a greater champion for thy truth than ever he was against it.

Mr. B[erridge] preached in his close this afternoon, though in great bodily weakness. But when he is weakest, God so strengthens him that it is surprising to what a distance his voice reaches. I have heard Mr. Whitefield speak as loud, but not with such a continued, strong, unbroken tenor.

Mon. 23. Mr. Keeling and I walked to Barford.[34] I was relating there how God had plucked such a brand as me out of the burning, but my voice was quickly stopped by rejoicing. And I have often found that nothing I can say makes so much impression on myself or others as thus repeating my own conversion.

The first time I saw Mr. B[erridge] was June 2, 1758. But I scarce thought of him again till June 7, as I was walking up to Luton Down. There an awful sense of God's presence fell upon me, and my voice grew louder and louder in proportion to the joy of my soul, with a strong impulse to pray for the success of Mr. B[erridge]'s labours. And such a foresight did the Lord give me of what he was bringing to pass through his ministry that I was quite overwhelmed for near an hour, till my voice was lost and only tears remained. And Oh! how graciously has the God of truth accomplished all those things! With what delight hast thou since caused me to 'walk

[34] The original text reads Barford, but in the *Works* (1774) this was altered (probably by a printer's error) to 'Bradford', which thereupon Wesley 'corrected' in the errata and his own personal copy to 'Bedford'; but this was twice as far from Everton as Great Barford, which Wesley himself visited on Feb. 1, 1761.

round the walls of thy Zion, to mark well her bulwarks, and count the towers thereof!'

Wednesday, August 1. A few of us spoke freely and largely to a brother who had been 'overtaken in a fault', and endeavoured to 'restore' him 'in the spirit of meekness'.[35] And we were much comforted over him, having great hope that God would restore his usefulness as well as his strength.

Thur. 2. I rode to Sheffield and preached at one to a large and quiet congregation. I was afterward desired to visit Mr. Dodge, curate of the new church.[36] I found him on the brink of eternity, rejoicing in God his Saviour.[37] Thence I went on to Rotherham and talked with five men and six women (as I had done with many others before in various places) who believe they are *saved from sin*. And this fact I believe, that they 'rejoice evermore, pray without ceasing, and in everything give thanks'.[38] I believe they feel nothing but love now. What they *will* do I leave to God.

Fri. 3. I preached at Gainsborough, in Sir Nevil Hickman's[39] great hall. It is full as large as the Weavers' Hall in Bristol. At two it was filled with a rude, wild multitude (a few of a better spirit excepted). Yet all but two or three gentlemen were attentive while I enforced our Lord's words, 'What shall it profit a man, if he shall gain the whole world and lose his own soul?'[40] I was walking back through a gaping staring crowd, when Sir Nevil came and thanked me for my sermon, to the no small amazement of his neighbours, who shrunk back as if they had seen a ghost. Thence I rode to North Scarle,[41] the last village in Lincolnshire, ten miles

[35] Gal. 6:1.

[36] The 'new church' was St. Paul's, Sheffield, consecrated in 1740. Nathaniel Dodge was not curate, however, of this church but of Greasbrough in the parish of Rotherham from 1755 until his death, which must have occurred in the next twelve months, as the next licensing to his curacy took place on Aug. 12, 1760 (Borthwick Institute of Historical Research, York, AB 13, p. 423; 14, p. 117). According to Everett, Sheffield Methodists were accustomed to go to Eccleshall to hear him (Everett, *Sheffield*, p. 136).

[37] See Luke 1:47.

[38] 1 Thess. 5:16-18.

[39] Sir Nevil George Hickman of Gainsborough, JP, succeeded his father in 1733 and died in 1781. Hickman is singled out for praise for securing protection for the harrassed Methodists of Scotter (see Apr. 23, 1766; cf. July 8, 1779). He is probably the upright magistrate of Apr. 6, 1764. Gainsborough was a market town and parish 15 miles north-west of Lincoln.

[40] Cf. Matt. 16:26.

[41] North Scarle was a parish 8 miles west of Lincoln and bordering on the county boundary. The society there existed before, if only just before, JW's visit, Methodism having been introduced by one of JW's Moorfields converts. In its turn, the North Scarle

short of Newark. Here a great multitude assembled from various parts, most of them wholly unacquainted with the ways of God; indeed to such a degree that, though I spoke as plain as I could on the first principles of religion, yet it seemed very many understood me no more than if I was talking Greek. O what a condition is the bulk of *reformed Christians* in, to this day!

Sat. 4. As we took horse, the rain began and accompanied us till we alighted in the evening. Sunday 5, between eight and nine, I reached Everton, faint and weary enough. During the prayers, as also during the sermon and the administration of the Sacrament, a few persons cried aloud. But it was not from sorrow or fear, but love and joy. The same I observed in several parts of the afternoon service. In the evening, I preached in Mr. Hicks's church. Two or three persons fell to the ground and were extremely convulsed, but none cried out. One or two were filled with strong consolation.

Mon. 6.[42] I talked largely with Ann Thorn[43] and two others who had been several times in trances. What they all agreed in was: (1) that when they 'went away' as they termed it, it was always at the time they were fullest of the love of God; (2) that it came upon them in a moment, without any previous notice, and took away all their senses and strength; (3) that there were some exceptions, but generally from that moment they were in another world, knowing nothing of what was done or said by all that were round about them.

About five in the afternoon I heard them singing hymns. Soon after, Mr. B[erridge] came up and told me Alice Miller (fifteen years old) was fallen into a trance. I went down immediately and found her sitting on a stool and leaning against the wall, with her eyes open and fixed upward. I made a motion as if going to strike, but they continued immovable. Her face showed an unspeakable

society was an evangelistic agency from Newark on the one side, to Navenby on the other. A. Watmough, *History of Methodism in the Neighbourhood and City of Lincoln* (London, 1829), pp. 13-14.

42 *Wesleyan Methodist Magazine* 134 (1911):787-90 gives a MS fragment in JW's hand that recounts Berridge's preaching, dated Aug. 5-12, which Curnock believed was torn from the notebook in which JW kept his journal; for another view see Introduction above (18:90-91). It adds to the text of the published Journal: 'I soon found Satan labouring to create a misunderstanding between Mr. Berridge and Mr. Hicks, but on Monday they talked freely together and the snare was broken.' There is also a much extended treatment of trances and an explicit statement of JW's own weak condition when he reached London.

43 For Ann Thorn's visions, see above, July 29, 1759. Berridge himself had written to JW on July 16, asking him not to publish Walsh's account of her; *Arminian Magazine* 3 (1780):612. This letter also gives an account of the revival in the Cambridge area.

mixture of reverence and love, while silent tears stole down her cheek. Her lips were a little open and sometimes moved, but not enough to cause any sound. I do not know whether I ever saw an human face look so beautiful. Sometimes it was covered with a smile, as from joy mixing with love and reverence. But the tears fell still, though not so fast. Her pulse was quite regular. In about half an hour, I observed her countenance change into the form of fear, pity, and distress. Then she burst into a flood of tears and cried out, 'Dear Lord! They *will* be damned! They will all be damned!' But in about five minutes her smiles returned, and only love and joy appeared in her face. About half an hour after six, I observed distress take place again; and soon after, she wept bitterly and cried out, 'Dear Lord, they *will* go to hell! The world *will* go to hell!' Soon after, she said, 'Cry aloud! Spare not!' And in a few moments her look was composed again and spoke a mixture of reverence, joy, and love. Then she said aloud, 'Give God the glory.' About seven, her senses returned. I asked, 'Where have you been?' 'I have been with my Saviour.' 'In heaven, or on earth?' 'I cannot tell, but I was in glory!' 'Why then did you cry?' 'Not for myself, but for the world; for I saw they were on the brink of hell.' 'Whom did you desire to give the glory to God?' 'Ministers that cry aloud to the world. Else they will be proud. And then God will leave them, and they will lose their own souls.'

I preached at eight on 'The wicked shall be turned into hell, and all the people that forget God.'[44] The whole congregation was earnestly attentive. But not above one or two cried out. And I did not observe any that fainted away, either then or in the morning. I have generally observed more or less of these outward symptoms to attend the beginning of a general work of God. So it was in New England, Scotland, Holland, Ireland, and many parts of England. But after a time they gradually decrease, and the work goes on more quietly and silently. Those whom it pleases God to employ in his work ought to be quite passive in this respect. They should *choose* nothing, but leave entirely to him all the circumstances of his own work.[45]

[44] Cf. Ps. 9:17 (BCP).

[45] In a letter to the Countess of Huntingdon on Mar. 10, 1759, JW had shown rather less equanimity about the change which was coming over the revival (see Telford, 4:57-58): 'I have found great satisfaction in conversing with those instruments whom God has lately raised up. But still, there is I know not what in them whom we have known from the beginning, and who have borne the burden and heat of the day, which we do not find in

Tue. 7. After preaching at four (because of the harvest), I took horse and rode easily to London. Indeed I wanted a little rest, having rode in seven months above four and twenty hundred miles.

Wed. 8. Our Conference began, the time of which was almost entirely employed in examining whether the spirit and lives of our preachers were suitable to their profession. On Saturday in the afternoon we concluded. Great was the unanimity and love that reigned among us. And if there were any who hoped or feared the contrary, they were happily disappointed.

Sun. 12. I was afraid to look forward to the work of the day, knowing my strength was not sufficient for it. But God looked to that, for though I was exceeding weak at Snowsfields in the morning, I was stronger at noon. And after preaching in the afternoon in the fields and meeting the society, I felt no weakness at all.

Mon. 13. I took a little ride to Croydon, one of the seats of the Archbishops of Canterbury.[46] Was it one of these who ordered many years ago (for the characters are of old standing) that dreadful inscription to be placed, just over the Communion Table: 'And now, ye priests, this commandment is for you. If ye will not hear, and if ye will not lay it to heart, to give glory unto my name, saith the Lord, I will even send a curse among you, and I will curse your blessings. Yea, I have cursed them already, because ye do not lay it to heart. Behold I will corrupt your seed and spread dung upon your faces, even the dung of your solemn feasts, and one shall take you away with it.'[47]

those who have risen up since, though they are upright of heart. Perhaps, too, those who have but lately come into the harvest are led to think and speak more largely of justification and the other first principles of the doctrine of Christ; and it may be proper of *them* so to do. Yet *we* find a thirst after something farther. We want to sink deeper and rise higher in the knowledge of God our Saviour. We want all helps for walking closely with him whom we have received, that we may the more speedily come to the measure of the stature of the fullness of Christ. Mr. Berridge appears to be one of the most simple as well as the most sensible men of all whom it has pleased God to employ in reviving primitive Christianity,' precisely because of his capacity to induce the phenomena of abnormal psychology, not worked by more technically doctrinal preaching.

[46] Dating in part from the twelfth century the house at Croydon became a favourite summer residence of the archbishops and an administrative centre for their estates in the Home Counties until it was sold in 1780; Pevsner, *Surrey* (London, 1972; rev. by B. Cherry), p. 183. Thomas Herring, Archbishop of Canterbury 1747–57, was attacked by a fever in 1753 from which he never completely recovered, and he retired from Lambeth (and public business) to the Croydon house. One of the consequences of the improvements at Croydon was that his successor, Matthew Hutton (primate 1757–58), never moved into Lambeth owing to a dispute with Herring's executors over dilapidations.

[47] Cf. Mal. 2:1-3.

The archbishop's palace is an ancient, venerable pile, and the gardens are extremely pleasant. The late archbishop had improved them at a large expense, but continual illness prevented his enjoying them, till after four years' constant pain he was called away, one may hope, to the garden of God.

I dined at Mr. B[elchier]'s[48] in Epsom, whose house and gardens lie in what was once a chalk pit. It is the most elegant spot I ever saw with my eyes, everything within doors and without being finished in the most exquisite taste. Surely nothing on earth can be more delightful. O what will the possessor *feel* when he cries out,

> Must I then leave thee, paradise? Then leave
> These happy shades, and mansions fit for Gods?[49]

Fri. 17. I spent an hour pleasantly and profitably at ——— ———'s. How gracious is God who still preserves him unconsumed in fire! How plain that with God all things are possible.[50] He can draw the sting either of wealth or death!

Sun. 19. I preached in the afternoon to an huge multitude in the fields, on 'Now God commandeth all men everywhere to repent.'[51] Monday 27, I rode to Bedford and about six preached on St. Peter's Green. None of the numerous congregation stood with their heads covered except the Germans.[52] Blessed be God that *I* have not so learned Christ![53] If *they* know no better I cannot help it.

Tue. 28. I rode on to Mr. Berridge's at Everton, and in the evening went to the church, but unusually heavy and hardly expecting to do any good there. I preached on those words in the Second Lesson, 'We know that we are of God.'[54] One sunk down,

[48] William Belchier, d. 1772, common councillor, banker, and MP for Southwark 1747 61, with whom JW had been in touch since at least 1748, and from whom he sought franks for the post (*Letters*, 26:283, 554 in this edn.). He owned the estate at Durdens, took down the house and rebuilt it, and it was burned down in 1755 (*Horace Walpole's Correspondence*, 35:211). A new house was completed only in 1764, known as Pit Place from the chalkpit in which it stood. Other visitors, contemporaneous with JW, were also struck by the beauty and completeness of the gardens (*WHS* 4 [1903]:68). Thomas, 2nd Lord Lyttelton, died in the house on Nov. 26, 1779, three days after being warned of his fate in a dream, a story which JW picked up on another visit; *Arminian Magazine* 9 (1786):199.

[49] Adapted from Milton's *Paradise Lost*, xi.269-71; see Aug. 1, 1778; and May 3, 1783.

[50] See Matt. 19:26, etc.

[51] Cf. Acts 17:30.

[52] On the Moravians in Bedford, see Oct. 8, 1753, n. 23 (20:476 in this edn.).

[53] See Eph. 4:20.

[54] 1 John 5:19.

and another, and another. Some cried aloud in agony of prayer. I would willingly have spent some time in prayer with them. But my voice failed, so that I was obliged to conclude the service, leaving many in the church crying and praying, but unable either to walk or stand. One young man and one young woman were brought with difficulty to Mr. B[erridge]'s house and continued there in violent agonies both of body and soul. When I came into the room the woman lay quiet, wrestling with God in silent prayer. But even the bodily convulsions of the young man were amazing. The heavings of his breast were beyond description—I suppose equal to the throes of a woman in travail. We called upon God to relieve his soul and body. And both were perfectly healed. He rejoiced in God with joy unspeakable,[55] and felt no pain or weakness or weariness. Presently after, the woman also was delivered and arose rejoicing in God her Saviour.[56]

Wed. 29. I rode to Lakenheath and spoke exceeding plain to an honest, drowsy people. Thursday 30, I preached at the Tabernacle in Norwich, to a large, rude, noisy congregation. I took knowledge what manner of teachers they had been accustomed to, and determined to *mend* them or *end* them. Accordingly, the next evening after sermon, I reminded them of two things: the one that it was not decent to begin talking aloud as soon as service was ended, and hurrying to and fro as in a bear-garden;[57] the other that it was a bad custom to gather into knots just after sermon and turn a place of worship into a coffee-house. I therefore desired that none would talk under that roof, but go quietly and silently away. And on Sunday, September 2, I had the pleasure to observe that all went as quietly away as if they had been accustomed to it for many years.

Mon. 3. I met the society at five and explained the nature and use of meeting in a class. Upon inquiry I found, we have now about five hundred members. But an hundred and fifty of these do not *pretend* to meet at all. Of those therefore I make no account. They hang on but by a single thread.

Tue. 4. I walked to Hempnall,[58] nine miles from Norwich, and preached at one o'clock. The ringleader of the mob came with his horn, as usual, before I began. But one quickly catched and threw

[55] See 1 Pet. 1:8.

[56] See Luke 1:47.

[57] *Works* (1774), 'a beer-garden'.

[58] 1764, 1791, 'Kemnal'—surely a printer's error; *Works* (1774), 'Hemnal'. Hempnall was a parish and former market town 9 miles south of Norwich.

away his horn, and in a few minutes he was deserted by all his companions, who were seriously and deeply attentive to the great truth, 'By grace ye are saved through faith.'[59]

Sun. 9. I met the society at seven and told them in plain terms that they were the most ignorant, self-conceited, self-willed, fickle, untractable, disorderly, disjointed society that I knew in the three kingdoms. And God applied it to their hearts, so that many were profited, but I do not find that one was offended.

At ten we had another happy opportunity, and many stubborn hearts were melted down. Just at two the great congregation met, and the power of God was again present to heal, though not so eminently as at five, while I was describing 'the peace that passeth all understanding'.[60] After preaching, I was desired to spend an hour with some whom I supposed to be of our own society. But I soon found my mistake—

Sensim medios delapsus in hostes.[61]

One in particular, warmly told me she could 'not like mine or Mr. Murlin's doctrine'[62]—it always threw her into heaviness. But in 'dear Mr. Cudworth's'[63] she could 'find comfort'. I desired we might pray. God quickly answered for himself. Her heart was broke in pieces. She was filled with love and grief and shame, but could only tell it by her eyes and her tears.

About this time I received a remarkable letter from abroad, an extract of which follows.[64]

Berlin, August 26, 1759

God has again wrought publicly in this place, in the presence of many thousand people. A soldier of the King's Guard was

[59] Eph. 2:8 (*Notes*). [60] Cf. Phil. 4:7.

[61] Adapted from Virgil, *Aeneid*, ii.377: 'I had unknowingly fallen into the midst of enemies.'

[62] John Murlin (1722–99), a Cornish carpenter, was converted under Methodist preaching in 1749, and subsequently became a class-leader and local preacher. He entered the itinerancy in 1754, and despite ill-health and the private means which would have enabled him to retire, he travelled until 1787 when he settled at High Wycombe, preaching actively in the district (see Oct. 16, 1788). In 1781, he published *Sacred Hymns on Various Subjects*, which had some success. He died some months after a paralytic stroke, the Conference *Minutes* of 1799 describing him as 'a primitive Methodist, a man of great integrity, sincerity and simplicity, who was, in general, so deeply affected with the subjects on which he preached that he obtained the name of "the weeping prophet"'. Jackson, *Early Methodist Preachers*, 3:292-306; Atmore, *Memorial*, pp. 288-91.

[63] On William Cudworth, see above, Mar. 25, 1759, n. 12.

[64] The source of this letter remains elusive.

sentenced to be hanged for desertion and theft. He was a wretch abandoned to all manner of wickedness. General K—— was much concerned for his soul. He earnestly desired me to take the charge of it, though we saw no prospect of success. I visited him the day he was condemned, being Thursday. He seemed quite careless and unconcerned. I endeavoured to convince him of sin but did not perceive any effect. I begged of him not to deceive his own soul but to consider the condition he was in. On Friday this began to sink into his heart, and on Saturday much more. Perceiving this, I much insisted on those words: 'This is a faithful saying, and worthy of all acceptation, that Christ Jesus came into the world to save sinners.' The effect was astonishing. He laid hold of them by faith, and not only his burden was gone, but he had such experience of the love of Christ as it is impossible to describe. His peace, triumph, and joy increased every hour till the night before his execution, and indeed was never more observable than when he was brought out of prison. In his way to the place of execution he praised God for dragging him as it were with chains to heaven. 'What,' said he, 'will God after all my hellish actions give me eternal life into the bargain?' The efficacy of the blood and death of Christ being made known to him by the Holy Ghost, he spoke of nothing but his wedding-day, which was to be this thirteenth of August. Everyone that looked upon him was struck. Officers and all were moved. Being entered into the ring, I once more prayed with him and gave him the last blessing. But the very instant he was to be turned off, Colonel H—— called out 'Pardon!' I was thunderstruck, and Mittelstadt protested it was to him like a ball shot through his body. He fainted away for some time. Being recovered, his first words were, 'Why was I not rather hanged, or even crucified, than pardoned? Why am I thus stopped in my course? I should now have been with Christ!' I was myself more afraid of him now than ever. But the grace of God was strong in his soul. And ever since it has continued the same. Yesterday I was informed, by one who went on purpose to inquire, that his whole employ during his confinement (which is to continue six months) is reading, praying, and comforting himself with the blood of Christ.

Mon. 10. We took horse at half-hour after four. Before eight it was as warm as it is usually at midsummer. And from ten we had the sun in our face all the way to Colchester. But we had the wind in our face too, or the heat would have been insupportable. I was in a fever from the moment I came into the house. But it did not hinder me from preaching on the green and afterwards meeting the society. I then lay down as soon as possible but could not sleep a quarter of an hour till between two and three in the morning. I do not know that I have lost a night's sleep before, sick or well, since I was six years old. But it is all one: God is able to give strength either with sleep or without it. I rose at my usual time and preached at five, without any faintness or drowsiness.

Thur. 13. We set out between four and five and rode to Dunmow,[65] about four and twenty miles. But here we were at a full stop. None could direct us any farther. So we were to cross the country as well as we could. But whenever we were at a loss (eight or ten times), we met someone to help us out. So about half an hour past one, we were come within sixteen miles of Sundon.[66]

An honest blunderer then undertook to direct us a nearer way. By his help we wandered up and down till our sixteen miles grew into six and twenty. However, we got to Sundon before seven, where a considerable number of people soon met, to whom I explained (what they seemed to know very little of) 'the grace of our Lord Jesus Christ'.[67]

Fri. 14. I returned to London. Saturday 15, having left orders for the immediate repairing of West Street Chapel, I went to see what they had done, and saw cause to praise God for this also. The main timbers were so rotten that in many places one might thrust his fingers into them. So that probably, had we delayed till spring, the whole building must have fallen to the ground.

Mon. 17. I went to Canterbury. Two hundred soldiers, I suppose, and a whole row of officers, attended in the evening. Their number was increased the next evening, and all behaved as men fearing God. Wednesday 19, I preached at Dover, in the new room which is just finished. Here also the hearers increase, some of whom are convinced, and others comforted daily. Thursday 20, I strongly applied at Canterbury, to the soldiers in particular, 'He that hath not the Son of God hath not life.'[68] The next day, in my return to London, I read Mr. Huygen's *Conjectures on the Planetary World.*[69] He surprised me. I think he clearly proves that the moon is not habitable; that there are neither

[65] Great Dunmow was a parish and former market town 12½ miles north-west of Chelmsford.

[66] To visit Mrs. Cole; see May 12, 1754, n. 64 (20:486 in this edn.).

[67] Rom. 16:20, etc.

[68] 1 John 5:12.

[69] Christian Huygens, a Dutch mathematician (1629–95), after stating at length the scholarly grounds for belief in the existence of living beings elsewhere in the universe, gives his own conclusion that it is unlikely that there are living beings anywhere else in the universe. *The Celestial Worlds Discover'd, or Conjectures concerning the Inhabitants, etc., of the Planets* (London, 1722), pp. 130-32. His final scepticism (p. 162) was as to the Cartesian

Rivers nor mountains on her spotty globe;[70]

that there is no sea, no water on her surface, nor any atmosphere. And hence he very rationally infers that 'neither are any of the secondary planets inhabited.' And who can prove that the primary are? I *know* the earth is. Of the rest I know nothing.

Sun. 23. A vast majority of the immense congregation in Moorfields were deeply serious. One such hour might convince any impartial man of the expediency of *field preaching*. What building, except St. Paul's Church, would contain such a congregation? And if it would, what human voice could have reached them there? By repeated observations I find I can command thrice the number in the open air [that][71] I can under a roof. And who can say the time for field preaching is over while (1) greater numbers than ever attend, (2) the converting as well as convincing power of God is eminently present with them?

Mon. 24. I preached about eight at Brentford, and in the evening at Basingstoke, to a people slow of heart and dull of understanding. Tuesday 25, I preached in the new house at Whitchurch, and at Salisbury in the evening. The new room there is, I think, the most complete in England. It strikes everyone of any taste that sees it—not with any single part, but an inexpressible *something* in the whole.

The militia from Hampshire being in town, a large number of them were at the preaching. But it was as music to an horse—such brutish behaviour have I seldom seen. The next evening they behaved, if possible, worse than before. However, many of them, I believe, were struck. For they came again in the morning and then appeared to be of quite another spirit, earnestly attending to what was spoken. Thursday 27, I had appointed to preach at seven in the evening at Bradford.[72] But when I came I found Mr. Hart[73] was to preach at six. So I delayed till the church service was

doctrine of the origin of planets, it being all that can reasonably be expected to attain sure knowledge of things as they are. For further comments by JW, see Sermon 103, 'What is Man?', II.8-10 (3:461-62 in this edn.).

[70] See Milton, *Paradise Lost*, i.291, where Satan's shield is likened to the enlarged orb of the moon as seen through the telescope. This passage is also quoted twice in Wesley's sermons and once in the conclusion to his *Survey of the Wisdom of God in the Creation*.

[71] Orig., 'than'.

[72] Bradford-on-Avon.

[73] Richard Hart (*c.* 1727–1808), vicar of St. George's, Bristol, 1759–1808, matriculated from Christ Church, Oxford, 1744; B.A., 1749. When in 1764, JW began to make attempts to unite the evangelical clergy, Richard Hart (who responded with the embarrassing proposal of an open debate) was among those to whom he wrote. Hart was

ended, that there might not appear (at least on *my* part) even the shadow of opposition between us.

Fri. 28. I reached Bristol. Sunday 30, the weather being fair and calm, I preached in the new square,[74] for the sake of many people who do not choose to come to the room. My text was, 'Him that cometh unto me I will in no wise cast out.'[75] I believe many found desires of coming to him. O that they may be brought to good effect!

Monday, October 1. All my leisure time during my stay at Bristol I employed in finishing the fourth volume of Discourses,[76] probably the last which I shall publish. Monday 15, I walked up to Knowle, a mile from Bristol, to see the French prisoners. Above eleven hundred of them, we were informed, were confined in that little place, without anything to lie on but a little dirty straw, or anything to cover them but a few foul thin rags, either by day or night, so that they died like rotten sheep. I was much affected, and preached in the evening on Exodus 23:9: 'Thou shalt not oppress a stranger; for ye know the heart of a stranger, seeing ye were strangers in the land of Egypt.' Eighteen pounds were contributed immediately, which were made up [to] four and twenty the next day. With this we bought linen and woollen cloth, which were made up into shirts, waistcoats, and breeches. Some dozen of stockings were added, all which were carefully distributed where there was the greatest want. Presently after, the Corporation of Bristol sent a large quantity of mattresses and blankets. And it was not long before contributions were set on foot at London[77] and in various parts of the kingdom. So that I believe from this time they were pretty well provided with all the necessaries of life.

Mon. 22. I left Bristol, and having preached at Shepton, Coleford, Frome, and Salisbury in my way, on Thursday 25,

also among the forty or fifty who received JW's printed circular advocating union in 1766, and one of only three who replied to it. See also *Christian Observer* 7 (1808):834.

[74] King Square.

[75] John 6:37.

[76] This was the fourth volume of JW's *Sermons on Several Occasions* (1760), for which see *Bibliography*, No. 131. It was advertised in the *Gentleman's Magazine* for Dec. 1759, though dated 1760. Besides seven sermons, it contained several tracts. In fact, JW published a further four volumes of sermons in 1788, and a ninth volume, consisting of sermons published in the *Arminian Magazine* after that date, was published posthumously in 1800.

[77] These contributions were stimulated by a letter JW wrote to *Lloyd's Evening Post* on Oct. 20, 1759, in which he gave an account of his inquiries into the conditions of the French prisoners at Knowle, concluding that their food and living conditions were satisfactory, but that clothing was in exceedingly short supply (see Telford, 4:73-74).

determined to try if I could do any good at Andover. The congregation at ten in the morning was small. In the evening their number was increased, and I think some of them went away crying out, 'God be merciful to me a sinner!'[78]

Fri. 26. I rode to Basingstoke. I was extremely tired when I came in but much less so after preaching. I then sent to inquire if there was a vacant place in any of the coaches which were going to London the next day. But they were all full, and I had promised to send back my mare to Bristol. The only way that remained was to take Joseph Jones's horse and let him ride behind one of the coaches. So I ordered the horse to be brought soon after four in the morning, and was waiting for the coach when a post-chaise drove by. I rode close after it, though it was so dark I could not see my horse's head. But I could *hear*, which was enough. About daybreak it drove away, but then I could see the road. It rained without intermission from the time I took horse till I came to the Foundery, so that I was wet through a great part of the day. But it did me no hurt at all.

Sun. 28. I found the ancient spirit in the congregation, both at Spitalfields and the Foundery. Tuesday 30, I preached at Deptford and rejoiced to find an increasing work there also. Wednesday and Thursday I spent in revising and perfecting a treatise on *Electricity*.[79] Friday, November 2, I spent an hour with that miracle of mercy, Miss ——, a clear proof that God *can*, even without external means, preserve a bush in the midst of the fire.[80]

Sun. 4. As I was applying those words, 'They neither marry nor are given in marriage. For neither can they die any more, for they are equal to angels,'[81] the power of God fell upon the congregation in a very uncommon manner. How seasonable! O how does God sweeten whatever cross we bear for his sake!

Mon. 12. I talked with J—— D——, a gentleman's coachman, an uncommon monument of mercy. Last year he was a violent persecutor of the truth, and of his wife for the sake of it. But the second or third time he heard for himself, he was thoroughly convinced. Soon after, he entered into the society and in six weeks found peace with God. Yet his natural tempers quickly revived, which made him restless after a thorough change. In spring this restlessness so increased that he was crying to God day

[78] Luke 18:13.

[79] John Wesley, *The Desideratum: or, Electricity made Plain and Useful* (1760); see *Bibliography*, No. 239; and vol. 17 in this edn.

[80] See Exod. 3:2.

[81] Cf. Luke 20:35-36.

and night, till on Sunday, May 27, he was utterly broken in pieces and ready to cast away the hope of it. But just as he received the bread in the Lord's Supper, the love of God filled his heart. And from that moment he had no doubt but has continued always rejoicing, always praying and praising God.

Sat. 17. I spent an hour agreeably and profitably with Lady G[ertrude] H[otham] and Sir C[harles] H[otham].[82] 'Tis well a few of the rich and noble are called.[83] O that God would increase their number! But I should rejoice (were it the will of God) if it were done by the ministry of others. If I might choose, I should still (as I have done hitherto) 'preach the gospel to the poor'.[84]

Mon. 19. I spent an hour with Mr. B——, who has escaped from Guadalupe,[85] as with the skin of his teeth.[86] He informed me that all the water they had in the voyage stunk intolerably, that the biscuit was full of maggots, and the beef mere carrion, so that none could bear to stand near a cask when it was opened. What wonder that the poor men died in troops! Who shall answer for their blood?

Tue. 22. I took horse between six and seven, in one of the coldest mornings I ever remember. We reached St. Alban's without much difficulty, but then the roads were all covered with snow. However, there was a beaten path, though slippery enough, till we turned into the by-road to Sundon. What we could have done there I cannot tell, for the snow lay deeper and deeper, had not a wagon gone awhile before us and marked the way for six miles to Mr. Cole's gate.

Fri. 23. The roads were so extremely slippery, it was with much

[82] Sir Charles Hotham, 6th Bart., died in 1767, having been predeceased by his wife, née Clara Clutterbuck, in 1759. His mother, Lady Gertrude, was the eldest daughter of the 3rd Earl of Chesterfield and died in 1775. The Hothams represented evangelical aristocracy of Puritan extraction. Lady Hotham was a correspondent of Whitefield, by whose agency her daughter was converted, and she and Sir Charles encouraged the musical ambitions of Charles Wesley's son, Charles, while he wrote an elaborate hymn on the death of the younger Lady Hotham in 1756 (George Whitefield, *The Works of the Reverend G. W. . . . to which is Prefixed an Account of His Life*, ed. John Gillies, 6 vols. [London, Dilly, 1771–72], 2:355-56; *CWJ*, 2:142, 327-33). It is clear that for a few years relations between the Hothams (the health of both of whom was precarious) and the Wesleys were warm and affectionate (*CWJ*, 2:239, 259; cf. A. M. W. Stirling, *The Hothams*, 2 vols. [London, 1918]). The initials 'C—— H——' are added only in the *Works* (1774); in 1764 (and in 1791, following 1764) JW omitted his surname, reading simply 'Sir ——'.

[83] See 1 Cor. 1:26.

[84] Luke 4:18.

[85] 1764 (and 1791), 'Mr. —— . . . from G——'.

[86] See Job 19:20.

difficulty we reached Bedford. We had a pretty large congregation, but the stench from the swine under the room was scarce supportable. Was ever a preaching-place over a hog-sty before? Surely they love the gospel who come to hear it in such a place.[87]

Sat. 24. We rode to Everton, Mr. Berridge being gone to preach before the university at Cambridge. Many people came to his house in the evening, and it was a season of great refreshment.

Sun. 25. I was a little afraid, my strength would not suffice for reading prayers and preaching, and administering the Lord's Supper alone to a large number of communicants. But all was well. Mr. Hicks began his own service early and came before I had ended my sermon. So we finished the whole before two, and I had time to breathe before the evening service.

In the afternoon God was eminently present with us, though rather to comfort than convince. But I observed a remarkable difference since I was here before as to the *manner* of the work. None now were in trances, none cried out, none fell down or were convulsed. Only some trembled exceedingly; a low murmur was heard. And many were refreshed with the 'multitude of peace'.[88]

The danger *was* to regard *extraordinary* circumstances too much, such as outcries, convulsions, visions, trances, as if these were *essential* to the inward work, so that it *could not* go on without them. Perhaps the danger *is* to regard them too little, to condemn them altogether, to imagine they had nothing of God in them and were an hindrance to his work. Whereas the truth is: (1) God suddenly and strongly convinced many that they were lost sinners, the *natural* consequence whereof were sudden outcries and strong bodily convulsions. (2) To strengthen and encourage them that believed and to make his work more apparent, he favoured several of them with divine dreams, others with trances and visions. (3) In some of these instances, after a time, nature mixed with grace. (4) Satan likewise mimicked *this work of God*, in order to discredit the *whole work*. And yet it is not wise to give up *this part*, any more than to give up the *whole*. At first it was doubtless wholly from God. It is partly so at this day. And he will enable us to discern how far in every case the work is *pure*, and where it *mixes* or *degenerates*.

Let us even suppose that in some few cases there was a mixture

[87] John Walsh had been there the previous year and found that 'many had left off hearing because hogs were kept under the room.' *Arminian Magazine* 3 (1780):104.
[88] Ps. 37:11 (BCP).

of *dissimulation*; that persons *pretended* to see or feel what they did not and *imitated* the cries or convulsive motions of those who were really overpowered by the Spirit of God. Yet even this should not make us either deny or undervalue the real work of the Spirit. The shadow is no disparagement of the substance, nor the counterfeit of the real diamond.

We may farther suppose that Satan will make these visions an *occasion* of pride. But what can be inferred from hence? Nothing but that we should guard against it, that we should diligently exhort all to be little in their own eyes, knowing that nothing avails with God but humble love. But still, to slight or censure visions in general would be both irrational and unchristian.

Mon. 26. In the evening, I preached in Mr. Hicks's church at Wrestlingworth and at ten the next morning. The people were deeply attentive, but none were so affected as when I was here last. In the evening Mr. B[erridge] returned from preaching before the university. In the midst of the sermon, he informed me, one person cried out aloud but was silent in a few moments. Several dropped down but made no noise, and the whole congregation, young and old, behaved with seriousness. God is strong as well as wise. Who knows what work he may have to do here also?

Wed. 28. I returned to London, and on Thursday the 29th, the day appointed for a General Thanksgiving,[89] preached again in the chapel near the Seven Dials,[90] both morning and afternoon. I believe the oldest man in England has not seen a Thanksgiving Day so observed before. It had the solemnity of the General Fast. All the shops were shut up. The people in the streets appeared, one and all, with an air of seriousness. The prayers, lessons, and whole public service, were admirably suited to the occasion. The prayer for our enemies, in particular, was extremely striking; perhaps it is the first instance of the kind in Europe. There was no noise, hurry, bonfires, fireworks in the evening—and no public diversions. This is indeed a Christian Holy-Day, a 'rejoicing unto

[89] Horace Walpole complained in 1759 that the church bells were worn threadbare with ringing for victories. Even in Europe, where things had gone badly, Ferdinand of Brunswick's defeat of the French at Minden enabled him to recover all the ground he had lost and save Ferderick the Great from the worst consequences of his defeats. In September, Wolfe captured Quebec. At sea, one French fleet was defeated in August by Boscawen at Lagos, and in November an invasion attempt was smashed by Hawke at Quiberon Bay.

[90] I.e., West Street Chapel.

the Lord'![91] The next day came the news that Sir Edward Hawke had dispersed the French fleet.[92]

Sunday, December 9. I had, for the first time, a love-feast for the whole society.[93] Wednesday 12, I began reading over the Greek Testament and the *Notes* with my brother and several others, carefully comparing the translation with the original and correcting or enlarging the notes as we saw occasion.[94]

The same day I spent part of the afternoon in the British Museum. There is a large library, a great number of curious manuscripts, many uncommon monuments of antiquity, and the whole collection of shells, butterflies, beetles, grasshoppers, etc., which the indefatigable Sir Hans Sloane, with such vast expense and labour, procured in a life of fourscore[95] years!

Fri. 14. I was at a *Christian* wedding, to which were invited only two or three relations and five clergymen, who spent part of the afternoon in a manner suitable to the solemn occasion.[96]

Wed. 19. I was desired to read over a chancery bill. The

[91] Cf. Ps. 2:11 (BCP).

[92] Edward Hawke (1705–81), in 1776 created Baron Hawke, had a most distinguished record and was created Rear Admiral of the White by special interposition of George II in 1747. At this time, after severe disputes with the admiralty, he was put in command of the western squadron and in an unprecedented action kept the port of Brest sealed for six months. After the victory he asked to be relieved and received the thanks of the Commons and a large pension for two lives.

[93] On this love-feast Tyerman comments, 'Hitherto none had been admitted to Methodist love-feasts except the members of the bands, that is, persons who were *justified*; now the members of the classes, that is, persons who were *penitent*, were allowed to join in the same privilege of Christian fellowship, and to evince brotherly affection by taking together "a little plain cake and water".' Tyerman, *John Wesley*, 2:341-42.

[94] This resulted in the definitive edition of JW's *Explanatory Notes upon the New Testament*, 3 vols. (3rd edn., 1760). See *Bibliography*, No. 209; and vols. 5-6 in this edn.

[95] Orig. 'fourteen', 1764, 1791, corrected in *Works*. Sir Hans Sloane (1660–1753), a physician, settled in practice in Bloomsbury Square in 1689, with eight hundred species of plants. He was Secretary of the Royal Society, 1693–1712, succeeding Isaac Newton as president, 1729–41. He had meanwhile published extensively in the field of natural history, and been President of the College of Physicians, 1719–30, attending on Queen Anne and George II. JW had doubtless come across him as a Georgia trustee. In 1741 he retired from practice and settled in Chelsea. He left his collections to the nation (at a price), and in 1753 an act was passed accepting the gift and appointing trustees to manage the collection. It was these trustees who moved the collection back to Bloomsbury and united it with the Cottonian Collection and Harleian MSS to form the basis of the holdings of the British Museum.

[96] That of Josiah Dornford of Deptford (1734–1810) with Eleanor Leyton (1736–90) at St. Dunstan's Fleet Street. The clergymen were Wm. Romaine (who officiated), Thomas Jones of Southwark, Thomas Maxfield, Charles Wesley, and JW, who gave the bride away. JW later buried Mrs. Dornford (see Jan. 17, 1790). *Wesleyan Methodist Magazine* 134 (1911):621-21; Eleanor Dornford, *Some Memoirs of the Life and Death of Mrs E. D.* (London, 1790).

occasion of it was this: 'A. B. tells C. D. that one who owed him thirty pounds wanted to borrow thirty more, and asked whether he thought the eighth part of such a ship, then at sea, was sufficient security. He said he thought it was. On this, A. B. lent the money. The ship came home. But through various accidents, the eighth part yielded only twenty pounds. A. B. on this, commenced a suit to make C. D. pay him the residue of his money.'

This worthy story is told in no less than an hundred and ten sheets of paper! C. D. answers, he 'advised to the best of' his 'judgment, not foreseeing those accidents whereby the share which cost two hundred pounds yielded no more than twenty.' This answer brought on fifteen sheets of exceptions, all which a quarter of a sheet might have contained! I desired the plaintiff and defendant to meet me the next day, both of whom were willing to stand to arbitration. And they readily agreed that C. D. should pay half his own costs, and A. B. the rest of the expense.

Fri. 21. I inquired into the particulars of a very remarkable story. A ship laden with wheat, and having no other ballast, about one in the morning on Sunday, November 18, the wind blowing hard, shifted her cargo and in half an hour sunk. Mr. Austin, the mate, leaped off her side as she sunk and, being an excellent swimmer, kept above water till he saw something floating toward him, which proved to be the capstan[97] of the ship. He got upon it and, although washed off several times, yet still recovered his seat and floated all day and all the following night. But on Monday morning he was quite exhausted and faint almost to death with thirst, having swallowed abundance of salt water. In this extremity he saw some apples floating toward him. He took up three, ate them, and was much strengthened. About noon Admiral Saunders's fleet came in sight, one of whose ships saw and took him up. He could not stand, but being blooded and put into a warm bed and fed with small broth, a spoonful or two at a time, he recovered strength apace and in a few days was as well as ever.

Sat. 22. I went to Colchester and, on Sunday 23, preached in the shell of the new house. It is twelve square and is the best building of the size for the voice that I know in England. Monday

[97] Orig., 'capstern'; made of wood, of course. The form 'capstern' is reported by the *OED* from 1624 to 1836, including this example from Wesley.

24, we did not set out till after seven, intending to ride about forty miles. But coming to Scole Inn[98] before three, we pushed on and before seven came safe to Norwich.

Thur. 27. I began visiting the society and found the greater part much changed from what they were a year ago. They are indeed fewer in number but are now of a teachable spirit, willing to be advised or even reproved. And if three hundred[99] of this spirit remain, they are worth all our labour.

Tuesday, January 1, 1760. We began the service at four in the morning. A great number attended, and God was in the midst, strengthening and refreshing their souls. Thursday 3, in the evening, while I was enforcing those awful words of the prophet, 'The harvest is past, the summer is ended, and we are not saved,'[1] a young woman, who had contained herself as long as she could, sunk down and cried aloud. I found this was a new thing in Norwich. The women about her got water and hartshorn[2] in abundance. But all would not do. When the service was ended I asked her, 'What do you want?' She immediately replied, 'Nothing but Christ.' And indeed what physician beside him is able to heal that sickness?

Fri. 4. I preached about one at Forncett to a much milder people than I left there, and in the evening at Kenninghall, where the antinomians have laboured hard in the devil's service. Yet all are not lost. A few are still left 'who walk not after the flesh, but after the spirit.'[3] Saturday 5, I preached in the evening at Colchester and, on Sunday 6, rode to Langham,[4] seven miles from thence, in such a day as I have seldom known, the north-east wind was so exceeding keen and drove the sleet full in our face. But this did not discourage the people, who flocked from all quarters. And those who took such pains to come were not sent empty away.

[98] Orig., 'Schole-Inn'. The Scole Inn was a posting station on the main road to Norwich, and is said to have been at one time the postal address for Diss, which lies just off the main road. It is described as 'a large brick building, adorned with imagery and carved work, in many places as large as life, and built in 1655. There was a round bed, like the great bed at Ware, large enough to hold 30 or 40 soldiers.' *WHS* 4 (1903):83.

[99] *Works* (1774), 'two hundred'.

[1] Jer. 8:20.

[2] I.e., smelling salts, the chief source of ammonia formerly being the substance obtained by rasping the horn of harts (*OED*).

[3] Rom. 8:1, 4.

[4] Langham was an elongated parish on the south bank of the river Stour, 6 miles north-east of Colchester.

Mon. 7. I returned to London and finished on the road the celebrated *Telemachus*.[5] Certainly it is wrote with admirable sense. But is it without fault? Is there not abundantly too much machinery? Are not the gods (such as they are) continually introduced without why or wherefore? And is not the work spun out too long? Drawn into mere French wire?[6] Would not twelve books have contained all the matter much better than four and twenty?

Sun. 13. I preached again in West Street Chapel, now enlarged and thoroughly repaired. When I took this eighteen years ago, I little thought the world would have borne us till now. But 'the right hand of the Lord hath the pre-eminence.'[7] Therefore we endure unto this day.

Wed. 16. One came to me, as she said, with a message from the Lord, to tell me, 'I was laying up treasures on earth, taking my ease, and minding only eating and drinking.' I told her, God knew me better. And if he had sent her, he would have sent her with a more proper message.

Fri. 18. I desired those who believed they were saved from sin (sixteen or seventeen in number) to meet me at noon, to whom I gave such cautions and instructions as I judged needful.[8] Nor did any of *these* pretend to be above man's teaching but received it with all thankfulness.

Thur. 24. I rode to Brentford, where after a stop of ten or twelve years the work of God is broke out afresh. I preached in a large place newly fitted up.[9] It was supposed there would be much disturbance, as a considerable number of rude, boisterous people

[5] François de Salignac de la Mothe Fénelon, *Les aventures de Telemaque, fils d'Ulysse* (The Hague, 1699). First published surreptitiously at the Hague in 1699, and afterwards in many languages (in Eng. from 1699).

[6] The *OED* cites Wesley's use of 'wire draw' ('to strain, force or wrest by subtle argument', *s.v.*, 3.c.; letter of May 14, 1765, to John Newton), which in the United States is known as 'nit-picking', but it has no mention of what is clearly a companion usage, probably arising (like 'taking French leave') from British-French enmity rather than any outstanding reputation among the French for being more proficient in the drawing out of very fine wire.

[7] Ps. 118:16 (BCP).

[8] Two years later, Wesley published a tract on Christian perfection with a title reminiscent of this entry, which probably incorporated his admonitions: *Cautions and Directions given to the Greatest Professors in the Methodist Societies* (1762); see *Bibliography*, No. 250; and vol. 12 in this edn.

[9] The meeting-house at Brentford was a rented structure which came to figure in JW's mind as an archetype of ecclesiastical pretentiousness. Late in life he conceived that the (very different) chapel at Alnwick so resembled it as to warrant description as 'a scarecrow'. See May 16, 24, 1788.

were gathered together for that purpose. But God overruled, and they all calmly and silently attended to his word. Surely 'the times and seasons' of sending his word effectually to any place God 'hath reserved in his own power.'[10]

Mon. 28. I began visiting the classes in London, and that with more exactness than ever before. After going through them, I found the society now contained about three and twenty hundred and fifty members, few of whom we could discern to be triflers, and none, we hope, live in any wilful sin.

Tuesday, February 5. I baptized a gentlewoman at the Foundery, and the peace she immediately found was a fresh proof that the outward sign, duly received, is always accompanied with the inward grace. Tuesday 12, after preaching at Deptford, I rode on to Welling, where I received (what few expected) an exceeding comfortable account of the death of Mr. Mason of Bexley. For many years he seemed to be utterly senseless, neither justified, nor even convinced of sin. But in his last sickness the God that heareth prayer broke in upon his soul. And the nearer death came, the more did he rejoice, to the astonishment of all that saw him.

Sat. 16. I spent an hour in the evening with a little company at Mr.——'s. I have not known so solemn an hour for a long season, nor so profitable to my own soul. Mysterious providence! Why am I cut off from those opportunities which of all others I most want? Especially considering the benefit I might *impart*, as well as that which I might *receive*, seeing they stand in as much need of *light* as I do of *heat*.

About this time we had a remarkable account from Yorkshire:

> On February 13 about thirty persons were met together in Otley (a town about twelve miles from Leeds) about eight o'clock in the evening, in order (as usual) to pray, sing hymns, and provoke one another to love and good works. After prayer was ended, when they proceeded to speak of the several states of their souls, some with deep sighs and groans complained of the burden they felt for the remains of indwelling sin, seeing in a clearer light than ever before the necessity of a deliverance from it.
>
> When they had spent the usual time together, a few went to their own houses. But the most remained upon their knees, groaning for the great and precious promises of God. One being desired to pray,

[10] Cf. Acts 1:7.

he no sooner began to lift up his voice to God than the Holy Ghost made intercession in all that were present, with groanings that could not be uttered. At length the travail of their souls burst out into loud and ardent cries. They had no doubt of the favour of God, but they could not rest while there was anything in them contrary to his nature. One cried out, in an exceeding great agony, 'Lord, deliver me from my sinful nature,' then a second, a third, and fourth. And while the person who prayed first was calling upon God in those words, 'Thou God of Abraham, Isaac, and Jacob, hear us for the sake of thy Son Jesus,' one was heard to say, 'Blessed be the Lord God for ever, for he hath cleansed my heart. Praise the Lord, O my soul, and all that is within me, praise his holy name.' Another said, 'I hold thee with a trembling hand but will not let thee go,' and in a little time cried out, 'Praise the Lord with me, for he hath cleansed my heart from sin.' Another cried, 'I am hanging over the pit of hell, by a slender thread'; a second, with loud and dismal shrieks, 'I am in hell; O save me, save me'; while a third said, with a far different voice, 'Blessed be the Lord, for he hath pardoned all my sins.' Thus they continued for the space of two hours, some praising and magnifying God, some crying to him for pardon or purity of heart, with the greatest agony of spirit. Before they parted, three believed God had fulfilled his word and 'cleansed them from all unrighteousness'.

The next evening they met again. And the Lord was again present to heal the broken in heart. One received remission of sins, and three more believed God had 'cleansed them from all sin'. And it is observable, these are all poor, illiterate creatures, of all others most incapable of counterfeiting and most unlikely to attempt it. But 'when' his 'word goeth forth, it giveth light and understanding to the simple.'[11]

Fri. 29. A great number of us waited upon God at five, at nine, and at one, with fasting and prayer. And at six in the evening, we met at the church in Spitalfields to renew our covenant with God. It was a blessed time. The windows of heaven were open,[12] and the skies poured down righteousness.[13]

Monday, March 3. I left London. It rained great part of the day, but so gently that we were not wet through, when about seven we came to Towcester. One person we found here whose soul God keeps alive, though he has scarce any in the town to converse

[11] Ps. 119:130 (BCP).
[12] See Isa. 24:18.
[13] See Isa. 45:8.

with.[14] Perhaps he is an earnest of a people that shall be born here and 'counted to the Lord for a generation'.[15]

Tue. 4. We came to Birmingham, where I rejoined several who had been long separated from their brethren, and left upwards of fifty resolved to stand together in the good, old path.

In the evening, I preached in the new house at Wednesbury;[16] few congregations exceed this either in number or seriousness. At five in the morning, the congregation far exceeded the morning congregation at the Foundery. Indeed, hunger after the word has been from the beginning the distinguishing mark of this people.

Thur. 6. I talked largely with M—— S—— and Eliz. Longmore.[17] The substance of what M—— S—— said was as follows:

> I was born April 8, 1736. My father died when I was between four and five, my mother when I was about eleven years old. I had little thought about religion, and seldom so much as went to church. But I had even then many troubles, which made me sometimes think of God and cry to him for help. When I was about seventeen, I was asked one Sunday to go and see a pit which was on fire and blazed out. It was near the house where Mr. James Jones[18] was then preaching. I was standing near the house when my brother persuaded me to go in. I liked what I heard, but it was above a year before I knew myself to be a lost sinner. For three weeks I was in deep distress, which made me cry to God day and night. I had comfort once or twice, but I checked it, being afraid of deceiving myself; till, as Mr. Johnson[19] was preaching one morning at five o'clock in Darlaston, my soul was so filled with the love of God that I had much ado to help crying out. I could only say, 'Why *me*, Lord, why *me*?' When I came home I was exceeding weak, having also a great pain in my head. But all was sweet; I did not wish it to be otherwise. I was happy in God all the day long. And so I was for several days. From this time I never committed any known sin,

[14] Apparently Samuel Basford who was converted in London, and with the assistance of a single young friend, Thomas Simons, created a small Methodist cause in Towcester. *Methodist Magazine* 24 (1801):476.

[15] Cf. Ps. 22:31 (BCP).

[16] The new chapel, opened in 1760, gave its name to Meeting Street, and remained in use till 1813. In this chapel Francis Asbury was converted, and his colleague in the American mission, Richard Whatcoat, also joined the society in 1758. E. A. Dingley, *Footsteps of John Wesley in Wednesbury* (London, 1938), p. 31.

[17] 1764, 'E—— L——', extended by *Works* (1774) to 'Eliz. Lymore', and the surname corrected in the errata and JW's personal copy to 'Longmore'. On Elizabeth Longmore (1730–70), see Mar. 18, 1770.

[18] See Feb. 18, 1744, n. 44 (20:10 in this edn.).

[19] On John Johnson, see above, May 5, 1757, n. 70.

nor ever lost the love of God, though I found abundance of temptations and many severe struggles. Yet I was more than conqueror over all and found them easier and easier.

About Christmas 1758, I was deeply convinced there was a greater salvation than I had attained. The more I saw of this and the more I prayed for it, the happier I was. And my desires and hopes were continually increasing for above a year.

On January 30, 1760, Mr. Fugill[20] talked with one who thought she had received that blessing. As she spoke, my heart burned within me, and my desire was enlarged beyond expression. I said to him, 'O sir, when shall I be able to say as she says?' He answered, 'Perhaps tonight.' I said, 'Nay, I am not earnest enough.' He replied, 'That thought may keep you from it.' I felt God was able and willing to give it *then*, and was unspeakably happy. In the evening as he was preaching, my heart was full, and more and more so, till I could contain no more. I wanted only to be alone, that I might pour out my soul before God; and when I came home, I could do nothing but praise and give him thanks. From that moment I have felt nothing but love in my heart; no sin of any kind. And I trust I shall never sin any more, nor any more offend God.[21] I never find any cloud between God and me; I walk in the light continually. I do 'rejoice evermore, and pray without ceasing.' I have no desire but to do and suffer the will of God. I aim at nothing but to please him. I am careful for nothing, but in all things make my requests known to him with thanksgiving. And I have a continual witness in myself that whatever I do, I do it to his glory.

Eliz. Longmore[22] said:

I was born in 1730. My mother died in childbed of me, my father when I was a year or two old. So I was brought up by the parish and taught nothing, not so much as to read. About eleven years old I was put out parish 'prentice, to a man and woman who used me

[20] William Fugill (d. 1800), born at Rothwell near Leeds, was an early and successful itinerant. 'But alas! he afterwards, by little and little, fell from his steadfastness and, falling into some grievous sins, he was excluded from the Methodist connection in . . . 1764. . . . At the Conference in 1767, he was tried again for a short time, but it too soon appeared that sin had the dominion over him, and consequently he was again put away from the connection. He then returned to Rothwell, where he spent the residue of his days in a state of poverty and disgrace.' Atmore, *Memorial*, pp. 147-48.

[21] *Works* (1774) reads: 'And I trust I shall never sin any more offend God. I never find any more, nor any more offend God.' This seems clearly to have been a double blunder by the printer, both repeating a phrase and reading 'sin' as 'find'. Wesley did not restore the reading of M. S.'s letter in his first edition, but made some kind of *ad hoc* sense in the errata and his personal copy by omitting 'sin any more offend God. I never', to read, 'And I trust I shall never find any more, nor any more offend God.'

[22] 1764, 1791, 'E—— L——'.

very harshly. I wanted much to learn to read, but they would not spare the time. I was about fourteen when I heard Mr. J[ohn] W[esley] preach at the Cross in Wednesbury. I immediately believed it was the right way, and begun to be very uneasy. I often wished I had died with my father or mother, fearing I should never be saved. But my convictions wore away by degrees, though still I could find no rest. About twenty I was married. My husband had sometimes heard the preaching, but not lately. Soon after, he began again, going with me constantly. I was now more and more convinced that I was a guilty, undone sinner. I cried to God day and night, laying down my work many times in a day. On Holy Thursday, 1756, I was sadly afraid of going to the Sacrament. However, I broke through and went. At the Lord's Table I found such a love as I cannot express. As soon as I came back, I went up into my chamber and kneeled down to prayer. In praying I heard a voice saying, 'Go in peace; thy sins are forgiven thee.'[23] My soul sunk into nothing before God and was filled with humble love. I loved God and all mankind, and thought no temptation could ever shake me more. But in a few days, being low and weak in body, I found hard thoughts of God. Yet I could never[24] give up my confidence that my sins were forgiven. Nor do I know that I ever committed any wilful sin after I was justified. About a year and half ago, Mr. Fugill came. One evening while he was preaching, I was convinced that my heart was still desperately wicked and needed to be wholly renewed. This made me sometimes afraid to die, lest I should be called before that change was wrought. But I had still hope at the bottom and never could doubt but that God was my God. In the meanwhile, my desire to be wholly renewed increased continually. And I was every day and every hour praying for it, whatever I was about. When my hopes prevailed I was happy; when my fears, I was quite cast down. Being convinced how little I loved God, I was grieved and ashamed before him.

On Friday, January 25, I took no food till the afternoon, though I had a child at my breast. I was much tempted to think I should never attain, and was quite uneasy. But the next morning, my uneasiness was gone, and I calmly waited for what I believed God would soon give. In the evening, I went to the preaching with a full expectation that he would meet me there. And so he did. As soon as Mr. Fugill began to speak I felt my soul was all love. I was so stayed on God as I never felt before and knew that I loved him with all my heart. When I came home, I could ask for nothing; I could only give thanks. And the witness that God had saved me from all my sins grew clearer every hour. On Wednesday, this was stronger than

[23] Luke 7:50, 48.

[24] *Works* (1774), 'not'.

ever. I have never since found my heart wander from God. When I have business to do, I just take a thought and do it, and it is gone, and my heart is with the Lord. I often in a day bow my knee to God, but my heart prays continually. He is never out of my thoughts; I see him always, although most at preaching and in my band and class. But I do not only *see* him, I *feel* him too, so as I cannot express. And the more I see and feel of God, the more I feel I am nothing. When I sleep, I sleep as in the arms of Jesus; and when I wake, my soul is full of praise, and it is as if all the angels were in the room round about me praising God. I never find any heaviness or coldness, and when I must go among the people of the world, God is as much with me as before, and I long for them, so as no tongue can tell. I am careful of every word I speak, and every look, and every thought. I search my heart again and again, and I can find nothing but love there. Indeed, I know if God left me a moment, I should fall. But I trust he will never leave me nor forsake me.

I observe, the spirit and experience of these two run exactly parallel. *Constant communion* with God the Father and Son *fills* their hearts with *humble love*. Now this is what I always did and do now mean by 'perfection'. And this I believe many have attained, on the same evidence that I believe many are justified. May God increase their number a thousandfold!

Fri. 7. I rode over to Dudley, formerly a den of lions. I was constrained to preach abroad. But no one opened his mouth, unless to pray or praise God. I believe the steady behaviour of the society has made an impression on most of the town.

Sat. 8. I was surprised at coming into Wolverhampton, which *is* what Dudley *was*, to find the people so still, many gaping and staring, but none speaking an uncivil word. 'Ay', said a well-meaning man, 'we shall not find them so civil by and by.' I wish these *croakers* would learn to hold their peace. I desire to hear no 'prophets of evil'.[25] What do they do but weaken the hands both of preachers and people, and transfuse their own cowardice into others?

But this prophet of evil was a false prophet too. For neither while I was preaching, nor after I had done, did anyone offer the least rudeness whatsoever. And we rode as quietly out of the town as we could have done out of London or Bristol.

Hence we went on to Burslem,[26] near Newcastle-under-

[25] Cf. 1 Kgs. 22:8.

[26] Orig., 'Borslam'. Burslem was a market town and parish 3 miles north of Newcastle-under-Lyme, already long celebrated for its earthenware manufacture.

Lyme,[27] a scattered town on the top of a hill, inhabited almost entirely by potters, a multitude of whom assembled at five in the evening. Deep attention sat on every face, though as yet accompanied with deep ignorance. But if the heart be toward God, he will in due time enlighten the understanding.

Sun. 9. I preached at eight to near double the number, though scarce half as many as came at five in the evening. Some of these seemed quite innocent of thought. Five or six were laughing and talking till I had near done, and one of them threw a clod of earth, which struck me on the side of the head. But it neither disturbed me nor the congregation.

Mon. 10. About nine I preached at Biddulph,[28] about eight miles north of Burslem. The earnestness of the whole congregation well rewarded me for my labour. Hence we had an extremely pleasant walk, three or four miles, to Congleton. Here we were accosted in a very different manner almost as soon as we entered the town, which caused some of our brethren to apprehend we should have rough treatment before we got out of it. That I left to God. They had procured the use of a meadow adjoining to the preaching-house, in a window of which they had fixed a kind of scaffold. Most of the congregation were deeply serious, so that three or four who took much pains to disturb them entirely lost their labour.

About seven in the evening, I preached at Stockport, where more and more hear the word of God and keep it. In the morning, we took horse at five but could find none to tell us which was the road to Leeds. So we rode on to Mottram.[29] Following the directions we received there, we rode up a mountain, and our path ended. We made toward a large house, and the gentleman sent a servant, who pointed out the way we were to take. But soon after, it divided, and an honest man bidding us keep to the right (meaning the left), we did so, till we came to the top of another high mountain, among several old stone quarries. Here that road ended. However, we went straight forward till we came to the brow. With great difficulty we led our horses down, and rode up a path on the opposite mountain. But at the top, this likewise ended. Still we thought it best to push forward. But my horse was

[27] Orig., 'Newcastle-under-Line'.

[28] Biddulph was a parish 3¼ miles south of Congleton.

[29] Mottram-in-Longdendale, a still entirely agricultural parish 7½ miles north-east of Stockport.

quickly embogged. After he had thrown me on one side and scrambled out himself, we endeavoured to walk down the mountain. But such a walk I never had before, for steepness and bogs and large stones intermixed. That we got to the bottom without hurt either to man or beast was little less than a miracle. But we were still at a loss, till we met a sensible man who directed us to Saddleworth.[30] In our inn here, we found one who had frequently heard me preach at Builth in Breconshire. I fear, to little purpose, for on my speaking a few words, he ran away in haste. But the whole family seemed to fear God. So we did not repent of our clambering up and down the mountains.

At six we reached Leeds sufficiently tired. But I forgot it as soon as I began to preach, and the spirit of the congregation comforted us over all our labour.

Wed. 12. Having desired that as many as could of the neighbouring towns, who believed they were saved from sin, would meet me, I spent the greatest part of this day in examining them one by one. The testimony of some I could not receive, but concerning the far greatest part it is plain (unless they could be supposed to tell wilful and deliberate lies): (1) that they *feel* no inward sin and, to the best of their knowledge, *commit* no outward sin; (2) that they *see* and *love* God every moment and 'pray, rejoice, give thanks evermore';[31] (3) that they have constantly as clear a *witness* from God of sanctification as they have of justification. Now in this I do rejoice and will rejoice, call it what you please. And I would to God thousands had experienced thus much—let them afterward experience as much more as God pleases.

Thur. 13. We rode over the mountains through furious wind and rain, which was ready to overthrow both man and beast. However, in the afternoon we came well to Manchester. On Friday the 14th, being the National Fast-Day, we had service at five, at seven, and at five in the evening. But I did not observe here anything of that solemnity with which the public fasts are observed in London. I was much out of order on Saturday, and not well on Sunday. However, having appointed to preach in Stockport at noon, I determined not to break my word. As it rained, our friends provided a post-chaise. When we were gone half a mile, one of the horses began to kick and rear, and would go no further. So we got out and walked on. But another driver

[30] Saddleworth was a chapelry in the parish of Rochdale, 12 miles west of Huddersfield.
[31] Cf. 1 Thess. 5:16-18.

brought the chaise after, and carried me to Stockport. A large congregation was waiting and received the word with all readiness of mind.[32] For some years the seed seemed to be here sown in vain, but at length it yields a good increase.

On the following days, I preached in several neighbouring towns, and on Wednesday evening at Liverpool. Thursday 20, I had a good deal of conversation with Mr. N[ewto]n.[33] His case is very peculiar. Our Church requires that clergymen should be men of learning and to this end have an university education. But how many have an university education and yet no learning at all! Yet these men are ordained! Meantime, one of eminent learning, as well as unblameable behaviour, cannot be ordained 'because he was not at the university'! What a mere farce is this! Who would believe that any Christian bishop would stoop to so poor an evasion!

Mon. 24. About noon I preached at Warrington. Many of 'the beasts of the people'[34] were present. But the bridle from above was in their teeth, so that they made not the least disturbance. At seven in the evening, I preached at Chester, but I was scarce able to open my eyes. They were much inflamed before I set out, and the inflammation was much increased by riding forty miles with a strong and cold wind exactly in my face. But in the evening I applied the eye-water made with *lapis calaminaris*,[35] which removed the disorder before morning.

Tue. 25. I rode to Mold in Flintshire. The wind was often ready to bear away both man and horse. But the earnest, serious congregation rewarded us for our trouble. Wednesday 26, about nine, I preached at Little Leigh,[36] a mile or two from Northwich. Many of the congregation scarce ever heard a Methodist before. But I trust they did not hear in vain.

[32] Acts 17:11.

[33] On John Newton and this encounter, see above, July 3, 1759, n. 4.

[34] Ps. 68:30 (BCP).

[35] A zinc carbonate (*OED*). From the first edn. of JW's *Primitive Physick* (1747) onward, this recipe was present:

> An excellent Eye-water.
>
> Heat half an ounce of *Lapis Calaminaris* red-hot, and quench it in half a pint of French white wine, and as much white rose-water. Then pound it fine and infuse it. Shake the bottle when you use it. It cures soreness, weakness, and most diseases of the eye. I have known it cure total blindness.

[36] Little Leigh was a small chapelry in the parish of Great Budworth 3½ miles north-west of Northwich.

Thur. 27. I rode to Liverpool in order to embark for Dublin. We were desired to be on board by nine on Saturday morning. But the wind falling and a fog coming on, we gained a little more time. So we had one more solemn opportunity in the evening. Sunday 30, the fog was gone and the wind fair. We took ship about nine and got under sail at noon, having only eight cabin passengers, seven of whom were our own company. So we prayed and sung and conversed at our own discretion. But a poor woman whom we permitted to come into the cabin gave us some uneasiness. She had been tapped for the dropsy in the infirmary but two days before. When I spoke to her concerning her soul, she gave but little answer, appearing to be serious and willing to hear, but totally uninstructed. She would eat nothing, but willingly accepted a dish or two of tea and two or three glasses of wine. The next morning she was extremely restless, continually moving from place to place to place, till the captain put a bed for her in the forecastle, on which she lay down about eight o'clock. A little after, she grew light-headed and began shrieking dreadfully. This she continued to do till about noon and then died. At night, the captain and all the sailors being present, we committed her body to the deep. On Tuesday noon, April 1, we landed safe at Dublin.

I never saw more numerous or more serious congregations in Ireland than we had all this week. On Easter Day, April 6, I introduced our English custom, beginning the service at four in the morning. Monday 7, I began speaking severally to the members of the society and was well-pleased to find so great a number of them much alive to God. One consequence of this is that the society is larger than it has been for several years. And no wonder, for where the real power of God is it naturally spreads wider and wider.

Thur. 10. I was sitting with a friend, when poor Mr. Cook came in. His eyes, his look, his hair standing

Like quills upon the fretful porcupine,[37]

his tattered gown, his whole person, as well as his speech, immediately bewrayed him. But he is quite an original and has so much vivacity, with touches of strong sense, that I do not wonder the gentlemen of the college, as he told me, have given him an

[37] Shakespeare, *Hamlet*, I.v.20.

apartment there. What a noble fabric lies here in ruins! What pity that when he first found himself a sinner, he had not one to speak to that understood his case and could teach him the only method of cure!

Sun. 13. At three in the afternoon, I preached in the Barrack Square, another kind of place than Ormandtown Green.[38] (So the word ought to be written.) No mob must show their heads here, for the soldiers would give them no quarter. Tuesday 15, I preached there again. But on Thursday, it being a rainy day, an offer was made me of the riding-house, a very large commodious building, designed by Lord Chesterfield[39] for a church but never used as such till now. A troop of soldiers was exercising there when I came. But this was clear gains. For the officers forbade any of them to go away before the sermon was ended.

Fri. 18. I went with Miss F[reeman][40] to see the French prisoners sent from Carrickfergus.[41] They were surprised at hearing as good French spoke in Dublin as they could have heard in Paris, and still more at being exhorted to heart-religion, to the 'faith that worketh by love'.[42]

Sun. 20. I appointed those of the society who desired to renew their covenant with God, which I had several times before explained, to meet me in the evening. And I believe of the five hundred and twelve members, hardly twelve were wanting.

Mon. 21. In riding to Rosmead I read Sir John Davies's historical relations concerning Ireland.[43] None who reads these can wonder that, fruitful as it is, it was always so thinly inhabited. For he makes it plain: (1) That *murder* was never *capital* among the native Irish. The murderer only paid a small fine to the chief of

[38] Usually called (even elsewhere in the *Journal*) Oxmantown Green. From his *Works* (1774), JW omitted the following parenthetical sentence and gave the spelling 'Ormandtown'.

[39] Philip Dormer Stanhope, 4th Earl of Chesterfield (1694–1773), politician and wit, Lord-lieutenant of Ireland 1745–46. In this brief period of office, further shortened by diplomatic service at The Hague and by illness in England, Chesterfield sought to preserve Ireland from the contagion of rebellion in 1745 by nonchalance and by relieving poverty by public works. Lecky, *Ireland*, 1:460-61.

[40] Miss Freeman was a lifelong favourite of the Wesley brothers, a London friend much prized on both social and spiritual grounds from her childhood, and one of the very few correspondents about the lack of whose letters JW became querulous. At this moment, she was travelling with him in Ireland. See JW's letter to Ebenezer Blackwell, through whom he often sent greetings to Miss Freeman, Apr. 26, 1760 in this edn.; and Telford, 4:94.

[41] On this episode, see below, May 5, 1760.

[42] Cf. Gal. 5:6.

[43] Sir John Davies (1569–1626), *A Discoverie of the True Causes why Ireland was never entirely subdued, nor brought under Obedience of the Crowne of England untill the Beginning of his Majesties happie Raigne* (London, 1612; and many other edns., including 1747).

his sept. (2) When the English settled here, still the Irish had no benefit of the English laws. They could not so much as sue an Englishman. So the English beat, plundered, yea, murdered them at pleasure. Hence, (3) arose continual wars between them, for three hundred and fifty years together. And hereby both the English and Irish natives were kept few, as well as poor. (4) When they were multiplied, during a peace of forty years from 1600 to 1641, the general massacre, with the ensuing war, again thinned their numbers, not so few as a million of men, women, and children, being destroyed in four years' time. (5) Great numbers have ever since, year by year, left the land merely for want of employment. (6) The gentry are continually driving away hundreds, yea thousands of them that remain, by throwing such quantities of arable land into pasture, which leaves them neither business nor food. This it is that now dispeoples many parts of Ireland, of Connaught in particular, which it is supposed has scarce half the inhabitants at this day which it had fourscore years ago.

Wed. 23. I rode to Newry and preached at seven in the evening to a numerous congregation. Sunday 27, we had a useful sermon at church. But they told me few attended the prayers in the afternoon. However, I resolved to set them the example, and the church was as full as in the forenoon. Of what importance is every step *we* take! Seeing so many are ready to follow us!

Mon. 28. I rode to Rathfriland,[44] seven Irish miles from Newry, a small town built on the top of a mountain, surrounded first by a deep valley and at a small distance by higher mountains. The Presbyterian minister had wrote to the popish priest 'to keep his people from hearing'. But they would not be kept. Protestants and Papists flocked together to the meadow where I preached, and sat on the grass still as night, while I exhorted them to 'Repent and believe the gospel.'[45] The same attention appeared in the whole congregation at Terryhoogan in the evening, where I spent a comfortable night in 'the prophet's chamber', nine foot long, seven broad, and six high. The ceiling, floor, and walls were all of the same marble—vulgarly called clay.

Thursday, May 1. I rode to Moira.[46] Soon after twelve,

[44] Rathfriland was a market town in Co. Down, 16½ miles west of Downpatrick.

[45] Cf. Mark 1:15.

[46] Orig., 'Moyra'. Moira was a parish 13 mile south-west of Belfast on the main road to Armagh.

standing on a tombstone near the church,[47] I called a considerable number of people to 'know God, and Jesus Christ, whom he hath sent'.[48] We were just opposite to the Earl of Moira's[49] house, the best finished of any I have seen in Ireland. It stands on a hill, with a large avenue in front, bounded by the church on the opposite hill. The other three sides are covered by orchards, gardens, and woods, in which are walks of various kinds.

General Flobert,[50] who commanded the French troops at Carrickfergus, was just gone from Lord Moira's. Major[-general] Bragelongue[51] was now there, a man of a fine person and extremely graceful behaviour. Both these affirmed that the French were all picked men, out of the King's Guards. That their commission was to land either at Londonderry or Carrickfergus, while Monsieur Conflans[52] landed in the south, and if they did not do this within three months, to return directly to France.

Fri. 2. In the evening, and morning and evening on Saturday, I preached at Lisburn. The people here (as Mr. Boston[53] said) are 'all ear'[54]—but who can find a way to their heart?

47 'At Moira, the rector having refused the request of the earl to allow Mr. Wesley to preach at the church, his lordship sent the bellman through the town to summon the people to the service'; JW's preaching from the tombstone did not bear fruit in the creation of a society for a number of years. Crookshank, *Ireland*, 1:143.

48 Cf. John 17:3.

49 John Rawdon (1720–93) of Rawdon Hall, Yorks., and Moira, Co. Down, was created Baron Rawdon of Moira in 1750, and Earl of Moira in 1762 (both in the Irish peerage); hence the confusion of titles in JW's narrative. His third wife, whom he married in 1752, was his cousin Elizabeth, daughter of the Countess of Huntingdon.

50 Orig., 'Flaubert'. N. de Flobert was in Spanish service when Louis XV made him an infantry brigadier on Apr. 13, 1759. He commanded eight hundred troops in Thurot's squadron, and the defeat of the latter after the Carrickfergus landing saved the failure of the expedition. Flobert returned to Spain and died there. J. Balteau, et al., *Dictionnaire de Biographie Française* (Paris, 1933–), 14:74.

51 Orig., 'Brajelon'. Christophe Bernard, Marquis de Bragelongue, who published the journal of this expedition at Paris, 1778.

52 Hubert, Comte de Conflans, (1690–1777), after a long naval career was made Vice Admiral of France in 1756, with command of an Atlantic squadron. His mission was to initiate attacks against Britain, but he fell to the superior strength and skill of Hawke and to insubordination in his own ranks.

53 Thomas Boston, the elder (1677–1732), minister of Simprin, Berwickshire (1699–1707), and of Ettrick (1707 till his death). Thomas Boston was one of the Scots proto-evangelists who brought Edward Fisher's *Marrow of Modern Divinity* (1643) back into fashion, and resisted the Act of the General Assembly in 1720 condemning the book as unscriptural, to the brink of secession.

54 Words of the Attendant Spirit in Milton, *Comus*, 506:

> . . . I was all ear,
> And took in strains that might create a soul
> Under the ribs of death.

Sun. 4. After preaching to a large congregation at seven, I hastened to Comber,[55] in order to be at church in time. As soon as service was ended I began, and four in five of the people behaved well. About six in the evening, I preached at Newtown, where there is usually the largest congregation in Ulster. But what avails 'the hearing ear'[56] without the 'understanding heart'?[57]

Mon. 5. After preaching in the market-place at Belfast to a people who 'care for none of these things',[58] we rode on, with a furious east wind right in our face, to Carrickfergus, where I willingly accepted of an invitation from a merchant in the town, Mr. Cobham, to lodge at his house; the rather when I understood that Mr. Cavenac,[59] the French lieutenant-general, was still there. I now received a very particular account of what had been lately transacted here. Mrs. Cobham said, 'My daughter came running in and said, "Mama, there are three Indiamen come into the bay, and I suppose my brothers are come in them" (who had been in the East Indies for some time). An hour after, she came in again and cried, "O mamma, they say they are Frenchmen. And they are landing, and their guns glitter in the sun."'

Mr. Cavenac informed me that Mr. Thurot[60] had received a thousand men out of the King's Guards, with orders to land

[55] Orig., 'Cumber'.

[56] Prov. 20:12.

[57] Prov. 8:5.

[58] Cf. Acts 18:17.

[59] Cavenac was described by JW to Blackwell as one 'who speaks Latin pretty readily. He is a Lieutenant Colonel of the King's Guards and a Knight of the Order of St. Louis. I found him not only a very sensible man but thoroughly instructed even in heart religion. One would think that the French King has sent these men on purpose to show what officers he has in his Army. I hope there are some such in the English army' (see Telford, 4:95-96). The grounds for JW's religious sympathies appear below, May 6, 1760. JW's fears of French invasion in Ireland were now borne out, when in February 1760, the French commander Thurot (see following note) captured Carrickfergus, a town whose fortifications were ruinous. A small force under Colonel Jennings made a fight of it but finally surrendered, according to Julian S. Corbett, unnecessarily; *England in the Seven Years' War* (London, 1907), p. 289. Thurot plundered the town and demanded contributions from Belfast. When British forces moved north, Thurot put to sea with the mayor and three of the principal inhabitants of Carrickfergus, including Willougby Chaplin, mayor of Carrickfergus 1742–45, 1751–52, 1757 (deputy mayor 1746–48, 1750, 1753, 1759–66, 1768), and George Spaight, deputy mayor in 1732, and mayor in 1734 and 1738. S. MacSkimin, *The History and Antiquities . . . of Carrickfergus* (Belfast, 1811), pp. 168-69. A full account of the action is given by MacSkimin, pp. 22-24, 138-43.

[60] François Thurot (1727–60), French seaman who earned the distinction, unusual in that age, of promotion from the ranks to the command of a squadron. In the Seven Years' War he threatened the naval installations at Portsmouth, and from 1757, cruised for two years off the coasts of Ireland and Scotland, disrupting British commerce and escaping pursuit by thirty English vessels. In October 1759, he left Dunkirk for a descent on British territory, although on Nov. 20, the great British victory over other French fleets ended the

in the north of Ireland at the same time that Monsieur Conflans landed in the south; that a storm drove him up to Bergen in Norway, from whence he could not get out till his ships were much damaged and his provisions consumed, nor could he there procure a supply at any price; that another storm drove him to sixty-six degrees north latitude, from whence he did not get back to Carrick Bay till all on board were almost famished, having only an ounce of bread per man daily; that they then landed merely to procure provisions.' I asked, 'Is it true that you had a design to burn the town?' He cried out, 'Jesu, Maria! We never had such a thought! To burn, to destroy, cannot enter into the heart or head of a good man.'

After they had landed (Mrs. Cobham and others informed me), they divided into two bodies. One of these marched up to the east gate, the other to the north. Twelve soldiers and a corporal were there on the wall, who fired upon them when they came near. Immediately General Flobert fell, having his leg broke by a musket-ball. The next in command, a young marquis, then led them on. When the English had fired four rounds, having no more ammunition, they retired, and the French entered the town and at the market-place met those who had come in at the east gate. When they had joined, they marched up to the castle (though the English there, who were an hundred and sixty-two in number, kept a constant fire), the gate of which was not barred, so that the marquis thrust it open and went in. Just then he was shot dead. Mr. Cavenac immediately took his place and drew up his men again. The English then desired a parley and articled to furnish them with provisions in six hours. But they could not perform it, there being little in the town. On this, Mr. Cavenac sent for Mr. Cobham and desired him to go up to Belfast and procure them, leaving his wife with the general as an hostage for his return. But the poor Frenchmen could not stay for this. At the time prefixed, they began[61] to serve themselves with meat and drink, having been in such want that they were glad to eat raw oats to sustain nature. They accordingly took all the food they could

danger of a major French invasion. Although Thurot was separated from three of his six ships by a storm, he landed his troops at Carrickfergus on Jan. 10, 1760, and took the town after a three-day siege. On Feb. 28, after four difficult months at sea, he was overtaken by the Royal Navy between the Isle of Man and the Mull of Galloway, and though now abandoned by all his other ships, joined battle, losing his life to a bullet in the chest. *Nouvelle Biographie Universelle*, 46 vols. (Didot, 1852–66), 45:324-26.

[61] 1764, 1791, 'They began presently'.

find, with some linen and wearing apparel. But they neither hurt nor affronted man, woman, or child, nor did any mischief for mischief's sake. Though they were sufficiently provoked, for many of the inhabitants affronted them without fear or wit, cursed them to their face, and even took up pokers or other things to strike them.

While Mrs. Cobham was with the general, a little plain-dressed man came in, to whom they all showed a particular respect. It struck into her mind, Is not this Mr. Thurot? Which was soon confirmed. She said to him, 'Sir, you seem much fatigued. Will you step to my house and refresh yourself?' He readily accepted the offer. She prepared a little veal, of which he ate moderately and drank three glasses of small, warm punch, after which he told her, 'I have not taken any food before, nor slept for eight and forty hours.' She asked, 'Sir, will you please to take a little rest now?' Observing he started, she added, 'I will answer, life for life, that none shall hurt you under my roof.' He said, 'Madam, I believe you. I accept the offer.' He desired that two of his men might lie on the floor by the bedside, slept about six hours and then, returning her many thanks, went aboard his ship.

Five days he was kept in the bay by contrary winds. When he sailed, he took the mayor of Carrick and another gentleman as hostages for the delivery of the French prisoners. The next morning, as he was walking the deck, he frequently started, without any visible cause, stopped[62] short, and said, 'I shall die today.' Awhile after, he said to one of the English, 'Sir, I see three ships. Pray take my glass and tell me freely, what you think they are?' He looked some time and said, 'I think they are English, and I guess they are about forty-gun ships.' He called his officers and said, 'Our ships are too foul[63] to fight at a distance: we must board them.' Accordingly, when they came up, after a short fire, he ran up close to Captain Elliot,[64] and Captain Scordee[65] with his four and twenty hussars immediately leaped on board. Almost instantly, nine of them lay dead, on which he was so enraged that he rushed forward with his sabre among the English, who seized his arms and carried him away. Meantime, his men that were left

62 Orig., all edns., 'stept', probably a misprint for 'stopt'.
63 I.e., entangled with each other; see *OED* under 'foul', III.18.
64 John Elliott, promoted captain, Apr. 5, 1757. Eventually Admiral of the Red, 1805.
65 'Orig., 'Scordeck'.

retired into their own ship. Thurot seeing this cried out, 'Why should we throw away the lives of the poor men?' and ordered to strike the colours. A man going up to do this was shot dead, as was likewise a second. And before a third could do it, Mr. Thurot himself was shot through the heart. So fell a brave man, giving yet another proof that 'there is no counsel or strength against the Lord.'[66]

[66] Cf. Prov. 21:30.

AN

EXTRACT

OF THE

Rev. Mr. John Wesley's

JOURNAL,

FROM

MAY 6, 1760, to OCT. 28, 1762.

BRISTOL:
PRINTED BY WILLIAM PINE, 1767.

To the Reader

I am sensible there are many particulars in the ensuing Journal which some serious persons will not believe and which others will turn to ridicule. But this I cannot help, unless by concealing those things which I believe it my bounden duty to declare. I cannot do otherwise while I am persuaded that this was a real work of God, and that he hath so wrought this and all 'his marvellous works, that they ought to be had in remembrance'.[1] I have only to desire that those who think differently from me will bear with me, as I do with them; and that those who think with me, that this was the most glorious work of God which has ever been wrought in our memory, may be encouraged to expect to be themselves partakers of all the great and precious promises, and that without delay, seeing 'Now is the accepted time! Now is the day of salvation!'[2]

London
Jan. 31, 1767

[1] Ps. 111:4 (BCP).
[2] Cf. 2 Cor. 6:2.

Journal

From May 6, 1760, to October 28, 1762

Tuesday, May 6. I had much conversation (at Carrickfergus) with Mons. Cavenac, the French General, not on the circumstances but the essence of religion. He seemed to startle at nothing, but said more than once, and with much emotion, 'Why, this is *my* religion! There is *no true religion* besides it.'

Wed. 7. I rode to Larne.[1] The rain, which had continued with little intermission for several days, stopped this afternoon, so that I had a very large as well as serious congregation. And I spoke to them with the utmost plainness. But I could not find the way to their hearts.

Thur. 8. We rode over the mountains to Ballymena,[2] and had just passed through the town when a man came running out of the field, called me by my name, and pressed me much to preach there. But I could not stay, having appointed one to meet me at Portglenone,[3] which he accordingly did, and brought me to Mr. Burrows, near Garvagh.[4]

Fri. 9. A little rest was acceptable. Saturday 10, I preached morning and evening in Mr. B[urrow]'s house to a well-behaved congregation, though of various denominations—churchmen, Papists, Presbyterians, Cameronians. One seceder likewise ventured in, but the moment he heard, 'Our Father which art in heaven', he ran away with all speed.

Sun. 11. We had such a congregation in the church as perhaps had not been there in this century. And I believe God reached

[1] Orig. , 'Larn'. Larne had received a severe fright from the news of the French landing at Carrickfergus and the report that they were marching on the town. 'The wife of the curate, the Rev. Henry Smith, had been a violent opponent of the Methodists; but it pleased the Lord now to impress her mind so deeply with the conviction that they were His people, that she . . . earnestly entreated an interest in their prayers . . . was led to become a member of the Society . . . and continued steadfast until her death, which was most triumphant.' Crookshank, *Ireland*, 1:141.

[2] Orig., 'Ballimena'. Ballymena was a market town in the parish of Kirkinriola, 21¼ miles north-west of Belfast.

[3] Orig., 'Portlo-nane'. Portglenone was a market town in the parish of Ahoghill, 32¾ miles north-west from Belfast.

[4] Orig., 'Garvah'. Garvagh was a market town in the parish of Errigal, 8 miles south of Coleraine.

some of their hearts; several were in tears. I spoke extremely plain, especially to those who were full of their own wisdom and righteousness.

Mon. 12. Returning through Ballymena, I preached in the market-house to a large concourse of people. And God was there of a truth. I have found no such spirit in any congregation since I left Dublin. Thence I rode to Moira[5] and preached to a very civil congregation. But there is no life in them!

Tue. 13. My Irish horse was thoroughly tired. However, with much difficulty, partly riding and partly walking, about eight in the evening I reached Cootehill. I preached in the house now and at five in the morning, but at eleven in the market-house, where I delivered my own soul to most of the Protestants in the town.

Having procured a fresh horse, I rode on to Belturbet,[6] a town in which there is neither Papist nor Presbyterian. But to supply that defect there are sabbath-breakers, drunkards, and common swearers in abundance. Thursday 15, we rode through a delightful country to Swanlinbar,[7] famed for its mineral waters. Soon after, my new horse began to tire, so that it was with much difficulty I got to Sligo.[8]

Fri. 16. I walked round the ruins of the abbey,[9] formerly one of the largest in the kingdom. The walls of it are standing, and three sides of the cloisters are entire. But you can scarce tread, either within or without, unless you will step upon skulls or human bones, which are everywhere scattered up and down as dung upon the earth.[10] Surely no other nation, Christian or heathen, would endure this!

[5] Moira was a town 13 miles south-west of Belfast on the road to Armagh.

[6] Belturbet was a market town divided between two parishes in Co. Cavan, 12 miles north-west of Cavan.

[7] Orig., 'Swadling-bar'. The town, situated in the parish of Kinawley, 8 miles north-west of Ballyconnell, had its origin in a rich iron mine worked in the neighbouring mountain of Cuilcagh by Messrs. Swan, Ling, and Barr.

[8] JW here found Methodism in so prosperous and socially respectable a state 'that he recommended some suitable place should be secured in which to hold services. Accordingly a large and commodious apartment was procured in a feudal castle.' Crookshank, *Ireland*, 1:144.

[9] Sligo Abbey, a Dominican foundation dating from 1252, was destroyed by fire in 1414, and the present ruins date mainly from the subsequent rebuilding, though the deeply splayed windows on the south side of the choir are of 13th century workmanship. The present ruinous state dates from 1641, though the cloisters on the north side of the nave remain perfect on three sides. Samuel Lewis, who appended his account of the abbey to that of the workhouse, was clearly as impressed as JW; see *A Topographical Dictionary of Ireland*, 2 vols. (2nd edn., London, 1846), 2:527.

[10] See Jer. 16:4.

In the evening, the congregation was a little disturbed by two or three giddy officers. I spoke to them and they stopped, but they soon recovered their spirits and behaved—as they used to do at church!

Sun. 18. I preached at nine to a large congregation, who all seemed to hear with understanding. At five in the evening, they were not less attentive, though abundantly more numerous. On Monday, we met for the last time, between four and five. Many were deeply affected, and all received the word 'with all readiness of mind'.[11] But which of these will 'bring forth fruit with patience'?[12] God only knoweth.

Mon. 19. We rode to Castlebar, where I preached in the evening. I was particularly concerned for the poor backsliders. It seems as if most of us said in our hearts, 'if they have a mind to go to hell, let them go.' Not so; rather let us pluck the 'brands', willing or unwilling, 'out of the burning'![13]

Thur. 22. I rode to Newport and preached at seven in the evening. I suppose all the Protestants in the town were present and many of the Papists, notwithstanding the prohibition and bitter curses of their priests. So God has spread the line from sea to sea, from Dublin on the east to this place on the western ocean.

May the 25th, being Whit Sunday, Mr. Ellison[14] desired me to assist him at the Lord's Supper. Tuesday 27, there was a remarkable trial here. A Swedish ship, being leaky, put into one of our harbours. The Irish, according to custom, ran to plunder her. A neighbouring gentleman hindered them, and for so doing demanded a fourth part of her cargo. And this, they say, *the law allows!* But where, meantime, is the law of God?

To hear this cause all the gentlemen of the country were come to Castlebar. It was to be heard in the court-house, where I preached. So they met an hour sooner and heard the sermon first. Who knows but even some of these may be found of him they sought not?

Wed. 28. I rode to Hollymount, and the next day to Aughrim,[15]

[11] Acts 17:11.

[12] Luke 8:15.

[13] Amos 4:11.

[14] On Thomas Ellison, see above, June 27, 1756, n. 32.

[15] It appears from a letter of the Hon. and Rev. Walter Shirley that JW wished to visit him at Loughrea, where he was rector, about 20 miles from Aughrim; *Arminian Magazine* 20 (1797):459. Shirley, however, was absent in England to assist the defence in the trial of his brother, the 4th Earl Ferrars (1720–60), before his peers (Charles Wesley was present in Westminster Hall). Ferrars was found guilty of the murder of the receiver of the rents of the trustees in whom his estates were vested, and failed with a plea of 'occasional insanity'; he was hung before an enormous crowd on May 5. Charles Wesley was in touch with

where were a people alive to God. I told them plainly what things they wanted still. And surely God will supply all their wants!

Trinity Sunday, June 1. I preached about nine in the market-house at Athlone, on 'There are three that bear record in heaven . . . , and these three are one.'[16] Afterwards, at the minister's desire,[17] I read prayers in the church, and in the evening preached on the Connaught side of the river, on 'Ye must be born again.'[18] Both Papists and Protestants attended. And some seemed cut to the heart.

Tue. 3. I met the classes and was agreeably surprised to find that bitterness against the Church, with which many were infected when I was here before, was now entirely over. Yet the deadness which it had occasioned remained, and I doubt it will not soon be removed.

Fri. 6. I preached in the evening at Ahascragh, where the bulk of the congregation were Papists. Yet the decency of their behaviour was such as might have made many Protestants ashamed.

Sun. 8. I rode over to Aughrim again. Understanding the rector[19] had none to assist in the service, I offered to read prayers for him, which he willingly accepted. Immediately after the church service, I preached to a numerous congregation, and returned to Athlone soon enough to speak once more to a large concourse of all ranks and religions. But great part of them were as bullocks unaccustomed to the yoke, neither taught of God, nor man.

Mon. 9. About one, I preached at Abbeyderg,[20] and then rode on to Longford. The town was so thronged by reason of the approaching fair that we had much ado to pass. But this increased the evening congregation much, among whom was Dr. Hort,[21]

Walter Shirley throughout, administering comfort and counsel. Thomas Jackson, *The Life of the Rev. Charles Wesley, M.A.*, 2 vols. (London, Mason, 1841), 2:167-78; hereafter, Jackson, *Charles Wesley.*

[16] 1 John 5:7.

[17] On Teare, the rector of Athlone, see May 7, 1749, n. 63 (20:270 in this edn.).

[18] John 3:7.

[19] The vicar of Aughrim, 1724–67, was William Crowe, who was also vicar of Killalaghton in 1730.

[20] Orig., 'Abidarrig'.

[21] Robert Hort, son of John Hort of Colne, Wilts., pleb. He matriculated from Brasenose College, Oxford in 1725, aged 16, graduating B.A. in 1729. He graduated from Trinity College, Dublin, M.A. in 1743, Hon. LL.D. in 1754. Rector of Templemichael, 1737–49, and of Longford, 1749–62, when he resigned to take preferment in England. He was probably a relative of Josiah Hort, Bishop of Kilmore and Ardagh 1727–41; Archbishop of Tuam 1742–51.

then rector of the parish, a learned, sensible, pious man and a pattern both for clergy and laity.

Tue. 10. I rode to Drumsna,[22] a village delightfully situated. Almost the whole town, Protestants and Papists, were present at the sermon in the evening, and a great part of them in the morning. But Oh! how few of them will bear fruit to perfection![23]

At noon William Ley,[24] James Glasbrook,[25] and I rode to Carrick upon Shannon. In less than an hour, an esquire and justice of the peace came down with a drum and what mob he could gather. I went into the garden with the congregation while he was making a speech to his followers in the street. He then attacked William Ley (who stood at the door), being armed with an halberd[26] and long sword, and ran at him with the halberd, but missing his thrust, he then struck at him and broke it short upon his wrist. Having made his way through the house to the other door, he was at a full stop. James Glasbrook held it fast on the other side. While he was endeavouring to force it open, one told him I was preaching in the garden. On this, he quitted the door in haste, ran round the house, and with part of his retinue climbed over the wall into the garden, and with a whole volley of oaths and curses declared, 'You shall not preach here today.' I told him, 'Sir, I do not intend it, for I have preached already.' This made him ready to tear the ground. Finding he was not to be reasoned with, I went into the house. Soon after, he revenged himself on James Glasbrook (by breaking the truncheon of his halberd on his arm) and on my hat, which he beat and kicked most valiantly. But a gentleman rescued it out of his hands, and we rode quietly out of the town.

After preaching to several of the intermediate societies[27] in the way, on Saturday 14, I came to Tyrrellspass and found several of our friends, who were come from various parts. Sunday 15, I preached at eight and at twelve (there being no service at the church). A heap of fine gay people came in their post-chaises to

22 Orig., 'Drumersnave'.

23 Luke 8:14.

24 An itinerant, now appointed to Ireland. He seems unsuccessfully to have pursued a curacy in the Church of England in 1766, and briefly became curate of Lakenheath in 1768, but was still a preacher in the mid-seventies (Telford, 6:5, 73; *CWJ*, 2:249, 263). It was through him that JW became acquainted with Professor Johan Hendrik Liden (1741–93), 'adjunct' in history at Lund, and librarian at Uppsala. *WHS*, 17 (1929):1-4.

25 An itinerant; see above, Mar. 28, 1758, n. 53.

26 Orig., 'halbert'.

27 The only place mentioned in the Sermon Register is Longford, but Drumsna, Edgeworthstown, and Mullingar, were also in this direction.

the evening preaching. I spoke very plain, but the words seemed to fly over them. 'Gallio cared for none of these things.'[28]

Mon. 16. I preached in the evening in the long shady walk at Edenderry to such a congregation as I had not[29] seen there for many years. And God gave an edge to his word, both this evening and the next morning. He *can* work even among these dry bones.

Wed. 18. I designed to preach in the market-house at Portarlington. But it was pre-engaged for a ball. So I preached, and with much comfort, in our own room, as also at five in the morning. I preached at ten, for the sake of the gentry. But it was too early—they could not rise *so soon.*

In the afternoon, I rode to Mountmellick. The rain was suspended in the evening, while I exhorted a large congregation to 'walk in the old paths'.[30] Many Papists appeared to be quite astonished, some of them almost persuaded to 'walk therein'.[31] The next evening, I preached in the market-place for the sake of the rich, who could hear there without impeachment to their honour. And some were deeply affected. Surely the thorns will not choke *all* the good seed![32]

Sat. 21. The congregation at Tullamore was near as large as at Mountmellick. At eight in the morning, Sunday 22, it was much increased, but much more at one. And I have reason to believe that God at this time touched several careless hearts. I rode from thence to Coolalough and found a congregation gathered from twenty miles round. It rained when I began to preach, but none offered to go away. And God did indeed 'send a gracious rain upon his inheritance'[33] and comforted the souls of his servants.

Mon. 23. Being the Quarterly Meeting,[34] the stewards from all the country societies were present, a company of settled, sensible men. Nothing is wanting in this kingdom but zealous, active preachers, tenacious of order and exact discipline.

Tue. 24. I took horse early, and at ten preached at Cloghan,[35] about twenty-four miles from Coolalough. We afterwards rode

[28] Acts 18:17 (*Notes*).
[29] *Works* (1774), 'as had not been'.
[30] Cf. Jer. 6:16.
[31] Ibid.
[32] See Matt. 13:7, etc.
[33] Cf. Ps. 68:9 (BCP).
[34] At this time the Quarterly Meeting was attended by stewards only, and was held here, in the country, because of the hospitality of Samuel Handy (see Apr. 5, 1748, n. 16; 20:217 in this edn.). JW's verdict on the state of the work was that 'in this kingdom nothing is wanting but a few more zealous and active labourers. James Morgan, John Johnson, and two or three more do their best; the rest spare themselves.' Telford, 4:100.
[35] Orig., 'Cloughan'. Cloghan was a village in the parish of Gallen, 4½ miles north-east of Banagher.

through Longford but did not stop, as the day was cool and pleasant. About two, we were unawares encompassed with a multitude of Papists, coming out of their mass-house.[36] One of them, knowing me, soon alarmed the rest, who set up a hideous roar and drew up in battle array. But we galloped through them and went on to Drumsna, where I preached in the evening, and the next day, Wednesday 25, rode on to Sligo.

Never did I see a fairer prospect of good here.[37] But blossoms are not fruit. As large, if not a larger, congregation than before was at the market-place in the evening. I was exceeding weary, having rode an extremely dull horse, but I soon forgot my weariness, seeing so many young and old, rich and poor, receiving the word with all gladness.

Thur. 26. I preached at five in a large commodious room, which has been procured since I was here last. I breakfasted at Mr. A[nderson]'s[38] and dined at Mr. K[nox's],[39] but two such families I have seldom seen. They had feared God for many years and served him in the best manner they knew. Nothing was wanting but that they should hear the 'more excellent way',[40] which they then embraced with all their heart.

Fri. 27. Our morning congregation was doubled. Mr. D——[41] did not fail to be there, though it seemed strange to him at first when mention was made of preaching at five in the morning. In the evening, we had a still larger congregation, and I believe God applied his word. Some trembled, others wept. Surely some of these shall know, 'there is balm in Gilead.'[42]

Sat. 28. At five, the congregation was larger than ever it had been at that hour. After breakfast I rode out with Mr. K[nox] and Mr. D., who, hearing I was ill-mounted, desired me to make use of one of his horses during my stay in Ireland.

In the evening (it being market day, so that the market-house was full of people), I wrote a line to the colonel, who readily gave

36 A derogatory term commonly used by Protestants in the seventeenth and eighteenth century, including Samuel Johnson, though not listed by him in *A Dictionary of the English Language*, 2 vols. (London, 1755).

37 All three contemporary editions read 'good than here', but in the errata to his *Works* (1774) and in a note in his own copy, Wesley removes 'than'.

38 John Anderson of Willowbrook, whose descendants remained attached to the Methodist society for many generations. Crookshank, *Ireland*, p. 144.

39 The original gives no clue, but the *Works* (1774) reads 'K——'. James Knox proved a disappointment, avoiding JW on his next visit, and in consequence, receiving a letter of rebuke from him in 1765, on which JW noted: 'He came to nothing.' See below, May 1, 1762; and Telford, 4:302-4.

40 1 Cor. 12:31.

41 Not identified.

42 Cf. Jer. 8:22.

me the liberty of preaching in the barrack-yard. He likewise came to hear himself, as did several of the officers. It was a solemn conclusion of the happiest birthday which I have known for many years.

Sun. 29. We had a solemn meeting of the society at five. At eight, I preached again in the barrack-yard. And I did not observe a trifler there. They all seemed to hear as for life. Today I saw an odd instance of the force of example. When we were at church in the morning, scarce anyone either sung or stood at the Psalms, so that I was almost alone there. But in the afternoon, almost everyone stood up, and most of them sung or endeavoured so to do. After service I went directly to the market-house and enforced those solemn words, 'What doth the Lord thy God require of thee, but to do justly, and to love mercy, and to walk humbly with thy God?'[43]

Mr. D—— had left us at six in the morning in order to serve his cure. But about ten at night, he came back and was with me soon after four, importuning me to stay another day. But as my journeys were fixed, I could not do that without disappointing several congregations. Now was the general call for the town of Sligo. And many did 'receive the word with joy'.[44] But the greatest part had 'no root in themselves'.[45] What fruit then could be expected from them?

Mon. 30. I have rarely seen so heavy rain in Europe as we had in the way to Tobercurry.[46] I was quickly wet to my toe's end,[47] but the day clearing, I was dry again in a few hours. We had a very large congregation at Castlebar in the evening, and many seemed 'almost persuaded to be Christians'.[48] Oh what does it avail *almost* to hit the mark? *Almost* to escape the damnation of hell?

Tuesday, July 1. We took horse about four. And it was well we did. For our seven and thirty Irish miles, so called, were little less than seventy English. I preached at a friend's house soon after three, and then, procuring a fresh horse about the size of a jackass, I rode on, with more ease than state, to Aughrim.

Wed. 2. We rode on to Eyrecourt,[49] where many threatened

[43] Mic. 6:8. [44] Luke 8:13. [45] Mark 4:17.

[46] Orig., 'Tubber-curraugh'. Tobercurry is a small market town 21¾ miles south-west of Sligo.

[47] *OED* lists but does not illustrate the combination 'toe-end', but does not list any such phrase as this.

[48] Cf. Acts 26:28.

[49] Eyrecourt, Co. Galway, a small town 7 miles west of Banagher, was the seat of the Eyre family. Colonel Stratford Eyre, here mentioned, had fought at Culloden, was renowned for emphatic Protestant views, and was appointed governor of Galway in 1747

great things, but all vanished into air. I preached at ten in the court-house. Col. Eyre was there, and several other persons of fashion. In the evening, I preached at Birr with more satisfaction than for several years, finding many more alive to God than ever and provoking one another to love and to good works.[50] I had purposed to set out early in the morning, but their love constrained me to stay a day longer. So I had leisure to complete the account of the societies. At present the societies in Connaught contain little more than two hundred members; those in Ulster, about two hundred and fifty; those in Leinster, a thousand.

Fri. 4. I took my ease, riding in a chaise to Limerick, where on Saturday 5, ten of us met in a little conference. By the blessing of God, we were all of one mind, particularly with regard to the Church. Even J[ames] D[eaves][51] has not now the least thought of leaving it, but attends there, be the minister good or bad. On Tuesday 8, having settled all our little affairs, we parted in much love.

Wed. 9. I rode over to Killeheen,[52] a German settlement, near twenty miles south of Limerick. It rained all the way, but the earnestness of the poor people made us quite forget it. In the evening, I preached to another colony of Germans at Ballingarrane.[53] The third is at Courtmatrix,[54] a mile from Killeheen. I suppose three such towns are scarce to be found again in England or Ireland. There is no cursing or swearing, no sabbath-breaking, no drunkenness, no alehouse in any of them. How will these poor foreigners rise up in the judgment against those that are round about them!

to hunt out friaries and unregistered priests (Lecky, *Ireland*, 1:347-48). He was a great hero of James Anthony Froude; see *The English in Ireland in the Eighteenth Century*, 3 vols. (London, 1872–74), 1:667-74. See also JW's next visit, Apr. 17, 1775.

50 See Heb. 10:24.

51 James Deaves entered the Irish itinerancy as a young zealot in 1753, serving at least at intervals until 1768. He settled at Waterford in 1784 (Crookshank, *Ireland*, 1:98, 391). By 1772, however, he was known as a 'sower of discord', though on a favourable view 'a troublesome man only to mongrel Methodists' (Telford, 5:321, 337; 7:131). Further trouble was in store, for Deaves had some kind of property in the Wexford chapel, there was trouble over the settlement of the chapel under the Deed Poll, and late in life JW declared, 'I will not, I dare not, draw the saw of controversy any longer; especially with James Deaves, who will dispute through a stone wall' (Telford, 8:132) 'for he has ten words to my one' (Telford, 7:280, 300; 8:152; Crookshank, *Ireland,* 1:455; see also May 28, 1789). By this time relations with the Established Church had added fuel to the fire.

52 Spelled 'Killiheen' on the first two occasions here, and Killeheen on the third. For the Palatines, see May 12, 1749, n. 75 (20:272 in this edn.).

53 Orig., 'Ballygarane'.

54 Orig., 'Court-mattrass'.

Fri. 11. I preached in the new house at Clare to a genteel congregation. What a contrast between these and the poor people at Killeheen! We had a still more genteel congregation the next morning at nine in the court-house at Ennis, to whom I spoke with all plainness. I did the same on Sunday morning, so if they hear me no more, I am clear of their blood. I took my leave of them at Clare in the afternoon, and in the evening returned to Limerick.

Wed. 16. I rode to Newmarket, which *was* another German settlement. But the poor settlers, with all their diligence and frugality, could not procure even the coarsest food to eat and the meanest raiment to put on, under their *merciful* landlords! So that most of these, as well as of those at Ballingarrane, have been forced to seek bread in other places—some of them in distant parts of Ireland, but the greater part in America.[55]

Thur. 17. I met the classes at Limerick and found a considerable decrease. And how can it be otherwise, when vice flows as a torrent, unless the children of God are all life, zeal, activity? In hopes of quickening them, I preached at seven in the old camp, to more than twice the usual congregation, which the two next evenings was more numerous still and equally attentive. I was well pleased to see a little army of soldiers there and not a few of their officers. Nor did they behave as unconcerned hearers, but like men that really desired to save their souls.

Sun. 20. I took my leave of that comfortable place, where some thousands of people were assembled. I have seen no such sight since I came to the kingdom. They not only filled all the lower ground, but completely covered the banks that surround it, though they stood as close as possible. I exhorted them to 'ask for the old paths and walk therein', that they might 'find rest to' their 'souls'.[56] We had afterwards a solemn meeting of the society, in confidence that God would revive his work.

Mon. 21. I left Limerick, and about noon preached at Shronell,[57] near a great house which a gentleman built many years ago. But he cannot yet afford to finish it, having only

[55] Notable among these emigrants were Philip Embury and Barbara Heck (1734–1804) who introduced Methodism into the American colonies (see above, June 23, 1758, n. 6). Barbara Heck emigrated to New York in this very year, 1760, inspired Embury to preach in 1760, and later became a United Empire Loyalist, moving on to Canada.

[56] Jer. 6:16.

[57] There were three chief seats at Shronell; this may have been Damer Court built by John Damer in the first half of the eighteenth century and demolished in 1776. Lewis, *Ireland*, 2:54.

thirty thousand a year and some hundred thousands in ready money!

> The beggars but a common lot deplore;
> The rich poor man's emphatically poor.[58]

At six, I preached at the camp near Caher,[59] to a large and serious congregation of soldiers. Thence we rode on to Clonmel, where I preached near the barracks at eight in the morning, to a wild, staring people, but quiet perforce—for the soldiers kept them in awe. We rode in the afternoon to Waterford, where our friends had procured a commodious place, enclosed on all sides.[60] I preached there three evenings, with great hope of doing good. Our large room was full every morning. O why should we despair of any souls whom God hath made?

Thur. 24. I looked over that well-wrote book, Mr. Smith's *State of the County and City of Waterford*.[61] He plainly shows that twelve hundred years ago Ireland was a flourishing kingdom. It seems to have been declining almost ever since, especially after it was torn into several independent kingdoms. Thenceforward, it grew more and more wild and barbarous for several hundred years. In Queen Elizabeth's time, it began to revive. And it increased greatly both in trade and inhabitants till the deadly blow, which commenced on October 23, 1641.[62] Three hundred thousand Protestants, by a moderate computation, were then destroyed in less than a year, and more than twice as many Papists within a few years following. Most of these were adults, and this was a loss which the nation has not recovered yet. Nay, it will probably require another century to restore the number of inhabitants it had before.

[58] Abraham Cowley, *Essays, Plays, and Sundry Verses*, ed. A. R. Waller (Cambridge, 1906), p. 437, Essay 'Of Avarice'. Cf. JW's Sermon 131, 'On the Danger of Increasing Riches', I.1; 4:179 in this edn.

[59] Orig., 'Caire'. Caher, or Cahir, was a market town and parish in Co. Tipperary, 7¾ miles west of Clonmel.

[60] This curious reference is to the first Methodist chapel, built in Factory Lane. Crookshank, *Ireland*, 1:147.

[61] Charles Smith, *The Antient and Present State of the County and City of Waterford*, 2 vols. (Dublin, 1746).

[62] The reference is to the Irish massacre. More recent comment holds that 'certainly several thousands were killed in cold blood and probably two or three times as many perished from exposure and deprivation'; it was, however, generally believed in England and Scotland that 'there had been a plot formed by the Irish for the universal extirpation of all British settlers.' Godfrey Davies, *The Early Stuarts, 1603–1660* (Oxford, Clarendon, 1937), p. 115.

Fri. 25. I preached once more near the barracks in Clonmel, and the next morning took horse at four. About eleven, the sun was scorching hot, till a little cloud rose and covered us till we were near Rathcormack. Here we rested two hours and then rode on (mostly shaded by flying clouds) to Cork.

Sun. 27. The house was well filled, but I expect small increase of the work of God till we preach abroad. Thursday 31, I rode to Bandon, but my good old friend, Mrs. Jones,[63] did not stay for my coming. She was released out of life some weeks ago, in the seventy-second year of her age. I preached as usual in the main street to a large and attentive congregation. And they were nearly doubled the next evening, yet all behaved with the utmost decency. The market obliged me to preach in the house on Saturday in the afternoon—a very neat and lightsome building. Having spent the time I proposed here, with much satisfaction, in the evening I returned to Cork.

Sunday, August the 3rd, I had wrote to the commanding officer for leave to preach near the barracks. But he was just gone out of town. So I was obliged once more to coop myself up in the room. Monday 4. Knowing by the experiment I made two years since, that it was an entertainment above the taste of our evening congregation, I read some select letters at five in the morning to those who desired to hear them. And many of them were not a little comforted and established in the ways of God.

Thur. 7. In the afternoon, I set out for Kinsale. In the way a violent storm drove us into a little hut, where a poor woman was very thankful for physical advice, and another for a little money to buy her food. The sky then clearing, we soon reached Kinsale, where I preached at six in the Exchange to a multitude of soldiers and not a few of the dull, careless townsfolk. At five in the morning, it being a field-day, the soldiers could not attend. But I had a large and serious congregation notwithstanding. Surely good might be done here also, would our preachers always preach in the Exchange, as they may without any molestation, instead of a little, ugly, dirty garret.

About nine, a sharp storm having put an end to their exercise, I went to the soldiers in the field. I stood so near the entrenchments of the fort that they could hear within as well as without. The sun indeed shone extremely hot on my head, but presently a cloud interposed. And when I began to be chill (for the wind was high

[63] See above, May 25, 1756, n. 15.

and sharp), it removed till I wanted it again. How easily may we see the hand of God in small things as well as great! And why should a little, pointless raillery make us ashamed to acknowledge it?

In the evening, I preached to the usual congregation in the main street at Bandon, on 'Her ways are ways of pleasantness,' and 'all her paths peace'.[64] The congregation was near twice as large at five in the morning as it was last week, when I preached an hour later. Sunday 10. After preaching at seven, in an house crowded within and without, I left this comfortable place and went back to Cork. I had a desire to preach abroad in the evening, but the weather would not permit. When the society met, a person hugely daubed with gold thrust violently in. By his appearance I should have judged him to be some nobleman. But I was afterward informed, it was Dr. Taylor.[65]

On Monday and Tuesday, I took an account of the society and was grieved, though not surprised, to find such a declension. I left two hundred and ninety members; I find only two hundred and thirty-three. And what will the end be, unless those that remain learn to bear one another's burdens? Adding to those in the other provinces, about six hundred who are in Munster, the whole number is a little above two thousand.

Our evening congregations this week were smaller than usual, as the gentry were engaged in a more important affair. A company of players were in town. However, many of them came on Friday—for a watch-night was newer to them than a comedy.

Mon. 18. Being advised from Dublin that Capt. Dansey[66] (with whom I desired to sail) would sail on the 19th or 20th, I took horse early and reached Clonmel between five and six in the evening. I took my usual stand near the barrack-gate but had abundantly more than my usual congregation, as it was the assize week, so that the town was extremely full of gentry as well as common people.

Tue. 19. We had many light showers, which cooled the air and laid the dust. We dined at Kilkenny, noble in ruins; I see no such remains of magnificence in the kingdom. The late Duke of Ormond's house[67] on the top of a rock hanging over the river, the

[64] Cf. Prov. 3:17.

[65] Not identified.

[66] Dansey and JW were clearly acquainted; JW, when in Dublin in 1758, had employed him to take a letter to his wife in Bristol. Telford, 4:23.

[67] On the 2nd Duke of Ormond, see June 15, 1750, n. 17 (20:345 in this edn.). Kilkenny Castle continued as a residence of the earls of Ormond.

ancient cathedral, and what is left of many grand buildings, yield a melancholy pleasure. Thus

> A little power, a little sway,
> A sunbeam in a winter's day,
> Is all the great and mighty have
> Between the cradle and the grave![68]

We lodged at Castledermot,[69] and reached Dublin on Wednesday 20, but Captain Dansey was not to sail this week. I then inquired for a Chester ship and found one which was expected to sail on Friday morning. But on Friday morning, the captain sent us word he 'must wait for General Montague'.[70] So in the afternoon, I rode over to the Skerries,[71] where the packet lay. But before I came thither, the wind, which was fair before, shifted to the east and blew a storm. I saw the hand of God and, after resting a while, rode cheerfully back to Dublin. It being the watch-night, I came just in time to spend a comfortable hour with the congregation. O how good it is to have no choice of our own, but to leave all things to the will of God!

Sat. 23. The captain of the Chester ship sent word, 'the general would not go,' and he 'would sail the next morning'. So we have one day more to spend in Ireland. Let us 'live this day as it were our last!'[72]

Sun. 24. At seven, I took leave of my friends, and about noon embarked in the *Nonpareil*[73] for Chester. We had forty or fifty passengers on board, half of whom were cabin passengers.[74] I was afraid we should have an uneasy time in the midst of such a crowd

[68] Adapted from John Dyer, *Gronger Hill*, pp. 89-92 (somewhat differently from above; cf. Dec. 29, 1758).

[69] Castledermot was a parish 7¼ miles south-east from Athy and 34 miles south-west from Dublin.

[70] Orig., ' Mountague'. Major-General Charles Montague, then serving in Ireland, *WHS*, 5 (1905):76.

[71] Orig., 'Skirries'. Skerries was a seaport and fishing town 18 miles north of Dublin, the anchorage protected by groups of islands called the Skerries.

[72] Cf. William Drummond of Hawthornden (1585–1649), 'Death's Last Will':

> Trust flattering life no more, redeem time past,
> And live each day as if it were thy last.

And cf. Sermon 126, 'On Worldly Folly', II:5, n.25 (4:136 in this edn.).

[73] Under Captain Jordan; cf. below, Apr. 2, 1762, n. 76.

[74] Among JW's travelling companions was the preacher Nicholas Manners whose account of the voyage is to be found in Bretherton, *Methodism in Chester*, p. 51.

of gentry. We sailed out with a fair wind, but at four in the afternoon, it failed and left us in a dead calm. I then made the gentlemen an offer of preaching, which they thankfully accepted. While I was preaching, the wind sprung up fair, but the next day we were becalmed again. In the afternoon, they desired me to give them another sermon, and again the wind sprung up while I was speaking and continued till, about noon on Tuesday, we landed at Parkgate.

Being in haste, I would not stay for my own horse, which I found could not land till low water. So I bought one, and having hired another, set forward without delay. We reached Whitchurch that evening. Wednesday 27, we breakfasted at Newport,[75] where, finding our horses begin to fail, we thought it best to take the Birmingham road, that if they should fail us altogether, we might stay among our friends. But they would go no farther than Wolverhampton, so we hired fresh horses there and immediately set out for Worcester. But one of them soon after fell, and gave me such a shock (though I did not quit my seat) that I was seized with a violent bleeding at the nose, which nothing we could apply would stop. So we were obliged to go a foot-pace for two miles and then stay at Broadwaters.[76]

Thur. 28. Soon after we set out, the other horse fell lame. An honest man at Worcester found this was caused by a bad shoe. A smith cured this by a new shoe, but at the same time, by paring the hoof too close, he effectually lamed the other foot, so that we had hard work to reach Gloucester. After resting here a while, we pushed on to Newport,[77] where I took a chaise and reached Bristol before eleven.

I spent the two following days with the preachers, who had been waiting for me all the week. And their love and unanimity was such as soon made me forget all my labour.[78]

Monday, September 1. I set out for Cornwall, preaching at Shepton, Middlezoy, and Tiverton in the way. Wednesday 3, I reached Launceston and found the small remains of a dead,

[75] Shropshire.

[76] Broadwaters is a hamlet one mile north-east of Kidderminster.

[77] Newport was a village in the parish of Berkeley, Glos., a posting place on the main road from Bristol to Gloucester, 18 miles from the former and 16 from the latter.

[78] This was probably the shortest Conference on record; the affection of the preachers was doubtless the sweeter as relations between the Wesley brothers were at this moment strained, while it is sufficient commentary on JW's relations with his wife, that having been separated from her for six months, he set out immediately after Conference for a month's tour in Cornwall (Charles indeed may not have been present; cf. Telford, 4:99-100).

scattered society. And no wonder, as they have had scarce any discipline, and only one sermon in a fortnight. On Friday 5, I found just such another society at Camelford. But their deadness here was owing to bitterness against each other. In the morning, I heard the contending parties face to face, and they resolved and promised on all sides to let past things be forgotten. O how few have learned to forgive 'one another, as God for Christ's sake hath forgiven' us![79]

Sat. 6. We had an exceeding lively congregation in the evening at Trewalder. Indeed, all the society stands well and 'adorns the doctrine of God our Saviour'.[80] Sunday 7. At eight, I preached again and was much comforted. I then rode to Port Isaac church and had the satisfaction of hearing an excellent sermon.[81] After service I preached at a small distance from the church to a numerous congregation, and to a far more numerous one in the town at five in the afternoon.

In examining this society, I found much reason to bless God on their behalf. They diligently observe all the rules of the society, with or without a preacher. They constantly attend the church and Sacrament, and meet together at the times appointed. The consequence is that thirty out of thirty-five, their whole number, continue to walk in the light of God's countenance.[82]

Mon. 8. A gentleman followed me to my inn at St. Columb[83] and carried me to his house, where were three or four more as friendly as himself.[84] One of them rode with me seven or eight miles and gave me a pleasing account of two young clergymen, Mr. C[ooper][85] and Mr. Philp,[86] who had the care of three

[79] Cf. Eph. 4:32.

[80] Cf. Titus 2:10.

[81] The rector of the collegiate church of St. Endellion was Mydhope Wallis, a somewhat distant friend of Samuel Walker of Truro; but this sermon may well have been preached by William Buckingham, curate there 1759–64 (said to be unlicensed), who was turned out of his curacy by the bishop for Methodist sympathies, and who later assisted both JW and the Countess of Huntingdon.

[82] See Ps. 89:15.

[83] Orig., 'Colomb's'.

[84] Probably William Rawlings, a friend of Samuel Walker of Truro, and a merchant of St. Columb, who, after moving to Padstow in 1770, did much for the commercial development of the place. Pearce, *Wesleys in Cornwall*, p. 133.

[85] Samuel Cooper, curate of Cubert, 1759–60. He was perhaps the one of that name who matriculated, aged 18, at Christ Church, 1754, and graduated B.A. in 1759. He officiated at Truro on a number of occasions after Walker's departure. Davies, *Cornish Evangelicals*, pp. 85-86.

[86] Orig., 'Phelps'. William Philp (*c.* 1727–62), matriculated at Exeter College, Oxford, 1747, but did not graduate; he succeeded James Vowler as curate of St. Agnes and Perranzabuloe in 1758, and died of fever. He is said to have 'been brought to a sense of

adjoining parishes. Surely God has a favour for the people of these parts! He gives them so serious, zealous, lively ministers.[87] By these and the Methodists together, the line is now laid, with no inconsiderable interruption, all along the north sea, from the eastern point of Cornwall to the Land's End. In a while, I trust, there will be no more cause on these coasts to accuse *Britannos hospitibus feros*.[88]

The congregation at St. Agnes in the evening was, I suppose, double to that at Port Isaac. We had near as many, Tuesday 9, at five in the morning, as the preaching-house could contain. Afterward I examined the society and was surprised and grieved to find that, out of ninety-eight persons, all but three or four had forsaken the Lord's Table. I told them my thoughts very plain; they seemed convinced, and promised no more to give place to the devil.[89]

Wed. 10. I had much conversation with Mr. Philp, a man of an humble, loving, tender spirit. Between him on the one hand and the Methodists on the other, most in the parish are now awakened. Let but our brethren have 'zeal according to knowledge',[90] and few will escape them both.

When I came to St. Ives, I was determined to preach abroad, but the wind was so high I could not stand where I had intended. But we found a little enclosure near it, one end of which was native rock, rising ten or twelve feet perpendicular, from which the ground fell with an easy descent. A jetting out of the rock, about four feet from the ground, gave me a very convenient pulpit. Here well-nigh the whole town, high and low, rich and poor, assembled together. Nor was there a word to be heard, or a smile seen, from one end of the congregation to the other. It was just the same the three following evenings. Indeed I was afraid on Saturday that the roaring of the sea, raised by the north wind, would have prevented their hearing. But God gave me so clear and strong a voice that I believe scarce one word was lost.

Sun. 14. At eight, I chose a large ground, the sloping side of a meadow, where the congregation stood, row above row, so that all might see as well as hear. It was a beautiful sight. Everyone

himself by Mr. Walker's means', and with Cooper, was a member of Walker's Clerical Club (Gillies, *Historical Collections*, 1:532).

87 Orig., 'preachers', altered in JW's *Works* (1774).

88 Horace, *Odes*, III.iv.33. 'Britons barbarous to strangers'. JW is thinking of the wreckers.

89 Eph. 4:27.

90 Cf. Rom. 10:2.

seemed to take to himself what was spoken. I believe every backslider in the town was there. And surely God was there to 'heal their backslidings'.[91]

I began at Zennor, as soon as the church service ended. I suppose scarce six persons went away. Seeing many there who did once run well, I addressed myself to them in particular. The spirit of mourning was soon poured out, and some of them wept bitterly. O that the Lord may yet return unto them and 'leave a blessing behind him'![92]

At five, I went once more into the ground at St. Ives and found such a congregation as I think was never seen in any place before (Gwennap excepted) in this county. Some of the chief of the town were now not in the skirts but in the thickest of the people. The clear sky, the setting sun, the smooth still water, all agreed with the state of the audience. Is anything too hard for God? May we not well say, in every sense,

> Thou dost the raging sea control,
> And smooth the prospect of the deep.
> Thou mak'st the sleeping billows roll;
> Thou mak'st the rolling billows sleep.[93]

Mon. 15. I inquired concerning the uncommon storm which was here on March 9, the last year. It began near the Land's End between nine and ten at night and went eastward, not above a mile broad, over St. Just, Morvah, Zennor, St. Ives, and Gwinear,[94] whence it turned northward over the sea. It uncovered all the houses in its way and was accompanied with impetuous rain. About a mile south-east from St. Ives, it tore up a rock, twelve or fourteen ton weight, from the top of a rising ground and whirled it down upon another, which it split through and at the same time dashed itself in pieces. It broke down the pinnacles of Gwinear church, which forced their way through the roof. And it was remarkable, the rain which attended it was as salt as any sea-water.

[91] Cf. Hos. 14:4.

[92] Joel 2:14.

[93] Cf. Tate and Brady, New Version, Ps. 89, st. 9, opening:

> Thou dost the lawless sea control,
> And change the prospect of the deep.

Note the influence of Virgil, *Aeneid*, I.65, 66.

[94] Gwinear was a parish 3¼ miles south-west from Camborne.

At one I preached in Madron[95] parish and then rode to St. Just. I have not seen such a congregation here for twice seven years. Abundance of backsliders being present, I chiefly applied to them. Some of them smiled at first, but it was not long before their mirth was turned into mourning. And I believe few, if any, went away without a witness from God that he 'willeth not the death of a sinner'.[96]

Tue. 16. At five the room was near full, and the great power of God was in the midst of them. It was now accompanied with one unusual effect: the mouth of those whom it most affected was literally stopped. Several of them came to me and could not speak one word; very few could utter three sentences. I re-joined to the society ten or eleven backsliders and added some new members. Here (as at Port Isaac, St. Agnes, and St. Ives) we are called to thankfulness; at most other places, to patience.

All the day it blew a storm, and in the evening, though the rain ceased, the furious wind continued. I ordered all the windows of the preaching-house to be set open so that most could hear without as well as within. I preached on 'He will not break the bruised reed, nor quench the smoking flax.'[97] And again God applied his word, both to wound and to heal them that were already wounded.

About this time I wrote the following letter.

To the Editor of the London Chronicle

Sept. 17, 1760

Sir,

As you sometimes insert things of a religious nature in your paper, I shall count it a favour if you will insert this.

Some years ago I published *A Letter to Mr. Law*,[98] and about the

[95] Orig., 'Maddern'. Elsewhere JW caps his story about the St. Just storm with another about Madron, taken from Joseph Hall (1574–1656), Bishop of Exeter (1697–41): 'Of this kind was that marvelous cure which was wrote upon a poor cripple, at St. Madern's in Cornwall, whereof, besides the attestation of many hundreds of neighbours, I took a strict examination in my last visitation. The man for sixteen years together, was obliged to walk upon his hands, by reason the sinews of his legs were so contracted. Upon an admonition in his dream to wash in a certain well he was suddenly so restored to his limbs that I saw him able to walk and get his own maintenance. The name of this cripple was John Trebble.' *Arminian Magazine*, quoted in Pearce, *Wesleys in Cornwall*, p. 135.

[96] Cf. BCP, Morning and Evening Prayer, Absolution.

[97] Cf. Isa. 42:3; Matt. 12:20.

[98] John Wesley, *A Letter to the Rev. Mr. Law. Occasioned by some of his late writings* (London, 1756), an *Extract* from which was reprinted in the *Preservative against Unsettled Notions in Religion* (Bristol, 1758). Vols. 13, 16 in this edn.

same time *An Address to the Clergy*.[99] Of the former, Mr. Law gives the following account in his *Collection of Letters*,[1] lately published.

'To answer Mr. Wesley's letter seems to be quite needless, because there is nothing substantial or properly argumentative in it. I was once a kind of oracle to Mr. W[esley]. I judged him to be much under the power of his *own spirit*. To this was owing the false censure which he published against the mystics, as enemies to good works, pp. 128, 130. His letter is such a juvenile composition of emptiness and pertness as is below the character of any man who had been serious in religion for half a month. It was not ability but necessity that put his pen into his hand. He had preached much against my books and forbid his people the use of them, and for a cover of all this he promised, from time to time, to write against them: therefore an answer was to be made at all adventures. He and the Pope conceive the same reasons for condemning the mystery revealed by Jacob Boehme.'[a]

[a] p. 190.

[99] London, 1756.

[1] *A Collection of Letters on the Most Interesting and Important Subjects, and on Several Occasions* (London, 1760). A footnote can do little more than indicate the grounds and occasion of this recrudescence of hostilities. JW's *Letter to the Rev. Mr. Law*, which some even of his intimate circle had considered unwise, had been written in the belief that Law's Boehmenite mysticism carried the same pastoral dangers as the Moravian 'stillness' JW had so long opposed, and was implicitly damaging to the sacramental and other virtues of institutional religion, for which, as a very young man, Law himself had made exalted claims. The same considerations led JW to compound the offence by including an *Extract* from the *Letter* in his *Preservative against Unsettled Notions in Religion.* Law made no public reply to JW but did not spare him in private correspondence to disciples and friends, and permitted two of his followers, Ward and Langcake, to publish many of these letters, cut, bowdlerized, and restitched, in the *Collection of Letters.* It was this publication which now stung JW into open reply. More generally the running warfare between them (ended by Law's death in 1761) clearly owed much to the mutual incomprehension of two utterly different men, sustaining entirely contrasting life-styles, though both engaged in holding together the doctrines of justification and sanctification according to their lights. JW's contact with Law had been made only in Law's second phase, when he became preoccupied with Christian Perfection; and he was deeply and permanently influenced by it. The disasters in Georgia, however, followed by conversion, convinced JW that he had found an impulse which was lacking in Law's burdensome ethical teaching, and this led to his first controversy in 1738 with Law (whom he never met again). Subsequently, Law deepened his own position by the study of Boehme, from whose influence JW was glad to have escaped, and with the Paracelsian intellectual setting of whose doctrines (as with that of Oetinger) he had no patience. The mutual contempt which developed between the two should not obscure the fact that JW went on republishing Law's works all his life and required the boys of Kingswood School, not merely to read, but to translate William Law's *A Practical Treatise upon Christian Perfection* (London, 1726) and *A Serious Call to a Devout and Holy Life* (London, 1729). For the question generally, see J. B. Green, *John Wesley and William Law* (London, 1945); E. W. Baker, *A Herald of the Evangelical Revival* (London, 1948); A. K. Walker, *William Law. His Life and Work* (London, 1973); *WHS* 37 (1969–70):78-82, 113-17, 143-50.

Of the latter, he gives this account. 'The pamphlet you sent is worse than no advice at all, but infinitely beyond Mr. Wesley's Babylonish *Address to the Clergy*, almost all of which is empty babble, fitter for an old *Grammarian* that was grown *blear-eyed* in mending dictionaries than for one who had tasted of the powers of the world to come.'[b]

I leave others to judge whether an answer to that letter be quite needless or no, and whether there be anything *substantial* in it; but certainly there is something *argumentative*. The very queries relating to Jacob's philosophy are arguments, though not in form, and perhaps most of them will be thought conclusive arguments by impartial readers. Let these likewise judge if there are not arguments in it (whether conclusive or no) relating to that entirely new system of divinity which he has *revealed* to the world.

It is true that Mr. Law, whom I love and reverence *now*, was *once* 'a kind of oracle to me'. He thinks I am still 'under the power of my *own spirit*', as opposed to the Spirit of God. If I am, yet my censure of the mystics is not at all owing to this but to my reverence for the oracles of God, which, while I was fond of them, I regarded less and less, till at length, finding I could not follow both, I exchanged the mystic writers for the scriptural.

It is sure, in exposing the philosophy of Boehme, I use ridicule as well as argument; and yet I trust I have, by the grace of God, been in some measure 'serious in religion', not 'half a month' only, but ever since I was six years old, which is now about half a century. I do not know that the Pope has condemned him at all, or that he has any reason so to do. My reason is this and no other: I think he contradicts Scripture, reason, and himself, and that he has seduced many unwary souls from the Bible way of salvation. A strong conviction of this, and a desire to guard others against that dangerous seduction, laid me under *a necessity* of writing that letter. I was under no other necessity, though I doubt not but Mr. Law *heard* I was and very seriously *believed* it. I very rarely mention his books in public, nor are they in the way of one in an hundred of those whom he terms 'my people', meaning, I suppose, the people called Methodists. I had therefore no temptation, any more than power, to 'forbid the use' of them to the Methodists in general. Whosoever informed Mr. Law of this wanted either ability or integrity.[2]

[b] P. 198.

[2] *Works* (1774) repeats this phrase, which is altered in the errata and in Wesley's manuscript notes in his own copy to 'either sense or honesty', an alteration of the text as found in the *London Chronicle* itself.

He is so deeply displeased with the *Address to the Clergy* because it speaks strongly in favour of learning. But still, if *this* part of it is only 'fit for an old *Grammarian,* grown *blear-eyed* in mending dictionaries', it will not follow that '*almost all* of it is mere empty babble'; for a large part of it much more strongly insists on a single eye and a clean heart. Heathen philosophers may term this 'empty babble', but let not Christians either account or call it so!

Wed. 17. The room at St. Just was quite full at five, and God gave us a parting blessing. At noon I preached on the cliff near Penzance, where no one now gives an uncivil word. Here I procured an account from [an] eyewitness of what happened the 27th of last month. A round pillar, narrowest at bottom, of a whitish colour, rose out of the sea near Mousehole and reached the clouds. One who was riding over the strand from Marazion to Penzance saw it stand for a short space and then move swiftly toward her, till the skirt of it touching her, the horse threw her and ran away. It had a strong sulphurous smell. It dragged with it abundance of sand and pebbles from the shore and then went over the land, carrying with it corn, furze, or whatever it found in its way. It was doubtless a kind of water-spout—but a water-spout on land, I believe, is seldom seen.

The storm drove us into the house at Newlyn also. Thursday 18. As we rode from thence, in less than half an hour we were wet to the skin. But when we came to Penhale the rain ceased, and the people flocking from all parts, we had a comfortable opportunity together. About six I preached near Helston.[3] The rain stopped till I had done, and soon after was as violent as before.

Fri. 19. I rode to Illogan. We had heavy rain before I began but scarce any while I was preaching. I learned several other particulars here relating to the water-spout. It was seen near Mousehole an hour before sunset. About sunset, it began travelling over the land, tearing up all the furze and shrubs it met. Near an hour after sunset, it passed (at the rate of four or five miles an hour) across Mr. Harris's[4] fields in Camborne, sweeping the ground as it went, about twenty yards diameter at

[3] Orig., 'Helstone'.

[4] See Sept. 16, 1744, n. 95 (20:40 in this edn.).

bottom and broader and broader up to the clouds. It made a noise like thunder, took up eighteen stacks of corn with a large haystack and the stones whereon it stood, and scattered them all abroad (but it was quite dry), and then passed over the cliff into the sea.

Sat. 20. In the evening I took my old stand in the main street at Redruth. A multitude of people, rich and poor, calmly attended. So is the roughest become one of the quietest towns in England.

Sun. 21. I preached in the same place at eight. Mr. C[ooper][5] of St. Cubert preached at the church both morning and afternoon, and strongly confirmed what I had spoken. At one, the day being mild and calm, we had the largest congregation of all. But it rained all the time I was preaching at Gwennap. We concluded the day with a love-feast, at which James Roberts, a tinner of St. Ives, related how God had dealt with his soul. He was one of the first society in St. Ives but soon relapsed into his old sin, drunkenness, and wallowed in it for two years, during which time he headed the mob who pulled down the preaching-house.[6] Not long after, he was standing with his partner, at Edward May's shop, when the preacher went by. His partner said, 'I will tell him I am a Methodist.' 'Nay', said Edward, 'your speech will bewray you.' James felt the word as a sword, thinking in himself, 'So does *my* speech now bewray *me!*' He turned and hastened home, fancying he heard the devil stepping after him all the way. For forty hours, he never closed his eyes nor tasted either meat or drink. He was then at his wit's end and went to the window, looking to drop into hell instantly, when he heard those words, 'I will be merciful to thy unrighteousness; thy sins and iniquities will I remember no more.'[7] All his load was gone, and he has now for many years walked worthy of the gospel.

Mon. 22. I preached at Penryn in the evening. It rained before and after, but not while I was preaching. While we were at prayer a sheet of light seemed to fill the yard, and *the voice of the Lord* was heard over our heads. This fixed the impression they had received upon the minds of many—as if it had said in express terms, 'Prepare to meet thy God!'[8]

On Wednesday evening, having (over and above meeting the societies) preached thirty times in eleven days, I found myself a

[5] Samuel Cooper; see above, Sept. 8, 1760, n. 85.
[6] See Apr. 5, 1744 (20:20-21 in this edn.).
[7] Cf. Heb. 8:12.
[8] Amos 4:12.

little exhausted, but a day's rest set me up. So on Friday 26, I preached at noon again near Liskeard. In the afternoon we had rain and wind enough, and when we came to Saltash no boat would venture out, so we were obliged to take up our lodgings there.

Sat. 27. Finding there was no hope of passing here, the wind being as high as ever, we determined to ride round by the *new bridge*.[9] The rain still fell on either side, but for near twenty miles we had not one drop and not a considerable shower all day. Soon after four in the afternoon, we came safe to Plymouth Dock.

I had but a melancholy prospect here, finding most of the people dead as stones. And when I took an account of the society, only thirty-four out of seventy were left. At seven in the evening and at five in the morning, I strongly exhorted them to return to God. At eight I did the same, and at five in the afternoon, and God made his word as an hammer. At the meeting of the society likewise, strong and effectual words were given me. Many were convinced afresh, many backsliders cut to the heart. And I left once more between sixty and seventy members.

Mon. 29. Being invited by the minister of Week St. Mary[10] to preach in his church, I crossed over the country and came thither about four in the afternoon. The congregation was large, considering the weather, and quite attentive and unconcerned. Hence I rode on to Mill House, and the next day to Cullompton where, finding the congregation waiting, I began preaching without delay and felt no weariness or want of strength till I had delivered my message to them.

Wednesday, October 1. After preaching at five, I examined the society and found them more alive to God than I had done for many years. About one I preached at Halberton,[11] and at Tiverton in the evening. The next morning I rode to Maiden Down, where the congregation was waiting for me. About noon I preached at

[9] The New Bridge at Gunnislake built, in fact, *c.* 1520. Charles Henderson and H. Coates, *Old Cornish Bridges and Streams* (London, 1928), p. 30 (photograph, plate 26).

[10] Orig., 'Mary Week'. The minister was John Turner; see June 18, 1745, n. 82 (20:69 in this edn.).

[11] Halberton, a parish 3½ miles east of Tiverton, provides in miniature an example of JW's familiar method. He now arrived a decade after the work had been begun by other preachers. Already a firm support for the society had been provided by the parents of Mrs. Anne Bale (1734–1806), who received the preachers 'and as soon as possible, provided a place, which they made into a preaching-house' and registered it as a Dissenting chapel. Subsequently the Bales themselves provided regular hospitality and a base for JW in his visits; cf. Yarm (above, July 6, 1759, n. 10). *Methodist Magazine* 31 (1808):509; *Wesleyan Methodist Magazine* 66 (1843):796-97.

Taunton. The rain lessened the congregation at Bridgwater, a dead, uncomfortable place at best. About seven, we set out thence for Bawdrip[12] in as dark a night as I ever saw. But God 'gave his angels charge over us', and we 'dashed not our foot against a stone'.[13]

I was surprised to see a congregation at five in the morning, to whom I spoke with much enlargement of heart. About one, I preached at Shepton Mallet, and about seven in the evening at Bristol.

Sun. 5. I perceived by the liveliness of the people that Mr. Gilbert's[14] labour had not been in vain. But I found some exercise too. And this is always to be expected among a large body of people; it being certain that as 'all men have not faith,'[15] so all believers have not wisdom.

Sun. 12. I visited the classes at Kingswood. Here only there is no increase. And yet where was there such a prospect till that weak man, John C[ennick],[16] confounded the poor people with strange doctrines? O what mischief may be done by one that means well! We see no end of it to this day.

In the afternoon I had appointed the children to meet at Bristol whose parents were of the society. Thirty of them came today, and above fifty more on the Sunday and Thursday following. About half of these I divided into four classes, two of boys and two of girls, and appointed proper leaders to meet them separate. I met them all together twice a week. And it was not long before God began to touch some of their hearts.

On Tuesday and Wednesday, I visited some of the societies in the country. On Thursday, I returned to Bristol, and in the afternoon preached a charity sermon in Newgate for the use of the poor prisoners.[17] What a change is in this place since I knew it

12 Orig., 'Baderipp'. Bawdrip was a small parish 3½ miles north-east from Bridgwater.

13 Cf. Ps. 91:11-12.

14 Nicholas Gilbert, said to be a son of Nathaniel Gilbert of Antigua, became an itinerant in 1744 (see above, Jan. 17, 1758, n. 29; Tyerman, *John Wesley*, 2:299). 'He was a man of deep piety, and possessed a sound and clear understanding in the things of God. A man of genuine simplicity, of great seriousness and integrity' (Atmore, *Memorial*, p. 156). Charles Wesley, writing that 'I look upon you as my brother, my son,' fought to keep him from unchurchly acts when three preachers gave the Sacrament at Norwich in 1760 (Jackson, *Charles Wesley*, 2:182-83). He died young at Bristol in 1763 (see below, Apr. 19, 1763).

15 2 Thess. 3:2.

16 Identified in *Works* (1774).

17 The *Bristol Chronicle* reported that at 3 p.m. on the 16th, a charity sermon was preached in Newgate for the relief of the debtors, and again on Friday 24th.

first! (1) Every part of it, above stairs and below, even *the pit* wherein the felons are confined at night is as clean and sweet as a gentleman's house, it being a rule that every prisoner wash and thoroughly cleanse his apartment twice a week. (2) Here is no fighting or brawling. If any think himself aggrieved, the cause is immediately referred to the keeper, who hears the contending parties face to face and decides the affair at once. (3) The usual grounds of quarreling are taken away, for it is very rarely that anyone cheats or wrongs another, as being sure, if anything of this kind is discovered, to be more closely confined. (4) Here is no drunkenness suffered, however advantageous it might be to the keeper and tapster. (5) Nor any whoredom, the women prisoners being narrowly observed and kept apart from the men, and no women of the town being now admitted, no, not at any price. (6) All possible care is taken to prevent idleness. Those who are willing to work at their callings are provided with tools and materials, partly by the keeper, who gives them credit at a moderate profit, partly by the alms occasionally given, which are divided with the utmost impartiality. Accordingly, at this time a shoemaker, a tailor, a brazier, and a coach-maker are all employed. (7) On the Lord's Day, they neither work nor play but dress themselves as clean as they can to attend the public service in the chapel, at which every person under the roof is present. None is excused unless sick, in which case he is provided both with proper advice and medicines. (8) To assist them in spirituals as well as temporals, they have a sermon preached every Sunday and Thursday. And a large Bible is chained on one side of the chapel, which any of the prisoners may read. By the blessing of God on these regulations, the whole prison has a new face. Nothing offends either the eye or ear, and the whole has the appearance of a quiet, serious family.[18]

On the three following days, I spoke severally to the members of the society. As many of them increase in worldly goods, the great danger I apprehend now is their relapsing into the spirit of the world. And then their religion is but a dream.

Wed. 22. Being informed that some neighbouring gentlemen had declared they would 'apprehend the next preacher who came to Pensford',[19] I rode over to give them the meeting. But none

[18] Wesley repeated this description of the improvements in Bristol Newgate in a letter to the *London Chronicle* on Jan. 2, 1761 (see below); *Works* (1774) omits the description here.

[19] Preaching at Pensford had been made impossible for nearly twenty years by the hostility of incumbent and mob (see Apr. 23 and May 7, 1739, and Mar. 19, 1742;

appeared. The house was more than filled with deeply attentive hearers. It seems the time is come at length for the Word of God to take root here also.

Fri. 24. I visited the French prisoners at Knowle and found many of them almost naked again. In hopes of provoking others to jealousy, I made another collection for them and ordered the money to be laid out in linen and waistcoats, which were given to those that were most in want.[20]

Sat. 25. King George was gathered to his fathers.[21] When will England have a better prince?

Many of us agreed to observe Friday the 31st as a day of fasting and prayer for the blessing of God upon our nation and in particular on his present Majesty.[22] We met at five, at nine, at one, and at half-hour past eight. I expected to be a little tired, but was more lively after twelve at night than I was at six in the morning.

Saturday, November 1. I had the pleasure of spending a little time with that venerable man, Mr. Walker of Truro.[23] I fear his physicians do not understand his case. If he recovers, it must be through an Almighty Physician.

Mon. 3. I left Bristol and took Bath, Bradford, and Frome, in my way to Salisbury, where I spent a day with much satisfaction. Friday 7, I preached about nine at Andover to a few dead stones, at one in Whitchurch, and in the evening at Basingstoke. The next day, Saturday 8, I was once more brought safe to London.

I spent about a fortnight, as usual, in examining the society, a heavy, but necessary, labour.

Mon. 17. I sent the following letter.

19:50-51, 55, 257 in this edn.). It had lately been resumed on the invitation of William Wait of Belton (1725–1806), who had been prevented from attending Methodist preaching at Kingswood, nine miles away, shortly after his marriage in 1759, by a riding accident involving his wife on the return journey. The Waits provided generous hospitality to the preachers, and were soon instrumental in getting a chapel built at Pensford; *Methodist Magazine* 131 (1908):130-34.

[20] The *Bristol Chronicle* (Oct. 23, 1760), p. 243, advertised a charity sermon by JW on their behalf for the following Sunday. For JW's earlier efforts for them see, above, Oct. 15, 1759, and n. 77.

[21] George II died suddenly, between 7 and 8 a.m., from a rupture of the right ventricle of the heart as he was preparing to go far a walk in the gardens. JW's comment reflects rather the shock of the event than the country traditions in which he had been bred. George III was a monarch much more to his taste.

[22] The day apparently was not designated as a national fast day.

[23] After prolonged infirmity, Samuel Walker died on July 19, 1761.

To the Editor of Lloyd's Evening Post

Nov. 17, 1760

Sir,[24]

In your last paper we had a letter from a very angry gentleman (though he says he had 'put himself into *as good humour* as possible') who *personates* a clergyman but is, I presume, in reality a retainer to the theatre. He is very warm against the people vulgarly termed 'Methodists'—'ridiculous impostors', 'religious buffoons', as he styles them; 'Saint Errants' (a pretty and quaint phrase) full of 'inconsiderateness, madness, melancholy, enthusiasm', teaching a 'knotty and unintelligible *system*' of religion, yea, a 'contradictory or self-contradicting'; nay, 'a mere illusion', a 'destructive scheme and of pernicious consequence', since 'an *hypothesis* is a very slippery foundation to hazard our *all* upon.'

Methinks the gentleman has a little mistaken his character; he seems to have exchanged the sock for the buskin. But, be this as it may, general charges prove nothing; let us come to particulars. Here they are. 'The basis of Methodism is the *Grace of Assurance*' (excuse a little impropriety of expression), '*Regeneration* being only a preparative to it'. Truly this is somewhat 'knotty and unintelligible'. I will endeavour to help him out. The fundamental doctrine of the people called Methodists is, Whosoever will be saved, before all things it is necessary that he hold the true faith: the faith which works by love, which, by means of the love of God and our neighbour, produces both inward and outward holiness. This faith is an evidence of things not seen; and he that thus believes is regenerate, or born of God. And he has the witness in himself (call it *assurance,* or what you please). The Spirit itself witnesses with his spirit that he is a child of God: 'from what Scripture' every one of these propositions 'is collected' any common concordance will show. 'This is the true portraiture of Methodism,' so called. 'A religion superior to this' (the love of God and man) none can 'enjoy', either in time or in eternity.

But the Methodists do not hold 'good works meritorious'. No, neither does ours or any other Protestant church. But meantime they hold it is their bounden duty, as they have time, to do good unto all men, and they know the day is coming wherein God will reward every man according to his works.

But they 'act with sullenness and sourness, and account innocent gaiety and cheerfulness a crime almost as heinous as sacrilege'. Who does? Name the men. I know them not and there-

[24] At the head of this letter as originally printed appeared the quotation: 'Spirat tragicum satis, et feliciter audet,' 'He has some tragic inspiration and is happy in his ventures.' Horace, *Epistles* II.i.166 (Loeb).

fore doubt the fact, though it is very possible you account that kind of gaiety innocent which I account both foolish and sinful.

I know none who denies that true religion, that is love, the love of God and our neighbour, 'elevates our spirits and renders our minds cheerful and serene'. It must, if it be accompanied, as we believe it always is, with peace and joy in the Holy Ghost, and if it produces a conscience void of offence toward God and toward man.

But they 'preach up religion only to accomplish a *lucrative* design, to *fleece* their hearers, to accumulate *wealth*, to *rob* and *plunder*, which they esteem meritorious'. We deny the fact. Who is able to prove it? Let the affirmer produce his witnesses, or retract.

This is the sum of your correspondent's charge, not one article of which can be proved. But whether it can or no, 'We have made them', says he, 'a theatrical scoff and the common jest and scorn of every chorister in the street.' It may be so, but whether you have done well herein may still admit of a question. However, you cannot but wish 'we had some formal court of judicature erected (happy Portugal and Spain!) to take cognizance of such matters.' Nay, *cur optas quod habes?*[25] Why do you wish for what you have already? The court is erected; the holy, devout playhouse is become 'the house of mercy'![26] And does take cognizance hereof 'of all pretenders to sanctity, and happily furnishes us with a discerning spirit to distinguish betwixt right and wrong'. But I do not stand to their sentence; I appeal to Scripture and reason, and by these alone consent to be judged. I am, sir,

Your humble servant,
John Wesley

Sat. 22. I was obliged to trouble him with another letter, as follows:

Sir,

Just as I had finished the letter published in your last Friday's paper, four tracts came to my hands: one wrote, or procured to be wrote, by Mrs. Downes;[27] one by a clergyman in the county of

[25] Horace, *Satires*, I.iii.126. Translated here by JW himself.

[26] Cf. Ps. 5:7. JW is of course alluding to this title as applied to the Court of Inquisition, but as the first sentence of the letter shows, he had reason to be irked by the theatre. In 1760, Samuel Foote (1720–77), described by the *D.N.B.* as 'actor and dramatist', and by Tyerman as 'the inimitable zany', published and staged his attack on Methodism in *The Minor; A Comedy* (Tyerman, *John Wesley*, 2:166). This piece, a failure in Dublin, succeeded in London (though public opposition led to the alteration of several passages), and it was followed in the press (though not on stage) by *The Methodist, a Comedy; being a continuation and completion of the plan of the "The Minor; A Comedy" written by Mr. Foote* (3rd edn., London, 1761), actually the work of Israel Pottinger.

[27] Mrs. Anne Downes (née Balguy) was the widow of John Downes (*c.* 1691–1759), rector of St. Michael, Wood Street (1746–59), and lecturer of St. Mary-le-Bow, who had

Durham;[28] the third by a gentleman of Cambridge;[29] and the fourth by a member (I suppose, dignitary) of the Church of Rome.[30] How gladly would I leave all these to themselves and let them say just what they please!—as my day is far spent, and my taste for controversy is utterly lost and gone. But this would not be doing justice to the world, who might take silence for a proof of guilt. I shall therefore say a word concerning each. I may, perhaps, some time say more to one or two of them.

The letter which goes under Mrs. Downes's name scarce deserves any notice at all, as there is nothing extraordinary in it but an extraordinary degree of virulence and scurrility. Two things only I remark concerning it (which I suppose the writer of it knew as well as me): (1) that my letter to Mr. Downes was both wrote and printed *before* Mr. Downes *died;* (2) that when I said *Tibi parvula res est* (your ability is small),[31] I had no view to his fortune, which I knew nothing of, but, as I there expressly say, to his wit, sense, and talents, as a writer.

The tract wrote by the gentleman in the north is far more bulky than this. But it is more considerable for its bulk than for its matter, being little more than a dull repetition of what was published some years ago, in *The Enthusiasm of the Methodists and Papists compared.*[32] I do not find the author adds anything new; unless we may bestow that epithet on a sermon annexed to his address, which, I presume,

published *Methodism Examined and Exposed* (London, 1759), to which JW had replied in *A Letter to the Rev. Mr. Downes* (London, 1759; 9:350-66 in this edn.). Mrs. Downes's tract says that 'there are four large tribes or families [of Methodists]: the Wheslers, the Whiflers, the Madmen and the Romancers (so called from their leaders, Wesley, Whitefield, Madan, and Romaine).'

28 Alexander Jephson, ordained deacon 1716 and priest 1718, claimed to be both B.A. and M.A., but from what university is unclear. He was rector of Crayke, Co. Durham, 1735 till his death in 1768. The tract was *A Friendly and Compassionate Address to all Serious and Well-disposed Methodists; in which their Principal Errors concerning the Doctrine of the New Birth . . . are largely displayed* (London, 1760).

29 John Green (*c.* 1707–79), scholar of St. John's College, Cambridge, 1724; B.D., 1739; M.A., 1731; D.D., 1749; fellow of St. John's, 1731–50; master of Corpus, 1750–64; Vice-Chancellor, 1757–58; Regius Professor of Divinity and rector of Somersham, 1749–56; chaplain to King, 1753–56; dean of Lincoln, 1756; Bishop of Lincoln, 1761–79; prebendary of St. Paul's 1771–79. His tract, signed Academicus, was entitled *The Principles and Practices of the Methodists Considered* (London, 1760).

30 A tract by Richard Challoner, *A Caveat against the Methodists, Showing how Unsafe it is for any Christian to Join Himself to their Society or to Adhere to their Teachers* (London, 1760; and five later edns.). E. H. Burton states both that it was by Richard Challoner and that it was written by Robert Manning; see Burton, *The Life and Times of Bishop Challoner, 1691–1781* (London, 1909), 2:17, 333-34. JW replied to this tract (see below, Feb. 19, 1761).

31 Horace, *Epistles,* I.xviii.29. In its original context, the quotation in fact signifies, 'Your means are but trifling' (Loeb).

32 By George Lavington, Bishop of Exeter, *The Enthusiasm of Methodists and Papists Compared,* in 3 parts (London, 1749–51).

will do neither good nor harm. So I leave the Durham gentleman, with Mrs. Downes, to himself and his admirers.

The author of the letter to Mr. Berridge is a more considerable writer. In many things I wholly agree with him, though not in admiring Dr. Taylor. But there is a bitterness even in him which I should not have expected in a gentleman and a scholar. So in the very first page I read, 'The Church, which most of your *graceless fraternity* have deserted'. Were the fact true (which it is not), yet is the expression to be commended? Surely Dr. G[reen] himself thinks it is not. I am sorry too for the unfairness of his quotations. For instance, he cites me[c] as speaking of 'faith shed abroad in men's hearts like lightning'. *Faith shed abroad* in men's hearts! I never used such an expression in my life: I do not talk after this rate. Again, he quotes, as from me[d] (so I presume, *Mr. W*[esley] means), 'A believer[33] does not pretend to add the least to what Christ has done.' But be these words whose they may, they are none of mine. I never spoke, wrote, no, nor read them before. Once more, is it well judged for any writer to show such an utter contempt of his opponents as you affect to do with regard to the whole body of people vulgarly termed 'Methodists'? 'You may keep up (say you) a little bush-fighting in controversy. You may skirmish a while with your feeble body of irregulars. But you must never trust to your skill in reasoning.'[e] Upon this I would ask, (1) If these are such poor, silly creatures, why does so wise a man set his wit to them? 'Shall the king of Israel go out against a flea?'[34] (2) If it should happen that any one of these silly bush-fighters steps out into the plain, engages hand to hand, and foils this champion by mere dint of reason, will not his defeat be so much the more shameful as it was more unexpected? But I say the less at present, not only because Mr. Berridge is able to answer for himself, but because the title-page bids me expect a letter more immediately addressed to myself.

The last tract, entitled, *A Caveat against the Methodists*, is, in reality, a Caveat against the Church of England; or rather, against all the churches in Europe who dissent from the Church of Rome. Nor do I apprehend the writer to be any more disgusted at the Methodists than at Protestants of every denomination, as he cannot but judge it equally unsafe to join to any society but that of Rome. Accordingly, all his arguments are levelled at the Reformed churches in general, and conclude just as well if you put the word 'Protestant' throughout in the place of the word 'Methodist'.

[c] P. 53. [d] P. 57. [e] P. 77.

---

[33] Orig., 'behaviour'.
[34] Cf. 1 Sam. 24:14.

Although, therefore, the author borrows my name to wound those who suspect nothing less, yet I am no more concerned to refute him than any other Protestant in England; and still the less, as those arguments are refuted over and over in books which are still common among us.

But is it possible any Protestants, nay, Protestant clergymen, should buy these tracts to give away? Is then the introducing popery the only way to overthrow Methodism? If they know this and choose popery as the smaller evil of the two, they are consistent with themselves. But if they do not intend this, I wish them more seriously to consider what they do.

I am, sir, your humble servant,
John Wesley

Mon. 24. I visited as many as I could of the sick. How much better is it, when it can be done, to *carry* relief to the poor than to *send* it! And that both for our own sake and theirs. For *theirs,* as it is so much more comfortable to them, and as we may then assist them in spirituals as well as temporals. And for *our own,* as it is far more apt to soften our heart and to make us *naturally care* for each other.

Monday, December 1, I went in the machine to Canterbury. In going and returning, I read over *The Christian Philosopher.*[35] It is a very extraordinary book, containing, among many (as some would be apt to term them) wild thoughts, several fine and striking observations not to be found in any other treatise.

Wed. 3. I rode to Dover. Who would have expected to find here some of the best singers in England? I found likewise what was better still, a serious, earnest people. There was a remarkable blessing among them, both in the evening and the morning, so that I did not regret the having been wet to the skin in my way to them.

Fri. 12. Having as far as Hyde Park Corner to go, I took a coach for part of the way, ordering the man to stop anywhere at the end of Piccadilly, next the Haymarket. He stopped exactly at the door of one of our friends, whose mother, above ninety years old, had

[35] It seems fairly certain that the work here mentioned is that by Cotton Mather (1663–1728), with the sub-title, *A Collection of the Best Discoveries in Nature, with Religious Improvements* (London, 1721), of which Wesley purchased a copy this year (now at Kingswood School, Bath). This volume he mentions as one of the sources of his *Survey of the Wisdom of God in the Creation* (Pref., §2). He also knew, however, Nicholas Robinson's work, *The Christian Philosopher; A Divine Essay of the Principles of Man's Universal Redemption* [Book 1] (London, 1741); see above, Feb. 10, 1757, n. 25; cf. Feb. 7, 1771.

long desired to see me, though I knew it not. She was exceedingly comforted and could not tell how to praise God enough for giving her the desire of her soul.

We observed Friday the 19th as a day of fasting and prayer for our king and country and the success of the gospel. And part of the answer immediately followed, in the remarkable increase of believers and in the strengthening of those who had before attained that precious faith 'unto all patience and long-suffering with joyfulness'.[36]

Sat. 20. In the evening I hastened back from Snowsfields to meet the penitents[37] (a congregation which I wish always to meet myself), and walked thither again at five in the morning. Blessed be God, I have no reason or pretence to *spare myself* yet. I preached a charity sermon in West Street Chapel both morning and afternoon. But many were obliged to go away, finding it impossible to get in. Is it novelty still which draws these from all parts? No, but the mighty power of God.

Today I sent the following letter:

For the Editor of Lloyd's Evening Post
To Mr. T. H., alias E. L., etc. etc.

What, my good friend again?[38] Only a little disguised with a new name and a few scraps of Latin? I hoped, indeed, you had been pretty well satisfied before, but since you desire to hear a little farther from me, I will add a few words and endeavour to set our little controversy in a still clearer light.

Last month you publicly attacked the people called Methodists, without either fear or wit. You charged them with 'madness, enthusiasm, self-contradiction, imposture', and what not? I considered each charge and, I conceive, refuted it to the satisfaction of all indifferent persons. You renewed the attack, not by *proving* anything, but *affirming* the same things over and over. I

[36] Col. 1:11.

[37] The Conference of 1744 had divided the Methodist people 'into the United Societies, the Bands, the Select Societies, and the Penitents. . . . The United Societies (which are the largest of all) consisted of awakened persons. Part of these, who were supposed to have had remission of sin, were more closely united in the Bands. Those in Bands, who seemed to walk in the light of God, composed the Select Societies. Those of them who had made shipwreck of the faith, met apart as penitents.' *John Bennet's Copy of the Minutes of . . . 1744, 1745, 1747, and 1748*, Publication 1 of the Wesley Historical Society (London, 1896), p. 19.

[38] JW here continues a controversy he had commenced in *Lloyd's Evening Post* on November 17, and in the *London Magazine* December 12. See Telford, 4:109-24.

replied and, without taking notice of the dull, low scurrility either of the first or second letter, confined myself to the merits of the cause and cleared away the dirt you had thrown.

You now heap together ten paragraphs more, most of which require very little answer. In the first, you say, 'Your *foolishness* is become the wonder and admiration of the public.' In the second, 'The *public* blushes for you, till you give a better solution to the articles demanded of you.' In the third, you cite my words; I still maintain 'the Bible, with the Liturgy and Homilies of our Church, and do not espouse any other principles but what are consonant to the Book of Common Prayer.' You keenly answer, 'Granted, Mr. Methodist—But whether or no you *would not* espouse other principles, if you durst, is evident from some *innovations* you have already introduced, which I shall attempt to *prove* in the subsequent part of my answer.' Indeed you won't. You neither *prove* nor *attempt* to prove that I '*would* espouse other principles if I durst'. However, you give me a deadly thrust—'You falsify the first article of the *Athanasian* Creed.' But how so? Why, I said, 'The fundamental doctrine of the people called Methodists is, Whosoever will be saved, before all things it is necessary that he hold the true faith.' Sir, shall I tell you a secret? It was for the readers of *your* class that I changed the hard word 'Catholic' into an easier.

In the fourth paragraph you say, 'Did you never use that phrase, "the grace of assurance"?' Never, that I remember, either in preaching or writing. Both your ears and eyes have been very *unhappy* if they informed you I did; and how many soever look either sorrowful or joyful, that will not prove the contrary. 'But produce your texts.' What, for a phrase I never use? 'I pray you, have me excused.'[39] But (as I said before) 'from what Scripture every one of my propositions is collected, any common concordance will show.' To save you trouble, I will for once point out those Scriptures. 'Whosoever will be saved must believe'—Mark 16:16; Acts 16:31. This 'faith works by love'—Gal. 5:6. It is 'an evidence of things not seen'—Heb. 11:1. 'He that believes is born of God'—1 John 5:1. 'He has the witness in himself'—ver. 10. 'The Spirit itself witnesses with his spirit that he is a child of God'—Rom. 8:15.

In the fifth, you say, 'You embrace any shift to twist words to your own meaning.' This is saying just nothing. Anyone may *say* this of anyone. To *prove* it is another point. In the sixth, you say, 'No Protestant divine ever taught your doctrine of assurance.' I hope you know no better, but 'tis strange you should not. Did you never see Bishop Hall's works? Was not he a Protestant divine? Was not

[39] Cf. Luke 14:18, 19.

Mr. Perkins? Bolton? Dr. Sibbs? Dr. Preston? Archbishop Leighton? Inquire a little farther and don't run thus hand over head, asserting you know not what. By 'assurance' (if we *must* use the expression) I mean 'a confidence which a man hath in God, that by the merits of Christ his sins are forgiven, and he reconciled to the favour of God'. Stop! Do not run your head into a noose again. These are the words of the Homily.

In the seventh, you grant 'that works are not *meritorious* unless accompanied with faith'. No, nor then neither. But pray don't talk of this any more till you know the difference between 'meritorious' and 'rewardable'; otherwise your ignorance will cause you to blunder on, without shame and without end.

In your eighth, you throw out a hard word, which somebody has helped you to, *thaumaturg*—what is it?—about *lay-preachers*. When you have answered the arguments in the *Farther Appeal to Men of Reason and Religion*,[40] I will say something more upon that head.

In the ninth, you say something no way material about the houses at Bristol, Kingswood, and Newcastle; and, in the last, you give me a fair challenge to a 'personal dispute'. Not so; you have fallen upon me in public, and to the public I appeal. Let all men, not any single umpire, judge whether I have not refuted your charge and cleared the people called Methodists from the foul aspersions which, without why or wherefore, you had thrown upon them. Let all my countrymen judge which of us have spoken the words of truth and soberness. Which has *reason* on his side? And which has treated the other with a *temper* suitable to the gospel?

If the general voice of mankind gives it against you, I hope you will be henceforth less flippant with your pen. I assure you, as little as you think of it, the Methodists are not such fools as you suppose. But their desire is to live peaceably with all men, and none desires this more than

John Wesley

About the close of this year I received a remarkable account from Ireland:

When Miss E—— was about fifteen, she frequently heard the preaching of the Methodists, so called. And though it made no deep impression, yet she retained a love for them ever after. About nineteen she was seized with a lingering illness. She then began to wrestle with God in prayer, that his love might be shed abroad in her heart. Then, said she, how freely could I give up all that is dear

[40] Published by Wesley in three parts (London, 1745); see 11:95-325 in this edn.

to me in this world! And from this very time she did not expect, nor indeed desire, to recover, but only to be cleansed from sin and to go to Christ.

Some who visited her said, 'O Miss, you need not fear; your innocence will bring you to heaven.' She earnestly replied, 'Unless the merits of Christ plead for me, and his nature be imparted to me, I can never enter there.' And she was incessantly breaking out into these and the like expressions: 'O that I knew my sins were forgiven! O that I was born again! My one wish is, to know God and to be with him eternally.'

She frequently sung or repeated that verse:

> O that he would himself impart,
> And fix his Eden in my heart,
> The sense of sin forgiven!
> How would I then throw off my load
> And walk delightfully with God,
> And follow Christ to heaven![41]

She had now an earnest desire to see some of the Methodists, and spoke to several, to ask some of those in Tullamore to visit her. At length her importunity prevailed, and James Kelly[42] was sent for. On his coming in she said, 'I am exceeding glad to see you. I have had a longing desire of it this month past. I believe the power of God is with you. If I had health and strength, there should not be a sermon preached or a prayer put up in your preaching-house, but I would be there.'

I told her, I hope the Spirit of the Lord will be your present and eternal comforter. She answered, 'I can find no comfort in anything but in God alone.' While she spoke her soul was melted down. The love of God was shed abroad in her heart, the tears ran down her cheeks, and she began to rejoice in God exceedingly. Her mother, seeing this, was fully convinced that there was more in religion than she had herself experienced, and began to pray, with many tears, that God would show her his salvation. This so affected me that I could not refrain from tears myself, so we all wept and prayed and sang praise together.

On my going to her a second time, I found her truly alive to God. 'Oh', she said, 'how I have longed to see you, that we may be happy in God together. Come let us sing an hymn.' I gave out,

[41] Charles Wesley, *Hymns for the Use of Families* (1767); see George Osborn, ed., *Poetical Works of John and Charles Wesley*, 13 vols. (London, 1868–72), 7:180.

[42] On James Kelly (1726–1807), see *Methodist Magazine* (Dublin edn.) 33 (1810):413-18.

Of him that did salvation bring
I could for ever think and sing.[43]

She sung all the time with exceeding joy. Afterwards she said, 'This is a weary world, but I have almost done with it. O how I long to be gone! Some people tell me I may recover, but I do not thank them: I do not count them my friends.' On my saying occasionally, 'There is no satisfaction for sin but that which Christ has made by his precious blood,' she answered, 'That is all the satisfaction I want, and I believe he both lived and died for *me*.'

After this she gave a strict charge that none should be admitted to see her but such as could speak for God, saying, 'I do not love to have a word spoken which is not to edification. O how unsuitable to me are all things which do not tend to the glory of my God!' On her spitting a large quantity of blood, one said, You are in great pain. She answered, 'I think little of it. My blessed Redeemer suffered greater pain for *me*.'

When I stood up to go away she said, 'I now take my leave of you. Perhaps we may not meet again in this world, but I trust we shall meet in heaven. I am going to God. O may it be soon! I now feel an heaven in my soul.'

The last time I came was on Sunday, Dec. 14. Hearing she was extremely ill and wanted rest, we did not go up, but after a while began singing below. She immediately heard, sat up in bed, and insisted on our being brought into the room and singing there. Many times she repeated these words, 'Come, Lord Jesus, come quickly!' And this she continued to do till on Wednesday the 17th she resigned her soul into the hands of her dear Redeemer.

January 2, 1761, I wrote the following letter:

To the Editor of the London Chronicle

Sir,

Of all the seats of woe on this side hell, few, I suppose, exceed or even equal Newgate. If any region of horror could exceed it a few years ago, Newgate in Bristol did, so great was the filth, the stench, the misery and wickedness which shocked all who had a spark of humanity left. How was I surprised, then, when I was there a few weeks ago: (1) Every part of it, above stairs and below, even *the pit* wherein the felons are confined at night is as clean and sweet as a gentleman's house, it being now a rule that every prisoner wash and

[43] The first couplet of a hymn popular at this time and included in many hymn books, Wesleyan and other. It has been attributed to Charles Wesley, even, it appears, by George Osborn who did not include it in *Poetical Works*; *WHS* 5 (1906):183-84.

clean his apartment thoroughly twice a week. (2) Here is no fighting or brawling. If any thinks himself ill-used, the cause is immediately referred to the keeper, who hears the contending parties face to face and decides the affair at once. (3) The usual grounds of quarreling are removed. For it is very rarely that anyone cheats or wrongs another, as being sure, if anything of this kind is discovered, to be committed to a closer confinement. (4) Here is no drunkenness suffered, however advantageous it might be to the keeper as well as the tapster. (5) Nor any whoredom, the women prisoners being narrowly observed and kept separate from the men; nor is any woman of the town *now* admitted, no, not at any price. (6) All possible care is taken to prevent idleness. Those who are willing to work at their callings are provided with tools and materials, partly by the keeper, who gives them credit at a very moderate profit, partly by the alms occasionally given, which are divided with the utmost prudence and impartiality. Accordingly, at this time, among others, a shoemaker, a tailor, a brazier, and a coach-maker are working at their several trades. (7) Only on the Lord's Day, they neither work nor play but dress themselves as clean as they can to attend the public services in the chapel, at which every person under the roof is present. None is excused unless sick, in which case he is provided gratis both with advice and medicines. (8) And in order to assist them in things of the greatest concern (besides a sermon every Sunday and Thursday), they have a large Bible chained on one side of the chapel, which any of the prisoners may read. By the blessing of God on these regulations, the prison now has a new face. Nothing offends either the eye or ear, and the whole has the appearance of a quiet, serious family.[44] And does not *the Keeper of Newgate deserve to be remembered, full as well as the man of Ross?*[45] May the Lord remember him in that day! Meantime, will no one follow his example? I am, sir, your humble servant,

John Wesley

Monday, January 5. This week I wrote to the author of the *Westminster Journal*[46] as follows:

[44] A nearly identical version of the description of Newgate to this point was given above, Oct. 16, 1760.

[45] On Abel Dagge, the keeper of Newgate, see Apr. 3, 1739, n. 94 (19:46 in this edn.). John Kyrle (1637–1724), English philanthropist born at Dymock, Glos., settled on the family property at Ross-on-Wye in Herts. and spent his time and fortune building churches and hospitals. He was styled "The Man of Ross" by Alexander Pope, who admired his character and charities; see *Moral Essays,* Epistle iii, line 250.

[46] This letter, dated Jan. 12, was also published in the *London Chronicle* (Jan. 15-17, 1761), p. 61, and is a reply to a letter published in the *Westminster Journal; or New Weekly Miscellany*.

Sir,

I hope you are a person of impartiality. If so, you will not insert what is urged on one side of a question only, but likewise what is offered on the other.

Your correspondent is, doubtless, a man of sense, and he seems to write in a good humour. But he is extremely little acquainted with the persons of whom he undertakes to give an account.

There is 'gone abroad', says he, 'an ungoverned spirit of enthusiasm, propagated by knaves and embraced by fools'. Suffer me now to address the gentleman himself. Sir, you may *call* me both a knave and a fool. But *prove* me either the one or the other, if you can. 'Why, you are an enthusiast.' What do you mean by the term? A believer in Jesus Christ? An asserter of his equality with the Father and of the entire Christian revelation? Do you mean one who maintains the antiquated doctrines of the new birth and justification by faith? Then I am an enthusiast. But if you mean anything else, either prove or retract the charge.

The enthusiasm which has lately gone abroad is faith which worketh by love. Does this 'endanger government itself'? Just the reverse. Fearing God, it honours the king. It teaches all men to be subject to the higher powers, not for wrath but for conscience' sake.

But 'no power in England ought to be independent of the Supreme Power.' Most true. Yet 'the Romanists own the authority of a Pope, independent of civil government.' They do, and thereby show their ignorance of the English constitution. 'In Great Britain we have many popes, for so I must call all who have the *souls and bodies* of their followers *devoted to them.*' Call them so and welcome. But this does not touch me; nor Mr. Whitefield, Jones,[47] or Romaine; nor any whom I am acquainted with: none of us have our followers thus *devoted to us.* Those who follow the advice we constantly give are devoted to God, not man. But 'the Methodist proclaims he can bring into the field twenty-five thousand men.' What Methodist? Where and when? Prove this fact, and I will allow you I am a Turk.

'But it is said, they are all good subjects. Perhaps they are, because under a Protestant government they have all the indulgence they can wish for.' And do you seriously wish for a popish government, to abridge them of that indulgence? 'But has not a bad use been made of this? [1] Has not the *decency* of religion

[47] Thomas Jones (1729–62) of St. Saviour's, Southwark, though weak in health proved to be a powerful preacher. In 1754 he had shared in the intercession meetings at the Countess of Huntingdon's.

been perverted?' Not in the least: the decency of religion is never so well advanced as by advancing inward and outward religion together. (2) 'Have not the minds of the vulgar been darkened to a total neglect of their civil and social duties?' Just the contrary: thousands in London, as well as elsewhere, have been enlightened to understand, and prevailed on to practise those duties, as they never did before. (3) 'Has not the peace of many families been ruined?' The lost peace of many families has been restored. In others, a furious opposition to true religion has occasioned division, as our Lord foretold it would. (4) 'Have not the circumstances of many industrious tradesmen been hurt?' I believe not. I know no instance. But I know an hundred tradesmen in London who began to be industrious since they began to fear God, and their circumstances, low enough till then, are now easy and affluent.

I am almost ashamed to spend time upon these threadbare objections, which have been answered over and over. But if they are advanced again, they must be answered again, lest silence should pass for guilt.

'But how can the government distinguish between tenderness of conscience and schemes of interest?' Nothing more easy. 'They may withdraw the licences of such.' Sir, you have forgot the question. Before they withdraw them, they are to distinguish whether they are such or no. And how are they to do this? 'Oh, 'tis very easy.' So you leave them as wise as they were before.

But 'the Methodist, who pretends to be of the Church of England in forms of worship and differs from her in point of doctrine, is not, let his pretences be what they will, a member of that Church.' Alas, sir, your friends will not thank you for this. You have broke their heads sadly. Is no man of the Church, let him pretend what he will, who differs from her in point of doctrine? *Au! absecro;*[48] *cave dixeris!*[49] I know not but you may stumble upon *scandalum magnatum.*[50] But stay: you will bring them off quickly. 'A truly good man may scruple signing and swearing to articles that his mind and reason cannot approve of.' But is he a truly good man who 'does not scruple' signing and swearing to articles which he cannot approve of? However, this doth not affect *us*, for we do not differ from our Church in point of doctrine. But all do who deny

48 Terence, *Eunuch*, 656: 'Gracious goodness!' (Loeb).

49 Terence, *Brothers*, 458: 'Don't name it!' (Loeb).

50 'Libel on persons of exalted rank'. '*Scandalum magnatum* is the special name of a *scandal* or wrong done to any high personage of the realm: and it is also a writ granted to receive damages thereupon.' Giles Jacob, *A New Law-Dictionary* (London, 1729), including a form of declaration to use in this case.

justification by faith. Therefore, according to you, they are no members of the Church of England.

'Methodist preachers', you allow, 'practise, sign, and swear whatever is required by law'—a very large concession—'but the reserves they have are incommunicable and unintelligible.' Favour us, sir, with a little proof of this; till then I must plead not guilty. In whatever I sign or swear to I have no reserve at all. And I have again and again communicated my thoughts, on most heads, to all mankind, I believe intelligibly—particularly in the *Appeals to Men of Reason and Religion.*

But 'if Methodism, as its professors pretend, be a new discovery in religion'—This is a grievous mistake. We pretend no such thing. We aver, it is the one, old religion: as old as the Reformation, as old as Christianity, as old as Moses, as old as Adam.

'They ought to discover the whole ingredients of which their nostrum is composed, and have it enrolled in the public register, to be perused by all the world.' It is done. The whole ingredients of Methodism, so called, have been discovered in print over and over. And they are enrolled in a public register, the Bible, from which we extracted them at first. 'Else they ought not to be tolerated.' We allow it and desire toleration on no other terms. 'Nor should they be suffered to add or alter one grain different from what is so registered.' Most certainly. We ought neither to add to, diminish, nor alter whatever is written in that book.

I wish, sir, before you write concerning the Methodists again you would candidly read some of their writings—common report is not a sure rule of judging. I should be unwilling to judge of *you* thereby.

To sum up the matter. The whole ingredients of our religion are love, joy, peace, long-suffering, gentleness, goodness, fidelity, meekness, temperance. Against these I think there is no law, and therefore I still apprehend they may be *tolerated,* at least in a Christian country.

I am, sir,
Your sincere well-wisher,
John Wesley[51]

Fri. 9. I rode to Sundon and preached in the evening, and the next evening at Bedford. Sunday 11, I read prayers and preached at Everton, both morning and afternoon. Monday 12, I rode to Colchester, and after spending two or three comfortable days, on Friday 16, went on to Bury [St. Edmunds].[52] I would gladly have

[51] For fuller notes and variant readings, see *Letters*, vol. 27 in this edn.
[52] Simply called 'Bury' by JW in most instances.

stayed a day or two here, had it been only on account of the severity of the weather, but I had work to do elsewhere. So I took horse, soon after preaching in the morning, Saturday 17, though as bitter an one as most I have known. I never before felt so piercing a wind as that which met us in riding out of the gate at daybreak. To think of looking up was a vain thing; I knew not whether I should not lose one of my eyes. The wind affected it as if I had received a severe blow, so that I had no use of it for a time. To mend the matter, having a very imperfect direction, we soon got out of our way. However, we hobbled on through miserable roads, till about three in the afternoon we got to Norwich.

Sun. 18. I met the society in the morning, and many of them went with me to the cathedral. At two, we had the largest congregation I ever saw at that hour. At five, the house was well filled, and just as long as I was speaking all were silent. But when I ceased the floods lifted up their voice; one would have thought Bedlam was broke loose. And thus it always is: the custom began in the reign of King Log[53] and continued ever since. The next evening the same hubbub began again, not among the mob, but the ordinary hearers. I desired them to stop, and reasoned the case with them. The effect was far greater than one could expect. The whole congregation went as quietly and silently away as they use to do at the Foundery in London.

Tue. 20. I inquired concerning Yarmouth, a large and populous town and as eminent both for wickedness and ignorance as even any seaport in England. Some had endeavoured to call them to repentance, but it was at the hazard of their lives. What could be done more? Why, last summer, God sent thither the regiment in which Howell Harris was an officer.[54] He

[53] Apparently a reference to Aesop's fable of the frogs desiring a king, to whom Jupiter first sent a log of wood, whom they rejected as too passive, and then a stork, who devoured them. The allusion here is obscure, but much clearer in Wesley's *Free Thoughts on the Present State of Public Affairs* (1770; see *Bibliography*, No. 325), for which, see the antepenultimate paragraph.

[54] The first Methodist preachers in Yarmouth were 'driven out of the town . . . narrowly escaping with their lives'; *Wesleyan Methodist Magazine* 48 (1825):308. Howell Harris, who found the place 'famous for licentiousness' was also roughly treated when, in the autumn of 1760, he arrived with the troop of men he had raised for the national defence, and also began to preach. His account of his experiences is given in T. Beynon, *Howell Harris, Reformer and Soldier, 1714–73* (Caernarvon, 1958), pp. 85-95. The success of his efforts led him to summon the assistance of the Methodist preachers, a society was formed, and a chapel rented. 'Two local preachers were raised up, who promised to be extensively useful, viz., Benjamin Worship, attorney, and John Simpson, woollen draper.' The former, however, became a Sandemanian, took the chapel and half the members in

preached every night, none daring to oppose him; and hereby a good seed was sown. Many were stirred up to seek God. And some of them now earnestly invited *me* to come over. I went this afternoon and preached in the evening. The house was presently more than filled. And instead of the tumult which was expected, all were as quiet as at London. Indeed, the word of God was quick and powerful among them, as it was again at six in the morning. At eleven I preached my farewell sermon. I saw none that was not deeply affected. O fair blossoms! But how many of these will 'bring forth fruit unto perfection'?[55]

In the afternoon, I rode back to Norwich and took an account of the society there. I found the persons who professed to meet in class were about three hundred and thirty. But many of them were as bullocks unaccustomed to the yoke. Where or what will they be a year hence?

Thur. 22. We had our first watch-night at the Tabernacle, at which I could not but observe, though I preached the law from the beginning of my sermon to the end, yet many were exceedingly comforted—so plain it is that God can send either terror or comfort to the heart, by whatever means it pleaseth him.

Sunday the 25th was a day of solemn rejoicing. Both at eight, at eleven, at two, and at five, God was eminently present in the congregation, filling their hearts with love and their mouths with praise.

In some of the following days I visited the country societies. Fri. 30. After preaching at the Foundery[56] in the evening, I met the bands as usual. While a poor woman was speaking a few artless words out of the fullness of her heart, a fire kindled and ran as flame among the stubble,[57] through the hearts of almost all that heard—so when God is pleased to work it matters not how weak or how mean the instrument!

Sat. 21 [i.e., 31]. I spent an hour with one who was as hot as any of 'the lambs'[58] at the Tabernacle. But she is now a calm, reasonable woman. Indeed, God has now breathed a spirit of love and peace[59] into all that remain united together. Those who are otherwise minded have left us.

1765 (see Oct. 22, 1783). Simpson also adopted Calvinist opinions, took the next place of worship to which the society moved and all but eight members. They continued to meet in a private kitchen, but Methodist preaching in Yarmouth ceased till 1780. A. Watmough, *A History of Methodism in . . . Yarmouth* (London, 1825), pp. 60-63.

55 Cf. Luke 8:14, and see below, May 3, 1761, and June 18, 1765.

56 I.e., in Norwich.

57 See Ps. 83:13-14.

58 I.e., James Wheatley's congregation.

59 See Gal. 5:22.

Sunday, February 1. Many were comforted and strengthened both at the Lord's Supper and at the evening service. I think all jealousies and misunderstandings are now vanished, and the whole society is well knit together. How long will they continue so, considering the unparalleled fickleness of the people in these parts? That God knows. However, he does work *now*, and we rejoice therein.

Mon. 2. I left them with a cheerful heart and rode on to Lakenheath. The congregation was large, but to this day there was no society. So after preaching, I explained the nature of a society and examined those who were willing to join together. Near half of them had known the love of God and seemed alive to him.

Tue. 3. About noon I preached at Harston, five miles beyond Cambridge. Here Mr. Berridge's[60] labour has not been in vain. Several have found peace with God. And a more artless, loving people I have seldom seen. They were gathered from all parts. It pleased God to give a manifestation of his love to one woman in the midst of the sermon. She praised God aloud and inflamed many hearts with love and thankfulness.

In the evening I preached at Melbourn, another small town about four miles from Harston. Many from Harston walked thither, and from the neighbouring villages. And surely God was in the midst of them, just as in our Bristol congregations at the beginning.

Hence, we rode on Ash Wednesday, February 4, to Mr. Hicks,[61] who showed me the way to his church at Wrestlingworth, where I exhorted a large and serious congregation, from the Scripture appointed for the Epistle, to 'rend their hearts, and not their garments, and turn unto the Lord their God'.[62]

In the evening, Mr. Berridge read prayers and I preached at Everton. The few of them are now affected as at first, the greater part having found peace with God. But there is a gradual increasing of the work in the souls of many believers.

Thur. 5. I called at Barford,[63] half-way to Bedford, and was agreeably surprised to meet J. C.[64] from London, who came to

[60] On the revival at Harston, see above, July 29, 1759.

[61] On William Hicks, vicar of Wrestlingworth, see above, Nov. 9, 1758, n. 79.

[62] Cf. Joel 2:13.

[63] Great Barford was a parish 6 miles east from Bedford.

[64] Thought to be Joshua Caldecott (1735–90), a member of the London Foundery Society and a frequent host of JW. George J. Stevenson, *City Road Chapel, London, and its Associations, Historical, Biographical, and Memorial* (London, Stevenson, 1872), p. 470.

Bedford the day before and walked over with Mr. Parker.[65] We had a far larger congregation than I expected—and all were deeply serious. I preached at Bedford in the evening, on Friday at Sundon, and on Saturday returned to London.

Monday 9 and the following days, I visited the classes. Friday 13, being the general fast-day, the chapel in West Street, as well as the rest, was thoroughly filled with serious hearers. Surely God is well-pleased with even these outward humiliations, as an acknowledgement that he is the disposer of all events. And they give some check, if it be but for a time, to the floods of ungodliness. Besides, we cannot doubt but there are some good men in most of the congregations then assembled. And we know 'the effectual fervent prayer even of one righteous man availeth much.'[66]

This week I published in the *London Chronicle* an answer to a tract entitled, *A Caveat against the Methodists.* It is here subjoined.

To the Editor of the London Chronicle

Feb. 19, 1761

Sir,

Is it not surprising that every person of understanding does not discern, at the very first view, that the tract entitled *A Caveat against the Methodists*[67] is, in reality, *A Caveat against the Protestants?* Do not the arguments conclude (if they conclude at all), not against the *Methodists* only, but against the *whole Body of Protestants?* The names indeed of Mr. Whitefield and Mr. Wesley are used, but this is mere finesse; greater men are designed, and all along are wounded through our sides.

I was long in hopes of seeing an answer to this artful performance from someone of more leisure, as well as abilities, and some whose name would have recommended his work; for that thought has something of truth in it:

O what a tuneful wonder seized the throng,
When Marlbro's conquering name alarmed the foe!
Had Whiznowisky[68] led the armies on,
The General's scarecrow name had foiled each blow.

[65] For William Parker, see Oct. 8, 1753, n. 23 (20:476 in this edn.).

[66] Cf. Jas. 5:16.

[67] On this tract, see above, Nov. 22, 1760, n. 30. For fuller details and the complete original text of Wesley's series of letters (the latter half of which he had apparently forgotten writing), see *Letters*, vol. 27 in this edn. For a provisional brief reply to the *Caveat*, see above, Nov. 22, 1760.

[68] When the elective Polish throne became vacant in 1668, Austria, France, Sweden, Brandenburg, and Russia all attempted to influence the succession. The Polish nobility

However, who knows but reason, for once, may be stronger than prejudice? And many may forget my 'scarecrow' name and mind not who speaks but what is spoken. I am pleading now, not for Methodists only, but for the whole body of Protestants. First, for the Church of England, then for the Protestants of every denomination. In doing which I shall first give the substance of each section of the Romish tract; secondly, answer and retort it upon the members of the Church of Rome. O that this may incite some more skilful advocate to supply *my lack of service!*

SECTION I

'The Methodists (Protestants) are not the people of God; they are not true Gospel Christians, nor is their *new-raised* society the true Church of Christ nor any part of it' (p. 3).

'This is demonstrated by the Word of God, marking out the people of God, the *true Church* of Christ, by such characters as cannot agree to the Methodists or *any other new-raised* sect or community' (ibid.).

'The Old Testament is full of prophecies relating to the Church. And the New Testament makes glorious promises to it and gives glorious characters of it' (p. 4).

'Now all these prophecies, promises, and characters point out a society founded by Christ himself, and by his commission propagated *throughout the world,* which should flourish till time should end, *ever one,* ever *holy,* ever *orthodox;* secured against error by the perpetual presence of Christ; ever directed by the spirit of truth; having a *perpetual succession* of pastors and teachers, divinely appointed and divinely assisted. But no part of this character is applicable to any *new-raised* sect, who have no succession from, or connection with that one, holy society; therefore *no modern* sect can be *any part* of the people of God' (p. 5).

I answer, It is true, 'all these promises, prophecies, and characters point out a society founded by Christ himself, and by his commission propagated throughout the world, which should flourish till time should end.'[f] And such is the Catholic Church, that is the *whole body* of men endued with faith, working by love, dispersed over the whole earth, in Europe, Asia, Africa, and

[f] The words of the *Caveat* are in *italics* [here shown by quotation marks].

responded to this situation by electing Michael Wisnowiecki (1640–73), a Polish-born magnate, who 'was undistinguished as a person' (see *The New Cambridge Modern History*, 14 vols. [Cambridge, University Press, 1957–79], 5:561). He was unable to resist the crumbling of royal power or the penetration of foreign influence; he became a tool of the pro-Habsburg party, and married the Habsburg Archduchess Eleonora.

America. And this Church is 'ever one'; in all ages and nations it is the one body of Christ; it is 'ever holy', for no unholy man can possibly be a member of it. It is 'ever orthodox'; so is every holy man, in all things necessary to salvation; 'secured against error', in things essential, 'by the perpetual presence of Christ'; and 'ever directed by the spirit of truth', in the truth that is after godliness. This Church has 'a perpetual succession of pastors and teachers, divinely appointed and divinely assisted'. And there has never been wanting, in the Reformed churches, such a succession of pastors and teachers, men both divinely appointed and divinely assisted; for they convert sinners to God, a work none can do unless God himself doth appoint them thereto and assist them therein; therefore *every part* of this character is 'applicable' to them. Their teachers are the proper successors of those who have delivered down, through all generations, the faith once delivered to the saints; and their members have true, spiritual communion with the *one, holy* society of true *believers.* Consequently, although they are not the *whole* 'people of God', yet are they an undeniable *part* of his people.

On the contrary, the Church of Rome, in its present form, was not 'founded by Christ himself'. All the doctrines and practices wherein she differs from us were not instituted by Christ; they were unknown to the ancient Church of Christ; they are unscriptural, *novel* corruptions; neither is *that* Church 'propagated throughout the world'. Therefore, if either antiquity or universality be essential thereto, the Church of Rome cannot be 'the true Church of Christ'.

Nor is the Church of Rome 'one'; it is not in unity with itself: it is to this day torn with numberless divisions. And it is impossible it should be 'the One Church' unless a part can be the whole, seeing the Asiatic, the African, and the Muscovite Churches (to name no more) never were contained in it.

Neither is it 'holy'. The generality of its members are no holier than Turks or heathens. You need not go far for proof of this. Look at the Romanists in London or Dublin. Are these the 'Holy', the only 'Holy' Church? Just such holiness is in the bottomless pit.

Nor is it *secured against error,* either *by Christ* or *his Spirit:* witness Pope against Pope, Council against Council, contradicting, anathematizing each other—the instances are too numerous to be recited.

Neither are the generality of her *pastors* and *teachers* either 'divinely appointed' or 'divinely assisted'. If God had sent them, he would confirm the word of his messengers. But he does not; they convert no sinners to God; they convert many to their own opinion but not to the knowledge or love of God. He that was a drunkard is a drunkard still; he that was filthy is filthy still; therefore, neither are they 'assisted' by him; so they and their flocks wallow in sin together. Consequently (whatever may be the case of some particular souls) it must be said, if your own marks be true, the Roman Catholics, in general, are not 'the people of God'.

It may be proper to add here the Second Section, which is all I had leisure to write, though it was not published till the following week:

SECTION II [g]

'The Methodist (Protestant) teachers are not the true ministers of Christ; nor are they called or sent by him' (p. 6).

'This appears from what has been already demonstrated. For if the Protestants are not the true people of Christ, their ministers cannot be the true ministers of Christ' (ibid.).

[. . .][69] Farther, 'The true ministers came down by succession from the apostles. But the Protestant teachers do not.' Therefore they 'are not the true ministers of Christ' (ibid.).

'All power in the Church of Christ comes from him, so that whoever, without a commission from him, intrudes into the pastoral office, is a thief and a robber. Now the commission can be conveyed but two ways, either immediately from God himself, as it was to the apostles, or from men who have the authority handed down to them from the apostles.

'But this commission has not been conveyed to Protestant preachers, either of these ways. Not immediately from God himself, for how do they prove it? By what miracles? Neither by men deriving authority from the apostles, through the channel of the Church. And they stand divided in communion from all churches that have any pretensions to antiquity. Their doctrine of justification by faith alone was anathematized at its first appearance by the "undoubted heirs of the apostles, the pastors of the apostolic churches"; consequently they are sent by no other but him who sent all the false prophets from the beginning' (pp. 8, 9).

I answer, 'from what has been already demonstrated', that nothing will follow, for you have demonstrated just nothing.

Now for your 'farther' proof, 'the true ministers came down by succession from the apostles.' So do the Protestant ministers, if the

[g] P. 180 [actually p. 203, *London Chronicle,* Feb. 26-28, 1761; in spite of his disclaimer, Wesley also published Sections III and IV; see *Letters*, vol. 27 in this edn.].

[69] Wesley here omits two paragraphs from the original.

Romish do, the English in particular, as even one of yourselves, F. Courayer,[70] has irrefragably proved.

'All power in the Church of Christ comes from him; either immediately from himself, or from men who have the authority handed down to them from the apostles. But this commission has not been conveyed to the Protestant preachers, either of these ways. Not immediately, for by what miracles do they prove it?' So said Cardinal Bellarmine[71] long ago. Neither 'by men deriving authority from the apostles'. Read F. Courayer and know better. Neither are the Protestants 'divided from' any churches who have true 'pretensions to antiquity'. But 'their doctrine of justification by faith alone was anathematized at its first appearance by the undoubted heirs of the apostles, the pastors of the apostolic Church.' By the prelates at the Council of Trent it was, who thereby anathematized the Apostle Paul, to all intents and purposes. Here you throw off the mask; otherwise you might have passed for a Protestant a little longer. 'Consequently they are sent by no other but him who sent all the false prophets from the beginning.' Sir, we thank you. This is really a very modest assertion for the subject of a Protestant king.

But to turn the tables. I said, 'If the Romish bishops do.' For this I absolutely deny. I deny that the Romish bishops came down by *uninterrupted* succession from the apostles. I never could see it proved, and I am persuaded I never shall. But unless this is proved, your own pastors, on *your* principles, are no pastors at all.

But farther. It is a doctrine of *your* church that the intention of the administrator is essential to the validity of the sacraments which are administered by him. Now, are you assured of the intention of every priest from whom you have received the Host? If not, you do not know but what you received as the Sacrament of the Altar was no sacrament at all. Are you assured of the intention of the priest

[70] Pierre François Le Courayer, *Defence of the Validity of English Ordinations and of the Succession of Bishops in the Church of England*. Eng. trans. Daniel Williams (London, 1725). Original French edn. Nancy, 1723. Courayer (1681–1776) was one of the French priests, who, though not Jansenist, appealed against the bull *Unigenitus* on grounds of justice, and hence became known as anti-constitutionaries. William Wake negotiated for a possible union between the Anglican and Gallican churches with the group, and assisted Courayer with the studies of Anglican orders which led to the production of this book. The book created such public animosity, however, that he had to flee to England. There he lived the rest of his life writing and being suspected of Socinianism, but never pretending to have been converted to Anglicanism.

[71] St. Robert Bellarmine (1542–1621), Jesuit theologian and controversialist. He was made a cardinal in 1599 and was Archbishop of Capua, 1602–5. One of the great exponents of Tridentine Catholicism, he became entitled to the appellation 'Venerable' in 1627, but further recognition was delayed till his canonization in 1630, owing to his minimizing view of papal authority.

who baptized you? If not, perhaps you are not baptized at all. To come close to the point in hand: if *you* pass for a priest, are you sure of the intention of the bishop that ordained you? If not, you may happen to be no priest, and so all *your* ministry is nothing worth. Nay, by the same rule, he may happen to be no bishop. And who can tell how often this has been the case? But if there has been only one instance in a thousand years, what becomes of your *uninterrupted* succession?

This *ad hominem.* But I have a word more *ad rem.* Can a man teach what he does not know? Is it possible a man should teach others what he does not know himself? Certainly it is not. Can a priest then teach his hearers the way to heaven, marked out in our Lord's Sermon on the Mount, if he does not know or understand the way himself? Nothing is more impossible. But how many of your priests know nothing about it? What avails then their *commission* to teach what they cannot teach, because they know it not? Did God then send these men on a fool's errand—send them to do what they cannot do? O say not so! And what will be the event of their attempting to teach they know not what? Why, 'If the blind lead the blind, both shall fall into the pit.'[72]

Sat. 21. I spent some hours with Mr. L[loyd] and Mr. I'Anson, in order to prevent another chancery suit.[73] And though the matter[74] could not then be fully adjusted, yet the suit did not go on.

Tue. 24. I retired to Lewisham and transcribed the list of the society. About an hundred and sixty I left out, to whom[75] I can do no good at present. The number of those which now remain is two thousand three hundred and seventy-five.

Fri. 27. At twelve I met about thirty persons who had experienced a deep work of God. And I appointed an hour for meeting them every week. Whether they are 'saved from sin' or

72 Matt. 15:14.

73 Lloyd and I'Anson were legal advisers of the Wesley brothers (indeed, the reference to 'another chancery suit' may be explained by a letter of Bryan I'Anson on Kingswood School business in 1752); *WHS* 3 (1901):68-70. But two I'Anson brothers with a legal practice in Westminster and a seat at Southborough, Kent, were also intimate friends of the Wesleys. They were Sir Thomas I'Anson (d. 1773; Hutchins says 1764) and Bryan I'Anson, here mentioned (d. 1775). (*WHS* 5 [1906]:230-37; E. Hasted, *History and Topographical Survey of the County of Kent*, 12 vols. [2nd edn., Canterbury, 1797–1803; repr. East Ardsley, 1972], 2:341-42; 5:237; J. Hutchins, *History and Antiquities of Dorset*, 2 vols. [London, 1774], 1:546.) The preaching supported by Sir Thomas I'Anson in his house and neighbourhood appears to have given the first entrée to evangelicalism in Tunbridge Wells. Seymour, *Huntingdon*, 2:124.

74 Orig., 'And the matters', altered in *Works* (1774).

75 Orig., 'which', altered in *Works* (1774).

no, they are certainly full of faith and love, and peculiarly helpful to my soul.

Sunday, March 1. We had a happy love-feast at the chapel. Many of our brethren spoke plainly and artlessly[76] what God had done for their souls. I think none were offended, but many were strengthened and comforted.

Wed. 4. I was scarce come into the room where a few believers were met together, when one began to tremble exceedingly and soon after sunk to the floor. After a violent struggle, she burst out into prayer, which was quickly changed into praise. She then declared, 'The Lamb of God has taken away *all* my sins.' She spoke many strange words to the same effect, rejoicing with joy unspeakable.

Fri. 6. I met again with those who believe God has delivered them from the root of bitterness. Their number increases daily. I know not if fifteen or sixteen have not received the blessing this week.

Mon. 9. I set out early, and about noon preached at High Wycombe, where the dry bones began to shake again. In the afternoon I rode on to Oxford and spent an agreeable evening with Mr. H——.[77] His openness and frankness of behaviour were both pleasing and profitable. Such conversation I want, but I do not wonder it is offensive to men of nice ears.

Tue. 10. We rode to Evesham, where I found the poor, shattered society almost sunk into nothing. And no wonder, since they have been almost without help till Mr. Mather came.[78] In the

[76] Orig., 'artless', altered in *Works* (1774).

[77] Thomas Haweis (1733/34–1820), at this time curate to Joseph Jane at St. Mary Magdalen, Oxford. In his autobiography (Mitchell Library MS B1176, fol. 61-62), Haweis noted that the Wesley brothers and Whitefield treated him 'with particular affection . . . tho' I formed no connection with them. Mr. John Wesley. . . visited me at Oxford, and Mr. Jane received him very co[rdially].' JW's final comment was prophetic; Haweis was inhibited in the next year. He was among the evangelical clergy to whom JW appealed in 1764. A. S. Wood, *Thomas Haweis 1734–1820* (London, 1957), p. 76. I am grateful to Dr. Edwin Welch and Dr. J. D. Walsh for assistance with this note.

[78] Alexander Mather (1733–1800) was born at Brechin and converted under JW's preaching in London in 1754. JW tried him in various spiritual offices, before accepting him as an itinerant in 1757. Powerful in mind and body, Mather developed an apostolic reputation, and in 1792 succeeded as president of the connexion, only the second after JW's death. In 1788, Mather was one of three preachers ordained by JW without being sent out of the country, and it was widely believed by the party which wished to separate from the Church that he had created Mather a bishop with a view to ensuring a succession of ordinations after his death (see *Diary*, Aug. 7 and 8, 1788). Mather's nerve, however, seems to have failed, and in the immediate crisis he stood for the maintenance of the connexion's status as a society within the Church of England. W. Reginald Ward, 'The Legacy of John Wesley', in *Statesmen, Scholars, and Merchants*, ed. Anne Whitman,

evening I preached in the town hall. Both at this time and at five in the morning, God applied his word, and many found a desire to 'strengthen the things that remained'.[79] I designed to have rested on Wednesday, but finding that notice had been given of my preaching at Stanley,[80] we got thither, through roads almost impassable, about noon, and found more people than the house could contain. So I stood in the yard and proclaimed free salvation to a loving, simple people. Several were in tears, and all of them so thankful that I could not repent of my labour.

The congregation at Evesham in the evening was thrice as large as the night before. Indeed, many of them did not design to *hear*, or to let anyone else hear. But they were overruled and behaved with tolerable decency till the service was over. Then they roared amain. But I walked strai[gh]t through them. And none offered the least rudeness.

Thur. 12. About one, I preached at Redditch to a deeply serious congregation; about seven in the room at Birmingham, now far too small for the congregation.[81] Fri. 13. Many flocked together at five, and far more than the room would contain in the evening. Perhaps the time is come for the gospel to take root even in this barren soil.

Sat. 14. I rode to Wednesbury. Sun. 15. I made a shift to preach within at eight in the morning. But in the afternoon I knew not what to do, having a pain in my side and a sore throat. However, I resolved to speak as long as I could. I stood at one end of the house,[82] and the people (supposed to be eight or ten thousand) in the field adjoining. I spoke from, 'I count all things but loss for the excellency of the knowledge of Jesus Christ my Lord.'[83] When I had done speaking my complaints were gone. At the love-feast in the evening many, both men and women, spoke their experience, in a manner which affected all that heard. One in particular said, 'For seventeen or eighteen years I thought God

J. S. Bromley, and P. G. M. Dickson (Oxford, 1973), p. 338. His autobiography appears in Jackson, *Early Methodist Preachers*, 2:158-88. See also *Minutes of Conference* (1801), and Atmore, *Memorial*, pp. 256-66.

[79] Cf. Rev. 3:2.

[80] Stanley Pontlarge, a tiny parish 2¾ miles north-west of Winchcombe, the living being annexed to the vicarage of Toddington.

[81] Alexander Mather was now appointed to Birmingham, and there had been a great revival under his ministry. Sheldon, *Birmingham*, p. 20.

[82] The chapel in Meeting Street opened in 1760. *Methodist Recorder* (Apr. 25, 1901), pp. 13-14.

[83] Phil. 3:8.

had forgotten me. Neither I, nor any under my roof, could believe. But now, blessed be his name, he has taken me and all my house, and given me and my wife and our seven children to rejoice together in God our Saviour.'

Mon. 16. I intended to rest two or three days. But being pressed to visit Shrewsbury,[84] and having no other time, I rode over today, though upon a miserable beast. When I came in my head ached as well as my side. I found the door of the place where I was to preach surrounded by a numerous mob. But they seemed met only to stare. Few of them came in; almost all that did (a large number) behaved quietly and seriously.

Tue. 17. At five, the congregation was large and appeared not a little affected. The difficulty now was how to get back.[85] For I could not ride the horse on which I came. But this too was provided for. We met in the street with one who lent me *his* horse, which was so easy that I grew better and better till I came to Wolverhampton. None had yet preached abroad in this furious town,[86] but I was resolved, with God's help, to make a trial and ordered a table to be set in the inn-yard. Such a number of wild men I have seldom seen. But they gave me no disturbance, either while I preached, or when I afterwards[87] walked through the midst of them.

About five, I preached to a far larger congregation at Dudley, and all as quiet as at London. The scene is changed since the dirt and stones of this town were flying about me on every side![88]

Wed. 18. By talking with several at Wednesbury, I found God is carrying on his work here as at London. We have ground to hope, one prisoner was set at full liberty under the sermon on Saturday morning, another under that on Saturday evening. One or more received remission of sins on Sunday. On Monday morning another, and on Wednesday yet another believed 'the blood of Jesus Christ' had 'cleansed' him 'from all sin'.[89] In the

[84] Until John Fletcher became vicar of Madeley in October 1760, Methodism had made little impact on Shropshire. Five years later, Salop was a circuit and all the notable figures of the revival were appearing in the county. Here Fletcher is seen exploiting his first opportunity to bring in JW himself. R. F. Skinner, *Nonconformity in Shropshire 1662–1816* (Shrewsbury, 1964), pp. 57, 61.

[85] There was only a weekly coach from Shrewsbury to London (taking four days) via Wolverhampton, *WHS* 7 (1909):6.

[86] But one of Whitefield's preachers, William Allt, had faced the mob there in 1745, and Whitefield himself had preached there in the dark in 1753; see Luke Tyerman, *The Life of the Rev. George Whitefield*, 2 vols. (2nd edn., London, Hodder and Stoughton, 1890), 2:112, and Whitefield, *Works*, 3:35.

[87] 1774 added 'afterwards'.

[88] Cf. Oct. 24, 1749 (20:311 in this edn.).

[89] Cf. 1 John 1:7.

evening I could scarce think, but more than one heard him say, 'I will. Be thou clean!'[90] Indeed, so wonderfully was he present till near midnight as if he would have healed the whole congregation.

Thur. 19. After preaching at Bilbrook, I rode on to Burslem and preached at half-hour past five in an open place on the top of the hill to a large and attentive congregation, though it rained almost all the time and the air was extremely cold. The next morning, being Good Friday, I did not preach till eight. But even then, as well as in the evening, the cold considerably lessened the congregation. Such is human wisdom! So small are the things which divert mankind from what might be the means of their eternal salvation!

Sat. 21. About ten I preached at Biddulph,[91] and about six at Congleton. Sun. 22. About one, I preached at Macclesfield near the preaching-house. The congregation was large, though the wind was sharp. But it was more than doubled after the evening service, while I opened and enforced the solemn declaration, 'Him hath God exalted with his own right hand, to be a prince and a Saviour.'[92] In the evening I rode on to Manchester.

Mon. 23. After preaching at five, I hastened forward and reached Leeds about five in the evening, where I had desired all the preachers in those parts to meet me,[93] and an happy meeting we had both in the evening and morning. I afterwards inquired into the state of the societies in Yorkshire and Lincolnshire. I find the work of God increases on every side, but particularly in Lincolnshire, where there has been no work like this since the time I preached at Epworth on my father's tomb.

In the afternoon I talked with several of those who believe they are saved from sin. And after a close examination, I found reason to hope that fourteen of them were not deceived. In the evening, I

[90] Matt. 8:3, etc.

[91] JW's base here was provided by William Stonier of The Hurst, Biddulph. Stonier was a man of property, the chief trustee of the Congleton chapel, and an early and active local preacher. *WHS* 4 (1903):30; see also J. B. Dyson, *The History of Wesleyan Methodism in the Congleton Circuit* (London, Mason, 1856), pp. 69-70.

[92] Cf. Acts 5:31.

[93] To this odd gathering of Yorkshire preachers, Grimshaw was invited but did not attend. Though his principal discomfort with Wesley's Methodism at this time lay in the tendency he perceived in it to separate from the Church, his present ground for staying away was the incautious teaching about Christian perfection employed by some of the preachers (Whitehead, *Wesley*, 2:291-93). To correct these embarrassments seems to have been the object of the meeting; see below, July 13, 1761. It was only slightly bizarre that when, less than a week later, JW expounded perfection in Manchester, 'to many of them it seemed a new doctrine'; see below, Mar. 29, 1761.

expounded the thirteenth chapter of the First Epistle to the Corinthians and exhorted all to weigh themselves in that balance and see if they were not 'found wanting'.[94]

Wed. 25. I took horse early, breakfasted with Mr. Venn,[95] and about four in the afternoon came to Stockport. Finding the congregation waiting, I preached immediately and then rode on to Manchester, where I rested on Thursday. Fri. 27. I rode to Bridgefield,[96] in the midst of the Derbyshire mountains, and cried to a large congregation, 'If any man thirst, let him come unto me and drink.'[97] And they did indeed drink in the word, as the thirsty earth the showers. About six I preached at Stockport. Here I inquired after a young man who was some time since much in earnest for salvation. But it was not long before he grew quite cold and left the society. Within a few months after, he left the world, and that by his own hand! The next day I returned to Manchester.[98]

Sun. 29. We had an uncommon blessing, both morning and afternoon. In the evening I met the believers and strongly exhorted them to 'go on to perfection'.[99] To many of them it seemed a new doctrine. However, they all received it in love, and a flame was kindled which I trust neither men nor devils shall ever be able to quench.

Tue. 31. I rode to Altrincham. We had four rooms which opened into each other. But they would not near contain the congregation, so that many were obliged to stand without. I believe many were wounded, and some much comforted. Perhaps this town will not be quite so furious as it has been.

In the evening, we had abundance of genteel people at Manchester while I described 'faith' as 'the evidence of things not seen'.[1] I left Manchester in the morning, April 1, in a better condition than ever I knew it before: such is the shaking not only among the dry bones but likewise among the living souls.

About noon I preached at Little Leigh, and at Chester in the evening. Thur. 2. I rode over to Tattenhall,[2] eight or nine miles

[94] Cf. Dan. 5:27.

[95] On Henry Venn, see above, Feb. 27, 1759, n. 5.

[96] Perhaps Brookfield, a locality 2 miles north-west of Glossop.

[97] John 7:37.

[98] JW's conversation with Byrom on this visit is reported by the latter. *Wesleyan Methodist Magazine* 86 (1863):1104-6.

[99] Heb. 6:1 (*Notes*).

[1] Heb. 11:1.

[2] Tattenhall was a township and parish 7 miles south-east of Chester.

from Chester. When we came the town seemed to be all in an uproar. Yet when I began preaching (in the open air, the house not being large enough to contain one-quarter of the congregation) none opposed or made the least disturbance, the fear of God falling upon them. I think Tattenhall will be less bitter for the time to come. Well may Satan be angry with field preaching.

Fri. 3. I preached about one at Mold[3] in Flintshire and was again obliged to preach abroad, though the wind was exceeding rough. All were deeply attentive. I preached in the evening at Chester, and in the morning set out for Liverpool. I came thither (preaching at Warrington by the way) in the evening. The election[4] seemed to have driven the common sort of people out of their senses. But on Sunday, they were tolerably recovered, and the town looked like itself. I heard two useful sermons at our parish church,[5] one upon 'Follow peace with all men, and holiness,'[6] the other on, 'Blessed are the dead which die in the Lord.'[7] I pity those who 'can learn nothing at church'.

Mon. 13. I left them at Liverpool, a little increased in number but very considerably in strength, being now entirely united together in judgment as well as in affection.

About noon I preached to a serious congregation at Downall Green[8] near Wigan, but to a far more serious one in the evening at Bolton. I find few places like this. All disputes are forgot, and the Christians do indeed love one another.[9] When I visited the classes on Wednesday 15, I did not find a disorderly walker among them, no, nor a trifler. They appeared to be, one and all, seriously seeking salvation.

Thur. 16. After preaching at noon, I rode to Lower Darwen near Blackburn, where a large congregation behaved with deep seriousness. Leaving honest Mr. Grimshaw to preach in the morning, I set out early, and in the evening reached a little quiet house a few miles beyond Kendal, to which, I believe, we did not come in vain. The man of the house, having been long ill, was

[3] Orig., 'Mould'.

[4] Occasioned by the death of George II on Oct. 25, 1760.

[5] St. Nicholas's, Liverpool; see above, May 6, 1759, n. 44.

[6] Heb. 12:14.

[7] Rev. 14:13.

[8] Orig., 'Downah-green', altered in the 1774 (*Works*) to 'Downath-Green', but in the errata and Wesley's annotated copy of the *Works* to 'Downam Green'. Cf. above, May 9, 1759, n. 45.

[9] For the phrase, see letter to his mother, July 6, 1738 (*Letters*, 25:557 in this edn.); the substantive reference is to the healing of the disputes created by John Bennet.

thankful for advice with regard to his bodily disorder. And his guests appeared right willing to receive some advice with respect to their souls.

Sat. 18. We were soon lost on the mountains.[10] But in an hour we found a cottage and a good woman who bade her son, 'Take the galloway and guide them to the fell foot.' There we met a poor man just coming from a doctor who, I think, had quite mistaken his case. Perhaps this meeting us may save his life. He piloted us over the next mountain, the like to which I never beheld either in Wales or Germany. As we were climbing the third, a man overtook us who was going the same road. So he accompanied us till we were in a plain, level way, which in three hours brought us to Whitehaven.

Sun. 19. I preached morning and evening at the Gins[11] to far more people than the house would have contained. At one I preached in the assembly-room at Workington. The whole congregation behaved well—though I could not perceive that the greater part understood anything of the matter.

Wed. 22. About noon I preached at Branthwaite, and in the evening at Lorton. Who would imagine that Deism should find its way into the heart of these enormous mountains! Yet so it is. Yea, and one who once knew the love of God is a strenuous advocate for it.

Sat. 25. As the people at Whitehaven are usually full of zeal, right or wrong, I this evening showed them the nature of Christian zeal. Perhaps some of them may now distinguish the flame of love from a fire kindled in hell.

Sun. 26. I preached in the morning at the Gins, in the room at one, and about five at Cockermouth on the steps of the market-house. Even the genteel hearers were decent; many of the rest seemed deeply affected. The people of the town have never been uncivil. Surely they will not always be unfruitful.

Mon. 27. I preached at eight in the market-place at Wigton. The congregation, when I began, consisted of one woman, two boys, and three or four little girls. But in a quarter of an hour we

[10] JW's commentators are here as lost as he was, but it is probable that (by whatever route, with the help of the hardy Scottish horse) he got to the head of Little Langdale and made the crossing by Wrynose and Hard Knott passes, proceeding to Whitehaven by Boot (*WHS* 6 [1907]:33-34). Curnock's suggestion of the route via Keswick and the Whinlatter Pass is excluded by the fact that JW had made that crossing too often to be awestruck as he was now; see above, May 15, 1759.

[11] Once a village, now part of Whitehaven.

had most of the town. I was a good deal moved at the exquisite self-sufficiency which was visible in the countenance, air, and whole deportment of a considerable part of them. This constrained me to use a very uncommon plainness of speech. They bore it well. Who knows but some may profit?

Before noon we came to Solway Firth.[12] The guide told us it was not passable. But I resolved to try, and got over well. Having lost ourselves but twice or thrice in one of the most difficult roads I ever saw, we came to Moffat[13] in the evening. Tue. 28. We rode partly over the mountains, partly with mountains on either hand, between which was a clear, winding river, and about four in the afternoon reached Edinburgh.

Here I met Mr. Hopper, who had promised to preach in the evening, in a large room, lately an episcopal meeting-house.[14] Wednesday 29, it being extremely cold, I preached in the same room at seven. Some of the reputable hearers cried out in amaze, 'Why, this is sound doctrine! Is this *he* of whom Mr. Wh[itefield][15] used to *talk so?*' Talk as he will, I shall not retaliate.

I preached again in the evening, and the next day rode round by the Queensferry[16] to Dundee. But the wind being high, the boatmen could not, at least would not, pass. Nor could we pass the next day till between nine and ten. We then rode on through Montrose to Stonehaven. Here Mr. Memyss[17] met us and on Saturday morning brought us to his house at Aberdeen.

12 Orig., 'Solway-frith'.

13 Moffat was a town and parish 19 miles north-east of Dumfries.

14 JW had written to Hopper from his Leeds gathering in March that 'I cannot fix my route through Scotland till I hear from Mr. Gillies, but I expect to be in Aberdeen in four or five weeks' (Telford, 4:141-42; for Gillies, see Apr. 17, 1753, n. 15; 20:453 in this edn.). Hopper's own account of the Edinburgh occasion is that not he, but JW, preached, 'and the Lord gave his word success' (Jackson, *Early Methodist Preachers*, 1:211). Whether JW's reference to the 'episcopal meeting-house' was disingenuous or simply mistaken is not clear. There were two rooms in Bailie Fyfe's Close, an episcopal meeting-house which continued in use throughout the period of the Methodist presence there, 1761–65, and a disused dancing-school taken over by the Methodists, which became a printing-works when they moved into the Low Calton chapel. A. J. Hayes, *Edinburgh Methodism 1761–1975* (Edinburgh, 1976), pp. 2-3.

15 Orig., 'Mr. ——', altered in *Works* (1774) to 'Mr. Wh——'.

16 Orig.,'Queen's Ferry'. Queensferry was a tiny royal burgh and parish nine miles west from Edinburgh, named from the frequent crossings of the Forth at that place by Margaret, the queen of Malcolm Canmore. The ferry, originally private property, was at this time managed very inefficiently by a group of individuals. In 1809 an act was obtained greatly to improve the ferry by raising capital on a joint-stock principle and changing the management.

17 Orig., 'Memis'. John Memyss, a journeyman apothecary, joined the Methodists at Wrexham. The itinerant there, Thomas Olivers, believed he owed his life to Memyss's

In the afternoon, I sent to the Principal and Regent[18] to desire leave to preach in the College Close. This was readily granted, but as it began to rain I was desired to go into the hall. I suppose this is full an hundred feet long and seated all around. The congregation was large, notwithstanding the rain, and full as large at five in the morning. Sunday, May 3, I heard two useful sermons at the kirk, one preached by the Principal of the college, the other by the divinity professor.[19] A huge multitude afterwards gathered together in the College Close. And all that could hear seemed to receive the truth in love. I then added about twenty to the little society. Fair blossoms! But how many of these will bring forth fruit?[20]

Mon. 4. We had another large congregation at five. Before noon, twenty more came to me, desiring to cast in their lot with us and appearing to be cut to the heart.

About noon I took a walk to the King's College in Old Aberdeen. It has three sides of a square handsomely built, not unlike Queen's College in Oxford.[21] Going up to see the hall, we

gratuitous treatment (Jackson, *Early Methodist Preachers*, 2:52). Moving to Aberdeen *c.* 1747, Memyss joined the congregation of one of the evangelical ministers in the town, John Bisset (1692–1756), minister of the East Parish, Aberdeen, generally regarded as the founder of the Secession there and a critic of Whitefield. After Bisset's death in 1756, Memyss, now a doctor, urged on JW in London the need to provide evangelical preaching for the town. The result of this request was that Christopher Hopper was sent north, visited Aberdeen in 1759 and 1760, formed a society, and until just before this visit had 'a fair prospect of a great harvest . . . till men of corrupt minds stirred up the spirit of vain controversy.' C. Diack, *Sketch of Methodism in Aberdeen* (Aberdeen, 1901); Jackson, *Early Methodist Preachers*, 1:211. A satirical but informative account of JW's visit was published by the *Scots Magazine* (August 1763); repr. *WHS* 4 (1904):159-62.

[18] George Campbell (1719–96) was ordained minister of Banchory Ternon, Aberdeen, 1748, and became a well-known preacher. He became one of the ministers of Aberdeen, 1757. He was one of the founder members of the Philosophical Society, 1758, and in 1759 was appointed Principal of Marischal College by the influence of his distant relative, the Duke of Argyll (resigning on account of ill-health, 1792). In 1762 he published his *Dissertation on Miracles* (Edinburgh, 1762), one of the chief answers to Hume. In June 1771 he was elected divinity professor and minister of Carey Friars.

[19] Alexander Gerard (1728–95) was elected professor of philosophy at Marischal College, 1750–60, writing a prize-winning essay on taste. From 1760–71, he was professor of divinity, acting as moderator of the General Assembly in 1764. In 1771 he became professor of divinity at King's College, Aberdeen, writing an 'Essay on Genius' (1774). He was a member of the Aberdeen Philosophical Society. He was a royal chaplain, and a supporter of the moderate party in the Church.

[20] Cf. above, Jan. 20, 1761; June 18, 1765; and Dec. 2, 1771.

[21] The comparison with Queen's College is not now apparent since the oldest parts of King's College are much the older, and two sides of the quadrangle were rebuilt in the nineteenth century. The interior court, 108 feet square remains, however, and it may be this that stirred JW's recollections of Oxford. *Burrow's Guide to Aberdeen* (Aberdeen, 1917), p. 20.

found a large company of ladies with several gentlemen. They looked and spoke to one another, after which one of the gentlemen took courage and came to me. He said, 'We came last night to the College Close but could not hear, and should be extremely obliged if you would give us a short discourse here.' I knew not what God might have to do, and so began without delay on 'God was in Christ reconciling the world unto himself.'[22] I believe the word was not lost. It fell as dew on the tender grass.

In the afternoon I was walking in the library of the Marischal[23] College, when the Principal and the divinity professor came to me, and the latter invited me to his lodgings, where I spent an hour very agreeably. In the evening the eagerness of the people made them ready to trample each other under foot. It was some time before they were still enough to hear, but then they devoured every word. After preaching, Sir Archibald Grant[24] (whom business had called to town) sent and desired to speak to me. I could not then, but promised to wait upon him, with God's leave, in my return to Edinburgh.

Tue. 5. I accepted the Principal's invitation and spent an hour with him at his house. I observed no stiffness at all but the easy good breeding of a man of sense and learning. I suppose both he and all the professors, with some of the magistrates, attended in the evening. I set all the windows open, but the hall, notwithstanding, was as hot as a bagnio. But this did not hinder either the attention of the people or the blessing of God.

Wed. 6. We dined at Mr. Ogilvie's,[25] one of the ministers between whom the city is divided. A more open-hearted, friendly man I know not that I ever saw. And indeed I have scarce seen such a set of ministers in any town of Great Britain or Ireland.

At half-hour after six, I stood in the College Close and

[22] 2 Cor. 5:19.

[23] Orig., 'Mareshall'.

[24] Sir Archibald Grant (1696–1778) owes enduring fame as one of the most celebrated Scots agricultural improvers of the eighteenth century in part to two accidents: (1) that his estate papers have survived in detail and (2) that, having been expelled from the Commons in 1731 for a disgraceful fraud involving the funds of a charitable society, he took agricultural improvement seriously as a business instead of an acceptable form of conspicuous waste (like so many genteel improvers) .

[25] Orig., 'Ogilvey'. James Ogilvie (1695–1776), M.A., Aberdeen, 1724; minister of Inchtore, 1726–29; minister of Aberdeen from 1729; he opened the new West Church in 1755. He is described as 'a person of great prudence, strictly evangelical in his sentiments', and was what was termed 'a sweet-blooded man' with 'a very taking gift' (Scott, *Fasti*, 3, pt. 2, p. 465). For a providential incident related on this occasion to JW, see *Arminian Magazine* 7 (1784):608-9.

proclaimed 'Christ crucified'.[26] My voice was so strengthened that all could hear, and all were earnestly attentive. I have now 'cast' my 'bread upon the waters'; may I 'find it again after many days'.[27]

Thur. 7. Leaving near ninety members in the society, I rode over to Sir A. Grant's near Monymusk, about twenty miles north-west from Aberdeen. It lies in a fruitful and pleasant valley, much of which is owing to Sir Archibald's improvements, who has ploughed up abundance of waste ground and planted some millions of trees. His stately old house is surrounded by gardens and rows of trees, with a clear river on one side. And about a mile from his house he has laid out a small valley into walks and gardens, on one side of which the river runs. On each side rises a steep mountain, one rocky and bare, the other covered with trees, row above row, to the very top.

About six we went to the church. It was pretty well filled with such persons as we did not look for so near the highlands. But if we were surprised at their appearance, we were much more so at their singing. Thirty or forty sung an anthem after sermon, with such voices as well as judgment that I doubt whether[28] they could have been excelled at any cathedral in England.

Fri. 8. We rode to Glamis,[29] about sixty-four measured miles, and on Saturday 9 about sixty-six more to Edinburgh. I was tired; however, I would not disappoint the congregation, and God gave me strength according to my day.[30]

Sun. 10. I had designed to preach near the infirmary. But some of the managers would not suffer it. So I preached in our room morning and evening, even to the rich and honourable. And I bear them witness, they will *endure* plain dealing, whether they *profit* by it or not.

Mon. 11. I took my leave of Edinburgh for the present. The situation of the city on a hill shelving down on both sides, as well as to the east, with the stately castle upon a craggy rock on the west, is inexpressibly fine. And the main street so broad and finely paved, with the lofty houses on either hand (many of them seven or eight stories high) is far beyond any in Great Britain. But how can it be suffered that all manner of filth should still be thrown even into this street continually? Where are the magistracy, the

[26] 1 Cor. 1:23.
[27] Eccles. 11:1.
[28] Orig., 'where', altered 1774, 1791.
[29] Glamis is a parish and village 5½ miles south-west of Forfar.
[30] See Deut. 33:25.

gentry, the nobility of the land? Have they no concern for the honour of their nation? How long shall the capital city of Scotland, yea, and the chief street of it, stink worse than a common sewer? Will no lover of his country, or of decency and common sense, find a remedy for this?[31]

Holyrood House, at the entrance of Edinburgh, the ancient palace of the Scottish kings, is a noble structure. It was rebuilt and furnished by King Charles the Second. One side of it is a picture gallery, wherein are pictures of all the Scottish kings and an original one of the celebrated Queen Mary. It is scarce possible for any who looks at this to think her such a monster as some have painted her, nor indeed for any who considers the circumstances of her death, equal to that of an ancient martyr.[32]

I preached in the evening at Musselburgh,[33] and at five in the morning. Then we rode on to Haddington, where (the rain driving me in) I preached between nine and ten in provost Dickson's parlour.[34] About one, I preached at North Berwick, a pretty large town (close to the sea-shore), and at seven in the evening (the rain continuing), in the house at Dunbar.

Wednesday, May 13. It being a fair mild evening, I preached near the quay to most of the inhabitants of the town, and spoke full as plain as the evening before. Everyone seemed to receive it in love. Probably if there was regular preaching here, much good might be done.

Thur. 14. I set out early and preached at noon on the bowling-green at Berwick-upon-Tweed. In the evening I preached at Alnwick. Friday 15, abundance of soldiers came in, on their way to Germany. Many of these attended the preaching,

[31] There is an interesting balance in this thumb-nail sketch of Edinburgh. Visitors, right through the eighteenth century, tended to concentrate on JW's latter points, with such unanimity that the Town Council finally adopted James Craig's plan for the New Town in 1767, and were shamed into cleaning up at least the main streets of the Old. But the answer to JW's question as to where the upper orders were (put at a time when the density of population in the Old Town was approaching its peak), was—remarkably for a town in which at least the professional classes were more numerously represented than anywhere else and to which the gentry and nobility came in for the winter season—that they were not merely in the midst of the filth but in the same tenement buildings as the lower orders, though usually on the second and third floors.

[32] On the place of JW's Stuart romanticism in his general intellectual make-up, see Intro., 18:26-27 in this edn.

[33] Orig., 'Musselborough'.

[34] Despite this visit, Methodism was not established in Haddington till the early nineteenth century, where it lasted for fifty years (*WHS* 41 [1977]:43-52). Andrew Dickson, merchant, was provost of Haddington in 1733, 1750, 1754, and 1758. James Miller, *The Lamp of Lothian* (Haddington, 1844), p. 502.

to whom I could not but make a particular application. And who knows but what they have now heard may stand them in stead in a day of trial?

Sat. 16. One of our friends importuned me much to give them a sermon at Warkworth.[35] And a post-chaise came for me to the door, in which I found one waiting for me whom in the bloom of youth mere anguish of soul had brought to the gates of death. She told me the troubles which held her in on every side, from which she saw no way to escape. I told her, 'The way lies strait before you. What you want is the pure love of God. I believe, God will give it you shortly. Perhaps it is his good pleasure to make *you* a poor, bruised reed, the first witness here of that great salvation. Look for it *just as you are,* unfit, unworthy, unholy, by simple faith, every day, every hour.' She did feel the next day something she could not comprehend and knew not what to call it. In one of the trials which used to sink her to the earth, she was all calm, all peace and love, enjoying so deep a communion with God as nothing external could interrupt. Ah, thou child of affliction, of sorrow and pain, hath Jesus found out thee also? And he is able to find and bring back thy husband, as far as he is wandered out of the way.

About noon, I preached at Warkworth to a congregation as quiet and attentive as that at Alnwick. How long shall we forget that God can raise the dead? Were not *we* dead, till he quickened us?

A little above the town, on one side of the river, stand the remains of a magnificent castle. On the other side, toward the bottom of a steep hill, covered with wood, is an ancient chapel with several apartments adjoining to it, hewn in the solid rock. The windows, the pillars, the Communion Table, and several other parts, are entire. But where are the inhabitants? Gathered to their fathers; some of them, I hope, in Abraham's bosom,[36] till rocks and rivers and mountains flee away, and the dead, small and great, stand before God![37]

Sun. 17. I preached at eight in Alnwick, and about one at Alnmouth, a poor, barren place, where as yet there is no fruit of all

[35] Orig., 'Warksworth'. Warkworth was a township and parish, 7 miles south-east of Alnwick, dominated by the ruins of the castle. A castle of sorts seems to have existed since the twelfth century, though the moated mound on which it stands may be much older. John Hodgson, *History of Northumberland*, 6 vols., in 3 pts. (Newcastle, 1827–40), 5:18, 21.

[36] See Luke 16:22.

[37] Rev. 20:12.

the seed which has been sown. But there may be, since many are still willing to hear.

In the evening, a multitude of people and a little army of soldiers were gathered in the market-place at Alnwick. In the morning, they were to march for Germany. I hope some of them have 'put their armour on'.[38]

Mon. 18. At nine I preached to a large and serious congregation at Widdrington. Thence we rode to Morpeth.[39] As it was a rainy day, they expected me to preach in the room. But observing a large, covered place in the market-place, I went thither without delay. It was soon more than filled, and many, soldiers and others, stood on the outside, notwithstanding the rain. Why should we despair of doing good in any place because we do not see present fruit? At five I preached to the honest, simple-hearted colliers at Plessey, and before sunset reached Newcastle.

Tuesday the 19th was a day of rest. In the evening God was with us of a truth,[40] and many felt their hearts burn with fervent desire of being renewed in the whole image of God. The same flame was kindled at Gateshead Fell while I was opening and applying those words, 'Everyone that hath this hope in him purifieth himself even as he is pure.'[41]

Thur. 21. I was much struck with a story told by Ephraem Syrus.[42] I wonder it was never translated into English. It is as follows:

> My beloved brethren, I have a desire to relate to you what our brother Abraham did in his old age. This blessed man had a brother according to the flesh, who had an only child. When her father fell asleep she remained an orphan. Her friends brought her to him, being six years old. He ordered her to be placed in the outer cell; he himself abode in the inner. A little door was between them. He taught her the Psalms and the other Scriptures, and watched and sang with her. And as he lived an austere life, so did she, willingly profiting in every exercise and labouring to excel in all

[38] Cf. Eph. 6:11, 13; and Charles Wesley's 'Soldiers of Christ, Arise' ('The Whole Armour of God'), No. 258 in Wesley's *Collection of Hymns* (1780), 7:399-400 in this edn.

[39] Thomas Rankin, the itinerant, describes the latter portion of this service at which he 'was so struck with the power of God' as almost to collapse. *Arminian Magazine* 2 (1779):193-94.

[40] See 1 Cor. 14:25.

[41] 1 John 3:3 (*Notes*).

[42] Orig., 'Ephraim'. On Ephraem Syrus, see Mar. 4, 1747, n. 65.

virtues. The holy man often besought God for her with tears, that her heart might be fixed on God and not entangled with the care of worldly things—for her father had left her much wealth, which by his advice she gave to the poor. And she entreated him, saying, 'Pray for me, that I may be delivered from evil thoughts and from all the wiles and snares of the devil.' The blessed man rejoiced, seeing her good conversation and forwardness, and tears, her lowliness, meekness, quietness of spirit, and earnest love to God. And for twenty years she thus exercised herself with him as a fair lamb, a spotless dove.

When the twentieth year was fulfilled, the devil was mad against her and lay in wait to get her into his net. There was a man, in name *religious* but not in truth, who frequently came to consult Abraham. He saw the maid, and his heart burned within him. He lay in wait for her a whole year, till her heart was inflamed also. And opening the door of her cell, she went out to him and consented to his will. But no sooner had she committed wickedness than she rent her clothes, smote her breast, and thought of putting an end to her own life. For she said in herself, 'Now I am dead, and I have lost all my time and all my labour, and my austerity and my tears are perished, and I have destroyed my own soul, and I have brought sorrow upon the man of God and am become a laughing-stock to the devil. Why do I live any longer? Ah me, what have I done? Ah me, from whence, how low am I fallen! How shall I be hid? Where shall I go? Into what pit shall I cast myself? Where is the exhortation of the blessed man, "Keep thy soul spotless for thy immortal bride-groom"? I dare no more look up to heaven. I am lost, both to God and men. I dare not approach that holy man, sinner as I am and full of uncleanness. Were I to make such an attempt, surely fire would come out of that door and consume me. It is better for me to go where none knows me. For I am undone, and there is no salvation for me.' And rising up, she went straight to another city and became servant at an inn.

A little before this Abraham saw a vision: a dragon, great and terrible, rising out of his place. And coming to his cell, he found a dove and devoured it, and then returned to his place. The holy man, coming to himself, was much troubled, and wept bitterly and said, 'Thou, Lord knowest all things, and thou only knowest what this vision meaneth.' After two days he saw the same dragon again. And he came out of his place to the blessed man and, laying his head under Abraham's feet, burst asunder, and the dove was found alive in the dragon's belly.

Coming to himself, he called once and again, saying, 'Child, where art thou? Behold, here are two days that thou hast not opened thy mouth in the praise of God.' Finding that none answered and that she was not there, he perceived the vision related to her. And he groaned in spirit and said, 'O Saviour of the world, bring back this lamb into thy fold, that my gray hairs come not down with sorrow to the grave. Lord, despise not my supplication. But send down thy hand and take her out of the mouth of the dragon that hath devoured her.'

After a season he heard where she was, and having learned all things concerning her, he called one of his friends and said to him, 'Bring me an horse and the habit of a soldier.' And having put it on, with a large cap upon his head, he left his cell and rode away. Being come to the place he alighted and went in, and after a time said to the innkeeper, 'Friend, I have heard thou hast a beautiful damsel here. Call her to me, that I may rejoice with her.' Being called, she came. When the holy man saw her, in her harlot's attire, he was melting into tears. But he refrained himself, that she might not perceive it. After they sat down, she embraced him, and kissed his neck. And she smelled the smell of his cell, and called to mind past things, and groaning deeply said, 'Woe is me! What am I?' The innkeeper, being astonished, said, 'Mary, thou hast now been with us two years, and I never heard thee groan before or heard such a word from thee. What is come to thee?' She answered, 'Would I had died three years since; then I had been happy.'

Immediately Abraham said to him, 'Prepare us a supper, that we may rejoice together, for I am come from far, for *her* sake.' After supper she said to him, 'Let us go into the chamber.' And when they were come in he saw a bed made ready. And he sat upon it and said, 'Make fast the door.' She made it fast and came to him. Having taken hold of her, so that she could not run away, he took off his cap and said to her, weeping, 'My child, Mary, dost thou not know me? Am not I he that brought thee up? Mary, what is come to thee? Who hath destroyed thee, my daughter? Where are thy prayers and thy tears? Thy watching and holy exercise? My child, when thou hadst sinned, why didst thou not tell me, that I might have humbled myself for thee? My daughter, why hast thou done this? Why hast thou forsaken thy father?' She remained in his hands as a lifeless stone, till he said to her with tears, 'Dost thou not speak to me, my child, Mary? Dost thou not speak to me? Am I not come hither for thy sake? I have besought the Lord concerning thee.' Till midnight he continued exhorting and comforting her. Then, coming a little to herself, she said to him weeping, 'I cannot look at thee, for I am defiled with sin.' The blessed man replied, 'On me be thy sin; only come, let us go to our place.' She said to him, 'If it be possible for me to repent and if God can accept my repentance, I come; and I fall down and kiss thy steps, wetting them with my tears, that thou hast thus had compassion on me a forlorn wretch and art come hither to draw me out of the mire of sin.' And laying her head at his feet, she wept bitterly all the night, saying, 'What shall I render thee for all thy benefits?'

Early in the morning he set her upon the horse and went before her with great joy. And being come to his place, he put her in the inner cell, where she gladly resumed her former exercise, with sackcloth and ashes and much humiliation, with mourning and watching and ceaseless calling upon God. And the merciful Lord gave her a sign that he accepted her repentance, healing many that were sick through her prayers.

Holy Abraham lived ten years after, beholding her good conversation, and blessing and praising and magnifying God. Then, having lived seventy years, he slept in peace. Mary survived him thirty and five years, calling upon God night and day, insomuch that all who passed by glorified God, who saveth them that were gone astray.

Among the believers who met in the evening, God had kindled a vehement desire of his full salvation. Inquiring how it was that in all these parts we have scarce one living witness of this, I constantly received from every person one and the same answer, 'We see now, we sought it by our *works*. We never thought it was to come *gradually*. We never expected to receive it *in a moment*, by *faith*, as we did *justification*.'[43] What wonder is it then that you have been fighting all these years as one that 'beateth the air'.[44]

Fri. 22. I earnestly exhorted all who were sensible of their wants and athirst for holiness to look unto Jesus, to come to him *just as they were* and receive *all* his promises. And surely it will not be long before some of these also are fully saved by simple faith.

Sat. 23. I rode over to Plessey. I was wet through both going and coming, but I did not repent of my journey. Such a number gathered together, a great part of whom could rejoice in God. These were quite ripe for all the great and precious promises, which they received with all gladness.

Mon. 25. I rode to Shields and preached in an open place to a listening multitude. Many of them followed me to South Shields, where I preached in the evening to almost double the congregation. How ripe for the gospel are these also! What is wanting but more labourers?

'More! Why, is there not here (as in every parish in England)

[43] See Sermon 43, 'The Scripture Way of Salvation', III.17 (2:168-69 in this edn.).
[44] 1 Cor. 9:26.

a particular minister who takes care of all their souls?' There is one here who *takes charge* of all their souls;[45] what *care* of them he takes is another question. It may be, he neither knows nor cares whether they are going to heaven or hell. Does he ask man, woman, or child any question about it from one Christmas to the next? O what account will such a pastor give to the Great Shepherd in that day!

Tue. 26. I went on to Sunderland and in the evening preached in the new house. The next evening I preached at Monkwearmouth.[46]

Thur. 28. About noon I preached at Biddick, and the power of God was in the midst of his people; and more eminently at Sunderland in the evening. After preaching, I met the believers and exhorted them to 'go on to perfection'.[47] It pleased God to apply the plain words which were spoken, so that all were athirst for him. Objections vanished away, and a flame was kindled almost in every heart.

Sun. 31. I preached again, both morning and evening, in Monkwearmouth church.[48] But it would not near contain the people, many of whom were constrained to go away. After evening service, I hastened to Newcastle and exhorted a willing multitude to 'stand in the ways and see', and 'ask for the old paths' and 'walk therein'.[49]

In the week following, I preached at many little places round

[45] The perpetual curate of South Shields, 1754 till his death in 1775, aged 74, was Samuel Dennis, who matriculated at Christ Church in 1719, and became M.A. Dennis was non-resident, and assistant curates and a lecturer (William Radley) were appointed to the parish during his time. In 1750–51 he was curate of St. Mary Magdalen, and the holder of minor offices about Durham Cathedral where he was buried. According to C. M. Carlton, he was also rector of 'Beford', Yorks.; see C. M. Carlton, *The Monumental Inscriptions of the Cathedral, Parish Churches, Cemeteries of the City of Durham* (Durham, 1880), 1:61 (only 1 vol. published).

[46] Orig., 'Monk-were-mouth'.

[47] Heb. 6:1.

[48] Thomas Goodday (1705–68) matriculated at Queen's College, Oxford, 1736, aged 20, but did not graduate. He was perpetual curate of Monkwearmouth from 1744 (Auckland Subscription Book), and a devoted friend of the Wesleys. 'At this time the Methodists had no chapel in the place: they worshipped God in the upper room of a dwelling-house, adjoining the residence of Mr. Goodday . . . who had a private entrance to it. Mr. Goodday here constantly took his seat under the Methodist ministry; nor was he ever known to absent himself from hearing the plainest preacher, or the feeblest Exhorter. . . . [JW] usually occupied his church whenever he visited Sunderland'; see *Wesleyan Methodist Magazine*, 52 (1829):795-96. He was listed by William Fordyce as an author, see *The History and Antiquities of the County Palatine of Durham*, 2 vols. (Newcastle, 1855–57), 2:442.

[49] Cf. Jer. 6:16.

Newcastle. Friday, June 5, I went to Prudhoe, where there had been some jar in the society, occasioned by a few who had lately espoused and warmly defended a new opinion. I said not one word about it, but preached on 'there is joy in heaven over one sinner that repenteth, more than over ninety and nine just persons who need no repentance.'[50] Afterwards, perceiving their hearts were much softened, I met the society and exhorted them to beware of bitter zeal and to 'walk in love, as Christ also loved us'.[51] They were ashamed before God, and (for the present at least) their contentions were at an end.

In the evening, I preached at Nafferton and the next morning rode to Winlaton, where I had appointed to be between twelve and one. They placed the stand exactly fronting the sun, which shone very warm and very bright. But almost as soon as I began the clouds rose and shadowed us till I concluded. I preached at Swalwell at five to such a congregation as was never seen there before.

Mon. 8. I rode to Hexham and preached at noon in an open place near the church. Some expected there would be much disturbance, but there was none at all. We rode thence over the mountains to Allendale,[52] where I had not been for several years. After preaching and meeting the society, I took horse again and, crossing another chain of mountains, reached Weardale before eleven.

Thur. 9. I preached at nine but was obliged to stand abroad because of the multitude of people. The sun shone full in my face, but after having spent a short time in prayer I regarded it not. I then met the society and came just in time to prevent their all turning Dissenters, which they were on the point of doing, being quite disgusted at the curate,[53] whose life was no better than his doctrine.

At noon I preached in Teesdale. Most of the men are lead-miners, who a while ago were turned out of their work for following 'this way'.[54] By this means many of them got into far

[50] Cf. Luke 15:7.

[51] Cf. Eph. 5:2.

[52] JW had visited Allendale on two previous occasions, in 1748 and 1752, but after this visit, he never mentions the dale again.

[53] Thomas Coulthard was unlicensed perpetual curate of Allendale at a visitation in 1757, the previous perpetual curate having been buried there on 21 March 1756, as was Coulthard himself on 17 September 1779. He was apparently baptized in 1711, graduated M.A. at Glasgow in 1731, and was presented to the two livings of Edmondbyers and Muggleswick in 1743, which he also held till his death.

[54] Acts 9:2, etc.

better work. And some time after, their old master was glad to employ them again.

We had a long stage from hence to Swaledale,[55] where I found an earnest, loving, simple people, whom I likewise exhorted not to leave the Church, though they had not the best of ministers.[56] I then baptized a man and two women who had been bred among the Anabaptists, and I believe all of them received such a blessing therein as they were not able to express.

Wed. 10. I took horse at half-hour past three and reached Barnard Castle soon after six. I preached at eight in a ground adjoining to the town. Are these the people that a few years ago were like roaring lions?[57] They were now quiet as lambs, nor could several showers drive them away till I concluded. In the evening I preached at Brancepeth[58] near Bishop Auckland. Most of the congregation, though I stood in the street, were deeply attentive. Only one, a kind of gentleman, seemed displeased. But he had none to second him.

Fri. 12. We had one of the most solemn watch-nights at Newcastle which we have had for several years. Sat. 13. I rode once more to Sunderland and preached as usual to a numerous congregation. Sun. 14. After Mr. G[oodday] had read prayers, I spoke exceeding plain to as many as could crowd into the church. And out of so 'many that are called', will not some 'be chosen'?[59]

About three, I preached at Gateshead Fell; about five, at the Garth Heads[60]—at each place to a larger congregation than I ever saw there before. What a change is wrought in this whole country! And will it not be wrought in the whole kingdom?

Mon. 15. I rode to Durham, having appointed to preach there at noon. The meadow near the riverside was quite convenient,

[55] The destination was again determined by the prospect of hospitality. The Spensleys of Blades near Low Row, where the Methodist cause in Swaledale began, fitted up a cottage adjoining their house for preaching, and provided a home for JW. See *Methodist Recorder* (Winter, 1900):25.

[56] Timothy Dickonson, A.B. (*c.* 1711–82), vicar of Bolton-on-Swale, 1732–82, and Grinton, 1742–82. The church in Swaledale had by this date been reduced to a very low ebb by pluralism and a relative independence of episcopal oversight. Dickonson matriculated at Trinity College, Cambridge, in 1728, and graduated B.A., 1731–32. Thomas D. Whitaker, *A History of Richmondshire*, 2 vols. (London, 1823), 1:314.

[57] For JW's adventure with the Barnard Castle fire-engine on May 25, 1752, see 20:424 in this edn.

[58] Brancepeth was a township and parish 4¼ miles south-west of Durham.

[59] Cf. Matt. 20:16.

[60] Garth Heads was a street just to the north-west of the Keelman's Hospital.

and the small rain neither disturbed me nor the congregation.[61] In the afternoon I rode to Hartlepool. But I had much ado to preach. My strength was gone as well as my voice, and indeed they generally go together. Three days in a week I can preach thrice a day without hurting myself. But I had now far exceeded this, besides meeting classes and exhorting the societies. I was obliged to lie down good part of Tuesday; however, in the afternoon I preached at Sheraton,[62] and in the evening at Hartlepool again, though not without difficulty. Wednesday 17, I rode to Stockton, where a little before the time of preaching my voice and strength were restored at once. The next evening it began to rain just as I began to preach, but it was suspended till the service was over. It then rained again till eight in the morning.

Fri. 19. It was hard work to ride eight miles, so called, in two hours and an half, the rain beating hard upon us, and the by-road being exceeding slippery. But we forgot all this when we came to the Grange, so greatly was God present with his people. Thence we rode to Darlington.[63] Here we were under a difficulty again. Not half the people could come in, and the rain forbade my preaching without. But at one (the hour of preaching) the rain stopped and did not begin again till past two. So the people stood very conveniently in the yard. And many did not care to go away. When I went in, they crowded to the door and windows, and stayed till I took horse. At seven I preached at Yarm, and desired one of our brethren to take my place in the morning.

Sat. 20. At noon I applied those words, 'Now abide faith, hope, love; but the greatest of these is love.'[64]

This evening also it rained at Hutton Rudby[65] till seven, the hour of preaching. But God heard the prayer, and from the time I began we had only some scattering drops. After sermon, the

[61] Christopher Hopper describes how JW preached 'to a very large auditory. One poor man was favoured with a stone, and lost a little blood; but in the general they behaved tolerably well.' Jackson, *Early Methodist Preachers*, 1:211.

[62] Orig., 'Cherington', no doubt an error for Sheraton, a township in the parish of Monk Hesleden, 5 miles north-west of Hartlepool.

[63] The 'Grange' was Morton Grange, 2½ miles east of Darlington. The peaceful atmosphere in this area was soon disrupted by George Bell's prophecy of the end of the world. In 1763 George Story found that 'many people were much frightened; but their fears soon gave place to resentment, and they threatened to pull down the [meeting-]house. . . . Providentially I found in the Newcastle paper, a paragraph wherein Mr. Wesley disavowed all connection with Mr. Bell, and all credit to his prophecy. This I read to the people, which instantly quieted them.' *Arminian Magazine* 5 (1782):126.

[64] 1 Cor. 13:13 (*Notes*).

[65] Orig., 'Hutton-Rugby'.

society alone filled the new preaching-house. So mightily has the word of God prevailed since Alexander Mather laboured here.[66]

Sunday 21, I preached to a larger congregation than in the evening, on 'Behold what manner of love the Father hath bestowed upon us, that we should be called the children of God!'[67] I then rode to Osmotherley, where the minister read prayers seriously[68] and preached an useful sermon. After service, I began in the churchyard; I believe many were wounded and many comforted. After dinner, I called on Mr. Adams, who first invited me to Osmotherley.[69] He was reading the strange account of the two missionaries who have lately made such a figure—in the newspapers.[70] I suppose the whole account is just such another gross imposition upon the public as the man's gathering the people together to see him go into the quart bottle.[71] 'Men seven hundred years old!' And why not seven yards high? He that *can* believe it, let him believe it.

At five I preached at Potto, a mile from Hutton. When I began I was extremely weak. But God renewed my strength and so applied his word that it seemed as if *everyone must* believe it. But the Scripture cannot be broken. Some seed will still fall 'by the way-side', and some 'on stony ground'![72]

Mon. 22. I spoke one by one to the society at Hutton Rudby. They were about eighty in number, of whom near seventy were believers, and sixteen (probably) renewed in love. Here were two bands of children, one of boys and one of girls, most of whom

[66] As recently as 1759. Jackson, *Early Methodist Preachers*, 2:178.

[67] 1 John 3:1 (*Notes*).

[68] William Deason, see Mar. 1, 1747, n. 63 (20:161 in this edn.).

[69] On Thomas Adams, alias Watson, see Mar. 28, 1745, n. 34 (20:58 in this edn.).

[70] 'Two men arrived from Cologne who say they came from Damascus, are 700 years old, and are sent by heaven to call men to repentance. They foretell the dissolution of the world in 1771, understand Greek, Latin, Hebrew, and Chaldaic, and are sent to Rome for further examination'; *Gentleman's Magazine* 31 (1761):187. At Osmotherley (as the society book records) they further prophesied, 'Constantinople Destroy'd 1766: ye true god acknowledged by all nations in general, 1767: England overflow'd 1769: an earthquake all over ye world 1770: the fall of ye sun, mun and stars 1771: the globe of ye earth burnt 1772: ye universal judgement 1773.' JW would have approved the final note of the Osmotherley classleader: 'I believe it not: James Hunton.' *WHS* 3 (1901):94.

[71] In 1749 an advertisement (attributed to the Duke of Montague) appeared in the press announcing that a performer at the New Theatre in the Haymarket would in full public view get into a common wine-bottle. Obvious though the hoax was, the theatre was full, and attracted many of the upper orders, including the Duke of Cumberland. No performer appearing, the audience became riotous, troops were called out, and in the confusion Cumberland's diamond-hilted sword was stolen. *Wesleyan Methodist Magazine* 132 (1909):133.

[72] Mark 4:4-5.

were walking in the light. Four of those who seemed to be saved from sin were of one family, and all of them walked holy and unblameable,[73] adorning the doctrine of God their Saviour.[74]

At eleven I preached once more, though in great weakness of body, and met the stewards of all the societies. I then rode to Stokesley, and having examined the little society, went on for Guisborough. The sun was burning hot, but in a quarter of an hour a cloud interposed, and he troubled us no more. I was desired by a gentleman of the town to preach in the market-place. And there a table was placed for me. But it was in a bad neighbourhood. For there was so vehement a stench of stinking fish as was ready to suffocate me. And the people roared like the waves of the sea, but the voice of the Lord was mightier.[75] And in a few minutes, the whole multitude was still and seriously attended while I proclaimed 'Jesus Christ, made of God unto us wisdom, and righteousness, and sanctification, and redemption.'[76]

Tue. 23. I began about five near the same place and had a great part of the same audience. Yet they were not the same: the change might easily be read in their countenance. When we took horse and just faced the sun, it was hard work for man and beast. But about eight the wind shifted and, blowing in our face, kept us cool till we came to Whitby.

In the evening I preached on the top of the hill,[77] to which you ascend by an hundred, ninety and one steps. The congregation was exceeding large, and ninety-nine in an hundred were attentive. When I began, the sun shone full in my face, but he was soon clouded and shone no more till I had done.

After meeting the society, I talked with a sensible woman whose experience seemed peculiar. She said, 'A few days before Easter last I was deeply convinced of sin, and in Easter week I knew my sins were forgiven, and was filled with "joy and peace in believing".[78] But in about eighteen days I was convinced in a dream of the necessity of an higher salvation, and I mourned day and night in agony of desire to be thoroughly sanctified, till on the twenty-third day after my justification, I found a total change, together with a clear witness that the blood of Jesus had cleansed me from all unrighteousness.'

[73] Col. 1:22.
[74] See Titus 2:10.
[75] See Ps. 93:4.
[76] Cf. 1 Cor. 1:30.
[77] By the old church and abbey.
[78] Rom. 15:13.

Wed. 24. I walked round the old abbey, which both with regard to its size (being, I judge, an hundred yards long) and the workmanship of it, is one of the finest, if not the finest ruin in the kingdom. Hence we rode to Robin Hood's Bay, where I preached at six in the Lower Street near the quay. In the midst of the sermon a large cat, frighted out of a chamber, leaped down upon a woman's head and ran over the heads or shoulders of many more. But none of them moved or cried out, any more than if it had been a butterfly.

Thur. 25. I had a pleasant ride to Scarborough, the wind tempering the heat of the sun. I had designed to preach abroad in the evening, but the thunder, lightning, and rain prevented. However, I stood on a balcony, and several hundreds of people stood below and, notwithstanding the heavy rain, would not stir till I concluded.

Fri. 26. I rode to Hull and had there also the comfort of finding some witnesses of the great salvation. I was constrained to leave them early in the morning, on Saturday 27. At seven I preached in Beverley, about one in Pocklington, and at York in the evening, to far the genteelest audience I have had since I left Edinburgh.

Mon. 29. I met the classes and found many therein who were much alive to God. But many others were utterly dead, which sufficiently accounts for the society's not increasing. Wednesday, July 1, the stewards met from the societies in the country. In the evening we all wrestled with God for the revival of his work. Many found their hearts much enlarged herein and had confidence he would answer the prayer.

Thur. 2. I set out early for North Cave,[79] twenty computed miles from York. I preached there at nine to a deeply serious congregation, and was much refreshed. At two I preached to such another congregation at Thorpe, and concluded the day by preaching and meeting the society at Pocklington.

Fri. 3. We returned to York, where I was desired to call upon a poor prisoner in the castle. I had formerly occasion to take notice of an hideous monster called a *chancery bill.*[80] I now saw the fellow to it, called *a declaration.* The plain fact was this. Some time since, a man who lived near Yarm assisted others in running some brandy. His share was worth near four pounds. After he had wholly left off that bad work and was following his own business,

[79] North Cave was a township and parish 6 miles south from Market Weighton.
[80] See above, Dec. 19, 1759.

that of a weaver, he was arrested and sent to York jail. And not long after comes down *a declaration* 'that Jac. Wh—— had landed a vessel laded with brandy and geneva at the port of London, and sold them there, whereby he was indebted to his Majesty £577 and upwards.' And to tell this worthy story the lawyer takes up thirteen or fourteen sheets of trebly stamped paper.

O England, England! Will this reproach never be rolled away from thee? Is there anything like this to be found either among Papists, Turks, or heathens? In the name of truth, justice, mercy, and common sense, I ask, (1) Why do men lie for lying['s] sake? Is it only to keep their hands in? What need else of saying it was the port of London, when everyone knew the brandy was landed above three hundred miles from thence? What a monstrous *contempt of truth* does this show, or rather *hatred* to it! (2) Where is the *justice* of swelling four pounds into five hundred and seventy-seven? (3) Where is the *common sense* of taking up fourteen sheets to tell a story that may be told in ten lines? (4) Where is the *mercy* of thus grinding the face of the poor, thus sucking the blood of a poor, beggared prisoner? Would not this be execrable villainy, if the paper and writing together were only sixpence a sheet, when they have stripped him already of his little all and not left him fourteen groats in the world?

Sun. 5. Believing one hindrance of the work of God in York was the neglect of field preaching, I preached this morning at eight in an open place near the city walls. Abundance of people ran together, most of whom were deeply attentive. One or two only were angry and threw a few stones, but it was labour lost, for none regarded them.

Mon. 6. I rode to Tadcaster and preached within, the rain not suffering us to be abroad as I intended. In the evening I preached at Otley and afterward talked with many of the society. There is reason to believe that ten or twelve of these are filled with the love of God. I found one or two more the next day at Fewston,[81] a few miles north of Otley (where I preached at noon), whom God had raised up to witness the same good confession. And indeed, the whole congregation seemed just ripe for receiving all the promises.

Wed. 8. I rode to Knaresborough, where it was expected we should not meet with so friendly a reception. But the Lord is King.[82] Our own house being too small, I preached in the

[81] Fewston was a parish and township 7 miles north of Otley.

[82] See Ps. 10:16.

assembly-room. Most of the people looked wild enough when they came in. But they were tame before they went out and behaved as decently and seriously as the congregation at Otley.

Indeed, the mob never was so furious here as they were formerly at Otley, where the good magistrate *directed*, 'Do what you will to them, so you *break no bones*.' But may not a man cut his neighbour's throat without breaking his bones?

The remaining part of this week I preached at Guiseley, Bingley, and Keighley. Sunday 12, I had appointed to be at Haworth. But the church would not near contain the people, who came from all sides. However, Mr. Grimshaw had provided for this by fixing a scaffold on the outside of one[83] of the windows, through which I went after prayers, and the people likewise all went out into the churchyard. The afternoon congregation was larger still. What has God wrought in the midst of these rough mountains!

Mon. 13. At five, I preached on the manner of waiting for *perfect love*, the rather to satisfy Mr. Grimshaw, whom many had laboured to puzzle and perplex about it. So once more their bad labour was lost, and we were more united both in heart and judgment than ever.

At noon I preached in Colne, once inaccessible to the gospel, but now the yard I was in would not contain the people. I believe I might have preached at the cross without the least interruption.

About five, I preached at Padiham, another place eminent for all manner of wickedness. The multitude of people obliged me to stand in the yard of the preaching-house.[84] Over against me, at a little distance, sat some of the most impudent women I ever saw. Yet I am not sure that God did not reach their hearts. For

> They roared and would have blushed, if capable of shame.[85]

In the morning I preached at Burnley Wood Green,[86] on 'Be ye perfect, as your Father which is in heaven is perfect.'[87] Mr.

[83] Orig., 'some', corrected in the errata and Wesley's own copy of his *Works* (1774).

[84] For the 'stealthy' building of this meeting-house in 1759, see B. Moore, *History of Wesleyan Methodism in Burnley and East Lancashire* (Burnley, 1899), pp. 20-21.

[85] Cf. Samuel Wesley, Jun., *Poems on Several Occasions* (London, Say, 1736), 'The Battle of the Sexes', st. xxv, altering the opening 'He' to 'They'.

[86] Orig., 'Bentley Wood Green', no doubt an error for 'Burnley Wood Green', which lies between Padiham and Bacup. Burnley Wood is on the south side of the town. Burnley itself does not appear in the Journal until July 13, 1784, but a Methodist society was formed here in 1763.

[87] Cf. Matt. 5:48.

G[rimshaw] afterwards told me that *this perfection* he firmly believed and daily prayed for, namely, the love of God and man, producing all those fruits which are described in our Lord's Sermon upon the Mount.

About noon I preached at Bacup,[88] a village in Rossendale. The new preaching-house is large but not large enough to contain the congregation. Soon after five, I preached at Heptonstall. The society here had been greatly hurt by two leaders, getting into new opinions. One of them fell upon me directly for 'denying the righteousness of Christ'. On this we discoursed about an hour. The issue was, one of them was quite convinced, and the other (to my no small satisfaction) desired me to put a new leader in his place.

Wed. 15. About seven, I preached at Ewood, and about noon at Halifax. New opinions had done harm here also. But at this time all was quiet. I rode over to Bradford in the afternoon, where I found an Anabaptist teacher had perplexed and unsettled the minds of several.[89] But they are now less ignorant of Satan's devices.

Fri. 17. I rode to Birstall and was much comforted to find many of our first children in this county who are not yet weary of the good, old way. May they continue therein unto the day of the Lord Jesus!

Sat. 18. At one, I preached at South Royd.[90] The good people had placed the stand so that the sun, which was very hot, shone upon my head, and the wind, which was very cold, blew in my neck. But it was all one: I was on my Master's business. And great was our rejoicing in him.

Sun. 19. I preached in Birstall room at eight. At one, we had thousands upon thousands, the greatest part of whom were

[88] Orig., 'Baycup'. Bacup was a township in the parish of Whalley (later a chapelry in its own right), 6 miles east of Haslingden.

[89] William Crabtree (1720–1811), minister of the General Baptist Church, Scruton. The Yorkshire Baptists had never succumbed to the domination of the great hyper-Calvinists of the south, Gill and Brine. Some, like Fawcett and Jackson, had found no scruple against powerful evangelism in the Rossendale area just visited by JW; others, like Crabtree, were not too clear how they stood in relation to the great crux about offers of grace, and, though feeling obliged to tilt against Arminianism, regretted the bitterness controversy caused; W. R. Ward, 'The Baptists and the Transformation of the Church, 1780–1830', *Baptist Quarterly* 25 (1973):167-84; Isaac Mann, *Memoirs of the late Rev. Wm. Crabtree* (London, 1875).

[90] Perhaps Royd, a hamlet 4½ miles south-east of Penistone; more probably, South Royd, a hamlet in the parish of Kirkheaton, 2½ miles east of Huddersfield.

persons 'fearing God and working righteousness'.[91] I rode thence to Leeds in order to preach a funeral sermon for Mary Shent,[92] who after many severe conflicts died in great peace. It was one of the largest congregations which has been seen at Leeds, to whom I spoke very plain from part of the Gospel for the day, 'Give an account of thy stewardship, for thou mayest be no longer steward.'[93]

I hastened back to the love-feast at Birstall.[94] It was the first of the kind which had been there. Many were surprised when I told them, 'The very design of a love-feast is a free and familiar conversation, in which every man, yea, and woman, has liberty to speak whatever may be to the glory of God.' Several then did speak, and not in vain: the flame ran from heart to heart. Especially while one was declaring with all simplicity the manner wherein God, during the morning sermon (on those words, 'I will: be thou clean'),[95] had set her soul at full liberty. Two men also spoke to the same effect, and two others who had found peace with God. We then joyfully poured out our souls before God and praised him for his marvellous works.

Mon. 20. I came to a full explanation with that good man, Mr. V[enn].[96] Lord, if I *must* dispute, let it be with the children of the devil. Let me be at peace with *thy* children!

On Tuesday, Wednesday, and Thursday, I preached at the neighbouring towns. Friday 24, in speaking from those words, 'In

91 Cf. Acts 10:35.

92 Probably the wife of William Shent, ex-barber and itinerant; see June 2, 1753 (20:460 in this edn.).

93 Luke 16:2.

94 This, the first love-feast in the West Riding, attracted participants even from Bradford, 'who almost to their dying day were accustomed to speak of it as a peculiarly gracious season'; Stamp, *Historical notices of Wesleyan Methodism,* p. 42.

95 Matt. 8:3.

96 JW had a few days previously confessed his embarrassment in relation to Venn. 'Several years before he came to Huddersfield some of our preachers went thither, carrying their lives in their hands, and with great difficulty established a little earnest Society. These eagerly desire them to preach there still; not in opposition to Mr. Venn (whom they love, esteem, and constantly attend), but to supply what they do not find in his preaching. It is a tender point. Where there is a gospel ministry already, we do not desire to preach; but whether we can leave off preaching because such an one comes after, is another question, especially when those who are awakened and convinced by us beg and require the continuance of our assistance.' The immediate outcome of the present discussion was satisfactory: 'We have amicably compromised the affair of preaching. He is well pleased that the preachers should come once a month' (Telford, 4:160-61). But the embarrassment continued on both sides. To try to placate Venn, JW withdrew his preachers altogether in 1762; to secure the continuance of his own work in Huddersfield, Venn had to resort to building non-episcopal chapels (Telford, 4:215-18).

many things we offend all,' I observed: (1) As long as we live our soul is connected with the body. (2) As long as it is thus connected, it cannot think but by the help of bodily organs. (3) As long as these organs are imperfect, we are liable to mistakes, both speculative and practical. (4) Yea, and a mistake may occasion my loving a good man less than I ought, which is a defective, that is, a wrong temper. (5) For all these we need the atoning blood, as indeed for every defect or omission. Therefore, (6) all men have need to say daily, 'Forgive us our trespasses.'

About one, I preached at Bramley, where Jonas Rushford, about fourteen years old, gave me the following relation:

About this time last year I was desired by two of our neighbours to go with them to Mr. Crowther's at Skipton, who would not speak to *them* about a man that had been missing twenty weeks,[97] but bid them bring a boy twelve or thirteen years old. When we came in, he stood reading a book. He put me into a bed, with a looking-glass in my hand, and covered me all over. Then he asked me whom I had a mind to see. And I said, 'My mother.' I presently saw her with a lock of wool in her hand, standing just in the place, and the clothes she was in, as she told me afterwards. Then he bid me look again for the man that was missing, who was one of our neighbours. And I looked and saw him riding towards Idle, but he was very drunk. And he stopped at the alehouse and drank two pints more, and he pulled out a guinea to change. Two men stood by, a big man and a little man; and they went on before him and got two hedge-stakes. And when he came up, on Windle Common, at the top of the hill, they pulled him off his horse and killed him and threw him into a coal-pit. And I saw it all as plain as if I was close to them. And if I saw the men I should know them again.

We went back to Bradford that night, and the next day I went with our neighbours and showed them the spot where he was killed and the pit he was thrown into. And a man went down and brought him up. And it was as I had told them: his handkerchief was tied about his mouth and fastened behind his neck.

Is it improbable only, or flatly impossible, when all the circumstances are considered, that this should all be pure fiction? They that can believe this, may believe a man's getting into a bottle.[98]

97 *Works* (1774), 'days'.
98 The reference is to June 21, 1761, above.

From Bramley I rode to Kippax.[99] Mr. Venn came a little after we were gone into the church. Mr. Romaine read prayers. I preached on 'Christ crucified, to the Jews a stumbling-block, and to the Greeks foolishness'.[1] O why should they who agree in this great point fall out about smaller things!

Sat. 25. About one, I preached at Seacroft and found several who believed God had saved them from sin. In the evening, I talked with twelve or fourteen of these particularly. But I found not one who presumed to say that he did not need the atoning blood. Nor could I hear of any more than two persons that ever spoke in this manner. And these were soon after, *for that reason,* expelled out of Otley society.

Sun. 26. I preached at seven, on 'Lord, if thou wilt, thou canst make me clean.'[2] And Oh! what a flame did God kindle! Many were 'on fire to be dissolved in love'.[3]

About one, I preached to the usual congregation at Birstall. What a work is God working here also! Six in one class have within this week found peace with God; two this morning, in meeting the class. While I was praying on Sunday evening that God would give us a token for good, James Eastwood[4] was set at full liberty, as were William Wilson and Elizabeth his wife before, and Martha his daughter, with Agnes Gooddel, on the Wednesday after. To these were added Joseph Newsam and Richard Hellewell, sixteen years of age. So that the oldest of our believers now cry out, 'We never saw it before on this fashion.'[5]

Mon. 27. I preached at Staincross[6] about eleven, about five at Barley Hall,[7] the next morning at Sheffield. In the afternoon I rode on to Matlock Bath.[8] The valley which reaches from the

[99] Kippax was a substantial parish 6½ miles north-west of Pontefract. The constellation of evangelical clergy was occasioned by the fact that Lady Huntingdon's niece and friend, Mrs. Medhurst lived here (Seymour, *Huntingdon*, 1:290). Samuel Furly was acting briefly as curate of Kippax. He had been a friend of Venn at Cambridge and had briefly assisted Romaine in London immediately after his ordination (C. A. Hulbert, *Annals of the Church in Slaithwaite* [Huddersfield, 1864], p. 58; and see below, Apr. 19, 1764). The later vicar of Kippax, Edward Buckley (1743–83), was educated at Christ's College, Cambridge, B.A., 1766; M.A., 1769; priest, 1768; curate of Kippax and Hunslet, 1767–70; vicar of Kippax, 1770–83; he was nominated curate by Henry Crook, vicar of Kippax and curate of Hunslet, and helped to provide a meeting-house for the Methodists at Pontefract; *Methodist Recorder* (Dec. 17, 1908), p. 10.

[1] 1 Cor. 1:23. [2] Matt. 8:2. [3] Cf. 2 Pet. 3:12.

[4] He seems to have been briefly an itinerant. Everett, *Sheffield*, p. 186.

[5] Cf. Mark 2:12. [6] Staincross is a village 2 miles north of Barnsley.

[7] For Barley Hall, see June 15, 1742, n. 27 (19:278 in this edn.).

[8] Matlock Bath is 1 mile south of Matlock, and was just entering the period of its greatest popularity as a health resort. 'The waters were first applied to medicinal uses

town to the bath is pleasant beyond expression. In the bottom of this runs a little river, close to which a mountain rises, almost perpendicular, to an enormous height, part covered with green, part with ragged and naked rocks. On the other side, the mountain rises gradually, with tufts of trees here and there. The brow on both sides is fringed with trees, which seem to answer each other.

Many of our friends were come from various parts. At six, I preached standing under the hollow of a rock on one side of a small plain, on the other side of which was a tall mountain. There were many well-dressed hearers, this being the high season, and all of them behaved well. But as I walked back a gentleman-like man asked me, 'Why do you talk thus of *faith?—Stuff, nonsense.*' Upon inquiry, I found he was an eminent deist. What, has the plague crept into the Peak of Derbyshire?

Wed. 29. I preached at five near the Bath, in Woodseats at two, and in the evening at the end of the house in Sheffield to thrice as many people as it would have contained. Thursday and Friday, I preached at Rotherham in the shell of the new house, which is an octagon.[9] Pity our houses, where the ground will admit of it, should be built in any other form. The congregation was larger than ever, the society well united and much alive to God.

Saturday, August 1. I rode to Clayworth and, after preaching, laboured all I could to reconcile two brothers who had long been quarrelling about their inheritance. But it was labour lost. Indeed, the reason of the thing was clear, but passion is ever too hard for reason.

Hence, I went on to Misterton and both in the evening and morning spoke to a lifeless, money-getting people, in a sharper manner than ever I did before, and (I heard afterward) with good effect.

about the end of the seventeenth century, prior to which period the neighbourhood consisted of a few rude dwellings inhabited by miners.' Lewis, *England*, 3:244. Cf. G. Lipscomb, *A Description of Matlock Bath* (Birmingham, 1802).

[9] James Everett collected a story about this occasion from the itinerant, the elder Joseph Taylor, who had it from JW himself, of 'one of the most attentive hearers in the old octagon chapel in Rotherham he ever had—for, he continued, "while I was preaching in the octagon, the rabble drove in an ass—the animal stood in the aisle—turned up his eyes to the preacher—stood & looked—" & when he (Wesley) was done, the animal turned round and walked quietly out' (Methodist Archives, Tyerman MSS 2, fols. 26-27). The spiritual strength of the society, here reported by JW, was exemplified in a great revival the following year (Methodist Archives, Tyerman MSS 2, fol. 63). The Rotherham chapel was the first of the Methodist octagon chapels, the predominant style in the 1760s. At least fourteen were built before 1776. *WHS* 25 (1945):81-86.

Sun. 2. I had the satisfaction of hearing Mr. Madan[10] preach an excellent sermon at Haxey.[11] At two, I preached at Westwoodside to the largest congregation I ever saw in the Isle of Axholme, and to nearly the same at Epworth Cross, as soon as the church service was ended. After spending two days here, on Wednesday 5, I preached about nine at Ferry, and then rode on to Gainsborough. I preached in the old hall[12] to a mixed multitude, part civil, part rude as bears. We rode home through heavy rain, joined with much thunder and lightning, part of which was just over our heads. But 'the Lord sitteth above the water clouds.'[13] So we came safe, only very wet, to Epworth.

Thur. 6. I preached about nine at Hatfield Woodhouse,[14] and about one at Sykehouse to far the largest congregation which has been seen there for many years. Boast who will that 'Methodism (the revival of true religion) is just coming to nothing.' We know better things and are thankful to God for its continual increase.

Sat. 8. I preached at Winterton[15] to such a congregation as I suppose never met there before. From thence we rode on to Barrow,[16] where the mob was in readiness to receive us. But their hearts failed, so they gave only two or three huzzas and let us pass by unmolested.

As soon as I came out to preach we had another huzza. But as more and more of the angry ones came within hearing, they lost all their fierceness and sunk into calmness and attention. So I concluded my discourse with quietness and satisfaction. In the evening I preached at Grimsby, where I spent Sunday and Monday. Tuesday 11, I preached at two in Ludborough,[17] in the evening at Elkington.[18] The next morning we rode to Horncastle, where Satan's children had threatened terrible things. But they could go no farther than to give one feeble shout as we entered into the town. As the house would not contain the congregation, I preached on the outside of it. And there was no disturbance. Indeed a silly, pert man spoke twice or thrice, but none regarded him.

[10] On Martin Madan, see above, Dec. 19, 1758, n. 88.

[11] Orig., 'Haxley'.

[12] On this, see above, Aug. 3, 1759.

[13] Cf. Ps. 29:9 (BCP).

[14] Hatfield Woodhouse is a village 3 miles south of Thorne.

[15] Winterton was a parish 8¼ miles west from Barton-upon-Humber.

[16] Barrow upon Humber was a parish 3 miles east from Barton-upon-Humber.

[17] Orig., 'Lorborough'.

[18] North and South Elkington were parishes 3 miles and 2 miles, respectively, north-west from Louth.

About one, I preached at Sibsey,[19] on the edge of the Fens. There were a few wild colts here also. But all the rest (and they were not a few) were serious and deeply attentive. So were most of the congregation even at Boston, though much astonished, as not being used to field preaching.

Thur. 13. I took a walk through the town. I think it is not much smaller than Leeds,[20] but in general it is far better built. The church is indeed a fine building. It is larger, loftier, nay, and rather more lightsome, than even St. Peter's at Norwich. And the steeple is, I suppose, the highest tower in England,[21] nor less remarkable for the architecture than the height. The congregation in the evening was far more numerous than the day before. And I trust God fixed the arrows of conviction in not a few of their hearts.

We went forward after preaching at a friend's house about nine miles from Boston. Friday 14, we rode to Billingford,[22] and on Saturday to Norwich. After spending a few days here and a few more at Yarmouth and Colchester, on Saturday 22, I returned to London.

I found the work of God swiftly increasing here. The congregations in every place were larger than they had been for several years. Many were from day to day convinced of sin. Many found peace with God. Many backsliders were healed, yea filled with joy unspeakable. And many believers entered into such a rest as it had not before entered into their hearts to conceive. Meantime, the enemy was not wanting in his endeavours to sow tares among the good seed.[23] I saw this clearly but durst not use violence, lest in plucking up the tares I should root up the wheat also.[24]

Tuesday, September 1. Our Conference began,[25] and ended on Saturday. After spending a fortnight more in London and guarding both the preachers and people against running into

[19] Sibsey was a parish 5 miles north-east of Boston.

[20] JW's first-hand impressions misled him. The population of Boston at this date was about 3,500, that of Leeds nearly 30,000.

[21] Boston Stump, 272 feet high, overtops all English cathedral towers. *Boston and its Famous Stump* (Boston, 1929), p. 8.

[22] Orig., 'Bellingford'. Billingford was a Norfolk parish 3½ miles south-west of Foulsham.

[23] See Matt. 13:25.

[24] See Matt. 13:29.

[25] The Minutes of this Conference are lost, but it is clear from correspondence that among the subjects discussed was separation from the Church (Telford, 4:161-62). The signs of revival reported by JW were also observed by preachers at the Conference.

extremes on the one hand or the other, on Sunday 20, at night, I took the machine, and on Monday 21 came to Bristol.

Here likewise, I had the satisfaction to observe a considerable increase of the work of God. The congregations were exceeding large, and the people hungering and thirsting after righteousness.[26] And every day afforded us fresh instances of persons convinced of sin or converted to God. So that it seems God was pleased to pour out his spirit this year on every part both of England and Ireland—perhaps in a manner we had never seen before, certainly not for twenty years. O what pity that so many, even of the children of God, did not know the day of their visitation![27]

Sunday, Oct. 11. I preached at Kingswood, morning and afternoon, but not as I designed, under the sycamore-tree, because of the rain. In the ensuing week, I visited the societies in Somersetshire. Sunday 11, I observed God is reviving his work in Kingswood. The society, which had much decreased, being now increased again to near three hundred members, many of whom are now athirst for full redemption, which for some years they had almost forgot.

Tuesday 13, I preached at Newgate, at Kingswood in the afternoon, and in the evening at North Common.[28] Here a people are sprung up as it were out of the earth, most of them employed in the neighbouring brass-works. We took a view of these the next day, and one thing I learned here: the propriety of that expression, 'His feet were as fine brass, burning in a furnace.'[h] The brightness of this cannot easily be conceived. I have seen nothing like it but clear, white lightning.

Mon. 19. I desired all those to meet me who believed they were saved from sin. There were seventeen or eighteen. I examined them severally, as exactly as I could. And I could not find anything in their tempers (supposing they spoke true) any way contrary to their profession.

Wed. 21. I was desired by the condemned prisoners to give them one sermon more.[29] And on Thursday, Patrick Ward,[30] who was to die that day, sent to request I would administer the Sacrament to him. He was one and twenty years of age and had

[h] Rev. 1:15.

---

[26] See Matt. 5:6.
[27] See Luke 19:44.
[28] North Common is a locality 6 miles east of Bristol.
[29] At the Bristol Newgate.
[30] A poacher hanged for murder.

scarce ever a serious thought till he shot the man who went to take away his gun. From that instant, he felt a turn within and never swore an oath more. His whole behaviour in prison was serious and composed. He read, prayed, and wept much, especially after one of his fellow-prisoners had found peace with God.[31] His hope gradually increased till this day and was much strengthened at the Lord's Supper. But still he complained, 'I am not *afraid*, but I am not *desirous* to die. I do not find *that warmth* in my heart; I am not *sure* my sins are forgiven.' He went into the cart about twelve in calmness but mixed with sadness. But in a quarter of an hour, while he was wrestling with God in prayer (not seeming to know that anyone was near him), 'The Holy Ghost', said he, 'came upon me, and I knew that Christ was mine.' From that moment his whole deportment breathed a peace and joy beyond all utterance, till after having spent about ten minutes in private prayer, he gave the sign.

Sun. 25. I took a comfortable leave of Kingswood, leaving both the society and school in a flourishing state; and the next morning of Bristol, leaving the society larger than it had been for many years. Now let zeal as well as 'brotherly love continue',[32] and it will not decrease any more. Having travelled slowly through the intermediate societies, on Saturday 31, I came to London.

Sunday, November 1. I found the same spirit which I left here, both in the morning and evening service. Monday 2, at five, I began a course of sermons on Christian perfection. At seven, I began meeting the classes. Tue. 10. I found the society at Deptford more alive than ever, a sure consequence of which is their increasing in number. Thur. 12. I rode to Brentford. Here likewise God is at work, and sinners are converted to him. Sat. 14. I spent an hour with a little company near Grosvenor Square. For many years this has been the darkest, driest spot of all in or near London. But God has now watered the barren wilderness, and it is become a fruitful field.

Mon. 16. I retired to Lewisham,[33] having many things to write. Fri. 20. I spent an hour at St. George's Hospital. The behaviour of two or three patients there had done unspeakable good. Deep prejudice was torn up by the roots, and much goodwill to the truth had succeeded it. O what may not a single believer do who seeks nothing but the glory of God!

[31] John Cope, hanged for returning from transportation.

[32] Heb. 13:1.

[33] To the house of Ebenezer Blackwell.

Mon. 23. I went to Canterbury. The congregations were larger than I ever remember. And many found a deeper work of God in their hearts than ever they had known before. Thur. 26. I was desired to read part of Bishop Pontoppidan's *Natural History of Norway*.[34] I soon found he was a man of sense, yet credulous to an extreme. And therefore I was the less surprised when I came to his *craken* and *sea-serpent*. Of the former (an animal a mile round, to which a poor whale is no more than a gudgeon), he gives no proof or shadow of proof, nothing but vague, uncertain hearsays. 'Two sailors', he says, 'made oath of seeing part of the latter, seven or eight folds of his back.' But I did not talk with them myself, so I can lay little stress on their evidence. They might be *weak* men; they might be *frighted*—yea, they were, by their own confession. Or they might be men of *no conscience*—on any of which suppositions their testimony is nothing worth.

Sat. 28. We returned to London. Sun. 29. We had a comfortable love-feast, at which several declared the blessings they had found lately. We need not be careful by what *name* to call them, while *the thing* is beyond dispute. Many have, and many do daily experience an unspeakable change. After being deeply convinced of inbred sin, particularly of pride, anger, self-will, and unbelief, in a moment they *feel* all faith and love: no pride, no self-will, or anger. And from that moment they have continual fellowship with God, always rejoicing, praying, and giving thanks. Whoever ascribes such a change to the devil, I ascribe it to the Spirit of God. And I say, let whoever feels it wrought, cry to God that it may continue, which it will if he walks closely with God—otherwise it will not.

Preaching at Deptford, Welling, and Sevenoaks in my way, on Thursday, December 3, I came to Shoreham. There I read the celebrated life of St. Catherine of Genoa.[35] Mr. Lesley[36] calls one,

[34] Eric Pontoppidan, *The Natural History of Norway, Containing a Particular Account of the Temperature of the Air [&c.]*, trans. Andreas Berthelson (London, 1755). Pontoppidan (1698–1764) was Bishop of Bergen in Norway. Edvard Bull, et al., *Norsk Biografisk Leksikon* (Kristiania, 1921–23), 11:137-42.

[35] Orig., 'Katherine'. St. Catherine of Genoa, 1447–1510, a mystic notably studied in modern times by Friedrich von Hugel. Her spiritual doctrine is contained in the book *Vita e dottrina* (1551). A French version of this work appeared under the title *La Vie et les oeuvres spirituelles de S. Catherine d'Adency de Gennes* (Lyons, 1616; 2nd edn., Paris, 1666–67). There seems to have been no English version before that of New York, 1874.

[36] Perhaps William Aloysius Leslie (1641–1704), a Jesuit born in Aberdeenshire, who published a *Vita di S. Margharita, Regina di Scozia, raccolta da diversi autori* (Frome, 1675; and later edns.).

a devil of a saint; I am sure this was *a fool of a saint.* That is, if it was not the folly of her historian, who has aggrandized her into a mere idiot. Indeed, we seldom find a saint of God's making sainted by the Bishop of Rome. I preached at five to a small serious company and the next day returned to London.

Mon. 7. I rode to Colchester and had the satisfaction to find many of our brethren much alive to God. After confirming them as I could in the ways of God, on Thursday, I returned home. Sunday the 13th was a comfortable day, wherein several prisoners were set at liberty. Saturday 19, I visited many near Oxford Market and Grosvenor Square, and found God was still enlarging his work. More and more were convinced, converted to God, and built up day by day, and that notwithstanding the weakness of the instruments by whom God was pleased to work.

Mon. 21. I retired again to Lewisham and wrote *Farther Thoughts on Christian Perfection.*[37] Had the cautions given herein been observed, how much scandal had been prevented! And why were they not? Because my own familiar friend[38] was even now forming a party against me.

Fri. 25. We began, as usual, at four. A few days since, one who lived in known sin, finding heavy conviction, broke away and ran out, she knew not whither. She met one who offered her a shilling a week to come and take care of her child. She went gladly. The woman's husband, hearing her stir between three and four,[39] began cursing and swearing bitterly. His wife said, 'I wish thou wouldst go with her and see if anything will do *thee* good.' He did so. In the first hymn God broke his heart, and he was in tears all the rest of the service. How soon did God recompense this poor woman for taking the stranger in!

Sat. 26. I made a particular inquiry into the case of Mary Special,[40] a young woman then in Tottenham Court Road. She said,

> Four years since, I found much pain in my breasts, and afterward, hard lumps. Four months ago my left breast broke and kept running continually. Growing worse and worse, after some time I

[37] Published at London, 1763.

[38] Thomas Maxfield, see Nov. 2, 1751, n. 2 (20:406 in this edn.); and below, Dec. 29, 1761.

[39] To attend the 4 a.m. service at the Foundery.

[40] JW's London diary, Mar. 25, 1739, records '1 At Mr. Special's, religious talk with Nanny; dinner' (see 19:381 in this edn.).

was recommended to St. George's Hospital. I was let blood many times and took hemlock thrice a day, but I was no better, the pain and the lumps were the same, and both my breasts were quite hard and black as soot; when yesterday sennight I went to Mr. Owen's,[41] where there was a meeting for prayer. Mr. Bell[42] saw me and asked, 'Have you faith to be healed?' I said, 'Yes.' He prayed for me, and in a moment all my pain was gone. But the next day I felt a little pain again. I clapped my hands on my breasts and cried out, 'Lord, if thou wilt, thou canst make me whole.' It was gone. And from that hour I have had no pain, no soreness, no lumps or swelling, but both my breasts were perfectly well, and I have been so ever since.

Now here are plain facts: (1) She *was* ill; (2) she *is* well; (3) she became so in a moment. Which of these can, with any modesty, be denied?

Tue. 29. In order to remove some misunderstandings, I desired all the parties concerned to meet me. They did so; all but T[homas] M[axfiel]d, who flatly refused to come.[43] Is this only the first step toward a *separation?* Alas for the man! alas for the people![i]

Thur. 31. We concluded the year as usual with a solemn

[i] These were the words I wrote at the time.

---

[41] Daniel Owen, who in 1763 resigned along with George Bell. See below, Feb. 4, 1763.

[42] George Bell, an intimate of Daniel Owen and Thomas Maxfield, and bracketed with them by JW in his attempt to assess the doctrinal and disciplinary failings of the latter; see below, Nov. 1, 1762. 'George Bell . . . was a sergeant in the Life-guards. He was at one time unquestionably a man of piety, of deep communion with God, and of extraordinary zeal for the conversion of souls. But he was not a man of understanding: His imagination was lively, but his judgement weak' (Moore, *Wesley*, 2:222). He was converted in 1758, and professed sanctification in March 1761. JW was extremely loath to get rid of him, but had finally to do so (see below, Nov. 24, 1762; and Dec. 22, 1762). The spiritual healing which JW here gladly accepted, was a foretaste of increasingly extravagant claims: to raise the dead (*Arminian Magazine* 13 [1790]:42) and to foretell the end of the world for Feb. 28, 1783. On that day, JW preached against enthusiasm, 'went to bed at my usual time and was fast asleep by about ten o'clock'. According to Southey, Bell, 'passing from one extreme to another, the ignorant enthusiast became an ignorant infidel; turned fanatic in politics as he had done in religion; and having gone through all the degrees of disaffection and disloyalty, died, at a great age, a radical reformer.' Robert Southey, *The Life of Wesley and the Rise and Progress of Methodism*, Maurice H. Fitzgerald, ed., 2 vols. (London, 1925), 2:184; see also *Arminian Magazine* 3 (1780):674-76; and George J. Stevenson, *City Road Chapel, London, and its Associations, Historical, Biographical, and Memorial* (London, Stevenson, 1872), pp. 48, 80; hereafter, Stevenson, *City Road*.

[43] The difficulties continued, JW convinced both of Maxfield's essential wrongness and of the fact that God strangely blessed his work. On Jan. 5, 1763 (misdated 1762), JW wrote to Charles: 'If Thomas Maxfield continues as he is it is impossible he should long continue with us. But I live in hope of better things. Meantime, *festina lente*.' Telford, 4:199.

watch-night. O may we conclude our lives in the same manner, blessing and praising God!

Friday, January 1, 1762. We had, I believe, pretty near two thousand of the society at Spitalfields in the evening, where Mr. Berridge, Maxfield, and Colley[44] assisted me. And we found God was in the midst, while we devoted ourselves to him[45] in the most solemn and explicit manner.

Sat. 2. I set out for Everton in order to supply Mr. Berridge's church in his absence. In my way I preached at Rood Farm,[46] five and forty miles from London. Afterward, the moon shining bright, we had a pleasant ride to Everton.

Sun. 3. I read prayers and preached morning and evening to a numerous and lively congregation. I found the people in general were more settled than when I was here before. But they were in danger of running from east to west. Instead of thinking, as many then did, that none can[47] possibly have true faith but those that have trances or visions, they were now ready to think that whoever had anything of this kind had no faith.

Mon. 4. After preaching to a large congregation at Wrestlingworth, we rode on to Harston. I never preached a whole sermon by moonlight before. However, it was a solemn season—a season of holy mourning to some, to others of joy unspeakable.

Tue. 5. I preached in Harston at nine, and about eleven at Whittlesford,[48] three miles farther, to a people just ripe for 'Come unto me, all ye that are weary and heavy laden.'[49] In the afternoon we set out for Stoke, on the edge of Suffolk. As we rode through Haverhill, we were saluted with one huzza, the mob of that town having no kindness for Methodists. But all was quiet at Stoke, for Sir H[enry] A[rcher][50] will suffer no disturbance there. The congregation came from many miles round, and God was in the

[44] Benjamin Colley (d. 1767) of Tollerton, Yorks., was one of the enthusiasts with whom JW's policy of patience succeeded. Converted by the itinerant John Manners, he joined the Methodists in 1761, and receiving episcopal ordination, assisted JW as a clergyman in the London chapels. In 1762, 'he was carried away by the enthusiasm of George Bell and Thomas Maxfield,' but being reclaimed by Manners, he was appointed to Newcastle upon Tyne in 1763, and JW buried him four years later.

[45] Orig., 'ourselves'; 'to him' added only in errata and Wesley's personal notes to his *Works* (1774).

[46] Curnock notes 'near Biggleswade, on the road going to Potton'.

[47] Errata and Wesley's personal note in *Works* (1774), add 'can'.

[48] Orig., 'Wiltstow'. Whittlesford was a parish 7 miles south of Cambridge.

[49] Cf. Matt. 11:28.

[50] Alderman Sir Henry Archer, Kt., of Saffron Walden. He died June 11, 1770.

midst of them. Thus hearty prayers went up on every side. And many felt the answer to them.

Wed. 6. The largeness of the congregation at five showed they were not forgetful hearers. I preached longer than I am accustomed to do, but still they were not satisfied. Many crowded after me into the dwelling-house. After speaking a few words, I went to prayer. A cry began and soon spread through the whole company, so that my voice was lost. Two seemed to be distressed above all the rest. We continued wrestling with God till one of them had a good hope, and the other was 'filled with joy and peace in believing'.[51]

In the afternoon it blew a storm, by the favour of which we came into Haverhill quite unmolested. But, notwithstanding wind and rain, the people crowded so fast into the preaching-house that I judged it best to begin half an hour before the time, by which means it contained the greater part of them. Although they that could not come in made a little noise, it was a solemn and an happy season.

Thur. 7. Abundance of them came again at five and drank in every word. Here also, many followed me into the house and hardly knew how to part. At nine, I preached at Steeple Bumpstead,[52] three miles from Haverhill, to a considerably larger congregation. And all were serious. Hence we rode for Barkway, four miles from Royston. The preaching-place was exceeding large, yet it was well filled, and the people were wedged in as close as possible. And many of them found that God was there, to their unspeakable comfort.

Hence we rode to Barley, where I preached at one. A middle-aged woman dropped down at my side and cried aloud for mercy. It was not long before God put a new song in her mouth.[53] At six in the evening I preached at Melbourn. Here too God both wounded and healed.[54] I laid hold after preaching on a poor backslider, who quickly melted into tears and determined to return once more to him from whom she had deeply revolted.

[Fri. 8.] Here I talked at large with one who thinks he is renewed in love. Perhaps he is, but his understanding is so small, his experience so peculiar, and his expressions so uncouth, that I doubt very few will receive his testimony.

[51] Cf. Rom. 15:13.
[52] Orig., 'Steeple-Bumstead'.
[53] See Ps. 40:3.
[54] See Deut. 32:39.

Sat. 9. I rode to Potton. What has God wrought here since I saw this town twenty years ago![55] I could not then find a living Christian therein but wild beasts in abundance. Now here are many who know in whom they have believed,[56] and no one gives us an uncivil word! I preached at six to a very numerous and serious congregation. What have we to do to despair of any person or people?

Sun. 10. I preached at six in the morning to nearly the same congregation. I read prayers and preached, morning and afternoon, at Everton and gave the Sacrament to a large number of communicants. At four, we took horse and reached Grantchester a little before seven. Finding a little company met together, I spent half an hour with them exceedingly comfortably. And through the blessing of God I was no more tired when I went to bed than when I arose in the morning.

Mon. 11. The house was thoroughly filled at five, and that with serious and sensible hearers. I was sorry I had no more time at this place, especially as it was so near Cambridge, from whence many gentlemen used to come when any clergyman preached. But my work was fixed; so I took horse soon after preaching and rode to a village called Bottisham-Lode,[57] seven miles from Cambridge. Here a large congregation was soon assembled, and I had no sooner named my text, 'When they had nothing to pay, he frankly forgave them both,'[58] than a murmur ran through the whole people, and many of them were in tears. This concern increased as I went on, so that none appeared to be unmoved. One just by me cried with a bitter cry. But in a short time she shouted for joy. So did several others, so that it was not easy to tell whether more were wounded or comforted.

Hence we rode to Lakenheath and passed a comfortable night.

Tue. 12. Just as we set out the storm, which had been very high all night, brought on impetuous rain. It was a good providence (1) that we had now firm, sandy road, not clay and miry fields as yesterday; (2) that the wind was behind us—otherwise I believe it would have been impossible to go on. It was often ready to bear

55 JW's first mentioned visit to Potton on Feb. 16, 1747, in fact produced 'a serious congregation'; see 20:155 in this edn.

56 See 2 Tim. 1:12.

57 Orig., 'Botsam-lode'. Bottisham-Lode is a district of the parish of Bottisham, 6 miles east of Cambridge.

58 Luke 7:42.

away man and beast. However, in the afternoon we came safe to Norwich.

Wed. 10 [i.e., 13]. We rested from our labour. How can they who never labour taste the sweetness of rest? Fri. 15. I preached at Yarmouth. Sat. 16. I transcribed the society at Norwich. But two hundred of them I made no account of, as they met no class. About four hundred remained, half of whom appeared to be in earnest.

Tue. 19. I rode to Bury [St. Edmunds] and was glad to find a little, serious company still. But there cannot be much done here till we preach abroad, or at least in the heart of the town. We are now quite at one end, and people will not come from the other till they have first 'tasted the good word'.[59]

Thur. 21. I rode to Colchester and found a quiet, loving, regular society. After spending a day with them, on Saturday 23, I cheerfully returned to London.

Wed. 27. I had a striking proof that God *can* teach by whom he *will* teach. A man full of words but not of understanding, convinced me of what I could never see before, that *anima est ex traduce*[60]—that all the souls of his posterity, as well as their bodies, were in our first parent.

Friday, Feb. 5. I met at noon, as usual, those who believe they are saved from sin, and warned them of the *enthusiasm* which was breaking in by means of two or three weak though good men, who from a misconstrued text in the Revelation inferred that they should not die. They received the warning in much love. However, this gave great occasion of triumph to those who sought occasion, so that they rejoiced as though they had found great spoil.[61]

After preaching at Deptford, Welling, and Sevenoaks on Tuesday and Wednesday, I rode on to Sir Thomas I'Anson's[62] near Tunbridge and, between six and seven, preached in his large parlour, which opens likewise into the hall. The plain people were all attention: if the seed be watered, surely there will be some fruit.

[59] Heb. 6:5.

[60] 'The soul derives from the progenitor', i.e., *not* directly from the Creator. This view is known as traducianism, and is opposed to creationism. Wesley at first hesitantly espoused the creationist view, in his *Notes* on Heb. 12:9 (1755) and in his *Doctrine of Original Sin* (1757). The reading of *The True Original of the Soul* (see Nov. 7, 1770) swung him over to traducianism, and he accordingly revised his *Notes* on Heb. 12:9.

[61] See Ps. 119:162.

[62] On him and his seat at New Bounds, Southborough, see above, Feb. 21, 1761, n. 73.

Sun. 14. I buried the remains of Thomas Salmon, a good and useful man.[63] What was peculiar in his experience was, he did not know when he was justified, but he did know when he was renewed in love, that work being wrought in a most distinct manner. After this he continued about a year in constant love, joy, and peace. Then, after an illness of a few days, he cheerfully went to God.

Monday and the following days I spent in transcribing the list of the society. It never came up before to 2400; now it contains above 2700 members.

Sun. 28. We had a peculiar blessing at Spitalfields, while I was enforcing, 'Now is the day of salvation.'[64] Indeed there is always a blessing when we cut off all delay and come to God *now* by simple faith.

Friday, March 5. I had a long conversation with Joseph Rule, commonly called *the White Quaker*.[65] He appeared to be a calm, loving, sensible man and much devoted to God.

Mon. 8. I retired to Lewisham to answer Dr. Horne's ingenious sermon on justification by works.[66] O that I might dispute with no man! But if I *must* dispute, let it be with men of sense!

Thur. 11. I buried the remains of Mary Ramsey,[67] a true daughter of affliction, worn out by a cancer in her breast, with a variety of other disorders. To these was added for a time great

[63] Nothing is known of Thomas Salmon, and only speculation connects him with the other Salmons in JW's life, Matthew Salmon, a member of the Holy Club, Joseph Salmon of Nantwich (Matthew's nephew), Mrs. Jones (née Salmon), the friend of Elizabeth Ritchie, and the Salmon who helped build the chapel at Coleford, Som., and later fell on hard times. On all these, see Apr. 6, 1779.

[64] 2 Cor. 6:2.

[65] Joseph Rule (*c.* 1695–1770) was in early life a Thames waterman. He later joined the Society of Friends, wore white or undyed clothing, lived in a white cottage at Upton Lane, Essex, and preached in the streets of London from a small white Bible. In later life, he lived in Somerset and Wales, and in 1767, moved to Jordans, Bucks., where he died. *WHS* 1 (1901):165–66.

[66] The work which JW withdrew to Lewisham to answer was a university sermon by George Horne, *Works Wrought through Faith a Condition of our Salvation* (Oxford, 1761), JW's reply being *A Letter to the Rev. Mr. Horne* (London, 1762; 11:437-58 in this edn.). George Horne (1730–92) was elected fellow of Magdalen College, Oxford, in 1750, and spent most of his life there. Being a Hutchinsonian, Horne himself suffered the imputation of Methodism, and in later life, while JW warmly appreciated his *Commentary on the Psalms* (Oxford, 1784), Horne responded, when asked whether he had any objection to JW's preaching in his diocese, with the answer, 'None at all' (see Mar. 27, 1783, and Oct. 20, 1790). A court chaplain, 1771–81, and Vice-Chancellor in 1776, Horne was in the way of preferment, and became Dean of Canterbury in 1781, and Bishop of Norwich in 1790.

[67] She had been a member of one of the single women's bands at the Foundery in 1745. Stevenson, *City Road*, p. 35.

darkness of mind, the body pressing down the soul.[68] Yet she did not murmur or repine, much less charge God foolishly. It was not long before he restored the light of his countenance, and shortly after, she fell asleep.

Friday the 12th, the National Fast, was observed all over London with great solemnity. Surely God is well pleased even with this acknowledgement that he governs the world. And even the outward humiliation of a nation may be rewarded with outward blessings.

Mon. 15. I left London, though not without regret, and went slowly through the societies to Bristol. Sat. 27. I heard a large account of the children near Lawford's Gate which has made so much noise here.[69] The facts are too glaring to be denied. But how are they to be accounted for? By natural or supernatural agency? Contend who list about this.

Monday, March 29. I came to the New Passage a little before nine. The rain and wind increased much while we were on the water; however, we were safe on shore at ten. I preached about twelve in the new room at Chepstow.[70] One of the congregation was a neighbouring clergyman, who lived in the same staircase with me at Christ Church and was then far more serious than me.

[68] See Wisd. 9:15.

[69] Henry Durbin (1718–98), later one of the leaders of the Old Plan party in Bristol, posthumously published *A Narrative of Some Extraordinary Things that Happened to Mr. Richard Giles's Children, at the Lamb, without Lawford's Gate, Bristol, Supposed to be the Effect of Witchcraft* (Bristol, 1800). Durbin, a chemist, and uncle to Sir John Durbin, a Bristol alderman, investigated nightly attacks on two of the daughters of Richard Giles, landlord of the Lamb Inn near Lawford's Gate; they were bitten on the necks and arms, and their bedroom furniture upset; *WHS* 2 (1899):41-42. Other strange phenomena at the Lamb convinced Durbin that evil spirits were at work, and he became convinced that they were instigated by a witch at Mangotsfield, who had been paid by a business competitor of Giles (who had started a service of 'flying waggons' to London) to bewitch his family and wagons. This view was confirmed by the fact that one of Mr. Giles's flying wagons had suddenly stuck fast in the road at Hanton where eighteen horses had been required to move it, while another wagon had a trembling fit in Giles's own yard. Several clergy of the town now joined in the case, though Giles himself seems to have suspected foul play of a different order. On May 17, however, Giles was returning from Bath, and when he reached the point on the road where his wagons were usually affected, the harness broke, and he himself was taken ill and died a few days later. Durbin now was certain that he was a victim of witchcraft, and when attacks on the daughters began again, the Cunning Woman of Bedminster was called in, and she 'propounded a remedy for [the spirit's] summary overthrow which modern delicacy will not permit to be described' but proved triumphantly successful. J. Latimer, *The Annals of Bristol in the Eighteenth Century* (Bristol, 1893; repr. 1970), pp. 349-50.

[70] This new room may have been quite new, for on May 31, 1761, Howell Harris reports speaking at Chepstow 'to some that begin to meet in this town together'. Beynon, *Howell Harris*, p. 117.

Blessed be God, who has looked upon me at last! *Now* let me redeem the time!

In the afternoon we had such a storm of hail as I scarce ever saw in my life. The roads likewise were so extremely bad that we did not reach Hereford till past eight. Having been well battered both by hail, rain, and wind, I got to bed as soon as I could, but was waked many times by the clattering of the curtains; in the morning I found the casement wide open. But I was never the worse. I took horse at six with William Crane and Francis Walker.[71] The wind was piercing cold, and we had many showers of snow and rain, but the worst was, part of the road was scarce passable. So that at Church Stretton,[72] one of our horses lay down and would go no farther. However, William Crane and I pushed on, and before seven reached Shrewsbury.

A large company quickly gathered together. Many of them were wild enough. But the far greater part were calm and attentive, and came again at five in the morning.

Wed. 30. Having been invited to preach at Wem,[73] Mrs. Glynne[74] desired she might take me thither in a post-chaise. But in little more than an hour we were fast enough. However, the horses pulled till the traces broke. I should then have walked on had I been alone, though the mud was deep and the snow drove impetuously. But I could not leave my friend. So I waited patiently till the man had made shift to mend the traces. And the horses pulled amain, so that with much ado, not long after the time appointed, I came to Wem.

I came, but the person who invited me was gone—gone out of town at four in the morning. And I could find no one who seemed either to expect or desire my company. I inquired after the place where Mr. Mather preached—but it was filled with hemp. It

[71] Crane and Walker are here introduced as though they were itinerants; Walker indeed was (see July 15, 1745, n. 21; 20:80 in this edn.), but of Crane there is no other trace.

[72] Church Stretton was a market town and parish 12 miles south of Shrewsbury.

[73] Wem was a substantial market town and parish 10 miles north of Shrewsbury.

[74] Mrs. Bridget Glynne, née Lloyd (1708–99), was the widow of Edward Glynne of Glynne, Monts., who died in 1757. She now resided in Shrewsbury, and had been on intimate terms with John Fletcher since before his ordination, and exemplifies the way Fletcher's early influence helped to ensure JW a welcome in the Shrewsbury area. Her name appears in the earliest Methodist membership list in Shrewsbury, and there is a celebrated story of her intercession with her connexion, Lord Hereford, when he threatened to put Thomas Olivers in the stocks (Jackson, *Early Methodist Preachers*, 2:68-71). Lord Hereford provided hospitality for JW on a number of occasions. *WHS* 4 (1904):217-20.

remained only to go into the market-house, but neither any man,[75] woman, nor child cared to follow us, the north wind roared so loud on every side and poured in from every quarter. However, before I had done singing, two or three crept in, and after them two or three hundred. And the power of God was so present among them that I believe many forgot the storm.

The wind grew still higher in the afternoon, so that it was difficult to sit our horses. And it blew full in our face but could not prevent our reaching Chester in the evening. Though the warning was short, the room was full; and full of serious earnest hearers, many of whom expressed a longing desire for the whole salvation of God.

Here I rested on Thursday. Friday, April 1, I rode to Parkgate and found several ships, but the wind was contrary. I preached at five in the small house they have just built, and the hearers were remarkably serious. I gave notice of preaching at five in the morning. But at half-hour after four one brought us word that the wind was come fair, and Captain Jordan[76] would sail in less than an hour. We were soon in the ship, wherein we found about threescore passengers. The sun shone bright, the wind was moderate, the sea smooth, and we wanted nothing but room to stir ourselves, the cabin being filled with hops, so that we could not get into it but by climbing over them on our hands and knees. In the afternoon we were abreast of Holyhead. But the scene was quickly changed. The wind rose higher and higher, and by seven o'clock blew a storm. The sea broke over us continually and sometimes covered the ship, which both pitched and rolled in an uncommon manner. So I was informed, for, being a little sick, I lay down at six and slept with little intermission till near six in the morning. We were then near Dublin Bay, where we went into a boat which carried us to Dunleary. There we met with a chaise just ready, in which we went to Dublin.

I found much liberty of spirit in the evening while I was enforcing, 'Now is the day of salvation.'[77] The congregation was uncommonly large in the morning and seemed to be much alive. Many children, I find, are 'brought to the birth'. And shall there not be strength to bring forth?[78]

[75] Orig. omits 'man', which JW added in *Works* (1774).
[76] With whom JW had sailed from Dublin; see Aug. 24, 1760, and n. 73.
[77] 2 Cor. 6:2.
[78] Cf. Isa. 66:9.

It was at this time that Mr. Grimshaw fell asleep.[79] He was born Sept. 3, 1708, at Brindle, six miles south of Preston in Lancashire, and educated at the schools of Blackburn and Heskin in the same county. Even then the thoughts of death and judgment made some impression upon him. At eighteen, he was admitted at Christ's College in Cambridge. Here bad example so carried him away that for more than two years he seemed utterly to have lost all sense of seriousness, which did not revive till the day he was ordained deacon, in the year 1731. On that day he was much affected with the sense of the importance of the ministerial office. And this was increased by his conversing with some at Rochdale who met once a week to read, and sing, and pray. But on his removal to Todmorden soon after, he quite dropped his pious acquaintance, conformed to the world, followed all its diversions, and contented himself with 'doing his duty' on Sundays.

But about the year 1734, he began to think seriously again. He left off all his diversions, he began to catechise the young people, to preach the absolute necessity of a devout life, and to visit his people, not in order to be merry with them, as before, but to press them to seek the salvation of their souls.

At this period also, he began himself to pray in secret four times a day. And the God of all grace, who prepared his heart to pray, soon gave the answer to his prayer; not indeed as he expected, not in joy or peace, but by bringing upon him very strong and painful convictions of his own guilt and helplessness and misery; by discovering to him what he did not suspect before, that his heart was deceitful and desperately wicked; and what was more afflicting still, that all his duties and labours could not procure him pardon, or gain him a title to eternal life. In this trouble he continued more than three years, not acquainting anyone with the distress he suffered, till one day (in 1742), being in the utmost agony of mind, there was clearly represented to him Jesus Christ pleading for him with God the Father and gaining a free pardon for him. In that moment all his fears vanished away, and he was filled with joy unspeakable. 'I was now', says he, 'willing to renounce myself and to embrace Christ for my all in all. O what light and comfort did I enjoy in my own soul, and what a taste of the pardoning love of God!'

All this time he was an entire stranger to the people called Methodists, whom afterwards he thought it his duty to countenance and to labour with them in his neighbourhood. He

[79] In fact Grimshaw died Apr. 7, 1763, an indication of how Wesley would often insert documents in his *Journal* at a much later period. This extract was not published until 1767. This biography is in fact a characteristic abridgement of the 'Sketch' added to Henry Venn's funeral sermon for Grimshaw, with one minor addition—again incorrectly placed.

was an entire stranger also to all their writings till he came to Haworth, May 26 of this year [i.e., 1742]. And the good effects of his preaching soon became visible. Many of his flock were brought into deep concern for salvation and were, in a little time after, filled with peace and joy through believing. And, as in ancient times, the whole congregation have been often seen in tears on account of their provocations against God, and under a sense of his goodness in yet sparing them.

His lively manner of representing the truths of God could not fail of being much talked of and bringing many hundreds out of curiosity to Haworth church, who received so much benefit by what they heard that, when the novelty was long over, the church continued to be full of people, many of whom came from far, and this for twenty years together.

Mr. Grimshaw was now too happy himself in the knowledge of Christ to rest satisfied without taking every method he thought likely to spread the knowledge of his God and Saviour. And as the very indigent constantly make their want of better clothes to appear in, an excuse for not coming to church in the daytime, he contrived, for them chiefly, a lecture on Sunday evenings, though he had preached twice in the day before. God was pleased to give great success to these attempts, which animated him still more to spend and be spent for Christ. So the next year he began a method, which was continued by him for ever after, of preaching in each of the four hamlets he had under his care three times every month. By this means, the old and infirm who could not attend the church had the truth of God brought to their houses, and many who were so profane as to make the distance from the house of God a reason for scarce ever coming to it were allured to hear. By this time the great labour with which he instructed his own people, the holiness of his conversation, and the benefit which very many from the neighbouring parishes had obtained by attending his ministry, concurred to bring upon him many earnest entreaties to come to their houses, who lived in neighbouring parishes, and expound the word of God to souls as ignorant as they had been themselves. This request he did not dare to refuse, so that while he provided abundantly for his own flock, he annually found opportunities of preaching near three hundred times to congregations in other parts.

And for a course of fifteen years or upwards, he used to preach every week, fifteen, twenty, and sometimes thirty times, besides visiting the sick and other occasional duties of his function. It is not easy to ascribe such unwearied diligence, chiefly among the poor, to any motive but the real one. He thought he would never keep silence while he could speak to the honour of that God who had done so much for his soul. And while he saw sinners perishing for lack of knowledge, and no one breaking to them the bread of life, he was constrained, notwithstanding the reluctance he felt within, to give up his name to still greater reproach, as well as all his time and strength to the work of the ministry.

During this intense application to what was the delight of his heart, God was exceeding favourable to him. In sixteen years he was only once suspended from his labour by sickness, though he dared all weathers upon the bleak mountains and used his body with less compassion than a merciful man would use his beast. His soul at various times enjoyed large manifestations of God's love, and he drank deep into his spirit. His cup ran over, and at some seasons his faith was so strong and his hope so abundant that higher degrees of spiritual delight would have overpowered his mortal frame.

In this manner Mr. Grimshaw employed all his powers and talents even to his last illness. And his labours were not in vain in the Lord. He saw an effectual change take place in many of his flock and a restraint from the commission of sin brought upon the parish in general. He saw the name of Jesus exalted and many souls happy in the knowledge of him and walking as became the gospel. Happy he was himself, in being kept by the power of God unblameable in his conversation. Happy in being beloved in several of the last years of his life by everyone in his parish, who, whether they would be persuaded by him to forsake the evil of their ways or no, had no doubt that Mr. Grimshaw was their cordial friend. Hence, at his departure, a general concern was visible through his parish. Hence his body was interred with what is more ennobling than all the pomp of a royal funeral, for he was followed to the grave by a great multitude, with affectionate sighs and many tears; who cannot still hear his much-loved name without weeping for the guide of their souls, to whom each of them was dear as children to their father.

His behaviour throughout his last sickness was of a piece with the last twenty years of his life; from the very first attack of his fever he welcomed its approach. His intimate knowledge of Christ abolished all the reluctance nature feels to a dissolution, and, triumphing in him who is the resurrection and the life, he departed April 7th, in the fifty-fifth year of his age and the twenty-first of his eminent usefulness.

It may not be unacceptable to subjoin here one of his plain, rough letters, to the society in London.

Haworth, Jan. 9, 1760

My dear Brethren,

Grace, mercy, and peace be to you from God our Father and from our Lord Jesus. It is well with four sorts of people that you have had, or now have, to do with. It is well with those of you 'in Christ, who are gone to God.' It is well with those of you 'in Christ, who are not gone to God.' It is well with those who earnestly 'long to be in Christ', that they may go to God. It is well for those who 'neither desire to be in Christ, nor to go to God.' And 'tis only bad with such who, being out of Christ, are gone to the devil. These 'tis best to let alone and say no more about them.

But to be sure, it is well with the other four. It is well with those of you who being 'in Christ, are gone to God'. You ministers and members of Christ have no more doubt or pain about them. They are now, and for ever, out of the reach of the world, flesh, and devil. They are gone 'where the wicked cease from troubling, and where the weary are at rest.' They are sweetly reposed in Abraham's bosom. They dwell in his presence who hath redeemed them, where 'there is fullness of joy, and pleasures for evermore.' They are waiting the joyful morning of the resurrection, when their vile bodies shall be made like unto his glorious body, shall be re-united to their souls, shall receive the joyful sentence and 'inherit the kingdom prepared for them from the foundation of the world'.

It is well also with those of you who are 'in Christ, though not gone to God'. You live next door to them. Heaven is begun with you, too. The kingdom of God is within you. You feel it. This is a kingdom of righteousness and peace and joy in the Holy Ghost. It is begun in grace and shall terminate in glory. Yea, it is Christ within you the hope of glory. Christ the rock, the foundation, laid in your hearts. Hope in the middle, and glory at the top. Christ, hope, glory; Christ, hope, glory. You are washed in the blood of the Lamb, justified, sanctified; and shall shortly be glorified. Yea, your lives are already 'hid with Christ in God'. You have your conversation already in heaven. Already you 'sit in heavenly places in Christ Jesus'. What heavenly sentences are these! What can come nearer paradise? Bless the Lord, O ye happy souls, and let all that is within you bless his holy name. Sing unto the Lord, so long as you live, and praise your God while you have your being. And how long will that be? Through the endless ages of a glorious eternity.

O my dear brothers and sisters, this is my hope and this is my purpose. But to whom and to what are we indebted for all this, and infinitely more than all the tongues and hearts of men or angels can tell or conceive? To our Redeemer only and to his merits. Christ within us is Jesus to us. We were poor, lost, helpless sinners, aliens from the commonwealth of Israel, and children of wrath. But Jesus lived, and Jesus died, the just for the unjust, to bring us to the enjoyment of it.

And what does all this require at our hands? Why, infinitely more than we can render him to all eternity. However, let us praise and glorify God in the best manner and with the best member that we have. Let us do it constantly, cordially, cheerfully, so long as we live, and then no doubt we shall do it in heaven for ever.

Keep close, I beseech you, to every means of grace. Strive to walk in all the ordinances and commandments of God blameless, giving all diligence to make your calling and election sure. Add to your faith virtue, to virtue knowledge, to knowledge temperance, to temperance patience, to patience godliness, to godliness brotherly kindness, to brotherly kindness charity. For 'if these things', says St. Peter, 'be in you and abound, they make you that you shall neither be barren nor unfruitful in the knowledge of our Lord Jesus Christ.' Thus you will give the best token of your thankfulness to him for what he hath done for your souls, and you shall not long hence in heaven sing his praise with your happy brethren, gone thither before you.

It is well likewise with all those of you who do truly 'desire to be in Christ', that you may go to God. Surely he owns you. Your desires are from him; you shall enjoy his favour. By and by you shall have peace with him through our Lord Jesus Christ. Go forth by the footsteps of the flock, and feed ye by the shepherd's tents. Be constant in every means of grace. He will be found of them that diligently seek him. Blessed are they that mourn, for they shall be comforted. Though your sins be never so many, never so monstrous, all shall be forgiven. He will have mercy upon you and will abundantly pardon. For where sin hath abounded, grace doth much more abound. He who hath begun this good work in you will accomplish it to your eternal good and his eternal glory. Therefore doubt not, fear not. A broken and a contrite heart God will not despise. The deeper is your sorrow, the nearer is your joy. Your extremity is God's opportunity. 'Tis usually darkest before daybreak. You shall shortly find pardon, peace, and plenteous redemption, and at last rejoice in the common and glorious salvation of his saints.

And lastly, it is well for you who 'neither truly desire to be in Christ', nor to go to God. For 'tis well for you that you are out of hell. 'Tis well your day of grace is not utterly past. Behold, now is your accepted time; behold, now is the day of your salvation! O that you employ the remainder of it in working out your salvation with fear and trembling. Now is faith to be had, saving faith. Now you may be washed from all your sins in the Redeemer's blood, justified, sanctified, and prepared for heaven. Take, I beseech you, the time while the time is. You have now the means of grace to use, the ordinances of God to enjoy, his Word to read and hear, his ministers to instruct you, and his members to converse with. You know not what a day may bring forth. You may die suddenly. As death leaves you, judgment will find you. And if you die as you are, 'out of Christ', void of true faith, unregenerate, unsanctified, snares, fire and brimstone, storm and tempest God will rain upon you as your eternal, intolerable portion to drink (Ps. 11:7 [BCP]).

Suffer me therefore thus far, one and all of you. God's glory and your everlasting welfare is all I aim at. What I look for in return from you is, I confess, much more than I deserve, your prayers. Pray for me and I will pray for you, who am,

Your affectionate brother,
W. Grimshaw

Friday 9 (being Good Friday), I had almost lost my voice by a cold. However, I spoke as I could, till before twelve (it being a watch-night), I could speak near as well as ever.

On Easter Day we had uncommon congregations, as indeed we have had all the week. And I observed a more staid[80] and solid behaviour in most than is usual in this kingdom. Monday and Tuesday, I was employed in visiting the classes, and I was much comforted among them, there was such an hunger and thirst in all who had tasted of the grace of God, after a full renewal in his image.

Sun. 18.[81] As often as I have been here, I never saw the house thoroughly filled before. And the multitude did not come together in vain. I think many will remember this day.

Mon. 19. I left Dublin. And I could look back with satisfaction on the days I had spent therein. I had reason to believe that God had been at work in a very uncommon manner. Many of those who once contradicted and blasphemed were now convinced of the truth as it is in Jesus.[82] Many who had long revolted from God had returned to him with full purpose of heart. Several mourners had found peace with God, and some believe he has saved them from all sin. Many more are all on fire for this salvation, and a spirit of love runs through the whole people.

I came in the evening to Newry, where I found a far different

[80] Orig., 'stayed'.

[81] A fuller account of the events of the previous fortnight, broken up in JW's account by the Grimshaw obituary, is given in Crookshank, *Ireland*, 1:154-56, from Thomas Garret's diary. For Garret, see ibid., 1:123; and below, July 28, 1762.

[82] See Eph. 4:21.

face of things. Offences had broke the society in pieces, only two and thirty being left of near an hundred. But God has a few names left here also. Let these stand firm, and God will maintain his own cause.

Wed. 21. I rode to Carrickfergus. The violent rain kept away the delicate and curious hearers. For the sake of these, I delayed the morning preaching till a quarter before nine. But it was too early still for a great part of the town, who could not possibly rise before ten. I added a few members to the society and left them in peace and love.

Where to preach in Belfast, I did not know. It was too wet to preach abroad. And a dancing-master was busily employed in the upper part of the market-house, till at twelve the sovereign drove him out by holding his court there.[83] While he was above I began below, to a very serious and attentive audience. But they were all poor—the rich of Belfast 'cared for none of these things'.[84]

After dinner we rode to Newtown[ards] and found another poor, shattered society, reduced from fifty to eighteen members, and most of those cold enough. In the evening, I preached to a large congregation in the market-house on 'I will heal their backsliding.'[85] God fulfilled his Word. Many were healed, and many more deeply wounded. I had full employment among them the next day. And on Saturday 24, I left between thirty and forty members full of desire, and hope, and earnest resolutions not to be 'almost, but altogether Christians'.[86]

About ten I preached at Comber, and then rode to Lisburn, where in the evening I had many rich and genteel hearers. Sun. 25. The congregation was larger in the morning than the evening before, and many appeared to be deeply wounded. O may none heal their wound slightly.[87] But far the largest congregation of all met in the evening, and yet I saw not a scoffer, no, nor trifler among them.

Mon. 26. In the evening I preached to a large congregation in

[83] In the seventeenth and eighteenth centuries, the corporation of Belfast was 'styled, "The Sovereign, Free Burgesses and Commons of the Borough of Belfast" and . . . consisted of a sovereign, lord of the castle, constable of the castle, twelve other free burgesses, and an unlimited number of freemen, assisted by a town-clerk and two sergeants-at-mace. The sovereign was chosen annually on the 24th of June by the free burgesses, from three of their own body nominated by the lord of the castle, and was sworn into office before the lord . . . on Michaelmas-day.' This arrangement continued till the Act for the Regulation of Municipal Corporations, 3 & 4 Vict.c.108. Lewis, *Ireland*, 1:189.

[84] Acts 18:17 (*Notes*).

[85] Hos. 14:4.

[86] Cf. Acts 26:28.

[87] See Jer. 6:14.

the market-house at Lurgan.[88] I now embraced the opportunity, which I had long desired, of talking with Mr. Miller, the contriver of that statue which was in Lurgan when I was there before.[89] It was the figure of an old man, standing in a case, with a curtain drawn before him, over against a clock which stood on the other side of the room. Every time the clock struck, he opened the door with one hand, drew back the curtain with the other, turned his head, as if looking round on the company, and then said with a clear, loud, articulate voice, 'Past, one, two, three,' and so on. But so many came to see this (the like of which all allowed was not to be seen in Europe) that Mr. Miller was in danger of being ruined, not having time to attend his own business. So, as none offered to purchase it or to reward him for his pains, he took the whole machine in pieces; nor has he any thought of ever making anything of the kind again.

Tue. 27. I preached in Lurgan at five, in Terryhoogan[90] at ten, and at two in the market-house at Richhill.[91] I have rarely seen so serious a congregation at a new place. At six, I preached in the new preaching-house at Clonmain,[92] the largest in the north of Ireland. And the people were all alive, being stirred up by Mr. Ryan,[93] once an attorney but now living upon his own estate.

[88] This brief entry conceals both the way in which a market for JW's services was created, and the way in which he put it to institutional advantage. A young lady (later Mrs. Whitestone of Dublin) then resident in Lurgan describes how 'the news of Mr. Wesley's visit spread abroad, and so many flocked to hear, that he, seeing this, appointed two of his preachers to visit the town alternately, once a fortnight, which led to the introduction of Methodism.' Crookshank, *Ireland*, 1:157.

[89] William Miller (d. 1779) was a woollen-draper in Lurgan. He did not abandon his project of a speaking statue and, on a later visit by JW (see June 14, 1773), proposed to build two which should speak and sing hymns alternately. He was not a Methodist, but when in 1778 a small dwelling-house in Lurgan was fitted up as a Methodist chapel, Miller, 'a curious artist . . . painted an angel, pointing to Rev. xxii.17: "The Spirit and bride, say, Come . . . ," [and] the picture was placed above the pulpit' (*Wesleyan Methodist Magazine* 50 [1827]:801; *WHS* 21 [1938]:192-94). Another of his pictures portrayed George Whitefield preaching in the timber-yard at Lurgan surrounded by the local people. W. J. Piggot, 'The Miller family of Lurgan', *Ulster Journal of Archaeology* 12 (1906):141-42.

[90] Orig., 'Terry-hugan'.

[91] Richhill was a small town 4 miles east of Armagh. 'The market-house, a substantial and commodious building, was erected in 1753 by W. Richardson, Esq.,' whose family were proprietors of the town. Lewis, *Ireland*, 2:472.

[92] Orig., 'Clanmain'. Clonmain was one of the minor estates in the parish of Loughgall, 4 miles north-east of Armagh, belonging to Thomas Ryan.

[93] Thomas Ryan was later an itinerant for a time (see below, May 6 and 10, 1765; and W. Myles, *A Chronological History of the People Called Methodists* [Liverpool, 1800], p. 453). He had been converted in a Methodist service on a visit to England. Crookshank, *Ireland*, 1:150.

Wed. 28. The rain kept off the curious hearers, so that we had few in the evening, but earnest souls. After sermon we had a love-feast. It was a wonderful time. God poured out his spirit abundantly. Many were filled with consolation, particularly two who had come from Lisburn (three and twenty Irish miles), one a lifeless backslider, the other a girl of sixteen, who had been some time slightly convinced of sin. God restored him to the light of his countenance and gave her a clear evidence of his love—and indeed, in so uncommon a manner that it seemed her soul was all love. One of our brethren was constrained openly to declare, he believed God had wrought *this change* in him. I trust he will not lightly cast away the gift which God has given him. In the morning I left them rejoicing and praising God, and rode to Monaghan.

The commotions in Munster[94] having now alarmed all Ireland, we had hardly alighted when some wise persons informed the provost there were three strange sort of men come to the King's Arms. So the provost with his officers came without delay to secure the north from so imminent a danger. I was just come out when I was required to return into the house. The provost asked me many questions, and perhaps the affair might have turned serious had I not had two letters with me which I had lately received, one from the Bishop of Londonderry,[95] the other from the Earl of Moira.[96] Upon reading these he excused himself for the trouble he had given and wished me a good journey.

Between six and seven I preached at Cootehill, and in the morning rode on to Enniskillen,[97] the situation of which is both

[94] Catholic resurgence was beginning on two fronts. The Catholic Committee was founded in 1760 to obtain by constitutional means some social justice for the depressed majority, and some political recognition for the middle class. At the same time agrarian discontent, Protestant (Oakboys) and Catholic (Whiteboys), became open, the latter concentrated mainly in Munster and Leinster. This led in 1766 to the judicial murder of Fr. Nicholas Sheehy on a charge of killing a renegade Whiteboy. At this level and at that of the Catholic Committee, the leadership of the Catholic cause was passing from the passive remnant of the Catholic aristocracy into more active hands. Cf. June 14, 1762.

[95] William Barnard (*c.* 1697–1768) was educated at Westminster and Trinity College, Cambridge, where he graduated M.A. in 1724, D.D. in 1740. As rector of Esher, Surrey (1726), he was put into the way of preferment by becoming chaplain to the Duke of Newcastle. He was chaplain to the King in 1728, and vicar of St. Bride's, Fleet Street, 1729–47. He became dean of Rochester, 1743; Bishop of Raphoe, 1744; and Bishop of Derry, 1747. Cordial letters of his to JW are printed in Crookshank, *Ireland*, 1:148; and Whitehead, *Wesley*, 2:292-93.

[96] See above, May 1, 1760. John Rawdon, Baron Rawdon of Moira, was created Earl of Moira in the Irish peerage on Jan. 30, 1762.

[97] Enniskillen was a borough, market town, and parish and chief town of Co. Fermanagh.

pleasant and strong, as it is surrounded by a deep and broad river. But fortifications it has none, no, nor so much as an old castle. The inhabitants glory that they have no Papist in the town.

After riding round and round we came in the evening to a lone house called Carrickabwheehan.[98] It laid in the midst of horrid mountains[99] and had no very promising appearance. However, it afforded corn for our horses and potatoes for ourselves. So we made an hearty supper, called in as many as pleased of the family to prayers, and, though we had no fastening either for our door or our windows, slept in peace.

Saturday, May 1. We took horse at five. The north-east wind would have suited the first of January. And we had soaking rain on *the black mountains.* However, before noon we came well to Sligo.

None in Sligo, when I was there last,[1] professed so much love to me as Mr. Knox's family.[2] They would willingly have had me with them morning, noon, and night, and omitted no possible mark of affection. But what a change! Mrs. K[nox] went into the country the day before I came. Her brother and his wife set out for Dublin at the same time. He himself and the rest of his family saw me, that is, at church, because they could not help it:

> But wondered at the strange man's face,
> As one they ne'er had known.[3]

[98] Orig., 'Carrick-a-biggan'; see *WHS* 11 (1917):15-16.

[99] This phrase recalls a passage in Sermon 56, 'God's Approbation of His Works', I.2, and a curious eighteenth-century theological controversy. JW describes how, after the creation and before the deluge, 'the *earth* was good: the whole surface of it was beautiful in an high degree. . . . [God] adorned it with flowers of every hue, and with shrubs and trees of every kind. And every part was fertile as well as beautiful: it was nowhere deformed by rough or rugged rocks; it did not shock the view with horrid precipices, huge chasms or dreary caverns. . . . But we have not any authority to say, with some learned and ingenious authors, that there were no mountains on the original earth, no unevenness on its surface.' The principal representative of this view was Thomas Burnet (1635?–1715), master of the Charterhouse, JW's old school, who argued that the world was like a gigantic egg; the shell was crushed at the deluge, the internal waters burst out, while the fragments of the shell formed the mountains. Though JW found scriptural grounds for rejecting this view, how nearly his sensibilities resembled those of Burnet comes out in his conclusion that the original mountain-sides were not 'abrupt, or difficult of ascent. It is highly probable that they rose and fell by almost insensible degrees.' *Sermons,* 2:389, in this edn.

[1] See above (also for the Knox family), June 26, 1760.

[2] 'Knox' inserted in *Works* (1774), only. This was the family of the Rev. John Knox, whose son Alexander was one of Wesley's favourite correspondents, and an important literary figure.

[3] Adapted from William Congreve, *Doris*, in *Complete Works of William Congreve*, ed. Montague Summers (London, 1923), 4:143.

I am sorry for *their* sake, not my own. Perhaps they may wish to see me when it is too late.

Sun. 2. I preached in the market-house morning and evening. Abundance of the dragoons were there, so were many of the officers, who behaved with uncommon seriousness.

Mon. 3. In the evening a company of players began acting in the upper part of the market-house, just as we began singing in the lower. The case of these is remarkable. The Presbyterians for a long time had their public worship here. But when the strollers came to town, they were turned out and from that time had no public worship at all. On Tuesday evening the lower part too was occupied by buyers and sellers of oatmeal. But as soon as I began, the people quitted their sacks and listened to business of greater importance.

On the following days, I preached at Carrick-on-Shannon,[4] Drumsna, Cleggill, Longford, and Abbeyderg. Sat. 8. Calling on a friend in our way, we had not sat down before several of the neighbours, Papists as well as Protestants, came in, supposing I was to preach. I was not willing to disappoint them. And they all listened with deep attention.

Hence I rode to Athlone. I intended on Sunday 9 to preach abroad as usual. But the sharp wind made it impracticable and obliged me to keep in the house. The congregations, however, were large, both morning and evening, and I found a little fruit of my labour.

Thur. 13. I was in hopes even the Papists here had at length a shepherd who cared for their souls. He was stricter than any of his predecessors and was esteemed a man of piety as well as learning. Accordingly he had given them strict orders not to *work* on the Lord's Day. But I found he allowed them to *play* as much as they pleased, at cards in particular; nay, and averred it was their '*duty* so to do', to 'refresh both' their 'bodies and minds'. Alas for the blind leader of the blind.[5] Has not *he* the greater sin!

Sun. 16. I had observed to the society last week that I had not seen one congregation ever in Ireland behave so ill at church as that at Athlone, laughing, talking, and staring about during the whole service. I had added, 'This is *your* fault, for if you had attended the church as you ought to have done, *your* presence

[4] Here he was the guest of Glover Laird who founded a long-lasting Methodist dynasty.

[5] See Matt. 15:14, etc.

and example would not have failed to influence the whole congregation.' And so it appeared. I saw not one today either laughing, talking, or staring about, but a remarkable seriousness was spread from the one end of the church to the other.

Mon. 17. I preached at Ahascragh to all the Protestants in or near the town. But their priests would not suffer the Papists to come. What could a magistrate do in this case? Doubtless he might tell the priest, 'Sir, as you *enjoy* liberty of conscience, you shall *allow* it to others. You are not persecuted yourself; you shall not persecute them.'

Tue. 18. I preached at Ballinasloe[6] about ten in the morning, and in the evening at Aughrim. Thur. 20. I rode on to Hollymount. The sun was extremely hot, so that I was much exhausted. But after a little rest, I preached in the churchyard without any weariness.

Fri. 21. I preached at Ballycarra[7] church at ten to a deeply serious congregation, and in the court-house at Castlebar in the evening. Sun. 23. The chief family in the town[8] made a part of our congregation. And whether they received any benefit thereby or no, their example may bring others who *will* receive it.

Mon. 24. I went with two friends to see one of the greatest natural wonders in Ireland, Mount Eagle, vulgarly called Croagh Patrick.[9] The foot of it is fourteen miles from Castlebar. There we left our horses and procured a guide. It was just twelve when we alighted, the sun was burning hot and we had not a breath of wind. Part of the ascent was a good deal steeper than an ordinary pair of stairs. About two we gained the top, which is an oval, grassy plain about an hundred and fifty yards in length and seventy or eighty in breadth. The upper part of the mountain much resembles the Pike of Tenerife.[10] I think it cannot rise much less than a mile perpendicular from the plain below.[11] There is an

[6] Ballinasloe was a market town in Co. Roscommon, 12 miles south-west of Athlone. Here, too, JW had formed a connection with a devout man of property, Mr. John Knight, who survived into the 1820s to an age of 90. Crookshank, *Ireland*, 1:159.

[7] Orig., 'Balcarrow' Ballycarra is a hamlet in Co. Mayo, 6 miles south-east of Castlebar.

[8] That of Sir Charles Bingham, 7th Bart. (1735–99), M.P. for Co. Mayo, 1761–76, who was created Baron Lucan of Castlebar, 1776, and Earl of Lucan, 1795, both in the Irish peerage.

[9] Orig., 'Crow-Patrick'; located to the south of Westport Bay.

[10] Orig., 'Tenariff'. JW does not mention visiting the Canary Islands, and this observation presumably depends on his seeing an engraving.

[11] It is characteristic of JW's attitude toward mountains that he more than doubles the true height of 2510 feet.

immense prospect, on one side toward the sea and on the other over the land. But as most of it is waste and uncultivated, the prospect is not very pleasing.

At seven in the evening I preached at Westport[12], and at six in the morning. I then returned to Newport and began reading prayers at ten. After sermon, I had a little conversation with Lord Mounteagle,[13] an extremely sensible man, and would gladly have stayed with him longer, but that I had promised to be at Castlebar. Where in the evening I preached my farewell sermon to a numerous congregation.

Wed. 26. We took horse at four, to enjoy the cool of the morning. At seven the sun was warm enough—I verily think, as warm as in Georgia. We could not have borne it, but the wind was in our face. However, in the afternoon we got well to Galway. There was a small society here, and (what is not common) all of them were young women. Between seven and eight, I began preaching in the court-house, to a mixed multitude of Papists and Protestants, rich and poor, who appeared to be utterly astonished. At five in the morning, I preached again and spoke as plain as I possibly could. But to the far greater part it seemed to be only 'as the sound of many waters'.[14]

Thur. 27. We had another Georgian day. But having the wind again, full in our face, after riding about fifty English miles we got well to Ennis in the afternoon. Many being ready to make a disturbance at the court-house, I left them to themselves and preached over against Mr. Bindon's[15] house in great quietness.

Fri. 28. I was informed that a few days before two of Mr. B[indon]'s maids went to bathe (as the women here frequently do) in the river near his house. The water was not above a yard deep, but there was a deep hole at a little distance. As one of them dashed water at the other, she, endeavouring to avoid it, slipped into the hole, and the first, striving to help her, slipped in too; nor was either of them seen any more till their bodies floated upon the water. Yet after some hours, one of them was brought to life. But the other could not be recovered.

12 Orig., 'Newport', altered only in the errata and personal notes to JW's *Works* (1774). Westport was a seaport and market town developed for herring-fishing in 1780.

13 John Browne, of Westport, Co. Mayo (1709–76), was M.P. for Castlebar, 1744–60, and Governor of Mayo. In September 1760 he was created Baron Monteagle of Westport; in 1768, Viscount Westport; and 1771, Earl of Altament, all in the Irish peerage. Mount Eagle is the English name for Croagh Patrick.

14 Rev. 1:15.

15 See above, June 29, 1758, n. 10.

The violent heat, which had continued for eight days, was now at an end, the wind turning north. So on Saturday 29, we had a pleasant ride to Limerick. Sun. 30. I preached in the old camp. The pleasantness of the place, the calmness of the evening, and the convenient distance from the town, all conspired to draw the people together, who flocked from every quarter. Many officers, as well as abundance of soldiers,[16] were among them and behaved with the utmost decency. I preached the following evenings at the same place, and that in great measure for the sake of the soldiers, it being within a musket-shot of the place where they were exercising. Nay, two evenings an officer ordered a large body to exercise on the very spot. But the moment I began, they laid down their arms and joined the rest of the congregation.

Friday, June 4. I preached at noon in Ballingarrane, to a large congregation, chiefly of Palatines.[17] And so at Newmarket in the evening and the morning following. These have quite a different look from the natives of the country, as well as a different temper. They are a serious, thinking people. And their diligence turns all their land into a garden.

Mon. 7. I met a large number of children, just as much acquainted with God and with the things of God as 'a wild ass's colt',[18] and just as much concerned about them. And yet who can believe that these pretty little creatures have 'the wrath of God abiding on them'?[19]

Numberless crowds ran together about this time to see the execution of the poor deserter. And I believe some of them retained serious impressions—for near four and twenty hours! But it was not so with the soldiers; although they walked one by one close to the bleeding, mangled carcase, most of them were as merry within six hours as if they had only seen a puppet-show.

Tue. 8. I visited the classes and wondered to find no witness of the great salvation. Surely the flame which is kindled in Dublin will not stop there. The next evening, God did indeed kindle it

[16] Among them was John Dillon (d. 1769), who had been born in the army and had served in it since he was fourteen. He began to suffer religious anxieties after being taken prisoner at Fontenoy (1745), and many years later was converted under Methodist preaching and became a member of the society at Cork. He had a great reputation in Ireland for lively spirituality, and in 1765 he was taken into the itinerancy (Atmore, *Memorial*, pp. 105-8). JW published *A Short Account of John Dillon* (Bristol, 1771).

[17] See May 12, 1749, n. 75 (20:272 in this edn.).

[18] Job 11:12.

[19] Cf. John 3:36.

here: a cry went up on every side, and the lively believers seemed all on fire to be 'cleansed from all unrighteousness'.[20]

On Friday and Saturday, I had much conversation with a very noted person. But I found none in town who expected that any good could be done to such a sinner as him! *Such a sinner?* Why, were we not all *such?* We were *dead in sin.* And is he more than dead?

Sun. 13. Being informed I had shot over the heads of the soldiers, who did not 'understand anything but hell and damnation', I took my leave of them this evening by strongly applying the story of Dives and Lazarus. They seemed to understand this, and all but two or three boy-officers behaved as men fearing God.

Mon. 14. I rode to Cork. Here I procured an exact account of the late commotions. About the beginning of December last, a few men met by night near Nenagh, in the county of Limerick, and threw down the fences of some commons which had been lately enclosed. Near the same time others met in the county of Tipperary, of Waterford, and of Cork. As no one offered to suppress or hinder them, they increased in number continually and called themselves *Whiteboys*, wearing white cockades and white linen frocks. In February, there were five or six parties of them, two or three hundred men in each, who moved up and down, chiefly in the night—but for what end did not appear. Only they levelled a few fences, dug up some grounds, and hamstrung some cattle, perhaps fifty or sixty in all. One body of them came into Clogheen,[21] of about five hundred foot and two hundred horse. They moved as exactly as regular troops and appeared to be thoroughly disciplined. They now sent letters to several gentlemen, threatening to pull down their houses. They compelled everyone they met to take an oath 'to be true to Queen *Sive*'[22] (whatever that meant) and the *Whiteboys*, not to reveal their secrets, and to join them when called upon'. It was supposed eight or ten thousand were now actually risen, many of them well-armed, and that a far greater number were ready to rise whenever they should be called upon. Those who refused to swear, they threatened to bury alive. Two or three they did bury

[20] Cf. 1 John 1:9.

[21] Orig., 'Clohean', changed in 1774 to 'Cloheen'. Clogheen was a market town in Co. Tipperary, 11½ miles south-west of Clonmel.

[22] The Whiteboy movement was treated by Froude as an aspect of 'the revival of the Celts', and Sive Oulteagh was the assumed name of their leader.

up to the neck and left them, where they must quickly have perished had they not been found in time by some travelling by. At length toward Easter, a body of troops, chiefly light horse, were sent against them. Many were apprehended and committed to jail; the rest of them disappeared. This is the plain, naked fact, which has been so variously represented.

Thur. 17. I rode about thirty English miles, through a pleasant and well-cultivated country, to Youghal.[23] It is finely situated on the side of an hill, so as to command a wide sea-prospect. I preached in the evening at the Exchange. Abundance of people attended, as did the far greater part of them at five o'clock in the morning. I returned to Cork on Friday. Sunday 20, at the desire of Captain Taylor,[24] I went to Passage and preached to many of the town's people and as many of the sailors as could attend. On Monday and Tuesday, I visited the classes and observed what was very uncommon—in two years there was neither any increase nor any decrease in this society. Two hundred and thirty-three members I left, and two hundred and thirty-three I find.

Thur. 24. I rode to Kinsale and preached in the Exchange to a considerable number of attentive hearers. In the afternoon, I rode to Bandon and found the society much lessened and dead enough. Yet the congregation in the main street was remarkably large as well as deeply attentive. So it was on Friday. Saturday 26, I visited the classes and exhorted them to 'be zealous and repent'.[25] The word sunk into their hearts, so that when we met in the evening they did not seem to be the same persons. They appeared to breathe quite another spirit, everyone stirring up his neighbour. I know not when I have seen so deep and general an impression made in so short a time.

Sun. 27. I returned to Cork, and in the afternoon preached on the Barrack Hill. The congregation was such as I had not seen at Cork for at least twelve years. One soldier made some noise, but the commanding officer soon ordered him into custody. The top of the walls, being covered with soldiers, made a solemn appearance. Let this preaching be continued, and the work of God will quickly revive at Cork.

On Monday and Tuesday, the congregation at the house was

[23] Youghal was a seaport, borough, market town, and parish, 29 miles east of Cork.

[24] Perhaps Captain Richard Taylor with whom JW later sailed from Dublin. *WHS* 5 (1905):77-78.

[25] Cf. Rev. 3:19.

far larger than on any weekday before. And there was much life among the people, which perhaps was[26] increased by the epidemic disorder. This generally attacked first the head, afterward the throat and the breast. Mr. Jones, who had been drooping for some time, was seized with this three weeks since. While I was at Youghal, he sent for a physician, who applied a blister to his head. In two or three days, a second physician was called in, who told his relations he was better and better. Returning from Bandon and observing what was prescribed, I could not help saying, 'When a fever neither intermits nor remits the bark is no better than poison.' At hearing this, the doctors were much displeased and declared again he was 'a great deal better'. On Wednesday morning, a little before two, his spirit returned to God.

So died honest Thomas Jones, *secundum artem!*[27] A man whom God raised from nothing, by a blessing on his unwearied diligence, to a plentiful fortune. Yet when riches increased on every side, he did not set his heart upon them. Some years since, he retired from business but was still fully employed in building and in doing good. His natural temper was rough and so was his speech, which occasioned him many trials. But notwithstanding this, he was generous and compassionate, and never weary of well-doing. From the beginning of his illness he was continually in prayer, for some time with much fear and distress. But I saw no signs of this after I came from Bandon. I believe his fears were then all scattered, and he waited with calm, though earnest, desire for the salvation of God.

Wed. 30. I rode to Limerick. I had promised to come again if our brethren found a convenient place to build a preaching-house. One now offered, proper in all respects. Saturday, July 3, I met the society and inquired what each was willing to subscribe. A considerable sum was subscribed immediately.

Sunday 4 was a day of solemn joy, equal to any I had seen in Dublin. At the love-feast in the evening, it appeared that God had now visited Limerick also. Five persons desired to return thanks to God for a clear sense of his pardoning love, several others for an increase of faith and for deliverance from doubts and fears. And two gave a plain, simple account of the manner wherein God

[26] Orig., 'who perhaps were'.

[27] I.e., 'following accustomed [medical] practice'. Thomas Jones was one of the sufferers in the Cork riots; see July 20, 1749, n. 34 (20:285 in this edn.).

had cleansed their hearts, so that they now felt no anger, pride, or self-will, but continual love and prayer and praise.

Mon. 5. I rode to Clonmel and preached in the evening near the barrack-gate to a wild, staring multitude, many of whom would have been rude enough, but they stood in awe of the soldiers. Tuesday 6, I rode to Carrick on Suir.[28] Having been informed there was one family here also wherein both the man and his wife feared God, I immediately sent to the house. The woman presently came, from whom I learned that her husband died the Saturday before and left her with nothing but four little children and an unshaken confidence in God. Her words, her look, her whole carriage, were of a piece and showed the dignity of Christian sorrow. I could not but admire that God should send *me* just at such a time! And her tears were turned into tears of joy.[29]

In the evening, I preached at Waterford in a court adjoining to the main street. Wed. 7. Four of the *Whiteboys,* lately condemned for breaking open houses, were executed. They were all, notwithstanding the absolution of their priest, ready to die for fear of death. Two or three of them laid fast hold on the ladder and could not be *persuaded* to let it go. One in particular gave such violent shrieks as might be heard near a mile off. O what but love can cast out the fear of death! And how inexpressibly miserable is that bondage!

On this and the two following days God remembered poor Waterford also. Several backsliders were healed; many awoke out of sleep. And some mightily rejoiced in God their Saviour.[30]

Sat. 10. We rode to Kilkenny, one of the pleasantest and the most ancient cities in the kingdom and not inferior to any at all in wickedness or in hatred to 'this way'.[31] I was therefore glad of a permission to preach in the town hall, where a small, serious company attended in the evening. Sun. 11. I went to the cathedral, one of the best built which I have seen in Ireland. The pillars are all of black marble. But the late bishop[32] ordered them

28 Orig., 'Carrick on Sure'.

29 Cf. Ps. 126:5.

30 Cf. Luke 1:47.

31 Acts 9:2.

32 Edward Maurice, Scholar of Trinity College, Dublin, 1709; B.A., 1711; Bishop of Ossory, 1754–56 (his death). Maurice had been precentor of Ossory since 1716. He produced (unpublished) versions of Homer's *Iliad* and *Odyssey* in blank verse and bequeathed his books to the diocesan library.

to be whitewashed! Indeed, marble is so plentiful near this town that the very streets are paved with it.

At six in the evening, I began preaching in the old bowling-green near the castle. Abundance of people, Protestants and Papists, gathered from all parts. They were very still during the former part of the sermon. Then the Papists ran together, set up a shout, and would have gone further, but they were restrained, they knew not how. I turned to them and said, 'Be silent, or be gone!' Their noise ceased, and we heard them no more. So I resumed, and went on with my discourse, and concluded without interruption.

When I came out of the green, they gathered again and gnashed upon me with their teeth.[33] One cried out, 'O what is Kilkenny come to!' But they could go no farther. Only two or three large stones were thrown, but none was hurt save he that threw them. For as he was going to throw again, one seized him by the neck and gave him a kick and a cuff, which spoiled his diversion.

Mon. 12. I went to Dunmore Cave, three or four miles from Kilkenny.[34] It is full as remarkable as Poole's Hole, or any other in The Peak. The opening is round, parallel to the horizon, and seventy or eighty yards across. In the midst of this there is a kind of arch, twenty or thirty feet high. By this you enter into the first cave, nearly round and forty or fifty foot in diameter. It is encompassed with spar stones, just like those on the sides of Poole's Hole. On one side of the cave is a narrow passage which goes under the rock two or three hundred yards; on the other, an hollow which no one has ever been able to find an end of. I suppose this[35] hole too, as well as many others, was formed by the waters of the deluge, retreating into the great abyss, with which probably it communicates.

Tue. 13. I rode to Birr. About forty persons attended in the evening, and half as many in the morning. I saw there was but one way to do any good. So in the evening I preached abroad. I had then hundreds of hearers, and God himself spoke to many a cold heart. The next morning at five the room was full, and light

[33] Ps. 35:16.

[34] In fact 7 miles from Kilkenny; *WHS* 7 (1910):122. Dunmore Cave consists of a series of limestone caverns opening from one to another, all with stalactites. It is still on the tourist round. L. R. Muirhead, ed., *Blue Guide: Ireland*, 3 vols. (London, 1962), pp. 84-85.

[35] Orig., 'the', altered to 'this' in the errata and personal notes to JW's *Works* (1774).

sprung out of darkness, so that many poor, withered souls began to revive and rejoice again in God their Saviour.

Thur. 15. I took my old standing in the market-place at Mountmellick. But the next evening the rain drove us into the market-house. Afterward we had a joyful love-feast. Indeed, hitherto God has been pleased to mark all our way with blessings.

Sat. 17. I went on to poor dead Portarlington. And no wonder it should be so, while the preachers coop themselves up in a room with twenty or thirty hearers. I went straight to the market-place and cried aloud, 'Hearken! Behold a sower went forth to sow.'[36] God made his word 'quick and powerful' and 'sharp as a two-edged sword'.[37] Abundantly more than the room could contain were present at five in the morning. At eight, I began in the market-place again on 'How shall I give thee up, Ephraim?'[38] Solemn attention sat on every face, and God repeated his call to many hearts.

In the evening I preached in the market-place at Tullamore. Mon. 19. Between two and three in the morning was such thunder and lightning as I never knew in Europe. The crack and the flash were in the same instant. Most of the houses shook, and yet no hurt was done in the whole town. But some good was done, for at five o'clock the preaching-house was quite filled. And the inward 'voice of the Lord' was 'mighty in operation'; this also was 'a glorious voice'![39]

Tue. 20. We had our quarterly meeting at Coolalough. On Wednesday I preached at Clara, Thursday 22 at Tyrrellspass, and on Friday went on to Edenderry. Here I found some who had been long labouring in the fire and toiling to *work themselves* into holiness. To show them a more excellent way, I preached on Rom. 10:6-8. They found this was the very thing they wanted, and at the meeting of the society God confirmed the word of his grace in so powerful a manner that many wondered how they could help believing.

Sat. 24. I rode to Dublin and found the flame not only continuing but increasing. The congregation used to be small on Saturday night, but it was as large now as formerly on Sunday. Monday 26, at five in the morning, the congregation was larger than it used to be in the evening. And in these two days and an half, four persons gave thanks for a sense of God's pardoning

[36] Matt. 13:3.
[37] Cf. Heb. 4:12.
[38] Hos. 11:8.
[39] Ps. 29:4 (BCP).

mercy, and seven (among whom were a mother and her daughter) for being 'perfected in love'.[40]

The person by whom chiefly it had pleased God to work this wonderful work was John Manners,[41] a plain man of middling sense, and not eloquent but rather rude in speech—one who had never before been remarkably useful but seemed to be raised up for this single work. As soon as it was done, he fell into a consumption, languished a while, and died.

I now found he had not at all exceeded the truth in the accounts he had sent me from time to time. In one of his first letters after I left the town he says,

> The work here is such as I never expected to see. Some are justified or sanctified almost every day. This week three or four were justified, and as many, if not more, renewed in love. The people are all on fire. Such a day as last Sunday I never saw. While I was at prayer in the society, the power of the Lord overshadowed us, and some cried out, 'Lord, I *can* believe.' The cry soon became general, with strong prayers. Twice I attempted to sing, but my voice could not be heard. I then desired them to restrain themselves and, in stillness and composure, to wait for the blessing; on which all but two or three, who could not refrain, came into a solemn silence. I prayed again, and the softening power of grace was felt in many hearts. Our congregations increase much, and I have no doubt but we shall see greater things than these.

Four days after, he writes,

> The work of God increases every day. There is hardly a day but some are justified or sanctified or both. On Thursday three came and told me that 'the blood of Jesus Christ' had 'cleansed *them* from all sin'. One of them told me she had been justified seven years and had been five years convinced of the necessity of sanctification. But this *easy* conviction availed not. A fortnight since, she was seized with so *keen* a conviction as gave her no rest till God had sanctified her and witnessed it to her heart.

Three days after (May 11), he writes thus:

[40] Cf. 1 John 2:5.

[41] John Manners (1731–64) was born near Malton, and converted under Methodist preaching, 1754–55. It is not known when he commenced to itinerate, but the present revival in Dublin was remembered as the most spectacular episode of his career. Atmore, *Memorial*, pp. 247-50; *Arminian Magazine* 3 (1780):275-76.

God still continues his marvellous loving-kindness to us. On Sunday last Dor[othea] King[42] entered into *the rest.* She had been seeking it for some time. But her convictions and desires grew stronger and stronger as the hour approached. A while ago she told me, she grew worse and worse, and her inward conflicts were greater than ever. But on the Lord's Day she felt an entire change while these words were spoke to her heart, 'Thou art all fair, my love; there is no spot in thee.'[43] She now walks in sweet peace and rejoices evermore. Her father received the blessing a few days before her and is exceeding happy.

The fire catches all that come near. An old soldier[44] in his return from Germany to the north of Ireland fell in one night with these wrestling Jacobs, to his great astonishment. He was justified seventeen years ago but afterward fell from it for five years. As he was going to Germany, in the beginning of the war, the Lord healed him in Dublin, and in spite of all the distresses of a severe campaign, he walked in the light continually. On his return through London, he was convinced of the necessity of sanctification. And soon after he came hither, his heart was broken in pieces while he was with a little company who meet daily for prayer. One evening as they were going away, he stopped them and begged they would not go till the Lord had blessed him. They kneeled down again and did not cease wrestling with God till he had a witness that he was saved from all sin.

The case of Mr. Timmins[45] is no less remarkable. He had been a notorious sinner. He was deeply wounded two months since. Ten

[42] Dorothea King (1732–1817) was one of the legendary characters of early Dublin Methodism. The daughter of a merchant, Thomas Garrett, said to be of Dutch origin, but settled in Dublin and in the clutches of a creditor called King, she married the latter at the age of sixteen as the only way to save her father from prison. The marriage proved to be cruel as well as unhappy and ended in separation. Deeply impressed by Whitefield on one of his visits to Dublin, both she and her father were in due course converted. It was now that she entered 'the rest' of perfect of love, a lifelong blessing. She became a class leader of great spiritual repute, and in 1784 married the retired itinerant John Johnson at Lisburn; see Crookshank, *Ireland,* 1:123, 384, 387: C. H. Crookshank, *Memorable Women of Irish Methodism in the Last Century* (London, 1882), pp. 53-62; see above, May 5, 1757, n. 70. Four of her letters to JW were published in *Arminian Magazine* 4 (1781):501-4.

[43] S. of S. 4:7.

[44] William Price (died March 1795) as a young man served in the Enniskillen Dragoons at Dettingen and Fontenoy, and was converted by the influence of John Haime (see Feb. 2, 1744, n. 39; 20:9 in this edn.). As the passage relates he found it hard to sustain his profession in a hostile environment, and even after this latest impulse, he was discouraged to find himself without a single companion of like mind when he returned to Fermanagh in 1762. He then invited the preacher John Smith to Tonyloman, and from his efforts a Methodist society was formed, with Price as its first member and class leader, in which office he continued active to within a few months of his death. Crookshank, *Ireland,* 1:173, 192; Thomas Ridgeway, 'Account of Thomas Price', *Arminian Magazine* 19 (1796):503 [misnumbered 453].

days ago, on a Friday, God spake peace to his soul. The Sunday following, after a violent struggle, he sunk down as dead. He was cold as clay. After about ten minutes he came to himself and cried, 'A new heart, a new heart!' He said he felt himself 'in an instant entirely emptied of sin and filled with God'. Brother Barry[46] likewise had been justified but a few days before God gave him purity of heart.

May 15 he writes,

God still makes me a messenger of good tidings. His work goes on. Our last night's meeting was remarkable for the presence and power of God, while several were relating what he had done. One said, 'All that day in which God delivered me, I felt the blessing just at hand but could not open my heart to receive it. I was fast shut up till under the sermon in the evening I felt God open my heart, remove the bar of unbelief, and give me power to receive the blessing freely.'

There are now three places in the city wherein as many as have opportunity assemble day and night to pour out their souls before God for the continuance and enlargement of his work.

May 29:

Since my last account many have been sanctified and several justified. One of the former is Wm. Moore.[47] He was a long time struggling for the blessing. And one night he was resolved not to go to bed without it. He continued wrestling with God for two hours, when he felt a glorious change and the Spirit of God witnessing that the work was done.

[45] It may well have been his widow whom JW was trying to place in the Widow's House in 1787; Telford, 7:380-81.

[46] Perhaps a member of the Barry family of Bandon, which became Methodist about this time, and in due course sent John Barry into the Methodist ministry and William Barry into that of the Establishment. *WHS* 16 (1928):147-48.

[47] Orig., 'Moor'. William Moore was admitted to the itinerancy on trial in 1774, but in 1782 had to be warned to keep clear of the separatists at Bath (Telford, 7:123). In 1784 he was dissatisfied at finding no place in the Deed of Declaration and, being appointed to Plymouth, hired a preaching place there, took forty of the members, and appealed to the public in a pamphlet (Tyerman, *John Wesley*, 3:459); he 'wrote a strong letter to Mr. Wesley in vindication of his conduct on the ground "that spiritual justice was not done to the people; that by denying them the ordinances we obliged them to go to strange pastures where they were not properly fed . . . and that because these ordinances were not administered among us, many (I believe, the greater number) of our Societies did not receive the Lord's Supper *at all*"'; *WHS* 18 (1931):22, 24. Adam Clarke and JW himself (see Feb. 25, 1785) were hastily dispatched to Plymouth to seal the breach, and Moore is last heard of trying to create a separation near Pembroke where he had served 1779–81.

We begin now to meet with opposition from every quarter. Some say, 'This is rank enthusiasm'; others, that it is 'either[48] a cheat or mere pride'; others, that it is 'a new thing' and that they 'can find no such thing in the Bible'.

June 3:

The Lord increases his work in proportion to the opposition it meets with. Between Monday morning and Tuesday night I have had eight bills of thanksgiving: for two justified, three renewed in love, and three backsliders healed.

June 15:

There is no end of the mercies of God. Three days of this week are gone, in which God has justified five sinners. On Sunday in the afternoon I preached at three in the Barrack Square. And a more solemn time I have not seen. The hearers were as many as my voice could reach, and all remarkably attentive.

In the evening a cry ran through the society, and four were justified that night. Two of these, Alexander Tate[49] and his wife, were but lately joined. The power of God first seized her and constrained her to cry aloud till she heard the still, small voice. He continued calling upon God and would not cease before God answered him also in the joy of his heart.

Saturday, June 19:

We have had eight this week whose sins are blotted out, and two more have entered into that rest. One of them says she has enjoyed the love of God nine years but felt as great a difference between that state and the state she is now in as if her soul was taken into heaven!

June 26:

Last week eleven were justified, or sanctified, and this week eleven more, eight of whom received remission of sins, and three a clean heart. And a troop are waiting for the moving of the water. Among them whom the power of God has seized lately are two eminent sinners, each of whom lived with a woman to whom he was never married. One of them already rejoices in God; the other

[48] Orig., 'rather', altered in *Works* (1774).

[49] For his progress, see below, July 29, 1762. JW dined with him in 1783; see *Diary*, Apr. 21, 1783.

mourns and will not be comforted. But the women are gone; they put away the accursed thing immediately.

I had much fear about the children, lest our labour should be lost upon them. But I find we shall reap, if we faint not. Margaret Roper, about eight years old, has been thoughtful for some time. The other day, while they were at family prayer, she burst into tears and wept bitterly. They asked what was the matter. She said she was 'a great sinner and durst not pray'. They bade her go to bed. She no sooner came into the chamber than she began crying and clapping her hands, so that they heard her across the street. But God soon bound up her broken heart. Being asked how she felt herself, she said, 'Ten times better. Now I can love God. I wish you would sit up and sing with me all night.' She has been happy ever since and as serious as one of forty.

July 3:

Our joy is now quite full. The flame rises higher and higher. Since Saturday last, eight sinners more are freely justified, and two more renewed in love. Our house was once large enough; now it is scarce able to contain us. And we have not many in the society who are not either wrestling with God for his love or rejoicing therein.

Thus far the account of John Manners, quite unadorned, but plain and sensible.

Upon farther examination, I found three or four and forty in Dublin who seemed to enjoy the pure love of God. At least forty of these had been set at liberty within four months. Some others, who had received the same blessing, were removed out of the city. The same, if not a larger number, had found remission of sins. Nor was the hand of the Lord shortened yet: he still wrought as swiftly as ever.

In some respects the work of God in this place was more remarkable than even that in London. (1) It is far greater in proportion to the time and to the number of people. That society had above seven and twenty hundred members; this, not a fifth part of the number. Six months after the flame broke out there, we had about thirty witnesses of the great salvation. In Dublin there were above forty in less than four months. (2) The work was more pure. In all this time, while they were mildly and tenderly treated, there were none of them headstrong or unadvisable, none that were wiser than their teachers, none who dreamed of being immortal or infallibly incapable of temptation; in short, no whimsical or enthusiastic persons. All were calm and sober-minded.[50]

I know, several of these were in process of time 'moved from their steadfastness'.[51] I am nothing surprised at this; it was no more than might be expected. I rather wonder that more were not moved. Nor does this in any degree alter my judgment concerning the great work which God then wrought.

Tue. 27. I received a comfortable letter from Edenderry:[52] 'When you came hither, Satan had gained such an advantage over us that few even of the society would read your sermons, saying they were nothing but the law. But God has now taught us better.' His power fell upon us first in the preaching but abundantly more when the society met. At that time many who were in heaviness were filled with consolation. And two of the old believers were constrained to declare, they believed God had cleansed them from all sin.

Wed. 28.[53] I received farther accounts from Limerick; one letter ran thus:

July 20, 1762

There is a glorious work going on at Limerick. Twelve or fourteen have a clear sense of being renewed. Several have been justified this week; and on Sunday night, at the meeting of the society, there was such a cry as I scarce ever heard before, such confession of sins, such pleading with the Lord, and such a spirit of prayer, as if the Lord himself had been visibly present among us. Some received remission of sins, and several were just brought to the birth. All were in floods of tears; they trembled, they cried, they prayed, they roared aloud, all of them lying on the ground. I began to sing, yet they could not rise but sang as they lay along. When we concluded, some of them could not go away but stayed in the house

[50] JW's second thoughts on all this are given in a tail-piece to this Journal, below, Oct. 28, 1762. A further attempt to hold together reason and faith was made in Sermon 70, 'The Case of Reason Impartially Considered' (2:587-600 in this edn.).

[51] Cf. 2 Pet. 3:17.

[52] JW's first experience of Edenderry had been *un*comfortable; see Apr. 16, 1748: 'But still there is no such work as I look for. I see nothing yet but drops before a shower' (20:219 in this edn.).

[53] Orig., '18'. To the surprise of Wesleyan commentators, JW was too full of the revival to note that on July 28-29, 1762, the Irish Conference was held in Dublin (Curnock, 4:521, n. 1). It is recorded in Thomas Garret's Diary: 'July 28. Have had a good time of it since Mr. Wesley and the preachers came amongst us. 29th. Last night was a watchnight, when we had nine or ten preachers, the greatest number I remember to have seen at one time—Messrs. J. Wesley, Manners, Kead, Swindells, Deaves, Davis, Roberts, Guildford, Lee, and Harris' (Crookshank, *Ireland.* 1:165).

all night. And, blessed be our Lord, they all hitherto walk worthy of their calling.

Another writes,

> I will just tell you, the Lord has made your last visit to us a great blessing. Such times were never before in Limerick. The fire which broke out before you left us is now spreading on every side. Four were happy before you left us; several others can now rejoice evermore and pray without ceasing. And this certainly they could not do did they not love God with all their heart.

A third letter, dated July 25, says,

> Blessed be God, his word runs swiftly. Last night his power was present indeed; and another was assured that God, who had before forgiven his sins, had now 'cleansed *him* from all unrighteousness'. There are now ten women and thirteen men who witness the same confession. And their lives agree thereto. Eight have lately received the remission of their sins. And many are on the full stretch for God and just ready to step into the pool.

Hence it appears that in proportion to the time, which was only three or four weeks, and the number of hearers (not one half, if a third part) the work of God was greater in Limerick than even in Dublin itself.

Thur. 29. I was informed of a remarkable instance of divine mercy. An harmless, unawakened young woman came to one of the meetings for prayer in Dublin. While they were praying, she felt herself a sinner and began crying aloud for mercy. And when they rose to go away she cried with a bitter cry, 'What, must I go without Christ?' They began praying again, and in a short time she was as loud in praising God for his pardoning mercy.

No less remarkable was the case of Alexander Tate.[54] He and his wife were present where a few were met for prayer. Her sorrow was quickly turned into joy. Her husband, who was before little awakened, was just then cut to the heart and felt the wrath of God abiding on him. Nor did he cease crying to God till his prayers and tears were swallowed up in thanksgiving. So here are two instances of persons both convinced and converted in the same hour.

[54] See above, July 24, 1762, at n. 49.

Sat. 31. Although I never before felt such an union of heart with the people of Dublin, yet believing my present work in Ireland was ended, I cheerfully commended them to God and embarked on board the *Dorset* for Parkgate. We weighed anchor at eight in the evening. Between nine and ten on Sunday morning [August 1], the captain[55] asked me if I would not 'go to prayers with them'. All who were able to creep out were willingly present. After prayers I preached on Prov. 3:17. We had scarce any wind when I began. But while I was preaching, it sprung up and brought us to Parkgate between six and seven.

Mon. 2. I rode on to Chester. Never was the society in such a state before. Their jars and contentions were at an end, and I found nothing but peace and love among them. About twelve of them believed they were saved from sin, and their lives did not contradict their profession. Most of the rest were strongly athirst for God and looking for him continually.

Tue. 3. I was desired to preach at Northwich. And one had stuck up notices in all parts of the town. But what place had they for me to preach in? Only a little room which would hold about fifty people.[56] Between twelve and one they gathered from all parts, noisy and rude enough.[57] I could not stand in the yard without just facing the sun. So I stood at the casement, that those without might hear, that is, if they had a mind to it. But a great part of them had no such intention. They came only either for sport or mischief. However, they were pretty quiet till I had done. Our friends would then have persuaded me to stay till the mob was dispersed. But as they grew louder and louder, I judged it best to walk immediately through the midst of them. Many things were thrown, but nothing touched me till I took horse and rode to Manchester.

Here I received letters from Congleton in Cheshire and Burslem in Staffordshire. Part of the former ran thus:

August 1, 1762

The work of God for some time stood still here. But at the love-feast on the 21st of March last (glory for ever be to God!),

[55] Captain Caulder; *WHS* 5 (1905):75-78.

[56] The old Congregational chapel, Crown Street, later Hobson's print works, which was rented from the decayed Independent cause, 1760–66, when it was repossessed. *WHS* 22 (1939):41.

[57] This was probably the occasion when the mob tried to throw the itinerant John Morris, who was with JW, from his horse over the bridge. *Arminian Magazine* 18 (1795):76; *Wesleyan Methodist Magazine* 53 (1830):857.

there was an outpouring of his spirit among us. Five persons were assured of their acceptance with God, of whom by his free grace I was one; four believed he had not only *forgiven* their *sins*, but likewise 'cleansed them from all unrighteousness'. Many more have since found him gracious and merciful, nor is his hand yet stayed at all.

Part of the other is as follows:

Before Mr. Furz[58] came into these parts, we were biting and devouring one another. And many who once had known God were 'in their works denying him'. The society in general was cold and dead, and only two were converted to God in a whole year. But, glory be to God, the case is now altered. Those grievances are removed. The power of God is present with us, and the fire of his love is kindled among us. We are very weak, but blessed be God we are all alive. Many are crying out in the bitterness of their souls, 'God be merciful to me a sinner.' Sometimes we have had two, at other times six or seven justified in one week. Others find the very remains of sin destroyed and wait to be 'filled with all the fullness of God'.

Wed. 4. I rode to Liverpool, where also was such a work of God as had never been known there before. We had a surprising congregation in the evening, and, as it seemed, all athirst for God. This, I found, had begun here likewise in the latter end of March. And from that time it had continually increased till, a little before I came, nine were justified in one hour. The next morning I spoke severally with those who believed they were sanctified. They were fifty-one in all: twenty-one men, twenty-one widows or married women, and nine young women or children. In one of these, the change was wrought three weeks after she was justified; in three, seven days after it; in one, five days; and in Sus.[59] Lutwich, aged fourteen, two days only. I asked Hannah Blakeley, aged eleven, 'What do you want now?' She said, with amazing energy, the tears

[58] John Furz (1717–1800), born at Wilton, near Salisbury, was powerfully afflicted by religious fears at an early age, and unable to quiet them in the Church or Dissent. But he found relief in preaching, and was taken into the Methodist itinerancy in 1758. Though quoted by JW as writing from Burslem, it was at Congleton that some of the most spectacular conversions of his career were achieved (Atmore, *Memorial*, pp. 148-54). JW noted in 1780 that 'John Furz is fairly worn out; he is hardly able to preach at all'; he became a supernumerary the following year, and was senile some years before his death. Telford, 7:19, 68; Jackson, *Early Methodist Preachers*, 5:108-34.

[59] *Works* (1774), 'S.'; JW's 'A Short History of the People called Methodists' (1781), §93, 'Samuel'.

running down her cheeks, 'Nothing in this world; nothing but more of my Jesus.' How often 'out of the mouth of babes and sucklings dost thou perfect praise'![60]

Fri. 6. I was informed of the flame which had broken out at Bolton. One writing to Mr. Furz described a little of it in the following words:

> Glory be to God, he is doing wonders among us. Since you left us there have been seven (if not more) justified, and six sanctified at one meeting. Two of these were (I think) justified and sanctified in less than three days. O what a meeting was our last class-meeting! In three minutes or less, God quite unexpectedly convinced an old opposer of the truth and wounded many. I never felt the abiding presence of God so exceeding powerful before.

I preached at Macclesfield in the evening, to a people ready prepared for the Lord. An impetuous shower began just as we came into the town, but it did us no hurt. Inquiring how the revival here began, I received the following account. In March last, after a long season of dryness and barrenness, one Monday night John Oldham preached.[61] When he had done and was going away, a man fell down and cried aloud for mercy. In a short time so did several others. He came back and wrestled with God in prayer for them. About twelve he retired, leaving some of the brethren, who resolved to wrestle on till they had an answer of peace. They continued in prayer till six in the morning, and nine prisoners were set at liberty.

They met again the next night, and six or seven more were filled with peace and joy in believing. So were one or two more every night till the Monday following, when there was another general shower of grace. And many believed that 'the blood of Christ had cleansed them from all sin.'[62]

I spoke to these (forty in all) one by one. Some of them said they received that blessing ten days, some seven, some four, some three days after they found peace with God. And two of them the next day. What marvel? Since one day is with God as a thousand years.[63]

60 Cf. Matt. 21:16.

61 John Oldham (d. 1769) was born in Manchester and became one of the first of JW's itinerants. He ran into considerable opposition to his insistence on 'full, free and present salvation from all sin', and, infirm in health, lived on the brink of eternity for some years before his death. See Benjamin Smith, *Methodism in Macclesfield* (London, Wesleyan Conference Office, 1875), p. 62.

62 Cf. 1 John 1:7.

63 See 2 Pet. 3:8.

The case of Ann Hooly[64] was peculiar. She had often declared, 'The Methodists' God shall not be my God. I will sooner go to hell than I will go to heaven in their way.' She was standing in the street with two young women, when John Oldham, passing by, spoke to one and the other and went on. She burst into tears and said, 'What, am I so great a sinner that he won't speak to me?' About twelve, he was sent for in all haste. He found her in deep distress, but continued in prayer till all her trouble was gone, and her spirit rejoiced in God her Saviour. Yet three nights after, she was in much distress again, crying, 'I have a wicked heart, and I cannot rest till God takes it away.' He did so in a few hours. Ever since, she has been a pattern to all the young people in the town. She was thirteen years old. In about a year, her spirit returned to God.

Sat. 7. I made one more trial at Northwich, preaching in Mr. Page's yard. Abundance of people flocked together, nor did anyone oppose or make the least disturbance. And when I afterward rode quite through the town, I had not one uncivil word.

In the evening I spoke with those at Manchester who believed God had cleansed their hearts. They were sixty-three in number, to about sixty of whom I could not find there was any reasonable objection.

Mon. 9. I preached at Elland[65] and Birstall in my way to Leeds, where our Conference[66] began on Tuesday morning. And we had great reason to praise God for his gracious presence, from the beginning to the end.

Sun. 15. I preached about one at Birstall, and in the morning and evening at Leeds. I then rode about eighteen miles. On Monday morning I preached at Sheffield, and in the evening came to Derby.[67] I had sent word that I did not intend to preach.

[64] At the time of her conversion Ann Hooley was twelve or thirteen, and two years later JW declared he had 'seldom known so devoted a soul as Sister Hooley . . . who was sanctified within nine days after she was convinced of sin . . . and I believe was never afterwards heard to speak an improper word. . . . Her look struck an awe into all that saw her.' Smith, *Macclesfield*, p. 70; Telford, 4:268.

[65] Elland was a chapelry in the parish of Halifax, 3 miles south-east of that town.

[66] Like the Irish Conference, the English Conference of 1762 has sunk into obscurity, being recalled only by George Story's reminiscence of JW's edifying sermons and of the shortage of itinerants which led to his being asked to offer himself for the work. Jackson, *Early Methodist Preachers*, 5:237-38.

[67] This entry is a further example of JW's itinerary being influenced by the offer of hospitality and a base to work from. Methodism had been introduced into Derby only the previous year with the arrival of Mr. & Mrs. Dobinson and their friend Mrs. Sarah

But after I had rested awhile in my chamber, coming down and finding the house full of people, I spoke to them half an hour in a familiar manner and then spent some time in prayer. I believe God touched some of their hearts. Indeed, it seemed none were unmoved.

Tue. 17. We rode to Northampton, the next day to Sundon, and on Thursday 19 to London. Fri. 20. As I expected, the sower of tares had not been idle during my five months' absence. But I believe great part of his work was undone in one hour when we met at West Street. I pointed out to those who had more heat than light the snares which they had well-nigh fallen into. And hitherto they were of an humble, teachable spirit. So for the present the snare was broken.

Sat. 21. My brother and I had a long conversation with Mr. Maxfield[68] and freely told him whatever we disliked. In some things we found he had been blamed without cause; others he promised to alter. So we were thoroughly satisfied with the conversation, believing all misunderstandings were now removed.

Mon. 23. I set out and on Tuesday reached Bristol. After spending two days there, on Friday 27, I set out for the west and, having preached at Shepton and Middlezoy in the way, came on Saturday to Exeter. When I began the service there, the congregation (beside ourselves) were two women and one man. Before I had done, the room was about half full. This comes of omitting field preaching.

Sun. 29. I preached at eight on Southernhay[69] Green to an

Crosby. Mr. Dobinson appears to have been a London Methodist whose wife was awakened to religious anguish by the preaching, first of William Romaine, and then of JW at the Foundery. Mr. Dobinson secured her release from distress and aided her conversion by obtaining the ministrations of a devout widow and class-leader, Mrs. Crosby. When business took Mr. Dobinson to Derby in 1761, the three moved together, he acting as a local preacher, and Mrs. Crosby (said to be the original of Sarah Williamson in *Adam Bede*) gathering a class of two hundred. Yet there were 'many threatenings from some of the magistrates and much opposition and discouragement in various ways', and JW's visit was a way of securing an impulse and some recognition for a promising cause. On this circle generally, see *Methodist Magazine* 26 (1803):557-66; 29 (1806):418-22, 465-73, 517-21, 563-68, 611-17; *Wesleyan Methodist Magazine* 53 (1830):786; *WHS* 14 (1924):104-9; 15 (1926):109-12; 27 (1949):76-82; 28 (1952):161. For JW's next visit to Derby, see below, Mar. 27, 1764.

68 For Thomas Maxfield and the difficulties occasioned by him, see May 21, 1739, n. 5 (19:61 in this edn.); Nov. 2, 1751, n. 2 (20:406 in this edn.); and above, Dec. 29, 1761, n. 43.

69 Orig., 'Southney-Green'.

extremely quiet congregation. At the cathedral we had an useful sermon, and the whole service was performed with great seriousness and decency. Such an organ I never saw or heard before, so large,[70] beautiful, and so finely toned. And the music of 'Glory be to God in the highest,' I think, exceeded the *Messiah* itself. I was well pleased to partake of the Lord's Supper with my old opponent, Bishop Lavington.[71] O may we sit down together in the kingdom of our Father!

At five, I went to Southernhay Green again and found a multitude of people. But a lewd, profane, drunken vagabond had so stirred up many of the baser sort that there was much noise, hurry, and confusion. While I was preaching, several things were thrown, and much pains taken to overturn the table. And after I concluded, many endeavoured to throw me down, but I walked through the midst and left them.

Mon. 30. We rode to Plymouth Dock. Wednesday, Sept. [1,] I came about two to Polperro,[72] a little village four hours' ride from Plymouth Passage, surrounded with huge mountains. However, abundance of people had found the way thither. And so had Satan too. For an old, grey-headed sinner was bitterly cursing *all the Methodists* just as we came into the town. However, God gave his blessing both to us and the congregation.

In the evening I preached at Methrose,[73] the next evening in St. Austell, and on Friday [3] at Mevagissey. Saturday [4], after preaching in Grampound, I rode on to Truro. I almost expected there would be some disturbance, as it was market-day, and I stood in the street at a small distance from the market. But all was quiet. Indeed, both persecution and popular tumult seem to be forgotten in Cornwall.

Sun. [5]. As I was enforcing in the same place those solemn words, 'God forbid that I should glory, save in the cross of our Lord Jesus Christ,'[74] a poor man began to make some tumult. But

[70] This organ was built by John Loosemore in 1665, enlarged in 1713, and rebuilt by Jordan in 1741. It had a great reputation for the excellence of its tone and for its being the first English organ to be provided with a double diapason. Samuel Sebastian Wesley, Charles Wesley's grandson, was organist 1835–41. Orig. omits 'large', added only in *Works* (1774).

[71] On whom, see Nov. 19, 1751, n. 6 (20:407 in this edn.); the bishop died a fortnight later, Sept. 13.

[72] Orig., 'Poleperrow'. Polperro was a fishing village and market town 5 miles east of Fowey.

[73] Orig., 'Medras'; cf. Sept. 26, 1757, 'Medros'.

[74] Gal. 6:14.

many cried out, 'Constables, take him away.' They did so, and the hurry was over. At one, I preached in the main street at Redruth, where rich and poor were equally attentive. The wind was so high at five that I could not stand in the usual place at Gwennap. But at a small distance was a hollow, capable of containing many thousand people.[75] I stood on one side of this amphitheatre toward the top, with the people beneath and on all sides, and enlarged on those words in the Gospel for the day (Luke 10:23[-4]), 'Blessed are the eyes which see the things that ye see, [. . .] and hear the things that ye hear.'[76]

Monday [6] I preached at Penryn, Tuesday [7][77] at Porkellis about one o'clock. Thence I rode on to Mullion,[78] near the Lizard Point. A man who *was* a sinner gladly received us. For he knew God had received him, having been deeply convinced of sin the last time I preached near Helston and, not long after, filled with peace and joy in the Holy Ghost.

A flame was kindled almost as soon as I began to speak, which increased more and more all the time I was preaching, as well as during the meeting of the society. How tender are the hearts of this people! Such is the advantage of true, Christian simplicity!

Wed. 8. The congregation at St. John's,[79] near Helston, was thrice as large as when I was there before. The next day, I preached at Crowan at noon and at Penhale (in Breage) in the evening. Fri. 10. I preached on St. Hilary Downs to a congregation gathered from all parts. Abundance of them were athirst for God, and he did not deceive their hope. The cry of the mourners went up before him, and he sent down an answer of peace.

Sat. 11. I preached at one on the cliff near Penzance, and in the evening at Newlyn. Sun. 12. At eight, God was in the midst, and many hearts were broken in pieces. Between one and two, I preached at Sancreed[80] where I never was before. Abundance of

[75] Gwennap Pit was an amphitheatre formed either by mining subsidence or by surface mining operations or both. It was improved by levelling and cutting circular terraces of seats in 1806. In 1799 all-day Methodist preaching was established on Gwennap Green as a rival attraction to a sports meeting, and, the sports meeting having succumbed to this competition, annual revival gatherings were held in the improved pit from 1807 onwards.

[76] BCP, Gospel for the Thirteenth Sunday after Trinity.

[77] In orig., Sept. 1-7 are incorrectly dated 2-8.

[78] Mullion was a village 5 miles south of Helston.

[79] St. John's was a village near Helston.

[80] Orig., 'St. Creet'. According to the preacher Richard Rodda (1743–1815), there had been preaching in his father's house at Sancreed since 1750. Pearce, *Wesleys in Cornwall*, p. 139, n. 127.

strangers came from every side, and I believe not many went empty away. Hence we rode to St. Just, where I spent two comfortable nights, the congregations being very large, evening and morning. Tue. 14. I preached in Lelant about one, and in the evening near the quay at St. Ives. Two or three pretty butterflies came and looked and smiled and went away. But all the rest of the numerous congregation behaved with the utmost seriousness.

Wed. 15. We had our Quarterly Meeting. The next day I appointed the children to meet. I expected twenty, but I suppose we had fourscore—all of them wanting, many desiring, instruction.

The more I converse with the believers in Cornwall, the more I am convinced that they have sustained great loss for want of hearing the doctrine of Christian perfection clearly and strongly enforced. I see, wherever this is not done, the believers grow dead and cold. Nor can this be prevented but by keeping up in them an hourly expectation of being perfected in love. I say, an 'hourly expectation'; for to expect it at *death*, or *some time hence*, is much the same as not expecting it at all.

Fri. 17. At one, I preached in Illogan; at six near Redruth at a gentleman's house,[81] in a large court shaded with trees. It was so calm that hardly a leaf moved. Saturday 18, I preached once more in the street at Redruth, and in St. Agnes in the evening. I preached again at eight in the morning, and afterwards heard an excellent sermon at church, preached by the rector, Mr. Walker,[82] elder brother to the late Mr. Walker of Truro. He likewise gave notice of his design to preach in the afternoon a funeral sermon for Mr. Philp, his late curate,[83] a man eminently humble, serious, and zealous for God. He was snatched away by a fever three weeks since, as was his predecessor, Mr. Vowler,[84] three or four years before—another upright, zealous servant of God, and indefatigable in his labour. How strange a providence is this! Who can account for it? Did the God of love take them away that

81 The home of William Jenkin (1738-1820) who, between the death of his first wife in 1784 and his marriage in 1790 to a Quaker, himself joined the Society of Friends. At the age of 54, he was made steward of the Lanhydrock estate, which consisted of twenty-six manors. For a memoir and his correspondence, see A. K. Hamilton Jenkin, *News from Cornwall* (London, 1951).

82 James Walker (*c.* 1712–93) matriculated from Merton College, Oxford, 1737; graduated B.C.L., 1739. He was vicar of Perranzabuloe and St. Agnes from 1739 till his death, and from 1752 also held Lanlivery.

83 Orig., 'Phelps'. On William Philp, see above, Sept. 8, 1760, n. 86.

84 See above, Sept. 3, 1757, n. 74.

they might not out of zeal for him continue to oppose their fellow-labourers in the gospel?

Mr. Walker gave him his due praise in a strong and pathetic sermon, well wrote and well pronounced, concluding with, 'God grant *me* (and I believe you will all join in the petition) like him to live, like him to die.'

Just as the service was ended it began to rain. The wind also was exceeding high. This created some difficulty. No house could contain the people, neither could I preach, as before, on the top of the hill. I therefore made an halt at the bottom. The congregation gathered round me in a few minutes. We were tolerably sheltered from the wind, and the rain ceased till I had done. I particularly advised all that feared God to confirm their love to each other, and to provoke each other, not to doubtful disputations, but to love and to good works.

The night came on soon after we were on horseback, and we had eight miles to ride. In about half an hour it was so dark I could not see my hand, and it rained incessantly. However, a little after eight, God brought us safe to Cubert.[85] I preached at the church town the next day, and on Tuesday 21, rode on to Port Isaac. Here the stewards of the eastern circuit met. What a change is wrought in one year's time! That detestable practice of cheating the king[86] is no more found in our societies. And since that accursed thing has been put away, the work of God has everywhere increased. This society, in particular, is more than doubled, and they are all alive to God. Fri. 24. About two, I preached at Trewalder and found God was there also, but more abundantly at Camelford in the evening, as well as at five on Saturday morning. In the afternoon, the rain intermitting, I preached in the market-place. And it was a solemn season.

Sun. 26. After preaching at eight, I left Camelford, now one of the liveliest places in Cornwall. About noon, I preached at Trewint. It was fifteen years since I preached there before.[87] Hence I rode to Launceston, to a people as dead as those at

[85] Orig., 'St. Kubert'. Pearce notes that the dedication of the parish church was altered from Cubert to Cuthbert in the 14th century, and the parish was commonly called by its newer name in the eighteenth century. But St. Cubertus, probably a local saint, was the older form of the parish name and Cubert is now the one in general use. Pearce, *Wesleys in Cornwall*, p. 142; cf. Sept. 7, 1765, where JW says the true spelling is 'Cuthbert'.

[86] Smuggling.

[87] See July 15, 1745 (20:80 in this edn.).

Camelford were once. Yet how soon may these also be quickened, by the voice that raiseth the dead!

Mon. 27. I rode to Week St. Mary.[88] It was a kind of fair-day, and the people were come [from] far and near for wrestling and other diversions. But they found a better way of employing their time. For young and old flocked to church from all quarters. The next day I preached at Mill House, on Wednesday at Cullompton, and on Thursday 30 in the market-house at Tiverton.

About midnight I was waked by loud thunder, which continued about a quarter of an hour at Tiverton. In other places, we were afterwards informed, it continued great part of the night. Yet by comparing various accounts, I found the main shock was at the same time for near an hundred miles. So it seems there was a train of clouds for at least that space, which by an electrical touch were all discharged at once.

Friday, October 1. I preached at Taunton and Shepton Mallet, and on Saturday 2, rode on to Bristol. In the two following weeks, I visited as many as I could of the societies in the country, as well as regulated those of Bristol and Kingswood. Sat. 16.[89] Being informed that James Oddie,[90] coming to Bristol, was stopped at Newport by a pleuritic fever, I went to him directly. He recovered from that hour, and in two or three days followed me to Bristol.

The next week, I went to many of the societies in Somersetshire. Mon. 25. I preached at one in the shell of the new house at Shepton Mallet. In digging the foundation they found a quarry of stone which was more than sufficient for the house.[91] Thence I rode to Wincanton. The rain prevented my preaching abroad. So I willingly accepted the offer of a large meeting-

[88] Orig., 'Mary-Week'.

[89] Orig., '19'. Sat. 9 would seem possible, but there is an extant letter by JW from Bristol with that date, and Sat. 16, in any case, seems to fit the context somewhat better.

[90] James Oddie (*c.* 1730–90) was an itinerant for nineteen years (latterly as a supernumerary) until 1771, when he retired to enter business (his business activities having caused Conference to forbid them to preachers in 1768). However, he contrived to preach and lead a class till 1788. He married, firstly, the widow of Thomas Thompson (she died in 1782), secondly, the widow of Thomas Colbeck of Keighley, but that marriage ended in separation. Atmore (p. 300) regarded him as 'an awful proof . . . of the dreadful consequences of leaving the path of duty', but Laycock took a kindlier view. J. W. Laycock, *Methodist Heroes in the Great Haworth Round* (Keighley, Wadsworth, 1909), pp. 172-74, 360-65; see also *Arminian Magazine* 3 (1780):335-37.

[91] The chapel (now opened by JW) may have been carefully sited for 'such was the indigence of the people, that they continued for some years to worship in it with no other than an earthen floor using benches without backs.' *Wesleyan Methodist Magazine* 50 (1827):284-85.

house,[92] where I preached to a crowded audience with much satisfaction, and again at seven in the morning.

Abundance of rain fell in the night, so that in the morning we were blocked up, the river which runs by the side of the town not being fordable. At length we made a shift to lead our horses over the foot-bridge. I preached at Coleford about noon, and at Bristol in the evening.

Thur. 28. One who had adorned the gospel in life and in death having desired that I should preach her funeral sermon, I went with a few friends to the house and sang before the body to the [New] Room. I did this the rather to show my approbation of that solemn custom and to encourage others to follow it. As we walked, our company swiftly increased, so that we had a very numerous congregation at the room. And who can tell but some of these may bless God for it to all eternity?

Many years ago my brother frequently said, 'Your day of Pentecost is not fully come. But I doubt not it will, and you will then hear of persons sanctified as frequently as you do now of persons justified.' Any unprejudiced reader may observe that it was now fully come. And accordingly, we did hear of persons sanctified in London and most other parts of England, and in Dublin and many other parts of Ireland, as frequently as of persons justified, although instances of the latter were far more frequent than they had been for twenty years before. That many of these did not retain the gift of God is no proof that it was not given them. That many do retain it at this day is matter of praise and thanksgiving. And many of them are gone to him whom they loved, praising him with *their* latest breath; just in the spirit of Ann Steed, the first witness in Bristol of the great salvation, who being worn out with sickness and racking pain, after she had commended to God all that were round her, lifted up her eyes, cried aloud, 'Glory! Hallelujah,' and died.

[92] On early Methodism in Wincanton and its uncertain relations with the Dissenting meeting, see Jackson, *Early Methodist Preachers*, 5:124-25.

AN

EXTRACT

OF THE

Rev. Mr. JOHN WESLEY'S

JOURNAL,

From *October* 29, 1762, to *May* 25, 1765.

XII.

BRISTOL:
Printed by WILLIAM PINE, in WINE-STREET.

M.DCC.LXVIII.

Journal

From October 29, 1762, to May 25, 1765

Friday, October 29, 1762, I left Bristol, and the next day came to London. Monday, November 1, I went down to Canterbury. Here I seriously reflected on some late occurrences and, after weighing the matter thoroughly, wrote as follows:[1]

Without any preface or ceremony, which is needless between you and me, I will simply and plainly tell what I dislike in your doctrine, spirit, or outward behaviour. When I say *yours,* I include brother Bell and Owen, and those who are most closely connected with them.

(1) I like your doctrine of *perfection,* or pure love—love excluding sin. Your insisting that it is merely by *faith;* that consequently it is *instantaneous* (though preceded and followed by a gradual work), and that it may be *now,* at this instant.

But I dislike your supposing man may be as perfect 'as an angel'; that he can be *absolutely* perfect; that he can be *infallible,* or above being *tempted;* or that the moment he is pure in heart he *cannot fall* from it.

I dislike the saying, This was not known or taught among us till within two or three years. I grant, *You* did not know it. You have over and over denied instantaneous sanctification to *me.* But I have known and taught it (and so has my brother, as our writings show)[2] above these twenty years.

[1] This letter was clearly written to Thomas Maxfield and is referred to below in the letter JW included in the *Journal* (Apr. 23, 1763). He there describes how he 'found the society in an uproar, and several of Mr. M[axfield]'s friends formed into a detached body. Enthusiasm, pride and great uncharitableness appeared in many who once had much grace,' a view very precisely echoed by Fletcher of Madeley: 'I have a particular regard for Mr. Maxfield and Mr. Bell: both of them are my correspondents. I am strongly prejudiced in favour of the witnesses, and do not willingly receive what is said against them; but allowing that what is reported is one half mere exaggeration, the tenth part of the rest shows that spiritual pride, presumption, arrogance, stubbornness, party spirit, uncharitableness, prophetic mistakes—in short *every sinew* of enthusiasm is now at work in many of that body. I do not credit anyone's bare word, but I ground my sentiments on Bell's own letters.' *Arminian Magazine* 18 (1795):50.

[2] Orig., 'brother, as well as our writings show', where possibly the second 'as' is redundant; *Works* (1774) omits 'as well'. In fact, in reaction to Thomas Maxfield's extravagances, Charles Wesley had begun to change his views on Christian perfection and

I dislike your directly or indirectly depreciating justification: saying a justified person is not 'in Christ',[3] is not 'born of God',[4] is not 'a new creature',[5] has not a 'new heart',[6] is not 'sanctified',[7] not a 'temple of the Holy Ghost';[8] or that he 'cannot please God',[9] or cannot 'grow in grace'.[10]

I dislike your saying that one saved from sin needs nothing more than 'looking to Jesus',[11] needs not to hear or think of anything else—'Believe, believe' is enough—that he needs no *self-examination,* no times of *private prayer;* needs not mind *little,* or *outward* things; and that he *cannot be taught* by any person who is not in the same state.

I dislike your affirming that justified persons in general persecute them that are saved from sin, that *they* have persecuted *you* on *this* account, and that for *two years* past *you* have been more persecuted by 'the two brothers' than ever you was by the world in all your life.

(2) As to your spirit, I like your confidence in God and your zeal for the salvation of souls.[12]

But I dislike something which has the appearance of *pride,* of overvaluing yourselves and undervaluing others, particularly the preachers, thinking not only that they are *blind* and that they are not sent of God, but even that they are *dead,* dead to God, and walking in the way to hell; that 'they are going *one* way,' you *another;* that 'they have *no life* in' them! Your speaking of *yourselves* as though *you* were the *only men* who knew and taught the gospel; and as if not only *all the clergy* but *all the Methodists* besides, were in utter darkness.

had been taken to task by his brother. In his *Short Hymns on Select Passages of the Holy Scriptures* (1762) Charles Wesley had begun to speak of a more exalted view of Christian perfection, a state 'not to be obtained by a present act of faith in the mercy, truth, and power of God; but is rather the result of severe discipline, comprehending affliction, temptation, long-continued labour, and the persevering exercise of faith in seasons of spiritual darkness', and hence regarded those who witnessed to the time they had already been made perfect in love as deluded. To this, JW, whose troubles had been increased by unguarded expressions in Charles's earlier hymns, boldly replied: 'That perfection which I believe, I can boldly preach, because I think I see five hundred witnesses of it. Of that perfection which you preach, you think you do not see any witness at all.' Jackson, *Charles Wesley*, 2:208-9; cf. JW's letter to Charles, September 1762, in Telford, 4:187.

[3] Rom. 16:7, etc.

[4] 1 John 3:9, etc.

[5] Gal. 6:15.

[6] Ezek. 18:31, etc.

[7] John 17:19, etc.

[8] 1 Cor. 6 :19.

[9] Rom. 8:8.

[10] 2 Pet. 3:18.

[11] Heb. 12:2 (*Notes*).

[12] See 1 Pet. 1:9.

I dislike something that has the appearance of *enthusiasm:* overvaluing *feelings* and *inward impressions;* mistaking the mere work of *imagination* for the voice of the Spirit; expecting the end without the means; and undervaluing *reason, knowledge,* and *wisdom,* in general.

I dislike something that has the appearance of *antinomianism:* not magnifying the law and making it honourable; not enough valuing *tenderness of conscience,* and exact *watchfulness* in order thereto; using *faith* rather as contradistinguished from *holiness* than as productive of it.

But what I most of all dislike is your *littleness of love* to your brethren, to your own society: your want of *union of heart* with them and 'bowels of mercies'[13] toward them; your want of *meekness, gentleness, long-suffering,*[14] your 'impatience of contradiction';[15] your counting every man your enemy that reproves or admonishes you in love; your *bigotry* and *narrowness* of spirit, loving in a manner only those that love *you;* your *censoriousness,* proneness to *think hardly* of all who do not exactly agree with you: in one word, your *divisive spirit.* Indeed, I do not believe that any of you either design or desire a separation. But you do not enough *fear, abhor,* and *detest* it, shuddering at the very thought. And all the preceding tempers tend to it and gradually prepare you for it. Observe, I tell you before! God grant you may immediately and affectionately take the warning!

(3) As to your outward behaviour, I like the general tenor of your life, devoted to God and spent in doing good.

But I dislike your slighting any, the[16] very least, rules of the bands or society and your doing anything that tends to hinder others from exactly observing them. Therefore,

I dislike your appointing such meetings as hinder others from attending either the public preaching or their class or band, or any other meeting which the rules[17] of the society or their office requires them to attend.

I dislike your spending so *much time* in several meetings, as many that attend can ill spare from the other duties of their calling, unless they omit either the preaching or their class or band. This naturally tends to dissolve our society by cutting the sinews of it.

As to your more public meetings, I like the praying fervently and largely for all the blessings of God. And I know much good has been done hereby and hope much more will be done.

[13] Col. 3:12.
[14] Cf. ibid.
[15] Cf. Heb. 12:3.
[16] Orig., 'your', altered to 'the' in *Works* (1774).
[17] Orig., 'rule', altered in *Works* (1774).

But I dislike several things therein: (i) the singing or speaking or praying of several at once; (ii) the praying to the Son of God only, or more than to the Father; (iii) the using improper expressions in prayer: sometimes too bold, if not irreverent, sometimes too pompous and magnificent, extolling yourselves rather than God and telling him what you *are*, not what you *want;* (iv) using poor, flat, bald hymns; (v) the never kneeling at prayer; (vi) your using postures or gestures highly indecent; (vii) your screaming, even so as to make the words unintelligible; (viii) your affirming people *will* be justified or sanctified just now; (ix) the affirming *they are*, when they are not; (x) the bidding them say, I believe; (xi) the bitterly condemning any that oppose, calling them wolves, etc., and pronouncing them hypocrites or not justified.

Read this calmly and impartially before the Lord in prayer. So shall the evil cease and the good remain. And you will then be more than ever united to

Your affectionate brother,
J. Wesley

Canterbury, Nov. 2, 1762

Sat. 6. Having had more satisfaction here than I had had[18] for many years, I cheerfully commended the little flock to God. In the way to London I read *The Death of Abel.*[19] That manner of writing, in 'prose run mad',[20] I cordially dislike. Yet with all that disadvantage, it is excellent in its kind—as much above most modern poems as it is below *Paradise Lost.*

I had hopes of seeing a friend at Lewisham[21] in my way. And so I did—but it was in her coffin. It is well, since she finished her course with joy. In due time I shall see her in glory.

Mon. 8. I began visiting the classes, in many of which we had hot spirits to deal with. Some were vehement for, some against,

[18] Orig., 'I had'; second 'had' added in *Works* (1774).

[19] Saloman Gersner, *The Death of Abel*, trans. Mary Collyer (London, 1761). Gersner (1730–88), born in Zurich, was later a member of the town council and a cantonal officer there. A bookseller, painter, and poet much translated into English, he was also in close touch with Hagedorn and Wieland.

[20] Alexander Pope, *An Epistle from Mr. Pope to Dr. Arbuthnot* (London, 1734), line 187: 'It is not poetry at all, but prose run mad.'

[21] In the Methodist Archives, Manchester, is a copy of this *Journal* with lavish annotations (unfortunately many of them severely damaged in binding at some time), in the hand of Edward Perronet. It will hereafter be termed the 'E. Perronet MS'. At this point the E. Perronet MS notes 'Mrs. Dewell'. Hannah Dewal, on whose death Charles Wesley wrote a hymn, died Nov. 12, 1762. *CWJ*, 2:240, 379-83; see John Biddulph Martin, *'The Grasshopper' in Lombard Street* (London, Leadenhall Press, 1892), p. 68.

the meetings for prayer which were in several parts of the town. I said little, being afraid of taking any step which I might afterwards repent of. One I heard of on Friday, and five on Saturday, who if I did not act as *they* thought best 'would leave the society'.

Tue. 16. I preached at Deptford and Welling and, Wednesday 17, rode on to Sevenoaks. But it was with much difficulty, for it was a sharp frost, and our horses could very hardly keep their feet. Here likewise, I found several who believed that God had 'cleansed' them 'from all sin'.[22] And all of them (except perhaps one) 'lived so that one might believe them'.

Fri. 19. I called upon Jane Cooper,[23] praising God in the fires. The next day I saw her for the last time, 'in everything giving thanks',[24] and overcoming all by the blood of the Lamb.[25] A day or two after, she fell asleep.

From Monday the 22nd to Friday 26th, I was employed in answering the Bishop of Gloucester's book.[26] Wednesday 24, being determined to hear for myself, I stood where I could hear and see without being seen. George Bell prayed, in the whole, pretty near an hour. His fervour of spirit I could not but admire. I afterwards told him what I did not admire: namely, (1) his screaming every now and then in so strange a manner that one could scarce tell what he said; (2) his thinking he had the

22 Cf. 1 John 1:7.

23 Jane Cooper was a model of Christian attainment JW could ill afford to lose in the middle of the controversy on Christian perfection. In 1764, he published *Letters wrote by Jane Cooper* with a preface insisting that 'all here is strong sterling sense, strictly agreeable to sound reason. Here are no extravagant flights, no mystic reveries, no unscriptural enthusiasm. . . . And such an inexpressible sweetness runs through the whole, as art would in vain strive to imitate' (Jackson, 14:245-46). He included a substantial account of her experience and death in his *Plain Account of Christian Perfection* and continued to speak warmly of her to the end of his life. See Jackson, 2:409-14; and Sept. 1, 1790.

24 Cf. 1 Thess. 5:18.

25 See Rev. 12:11.

26 William Warburton was Bishop of Gloucester, 1760–79. His *Doctrine of Grace: or The Office and Operations of the Holy Spirit Vindicated from the Insults of Infidelity, and the Abuses of Fanaticism* (London, 1763) went through three editions in the year. It accused JW of 'laying claim to almost every apostolic gift in as full and ample a manner as they were possessed of old' and advanced views on the Holy Spirit to which JW objected. Warburton sent JW the MS in advance, which he corrected and returned, with contemptuous comments to his brother on Warburton's scholarship. JW wrote a long and careful reply to the bishop, which was published in March 1763, denying that he laid claim to all the apostolic gifts, and denying also that he inferred from the Jansenist miracles in France, which followed in the wake of the Bull *Unigenitus*, that 'right opinions are but a slender part of religion, if any part of it at all'; letter of Jan. 5, 1763, Telford, 4:199; and see Jan. 11, 1750, n. 11 (20:317-18 in this edn.); see also 11:465-538 in this edn., and Telford, 4:338-84.

miraculous discernment of spirits;[27] and (3) his sharply condemning his opposers.

Thur. 25. I buried the remains of Jane Cooper, a pattern of all holiness and of the wisdom which is from above, who was snatched hence before she had lived five and twenty years. In good time! God, who knew the tenderness of her spirit, took her 'away from the evil to come'.[28]

Mon. 29. I retired to transcribe my Answer to Bishop Warburton. My fragments of time I employed in reading and carefully considering the lives of Magdalen de Pazzi and some other eminent Romish saints.[29] I could not but observe: (1) that many things related therein are highly improbable; I fear the relators did not scruple lying *for the Church* or for the credit of their Order; (2) that many of their reputed virtues were really no virtues at all, being no fruits of the love of God or man and no part of the mind which was in Christ Jesus;[30] (3) that[31] many of their applauded actions were neither commendable nor imitable; (4) that what was really good in their tempers or lives was so deeply tinctured with enthusiasm that most readers would be far more likely to receive hurt than good from these accounts of them.

Saturday, [December] 4. At the desire of Mr. Maxfield[32] and the *seeming* desire of themselves, I baptized two foreigners (one of them in a Turkish habit) who professed themselves to have been Turks.[33] On this I then remarked: 'They *may be* what they profess, but I wait for farther evidence. Their story is extremely plausible: it may be true, or it may not.'

Sun. 5. To take away one ground of contention from many well-meaning people, in preaching on, 'The kingdom of heaven is like a grain of mustard seed,'[34] I endeavoured to show at large in what sense sanctification is gradual and in what sense it's

[27] See 1 Cor. 12:10.

[28] Isa. 57:1.

[29] St. Mary Magdalen de' Pazzi (1566–1607), born of a noble Florentine family and precociously pious, was attracted to the Carmelite order because of its privilege of daily Communion, and entered it at the age of 16. In 1584, when apparently on the point of death, she began a series of ecstatic experiences whose number, intensity, and variety were to fill her works and to give her the title of the Ecstatic Saint. She was canonized in 1669. *WHS* 4 (1904):137.

[30] See Phil. 2:5.

[31] Orig., 'Yet' (probably a misreading of 'yt' in the MS), altered in *Works* (1774).

[32] The full name is added only in the errata and Wesley's manuscript note to his *Works* (1774).

[33] They proved to have been impostors; see below, Jan. 5, 1763.

[34] Matt. 13:31.

instantaneous. And (for the present at least) many were delivered from vain reasonings and disputings.

Monday 6 and the following days, I corrected the Notes upon the Revelation. O how little do we *know* of this deep book! At least, how little do *I* know! I can barely conjecture, nor affirm any one point, concerning that part of it which is yet unfulfilled.

Wed. 8. I had a second opportunity of hearing George Bell. 'I believe part of what he said was from God (this was my reflection *at that time*), part from an heated imagination. But as he did not *scream*, and there was nothing dangerously wrong, I do[35] not yet see cause to hinder him.'

All this time I observed a few of our brethren were diligently propagating that principle 'that none can teach those who are renewed in love, unless he be in the state himself.' I saw the tendency of this, but I saw that violent remedies would not avail.[36]

Mon. 13. I mentioned this to some of my friends and told them what would be the consequence. But they could not believe it. So I let it rest, only desiring them to remember I had told them before.

Sun. 19. From Matt. 18:3, I endeavoured to show those who use the word without understanding it what Christian 'simplicity' properly is and what it is not. It is not ignorance or folly; it is not enthusiasm or credulity. It is faith, humility, willingness to be taught, and freedom from evil reasonings.

Tue. 21. I had an opportunity of looking over the register of St. Luke's Hospital.[37] And I was surprised to observe that three in four (at least) of those who are admitted receive a cure. I doubt this is not the case of any other lunatic hospital, either in Great Britain or Ireland.

Wed. 22. I heard George Bell once more and was convinced he must not continue to pray at the Foundery. The reproach of

[35] Altered in *Works* (1774) to 'did'.

[36] In a letter to his brother on Dec. 11, 1762, JW noted that 'for eighteen or twenty days I heard with both ears, but rarely opened my mouth'; but finding 'the meeting in Beech Lane . . . like a bear-garden; full of noise, brawling, cursing, swearing, blasphemy and confusion', he moved it to the Foundery, experienced an immediate improvement of order, and continued hopeful of the good it accomplished (Telford, 4:196).

[37] St. Luke's Hospital for Lunatics 'was established by voluntary contributions, in the year 1751, for the reception of lunatics, and was intended both as an aid and as an improvement upon what Bethlehem Hospital then was' (see Aug. 23, 1740, n. 53; 19:166 in this edn.). 'The first hospital was erected . . . at the north-west corner of Finsbury Square.' Its success was such that a much larger scheme was commenced in Old Street in 1782. James Elmes, *A Topographical Dictionary of London* (London, 1831), p. 280.

Christ I am willing to bear, but not the reproach of enthusiasm,[38] if I can help it.

Sat. 25. We met at the chapel in Spitalfields to renew our covenant with God. And he did indeed appear in the midst of the congregation and answer as it were by fire.

Sun. 26. That I might do nothing hastily, I permitted George Bell to be once more (this evening) at the chapel in West Street, and once more (on Wednesday evening) at the Foundery. But it was worse and worse. He now spoke as from God, what I knew God had not spoken. I therefore desired that he would come thither no more.

I well hoped this would a little repress the impetuosity of a few good but mistaken men; especially considering the case of Benjamin Harris, the most impetuous of them all. A week or two ago, as he was working in his garden, he was struck raving mad. He continued so till Tuesday, December 21, when he lay still and sensible, but could not speak, till on Wednesday morning his spirit returned to God.

Friday 31. I now stood and looked back on the past year—a year of uncommon trials and uncommon blessings. Abundance have been convinced of sin; very many have found peace with God. And in London only, I believe full two hundred have been brought into glorious liberty. And yet I have had more care and trouble in six months than in several years preceding. What the end will be I know not. But it is enough that God knoweth.

Saturday, January 1, 1763. A woman told me: 'Sir, I employ several men. Now if one of my servants will not follow my direction, is it not right for me to discard him at once? Pray, do *you* apply this to Mr. Bell?' I answered: 'It is right to discard such a *servant.* But what would you do if he were your *son?*'[39]

Wed. 3 [i.e., 5]. Having procured one who understood Spanish to interpret, I had a long conversation with the supposed Turks. One account they gave of themselves then; a second they soon

[38] The cleft stick in which Wesley felt himself caught is neatly summarized in his introduction to the year 1762 in 'A Short History of the People called Methodists', §87: 'I met . . . those who believed they were saved from sin, and warned them of the enthusiasm that was breaking in by means of two or three weak, though good men. . . . [But] this year, from the beginning to the end, was a year never to be forgotten. . . . Such a multitude of sinners were converted from the error of their ways . . . and so many were filled with pure love' (9:476 in this edn.). The wheat as well as the tares abounded even in the ministry of men like Maxfield and Bell.

[39] In this case, the son in the gospel was Thomas Maxfield.

after gave to Mrs. G. I observed the account now given, which I read over to them, in some particulars differed from both. This increased my fear, though I still hoped the best, till Mr. B[lackwell][40] procured a Jew to talk with them, who understood both Turkish and Spanish, upon whose questioning them thoroughly they contradicted all the accounts given before. And upon the elder of them[41] mentioning Solomon Selim, a Jewish merchant of Amsterdam, one who knew him wrote to Solomon about him; who answered, he had 'known him upwards of fourteen years'; that he was 'a Spanish Jew, a physician by profession'; that some years since, he had cured him of a dangerous illness, in gratitude for which he had given him ten pounds, to carry him over to England.[42]

Fri. 7. I desired George Bell, with two or three of his friends, to meet me with one or two others.[43] We took much pains to convince him of his mistakes, particularly that which he had lately adopted, 'that the end of the world was to be on February the 28th', which at first he had earnestly withstood. But we could make no impression upon him at all. He was as unmoved as a rock.

Sun. 9. I endeavoured (from 1 Cor. 12:11 and the following verses) to guard the sincere against all thoughts of separating from their brethren, by showing what need all the members of the body have of each other. But those who wanted the caution most turned all into poison.

Mon. 10. I rode to Shoreham and paid the last office of love to Mrs. Perronet.[44] Wednesday 12, I returned to London, and the next day strongly enforced on a large congregation at the

[40] Identified in E. Perronet MS. [41] Orig., 'elders', altered in *Works* (1774).

[42] The last mention of this 'Turk' suggested an even more contorted story: 'He is an exquisite wretch; was originally a Spanish Jew, afterwards a Turk, then a Papist, then a Jew again, then a Protestant, and now at last (under Mr. Lombardi's wing) a zealous Papist! Concerning his companion we are still in doubt.' Letter to Charles, Feb. 26, 1763, Telford, 4:203.

[43] JW related the upshot of this meeting in a letter to the editor of the *London Chronicle* on Jan. 7, explaining that he had allowed Bell and his friends limited use of the premises at the Foundery and West Street in order to be sure he understood their views, and that he had now denied them access (*London Chronicle* [Jan. 15-18, 1763], p. 63; cf. p. 34). On Feb. 9, he wrote again to report that Bell was no longer a member of his society, and that he (JW) did 'not believe either that the end of the world or any signal calamity will be on the 28th instant' (*London Chronicle* [Feb. 8-10, 1763], p. 143; Telford, 4:200, 203). Bell waited on a mound near St. Luke's Hospital for that ultimate cataclysm, but before the event was arrested and imprisoned. *London Chronicle* (Feb. 26–Mar.1, 1763), p. 207.

[44] I.e., he administered Holy Communion. Charity Perronet, the daughter of Thomas Goodhew, of Clerkenwell, had married Vincent Perronet in 1718, and died on Feb. 5, 1763, aged 73. JW then buried her; see below, Feb. 11, 1763.

Foundery the words of Isaiah (never more needful), 'He that believeth shall not make haste.'[45]

Mon. 17. I rode to Lewisham and wrote my sermon to be preached before the Society for Reformation of Manners.[46] Sunday 23. In order to check if not stop a growing evil, I preached on 'Judge not, that ye be not judged.'[47] But it had just the contrary effect on many, who construed it into a satire upon G. Bell, one of whose friends said, 'If the devil himself had been in the pulpit he would not have preached such a sermon.'

All this time I did not want information from all quarters 'that Mr. M[axfield] was at the bottom of all this; that he was the life of the cause; that[48] he was continually spiriting up all with whom he was intimate against me; that he told them I was not capable of teaching them and insinuated that none was but himself; and that the inevitable consequence must be a division in the society.'

Yet I was not without hope that by bearing all things I should overcome evil with good, till on Tuesday 25, while I was sitting with many of our brethren, Mrs. Coventry (then quite intimate with Mr. M[axfield]) came in, threw down her ticket, with those of her husband, daughters, and servants, and said they would 'hear *two doctrines* no longer'. They had often said before, 'Mr. M[axfield] preached *perfection,* but Mr. W[esley] pulled it down.' So I did: that perfection of Benjamin Harris, G. Bell, and all who abetted them. So the breach is made! The water is let out. Let those who can, gather it up.

I think it was on Friday the 28th that I received a letter from John Fox and another from John and Elizabeth Dixon, declaring the same thing. Friday, February 4, Daniel Owen and G. Bell told me they should 'stay in the society no longer'.[49] The next day Robert Lee, with five or six of his friends, spake to the same effect.

I now seriously considered whether it was in my power to have prevented this. I did not see that it was; for though I had heard from time to time many objections to Mr. M[axfield]'s conduct, there was no possibility of clearing them up. Above a year ago, I

[45] Isa. 28:16.

[46] This sermon was preached on Jan. 30 and published immediately afterwards (Sermon 52, 2:299-323 in this edn.). This society had been revived in 1757, and nearly half its 160 members were followers of JW or Whitefield. Tyerman, *John Wesley*, 2:469.

[47] Matt. 7:1.

[48] Orig., 'yet'; cf. Nov. 29, 1762, n.31.

[49] See above, Dec. 26, 1761, nn. 41, 42.

desired him to meet me with some that accused him, that I might hear them face to face. But his answer was as follows:

Dec. 28, 1761

I have considered the thing, since you spoke to me about meeting at Mrs. March's. And I don't think to be there, or to meet them at any time. It is enough that I was arraigned at the Conference. (At which I earnestly defended him and silenced all his accusers.)[50] I am not convinced that it is my duty to make James Morgan,[51] etc. my judges. If you, sir, or any one of them, have anything to say to me *alone,* I will answer as far as I see good.

The next month I wrote him a long letter, telling him mildly all I heard or feared concerning him. He took it as a deep affront and in consequence thereof wrote as follows:

Jan. 14, 1762

If you call me proud or humble, angry or meek, it seems to sit much the same on my heart. If you call me John or Judas, Moses or Korah, I am content. As to a separation, I have no such thought, if you have, and now (as it were) squeeze blood out of a stone, be it to yourself.

Several months after, hearing some rumours, I again wrote to him freely. In his answer were the following words:

Sept. 23, 1762

Experience teaches me daily that they that preach *salvation from the nature of sin* will have the same treatment from the others as they had and have from the world. But I am willing to bear it.

Your brother is gone out of town. Had he stayed much longer and continued, Sunday after Sunday, to hinder me from preaching, he would have forced me to have got a place to preach in where I should not have heard what I think the highest truths contradicted.

In his next letter he explained himself a little farther:

Oct. 16, 1762

We have great opposition on every side. Nature, the world, and the devil will never be reconciled to Christian perfection. But the

[50] E. Perronet MS: 'It was this very thing that made him at last turn accuser himself.'
[51] See above, Aug. 11, 1756, n. 77.

great wonder is that Christians will not be reconciled to it; all, almost everyone who call themselves ministers of Christ, or preachers of Christ, contend for sin to remain in the heart as long as we live, as though it were the only thing Christ delighted to behold in his members.

I long to have *your* heart set at full liberty. I know you will *then see things* in a wonderful different light from what it is *possible* to *see them before.*

The day after the first separation, viz., Jan. 26, I wrote him the following note:

My dear Brother,

For many years I and all the preachers in connection with me have taught that every believer may and ought to grow in grace. Lately you have taught or seemed to teach the contrary. The effect of this is, when I speak as I have done from the beginning those who believe what *you* say will not bear it. Nay, they will renounce connexion with us—as Mr. and Mrs. Coventry did last night. This breach lies wholly upon *you.* You have contradicted what I taught from the beginning. Hence it is that many cannot bear it, but when I speak as I always have done, they separate from the society. Is this for *your* honour, or to the glory of God?

O Tommy, seek counsel, not from man, but God; not from brother B[ell], but Jesus Christ!

I am,
Your affectionate brother,
J. W.

Things now ripened apace for a farther separation, to prevent which (if it were possible), I desired all our preachers, as they had time, to be present at all meetings when I could not myself, particularly at the Friday meeting in the chapel at West Street. At this Mr. M[axfield] was highly offended and wrote to me as follows:

Feb. 5, 1763

I wrote to you to ask if those who before met at brother Guilford's[52] might not meet in the chapel. Soon after you came to

[52] Joseph Guilford, an ex-soldier with the voice of Boanerges, was converted under the preaching of Thomas Olivers at the Foundery and began to travel in 1761 (Jackson, *Early Methodist Preachers*, 2:78). 'Some disagreeable circumstances attending his second marriage, it was judged expedient (especially considering his age) that he should become a Local Preacher' in 1774 (Atmore, *Memorial*, p. 170). He died in 1777, being buried by JW

town, the preachers were brought into the meeting, though you told me again and again, they should not come. (True; but since I said this, there has been an entire change in the situation of things.) Had I known this I would rather have paid for a room out of my own pocket. I am not speaking of the people that met at the Foundery before, though I let some of them come to that meeting. . . . If you intend to have the preachers there to watch, and others that *I think very unfit*, and will not give me liberty to give leave to some that *I think fit* to be there, I shall not think it my duty to meet them.

So from this time he kept a separate meeting elsewhere.[53]

Sun. 6. Knowing many were greatly tempted on occasion of these occurrences, I preached on 1 Cor. 10:13. 'God is faithful, who will not suffer you to be tempted above that ye are able; but will with every temptation also make a way to escape, that ye may be able to bear it.' In the evening, we had a love-feast at which many spoke with all simplicity. And their words were like fire. I hardly know when we have had so refreshing a season.

Mon. 7. One who is very intimate with them that had left us, told me in plain terms, 'Sir, the case lies here: they say, *You* are only an hypocrite, and *therefore* they can have no fellowship with you.'

So now the wonder is over. First it was *revealed* to them that *all the people* were dead to God. Then they saw that *all the preachers* were so, too—only for a time they excepted *me.* At last they *discern* me to be *blind and dead* too. Now let him help them that can!

Thur. 10. I rode to Brentford, expecting to find disagreeable work there also. But I was happily disappointed. Not one seemed inclined to leave the society, and some were added to it. And the congregation was not only quiet but more deeply attentive than is usual in this place.

Hence, I rode on Friday 11 to Shoreham and buried the remains of Mrs. P[erronet], who after a long, distressing illness, on Saturday the 5th instant fell asleep.

Sat. 12. I visited the classes at Snowsfields, where I was told

on May 18, Whit-Sunday, and commemorated by a graceful and affectionate tribute in the *Journal* and *Arminian Magazine* 7 (1784):23. The reference here is to a holiness revival, prayed into being in his house. The meetings are described in Henry Moore, *Life of Mrs. Mary Fletcher*, 2 vols. (2nd edn., London, 1818), 1:36-37.

[53] Maxfield preached at the Snowsfields chapel for two or three years, then removed to Ropemaker Alley, Little Moorfields, and then to Princes Street, Moorfields. Wilson, *Dissenting Churches*, 3:418; 4:283.

many would go away. But the time is not come. As yet we have lost none—though some are held as by a single hair.

Tue. 15. I rode to Deptford and found the society there united in faith and love. During the sermon in the afternoon, one poor mourner found peace with God. In the evening I preached at Welling, and on [Wed. 16], rode on to Sevenoaks. Here I was grieved to find one who 'did run well'[54] quite hardened by the deceitfulness of sin.[55] But in the evening, God looked upon him once more and melted him into tears of love.

Thur. 17. Light from above broke into the heart of another hard-hearted sinner.[56] At the same time, many were delivered from doubts and fears, and 'knew the things which were freely given them of God'.[57] On Friday I returned to London.

Mon. 21. Observing the terror occasioned by that wonderful prophecy[58] to spread far and wide, I endeavoured to draw some good therefrom, by strongly exhorting the congregation at Wapping to 'seek the Lord while he might be found.'[59] But at the same time I thought it incumbent upon me to declare (as indeed I had done from the hour I heard it) that 'it *must* be false, if the Bible be true.'

The three next days I spent in the tedious work of transcribing the names of the society. I found about thirty of those who thought they were saved from sin had separated from their brethren. But above four hundred who witnessed the same confession seemed more united than ever.

Mon. 28. Preaching in the evening at Spitalfields on 'Prepare to meet thy God,'[60] I largely showed the utter absurdity of the supposition that the world was to end that night. But notwithstanding all I could say, many were afraid to go to bed, and some wandered about in the fields, being persuaded that if the world did not end, at least London would be swallowed up by an earthquake. I went to bed at my usual time and was fast asleep about ten o'clock.'[61]

[54] Gal. 5:7. 'Thurs. 17' in all edns. must surely be 'Wed. 16'.

[55] E. Perronet MS: 'Mr. Parker', written in Byrom's shorthand.

[56] Ibid., 'Jo. Marsh.'

[57] Cf. 1 Cor. 2:12.

[58] See above, Jan. 7, 1763.

[59] Cf. Isa. 55:6.

[60] Amos 4:12.

[61] JW's peaceful sleep did not spare him the necessity of further letters to the press and to individuals like Lady Huntingdon, dissociating his movement from Bell's views. Letters of Mar. 18, 20, 1763, Telford, 4:205-6.

Monday, March 8. I took the machine for Norwich and, after spending a few quiet, comfortable days in Norwich, Yarmouth, and Colchester, without any jar or contention, on Saturday the 19th returned to London.

Mon. 28. I retired to Lewisham and wrote the sermon *On Sin in Believers*[62] in order to remove a mistake which some were labouring to propagate, that there is no sin in any that are justified.

Monday, April 11. Leaving things, as I thought, tolerably well settled in London, I took the machine for Bristol, where on Tuesday 19, I paid the last office of love to Nicholas Gilbert,[63] who was a good man and an excellent preacher, and likely to have been of great use. But God saw it best to snatch him hence by a fever in the dawn of his usefulness.

Sat. 23. I returned to London. On Thursday 28, I was at Westminster, where I had appointed to preach, when word was brought me, about five in the afternoon, 'that Mr. M[axfield] *would not* preach at the Foundery'. So the breach is made. But I am clear. I have done all I possibly could to prevent it. I walked immediately away and preached myself on, 'If I am bereaved of my children, I am bereaved.'[64]

That I may conclude this melancholy subject at once [and][65] have no need to resume it any more, I add a letter which I wrote some time after for the information of a friend:

> At your instance I undertake the irksome task of looking back upon things which I wish to forget for ever. I have had innumerable proofs (though such as it would now be an endless task to collect together) of all the facts which I recite. And I recite them as briefly as[66] possible, because I do not desire to aggravate anything, but barely to place it in a true light.
>
> 1. Mr. Maxfield was justified while I was praying with him in Baldwin Street, Bristol.[67]

[62] JW published this sermon in April 1763; see Sermon 13, 'On Sin in Believers' (1:317-34 in this edn.); and *Bibliography*, No. 257.

[63] See above, Oct. 5, 1760, n. 14.

[64] Gen. 43:14. Atmore relates how 'he feelingly and with tears preached from that pathetic passage' (Atmore, *Memorial*, p. 268).

[65] Orig., 'I', altered to '&' in E. Perronet MS.

[66] *Works* (1774) adds 'briefly as'.

[67] E. Perronet MS: 'In Mr. Mxfld's own Acco[un]t of himself (see Intro. Letter to Narrative, 1767), he was first awakend by Mr. Whitfield's Preach[in]g at Bristol.' This section is across the foot of p. 17. Most of the notes are in the margin, and very defective because of the trimmed pages.

2. Not long after, he was employed by me as a preacher in London.

3. Hereby he had access to Mrs. Maxfield,[68] whom otherwise he was never likely to see, much less to marry; from whence all his outward prosperity had its rise.[69]

4. He was by *me* (by those who did it at *my* instance) recommended to the Bishop of Derry[70] to be ordained priest, who told him then (I had it from his own mouth), 'Mr. M[axfield], I ordain *you* to assist that good man, that he may not work himself to death.'

5. When a few years ago many censured him much, I continually and strenuously defended him, though to the disgusting several of the preachers and a great number of the people.

6. I disgusted them, not barely by defending him but by commending him in strong terms from time to time, both in public and private, with regard to his uprightness, as well as usefulness.

7. All this time Mr. M[axfield] was complaining (of which I was frequently informed by those to whom he spoke) that he was 'never so ill represented[71] by the rabble in Cornwall' as by *me* and my brother.

8. Four or five years since, a few persons were appointed to meet weekly at the Foundery. When I left London, I left these under Mr. M[axfield]'s care, desiring them to regard *him* just as they did *me.*

9. Not long after I was gone, some of these had dreams, visions, or impressions, as they thought from God. Mr. M[axfield] did not put a stop to these. Rather he encouraged them.

10. When I returned, I opposed them with my might, and in a short time heard no more of them. Meanwhile, I defended and commended Mr. M[axfield] as before and, when I left the town again, left them again under his care.

11. Presently visions and revelations returned. Mr. M[axfield] did not discourage them. Herewith was now joined a contempt of such as had them not, with a belief that they were proofs of the highest grace.

12. Some of our preachers opposed them roughly. At this, they took fire and refused to hear them preach but crowded after Mr. M[axfield]. He took no pains to quench the fire, but rather availed himself of it to disunite them from other preachers and attach them

68 Elizabeth, née Branford, see May 21, 1739, n. 5 (19:61 in this edn.).

69 E. Perronet MS adds in the same line: 'Like the Egg that had the Chicken, the Ch[icken] an egg, etc.'

70 Orig., 'D——'.

71 *Works* (1774), 'persecuted'.

to himself. He likewise continually told them they were 'not to be *taught by man*', especially by those who had *less grace than themselves.* I was told of this likewise from time to time. But he denied it. And I would not believe evil of *my friend.*

13. When I returned in October 1762,[72] I found the society in an uproar and several of Mr. M[axfield]'s most intimate friends formed into a detached body. Enthusiasm, pride, and great uncharitableness appeared in many who once had much grace. I very tenderly reproved them. They would not bear it. One of them, Mrs. C[oventry],[73] cried out, 'We will not be browbeaten any longer; we will *throw off the mask.*' Accordingly a few days after, she came and, before an hundred persons, brought me hers and her husband's tickets and said, 'Sir, we will have no more to do with *you*; Mr. *M*[axfield] is our teacher.'[74] Soon after, several more left the society (one of whom was George Bell), saying, '*Blind John* is not capable of teaching *us*; we will keep to Mr. *M.*'

14. From the time that I heard of George Bell's prophecy I explicitly declared against it, both in private in the society, in preaching, over and over, and at length in the public papers. Mr. M. made no such declaration.[75] I have reason to think, he believed it. I know many of his friends did, and several of them sat up the last of February, at the house of his most intimate friend, Mr. Biggs,[76] in full expectation of the accomplishment.

15. About this time one of our stewards, who at *my desire* took the chapel in Snowsfields *for my use*, sent me word, 'The chapel was *his*, and Mr. Bell should exhort there whether I would or no.' Upon this, I desired the next preacher there to inform the congregation that while things stood thus, neither I nor our preachers could in conscience preach there any more.

16. Nevertheless, Mr. M. did preach there. On this, I sent him a note, desiring him not to do it and adding, 'If you do, you thereby renounce connexion with *me.*'

17. Receiving this, he said, 'I *will* preach at Snowsfields.' He did so and *thereby* renounced connexion. On *this* point and no other we divided. By *this* act the knot was cut. Resolving to do this, he told Mr. Clementson, 'I am to preach at the Foundery no more.

[72] Orig., '1763'.

[73] E. Perronet MS: 'Dam[e] Covent[ry]'.

[74] See above, Jan. 25-27, 1763.

[75] Maxfield, however, in his *Vindication* (1767) says that at Wapping, after Bell had done speaking, 'I stood up and set aside all that he had said about it.'

[76] For the difficulties of identifying this Biggs, see *Letters* (26:388, n. 13, in this edn.). There is a reference to a meeting at brother Biggs's in 1761 in Henry Moore, *Life of Mrs. Mary Fletcher* (20th edn., London, 1890), p. 373. There seems no reason to associate this Biggs with the Benjamin Biggs of Whitehaven, 'a favourite servant of Sir James Lowther', who for a few years had been the travelling companion of the preacher John Murlin. Jackson, *Early Methodist Preachers*, 3:298.

18. From this time, he has spoke all manner of evil of *me,* his father, his friend, his greatest earthly benefactor. I cite Mr. F[letcher][77] for one witness of this and Mr. M[ada]n[78] for another. Did he speak evil of me to Mr. F—— one day only? Nay, but every day, for six weeks together. To Mr. M——n he said (among a thousand other things, which he had been twenty years raking together), 'Mr. W. *believed and countenanced all* which Mr. Bell said. And the *reason* of our parting was *this.* He said to me one day, "Tommy, I will tell the people, You are the greatest gospel preacher in England. And you shall tell them, I am the greatest." For *refusing to do this* Mr. W. put me away!'

Now with perfect calmness, and I verily think without the least touch of prejudice, I refer it to your own judgment, what connexion I ought to have with Mr. M., either till I am satisfied these things are not so, or till he is thoroughly sensible of his fault.[79]

Monday, May 2, and the following days, I was fully employed in visiting the society and settling the minds of those who had been confused and distressed by a thousand misrepresentations. Indeed, a flood of calumny and evil-speaking (as was easily foreseen) was poured out on every side. My point was still, to go straight forward in the work whereto I am called.

Mon. 16. Setting out a month later than usual, I judged it needful to make the more haste. So I took post-chaises,[80] and by that means easily reached Newcastle on Wednesday 18. Thence, I went on at leisure and came to Edinburgh on Saturday 21. The next day I had the satisfaction of spending a little time with Mr. Whitefield. Humanly speaking, he is worn out.[81] But we have to do with him who hath all power in heaven and earth.

Mon. 23. I rode to Forfar, and on Tuesday the 24th, rode on to Aberdeen.

Wed. 25 I inquired into the state of things here. Surely never

77 For Fletcher's views, see above, Nov. 1, 1762, n. 1.

78 On Martin Madan, see above, Dec. 19, 1758, n. 88.

79 Recipient not known.

80 This very explicit reference, following so quickly upon those of March 8 and April 11, shows JW quickly adapting himself to improved methods of transport (see above, Mar. 8 and Apr. 11, 1763).

81 Though still preaching actively, Whitefield had been in a more or less invalid condition for a couple of years. As the Seven Years War drew to its close he was, however, determined to return to America. He was delayed, first by the need to reply to the polemics of Warburton, and now by illness. On June 4 he sailed, and before long the English press carried (very premature) reports of his death (Tyerman, *Whitefield*, 2:465). Whitefield survived till 1770, meeting his end on yet another visit to America.

was there a more open door.[82] The four ministers of Aberdeen, the minister of the adjoining town, and the three ministers of Old Aberdeen,[83] hitherto seem to have no dislike, but rather to 'wish' us 'good luck in the name of the Lord'.[84] Most of the town's people as yet seem to wish us well, so that there is no open opposition of any kind. Oh! what spirit ought a preacher to be of, that he may be able to bear all this sunshine!

About noon I went to Gordon's Hospital,[85] built near the town for poor children. It is an exceeding handsome building and (what is not common) kept exceeding clean. The gardens are pleasant, well laid out, and in extremely good order. But the old bachelor who founded it has expressly provided that no woman should ever be there.

At seven, the evening being fair and mild, I preached to a multitude of people in the College Close on 'Stand in the ways and see, and ask for the old paths.'[86] But the next evening, the weather being raw and cold, I preached in the College Hall. What an amazing willingness to hear runs through this whole kingdom! There want only a few zealous, active labourers, who desire nothing but God, and they might soon carry the gospel through all this country,[87] even as high as the Orkneys.

[82] A full and friendly account of JW's visit to Aberdeen was written locally and published in the *Scots Magazine* (August 1763; repr. in *WHS* 4 [1904]:159-62). The Methodist peculiarities which it stressed were JW's desire for 'the keeping a love-feast at every full moon' and the fact that Methodists used 'none of the versions of David's psalms, but only hymns composed by themselves, in their public worship'.

[83] Aberdeen at this time was divided among three charges held respectively by James Ogilvie (1694–1776), George Campbell (1719–96), and Thomas Forbes (1729–83), and Greyfriars held by Alexander Gerard (1727–95). There was a chapel at Footdu held by William Bisset (1736–73). Old Macher was divided between two charges held by James Mitchel (1701–73) and Patrick Duff (1727–84).

[84] Ps. 129:8 (BCP).

[85] Robert Gordon, merchant, who died in 1732, worth over £10,000, conveyed his whole property in 1729 to the provost, baillies, town council, and ministers of Aberdeen, in trust for building a hospital for the maintenance and education of young boys of indigent parents and putting them to trades and employments. The building designed by James Gibbs was not ready for the reception of boys till 1750, when 30 were admitted; the number had increased to 80 by the early years of the nineteenth century. William Kennedy, *Annals of Aberdeen, from the Reign of King William the Lion to the End of . . . 1818; with an Account of the City, Cathedral, and University of Old Aberdeen*, 2 vols. (London, 1818), 2:140-41.

[86] Cf. Jer. 6:16.

[87] The revival in north-east Scotland had begun at Nigg, before the events at Cambuslang and Kilsyth in central Scotland and at Golspie and numerous other places had continued much longer. In this part of the world, the struggle between episcopacy and Presbyterianism was at its toughest, and JW reports the situation after the first skirmishes had been won in the battle, which ended in capturing the whole of the Highlands for

Fri. 27. I set out for Edinburgh again. About one, I preached at Brechin. All were deeply attentive. Perhaps a few may not be forgetful hearers. Afterwards we rode on to Broughty Castle, two or three miles below Dundee. We were in hopes of passing the river here, though we could not at the town. But we found our horses could not pass till eleven or twelve at night. So we judged it would be best to go over ourselves and leave them behind. In a little time, we procured a kind of a boat, about half as long as a London wherry and three or four feet broad. Soon after we had put off, I perceived it leaked on all sides, nor had we anything to lade[88] out the water. When we came toward the middle of the river, which was three miles over, the wind being high and the water rough, our boatmen seemed a little surprised. But we encouraged them to *pull away,* and in less than half an hour we landed safe. Our horses were brought after us. And the next day we rode on to Kinghorn Ferry and had a pleasant passage to Leith.

Sun. 29. I preached at seven in the High School yard at Edinburgh. It being the time of the General Assembly, which drew together, not the ministers only, but abundance of the nobility and gentry, many of both sorts were present;[89] but abundantly more at five in the afternoon. I spake as plain as ever I did in my life. But I never knew any in Scotland offended at *plain dealing.* In this respect the North Britons are a pattern to all mankind.

Mon. 30. I rode to Dunbar. In the evening it was very cold, and the wind was exceeding high. Nevertheless, I would not pen myself up in the room but resolved to preach in the open air. We saw the fruit: many attended, notwithstanding the cold, who never set foot in the room. And I am still persuaded, much good will be done here, if we have zeal and patience.

Tue. 31. I rode to Alnwick and was much refreshed among a people who have not the form only, but the spirit of religion, fellowship with God, the living power of faith divine. Wednesday, June 1, I went on to Morpeth and preached in a ground near the

evangelical religion, and establishing Rosshire as the home of the 'Fathers', the Holy Land of Highland evangelicalism.

[88] For this archaic usage, meaning to bail or scoop out water with a ladle, see *OED*, Lade, v.II.

[89] Among them was Lady Frances Gardiner, the widow of the legendary Colonel Gardiner who fell at Prestonpans, who wrote gracefully to JW on the occasion. Moore, *Wesley*, 2:249.

town to far the most serious congregation which I had ever seen there. At one, I preached to the loving colliers in Plessey, and in the evening at Newcastle.

Sat. 3. I rode, though much out of order, to Sunderland and preached in the evening at the room. I was much worse in the night, but toward morning, fell into a sound sleep and was refreshed. Sun. 4. I designed to preach abroad this morning, but the wind and rain hindered. So at eight, I preached in the room again, purposing to preach in the street at noon. But Mr. Goodday[90] sent me word he 'was taken ill in the night' and begged I would 'supply his church'. So at ten, I began reading prayers, though I was so exceeding weak that my voice could scarce be heard. But as I went on I grew stronger, and before I had half done preaching, I suppose all the church could hear.

The wind drove us into the house at Newcastle likewise, that is, as many as the house would contain. But great numbers were constrained to stand in the yard. However, I suppose all could hear. For my weakness was entirely gone, while I was enforcing those important words, 'If thou canst believe, all things are possible to him that believeth.'[91]

Mon. 5. I rode to Barnard Castle and preached in the evening, but to such a congregation, not only with respect to number but to seriousness and composure, as I never saw there before. I intended after preaching to meet the society, but the bulk of the people were so eager to hear more that I could not forbear letting in almost as many as the room would hold. And it was a day of God's power. They all seemed to take the kingdom by violence, while they besieged heaven with vehement prayer.

Tue. 6. So deep and general was the impression now made upon the people, that even at five in the morning I was obliged to preach abroad by the numbers who flocked to hear, although the northerly wind occasioned the air to be exceeding sharp. A little after preaching, one came to me who believed God had just set her soul at full liberty. She had been clearly justified long before but said the change she now experienced was 'extremely different' from what she experienced then, 'as different as the noonday light from that of daybreak'; that she now 'felt her soul

[90] Orig., 'Mr. G', expanded in *Works* (1774) to 'Mr. Goodday', i.e., Rev. Thomas Goodday, vicar of Monkwearmouth; cf. May 31, 1761, n. 48, above. E. Perronet MS: 'Mr. Gooday—a sensible man and a friendly—but devoted to Passions—now gone into Eternity!'

[91] Mark 9:23.

all love and quite swallowed up in God'. Now suppose, ten weeks or ten months hence, this person should be cold or dead; shall I say, 'She *deceived* herself; this was merely the work of her own *imagination*'? Not at all; I have no right so to judge, nor authority to speak. I will rather say, 'She was *unfaithful* to the grace of God, and so *cast away* what was *really given*.'

Therefore, that way of talking which has been very common, of 'staying to see if the gift be really given', which some take to be exceeding wise, I take to be exceeding foolish.[92] If a man says, 'I now feel nothing but love,' and I know him to be an honest man, I believe him. What then should I 'stay to see'? Not whether he *has* such a blessing, but whether he will *keep* it.

There is something remarkable in the manner wherein God revived his work in these parts. A few months ago the generality of people in this circuit were exceeding lifeless. Samuel Meggot perceiving[93] this, advised the society at Barnard Castle to observe every Friday with fasting and prayer. The very first Friday they met together, God broke in upon them in a wonderful manner. And his work has been increasing among them ever since. The neighbouring societies heard of this, agreed to follow the same rule, and soon experienced the same blessing. Is not the neglect of this plain duty—I mean, fasting, ranked by our Lord with almsgiving and prayer—one general occasion of deadness among Christians? Can anyone willingly neglect it and be guiltless?

In the evening I preached at Yarm. But I found the good doctrine of Christian perfection had not been heard of there for some time. The wildness of our poor brethren in London has put it out of countenance above two hundred miles off. So these strange advocates for perfection have given it a deeper wound than all its enemies together could do!

Wed. 8. Just as I began preaching (in the open air, the room being too small even for the morning congregation) the rain began. But it stopped in two or three minutes, I am persuaded, in answer to the prayer of faith. Incidents of the same kind I have seen abundance of times, and particularly in this journey. And they are nothing strange to them who seriously believe, 'The very hairs of your head are all numbered.'[94]

[92] E. Perronet MS: 'Then your own Brother is one of those *foolish* critics, and 'tis certain he can never *lose* what he never *had*. But surely 'tis equally certain that he may th[ink] he has attained that he never did.'

[93] Orig., 'observing', altered in *Works* (1774).

[94] Matt. 10:30.

After preaching at Potto about noon, I rode to Thirsk, intending to preach near the house where I alighted. But several gentlemen of the town sent to desire I would preach in the market-place. I did so, to a numerous congregation, most of whom were deeply attentive. I hastened away after preaching, and between nine and ten, came to York.

Sat. 11. I rode to Epworth and preached at seven in the market-place. Sunday 12, I preached at the room in the morning, in the afternoon at the market-place, and about one to the congregation gathered from all parts in Haxey parish near Westwoodside.[95] At every place, I endeavoured to settle the minds of the poor people who had been not a little harassed by a new doctrine, which honest Jonathan C[atlow][96] and his converts had industriously propagated among them—'That there is *no sin* in believers, but the moment we believe, sin is destroyed, root and branch.' I trust this plague also is stayed. But how ought those unstable ones to be ashamed, who are so easily 'tossed about with every wind of doctrine'![97]

I had desired Samuel Meggot to give me some farther account of the late work of God at Barnard Castle. Part of his answer was as follows:

June 7, 1763

Within ten weeks at least twenty persons in this town have found peace with God, and twenty-eight the pure love of God. This morning, before you left us, one found peace, and one the second blessing, and after you was gone, two more received it. One of these had belonged to the society before, but after he turned back had bitterly persecuted his wife, particularly after she professed the being saved from sin. May 29, he came, in a furious rage, to drag her out of the society. One cried out, 'Let us go to prayer for him.' Presently he ran away, and his wife went home. Not long after, he came in like a madman and swore he would be the death of her. One said, 'Are you not afraid lest God should smite you?' He answered, 'No, let God do his worst. I will make an end of her and the brats, and myself too, and we will all go to hell together.' His wife and children fell down and broke out into prayer. His countenance changed, and he was quiet as a lamb. But it was not

[95] Westwoodside is a village 3 miles south-west of Epworth.

[96] Name supplied in E. Perronet MS. For Jonathan Catlow and his propensity to preach in his sleep, see June 2, 1753, and n. 50 (20:460 in this edn.).

[97] Cf. Eph. 4:14.

long before an horrible dread overwhelmed him; he was sore distressed. The hand of God was upon him and gave him no rest, day or night. On Tuesday in the afternoon, he went to her who prayed for him when he came to drag his wife out, begging her with a shower of tears to pray for his deliverance. On Thursday, he wrestled with God till he was as wet all over with sweat as if he had been dipped in water. But that evening God wiped away his tears and filled him with joy unspeakable.

This morning, while brother Story was at prayer,[98] God gave him a witness in himself that he had purified his heart. When he was risen from his knees, he could not help declaring it. He now ran to his wife, not to kill her but to catch her in his arms, that they might praise God and weep over one another with tears of joy and love.

Monday 13. Even in Epworth a few faithful servants of Satan were left who would not leave any stone unturned to support his tottering kingdom. A kind of gentleman got a little party together and took huge pains to disturb the congregation. He hired a company of boys to shout, and made a poor man exceeding drunk, who bawled out much ribaldry and nonsense, while he himself played the French horn. But he had little fruit of his labour. I spoke a few words to this champion, and he disappeared. The congregation was not at all disturbed, but quietly attended to the end.

Wed. 15. I rode to Doncaster and at ten, standing in an open place, exhorted a wild yet civil multitude to 'seek the Lord while he might be found'.[99] Thence I went on to Leeds and declared to a large congregation, 'Now is the day of salvation.'[1]

Thursday 16, at five in the evening, I preached at Dewsbury, and on Friday 17, reached Manchester. Here I received a

[98] George Story (1738-1818) of Harthill, West Riding, had a devout if dull upbringing, was converted at the age of ten when news of the revival in Sheffield reached his village, but was subsequently vexed by the predestination question. Beginning work in the bookselling and printing trade, he read voraciously and was attracted by the Enlightenment. Drawn into Methodist circles by his mother's Methodist conversion, he 'immediately broke off all connection with [his] companions, threw [his] useless books into the fire, and sought the Lord with all [his] might'. He is said to have been the first preacher admitted to the Methodist connexion on trial, and in February 1763, he took up this, his first, appointment to the Dales Circuit and was immediately involved in quieting the repercussions in Darlington of George Bell's prophecy of the end of the world. In 1792 and for some years afterward, he served as connexional editor and superintendent of the printing office. Jackson, *Early Methodist Preachers*, 5:218-40.

[99] Cf. Isa. 55:6.

[1] 2 Cor. 6:2.

particular account of a remarkable incident.[2] An eminent drunkard of Congleton used to divert himself, whenever there was preaching there, by standing over against the house, cursing and swearing at the preacher. One evening he had a fancy to step in and 'hear what the man had to say'. He did so, but it made him so uneasy that he could not sleep all night. In the morning, he was more uneasy still; he walked in the fields, but all in vain, till it came in his mind to go to one of his merry companions, who was always ready to abuse the Methodists. He told him how he was and asked what he should do. 'Do?' said Samuel, 'Go and join the society. I will, for I was never so uneasy in my life.' They did so without delay. But presently David cried out, 'I am sorry I joined, for I shall get drunk again, and they will turn me out.' However, he stood firm for four days. On the fifth, he was persuaded by his old companions to 'take one pint', and then another and another, till one of them said, 'See, here is a Methodist drunk!' David started up and knocked him over, chair and all. He then drove the rest out of the house, caught up the landlady, carried her out, threw her in the kennel,[3] went back to the house, broke down the door, threw it into the street, and then ran into the fields, tore his hair, and rolled up and down on the ground. In a day or two was a love-feast; he stole in, getting behind, that none might see him. While Mr. Furz[4] was at prayer, he was seized with a dreadful agony, both of body and mind. This caused many to wrestle with God for him. In a while he sprung up on his feet, stretched out his hands, and cried aloud, 'All my sins are forgiven!' At the same instant, one on the other side of the room cried out, 'Jesus is mine! And he has taken away all my sins.' This was Samuel H——. David burst through the people, caught him in his arms, and said, 'Come, let us sing the Virgin Mary's song; I *never could sing it before.* "My soul doth magnify the Lord, and my spirit doth rejoice in God my Saviour."'[5] And their following behaviour plainly showed the reality of their profession.

Sat. 18. I found the work of God was still greatly increasing here—although many stumbling-blocks had been thrown in the way, and some by those who were once strong in grace. But this is no wonder; I rather wonder that there are not abundantly more.

[2] This story is more fully related by John Furz himself; see Jackson, *Early Methodist Preachers*, 5:128-30.

[3] I.e., the gutter; cf. Sermon 52, *The Reformation of Manners*, I.5, and n. 23 (2:306 in this edn.).

[4] On John Furz, see above, Aug. 3, 1762, n. 58.

[5] Cf. Luke 1:46-47.

And so there would be, but that Satan is not able to go beyond his chain.[6]

Mon. 20. I preached at Macclesfield[7] about noon. As I had not been well and was not quite recovered, our brethren insisted on sending me in a chaise to Burslem.[8] Between four and five, I quitted the chaise and took my horse. Presently after, hearing a cry, I looked back and saw the chaise upside down (the wheel having violently struck against a stone) and well-nigh dashed it in pieces. About seven, I preached to a large congregation at Burslem. These poor potters, four years ago, were as wild and ignorant as any of the colliers in Kingswood. Lord, thou hast 'power over thy own clay'![9]

Tue. 21. I rode to Birmingham,[10] and on Thursday to Towcester. I would willingly have rested there, but our brethren desiring me to go a little farther, I walked on (about three miles) to Whittlebury. Here I found a truly loving and simple people. I preached at the side of the new preaching-house.[11] I suppose most of the town were present. Friday 24, I took horse early, and in the afternoon came once more safe to London.

About this time I received the following letter:[12]

> God is the same yesterday, today, and forever! He was, is, and will be all in all! Being a *minute* part of the *whole*, let me consider

[6] Cf. John and Charles Wesley, *Hymns and Sacred Poems* (1742), p. 275 (*Poetical Works*, 11:334 in this edn.); and *Collection of Hymns* (1780), no. 271:9-10 (7:419 in this edn.):

> In vain doth Satan rage his hour,
> Beyond his chain he cannot go.

The theme comes from Rev. 20:1-3.

[7] Orig., 'Maxfield'.

[8] Orig., 'Borslem'.

[9] Cf. Rom. 9:21.

[10] On this occasion JW was accompanied by a new friend, Matthew Mayer of Portwood Hall, Stockport (1740–1814), in whose charge he left the circuit for a week, while he went off with the itinerant. This acquaintanceship, forged on JW's journey from Manchester to Macclesfield, is doubly noteworthy. It lasted throughout JW's life, and Mayer's house provided him and other preachers with one of the most useful of the bases they were accumulating around the country. Moreover, Matthew Mayer was one of the most notable local preachers and evangelists Methodism ever had. After a painful three-year *Busskampf*, which began in 1759, he became celebrated through the north-west as a preacher, spiritual adviser, and (by no means sympathizing with the growing denominational consciousness of the preachers after JW's death) as a founding father of the greatest of all nondenominational Sunday schools at Stockport. *Methodist Magazine* 39 (1816):3-11, 161-70, 241-51; W. R. Ward, *Religion and Society* (London, Batsford, 1972), pp. 32-33.

[11] William Myles, *A Chronological History of the People Called Methodists*, 3rd edn. (London, 1803), p. 330, gives Whittlebury chapel, Northants., built 1763.

[12] Sender unknown.

myself *alone.* Where was I before my parents were born? In the *mind* of him who is *all in all.* It was God alone that gave me a being amongst the *human* race. He appointed the *country* in which I should begin my existence. My *parents* were also his choice. Their *situation* in mind, body, and estate was fully known to him. My parents are answerable for my education in infancy. My *capacity* was from above. That I improved so little was mostly owing to my connections, but partly to my own inattention or idleness. In most things, whilst an infant, whether good or evil, I was certainly *passive,* i.e., I was instructed or led by others, and so acted right or wrong. In all the incidents of life, whether sickness, health, escapes, crosses, spiritual or temporal advantages or disadvantages, I can trace *nothing* of *myself* during my childhood. And till I became a subject to my *own will,* perhaps I was innocent in the eyes of infinite justice; for the blood of Jesus Christ certainly cleanseth from all original sin and presents all *spotless* who die free from the guilt of actual transgression.

At what time I became a subject to my *own will* I cannot ascertain, but from that time in many things I *offended.* First, against my *parents;* next, against God! And that I was preserved from outward evils was not owing to the *purity of my own will,* but the grace of Christ overruling and preventing me.

My *natural will* ever cleaved to *evil,* and if I had ever any *good* in me, it came from above. What is called 'good nature' is a divine gift and not from the corrupt root. My *will* could not produce good, and in various instances it was in a manner annihilated, before *grace* could fix any good in me. In other words, my *will* acts from the motions of the *Old Adam,* where I transgress; but what is good in me is from the grace of Christ working, whilst my *own will* is made *passive* or *unresisting.* Thus my life has been so far holy, as I gave up my *own will* and lived in God, who is *all in all.*

From the time I could sin, I trace the divine goodness in preserving me from innumerable evils into which my own will would have led me. The unknown temptations and evils perhaps are infinitely more numerous than the *known.* If my *will* was only *not resisting,* when I received or did any good, how little was it concerned in my conviction, my conversion, my peace, and the sphere of life I engaged in, after receiving such divine blessings? My concern about my soul's welfare, the *time* of my conversion, the *ministers* raised up to be the instruments of it, the place of my first hearing the gospel, and various other circumstances that instrumentally brought about those great and blessed events in my life, were no more from anything in myself than my birth and education. Rather, *my will* was overpowered, and *grace* triumphed over it.

From these reflections I conclude that whatever blessings I have enjoyed as to parents, country, education, employments, conversion, connections in life, or any exterior or interior circumstance. . . . All came from God, who is all in all! And whatever in my past life is matter of repentance and lamentation has arose chiefly from *my corrupt will,* though partly from a defective judgment, ever prone to err! So that upon the whole, I have great cause to be thankful that God has been so much the all in all of my life; at the same time, I must bewail that I ever followed my own corrupt will in anything.

My present state of life, I believe, is from God! In a bad state of health, out of employment, and retired from all engagements in the world. I use the means for my recovery, and it is not from any evil principle that I am a cipher; but I cannot yet obtain health, business, or a sphere of usefulness. Nor can I ascertain how far I am culpable as to being what I am. My present duty is, *submission* to the divine will. I study for improvement and pray for such blessings as I want. Is not God *all in all* as to my present state? I have no desire so strong as this, Let thy blessed will be done in and upon me. And the prayer which governs my soul continually is, O may *my will* die day by day, and may God in Christ Jesus be all in all to me and in me and mine, during our life, in our last moments, and to all eternity! Amen.

Finding it was not expedient to leave London during the ferment which still continued by reason of Mr. M[axfield]'s separation from us, I determined not to remove from it before the Conference.[13] This began on Tuesday, July 19, and ended on Saturday 23. And it was a great blessing that we had peace among ourselves, while so many were making themselves ready for battle.

Monday, August 1. I began visiting the classes again and found less loss than might reasonably have been expected, as most of those who had left us spake all manner of evil, without either fear

[13] This Conference, which was probably an important one, is known only from anecdotes about it told by John Pawson and from the inference that most of the changes recorded in the second edition of the *Large Minutes* issued in this year were its work (Jackson, *Early Methodist Preachers*, 4:26-27; *Methodist Magazine* 27 [1804]:269-70; *Minutes of Conference, 1862*, Appendix). Prominent among the changes were the attempt to mobilize the resources of the connexion to secure chapel debts, and the provision that appointments to Methodist pulpits after the deaths of the Wesley brothers and Grimshaw should be in the hands of Conference. A further effort was made to shore up the Church connection, and a Preacher's Fund established to provide for preachers in their old age and for their widows. Howell Harris, who was present, was instrumental in putting down an attempt 'by some of the preachers . . . to call in question the power exercised over them and their Societies'. J. S. Simon, *John Wesley, the Master-Builder* (London, 1927), pp. 138-43.

or shame! Poor creatures! Yet 'he that betrayed'[14] them into this, 'hath the greater sin'.[15]

Mon. 15. I went in the one-day machine to Bath, where one of our friends from Bristol met me (as I had desired) in the afternoon and took me thither in a post-chaise. Wed. 17. Being informed that the boat at the Old Passage would go over at six o'clock, I took horse at four and came to the passage a few minutes after six. But they told us they would not pass till twelve, and I had appointed to preach in Chepstow at eleven. So we thought it best to try the New Passage. We came thither at seven and might probably have stayed till noon, had not an herd of oxen come just in time to the other side. In the boat which brought them over, we crossed the water and got to Chepstow between ten and eleven. As it had rained almost all the day, the house contained the congregation. Hence, we rode to Coleford. The wind being high, I consented to preach in their new room. But large as it was, it would not contain the people, who appeared to be not a little affected; of which they gave a sufficient proof by filling the room at five in the morning.

Thur. 18. We breakfasted at a friend's, a mile or two from Monmouth, and rode to Crickhowell, where I intended to dine, but I found other work to do. Notice had been given that I would preach, and some were come many miles to hear. So I began without delay, and I did not observe one light or inattentive person in the congregation. When we came to Brecon, we found it was the assize week, so that I could not have the town hall, as before, the court being to sit there at the very time when I had appointed to preach. So I preached at Mr. James's door,[16] and all the people behaved as in the presence of God.

Fri. 19. I preached near the market-place, and afterwards rode over to Trevecca. Howell Harris's house is one of the most elegant places which I have seen in Wales.[17] The little chapel and

[14] Matt. 26:48.

[15] John 19:11.

[16] Probably Thomas James, the Brecon attorney, at whose house the Brecon society first met. Williams, *Wesley in Wales*, p. 63.

[17] For the extensive building which had gone on in Trevecca since JW's last visit, see above Mar. 21, 1756. Howell Harris, who on July 25 had sought to secure a visit from JW in the cause of 'striving to remove prejudices', records that JW 'graced our chapel with an excellent exposition on the history of David killing Goliath. We were happy at dinner. . . . I went with him to Brecon with my wife, Hannah, and Betty to show our love to him openly. He preached in the Street an excellent sermon. I had freedom to press on him to stand firm in the Established Church.' Beynon, *Howell Harris*, pp. 186, 192.

all things round about it are finished in an uncommon taste, and the gardens, orchards, fishponds, and mount adjoining, make the place a little paradise. He thanks God for these things and looks through them. About six score persons are now in the family—all diligent, all constantly employed, all fearing God and working righteousness.[18] I preached at ten to a crowded audience, and in the evening at Brecon again; but to the poor only—the rich (a very few excepted) were otherwise employed.

Sat. 20. We took horse at four and rode through one of the pleasantest countries in the world. When we came to Trecastle, we had rode fifty miles in Monmouthshire and Brecknockshire. And I will be bold to say, all England does not afford such a line of fifty miles length for fields, meadows, woods, brooks, and gently-rising mountains, fruitful to the very top. Carmarthenshire, into which we came soon after, has at least as fruitful a soil. But it is not so pleasant, because it has fewer mountains, though abundance of brooks and rivers. About five, I preached on the green at Carmarthen[19] to a large number of deeply attentive people. Here two gentlemen[20] from Pembroke met me, with whom we rode to St. Clears,[21] intending to lodge there, but the inn was quite full. So we concluded to try for Laugharne,[22] though we knew not the way, and it was now quite dark. Just then came up an honest man who was riding thither, and we willingly bore him company.

Sun. 21. It rained almost all the morning. However, we reached Tenby[23] about eleven. The rain then ceased, and I preached at the cross to a congregation gathered from many miles round. The sun broke out several times and shone hot in my face, but never for two minutes together. About five, I preached to a far

[18] See Acts 10:35.

[19] This was described in 1915 as 'an open strip of land at the end of the castle courtyard, facing the bridge over the river Tywi, and enclosed within living memory'. *WHS* 10 (1915):89.

[20] One of them may have been John Barnes, paymaster of the fort at Pembroke and former Moravian 'who first introduced Mr. Wesley's party into Pembrokeshire' (*WHS* 12 [1919]:46-47). In 1765, he produced *The Christian's Pocket Companion* with an introduction by JW; Williams, *Wesley in Wales*, p. 64, n. 2.

[21] Orig., 'St. Clare'. St. Clears was a parish 9 miles west from Carmarthen on the main road to Haverfordwest.

[22] Orig., 'Larn'. Laugharne was a seaport, market town, and parish 12½ miles south-west from Carmarthen.

[23] Tenby was a seaport, market town, and parish 11 miles east of Pembroke.

larger congregation at Pembroke.[24] A few gay people behaved ill at the beginning. But in a short time they lost their gaiety and were as serious as their neighbours.

Wed. 24. I rode over to Haverfordwest.[25] Finding it was the assize week, I was afraid the bulk of the people would be too busy to think about hearing sermons. But I was mistaken: I have not seen so numerous a congregation since I set out of London. And they were, one and all, deeply attentive. Surely some will bring forth fruit.

Thur. 25. I was more convinced than ever that the preaching like an apostle, without joining together those that are awakened and training them up in the ways of God, is only begetting children for the murderer. How much preaching has there been for these twenty years all over Pembrokeshire![26] But no *regular societies*, no discipline, no order or connection. And the consequence is that nine in ten of the once awakened are now faster asleep than ever.

Fri. 26. We designed to take horse at four. But the rain poured down so that one could scarce look out. About six, however, we set out and rode through heavy rain to St. Clears. Having then little hopes of crossing the sands, we determined to go round by Carmarthen. But the ostler[27] told us, we might save several miles by going to Llanstephan's Ferry.[28] We came thither about noon, where a good woman informed us the boat was aground and would not pass till the evening. So we judged it best to go by Carmarthen still. But when we had rode three or four miles, I recollected that I had heard speak of a ford which would save us

[24] Pembroke was a borough, market town, and seaport 6 miles south-east from Milford Haven, rescued from long decay only by the transfer of the government dockyard from Milford Haven in 1814.

[25] 'Aug. 23, 1763. Br. Nyberg at his return to Haverfordwest heard that Mr. John Wesley has yesterday notified by the Town-Crier that he would preach in this town next Wednesday (at the very hour of our preaching), tho' he has not one acquaintance here' (G. M. Roberts, 'Gleanings from the Moravian Records, Haverfordwest', quoted in Williams, *Wesley in Wales*, p. 65, n. 1). Haverfordwest was a seaport, borough, and market town 10½ miles north of Pembroke.

[26] Williams notes that, although the Moravians and Welsh Calvinistic Methodists had been active in South Pembrokeshire over this period, there is no evidence that JW's preachers had been there for so long. Williams, *Wesley in Wales*, p. 65, n.2.

[27] Orig., 'hostler'; see Mar. 11, 1738, n. 55 (18:229 in this edn.).

[28] Orig., 'Llansteffan's'. Llanstephan was a parish 8 miles south-west from Carmarthen; the ferry crossed the river Towy to the village of Ferryside. Lewis, *Wales*, 2:104.

some miles riding. We inquired of an old man, who soon mounted his horse, showed us the way, and rode through the river before us.[29]

Soon after, my mare dropped a shoe, which occasioned so much loss of time that we could not ride the sands but were obliged to go round through a miserable road to Llanelli.[30] To mend the matter, our guide lost his way, both before we came to Llanelli and after, so that it was as much as we could do to reach Loughor[31] Ferry a little after sunset. Knowing it was impossible then to preach at Penrice as we designed,[32] we went on straight to Swansea.

Sat. 27. I preached at seven, to one or two hundred people, many of whom seemed full of good desires. But as there is no society, I expect no deep or lasting work.

Mr. Evans[33] now gave me an account from his own knowledge of what has made a great noise in Wales. 'It is common in the congregations attended by Mr. W[illiam] W[illiams][34] and one or two other clergymen, after the preaching is over, for anyone that has a mind to give out a verse of an hymn. This they sing over and over with all their might, perhaps above thirty, yea, forty times. Meanwhile the bodies of two or three, sometimes ten or twelve, are violently agitated, and they leap up and down, in all manner of postures, frequently for hours together.' I think there needs no great penetration to understand this. They are honest, upright men, who really feel the love of God in their hearts. But they have little experience, either of the ways of God or the devices of

[29] For a fuller account of this journey, see *Arminian Magazine* 3 (1780):384.

[30] Orig., 'Lanellos'. Llanelli was a borough, seaport, market town, and parish 15 miles south-east from Carmarthen on the road to Swansea.

[31] Orig., 'Bocher'. Loughor was a borough and parish 7 miles north-west from Swansea. The ferry was replaced by a bridge in the 1830s.

[32] Orig., 'to reach at Penreese, as we designed', altered in 1789 to, 'to reach Penreese, as was designed', although it seems fairly clear that 'reach' was simply a misprint for 'preach' (see Williams, *Wesley in Wales*, p. 66, n. 2). The spelling in each contemporary edition is doubtless a clue to the pronunciation. Penrice was a small parish 13 miles west from Swansea.

[33] Doubtless William Evans, whom JW had met on his last visit to these parts; see above, Aug. 29, 1758, n. 46.

[34] E. Perronet MS: 'Wm. Wms., whom the Welch always call "Billy Wms."'—i. e., William Williams, Pantycelyn, whose collection of hymns, *Caniadau y rhai sydd ar y Môr o Wydr* (Aberhonddu, 1773), occasioned the revival which broke out at Llangeitho and then spread to many other parts of Wales; see Mar. 3, 1748, n. 92 (20:211 in this edn.); see also Williams, *Wesley in Wales*, p. 66, n. 4.

Satan. So he serves himself of their simplicity, in order to wear them out and to bring a discredit on the work of God.[35]

About two, I preached at Cowbridge in the assembly-room, and then went on to Llandaff.[36] The congregation was waiting, so I began without delay, explaining to them 'the righteousness of faith'.[37] A man had need to be all fire who comes into these parts, where almost everyone is cold as ice. Yet God is able to warm their hearts and make rivers run in the dry places.

Sun. 28. I preached once more in W[envoe][38] Church, but it was hard work. Mr. H[odges][39] read the prayers (not as he did once, with such fervour and solemnity as struck almost every hearer, but) like one reading an old song, in a cold, dry, careless manner. And there was no singing at all. O what life was here once! But now there is not one spark left!

Thence, I rode to Cardiff and found the society in as ruinous a condition as the castle. The same poison of *mysticism* has well-nigh extinguished the last spark of life here also. I preached in the town hall on, 'Now God commandeth all men everywhere to repent.'[40] There was a little shaking among the dry bones. Possibly some of them may yet 'come together and live'.[41]

Mon. 29. At noon, I preached again at Llandaff, and in the evening at Aberthaw.[42] I found the most life in this congregation that I have found anywhere in Glamorganshire. We lodged at F[onmon][43] Castle—so agreeable once! But how is the scene

[35] JW had of course encountered similar manifestations in his earliest preaching at Bristol in 1739, and was reminded of these events in Wales by later outbreaks in Derbyshire. See Apr. 3, 1786.

[36] Probably to Llandaff Court (now the Cathedral School), where an Arminian Methodist society seems to have met. JW's host was Thomas Matthews (who died in 1798), who had married Diana, the daughter of Robert Jones of Fonman, and was grandson of Admiral Thomas Matthews (see Apr. 5, 1744, n. 92 [20:20 in this edn.]; George Mervyn Williams, *A List of the Names and Residences of the High Sheriffs of the County of Glamorgan, from 1541 to 1966* [Llanharan, Williams, 1966], pp. 67-68). Llandaff, described as 'an ancient and decayed city or parish' was 2 miles north-west of Cardiff.

[37] Rom. 4:11, etc.

[38] E. Perronet MS: 'Wenvoe—about six miles from Cardiff, of which a very good, sensible man, Mr. Hodges, has been minister for many years, during the last twenty of which he has commenced *mystic.*'

[39] For John Hodges, see Oct. 18, 1741, n. 49 (19:233 in this edn.). It is thought that the society at Wenvoe had come to an end some eight years before.

[40] Cf. Acts 17:30.

[41] Cf. Ezek. 37:7, 9.

[42] Aberthaw was a small seaport and hamlet 7 miles south-east of Cowbridge, divided into two portions, East and West, by the River Thaw.

[43] No name is present in the original, and *Works* (1774) adds only 'F——'. When Robert Jones III came of age and inherited the home, he did not maintain his parents' evangelical

changed! How dull and unlovely is every place where there is nothing of God.

Thur. [i.e., Tue.] 30. I preached in the castle at Cardiff and endeavoured to lift up the hands that hung down.[44] A few seemed to awake and shake themselves from the dust.[45] Let these go on, and more will follow.

I came to Chepstow, Friday [i.e., Wednesday] 31, just at noon, and began preaching immediately at Mr. Cheek's[46] door. The sun shone full in my face, extremely hot, but in two or three minutes the clouds covered it. The congregation was large and behaved well; perhaps some may be 'doers of the word'.[47] When we went into the boat at the Old Passage, it was a dead calm. But the wind sprung up in a few minutes, so that we reached Bristol in good time.

Thursday, September 1. I began expounding a second time, after an interval of above twenty years, the first Epistle of St. John.[48] How plain, how full, and how deep a compendium of genuine Christianity!

Sat. 3. I went on in describing the one undivided 'fruit of the spirit',[49] one part of which men are continually labouring to separate from the other. But it cannot be: none can retain *peace* or *joy* without *meekness* and *long-suffering;* nay, nor without *fidelity* and *temperance.* Unless we have the whole, we cannot long retain any part of it.

Sun. 4. I preached on the quay, when multitudes attended, who would not have come to the other end of the city. In the afternoon, I preached near the new square.[50] I find no other way to reach the outcasts of men. And this way God has owned and *does* still own, both by the conviction and conversion of sinners.

Wed. 7. I preached at Pensford about eight, and it began raining almost as soon as I began preaching. But I think none went away. At noon, I preached at Shepton Mallet to a numerous, nay, and serious congregation, and about six, in a meadow at Wincanton. I suppose this was the first field preaching which had

faith and conduct (see above, Aug. 23, 1758, n. 37). E. Perronet MS: 'Fonmon, the seat of Robt. Jones, Esq., *now* the rendezvous of Welch oxen, alas, and *curates.*'

[44] See Heb. 12:12.

[45] See Isa. 52:2.

[46] Moseley Cheek, who from 1765 to 1768 was one of Wesley's preachers and then became incumbent of St. Stephen's, Salford.

[47] Jas. 1:22.

[48] It had been in fact over twenty-four years since Apr. 6, 1739, when JW had begun a series of sermons at Bristol on this Epistle, only four days after the beginning of the revival.

[49] Gal. 5:22.

[50] I.e., King Square.

been there. However, the people were all quiet, and the greater part deeply attentive.

Thur. 8. At nine, I preached in the same place to a far more serious audience. Between eleven and twelve, I preached at Westcombe, and in the evening at Frome. How zealous to hear are these people! And yet how little do they profit by hearing! I think this will not always be the case. By and by we shall rejoice over them.

Wed. 14. I preached at Bath, on 'Now is the day of salvation.'[51] I was afterwards not a little refreshed by the conversation of one lately come from London, notwithstanding an irregularity of thought almost peculiar to herself.[52] How much preferable is her *irregular warmth* to the *cold wisdom* of them that despise her! How gladly would I be as she is, taking her *wildness* and *fervour* together!

In the evening the congregation at Coleford was all alive, and great part of them were present again in the morning. The next evening we had a love-feast, at which many were not able to contain their joy and desire but were constrained to cry aloud and praise God for the abundance of his mercies.

Sat. 17. I preached on the green at Bedminster. I am apt to think many of the hearers scarce ever heard a Methodist before, or perhaps any other preacher. What but field preaching could reach these poor sinners? And are not *their* souls also precious in the sight of God?

Sun. 18. I preached in the morning in Princess Street to a numerous congregation. Two or three gentlemen, so called, laughed at first. But in a few minutes they were as serious as the rest. On Monday evening, I gave our brethren a solemn caution, not to 'love the world, neither the things of the world'.[53] This will be their grand danger. As they are industrious and frugal, they must needs increase in goods. This appears already: in London, Bristol, and most other trading towns, those who are in business have increased in substance sevenfold, some of them twenty, yea, an hundredfold. What need then have these of the strongest warnings lest they be entangled therein and perish?[54]

[51] 2 Cor. 6:2.

[52] E. Perronet MS: 'This, I believe, was the later famous Mrs. Garbrand of the Strand near Brentford—whose *chief* accomplishments were her intemperate love. . . .' See *WHS* 7 (1909):73-78; and Curnock, 5:94, n. 4, for another identification; see also *Arminian Magazine* 4 (1781):52; and letter of Sept. 29, 1764, in Telford, 4:265.

[53] Cf. 1 John 2:15.

[54] See 2 Pet. 2:20.

Fri. 23. I preached at Bath. Riding home, we saw a coffin carrying into St. George's Church, with many children attending it. When we came near we found they were our own children,[55] attending the corpse of one of their schoolfellows who had died of the smallpox. And God thereby touched many of their hearts in a manner they never knew before.

Mon. 26. I preached to the prisoners in Newgate, and in the afternoon rode over to Kingswood, where I had a solemn watch-night and an opportunity of speaking closely to the children. One is dead; two recovered; seven are[56] ill still. And the hearts of all are like melting wax.

Tue. 27. I took leave of the congregation at Bristol[57] by opening and applying those words (by which no flesh living shall be justified) 'Thou shalt love thy neighbour as thyself.'[58] I believe an eminent deist[59] who was present will not easily forget that hour. He was (then at least) deeply affected and felt he stood in need of 'an advocate with the Father'.[60]

Wednesday and Thursday evening I spent at Salisbury, and with no small satisfaction. Friday 30, I preached about one at Whitchurch, and then rode to Basingstoke. Even here there is at length some prospect of doing good. A large number of people attended, to whom God enabled me to speak strong words. And they seemed to sink into the hearts of the hearers.

Saturday, October 1. I returned to London and found our house in ruins, great part of it being taken down, in order to a thorough repair. But as much remained as I wanted—six foot square suffices me by day or by night.

I now received a very strange account from a man of sense, as well as integrity:[61]

> I asked M. S. many questions before she would give me any answer. At length, after much persuasion, she said, 'On old

55 Of Kingswood School.

56 'Are' is added only in the errata and MS notes to *Works* (1774).

57 A pastoral letter written by JW to the societies in Bristol soon after this time, counselling them, among other things, to avoid taking bribes in the forthcoming general election and to be constant in attendance on the means of grace, was printed in *Wesleyan Methodist Magazine* 60 (1837):822-24.

58 Matt. 22:39.

59 E. Perronet MS: 'Old Mr. Ford the surgeon'. James Ford of Bristol, doctor, father of Gilbert Ford who matriculated from Christ Church in 1767.

60 1 John 2:1.

61 E. Perronet MS: 'NB. Which ought to have been suppressed, come from whom it would . . .' (remainder difficult to decipher).

Michaelmas Day was three years I was sitting by myself at my father's with a Bible before me, and one whom I took to be my uncle came into the room and sat down by me. He talked to me some time till, not liking his discourse, I looked more carefully at him. He was dressed like my uncle, but I observed one of his feet was just like that of an ox. Then I was much frighted, and he began torturing me sadly and told me he would torture me ten times more if I would not swear to kill my father, which at last I did. He said he would come again, on that day four years, between half hour past two and three o'clock.

'I have several times since strove to write this down, but when I did, the use of my hand was taken from me. I strove to speak it, but whenever I did my speech was taken from me. And I am afraid I shall be tormented a deal more for what I have spoken now.'

Presently she fell into such a fit as was dreadful to look upon. One would have thought she would be torn in pieces. Several persons could scarce hold her, till after a time she sunk down as dead.

From that Michaelmas Day, she was continually tormented with the thought of killing her father, as likewise of killing herself, which she often attempted but was as often hindered. Once she attempted to cut her own throat; once to throw herself into Rosamond's Pond;[62] several times to strangle herself, which once or twice was with much difficulty prevented.

Her brother, fearing lest she should at last succeed in her attempt and finding her fits come more frequently, got a straight waistcoat made for her, such as they use at Bedlam. It was made of strong ticking, with two straps on the shoulders, to fasten her down to the bed—one across her breast, another across her middle, and another across her knees. One likewise was buckled on each leg and fastened to the side of the bed. The arms of the waistcoat drew over her fingers and fastened like a purse. In a few minutes after she was thus secured, her brother, coming to the bed, found she was gone. After some time he found she was up the chimney, so high that he could scarce touch her feet. When Mary Loftis[63] called her, she came down, having her hands as fast as ever.

The night after, I fastened her arms to her body with new straps over and above the rest. She looked at me and laughed, th[e]n gave her hands a slight turn, and all the fastenings were off.

In the morning Mr. Spark[s][64] came. On our telling him this he

[62] A pool which then existed in St. James's Park, lying across what is now Birdcage Walk.

[63] Orig., 'M. L——s'; *Works* (1774), 'Mary Lary', but the errata and MS notes to *Works*, 'Mary Loftis'.

[64] Sparks, a ministerial visitor at Newgate, had been a close friend of Charles Wesley in 1739; *CWJ*, 1:101, 115-27, 134, 137, 139.

said, 'But I will take upon me to fasten her so that she shall not get loose.' Accordingly he sent for some girth-web, with which he fastened her arms to her sides, first above her elbows round her body, then below her elbows; then he put it round each wrist and braced[65] them down to each side of the bedstead. After this she was quiet a night and a day. Then all this was off like the rest.

After this we did not tie her down any more, only watched over her night and day. I asked the physician that attended her whether [it] was a natural disorder. He said, 'Partly natural, partly diabolical.' We then judged there was no remedy but prayer, which was made for her, or with her, continually, though while any were praying with her, she was tormented more than ever.

The Friday before Michaelmas Day last, Mr. W.[66] came to see her. He asked, Do you know me? She said, 'No, you all appear to me like blackamoors.' But do not you know my voice? 'No, I know no one's voice, except Molly L[oftis].' Do you pray God to help you? 'No, I can't pray. God will never help *me.* I belong to the devil, and he will have me. He will take me, body and soul, on Monday.' Would you have *me* pray for you? 'No indeed. For when people pray, he torments me worse than ever.' In her fits she was first convulsed all over, seeming in an agony of pain and screaming terribly. Then she began cursing, swearing, and blaspheming in the most horrid manner. Then she burst into vehement fits of laughter; then sunk down as dead. All this time she was quite senseless; then she fetched a deep sigh and recovered her sense and understanding—but was so weak that she could not speak to be heard, unless you put your ear almost close to her mouth.

When Mr. W. began praying she began screaming, so that a mob quickly gathered about the house. However, he prayed on, till the convulsions and screaming ceased, and she came to her senses much sooner than usual. What most surprised us was that she continued in her senses and, soon after, began to pray herself.

On Sunday evening Mr. W. came again, asked her many questions, pressed her to call upon God for power to believe, and then prayed with her. She then began to pray again and continued in her senses longer than she had done for a month before, but still insisted the devil would come the next day between two and three and take her away.

[65] Orig., 'blockaded', altered in *Works* (1774).

[66] John Wesley; note the alternative first person later in the letter.

She begged me to sit up with her that night, which I willingly did. About four in the morning, she burst out into a flood of tears, crying, 'What shall I do, what shall I do? I cannot stand this day. This day I shall be lost.' I went to prayer with her and exhorted her to pray for faith, and her agony ceased.

About half hour after ten, ten of us came together, as we had agreed the day before. I said, 'Is there any among you who does not believe that God is able and willing to deliver this soul?' They answered with one voice, 'We believe he both can and will deliver her this day.' I then fastened her down to the bed on both sides and set two on each side to hold her if need were. We began laying her before the Lord and claiming his promise on her behalf. Immediately Satan raged vehemently. He caused her to roar in an uncommon manner, then to shriek, so that it went through our heads, then to bark like a dog. Then her face was distorted to an amazing degree, her mouth being drawn from ear to ear, and her eyes turned opposite ways and starting as if they would start out of her head. Presently, her throat was so convulsed that she appeared to be quite strangled. Then the convulsions were in her bowels, and her body swelled as if ready to burst. At other times, she was stiff from head to foot as an iron bar, being at the same time wholly deprived of her senses and motion, not even breathing at all. Soon after, her body was so writhed, one would have thought all her bones must be dislocated.

We continued in prayer, one after another, till about twelve o'clock. One then said, 'I must go; I can stay no longer.' Another and another said the same, till we were upon the point of breaking up. I said, 'What is this? Will you all give place to the devil? Are you still ignorant of Satan's devices? Shall we leave this poor soul in his hands?' Presently the cloud vanished away. We all saw the snare and resolved to wrestle with God till we had the petition we asked of him. We began singing an hymn and quickly found his Spirit was in the midst of us. But the more earnestly we prayed, the more violently the enemy raged. It was with great difficulty that four of us could hold her down; frequently we thought she would have been torn out of our arms. By her looks and motions we judged she saw him in a visible shape. She laid fast hold on Molly L[ofti]s and me with inexpressible eagerness and soon burst into a flood of tears, crying, 'Lord, save, or I perish. I *will* believe. Lord, give me power to believe, help my unbelief.' Afterwards she lay quiet for about fifteen minutes. I then asked, 'Do you now believe Christ will save you? And have you a desire to pray to him?' She answered, 'I have a little desire, but I want power to believe.' We bid her keep asking for the power and looking unto Jesus. I then gave out an hymn, and she earnestly sung with us those words:

O Sun of Righteousness, arise
With healing in thy wing!
To my diseased, my fainting soul,
Life and salvation bring.

I now looked at my watch and told her, 'It is half hour past two. This is the time when the devil said he would come for you.' But, blessed be God, instead of a tormentor, he sent a comforter. Jesus appeared to her soul and rebuked the enemy, though still some fear remained. But at three it was all gone, and she mightily rejoiced in the God of her salvation. It was a glorious sight. Her fierce countenance was changed, and she looked innocent as a child. And we all partook of the blessing. For Jesus filled our souls with a love which no tongue can express. We then offered up our joint praises to God for his unspeakable mercies, and left her full of faith and love and joy in God her Saviour.

Sun. 2. All this week I endeavoured to confirm those who had been shaken as to the important doctrine of Christian perfection, either by its wild defenders or wise opposers, who much availed themselves of that wildness. It must needs be that such offences will come. But 'woe unto him by whom the offence cometh!'[67]

Mon. 10. I set out for Norwich, taking Hertford[68] in my way, where I began preaching between ten and eleven. Those who expected disturbance were happily disappointed, for the whole congregation was quiet and attentive. I doubt not but much good may be done even here, if our brethren *live* what we *preach.*

In the evening, I preached in the New Room at Bedford, where we at last see some fruit of our labour. Tue. 11. I rode through miserable roads to Cambridge, and thence to Lakenheath. The next day, I reached Norwich and found much of the presence of God in the congregation, both this evening and the next day. On Friday evening, I read to them all the rules of the society, adding, 'Those who are resolved to keep these rules may continue with us, and those only.' I then related what I had done since I came to Norwich first, and what I *would do* for the time to come; particularly, that I would immediately put a stop to preaching in

[67] Cf. Matt. 18:7.

[68] Hertford was a borough, market, and county town 21 miles north of London. The revival in Hertfordshire seems to have commenced a little earlier with the work of Berridge and Hicks, and JW had taken note of their success. This was his first visit to Hertford, and, when he began regular visits to the county in the 1780s, his base was not the county town but Hinxworth Hall. *Wesleyan Methodist Magazine* 107 (1884):607-8.

the time of church service. I added, 'For many years I have had more trouble with this society than with half the societies in England put together. With God's help I will try you one year longer. And I hope you will bring forth better fruit.'

Sun. 16. Notwithstanding the notice I had given over and over, abundance of people came to the Tabernacle at two in the afternoon, the usual time of preaching. And many of these *lambs* roared like lions.[69] But it was no more than I expected. Mon. 17. I found at Yarmouth a little, loving, earnest company. In the evening, both the house and the yard were pretty well filled with attentive hearers. Tue. 18. I read over that surprising book, *The Life of Mr. William Lilly*.[70] If he believed himself, as he really seems to have done, was ever man so deluded? Persuaded that Hermeli, the queen of the Fairies, Micol Regina Pygmaeorum and their fellows, were good angels! How amazing is this! And is it not still more amazing that some of the greatest and most sensible men in the nation should, not only not scruple to employ him, but be his fast friends upon all occasions?

Wed. 19. I returned to Norwich and found the ferment a little abated. I was much pleased with the leaders in the evening, a company of steady, lively, zealous persons—and indeed with most of the society with whom I have conversed, none of whom seem to have lost ground since I was here last.

Sun. 23. I met the society for the first time, immediately after the morning preaching. Afterwards I went to church, with a considerable number of the people, several of whom I suppose had not been within those walls for many years. I was glad to hear a plain, useful sermon, and especially for the sake of those who, if they had been offended at first, would hardly have come any more. In the evening God made bare his arm,[71] and his word was sharp as a two-edged sword.[72] Before I had concluded my sermon the mob made a little disturbance. But let us only get the *lambs* in order, and I will quickly tame the *bears*.

Mon. 24. I rode to Bury [St. Edmunds]. Here the mob had for some time reigned lords paramount. But a strange gentleman

[69] James Wheatley's followers in Norwich had been known as his 'dear lambs'. Tyerman, *John Wesley*, 2:126.

[70] William Lilly, *History of His Life and Times, 1602–84, written by himself* (London, 1715). William Lilly was an astrologer who had attempted to serve Charles I while ostensibly serving parliament. JW had first read this book as an undergraduate.

[71] See Isa. 52:10.

[72] See Heb. 4:12.

from London, who was present one evening when they were in high spirits, took them in hand and prosecuted the matter so effectually that they were quelled at once.

Tue. 25. I rode to Colchester and found a strange ferment in the society, occasioned by the imprudence[73] of —— ——, who had kindled a flame which he could not quench and set every man's sword against his brother.[74] I heard them all face to face, but to no purpose. They regarded neither Scripture nor reason. But on Thursday evening at the meeting of the society, God was entreated for them. The stony hearts were broken; anger, revenge, evil surmising fled away. The hearts of all were again united together, and his banner over us was love.[75]

It may be of use to insert part of a letter[76] which I received about this time.

> I was reading your *Notes* on Heb. 12[77] a while since; I was struck with your exposition of the ninth verse. 'Perhaps these expressions, "fathers of our flesh" and "Father of spirits", intimate that our earthly fathers are only the parents of our bodies, our souls not being derived from them, but rather created by the immediate power of God and infused into the body from age to age.'[78] But meeting with a curious old book which asserts a contrary doctrine, I hope you will pardon my freedom in transcribing and begging your thoughts upon it.
>
> 'That souls are not immediately infused by God, but mediately propagated by the parent, is proved, (1) from the divine rest, Gen. 2:2, "And he rested on the seventh day, from all the work which he had made"; (2) from the blessing mentioned Gen. 1:28, "And God blessed them, and said unto them, Be fruitful, and multiply," for this does not relate to a part, but to the whole of man; (3) from the generation of Seth, Gen. 5:3, "And Adam . . . begat a son in his own likeness, after his image," for this image principally consisted in the soul; (4) from the procession of the soul from the parent mentioned, Gen. 16:26, "All the souls . . . which came out of his loins"; (5) from the very consideration of sin, for they are infused (i) either pure, and then, i, they will either be free from original sin, the primary seat of which is the soul, and so God will be cruel in condemning the soul for what it is not guilty of; or, ii, we must suppose the impure body to pollute the soul, which is absurd. Or

[73] Orig., 'impudence', corrected in *Works* (1774).
[74] See Ezek. 38:21.
[75] See S. of S. 2:4.
[76] Writer unknown.
[77] *Works* (1774) alters to, 'In reading your note on Heb. 12:9'.
[78] This is the reading of the 1755 edition of the *Notes*.

(ii) they are infused impure, and in that case God will be the cause of impurity, which is impossible. This is further proved from the doctrine of regeneration; for that which is regenerated was also generated or begotten, but the whole man is regenerated, therefore the whole man is generated. Compare John 3:6, "That which is born of the flesh is flesh, and that which is born of the Spirit is spirit"; and Eph. 4:23, "And be renewed in the spirit of your mind."

'That the human soul is propagated by the parents together with the body is further proved, (1) by the creation of Eve, whose soul is not said to have been breathed into her by God; (2) from the confession of David, Ps. 51:2, "Behold, I was shapen in iniquity, and in sin did my mother conceive me," which words cannot possibly relate to the body only; (3) from our redemption; what Christ did not assume, he did not redeem; if therefore he did not assume his soul together with his body from the Virgin Mary, our souls are not redeemed by Christ, which is evidently false; (4) from similar expressions (Job 10:8, "Thine hands have made and fashioned me," and Ps. 139:13, "For thou hast possessed my reins, Thou hast covered me in my mother's womb") where God is said to have formed us with his own hands, which yet is no otherwise done than mediately by generation; (5) from the nature of the begetter and the begotten; they are of one species, but the man who begets consisting of a soul and body, and a body without a soul, are not of one species.

'Again, supposing the soul to be infused by the Deity, either (first) it will be free from sin, and so God himself will be accused as guilty of injustice in condemning a pure spirit, and in infusing it into an impure body; or (2) he will be accounted the author of the soul's pollution, by uniting it, a pure spirit, to an impure body, in order that it should be polluted; (3) a double absurdity will follow upon this supposition, viz., (1) the organical parts of man only will be slaves to sin; (2) the immortal spirit would be corrupted by the mortal body; (3) or, if the soul being thus infused, it be polluted by sin, it will follow that God is expressly assigned to be the cause of sin, which is the highest blasphemy.'[79]

Fri. 28. At the request of the little society there, I rode round by Braintree. Here I met with one who was well acquainted with the

[79] JW's revision of his *Explanatory Notes* during 1760-62 introduced some minor revisions into his note on Heb. 12:19, thereby qualifying his creationist view and moving a step toward allowing the possibility of a modified traducianism, which this anonymous writer clearly supports. See above, Jan. 27, 1762; and below, Nov. 7, 1770; see also his 'On the Origin of the Soul' (1782), opening paragraphs and note.

Honourable Mr. [Shirley].[80] If he answers the character Mr. S——[81] gives, he is one of the most amiable men in the world. O what keeps us apart? Why cannot we openly give each other the right hand of fellowship?

Sat. 29. I returned to London. Sun. 30. I now, for the first time, spoke to the society freely concerning Mr. M[axfield], both with regard to his *injustice* in the affair of Snowsfields and his almost unparalleled ingratitude to *me*.[82] But I never expect one that is false to God to be true to an human friend.

Wed.[83] November 2. I spent an agreeable hour with old, venerable Mr.——.[84] How striking is a man of sense, learning, and piety, when he has well-nigh finished his course and yet retains all his faculties unimpaired! His grey hairs are indeed 'a crown of honour'.[85]

In this neighbourhood, I learned the particulars of a remarkable occurrence. On Friday, August 19, a gentleman who was at Lisbon during the great earthquake, walking with his friend near Brighthelmstone in Sussex and looking south-west toward the sea, cried out, 'God grant the wind may rise! Other-

[80] E. Perronet MS: 'Mr. Shirley'; i.e., the Hon. Rev. Walter Shirley, cousin of the Countess of Huntingdon; see above, June 6, 1758, n. 14; and May 28, 1760, n. 15.

[81] Orig., 'Mr. ——', altered in *Works* (1774) to 'Mr. S——', probably the Rev. Walter Sellon, for whom the Countess of Huntingdon obtained ordination; see June 12, 1751, n. 3 (20:392 in this edn.).

[82] In his *Vindication* (1767), Maxfield insisted that JW had abandoned the Snowsfield chapel, which was closed for a time, and that he was invited by Mr. Arvin, the lease holder of the property, to preach there. He also denied charges of enthusiasm.

[83] Orig., 'Saturday'.

[84] This may have been, as Curnock supposed, the Rev. Jacob Chapman (d. 1795), the Presbyterian minister at Staplehurst, Kent, who appears again below, Dec. 7, 1763. Against this view is the fact that Chapman had anything but 'finished his course' and that JW writes on Dec. 7 as if he were making a first visit. On the other hand, Chapman had been in the ministry since at least 1740, and had been at Staplehurst at least since 1747. In his youth suspected of unorthodoxy, Chapman carried into another age memories of personal intimacy with Doddridge and Watts, became a member of the Methodist society, and from 1762, the host of JW and his assistants; *Calendar of Doddridge Correspondence*, No. 603. A number of his letters to JW were printed in the *Arminian Magazine* 5 (1782):550, 666; 6 (1783):556; 7 (1784):113, 387, the last of which recalled that 'the name "Methodist"' was not a new name never before given to any religious people. Dr. Calamy, in one of his volumes of the *Ejected Ministers*, observes, 'They called those who stood up for God, Methodists. It is very remarkable that this was in the time of your own grandfather, John Wesley.' One of his oddities was that he would perform no spiritual exercises when Methodist preachers were to hand. Edmund Calamy, *An Abridgement of Mr. Baxter's History of his Life and Times; with an account of the Ministers, &c., who were ejected after the Restoration of King Charles II* (London, 1702; 2nd edn., 1713); *Methodist Magazine* 44 (1821):881-84.

[85] Cf. Ps. 8:5.

wise we shall have an earthquake quickly. Just so the clouds whirled to and fro, and so the sky looked that day at Lisbon.' Presently, the wind did rise and brought an impetuous storm of rain and large hail. Some of the hailstones were larger than hen-eggs. It moved in a line about four miles broad, making strange havoc, as it passed quite over the land till it fell into the river not far from Sheerness. And wherever it passed it left an hot sulphurous stream, such as almost suffocated those it reached.

Thur. 3. I returned to London. Sat. 5. I spent some time with my old friend John Gambold.[86] Who but Count Zinzendorf[87] could have separated such friends as we were? Shall we never unite again?

Sun. 13. I found much of the power of God in preaching, but far more at the Lord's Table. At the same time one who had been wandering from God for many years and would fain have been with us, but could not, found that the Spirit of God was not hindered or confined to one place. He found out ——, the poor backslider, in his own house and revealed Christ anew in his heart.

Tue. 15. I visited Joseph Norbury, a good old soldier of Jesus Christ.[88] I found him just on the wing for paradise, having rattled in the throat for some time. But his speech was restored when I came in, and he mightily praised God for all his mercies. This was his last testimony for[89] a good Master. Soon after, he fell asleep.

On Friday, I finished visiting the classes and observed that since February last an hundred and seventy-five persons have been separated from us. An hundred and six[90] left us on Mr. M[axfield]'s account—few of them will return till they are deeply humbled.

Here, I stood and looked back on the late occurrences. Before Thomas Walsh left England,[91] God began that great work which

[86] Orig., 'J. G.', expanded to 'John Gambold' in the errata and 'J. Gambold' in the MS notes to *Works* (1774). On Gambold, now a Moravian bishop, see Feb. 18, 1738, n. 28 (18:225 in this edn.).

[87] Orig., '——', altered to 'Count Z——' in *Works* (1774), with the latter expanded to 'Zinzendorf' in Wesley's MS notes thereon, but not in the errata. In the first edition of 1768, Edward Perronet filled in the blank differently: '*Moravians*—or the D[evil]'.

[88] See 2 Tim. 2:3.

[89] Orig., 'of', altered in *Works* (1774).

[90] Atmore put the number at two hundred, including some of JW's 'choicest friends'. 'Some who knew Mr. Wesley well, have declared that this was the heaviest trial that ever befell him.' For some time before Maxfield's death in 1784, relations between him and the Methodists thawed. Atmore, *Memorial*, pp. 268-69.

[91] In April 1758.

has continued ever since without any considerable intermission. During the whole time, many have been convinced of sin, many justified, and many backsliders healed. But the peculiar work of this season has been what St. Paul calls 'the perfecting of the saints'.[92] Many persons in London, in Bristol, in York, and in various parts both of England and Ireland, have experienced so deep and universal a change as it had not before entered into their hearts to conceive. After a deep conviction of inbred sin, of their total fall from God, they have been so filled with faith and love (and generally in a moment), that sin vanished, and they found from that time no pride, anger, desire, or unbelief. They could rejoice evermore, pray without ceasing, and in everything give thanks.[93] Now whether we call this the *destruction* or *suspension* of sin, it is a glorious work of God—such work, as considering both the depth and extent of it, we never saw in these kingdoms before.

'Tis possible some who spoke in this manner were mistaken, and 'tis certain some have lost what they then received. A few (very few compared to the whole number) first gave way to enthusiasm, then to pride, next to prejudice and offence, and at last separated from their brethren. But although this laid a huge stumbling-block in the way, still the work of God went on. Nor has it ceased to this day in any of its branches. God still convinces, justifies, sanctifies. We have lost only the dross, the enthusiasm, the prejudice and offence. The pure gold remains, faith working by love,[94] and we have ground to believe, increases daily.

Mon. 21. I buried the remains of Joseph Norbury, a faithful witness of Jesus Christ. For about three years he has humbly and boldly testified that God had saved him from *all sin.* And his whole spirit and behaviour, in life and death, made his testimony beyond exception. Dec. 1. All the leisure hours I had in this and the following months, during the time I was in London, I spent in reading over our works with the preachers, considering what objections had been made and correcting whatever we judged wrong, either in the matter or expression.

Monday, December 5. I rode to Shoreham and preached in the evening to a more than usually serious company. The next evening they were considerably increased. The smallpox, just broke out in the town, has made many of them thoughtful. O let not the impression pass away as the morning dew!

[92] Eph. 4:12.

[93] See 1 Thess. 5:16-18.

[94] See Gal. 5:6.

Wed. 7. I rode to Staplehurst, where Mr. Ch[apman],[95] who loves all that love Christ, received us gladly. At six the congregation, gathered from many miles round, seemed just ripe for the gospel, so that (contrary to my custom in a new place) I spoke merely of 'the grace of our Lord Jesus Christ'. Thursday 8, in returning to London, I was thoroughly wet, but it did me no hurt at all.

Fri. 16. I spent an agreeable hour, and not unprofitably, in conversation with my old friend John Gambold.[96] O how gladly could I join heart and hand again! But alas! 'thy heart is' not 'as my heart'![97]

Sat. 17. I dined at Dr. G[ifford]'s,[98] as friendly and courteous as Dr. Doddridge himself. How amiable is courtesy joined with sincerity! Why should they ever be divided?

Wed. 21. I took my leave of the Bull and Mouth,[99] a barren, uncomfortable place, where much pains has been taken for several years, I fear to little purpose. Thur. 22. I spent a little time in a visit to Mr. M——,[1] twenty years ago a zealous and useful magistrate, now a picture of human nature in disgrace—feeble in body and mind, slow of speech and of understanding. Lord, let me not live to be useless!

Mon. 26. I began preaching at a large commodious place in Bartholomew Close.[2] I preached there again on Wednesday, and at both times with peculiar liberty of spirit. At every place this week I endeavoured to prepare our brethren for renewing their covenant with God.

Sunday, January the first, 1764, we met in the evening for that solemn purpose. I believe the number of those that met was considerably larger than it was last year. And so was the blessing; truly 'the consolations of God' were 'not small with us'.[3] Many

[95] E. Perronet MS: 'Chapman'. On Jacob Chapman, see above, Nov. 2, 1763, n. 84.

[96] Orig., 'John G.', expanded in *Works* (1774). On John Gambold, see above, Nov. 3, 1763, n. 86.

[97] Cf. 2 Kgs. 10:15, and Sermon No. 39, 'Catholic Spirit', 2:79-95 in this edn.

[98] E. Perronet MS: 'Gifford's'. Andrew Gifford (1700–84), Baptist minister at Eagle Street, London 1730–84, and a numismatist whose collection of coins was bought by George II. Gifford was chaplain to Sir Richard and Lady Ellice, 1731–45, and his connections in the world of politics secured him appointment as assistant librarian to the British Museum.

[99] On this meeting-house, see above, Sept. 10, 1756, n. 96.

[1] As yet unidentified.

[2] An old Presbyterian meeting in Middlesex Court, part of a large building called Middlesex House. Wilson says, 'Mr. Wesley occupied the place only a short time, and was succeeded by Mr. [James Relly].' Wilson, *Dissenting Churches*, 3:385.

[3] Cf. Job 15:11.

were filled with peace and joy, many with holy fear, and several backsliders were healed.

On some of the following days, I visited the little societies near London. Thursday 12, I preached at Mitcham, and in the afternoon rode to Dorking.[4] But the gentleman to whose house I was invited seemed to have no desire I should preach. So that evening I had nothing to do. Friday 13, I went at noon into the street and, in a broad place not far from the market-place, proclaimed 'the grace of our Lord Jesus Christ'.[5] At first, two or three little children were the whole of my congregation. But it quickly increased, though the air was sharp and the ground exceeding wet. And all behaved well but three or four grumbling men, who stood so far off that they disturbed none but themselves.

I had purposed to preach there again in the morning, but a violent storm made it impracticable. So, after preaching at Mitcham in the way, I rode back to London.

Mon. 16. I rode to High Wycombe and preached to a more numerous and serious congregation than ever I saw there before. Shall there be yet another day of visitation to this careless people?

A large number was present at five in the morning. But my face and gums were so swelled, I could hardly speak. After I took horse, they grew worse and worse, till it began to rain. I was then persuaded to put on an oil-case hood, which (the wind being very high) kept rubbing continually on my cheek, till both pain and swelling were gone.

Between twelve and one, we crossed Eynsham Ferry.[6] The water was like a sea on both sides. I asked the ferryman, 'Can we ride the causeway?' He said, 'Yes, sir, if you keep in the middle.' But this was the difficulty, as the whole causeway was covered with water to a considerable depth. And this in many parts ran over the causeway with the swiftness and violence of a sluice. Once my mare lost both her fore feet, but she gave a spring and recovered the causeway. Otherwise we must have taken a swim, for the water on either side was ten or twelve feet deep. However,

[4] Orig., 'Darking'. Methodism is said to have been introduced into Dorking at the invitation of a Mr. Rose. T. R. Grantham, *Dorking Congregationalism 1662–1912* (Dorking, 1913), p. 12.

[5] 2 Cor. 8:9.

[6] Orig., 'Ensham'. Eynsham was a parish 6 miles north-west of Oxford; the ferry was later replaced by a toll bridge.

after one or two plunges more, we got through and came safe to Witney.[7]

The congregation in the evening, as well as the next day, was both large and deeply attentive. This is such a people as I have not seen, so remarkably diligent in business and at the same time of so quiet a spirit and so calm and civil in their behaviour.

Thur. 19. I rode through Oxford to Henley. The people here bear no resemblance to those of Witney. I found a wild staring congregation, many of them void both of common sense and common decency. I spoke exceeding plain to them all and reproved some of them sharply. Fri. 20. I took (probably my final)[8] leave of Henley and returned to London.

Mon. 23. I rode to Sundon and preached in the evening to a very quiet and very stupid people. How plain is it that even to enlighten the understanding is beyond the power of man! After all our preaching here, even those who have constantly attended, no more understand us than if we had preached in Greek.

Thur. 26. Returning from Bedford, I tried another way to reach them. I preached on 'Where their worm dieth not, and their fire is not quenched',[9] and set before them the terrors of the Lord in the strongest manner I was able. It seemed to be the very thing they wanted. They not only listened with the deepest attention, but appeared to be more affected than I had ever seen them by any discourse whatever.

Wednesday, February 1. I buried the remains of William Hurd,[10] a son of affliction for many years, continually struggling with inward and outward trials. But his end was peace.

Thursday, February 2. I preached again in the Foundery, which had been repairing for several weeks. It is not only firm and safe (whereas before, the main timbers were quite destroyed) but clean and decent, and capable of receiving several hundreds more.[11]

Sun. 5. I began Mr. Hartley's ingenious 'Defence of the Mystic

[7] Witney was a substantial market town and parish, noted for the manufacture of blankets, 10 miles west of Oxford.

[8] The Journal records further visits to Henley on Nov. 7, 1768; and Oct. 16, 1769; and the diary visits on Oct. 10, 1785; and Oct. 26, 1789.

[9] Mark 9:44, etc.

[10] See above, Jan. 28, 1758, n. 32.

[11] Charles Wesley put the additional accommodation at five or six hundred, but then he wildly exaggerated the existing accommodation 'to above five thousand'. *CWJ*, 2:245.

Writers'.[12] But it does not satisfy *me.* I must still object (1) to their *sentiments.* The chief of them do not appear to me to have any conception of Church communion. Again, they slight not only works of piety, the ordinances of God, but even works of mercy. And yet most of them, yea, all that I have seen, hold justification by works. In general, they are 'wise above what is written',[13] indulging themselves in many unscriptural speculations. I object (2) to their *spirit,* that most of them are of a dark, shy, reserved, unsociable temper. And that they are apt to *despise* all who differ from them as carnal, unenlightened men. I object (3) to their whole *phraseology.* It is both unscriptural and affectedly mysterious. I say, 'affectedly'. For this does not necessarily result from the nature of the things spoken of. St. John speaks as high and as deep things as Jacob Behmen. Why then does not Jacob speak as plain as him?

Mon. 6. I opened the New Chapel at Wapping, well-filled with deeply attentive hearers. Thur. 16. I once more took a serious walk through the tombs in Westminster Abbey. What heaps of unmeaning stone and marble! But there was one tomb which showed common sense—that beautiful figure of Mr. Nightingale, endeavouring to screen his lovely wife from *death.*[14] Here indeed the marble seems to *speak,* and statues appear only not *alive.*

After taking Brentford, Deptford, Welling, and Sevenoaks, in my way, on Thursday 23, I rode to Sir Thomas I'Anson's[15] (at New Bounds, two miles beyond Tunbridge), just quivering on the verge of life, helpless as a child, but (as it seems) greatly

[12] Thomas Hartley, *Paradise Restored: or, A Testimony to the Doctrine of the Blessed Millenium, with some considerations on its approaching advent from the signs of the times. To which is added, A Short Defence of the Mystical Writers* (London, 1764). Hartley (*c.* 1709–84), rector of Winwick, Northants., 1744–70, had been regarded as one of the evangelical clergy, to be mentioned in the same breath as Hervey and Baddeley, and the present work was in a sense one of the evangelical replies to Warburton (Seymour, *Huntingdon,* 1:167). Before the decade was out, he had commenced his life's work as a translator and expositor of Swedenborg. On Mar. 27, 1764, JW expostulated to him in a private letter subscribed 'your still affectionate brother'. Telford, 4:234-35.

[13] Cf. 1 Cor. 4:6.

[14] Lady Elizabeth Nightingale was the eldest sister of the Countess of Huntingdon; it is clear from other comment that JW was much affected by Roubiliac's sculpture (see Feb. 25, 1771). Pevsner, who quotes JW on this work more than once, is less enthusiastic: 'One may grumble at so sensational effect in so noble and restrained a building, and also from the Christian point of view, at such a cruel representation of the grave's victory and death's sting,' but adds, 'whatever one's reaction to the conceit, on the sculptural mastery there can be no two voices.' Pevsner, *London,* 1:381, 410.

[15] See above, Feb. 21, 1761, n. 73.

profited by this severe dispensation. The hall, staircase, and adjoining rooms, just contained the people in the evening. One poor backslider, whom Providence had brought thither, was exceedingly wounded. I left her resolved to set out once more, if haply God might heal her.

Fri. 24. I returned to London. Wed. 29. I heard *Judith*, an oratorio performed at the Lock.[16] Some parts of it were exceeding fine. But there are two things in all modern pieces of music which I could never reconcile to common sense: one is singing the same words ten times over; the other, singing different words by different persons at one and the same time. And this in the most solemn addresses to God, whether by way of prayer or of thanksgiving. This can never be defended, by all the musicians in Europe, till reason is quite out of date.

Monday, March 12. I set out for Bristol. Fri. 16. I met several serious clergymen. I have long desired that there might be an open, avowed union between all who preach those fundamental truths, original sin and justification by faith, producing inward and outward holiness. But all my endeavours have been hitherto ineffectual.[17] God's time is not fully come.

Mon. 19. I set out for the north. We reached Stroud about two in the afternoon. How many years were we beating the air in this place! One wrong-headed man pulling down all we could build up. But since he is gone, the Word of God takes root, and the society increases both in number and strength. Tue. 20. At seven I preached in Painswick. For many years an honest, disputing man, greatly hindered the work of God here also, subverting the souls that were just setting out for heaven. But since God took him to himself, his Word has free course, and many sinners are

[16] Madan (who introduced elaborate music in the services at the Lock Hospital, Hyde Park Corner, to which he was chaplain) and Haweis arranged an annual performance of oratorio there, which JW attended in this and the following year (below, Feb. 13, 1765). *Judith*, a work by Thomas Arne, had been first performed in 1761 and, though affording the first occasion in England for the admittance of women singers to the chorus, was not a success. Sadie, Stanley, eds., *The New Grove Dictionary of Music and Musicians*, 20 vols. (London, Macmillan, 1980), 11:452.

[17] This was an episode in the campaign Wesley had been waging since 1758 to unite considerable numbers of evangelical clergy behind his movement, a campaign which had been energetically supported since the last Conference by Howell Harris. After a conversation with the Countess of Huntingdon and a visit to Dr. Richard Conyers at Helmsley, he wrote a circular to evangelical clergy on Apr. 19, 1764 (Telford, 4:235-39). His hopes continued high till 1766, when a printed circular based on this letter elicited only three replies. For a fuller account of this subject, see Frank Baker, *John Wesley and the Church of England* (London, Epworth Press, 1970), pp. 180-96.

converted to him. We rode hence over the top of the bleak mountains to Stanley, where an earnest congregation was waiting. From Stanley to Evesham we were to go as we could, the lanes being scarce passable. However, at length we got through. I never before saw so quiet a congregation in the town hall, nor yet so numerous. I designed afterwards to meet the society at our room. But the people were so eager to hear, that I knew not how to keep them out. So we had a large congregation again. And again God gave us his blessing.

Wed. 21. After riding about two hours and an half from Evesham, we stopped at a little village. We easily perceived, by the marks he had left, that the man of the house had been beating his wife. I took occasion from thence to speak strongly to her concerning the hand of God and his design in all afflictions. It seemed to be a word in season. She appeared to be not only thankful, but deeply affected.

We had an exceeding large congregation at Birmingham, in what was formerly the play-house.[18] Happy would it be if all the play-houses in the kingdom were converted to so good an use. After service, the mob gathered, and threw some dirt and stones at those who were going out. But it is probable, they will soon be calmed, as some of them are in jail already. A few endeavoured to make a disturbance the next evening during the preaching. But it was lost labour—the congregation *would* not be diverted from 'taking earnest heed to the things that were spoken'.[19]

Fri. 23. I rode to Dudley, formerly a den of lions,[20] but now as quiet as Bristol. They had just finished their preaching-house, which was thoroughly filled; and I saw no trifler, but many in tears. Here I met with a remarkable account of a child, the substance of which was as follows.

> John B——, about ten years old, was some time since taken ill. He often asked how it was to die. His sister told him, 'Some children know God. And then they are not afraid to die.' He said, 'What, children as little as me?' She answered, 'Your sister Patty

[18] The Birmingham circuit enjoyed a considerable revival in 1763, and hired the theatre off Moor Street. As it was still some time before protection from magistrates could be obtained, they suffered continuous violence from the mob. Sheldon, *Birmingham*, pp. 21-22.

[19] Cf. Heb. 2:1.

[20] For an account of the early violence at Dudley, see *Wesleyan Methodist Magazine* 46 (1823):569.

did, and she was less than you'—at which he seemed to be much affected. Sunday was fortnight he took his bed, but was not able to sleep. Soon after, he said, 'We shall soon be with angels and archangels in heaven. What signifies this wicked world? Who would want to live here that might live with Christ?' The maid said, 'I wish I was married to Christ.' He said, 'Being married to Christ is coming to Christ and keeping with him. All may come to him. I'm happy, I'm happy.' His sister asked, 'Do you love God?' He answered, 'Yes, that I do.' She asked, 'And do you think God loves *you?*' He replied, 'Yes, I know he does.'

The next evening she said, 'How are you, Jacky, when you are so happy?' He said, stroking his breast down with his hand, 'Why, like as if God was in me. O my sister, what an happy thing it was that I came to Dudley! I am quite happy when I am saying my prayers. And when I think on God, I can almost see into heaven.'

Tuesday night last she asked, 'Are you afraid to die?' He said, 'I have seen the time that I was. But now I am not a bit afraid of death, or hell, or judgment, for Christ is mine. I know Christ is my own. He says, What would you have? I would get to heaven, I will get to heaven as soon as I can. And as well as I love you all, when I am once got to heaven, I would not come to you again for ten thousand worlds.' Soon after, he said, 'If God would let me do as the angels do, I would come and watch over you. I will, if God will let me; and when you are ready I will come and fetch you to heaven. Yea, if God would let me, I would fly all over the world to fetch souls to heaven.'

He asked his cousin if she had 'seen the king'. And added, 'I have. Indeed I have not seen King George, but I have seen a better king—for I have seen the King of heaven and earth.' His health since that time has been in some measure recovered. But he continues in the same spirit.

Sat. 24. We came once more to our old flock at Wednesbury. The congregation differed from most that we have lately seen. It almost entirely consisted of such as had 'repented', if not also 'believed the gospel'.[21] Sunday 25, at eight, I preached in the room, though it would by no means contain the congregation. But the north-east wind was so extremely sharp that it was not practicable to preach abroad. At one it drove us likewise into the house at Darlaston[22]—that is, as many as it would contain. At five there was such a congregation at Wednesbury as I have not seen since I left London. But I found my voice would have

[21] Cf. Mark 1:15.

[22] Built in 1760. Jackson, *Early Methodist Preachers*, 2:179.

commanded twice the number, while I declared, 'The word is nigh thee, even in thy mouth and in thy heart; that is, the word of faith which we preach.'[23]

Mon. 26. I was desired to preach at Walsall. James Jones was alarmed at the motion,[24] apprehending there would be much disturbance. However, I determined to make the trial. Coming into the house, I met with a token for good. A woman was telling her neighbour why she came. 'I had a desire', said she, 'to hear this man, yet I durst not, because I heard so much ill of him. But this morning I dreamed I was praying earnestly, and I heard a voice saying, "See the eighth verse of the first chapter of St. John." I waked, and got my Bible and read, "He was not that light, but was sent to bear witness of that light." I got up and came away with all my heart.'

The house not being capable of containing the people, about seven I began preaching abroad. And there was no opposer, no, nor a trifler to be seen. All present were earnestly attentive. How is Walsall changed! How has God either tamed the wild beasts, or chained them up!

In the afternoon, I came to Ashby-de-la-Zouch. The house and yard contained the people tolerably well. I saw but one trifler among all, which I understood was an attorney. Poor man! If men *live* what I *preach*, 'the hope of' his 'gain is lost'.[25]

Wed. [i.e., Tue.] 27. We rode to Donnington, where a great multitude earnestly attended while I explained and enforced, 'God forbid that I should glory, save in the cross of our Lord Jesus Christ.'[26]

Hence, we rode to Derby. Mr. Dobinson[27] believed it would be best for me to preach in the market-place, as there seemed to be a general inclination in the town, even among the people of fashion, to hear me. He had mentioned it to the mayor, who said he did not 'apprehend there would be the least disturbance. But if there should be anything of the kind', he would 'take care to suppress it.' A multitude of people were gathered at five and were pretty quiet till I had named my text. Then 'the beasts of the people'[28] lifted up their voice, hollowing and shouting on every side.

[23] Rom. 10:8.

[24] I.e., 'proposal'. On James Jones, see Feb. 18, 1744, n. 44 (20:10 in this edn.).

[25] Cf. Acts 16:19.

[26] Gal. 6:14.

[27] On Dobinson, see above, Aug. 16, 1762, n. 67.

[28] Ps. 68:30 (BCP).

Finding it impossible to be heard, I walked softly away. An innumerable retinue followed me. But only a few pebble-stones were thrown, and no one hurt at all. Most of the rabble followed quite to Mr. D[obinson]'s house, but it seems, without any malice prepense.[29] For they stood stock still about an hour, and then quietly went away.

At seven, I met the society, with many others who earnestly desired to be present. In the morning, most of them came again with as many more as we could well make room for. And indeed they received the word gladly. God grant they may bring forth fruit!

Thur. [i.e., Wed.] 28. Between eleven and twelve, I preached at Alfreton,[30] twelve miles from Derby, and in the evening at Sheffield,[31] to many more than could hear, on 'Now is the day of salvation.'[32] In the morning, I gave an hearing to several of the society who were extremely angry at each other.[33] It surprised me to find what trifles they had stumbled at. But I hope their snare is broken.

In the evening, while I was enlarging upon 'the righteousness of faith',[34] the Word of God was quick and powerful. Many felt it in their inmost souls, one backslider in particular, who was then restored to all she had lost and, the next morning, believed she was *saved from sin.*

[29] Orig., 'propense', altered in *Works* (1774).

[30] Orig., 'Alferton'. Alfreton was a market town and parish 14 miles north-east of Derby.

[31] JW's base in Sheffield at this time was provided by Thomas Robinson, a manufacturer, who in 1763 had engaged in press controversy on the doctrine of assurance with an assistant minister at Sheffield, Rev. George Bayliffe (J. Hunter, *Hallamshire*, ed. A. Gatty [London, 1869], p. 272). In 1764, he moved away to Bridlington where he died in 1815, aged about 83. *Wesleyan Methodist Magazine* 49 (1826):295, 368-69.

[32] 2 Cor. 6:2.

[33] Ill will had gathered round JW's preacher in Sheffield, Thomas Bryant, who had entered the itinerancy in 1759. Himself an active outdoor evangelist, Bryant endeavoured to put down revivalism in the select band and, being among those ordained by the Greek bishop, Erasmus in 1763, refused to preach except in a gown and began to administer the sacraments (Tyerman MSS 3, fols. 22-23). Despite the satisfaction here expressed at his diplomacy, JW had concluded by July that Bryant must be got out of Sheffield and during the next few months ended his connexion with him (letters of July 5, 1764, and Jan. 13, 1765; Telford 4:288, 252). Bryant, however, took 'half of the Sheffield society . . . and some of the principal members', and the Scotland Street church was built for him there. In 1796, the year before he died, Bryant divided his congregation again by giving hospitality to Alexander Kilham, who succeeded him as pastor and brought the chapel back into the main current of Methodist history as the mother church of the New Connexion. *WHS* 21 (1938):113-15; 29 (1953):21.

[34] Rom. 4:13.

Fri. 30. I met those who believe God has 'redeemed' them 'from all their sins'.[35] They are about sixty in number. I could not learn that any among them walk unworthy of their profession. Many watch over them for evil, but they overcome evil with good.[36] I found nothing of self-conceit, stubbornness, impatience of contradiction, or London enthusiasm among them. They have better learned of him that was meek and lowly of heart,[37] to 'adorn the doctrine of God their Saviour'.[38]

In the evening, I preached in the new house at Rotherham on the sure foundation, 'Ye are saved through faith.'[39] It was a season of strong consolation to many. One who had been some time groaning for full redemption, now found power to believe that God had fulfilled her desire and set her heart at liberty.

Sat. 31. An odd circumstance occurred during the morning preaching. It was well only serious people were present. An ass walked gravely in at the gate, came up to the door of the house, lifted up his head, and stood stock still, in a posture of deep attention. Might not 'the dumb beast reprove'[40] many who have far less decency and not much more understanding?

At noon, I preached (the room being too small to contain the people)[41] in a yard near the bridge in Doncaster. The wind was high and exceeding sharp, and blew all the time on the side of my head. In the afternoon I was seized with a sore throat almost as soon as I came to Epworth. However, I preached, though with some difficulty; but afterward I could hardly speak. Being better the next day, Sunday, April 1, I preached about one at Westwoodside, and soon after four in the market-place at Epworth to a numerous congregation. At first, indeed, but few could hear. But the more I spoke, the more my voice was strengthened, till toward the close all my pain and weakness were gone, and all could hear distinctly.

Mon. 2. I had a day of rest. Tuesday 3, I preached about nine at Scotter,[42] a town six or seven miles east of Epworth, where a

[35] Cf. Ps. 130:8 (BCP).

[36] See Rom. 12:21.

[37] See Matt. 11:29.

[38] Cf. Titus 2:10.

[39] Eph. 2:8 (*Notes*).

[40] Cf. 2 Pet. 2:16 (*Notes*).

[41] The small society at Doncaster had moved from a private house to a small rented room in the Old Falcon-Yard, Marsh-Gate, in 1763. *Wesleyan Methodist Magazine* 51 (1828):740.

[42] Scotter was a parish 9 miles north-east of Gainsborough.

sudden flame is broke out, many being convinced of sin almost at once, and many justified. But there were many adversaries stirred up by a bad man who told them,[43] 'There is no law for Methodists.' Hence, continual riots followed, till after a while an upright magistrate[44] took the cause in hand, and so[45] managed both the rioters and him who set them at work that they have been quiet as lambs ever since.

Hence we rode to Grimsby, once the most dead, now the most lively, place in all the county. Here has been a large and swift increase both of the society and hearers, so that the house, though galleries are added, is still too small. In the morning, Wednesday 4, I explained at large the nature of Christian perfection. Many who had doubted of it before were fully satisfied. It remains only to *experience* what we believe.

In the evening, the mayor and all the gentry of the town were present. And so was our Lord in an uncommon manner. Some dropped down as dead, but after a while rejoiced with joy unspeakable.[46] One was carried away in violent fits. I went to her after the service. She was strongly convulsed from head to foot and shrieked out in a dreadful manner. The unclean spirit did tear her indeed, but his reign was not long. In the morning both her soul and body were healed, and she acknowledged both the justice and mercy of God.

Thur. 5. About eleven, I preached at Elsham.[47] The two persons who are the most zealous and active here are the steward and gardener of a gentleman, whom the minister persuaded to turn them off unless they would leave 'this way'.[48] He gave them a week to consider of it, at the end of which they calmly answered, 'Sir, we choose rather to want bread here than to want "a drop of water" hereafter.' He replied, 'Then follow your own conscience, so you do my business as well as formerly.'

Fri. 6. I preached at Ferry at nine in the morning, and in the evening; and about noon in Sir N[evil] H[ickman]'s[49] hall at

[43] Orig., 'But there are . . . who tells them', altered in errata and MS notes to *Works* (1774).

[44] Probably Sir Nevil Hickman of Gainsborough; see above, Aug. 3, 1759, n. 39; and below, Apr. 6, 1764; and Apr. 23, 1766.

[45] 'So' added only in *Works* (1774).

[46] See 1 Pet. 1:8.

[47] Elsham was a small parish on the Wolds, 2¾ miles north-west of Barnetby le Wold.

[48] Acts 9:2.

[49] Orig., 'Sir——'s', enlarged in *Works* (1774) to 'Sir N. H's'.

Gainsborough. Almost as soon as I began to speak a cock began to crow over my head. But he was quickly dislodged, and the whole congregation, rich and poor, were quiet and attentive.

Sun. 8. I set out for Misterton, though the common road was impassable, being all under water. But we found a way to ride round. I preached at eight, and I saw not one inattentive hearer. In our return, my mare rushing violently through a gate, struck my heel against the gate-post and left me behind her in an instant, laid on my back at full length. She stood still till I rose and mounted again, and neither of us was hurt at all.

Mon. 9. I had designed to go by Althorpe[50] Ferry and Winterton to Hull. But we had not gone far before the wind rose so, that we judged it would be impossible to pass the Trent at Althorpe. So we turned back and went by Owston[51] and Brigg.[52] The rain beat vehemently upon us all the way. When we came to Brigg, despairing of being able to cross the Humber, we thought it best to turn aside to Barrow. When I was here last, the mob was exceeding rude and noisy. But all the people were now quiet and attentive. I was much pleased with their spirit and their behaviour and could not be sorry for the storm.

Tue. 10. The wind abating, we took boat at Barton with two such brutes as I have seldom seen. Their blasphemy and stupid, gross obscenity were beyond all I ever heard. We first spoke to them mildly, but it had no effect. At length we were constrained to rebuke them sharply, and they kept themselves tolerably within bounds till we landed at Hull. I preached at five, two hours sooner than was expected. By this means we had tolerable room for the greatest part of them that came. And I believe not many of them came in vain.

Wed. 11. Between eight and nine, I began preaching at Beverley in a room which is newly taken. It was filled from end to end, and that with serious hearers. Perhaps even these may know the day of their visitation.[53]

About one, I began at Pocklington. Here likewise, all were quiet and listened with deep attention. When I came to York at five in the afternoon, I was fresher than at seven in the morning.

[50] Orig., 'Authorp'. Althorpe was a parish on the Trent, 4½ miles south-east of Crowle.

[51] Orig., 'Ouston', now Owston Ferry.

[52] Brigg, or Glandford Bridge, was a market town and chapelry in the parish of Wrawby, 24 miles north of Lincoln.

[53] See Isa. 10:3; Luke 19:44.

During the preaching, many were not a little comforted, and one old follower of Christ, more than seventy years of age, was now first enabled to 'call' him 'Lord'[54] by the Holy Ghost.

I found that a most remarkable deadness had overspread this people, insomuch that not one had received remission of sins for several months last past. Then it is high time for us to prophesy on these dry bones, that they may live.[55] At this I more immediately pointed in all my following discourses. And I have reason to believe, God spoke in his Word—to him be all the glory!

Thur. 12. I spent an hour with John Manners,[56] weak in body, but not[57] in spirit. He is fairly worn out in good service and calmly waits till his change shall come.

Sun. 15. In the evening, many even of the rich were present and seriously attentive. But Oh! how hardly shall these enter into the kingdom![58] How hardly escape from 'the desire of other things'![59]

Mon. 16. I preached at Tollerton[60] at one. The congregation was large and serious. Some were deeply affected and wept much. Many received comfort.

At six, I began preaching in the street at Thirsk. The congregation was exceeding large. Just as I named my text, 'What is a man profited if he shall gain the whole world and lose his own soul,'[61] a man on horseback, who had stopped to see what was the matter, changed colour and trembled. Probably he might have resolved to save his soul, had not his drunken companion dragged him away.

Tue. 17. In consequence of repeated invitations, I rode to Helmsley. When I came, Mr. Conyers[62] was not at home, but his

[54] Cf. 1 Cor. 12:3.

[55] See Ezek. 37:4-5.

[56] On John Manners, who died a few days later, see above, July 26, 1762, n. 41; and below, Apr. 28, 1764.

[57] Orig., 'hot', corrected in *Works* (1774).

[58] See Matt. 19:23, etc.

[59] Mark 4:19 (*Notes*).

[60] Tollerton, N. Yorks., was a small township in the parish of Alne, 4½ miles south from Easingwold.

[61] Matt. 16:26.

[62] Orig., 'H——' and 'Mr. ——'. More clues were offered in *Works* (1774): 'H——y' and 'Mr. C.', extended in the errata and MS notes to 'Hemsley' and 'Mr. Conyers'. (E. Perronet MS incorrectly guessed at 'Huddersfield' and 'Mr. Venn'). Richard Conyers (1725–86), scholar of Jesus College, Cambridge, 1745–46; M.A., 1749; LL.D., 1767; vicar of Helmsley, 1756–75; rector of Kirby Misperton, 1763–68; vicar of St. Paul's, Deptford, 1775–86. Conyers, a zealous and effective clergyman, suffered from a spiritual malaise from which he was delivered by a conversion experience on Christmas Day 1758.

housekeeper faintly asking me, I went in. By the books lying in the window and on the table, I easily perceived how he came to be so cold now, who was so warm a year ago. Not one of ours, either verse or prose, was to be seen, but several of another kind. O that our brethren were as zealous to make *Christians* as they are to make *Calvinists!*

He came home before dinner and soon convinced me that *the Philistines* had been upon him.[63] They had taken huge pains to prejudice him against *me,* and so successfully that he did not even ask me to preach. So I had thoughts of going on. But in the afternoon he altered his purpose, and I preached in the evening to a large congregation. He seemed quite surprised and was convinced *for the present* that things had been misrepresented. But how long will the conviction last? Perhaps till next summer.[64]

Wed. 18. I called upon another serious clergyman, vicar of a little town near Pickering.[65] He immediately told me how he had been received by warm men to 'doubtful disputations'.[66] He said, this had for a time much hurt his soul, but that now the snare was broken.

About one, I preached at Snainton,[67] eight or nine miles beyond Pickering, to a small but deeply serious congregation. When I came to Scarborough, though the wind was very high and very sharp, the multitude of people constrained me to preach abroad. And all but a few noisy children behaved remarkably well.

Thur. 19. The room was filled at five. And the congregation this evening was larger than the last. How is the face of things changed here within a year or two! The society increased fourfold; most of them alive to God, and many *filled* with love. And all of them enjoy great quietness instead of noise and tumult, since God put it into the heart of an honest magistrate to 'still the madness of the people'.[68]

His ministry in a widely scattered parish was then notably blessed; within a few months he was in touch with JW, was one of the evangelical clergy from whom the latter hoped much, and on June 7, 1763, assured him that 'my house and heart are, and ever shall be, open to you' (Tyerman, *John Wesley*, 2:335-36, 473). As the present entry shows, this affection speedily cooled; however, see Feb. 17, 1783.

63 See Judg. 16:9, etc.

64 *Works* (1774), 'next month'.

65 Middleton, N. Yorks; cf. July 16, 1766. The vicar from 1763 till his death in 1782 was John King.

66 Rom. 14:1.

67 Snainton was a chapelry mostly in the parish of Brompton 9½ miles south-west from Scarborough.

68 Cf. Ps. 65:7 (BCP).

I wrote a letter today, which after some time I sent to forty or fifty clergymen,[69] with the little preface annexed:

[69] Curnock identified thirty-seven of these, of whom those not already identified were as follows (Curnock, 5:62-63, n. 2):

William Jesse, perpetual curate of West Bromwich, 1790–1814; matriculated from Trinity College, Oxford, 1757; B.A.,1761. In 1771, he was in Lincolnshire, described by Venn as 'a very excellent man, and seems appointed to evangelize the Wolds, the inhabitants of which are dark almost as the Indians.' He preached much for the Countess of Huntingdon, but withdrew from her connexion when the Spitalfields case led her to register her chapels as Dissenting chapels. He was appointed to West Bromwich by the interest of the evangelical Earl of Dartmouth, and subsequently became rector of Dowles and Ribblesford, Worcs., and chaplain to the Earl of Glasgow. Seymour, *Huntingdon*, 1:487; 2:314.

Thomas Adam (1701–84), presented to the rectory of Wintringham, 1724. He published various works of evangelical divinity while his posthumous *Private Thoughts on Religion and Other Subjects* (2nd edn., 1795) continued to arouse interest even in non-evangelical circles after his death.

William Talbot (*c.* 1719–74), of aristocratic lineage, vicar of Kineton, presented by Lord Chancellor Camden to the vicarage of St. Giles, Reading, 1767–74, one of the best Crown livings. As vicar of Kineton he itinerated widely, often in the service of the Countess of Huntingdon. Matriculated from Exeter College, Oxford, in 1737; B.A. and M.A., 1744.

John Riland (1736–1822), matriculated from Queen's College, Oxford, 1754; B.A., 1752; M.A., 1760. Curate of Sutton Coldfield; curate to Henry Venn in Huddersfield, 1773; first vicar of St. Mary's (Anglican) chapel, Birmingham, 1774; rector of Sutton Coldfield (1790–1822), the family living.

Edward Stillingfleet (*c.* 1732–95), great grandson of the bishop, perpetual curate, vicar of West Bromwich, 1757–82, and chaplain to the Earl of Dartmouth. Fellow of Merton College. Seymour, *Huntingdon*, 1:39.

John Johnson, curate-vicar of Cirencester.

John Andrews (born *c.* 1730), matriculated at Trinity College, Oxford, 1748; B.C.L. from St. Mary Hall; vicar of Stinchcomb.

Joseph Jane (1716–95), educated Westminster School and Christ Church; B.A., 1737; B.D., 1748. Senior student and tutor of Christ Church to 1747 (Richard Hart was his pupil). Curate of Cowley, 1747; curate of St. Thomas's, Oxford, 1747–48; vicar of St. Mary Magdalen, Oxford, 1748–63, where Haweis was his curate, 1757–62. Rector of Iron Acton, Glos., 1763–89. J. S. Reynolds, *The Evangelicals at Oxford, 1735–1871* (Oxford, Blackwell, 1953), p. 172; *WHS* 23 (1942):105-6.

Richard Symes, matriculated from Hart Hall, Oxford, 1740, aged 18; B.A., 1744. Rector of St. Werburgh's, Bristol (James Rouquet was his curate).

James Brown (*c.* 1730–91), matriculated from Trinity College, Oxford, 1748; B.A., 1752. Usher of Bristol Grammar School, 1759–64; lecturer of St. Nicholas Church, Bristol, to 1764; chaplain to the Duke of Atholl. Curate of Bradford; rector of Portishead, 1764–91; and vicar of Kingston, 1771–91.

John Richardson (*c.* 1735–91). Grimshaw's successor as perpetual curate of Haworth from 1763, 'a man of polished manners, unaffected piety, and of a mild and amiable disposition', and son of Joseph Richardson of Tideswell, Derbys., gent. He matriculated from Queen's College, Oxford, in 1757, graduating B.A. in 1761, and M.A. in 1764. He was curate of Huddersfield in 1762.

George Barnett (1734–93), as an assistant master at Truro Grammar School, came under the influence of Samuel Walker and felt drawn to the ministry of the Established Church; he went up to Oxford with Haweis. Ordained *c.* 1758, he went to

Rev. Sir,

Near two years and an half ago I wrote the following letter. You will please to observe, (1) that I propose no more therein than is the bounden duty of every Christian; (2) that *you* may comply with this proposal whether any other does or not. I myself have endeavoured so to do for many years, though I have been almost alone therein and although many, the more earnestly I 'talk of peace', the more zealously 'make themselves ready for battle'.[70]

I am, Rev. sir,
Your affectionate brother,
John Wesley

Dear Sir,[71]

It has pleased God to give you both the will and the power to do many things for his glory (although you are often ashamed you have done so little, and wish you could do a thousand times more). This induces me to mention to you what has been upon my mind for many years, and what I am persuaded would be much for the glory

be Venn's curate at Huddersfield, 1759–60. After a period of ill health, he became vicar of Elland (1761–93) and later founded the Elland Society for educating evangelical candidates for the ministry.

Samuel Furly (1722–95). Son of a wealthy London merchant, he became a friend of Venn at Cambridge. Matriculated from Queen's College, 1754; B.A., 1758; after occasionally assisting Romaine, he became incumbent of Lakenheath, curate of Kippax (to Henry Crooke), where he became acquainted with the Countess of Huntingdon; curate of Slaithwaite, a chapelry of Huddersfield, 1761–67; through the Countess, presented by Henry Thornton of Clapham to Roche, 1766–95; differed from JW on issues such as assurance; his sister married John Downes (see July 18, 1743, n. 30; 19:329 in this edn.). He was said to be 'a Boanerges rather than a Barnabas'. Seymour, *Huntingdon*, 2:2; Hulbert, *Church in Slaithwaite*, pp. 72-86; see also *Evangelical Magazine* (July 1797).

Roger Bentley, perhaps assisted Crook at Kippax. Probably admitted sizar at Sidney, Sussex, 1753, age 19. May have died vicar of Camberwell, 1795.

John King (*c.* 1724–1812), rector of Pertonhall, Beds., 1752–1800; Cowper's school fellow and husband of his correspondent, Mrs. King.

John Richardson (1734–92), educated for the Church at St. John's College, Cambridge; B.A., 1756; served curacies at Leek, where he is said to have fallen into 'some levities inconsistent with his profession which he afterwards lamented with much sorrow' (Venn), Battle Abbey, and Ewhurst near Rye, where he made contact with a Methodist society and deepened his religious experience. Being removed from his curacy he joined JW in 1762. Said by Venn, apparently in error, to have been minister of the meeting-house in Artillery Lane, Spitalfields, till his death.

The first edition includes Henry Crook, vicar of Kippax, 1758–70, Jonas Eastwood (headmaster of Kingswood and later assistant curate at Dewsbury, 1755; curate of Cleckheaton, 1757; and vicar of Whitechapel near Leeds), and also G. W. (Whitefield). Perronet adds Cooper (perpetual curate of Bengeworth), John Harmer, Anglican clergyman who is said to have worked with JW, 1766–72, and became curate of St. James's, Warrington, 1777, and Gwen. *WHS* 8 (1911):83.

[70] Cf. Job 15:24.

[71] E. Perronet MS: 'This Letter was originally wrote to Lord Dartmouth'.

of God, if it could once be effected. And I am in great hopes it will be, if you heartily undertake it, trusting in him alone.

Some years since, God began a great work in England, but the labourers were few. At first those few were of one heart, but it was not so long. First one fell off, then another, and another, till no two of us were left together in the work beside my brother and me. This prevented much good and occasioned much evil. It grieved our spirits and weakened our hands. It gave our common enemies huge occasion to blaspheme. It perplexed and puzzled many sincere Christians. It caused many to draw back to perdition.[72] It grieved the Holy Spirit of God.

As labourers increased, disunion increased. Offences were multiplied. And instead of coming nearer to, they stood farther and farther off from each other, till at length those who are not only brethren in Christ, but fellow-labourers in his gospel, had no more connection or fellowship with each other than Protestants have with Papists.

But ought this to be? Ought not those who are united to one common head and employed by him in one common work, to be united to each other? I speak now of those labourers who are ministers of the Church of England. These are chiefly

Mr. Perronet, Romaine, Newton, Shirley;
Mr. Downing, Jesse, Adam;
Mr. Talbot, Ryland,[73] Stillingfleet, Fletcher;
Mr. Johnson, Baddeley,[74] Andrews, Jane;
Mr. Hart, Symes, Brown, Rouquet;
Mr. Sellon;[75]
Mr. Venn, Richardson, Burnett,[76] Furly, Crooke;[77]
Mr. Eastwood,[78] Conyers, Bentley,[79] King;
Mr. Berridge, Hicks, G[eorge] W[hitefield],[80] J[ohn] W[esley],[81] C[harles] W[esley], John Richardson, Benjamin Colley.[82]

Not excluding any other clergymen who agree in these essentials:

I. Original sin,
II. Justification by faith,
III. Holiness of heart and life—provided their life be answerable to their doctrine.

72 See Heb. 10:39.
73 Orig., 'Riland'.
74 Orig., 'Baddily'.
75 E. Perronet MS adds: 'Cooper, Harmer, Gwen'.
76 Orig., 'Burnet'.
77 Orig., 'Crook'; *Works* (1774) omits.
78 *Works* (1774) omits.
79 Orig., 'Bently'.
80 *Works* (1774) omits.
81 *Works* (1774) omits.
82 *Works* (1774) omits.

'But *what union* would you desire among these?' Not an union in *opinions.* They might agree or disagree touching absolute decrees on the one hand and perfection on the other. Not an union in *expressions.* These may still speak of the 'imputed righteousness', and those of the 'merits' of Christ. Not an union with regard to *outward order.* Some may still remain *quite regular,* some *quite irregular,* and some *partly regular* and *partly irregular.* But these things being as they are, as each is persuaded in his own mind, is it not a most desirable thing, that we should

1. Remove hindrances out of the way? Not *judge* one another, not *envy* one another? Not be *displeased* at one another's *gifts* or *success,* even though greater than our own? Not *wait* for one another's halting, much less *wish* for it, or *rejoice* therein?

Never *speak* disrespectfully, slightly, coldly, or unkindly of each other; never *repeat* each other's faults, mistakes, or infirmities, much less *listen* for and *gather* them up; never say or do anything to hinder each other's usefulness, either directly or indirectly.

Is it not a most desirable thing that we should

2. *Love as brethren? Think well* of and *honour* one another? *Wish* all good, all grace, all gifts, all success, yea, greater than our own, to each other? *Expect* God will answer our wish, *rejoice* in every appearance thereof, and *praise* him for it? *Readily believe* good of each other, as readily as we once believed evil?

Speak respectfully, honourably, kindly of each other; *defend* each other's character; speak all the good we can of each other; recommend one another where we have influence; each *help* the other on in his work and *enlarge* his influence by all the honest means he[83] can.

This is the *union* which I have long sought after. And is it not the duty of every one of us so to do? Would it not be far better for *ourselves?* A means of promoting both our holiness and happiness? Would it not remove much *guilt* from those who have been faulty in any of these instances? And much *pain* from those who have kept themselves pure? Would it not be far better for the *people?* Who suffer severely from the clashings and contentions of their leaders. Which seldom fail to occasion many unprofitable, yea, hurtful disputes among them. Would it not be better even for the poor, blind *world,* robbing them of their sport, 'Oh, they cannot agree among themselves'? Would it not be better for the *whole work* of God, which would then deepen and widen on every side?

'But it will never be; it is utterly impossible.' Certainly it is *with men.* Who imagines *we* can do this? That it can be effected by any *human power?* All *nature* is against it, every infirmity, every *wrong*

[83] Orig., 'we', revised in the errata and MS notes to Works (1774).

temper and *passion;* love of honour and praise, of power, of pre-eminence; anger, resentment, pride; long-contracted habit, and prejudice lurking in ten thousand forms. The *devil* and all his angels are against it. For if this takes place, how shall his kingdom stand? All *the world*, all that know not God, are against it, though they may seem to favour it for a season. Let us settle this in our hearts, that we may be utterly cut off from all dependence on our own strength or wisdom.

But surely 'with God all things are possible.'[84] Therefore 'all things are possible to him that believeth.'[85] And this union is proposed only to them that believe, that show *their* faith by *their* works.

When Mr. C[onyers] was objecting the impossibility of ever effecting such an union, I went upstairs and, after a little prayer, opened Kempis on these words:

> *Expecta Dominum, viriliter age, [et confortare]; noli diffidere, noli discedere; sed corpus et animam expone constanter pro gloria Dei.*[86]

I am, dear sir,
Your affectionate servant,
J. W.

Scarborough,
April 19, 1764

I received three letters[87] in answer to this (though not at the same time), part of which I gladly subjoin.

Dear Sir,

I am not insensible of the happy consequences it might produce if 'those who agree in preaching that capital doctrine, "By grace ye are saved through faith," would maintain a free intercourse with

[84] Matt. 19:26.

[85] Mark 9:23.

[86] Kempis, *De imitatione Christi*, III.xxxv.3. Wesley's text is that of Rosweid (1634) and Merler (1682), both editions which Wesley himself used, not that of Castellio—he omits the phrase inserted in square brackets (see *Bibliography*, No. 4). His own 1735 revision of Worthington's translation of the passage reads: 'Wait upon the Lord, do manfully, be of good courage, do not despair, do not fly, but with constancy expose both *body* and *soul* for the glory of God.' It is probable that along with his Greek New Testament, Wesley carried his own Latin *Imitatio* around with him, along with other works, though a copy may well have been available in Conyers's study. The context, however, suggests that this was his personal copy and that it was used along with his New Testament for bibliomancy.

[87] Perhaps some of the others had been at the consultation JW had held on March 16 and felt no need to report their advice. JW's dismissal of the whole group in the *Minutes*, however, was crisp and entirely cavalier: 'only three vouchsafed me an answer. So I give this up. I can do no more. They are a rope of sand and such they will continue.' *Minutes of Conference* (1769), p. 87.

each other'. And if it could by any means be accomplished, it is doubtless an event most devoutly to be wished. It is what I always have shown the greatest readiness to, and what I have laboured at, for these several years past, within my little sphere; and though my success hitherto, through causes which I will not pretend to assign, has by no means equalled my hopes; yet I shall heartily rejoice if at length it may please God to make you the instrument of effecting so important a design. For my own part, I despise no man for his opinion; however, I may be most closely attached (as everyone is) to those whose judgment most nearly harmonizes with my own. And if I can bear anything, it is contradiction; so long as I am allowed the common liberty of answering for myself, without being treated with reproach or scorn for any heterodox notions I may be supposed to maintain.

I shall very gladly go halfway to London at any time to give a meeting to a number of ministers of any denomination that may be brought together with this pious intention; and, I think, I may answer for Mr. Johnson's concurrence.[88] Will you forgive me if for once I presume to suggest what (I apprehend) may be most conducive on such an occasion to our general profit and edification?

(1) Let one of the books of the New Testament be made choice of previous to our interview, for the subject of our conference when we meet; not with a view of displaying our critical talents on every word or verse that occurs, but of pointing out those things which necessarily enter into the plan of apostolical preaching. (2) Let everyone settle this in his heart beforehand, to expect contradiction, at the same time resolving to bear it calmly for the Lord's sake; and seeing we naturally carry about us an accursed spirit[89] of selfishness, pride, and impatience, that is ready to take fire at the most trivial offence, let us make it a point beforehand, daily to lament this our wretchedness of disposition at the throne of grace, earnestly beseeching the Lord to prepare us all for our intended conference, by enduing us with the spirit of meekness, forbearance, humility, and love. (3) Let everyone consent to renounce any favourite phrase, term, or mode of speech, that is not scriptural, if required so to do by those who dissent from him. Because whatever doctrine cannot maintain its ground, without the aid of humanly-invented words, is not of God.

I have unbosomed myself to you in the frankest manner, with a view to promote that happy intercourse which you wish to establish; and if you imagine it will answer any good purpose, you are

[88] John Johnson, curate of Cirencester.
[89] 1789 omits, 'we naturally . . . spirit'.

welcome to show this letter to any of the ministers you have had in your eye, and to disclose to them largely all you know of,

Dear sir,
Your affectionate friend and brother,
R[ichard] H[art][90]

Reverend and dear Sir,

I received your printed letter and should rejoice to see the union proposed therein to take place. But I must own I am an infidel concerning it. Daily experience convinces me more and more, that[91] the zeal for opinions and charity, *non bene conveniunt, nec in*[92] *una sede morantur.*[93] It has well-nigh destroyed all Christian love, zeal, and holiness among us. I have met with greater trials from these bigots within this twelvemonth than I have met with from all other opposers for fifteen years. Many that once would almost have plucked out their own eyes and given them to me, they are now ready to pluck out my eyes.

I really am tired of preaching to an ungrateful, gainsaying people. Pray for me, dear sir, for my hands hang down exceedingly.

I am your unworthy brother,
W[alter] S[ellon][94]

Shoreham

My reverend and dear Brother,

Yours of the 15th instant gave me both pain and pleasure.

I was highly delighted with your ardent wishes and endeavours for promoting the *spirit* of the *gospel* among the *preachers* and other *professors* of it, . . . but deeply concerned at the disappointment and opposition you have met with!

It has been always a *leading principle* with me (and I pray God confirm and strengthen it more and more) to *love* all those *labourers of Christ* who give proof by their *diligence,* their *holy* and *heavenly behaviour,* that they *love our Lord Jesus Christ in sincerity;* even though *their sentiments,* in many things, should differ from *mine.*

And therefore, though it be *absurd* to expect an entire *union*

[90] See Wesley's letter of May 16, 1764, to Lady Huntingdon, in response to a copy of the circular letter sent to her: 'I am much obliged to your Ladyship for your encouraging answer. . . . I have likewise received an exceeding friendly letter from Mr. Hart.' On Richard Hart, see above, Sept. 27, 1759, n. 73.

[91] *Works* (1774), here adds 'that' to the original.

[92] Orig., '*iri*', the misprint corrected only in the errata and MS notes to *Works* (1774).

[93] 'Do not well agree, and never remain together in the same place' (Thomas Jackson's trans.).

[94] E. Perronet MS: 'Sellon'.

of sentiments in all things, . . . yet the endeavouring, by every Christian method, to *keep the union of the Spirit in the bond of peace* . . . is the indispensable duty of all Christians. Where this *spiritual peace and union* are not, . . . there *faith working by love* . . . is not; and where this *divine faith* is wanting, . . . there *Christ* is *wanting;* there his *spirit* is *wanting;* and then, *neither circumcision* nor *uncircumcision will avail us anything!*

In this melancholy situation, whilst we are strangers to the *divine fruits* of the *Holy Spirit,* . . . let our *gifts* and *talents* be what they may; . . . let us *speak with the tongues of men and of angels;* we are yet *nothing* in the sight of God! Nay, though his *Spirit* should spread the *gospel* by our ministry in the hearts of thousands, yet our own souls will remain but a *barren wilderness!* And *Christ* may say, . . . '*I never knew you.*'

How ought we therefore always to pray . . . that the *peace of God may ever rule in our hearts;* . . . that we may be *rooted and grounded in love;* and that we may constantly *follow after the things which make for peace and things wherewith one may edify another!*

This is the *gospel of Jesus Christ!* And may God impress it thoroughly upon the *minds and hearts* of all! . . . And may the poor *despised flock grow in grace and in the knowledge of our Lord and Saviour Jesus Christ!*

I am, dear sir,
Yours most affectionately,
Vin. Perronet[95]

April 20, being Good Friday, we had a parting blessing at five. I then rode to Robin Hood's Bay and, about two, preached in the little square. A poor madman, literally such, came up to me just as I began, and sat down quietly till I had done. At six, I preached in the new house at Whitby, ill containing the congregation. Here God does still make bare his arm,[96] and sinners are continually converted to him.

Sat. 21. I visited one who was ill in bed and, after having buried seven of her family in six months, had just heard that the eighth, her beloved husband, was cast away at sea. I asked, 'Do not you fret at any of these things?' She said, with a lovely smile upon her pale cheek, 'O no! How can I fret at anything which is the will of God? Let him take all besides; he has given me himself. I love, I praise him every moment.' Let any that doubts of Christian perfection look on such a spectacle as this! One in such

[95] See Aug. 14, 1744, n. 74 (20:35 in this edn.).
[96] See Isa. 52:10.

circumstances rejoicing evermore and continually giving thanks.[97]

April 22 (Easter Day), I preached in the room at five and at eight. There were such a number of communicants at church as it was supposed had not been there these fifty years. In the evening, I preached under the cliff for the sake of those who were not able to get up the hill. The skirts of the congregation could not hear, though my voice was clear and loud. But the bulk of them seemed both to hear and understand. How ripe for the gospel is this place!

Mon. 23. After preaching at five, I met the select society, who seem all to have tasted of the same blessing. I then rode to Guisborough and, about eleven, preached in a meadow to a large and serious congregation; but not more serious than that in the street at Stokesley, to whom I declared in the afternoon, 'Jesus Christ, made of God unto us wisdom, righteousness, sanctification, and redemption.'[98] I was a little tired before I came to Hutton [Rudby]. But it was over when I saw the huge congregation; among them I found a greater blessing than either at Stokesley or Guisborough. I then met the society, gathered from all parts. Afterwards I met the select society. And when they were gone I was just as fresh as when I set out in the morning.

Tue. 24. I preached about noon at Potto, and in the evening in the new house at Yarm, by far the most elegant in England. A large congregation attended at five in the morning and seemed to be just ripe for the exhortation, 'Let us go on to perfection.'[99] I had indeed the satisfaction of finding most of the believers here athirst for full redemption.

In the evening, I preached at Stockton. The rain was suspended while I was enforcing those awful words, 'Now God commandeth all men everywhere to repent.'[1] Fri. 27. I was obliged to preach abroad at five, as also in Darlington at noon, and at Barnard Castle in the evening, where many hearts were bowed down before the Lord.

Sat. 28. I rode to Newcastle. Here I received a short letter from John Johnson[2] at York: 'This evening about a quarter before seven it pleased God to take to himself our dear brother, John

[97] See 1 Thess. 5:16, 18.
[98] Cf. 1 Cor. 1:30.
[99] Heb. 6:1 (*Notes*).
[1] Cf. Acts 17:30.
[2] Wesley's assistant; see above, May 5, 1757, n. 70.

Manners, after a time of remarkable affliction and as remarkable patience. He was clearly sensible to the last, as well as solidly happy, saying, "The way is quite clear; my heart is at liberty." '

Sun. 29. The ground being wet with heavy rain, I preached in the house both morning and evening. I soon found what spirit the people were of. No jar, no contention is here, but all are peaceably and lovingly striving together for the hope of the gospel. And what can hurt the Methodists, so called, but the Methodists? Only let them not fight one another, let not brother lift up sword against brother,[3] and 'no weapon formed against them shall prosper.'[4]

Mon. 30. I received a letter from Cornwall, wherein were these words: 'Yesterday I preached to a large congregation at St. John's. The occasion was this. One of our friends came into Mr. Thomas's a few days since. After speaking a little upon business, he said, "What need have we to watch!" Presently, sitting down, he added, "There is but one step between me and death," and died.'

Wednesday, May 2. I talked with M[argaret] L[ewen],[5] a remarkable monument of divine mercy. She is about two and twenty and has about six hundred pounds a year in her own hands. Some months since, God spoke peace to her soul while she was wrestling with him in private prayer. This was never entirely taken from her, even while she was almost alone. But she was often dull and faint, till she broke through all hindrances and joined heart and hand with the children of God.

Tue. 8. We rode over the wild moors to Wolsingham.[6] It proved to be the fair-day. So I had hearers from all parts. In the evening, I preached to the simple, loving earnest people at Barnard Castle. If all to whom we preach were of this spirit, what an harvest would ensue!

[3] See Isa. 19:2, etc. [4] Cf. Isa. 54:17.

[5] Margaret Lewen (*c.* 1742–66) had encountered JW for the first time at Durham, having some months previously been converted and joined the Methodist society. She already suffered from a heart disease, and her father, finding that JW's companionship and advice (he was shortly recommending reading to her) were more beneficial than medical treatment, encouraged her to go to London, where she lived with the female saints of the society there (Telford, 4:247-49). When JW fell from his horse late in 1765, she presented with him a chaise and pair, and in a will which occasioned considerable dispute, she left him £1000 (see Aug. 11, 1767). It is clear that the pious women of the London society took a severe view of her supposed propensity to worldliness, and were alleged to have forced on her death (Moore, *Mrs. Fletcher*, 1:78). JW also made a favourite correspondent of her niece Peggy Dale.

[6] Orig., 'Wessingham', corrected in *Works* (1774). Wolsingham was a Weardale parish and market town 16 miles west from Durham.

Wed. 9. I was invited to breakfast by Mr. F[ielding],[7] a neighbouring gentleman. I found we had been schoolfellows at the Charterhouse—and he remembered *me,* though I had forgot *him.* I spent a very agreeable hour with a serious as well as sensible man.

About noon, I preached to a large congregation in Teesdale, and to a still larger in Weardale[8] in the evening. The next day, after preaching at Prudhoe and Nafferton, I returned to Newcastle.

Tue. 15. I rode to South Shields and was persuaded to preach in the house. It was well I did, for about the middle of the sermon there was a violent shower. But it was quite fair at six while I preached in North Shields to a very large and yet very serious congregation. How is the scene changed since my brother preached here, when the people were ready to swallow him up![9] O what has God wrought in this land within four or five and twenty years!

Fri. 18. I received much satisfaction in conversing with the most honourable member of our society, Henry Jackson,[10] now in the ninety-fifth or ninety-sixth year of his age. He put me in mind of that venerable man, Mr. Eliot of New England,[11] who frequently used to say to his friends a few years before he went to God, 'My memory is gone; my understanding is gone, but I think I have more love than ever.'

Sat. 19. I preached to the poor colliers at Plessey,[12] who are still a pattern to all the county.[13] We rode home by a great house[14] I had

[7] Orig., 'Mr. ——', altered in *Works* (1774) to 'Mr. T—— (apparently a misprint), and in the errata and MS notes thereto to 'Mr. F——'. This was George Fielding, second son of Israel Fielding of Startforth Hall. He was a magistrate for both Yorkshire and County Durham, and he died in June, 1783, aged 82. I owe this information to the kindness of Mr. P. Attenbrough, the headmaster of Charterhouse.

[8] Where the first Methodist chapel had been built at High House in 1760.

[9] On June 16, 1743, Charles Wesley had a rough time at South Shields with a mob incited by the minister and church-wardens (*CWJ*, 1:314).

[10] It is clear from the letter of Jackson's daughter (see Feb. 23, 1766) that JW underestimated the age of this man (1666–1766), who was one of the trustees of the Orphan House.

[11] John Eliot (1604–90), celebrated as the Puritan missionary to the Indians. Born in England, Eliot went to Massachusetts in 1631, and served as pastor at Roxbury near Boston for the rest of his life. He organized fourteen towns of Christian Indians, a number gravely reduced by the war of 1675–76. His Bible in their tongue was the first to be printed in North America.

[12] Orig., 'P——'; *Works* (1774), 'Placey'.

[13] Orig., 'country', altered in *Works* (1774).

[14] Seaton Delaval, built by Sir John Vanbrugh for Admiral George Delaval, 1718–29, and one of his greatest works. The house had already suffered one fire in 1752, and was to

frequently heard of. The front is truly noble. In the house I saw nothing remarkable but what was remarkably bad—such pictures as an honest heathen would be ashamed to receive under his roof, unless he designed his wife and daughters should be common prostitutes. And this is the high fashion! What an abundant proof of the *taste* of the present age!

Sun. 20. Between eight and nine, I preached in Gateshead to a listening multitude. I believe their number was doubled at the Fell, about two in the afternoon. About five, I preached to such another congregation on the outside of Pandon Gate.[15] I know not that I ever before preached to three such congregations in one day,[16] such as obliged me to speak to the utmost extent of my voice, from the first word to the last. But it was all one. I was no more tired in the evening than if I had sat still all day.

Mon. 21. I took my leave of Newcastle, and about noon preached in the market-place at Morpeth. A few of the hearers were a little ludicrous at first, but their mirth was quickly spoiled. In the evening, I preached in the court-house at Alnwick, where I rested the next day. Wed. 23. I rode over the sands to Holy Island, once the famous see of a bishop, now the residence of a few poor families, who live chiefly by fishing.[17] At one side of the town are the ruins of the cathedral,[18] with an adjoining monastery. It appears to have been a lofty and elegant building, the middle aisle being almost entire. I preached in what was once the market-place, to almost all the inhabitants of the island, and distributed some little books among them, for which they were exceeding thankful. In the evening, I preached at Berwick-upon-Tweed; the next evening at Dunbar; and on Friday 25, about ten, at Haddington, in Provost D[ickson]'s yard,[19] to a very elegant congregation. But I expect little good will be done here. For we

suffer still worse from another in 1822; many of the furnishings which so aggrieved JW are no more to be seen. The features described by JW as 'noble' inspire more vigourous adjectives in Pevsner: 'cyclopean', 'ruthless', 'aggressive'. Pevsner, *Northumberland*, pp. 51, 287-88.

15 Pandon Gate was an entrance on the north-east of the Newcastle wall about 300 yards west of the Keelmen's Hospital.

16 Among those converted was William Potter, afterwards an important office-bearer in the Orphan House Society. He died in 1833. Stamp, *Orphan House*, p. 246.

17 And smuggling. *Arminian Magazine* 5 (1782):293.

18 There were bishops of Lindisfarne from 635 till 883, when the see was moved to Chester-le-Street. The church and monastery founded by St. Aidan, who arrived in 635, were important in the introduction of Celtic Christianity into Northumbria from Iona.

19 See above, May 11, 1761, n. 34.

begin at the wrong end. Religion must not go 'from the greatest to the least',[20] or the power would 'appear to be of men'.[21]

In the evening, I preached at Musselburgh, and the next, on the Calton Hill at Edinburgh. It being the time of the General Assembly, many of the ministers were there. The wind was high and sharp, and blew away a few delicate ones. But most of the congregation did not stir till I had concluded.

Sun. 27. At seven, I preached in the High School yard on the other side of the city. The morning was extremely cold. In the evening it blew a storm. However, having appointed to be on the Calton Hill, I began there to an huge congregation. At first the wind was a little troublesome, but I soon forgot it. And so did the people for an hour and half, in which I fully delivered my own soul.

Mon. 28. I spent some hours at the General Assembly, composed of about an hundred and fifty ministers. I was surprised to observe: (1) that *anyone* was admitted, even lads twelve or fourteen years old; (2) that the chief speakers were lawyers, six or seven on one side only; (3) that a single question took up the whole time, which when I went away seemed to be as far from a conclusion as ever, namely, 'Shall Mr. Lindsay be removed to Kilmarnock parish or not?'[22] The argument for it was, 'He has a large family, and this living is twice as good as his own.' The argument against it was, 'The people are resolved not to hear him and will leave the kirk if he comes.' If then the real point in view had been (as their law directs) *majus bonum Ecclesiae*,[23] instead of taking up five hours, the debate might have been determined in five minutes.

On Monday and Tuesday, I spoke to the members of the society severally. Thur. 31. I rode to Dundee and, about half an hour after six, preached on the side of a meadow near the town.

[20] Cf. Jer. 31:34, etc.

[21] Cf. Acts 5:38.

[22] On Nov. 30, 1762, William Lindsay (1732–74) was presented by the Earl of Glencairn to the second charge of Kilmarnock. A refusal to sustain the call or to grant the translation caused the case to be taken to the General Assemblies of 1763 and 1764, which sustained the one and granted the other. The opposition of the parishioners was so great, however, that the admission was made in a public house, July 12, 1764. The public prosecutor felt compelled to bring ten persons to trial before the Circuit Court at Ayr. Three of them, being found guilty of raising a tumult in and about the church, were sentenced to a month's imprisonment, then to be whipped through the streets of Ayr and find caution for a twelve months' good behaviour. Scott, *Fasti*, 2:175-76.

[23] 'The greater benefit of the Church' (Thomas Jackson).

Poor and rich attended. Indeed, there is seldom fear of wanting a congregation in Scotland. But the misfortune is, They *know everything*. So they *learn nothing*.[24]

Friday, June 1. I rode to Brechin, where Mr. Blair[25] received me in the most friendly manner. In the afternoon, I preached on the side of an hill near the town, where we soon forgot the cold. I trust there will be, not only a knowing, but a loving people in this place.

About seven, Mr. B[lair] was occasionally mentioning what had lately occurred in the next parish. I thought it worth a farther inquiry and therefore ordered our horses to be brought immediately. Mr. B[lair] guided us to Mr. Ogilvie's[26] house, the minister of the parish, who informed us that 'a strange disorder' had appeared in his parish 'between thirty and forty years ago', but that 'nothing of the kind' had been known there since, till some time in September last: 'A boy was then taken ill, and so continues still. In the end of January or beginning of February, many other children were taken, chiefly girls, and a few grown persons. They begin with an involuntary shaking of their hands and feet. Then their lips are convulsed, next their tongue, which seems to cleave to the roof of the mouth. Then the eyes are set, staring terribly, and the whole face variously distorted. Presently they start up, and jump ten, fifteen, or twenty times together straight upward, two, three, or more feet from the ground. Then they start forward and run with amazing swiftness, two, three, or five hundred yards. Frequently they run up like a cat to the top of an house and jump on the ridge of it, as on the ground. But wherever they are, they never fall or miss their footing at all. After they have run and jumped for some time, they drop down as dead. When they come to themselves, they usually tell when and where

[24] Christopher Hopper, who with his wife accompanied JW on this journey, noted, however, that 'many precious souls were awakened and added to the general assembly and church of the first-born which are enrolled in heaven.' Jackson, *Early Methodist Preachers*, 1:212.

[25] Orig. has 'Mr. B.', altered in *Works* (1774) to 'Mr. Blaire'. In 1758, Alexander Mather, a native of Brechin, was taken seriously ill there, was kindly attended by David Blair (1701–64), the minister of the second charge in Brechin, 1733–38, and of the first, 1738–69, and his son who was a physician (Jackson, *Early Methodist Preachers*, 2:177). This reference is probably to the father; in JW's next visit, May 2, 1766, it seems to be to the son. David Blair, the elder, was a zealous opponent of the Law of Patronage and is credited with 'having opened in 1760 the first sabbath-school in Scotland, perhaps in Britain'. Scott, *Fasti*, 2:813.

[26] Orig., 'Ogglevie's', altered in *Works* (1774) to 'Oglevie'. George Ogilvie, minister of Menmuir, 1745–79.

they shall be taken again—frequently, how often and where they shall jump and to what places they shall run.'

I asked, 'Are any of them near?' He said, 'Yes, at those houses.' We walked thither without delay. One of them was four years and half old, the other about eighteen. The child we found had had three or four fits that day, running and jumping like the rest, and in particular, leaping many times from a high table to the ground without the least hurt. The young woman was the only person of them all who used to keep her senses during the fit. In answer to many questions she said, 'I first feel a pain in my left foot, then in my head. Then my hands and feet shake, and I can't speak. And quickly I begin to jump or run.' While we were talking she cried out, 'Oh, I have a pain in my foot. It is in my hand. It is here, at the bending of my arm. Oh, my head, my head.' Immediately her arms were stretched out and were as an iron bar. I could not bend one of her fingers, and her body was bent backward, the lower part remaining quite erect, while her back formed exactly a half circle, her head hanging even with her hips. I was going to catch her, but one said, 'Sir, you may let her alone, for they never fall.' But I defy all mankind to account for her not falling, when the trunk of her body hung in that manner.

In many circumstances this case goes far beyond the famous one mentioned by Boerhaave,[27] particularly in that: their telling before, when and how they should be taken again. Whoever can account for this upon natural principles has my free leave. I cannot. I therefore believe, if this be in part a natural distemper, there is something preternatural too. Yet supposing this, I can easily conceive, Satan will so disguise *his* part therein that we cannot precisely determine which part of the disorder is natural and which preternatural.

Sat. 2. I rode to Aberdeen and preached in the evening in the College Hall, and at seven in the morning, Sunday 3. At four in the afternoon, I preached to a crowded audience in the College Kirk at Old Aberdeen. At seven I preached in the College Close at New Aberdeen. But the congregation was so exceeding large that many were not able to hear. However, many did hear and, I think, *feel* the application of 'Thou art not far from the kingdom of God.'[28]

[27] Hermann Boerhaave (1688–1738), physician, botanist, and chemist of Leyden, and the most famous clinical teacher of his age.

[28] Mark 12:34.

We want nothing here but a larger house. And the foundation of one is laid already.[29] It is true, we have little money, and the society is poor. But we know in whom we have believed.[30]

Thur. 7.[31] I rode over to Sir Archibald Grant's,[32] twelve computed miles from Aberdeen. 'Tis surprising to see how the country between is improved even within these three years. On every side the wild, dreary moors are ploughed up and covered with rising corn. All the ground near Sir Archibald's, in particular, is as well cultivated as most in England. About seven I preached. The kirk was pretty well filled, though upon short notice. Certainly this is a nation 'swift to hear' and 'slow to speak', though not 'slow to wrath'.[33]

Mr. Grant,[34] a gentleman from the county of Moray,[35] came in soon after us and, understanding we were going north, desired we would call at the Grange Green in our way. In the morning, Friday 8,[36] I rode to Oldmeldrum and preached in the market-place at noon to a large and serious congregation, among whom were the minister[37] and his wife. But I was more surprised to see a company of our friends from Aberdeen, several of whom had come on foot twelve old Scotch miles, and intended to walk back thither the same day. In the afternoon we rode on to Banff.[38] I had designed to preach, but the stormy weather would not permit. We set out early on Saturday morning and reached Nairn[39] in the evening. Sun. 10. About eight we reached Inverness. I could not preach abroad because of the rain, nor could I hear of any convenient room, so that I was afraid my coming hither would be in vain, all ways[40] seeming to be blocked up. At ten, I went to the

[29] This was the octagon chapel, opened later in the year; on June 13, JW preached in the shell.

[30] See 2 Tim. 1:12.

[31] Orig., '8'.

[32] Sir Archibald Grant of Monymusk, see above, May 4, 1761, n. 24.

[33] Jas. 1:19.

[34] Sir Lodowick Grant, who succeeded as 4th Bart. of Dalvey in 1772, received JW kindly at Grange Green in 1779 and 1784; he died in 1790.

[35] Orig., 'Murray'.

[36] Orig., '9'.

[37] The minister of Meldrum (1741–83) was John Likly (1717–83), who succeeded his father in the living and was rebuked by the Presbytery for simony.

[38] Banff was a substantial seaport, burgh, market town, and parish on the main road from Aberdeen to Inverness.

[39] Nairn was a royal burgh and parish 15½ miles north-east from Inverness.

[40] Orig., 'always', amended in *Works* (1774).

kirk. After service Mr. Fraser,[41] one of the ministers, invited us to dinner and then to drink tea. As we were drinking tea, he asked at what hour I would 'please to preach'. I said, 'At half hour past five.' The high kirk was filled in a very short time. And I have seldom found greater liberty of spirit. The other minister came afterwards to our inn and showed the most cordial affection. Were it only for this day, I should not have regretted the riding an hundred miles.

Mon. 11. A gentleman who lives three miles from the town invited me to his house, assuring me the minister of his parish would be glad if I would make use of his kirk. But time would not permit, as I had appointed to be at Aberdeen on Wednesday. All I could do was to preach once more at Inverness. I think the church was fuller now than before. And I could not but observe the remarkable behaviour of the whole congregation after service. Neither man, woman, nor child spoke one word all the way down the main street. Indeed, the seriousness of the people is the less surprising when it is considered that for at least an hundred years this town has had such a succession of pious ministers as very few in Great Britain have known.

After Edinburgh, Glasgow, and Aberdeen, I think Inverness is the largest town I have seen in Scotland. The main streets are broad and straight, the houses mostly old—but not very bad, nor very good. It stands in a pleasant and fruitful country, and has all things needful for life and godliness.[42] The people in general speak remarkably good English and are of a friendly, courteous behaviour.

About eleven we took horse. While we were dining at Nairn, the innkeeper said, 'Sir, the gentlemen of the town have read the little book you gave me on Saturday and would be glad if you would please to give them a sermon.' Upon my consenting, the bell was immediately rung, and the congregation was quickly in the kirk. O what a difference is there between south and north Britain! Everyone here at least loves to *hear* the Word of God. And none takes it into his head to speak one uncivil word to any for endeavouring to save their souls.

Doubting whether Mr. Grant was come home, Mr. Kershaw[43]

[41] Alexander Fraser (*c.* 1719–78), minister of the third charge in Inverness, 1754–63, and the second charge, 1763–78.

[42] See 2 Pet. 1:3.

[43] James Kershaw was among the first Methodist itinerants, but after a spell as an independent minister and returning to the itinerancy (Telford, 4:50), he ceased to travel in

called at the Grange Green near Forres,[44] while I rode forward. But Mr. Grant soon called me back. I have seldom seen a more agreeable place. The house is an old castle, which stands on a little hill, with a delightful prospect all four ways. And the hospitable master left nothing undone to make it still more agreeable. He showed us all his improvements, which are very considerable in every branch of husbandry. In his gardens many things were more forward than at Aberdeen, yea, or Newcastle. And how is it that none but one Highland gentleman has discovered that we have a tree in Britain, as easily raised as an ash, the wood of which is of full as fine a red as mahogany! Namely, the *laburnum*.[45] I defy any mahogany to exceed the chairs which he has lately made of this.

Thur. [i.e., Tue.] 12. We rode through the pleasant and fertile county of Moray to Elgin.[46] I never suspected before that there was any such country as this near an hundred and fifty miles beyond Edinburgh—a country which is supposed to have generally six weeks' more sunshine in a year than any part of Great Britain.

At Elgin are the ruins of a noble cathedral, the largest that I remember to have seen in the kingdom.[47] We rode thence to the Spey, the most rapid river next the Rhine that I ever saw. Though the water was not breast-high to our horses, they could very

1767, settled at Gainsborough, Lincs., 'and was famous in all that county for his quack medicines' (Atmore, *Memorial*, p. 237). He left a reputation among the preachers for instability ('stark, staring mad' in JW's phrase) and intellectual pretentiousness, and was the author of some memorably bad verse (Telford, 6:252, 254, 259). Indeed his book, *The Methodist; Attempted in Plain Metre* (1781), led to the decision that no preacher should print anything till it had been corrected by JW (Tyerman, *John Wesley*, 3:362). 'However, his earlier contributions to Methodist polemic were not thought disgraceful, and his late work, *The Grand Extensive Plan of Human Redemption, &c, in 12 Familiar Dialogues* (Louth, 1797), was 'generally esteemed as a masterly performance.' Green, *Anti-Methodist*, No. 362; *WHS* 11 (1917):71.

[44] Orig. 'Farras', altered in *Works* (1774). Sir Alan Grant, 5th Bart., bought in his father's lifetime Grange Hill, Co. Elgin, which he called Dalvey.

[45] Orig., '*liburnum*'; JW's reference given in *OED*. Curnock notes that much of the furniture of the house was made of laburnum.

[46] Elgin was a substantial burgh, market town, and parish 36 miles east of Inverness.

[47] Elgin Cathedral, founded by the Bishop of Moray in 1224, was burned down by the Wolf of Badenoch in reprisal for excommunication by a later bishop. It was restored, but in 1568 the Regent Morton ordered the lead to be stripped from the roof to pay his troops. Gradual decay culminated in major collapse in 1711. 'When entire, the cathedral had five towers, two at the west end, two at the east, and one stately tower rising from the centre; it was a splendid cruciform structure in the decorated style of English architecture, 264 feet in length . . . and the central tower was 198 feet high.' Samuel Lewis, *A Topographical Dictionary of Scotland*, 2 vols. (London, 1846), 1:399.

hardly keep their feet. We dined at Keith,[48] and rode on to Strathbogie,[49] much improved by the linen manufacture. All the country from Fochabers[50] to Strathbogie has little houses scattered up and down. And not only the valleys, but the mountains themselves are improved with the utmost care. There want only more trees to make them more pleasant than most of the mountains in England. The whole family at our inn, eleven or twelve in number, gladly joined with us in prayer at night. Indeed, so they did at every inn where we lodged. For among all the sins they have imported from England, the Scots have not yet learned, at least not the common people, to scoff at sacred things.

Wed. 13. We reached Aberdeen about one. Between six and seven, both this evening and the next, I preached in the shell of the new house and found it a time of much consolation. Fri. 15. We set out early and came to Dundee just as the boat was going off. We designed to lodge at the house on the other side, but could not get either meat, drink, or good words. So we were constrained to ride on to Cupar. After travelling near ninety miles, I found no weariness at all. Neither were our horses hurt. Thou, O Lord, dost save both man and beast![51]

Sat. 16. We had a ready passage at Kinghorn,[52] and in the evening I preached on the Calton Hill to a very large congregation. But a still larger assembled at seven on Sunday morning in the High School yard. Being afterwards informed that the Lord's Supper was to be administered in the West Kirk,[53] I knew not what to do. But at length I judged it best to embrace the opportunity, though I did not admire the manner of administration. After the usual morning service, the minister enumerated several sorts of sinners whom he forbade to approach. Two long tables were set on the sides of one aisle, covered with table-cloths. On each side of them a bench was placed for the people. Each table held four or five and thirty. Three ministers sat at the top, behind a cross-table, one of whom made a long exhortation,

[48] Keith was a parish and linen-making town 10½ miles north-west of Huntly.

[49] Strathbogie is the Bogie Valley to the south of Huntly.

[50] Orig., 'Fochaber'. Fochabers was a village 8 miles east of Elgin, and also the seat of the Dukes of Gordon.

[51] See Ps. 36:7 (BCP). Cupar (orig., 'Coupar') was a burgh, market town, and parish 9 miles west of St. Andrew's.

[52] Kinghorn was a royal burgh and parish in Fifeshire, 9 miles north of Edinburgh, across the Firth of Forth.

[53] St. Cuthbert's Parish Church. Henry Moore comments: 'He laid aside his last portion of bigotry, and partook of that holy ordinance.' Moore, *Wesley*, 2:250.

closed with the words of our Lord, and then, breaking the bread, gave it to him who sat on each side him. A piece of bread was then given to him who sat first on each of the four benches. He broke off a little piece and gave the bread to the next; so it went on, the deacons giving more when wanted. A cup was then given to the first person on each bench, and so by one to another. The minister continued his exhortation all the time they were receiving. Then four verses of the Twenty-second Psalm were sung, while new persons sat down at the tables. A second minister then prayed, consecrated, and exhorted. I was informed, the service usually lasted till five in the evening. How much more simple, as well as more solemn, is the service of the Church of England!

The evening congregation on the hill was far the largest I have seen in the kingdom—and the most deeply affected. Many were in tears; more seemed cut to the heart. Surely this time will not soon be forgotten. Will it not appear in the annals of eternity?

Mon. 18. I set out early and reached Wooler[54] about four in the afternoon. Some friends from Newcastle met me here and took me in a chaise to Whittingham.[55] Tue. 19. After preaching about noon at Morpeth, we went on to Newcastle. The fire had not gone out since I was here. I felt it as soon as I began to speak, and so, it seems, did the whole congregation. At five in the morning, the same spirit was in the midst of us, as well as at seven in the evening; but most of all at the Fell, while I was applying those words, 'Believe and thou shalt be saved.'[56]

Thur. 21. Leaving this[57] house of God, I rode to Carlisle. The day was extremely sultry, so that I was faint and feverish in the evening. However, the next day I got well to Whitehaven.

What has continually hurt this poor people is offence. I found the society now all in confusion because a woman had 'scolded with her neighbour', and another 'stole a twopenny loaf'. I talked largely with those who had been most offended, and they stood reproved. Sun. 24. About seven, I preached at the Gins, and the people flocked together from all quarters. The want of field preaching has been one cause of deadness here. I do not find any great increase of the work of God without it. If ever this is laid aside, I expect the whole work will gradually die away.

[54] Orig., 'Woller'.

[55] Whittingham was a small township and parish 8½ miles west from Alnwick.

[56] Cf. Acts 16:31.

[57] Orig., 'the'.

Mon. 25. I rode by Keswick to Kendal. The clouds shaded us most of the way, and the wind was just in our face; otherwise we should scarce have been able to bear the heat. A few years since, the fields here were white for the harvest.[58] But the poor people have since been so harassed by seceders and disputers of every kind that they are dry and dead as stones. Yet I think some of them felt the power of God this evening. And can he not 'out of these stones, raise up children unto Abraham'?[59]

Tue. 26. I preached abroad at five. And, I believe, not in vain. Between nine and ten we reached Black Burton,[60] where there was a general awakening till the jars between Mr. Ingham and Allen[61] laid the people asleep again. However, some are united again in a quiet, loving society, zealous of good works.[62] I preached about eleven. Thence we rode to Long Preston,[63] being still fanned by the wind and (unless a few minutes now and then) shaded by the clouds. The congregation was exceeding serious. Hence, I rode to Skipton,[64] where sometime since, no Methodist preacher could appear. I preached in the evening near the bridge without the least interruption. Nor did I find any weariness after preaching four times and riding fifty miles.

Wed. 27. I rode to Otley. In the evening we had a large congregation at the foot of the great mountain.[65] After preaching in the morning, I examined those who believe they are saved from sin. They are a little increased in number since I met them last, and some of them much increased in love. This evening I preached at Guiseley, the next at Keighley, and on Saturday 30,

[58] See John 4:35.

[59] Cf. Matt. 3:9.

[60] Orig., 'Black Barton'. Burton in Lonsdale was a small chapelry in the parish of Thornton in Lonsdale, 5½ miles south-east from Kirkby Lonsdale.

[61] For Ingham, see Oct. 14, 1735, n. 1 (18:136 in this edn.). James Allen (1734–1804) of Gayle, Yorks., became one of his chief assistants and preachers in 1752, and was ordained by him in 1756. When, in 1759, Ingham became interested in Sandemanianism, he sent Allen to Scotland to inquire of the sect, and he came back fully converted to their views. Ingham himself adopted Sandemanian views in 1760, but the disputes arising from the penetration of the new views did immense damage to Ingham's connexion, and in the breakup, Allen took a number of societies and ministered to them till his death (Luke Tyerman, *The Oxford Methodists* [London, Hodder and Stoughton, 1873], pp. 136, 138, 145; *Evangelical Magazine* [1814], p. 306). Allen matriculated at St. John's College, Cambridge, in 1751, but left after a year. He was the author of a hymnal.

[62] Titus 2:14.

[63] Long Preston was a township and parish 4 miles south from Settle.

[64] Skipton was a market town and parish 44 miles west of York. Methodism was indeed not introduced into Skipton till 1772, and then upon lay initiative. *Wesleyan Methodist Magazine* 45 (1822):752.

[65] The Chevin, a steep ridge south of Otley.

at Bradford. This was a place of contention for many years. But since the contentious have quitted us, all is peace. Sunday, July 1. I preached at seven to a more numerous congregation than I believe ever assembled there before. And all were serious as death. About one, I preached at Birstall, on 'Now is the day of salvation.'[66] The people stood by thousands, covering both the plain and the sides of the adjacent hill. It was a glorious opportunity. At five the congregation in Leeds was almost as large, but not so deeply affected.

Mon. 2. I gave a fair hearing to two of our brethren who had proved bankrupts. Such we immediately exclude from our society unless it plainly appears not to be their own fault. Both these were in a prosperous way till they fell into that wretched trade of bill-broking,[67] wherein no man continues long without being wholly ruined. By this means, not being sufficiently accurate in their accounts, they ran back without being sensible of it. Yet it was quite clear that I—— R—— is an honest man; I would *hope* the same concerning the other.

Tue. 3. I was reflecting on an odd circumstance which I cannot account for. I never relish a tune at first hearing, not till I have *almost* learned to sing it. And as I learn it more perfectly, I gradually lose my relish for it. I observe something similar in poetry; yea, in all the objects of imagination. I seldom relish verses at first hearing: till I have heard them over and over, they give me no pleasure, and they give me next to none when I have heard them a few times more, so as to be quite familiar. Just so a face or a picture, which does not strike me at first, becomes more pleasing as I grow more acquainted with it. But only to a certain point: for when I am too much acquainted it is no longer pleasing. O how imperfectly do we understand even the machine which we carry about us!

Thur. 5. I had the comfort of leaving our brethren at Leeds united in peace and love. About one, I preached in a meadow at Wakefield. At first the sun was inconvenient. But it was not many minutes before that inconvenience was removed by the clouds coming between. We had not only a larger, but a far more attentive, congregation than ever was seen here before. One, indeed, a kind of gentleman, was walking away with great unconcern when I spoke aloud, 'Does Gallio care for none of

[66] 2 Cor. 6:2.

[67] The earliest reference to 'bill-broking' in *OED*.

these things?[68] But where will you go with the wrath of God on your head and the curse of God on your back?' He stopped short, stood still, and went no farther till the sermon was ended.

In the evening, I preached on the top of the hill near Dewsbury, one of the pleasantest towns in England. The congregation was larger than ever before. They filled the preaching-house at five in the morning.

I had purposed to take horse early, to avoid the heat; but was detained till between nine and ten. It was then warm enough, there being no wind, and the sun shining full in our face. However, before one we got to Heptonstall, where I preached in the shell of the new house.[69] After service one brought his daughter to me who had been ill some months, just like those near Brechin.[70] Her sister was so two years since, and when that recovered, this was taken. How often must even physicians acknowledge spiritual agents, did not 'the nerves' help them out as a dead lift!

In the evening I preached at Halifax, where I had the pleasure of meeting Mr. Venn,[71] with whom in the morning, Saturday 7, I rode to Huddersfield and preached between eleven and twelve. The church[72] was pretty well filled, considering the short warning. At half-hour after one, we took horse. The sun shone burning hot, and the wind was in our back. But very soon the sky was overcast, and the wind changed and blew just in our face, all the way to Manchester. It was with difficulty that I preached in the evening, my voice being exceeding weak, as I had preached three times a day for ten days, and many of the times abroad.

Sun. 8. I rode to Stockport and preached at one on a green at the end of the town. A few wild young men strove to make a disturbance. But none regarded them. At five, I preached at Manchester on 'One thing is needful,'[73] and scarce knew how to leave off. At the meeting of the society, likewise, it pleased God to comfort us greatly. Mon. 9. The stewards from various parts gave a good account of the work of God among them, steadily increasing on every side. In the evening, curiosity brought to the house many *unbelievers,* in the proper sense, men who do not receive the Christian revelation. I preached on 'Thou shalt love

[68] See Acts 18:17.

[69] This was another octagonal building.

[70] The convulsions of these are described above, June 1, 1764.

[71] Orig., 'Mr. V——', amplified in *Works* (1774).

[72] I.e., Venn's church.

[73] Luke 10:42.

thy neighbour as thyself,'[74] and proved them sinners on their own principles. Some of the stout-hearted trembled. I hope to more purpose than poor Felix[75] did.

Wed. 11. I gave all our brethren a solemn warning not to 'love the world, or the things of the world'.[76] This is one way whereby Satan will surely endeavour to overthrow the present work of God. Riches swiftly increase on many Methodists, so called. What but the mighty power of God can hinder their 'setting' their 'hearts upon them'?[77] And if so, the life of God vanishes away.

About seven, I preached in the street at Bolton to twice or thrice as many as the room would have contained. It was a calm, still evening, and the congregation was as quiet as the season, though composed of awakened and unawakened, churchmen, Dissenters, and what not. As many as the house would well contain were present again at five in the morning. About seven in the evening, the multitude of people constrained me to preach in the street, though it rained. But in a very short time the rain stopped, and I strongly enforced our Lord's word, 'If thou canst believe, all things are possible to him that believeth.'[78]

After sermon one was mentioning a person who according to his account was disordered just like those in Scotland.[79] In the morning, Friday 13, her father brought her over. Soon after, she fell into a fit, but it was plainly natural. I judged it to be of the epileptic kind. When she fell into a second, I advised electrifying. The fit ceased by a very gentle shock. A third was removed in the same manner. And she was so well that her father found no difficulty in carrying her home behind him.

At ten I began to preach at Wigan, proverbially famous for all manner of wickedness.[80] As I preached abroad, we expected some disturbance, but there was none at all. A few were wild at first, but in a little space grew quiet and attentive. I did not find so civil a congregation as this the first time I preached at Bolton.

Today I wrote the following letter, which I desire may be seriously considered by those to whom it belongs:

[74] Matt. 22:39.
[75] Acts 24:25.
[76] Cf. 1 John 2:15.
[77] Cf. Ps. 62:10.
[78] Mark 9:23.
[79] See June 1, 1764.
[80] Even Wigan (a parish, borough, and market town 17 miles north-west of Manchester) improved in the long run; see Apr. 9, 1790.

Dear Sir,

There was one thing when I was with you that gave me pain. You are not in the society. But why not? Are there not sufficient arguments for it to move any reasonable man? Do you not hereby make an open confession of Christ, of what you really believe to be *his* work, and of those whom you judge to be in a proper sense *his* people and his messengers? By this means do not you encourage his people and strengthen the hands of his messengers? And is not this the way to enter into the spirit, and share the blessing, of a Christian community? Hereby likewise you may have the benefit of the advices and exhortations at the meeting of the society, and also of provoking one another, at the private meetings, to love and to good works.

The ordinary objections to such an union are of little weight with *you.* You are not afraid of the *expense.* You already give unto the Lord as much as you need do then. And you are not *ashamed* of the gospel of Christ, even in the midst of a crooked and perverse generation. Perhaps you will say, 'I am joined in *affection.*' True, but not to so good effect. This *joining half-way,* this being a friend to, but not a member of, the society, is by no means so open a confession of the work and servants of God. Many go thus far who dare not go farther, who are ashamed to bear the reproach of an entire union. Either *you* are ashamed or you are not. If you are, break through at once; if you are not, come into the light and do what those well-meaning cowards dare not do. This imperfect union is not so *encouraging* to the people, not so *strengthening* to the preachers. Rather it is weakening their hands, hindering their work, and laying a stumbling-block in the way of others; for what can any man think who knows you are so well acquainted with them and yet do not join in their society? What can he[81] think, but that you know them *too well* to come any nearer to them; that you know that kind of union to be *useless,* if not *hurtful.* And yet by this very union is the whole (external) work of God upheld throughout the nation, besides all the spiritual good which accrues to each member. O delay no longer, for the sake of the work, for the sake of the world, for the sake of your brethren. Join them inwardly and outwardly, heart and hand, for the sake of your own soul. There is something not easily explained in the 'fellowship of the Spirit',[82] which we enjoy with a society of living Christians. You have no need to give up your share therein and in the various blessings that result from it. You have no need to exclude yourself from the benefit of the advice and exhortations given from time to time. These are by no

[81] Orig., 'we', altered in the errata and MS notes to *Works* (1774).
[82] Phil. 2:1.

means to be despised, even supposing you have yourself more understanding than him that gives them. You need not lose the benefit of those prayers which experience shows are attended with a peculiar blessing. 'But I do not care to meet a class; I find no good in it.' Suppose you find even a dislike, a loathing, of it; may not this be natural or even diabolical? In spite of this, break through, make a fair trial. It is but a 'lion in the way'.[83] Meet only six times (with previous prayer) and see if it do not vanish away. But if it be a cross, still bear it for the sake of your brethren. 'But I want to gain my friends and relations.' If so, stand firm. If you give way, you hurt them, and they will press upon you the more. If you do not, you will probably gain them; otherwise you confirm both their wrong notions and wrong tempers. Because I love you I have spoken fully and freely; to know that I have not spoken in vain will be a great satisfaction to

Your affectionate brother,
J. W.

In the evening, I preached at Liverpool, and the next day, Sunday 15, the house was full enough. Many of the rich and fashionable were there and behaved with decency. Indeed, I have always observed more courtesy and humanity at Liverpool than at most seaports in England.

Mon. 16. In the evening, the house was fuller, if possible, than the night before. I preached on the 'One Thing Needful',[84] and the rich behaved as seriously as the poor. Only one young gentlewoman (I heard) laughed much. Poor thing! Doubtless she thought, 'I laugh prettily.'

Tue. 17. I preached at Warrington. But what a change! No opposer, nor no trifler now! Everyone heard as[85] for life, while I explained and applied, 'Why will ye die, O house of Israel?'[86]

In the evening, I preached in the little square adjoining to the preaching-house at Chester. There were many wild, rude people, but they were quite outnumbered by those who[87] were civil and attentive. And I believe some impression was made on the wildest. What can shake Satan's kingdom like *field preaching!*

Wed. 18. I should have been glad of a day of rest. But notice

[83] Prov. 26:13.
[84] Luke 10:42.
[85] Orig., 'us', altered in *Works* (1774).
[86] Ezek. 18:31.
[87] Orig., 'that', altered in *Works* (1774).

had been given of my preaching at noon near Tattenhall. The rain began almost as soon as we came in. So I could not preach abroad as I designed, but in a large commodious barn, where all that were present seemed to receive the Word of God with joy and reverence.

The congregation at Chester in the evening was more numerous and far more serious than the day before. There wants only a little more field preaching here, and Chester would be as quiet as London.

Thur. 19. After preaching at Little Leigh, I rode on to Macclesfield. Here I heard an agreeable account of Mrs. R[oe],[88] who was in the society at London from a child, but after she was married to a rich man, durst not own a poor, despised people. Last year she broke through and came to see *me.* A few words which I then spoke never left her, not even in the trying hour, during the illness which came a few months later. All her conversation was then in heaven, till feeling her strength quite exhausted, she said with a smile, 'Death, thou art welcome,' and resigned her spirit.

I preached about seven to an huge multitude of attentive hearers. Fri. 20. At noon, we made the same shift at Congleton as when I was here last. I stood in the window, having put as many women as it would contain into the house.[89] The rest, with the men, stood below in the meadow, and many of the townsmen, wild enough. I have scarce found such enlargement of heart since I came from Newcastle. The brutes resisted long but were at length overcome, not above five or six excepted. Surely 'man' shall not long 'have the upper hand';[90] God will get unto himself the victory.

[88] Mrs. Mary Roe, née Stockdale, (d. 1763), a former London Methodist, was the second wife of Charles Roe (1715–81), brother of Rev. James Roe (d. 1765), vicar of Macclesfield, and founder of copper works in the town. Roe did not allow her to join the Methodist society (and fiercely resisted the Methodist propensities of his children) but was concerned to maintain evangelical preaching. After his brother died in 1765, he brought in David Simpson as curate and in 1777 built Christ Church, Macclesfield, for him. Meanwhile, in 1770 Mrs. Roe's niece, Hester Anne Roe (1756–94), daughter of James Roe, had become a member of society. She became an intimate friend of JW, and her husband, James Rogers, being stationed at City Road when JW died, she attended him at the end. *A History of Macclesfield*, ed. C. S. Davies (Manchester, 1961), pp. 113-14, 330-32.

[89] This chapel was private property erected at the back of the house of a Mr. Troutbeck and owned by him. The space beyond it was then an open meadow where crowds, which the chapel could not contain, were in the habit of assembling, and sometimes hostile mobs as well. *WHS* 4 (1903):30; Dyson, *Congleton*, p. 65.

[90] Ps. 9:19 (BCP).

It rained all the day till seven in the evening, when I began preaching at Burslem. Even the poor potters here are a more civilized people than the 'better sort', so called, at Congleton. A few stood with their hats on, but none spoke a word or offered to make the least disturbance.

Sat. 21. I rode to Bilbrook, near Wolverhampton, and preached between two and three. Thence we went on to Madeley, an exceeding pleasant village encompassed with trees and hills. It was a great comfort to me to converse once more with a Methodist of the old stamp, denying himself, taking up his cross,[91] and resolved to be 'altogether a Christian'.[92]

Sun. 22. At ten, Mr. Fletcher read prayers, and I preached on those words in the Gospel, 'I am the good Shepherd; the good Shepherd layeth down his life for the sheep.'[93] The church would nothing near contain the congregation. But a window near the pulpit being taken down, those who could not come in stood in the churchyard, and I believe all could hear. The congregation, they said, used to be much smaller in the afternoon than in the morning. But I could not discern the least difference either in number or seriousness.

I found employment enough for the intermediate hours in praying with various companies who hung about the house, insatiably hungering and thirsting after the good word. Mr. Grimshaw, at his first coming to Haworth, had not such a prospect as this. There are many adversaries indeed, but yet they cannot 'shut the open and effectual door'.[94]

Mon. 23. The church was pretty well filled even at five, and many stood in the churchyard. In the evening, I preached at Shrewsbury to a large congregation, among whom were several men of fortune. I trust, though hitherto we seem to have been ploughing on the sand, there will at last be some fruit.

The next day I spent at Shrewsbury.[95] Wednesday 25, I took horse a little after four, and about two preached in the market-house at Llanidloes, two or three and forty miles from Shrewsbury. At three, we rode forward through the mountains to the Fountain Head.[96] I was for lodging there, but Mr. B——[97]

[91] See Matt. 16:24, etc.

[92] Cf. Acts 26:28-29.

[93] John 10:11 (*Notes*).

[94] Cf. 1 Cor. 16:9.

[95] This sentence is omitted from *Works* (1774) and 1789.

[96] Pen-ffynnon, an inn at Cwmystwyth, between Rhayader and Pontrhydygroes. Cf. Williams, *Wesley in Wales*, p. 68, n. 2.

[97] This is presumably one of the itinerants; there are no stationing minutes for this year.

being quite unwilling, we mounted again about seven. After having rode an hour, we found we were quite out of the way, having been wrong directed at setting out. We were then told to ride over some grounds, but our path soon ended in the edge of a bog. However, we got through to a little house, where an honest man instantly mounting his horse, galloped before us, up hill and down, till he brought us into a road which he said led straight to Ffair-rhos.[98] We rode on till another met us and said, 'No, this is the way to Aberystwyth. If you would go to Ffair-rhos, you must turn back and ride down to yonder bridge.' The master of a little house near the bridge[99] then directed us to the next village,[1] where we inquired again (it being past nine) and were once more set exactly wrong. Having wandered an hour upon the mountains through rocks and bogs and precipices, we with abundance of difficulty got back to the little house near the bridge. It was vain to think of rest there, it being full of drunken, roaring miners[2]—beside that there was but one bed in the house and neither grass nor hay nor corn to be had. So we hired one of them to walk with us to Ffair-rhos, though he was miserably drunk, till by falling all his length in a purling stream he came tolerably to his senses. Between eleven and twelve, we came to the inn, but neither here could we get any hay. When we were in bed, the good ostler and miner thought good to mount our beasts. I believe it was not long before we rose that they put them into the stable. But the mule was cut in several places, and my mare was bleeding like a pig, from a wound behind two inches deep, made, it seemed, by a stroke with a pitchfork. What to do we could not tell, till I remembered, I had a letter for one Mr. Nathaniel Williams,[3] whom upon inquiry I found to live but a mile off. We walked thither and found an 'Israelite indeed',[4] who gladly received both man and beast.

[98] Orig., 'Roes-Fair', incorrectly interpreted by Curnock as 'Rhos Fawr', a farm on the wrong road, leading to Aberystwyth. 'Roes-fair' (now 'Ffair-rhos') is 'on the route from Cwmystwyth to the Abbey farm near Strata Florida'. Williams, *Wesley in Wales*, pp. 68-69, n. 4.

[99] At Pontrhydygroes.

[1] Ysbyty Ystwyth.

[2] Lead miners, many of Cornish origin.

[3] The tenant of Mynachlog-fawr, Strata Florida, who visited Llangeitho to receive Holy Communion from Daniel Rowland. Both he and his brother William, who owned extensive sheep runs, became High Sheriffs of Cardiganshire in 1776 and 1751; Nathaniel was William's heir and succeeded him at Pant-y-siri. Williams, *Wesley in Wales*, p. 69, n. 3.

[4] John 1:47.

After I had got a little rest, Mr. W[illiams] desired me to give an exhortation to a few of his neighbours. None was more struck therewith than one of his own family, who before cared for none of these things.[5] He sent a servant with us after dinner to Tregaron, from whence we had a plain road to Lampeter.

Fri. 27. We rode through a lovely vale and over pleasant and fruitful hills to Carmarthen. Thence after a short bait, we went on to Pembroke and came before I was expected. So I rested that night, having not quite recovered [from] my journey from Shrewsbury to Ffair-rhos.

Sun. 29. The minister of St. Mary's[6] sent me word he was very willing I should preach in his church, but before service began the mayor sent to forbid it.[7] So he preached a very useful sermon himself. The mayor's behaviour so disgusted many of the gentry that they resolved to hear where they could. And accordingly flocked together in the evening from all parts of the town. And perhaps the taking up this cross may profit them more than my sermon in the church would have done.

Mon. 30. I rode to Haverfordwest. But no notice had been given, nor did any in the town know of my coming. However, after a short time, I walked up toward the castle and began singing an hymn. The people presently ran together from all quarters. They have curiosity at least. And some, I cannot doubt, were moved by a nobler principle. Were zealous and active labourers here, what an harvest might there be, even in this corner of the land!

We returned through heavy rain to Pembroke. Tue. 31. We set out for Glamorganshire and rode up and down steep and stony mountains, for about five hours, to Laugharne.[8] Having procured a pretty ready passage there, we went on to Llanstephan[9] Ferry, where we were in some danger of being swallowed up in the

[5] Acts 18:17.

[6] The minister of St. Mary's (Pembroke) was David Lewis.

[7] The diary of the Moravian, Laurentius Nyberg, casts some light on this action by Gwynne Davies, the mayor (Francis Green, ed., *West Wales Historical Records*, 14 vols. [Carmarthen, 1912–29], 5:124). Barnes, the paymaster at Pembroke Fort, was a Moravian turned Wesleyan. On Apr. 11, 1764, Nyberg reports 'there is a terrible confusion around Pembroke between Barnes and the followers of Whitefield and Wesley.' He also reports on July 30, 1764, 'J. Wesley preached a sermon in the pound near the Castle wall, in which he absurdly forgot the Saviour's death and sufferings altogether.' *WHS* 12 (1919):47; 15 (1925):63.

[8] Orig., 'Larn'.

[9] Orig., 'Llastuthan', changed to 'Llansteflan' in the errata and MS notes to *Works* (1774). See above, Aug. 26, 1763, n. 28.

mud before we could reach the water. Between one and two we reached Kidwelly,[10] having been more than seven hours on horseback, in which time we could have rode round by Carmarthen, with more ease both to man and beast. I have therefore taken my leave of these ferries, considering we save no time by crossing them (not even when we have a ready passage), and so have all the trouble, danger, and expense, clear gains. I wonder[11] that any man of common sense who has once made the experiment should ever ride from Pembroke to Swansea any other way than by Carmarthen.

An honest man at Kidwelly told us, there was no difficulty in riding the sands. So we rode on. In ten minutes one overtook us who used to guide persons over them. And it was well he did, or in all probability we had been swallowed up. The whole sands are at least ten miles over, with many streams of quicksands intermixed. But our guide was thoroughly acquainted with them and with the road on the other side. By his help, between five and six we came well tired to Oxwich[12] in Gower.

Gower is a large tract of land, bounded by Glamorgan[13] on the north-east, the sea on the south-west, and rivers on the other sides. Here all the people talk English and are in general the most plain, loving people in Wales. It is therefore no wonder that they receive the word with all readiness of heart.

Knowing they were scattered up and down, I had sent two persons on Sunday that they might be there early on Monday and so send notice of my coming all over the country. But they came to Oxwich scarce a quarter of an hour before me, so that the poor people had no notice at all. Nor was there any to take us in, the person with whom the preacher used to lodge being three miles out of town.[14] After I had stayed awhile in the street (for there was no public house), a poor woman gave me house-room. Having had nothing since breakfast, I was very willing to eat or drink, but she simply told me she had 'nothing in the house but a dram of

[10] Kidwelly was an incorporated market town and parish 9 miles south of Carmarthen.

[11] Orig., 'I wonder therefore', the latter word omitted in errata and MS notes to *Works* (1774).

[12] Orig., 'Oxwych'. Oxwich was a small parish 14 miles from Swansea via Penrice, 13 miles south-west across the sands.

[13] Orig., 'Brecknockshire'. Gower is a peninsula jutting out westward from Swansea toward the Bristol Channel.

[14] William Tucker of Horton, who later became the leader of a society which met in his own home.

gin'. However, I afterwards procured a dish of tea at another house and was much refreshed. About seven, I preached to a little company, and again in the morning. They were all attention, so that even for the sake of this handful of people I did not regret my labour.

Wednesday, August 1. It was with difficulty I reached Cowbridge about one, where the congregation was waiting. I found they had had heavy rain great part of the day; but very little fell upon us. Nor do I remember that from the beginning of March till now we have been in more than one heavy shower of rain, either in England, Scotland, or Wales.

I preached in the evening at Llandaff, and on Thursday 2, in the town hall at Cardiff. Saturday 4, we crossed at the New Passage and rode on to Bristol.

Sun. 5. I preached in Princes Street at eight, at two under the sycamore tree at Kingswood,[15] and at five near King Square in Bristol. How many thousands in this city do see in this 'their day, the things that belong to their peace'![16]

On Monday the 6th our Conference began.[17] The great point I now laboured for was a good understanding with all our brethren of the clergy who are heartily engaged in propagating vital religion. Sat. 11. I took chaise early in the morning and at night came safe to London.

Sun. 12. In the afternoon, I preached in Moorfields on those comfortable words, 'Believe in the Lord Jesus Christ, and thou shalt be saved.'[18] Thousands heard with calm and deep attention. This also hath God wrought!

Mon. 13. I was again as fully employed as at the Conference,

[15] Cf. June 26, 1739 (19:74 in this edn.).

[16] Cf. Luke 19:42.

[17] Though JW indicates that he was attempting to take further his irenical labours of the previous months, the Conference was to indicate both the impasse they had reached and the continuing difficulties of relations with Charles Wesley. To commentators a generation later, this Conference seemed prophetic of the strained relations with the Church of the mid–1790s. 'In the year 1764, twelve of those gentlemen [evangelical clergy] attended our conference in Bristol, in order to prevail with Mr. Wesley to withdraw the preachers from every parish where there was an awakened minister; and Mr. Charles Wesley honestly told us, that if he were a settled minister in any particular place, we should not preach there. To whom Mr. Hampson replied, "I would preach there, and never ask your leave, and should have as good a right to do so as you would have. . .". However, these gentlemen failed in their attempt that time; Mr. Wesley would not give up his societies to them.' J. Pawson, *Affectionate Address* (1795), p. 11; Myles, *Chronological History*, pp. 104-5.

[18] Acts 16:31.

in visiting classes from morning till night. Sat. 18. I preached for the first time in our new chapel at Snowsfields[19] on 'O how amiable are thy tabernacles, thou Lord of Hosts!'[20]

Sun. 19. Meeting with a pious and sensible man who was born in the Isle of Skye,[21] I said, 'Tell me freely: did you yourself ever know a *second-sighted* man?' He answered after a little pause, 'I have known more than one or two.' I said, 'But were they not deceivers? How do you know they were really such?' He replied, 'I have been in company with them when they dropped down as dead. Coming to themselves, they looked utterly amazed and said, "I have been in such a place, and I saw such and such persons" (perhaps fifty miles off) "die in such a manner." And when inquiry was made, I never could find that they were mistaken in one circumstance. But the reason why it is so hard for you to get any information concerning this is, those who have the *second-sight* count it a great misfortune. And it is thought a scandal to their family.'

Mon. 20. I went to Canterbury and opened our *new chapel*[22] by preaching on 'One thing is needful.'[23] How is it that many Protestants, even in England, do not know that no other *consecration* of church or chapel is *allowed*, much less *required*, in England, than the performance of public worship therein? This is the only consecration of any church in Great Britain which is *necessary*, or even *lawful*. It is true, Archbishop Laud composed a *Form of Consecration*, but it was never *allowed*, much less *established*, in England. Let this be remembered by all who talk so idly of preaching in *unconsecrated* places![24]

[19] Yet another octagonal building, erected on the initiative of Samuel Butcher, Leather-seller, Bermondsey.

[20] Cf. Ps. 84:1 (BCP).

[21] Orig., 'Skie'.

[22] This new chapel, known as 'the Round-house', was built at the top of King's Street of the materials made available for purchase by the demolition of St. Andrew's Church to improve the traffic flow. *Wesleyan Methodist Magazine* 60 (1837):423.

[23] Luke 10:42.

[24] 'The law . . . takes no notice of churches or chapels till they are consecrated by the bishop: but the canon law supposes that, with consent of the bishops, divine service may be performed and sacraments administered in churches and chapels not consecrated; inasmuch as it provides that a church shall have the privilege of immunity, in which the divine mysteries are celebrated, altho' it be not consecrated: and there are many licences to that effect (granted on special occasions) in our ecclesiastical records. And after a new church is erected, it may not be consecrated without a competent endowment. . . . In the Church of England, every bishop is left to his own discretion, as to the form of consecrating churches and chapels. . . . There was a form drawn up in the convocation, in the year 1661 (occasioned, as some think, by the offence taken at bishop Laud's

Wed. 22. I had designed to return to London, but being importuned to pay a visit first to Sandwich, I went over and preached about ten to a dull but attentive congregation. Immediately after service, we set out for Dover. In the way we were on the point of being dashed in pieces, the chariot wheels running within two or three inches or less of the edge of a bank ten or twelve feet high. I preached in Dover at two and returned time enough for the service at Canterbury. Thur. 23. I preached at Bethnal Green,[25] and in the evening at the Foundery.

Mon. 27. I saw a pattern of patience, John Matthews,[26] daily dying of a consumption, but in constant pain, weakness, weariness, and want of sleep, calmly giving himself up to God.

Sunday, September 2. After a toilsome yet comfortable day, I set out in the machine, and on Monday evening came to Bristol as fresh as I left London.

Mon. 10. I rode to Shepton Mallet and preached at noon on 'One thing is needful.'[27] Only one man, a common disturber, behaved amiss. I was constrained to rebuke him sharply. All the people turned their eyes upon him, and for once he was ashamed. In the evening, I preached at Bayford, near Wincanton, and at seven in the morning. Wednesday 12, I returned to Bristol, and at six in the evening preached on Redcliff Hill.[28] Many were here who I suppose never heard me before. And attention sat on every face.

Thur. 13. I spent an hour in Lord B[otecourt]'s[29] gardens, or

ceremonious manner of consecrating St. Katherine Creed Church in London [in 1630]), but this was not authorized or published. . . . Again in the year 1712 a form of consecrating churches and chapels and church yards or places of burial was sent down from the bishops to the lower house of convocation, which was agreed to with some alterations: which form, it is said, is now generally observed; but not having received the royal assent, was consequently not enjoined to be observed, nor then printed [though it is to be found in the collections of Wilkins and Gibson].' R. Burn, *Ecclesiastical Law* (London, 1763), 1:233-36, see also Feb. 28, 1772.

25 Orig., 'Bednel-Green', changed in 1774 to 'Bednal Green', and in 1789 to 'Bethnel Green'.

26 E. Perronet MS: 'This Gentleman married in 1767, Miss Vazeille, the only D[aughter] of Mr. M., who [remainder missing].' John Matthews was a London Methodist who had long been in JW's confidence and earned his glowing tributes on his death on Dec. 28, 1764 (Telford, 3:214; 4;153, 198). See below, Dec. 28, 1764; and Telford, 4:280.

27 Luke 10:42.

28 Orig., 'Redclift-hill'.

29 Orig., 'Lord ——'s', changed in *Works* (1774) to 'Lord B——'s'. Narborn Berkely of Stoke Gifford, M.P. for Gloucester 1741–63, having proved that he had inherited one third of the old Barony of Botecourt, which had been in abeyance since 1406, had the abeyance terminated in his favour in 1764. He died in 1770.

more properly woods. They are small to the late Duke of Kent's in Bedfordshire, and therefore not capable of so much variety. But for the size, it is not possible for anything of the kind to be more agreeable. And the situation, on the top of an high hill in one of the fruitfullest counties in England, gives them an advantage which even Stow gardens[30] have not. Yet happiness is not in these shades! And if it were, yet

How long? How soon will they upbraid
Their transitory master dead?[31]

Mon. 17. About noon I preached at Bath. The day before, Mr. Davis[32] had preached abroad. One fruit of this was, the congregation was larger now than I remember it to have been these seven years. Thence, I rode to Combe Grove,[33] an house built in a large grove on the side of an high, steep hill. I found Mrs. W——[34] the same still with regard to her liveliness but not her wildness; in this she was much altered. I preached at five to a small, serious congregation. And I believe few were sent empty away.

30 The comparison between the Duke of Kent's gardens at Wrest and the Cobham gardens at Stowe had occurred to JW in 1754; see June 20, 1754, n. 77 (20:487 in this edn.).

31 Cf. Horace, *Odes,* II.xiv.21-24, trans. Congreve, 11:49-50:

The rest shall live and flourish, to upbraid
Their transitory master dead.

Cf. July 1, 1767, where Wesley misquotes differently the line leading up to the memorable close: 'How soon, alas! will these upbraid. . . .' See Wesley's *Collection of Moral and Sacred Poems* (1744), 1:67.

32 Howel Davies (*c.* 1716–70) was converted by Howell Harris in 1737, while serving as schoolmaster at Talgarth, and, after studying under Griffith Jones, he was ordained priest in 1740. After holding curacies, he married an heiress, Catherine Poyer, in 1744, and went to live at Parke near Whitland. When she died, he married Elizabeth White and went to live at her home at Prendergast, where he became rector. Devoting most of his effort in later years to west Wales, he earned the title of 'Apostle of Pembrokeshire'. But from the beginning, he had maintained an active connection with the Welsh Calvinistic Methodists, and was also for many years a chaplain to the Countess of Huntingdon and, among others (now including JW), served the chapel she built at Bath. Having failed to secure a wider union among evangelical clergy, JW sought at least to secure closer cooperation with the Countess and Whitefield; of this, the present combined action with Davies at Bath was one of the fruits. Seymour, *Huntingdon*, 1:475-76.

33 There is a photo of Combe Grove in Curnock, 5:95.

34 Orig., 'Mrs. ——', to which E. Perronet MS adds the note 'Garbrand', as in the following paragraph. In *Works* (1774), Wesley clarifies slightly, to 'Mrs. W——'. Cf. the discussion above, Sept. 14, 1763, n. 52.

Two persons from London, who were at Bath for their health, had walked over to the preaching. Afterwards we all spent an hour in singing and serious conversation. The fire kindled more and more, till Mrs. ——[35] asked if I would give her 'leave to pray'. Such a prayer I never heard before; it was perfectly an original: odd and unconnected, made up of disjointed fragments—and yet like a flame of fire. Every sentence went through my heart, and I believe the heart of everyone present. For many months I have found nothing like it. It was good for *me* to be here.

Tue. 18. I preached again in the courtyard at seven, and it was now that one of the servants, who was in tears the night before, was thoroughly convinced that God had blotted out all her sins. About noon, I preached to a large congregation at Freshford, on 'Now is the day of salvation.'[36] A little before six, being determined to be no longer cooped up in the room at Bradford, I began in the main street, near the bridge. In a very short time a multitude of people ran together and listened with all attention, till an impetuous shower drove part of them away. The rest would not stir till I concluded. I then gave notice of meeting the society, but a crowd of people pressed in with them. Seeing their earnestness, I was unwilling to hinder, so we had quickly another large congregation. And I know not if we have had such a season at Bradford for twice seven years before.

Wed. 19. At five, we had such a congregation as does not use to meet here at that hour. At nine, I preached at Combe Grove and found again that God was there.

Is not this an instance of ten thousand of God's choosing the foolish things of the world to confound the wise?[37] Here is one that has not only a weak natural understanding, but an impetuosity of temper bordering upon madness. And hence both her sentiments are confused and her expressions odd and indigested. And yet not withstanding this, more of the real power of God attends these uncouth expressions than the sensible discourses of even good men, who have twenty times her understanding.

Thus I have many times known God attach his power to the words of extremely weak men. The humble overlooked the

[35] E. Perronet MS: 'The famous Mrs. Garbrand, late of Brentford—since dead—a visionary enthusiast and—*devotee*.'

[36] 2 Cor. 6:2.

[37] See 1 Cor. 1:27.

weakness of the men and rejoiced in the power of God. But all his power is unacknowledged, unfelt by those who stumble at the weakness of the instrument.

I reached Bristol time enough to preach in the evening upon Redcliff Hill. A malignant fever had lately broke out upon the very spot, which much increased the number and seriousness of the congregation.

Sat. 22. I was much refreshed by hearing the experience of Mary G——, once a determined enemy to the doctrine of perfection, opposing it with great eagerness and many reasons—but now an happy witness of it. During her hottest opposition she never could rest in any known sin. And this at length made both pride and anger so exceeding bitter to her that she could have no peace till she was fully delivered from them.

Sun. 23. I do not know whether we have had so large a congregation these twenty years as this evening at the New Square. Surely the wise world will not impute this to novelty—unless because the grace of God is ever new.

On Monday, Tuesday, and Wednesday, I visited the societies in Somersetshire. On the following days I met the classes in Bristol and narrowly inquired into the character and behaviour of each person—the rather because it had been strongly affirmed that there were many disorderly walkers in the society. I found a[38] woman and one man, who, I am afraid, deserved that character. Let anyone that is more clear-sighted than me find two more, and I will thank him.

Sun. 30. The whole society met in the evening and jointly renewed their covenant with God in the form recommended by Mr. Richard Alleine.[39] And many felt that God was there. It was 'a day of his power'[40] not to be forgotten, a day both of godly sorrow and strong consolation.

Monday, October 1. I left Bristol with joy, having seen the fruit of my labour. At noon, I preached at Combe Grove to a small congregation of earnest, simple people. I had designed to preach in the evening at Bradford in the same place I did before, but Mr. R——,[41] at whose door I then stood, had now altered his mind. So

[38] Orig., 'an', apparently an error for 'a', and so corrected in 1789, though *Works* (1774) alters to 'one'.

[39] Orig., 'Allen'. For the form of covenant, see vol. 8 in this edn.; and *Bibliography*, No. 412. On both, see above, Aug. 6, 1755, n. 82.

[40] Cf. Ps. 110:3.

[41] Perhaps Samuel Rayner; cf. Mar. 12, 1784.

I was constrained to preach in our own room to (comparatively) an handful of people.

Tue. 2. I breakfasted at the Devizes, with Mr. B——,[42] a black swan, an honest lawyer! Hence we rode through a most intricate road to Pewsey. I found a neighbouring gentleman had been there moving every stone to prevent my preaching. I was informed his first design was to raise a mob. Then he would have had the churchwardens interpose. Whether they intended it or no, I cannot tell, but they neither did nor said anything. The congregation filled a great part of the church[43] and were all deeply attentive. Surely good will be done in this place, if it be not prevented by a mixture of various doctrines. Wed. 3. I rode to Salisbury, and going slowly forward, on Saturday 6, I came to London.

Sun. 7. I preached in the morning at Snowsfields, and afterwards at West Street. We had a glorious opportunity at the Lord's Supper. The rocks were broken in pieces. At five, I preached in Moorfields to an huge multitude on 'Ye are saved through faith.'[44] A little before twelve I took the machine for Norwich. Mon. 8. We dined at Bury [St. Edmunds], where a gentlewoman came into the coach, with whom I spent most of the afternoon in close conversation and singing praises to God.

Tue. 9. I was desired to meet Mr. B——, and we had a good deal of conversation together. He seems to be a person of middling sense but a most unpleasing address. I would hope he has some little experience of religion, but it does not appear to advantage, as he is extremely hot, impetuous, overbearing, and impatient of contradiction. He hooked me unawares into a little dispute, but I cut it short as soon as possible, knowing neither was likely to convince the other. So we met and parted in peace.

Wed. 10. I went to Yarmouth, where the earnest congregation

[42] Thought to be Henry Samuel Biggs, an attorney of Devizes, who died in 1798.

[43] This opening, like that at Bath, probably owed much to the projected alliance with the Countess of Huntingdon. The rector of Pewsey (1763–1816), the Rev. Joseph Townshend (1739–1816)—matriculated from Clare Hall, Cambridge, 1758; B.A., 1762; M.A., 1765—was an intimate of hers and was dispatched by her on missionary journeys to Scotland and Ireland (Seymour, *Huntingdon*, 2:159). Townshend had obtained the living of Pewsey after acting as chaplain to the Duke of Atholl, and was remembered posthumously as a geologist. *WHS* 25 (1945):75-77; *Gentleman's Magazine*, N.S., 2 (1816):477.

[44] Eph. 2:8 (*Notes*).

was gathered at short warning. Thur. 11. I was desired to go to Lowestoft[45] in Suffolk, nine miles south-east of Yarmouth. The use of a large place had been offered, which would contain abundance of people. But when I was come Mr. Romaine[46] had changed his mind. So I preached in the open air. A wilder congregation I have not seen, but the bridle was in their teeth. All attended, and a considerable part seemed to understand something of what was spoken. Nor did any behave uncivilly when I had done—and I believe a few did not lose their labour.

It was easy in the evening to observe the different spirit of the congregation at Yarmouth. Almost all seemed to feel the power of God, and many were 'filled with consolation'.[47]

Fri. 11. I returned to Norwich and inquired into the state of the society. I have seen no people in all England or Ireland so changeable as this. This society in 1755 consisted of eighty-three members; two years after, of an hundred and thirty-four; in 1758, it was shrunk to an hundred and ten. In March 1759, we took the Tabernacle, and within a month the society was increased to above seven hundred and sixty. But nearly five hundred of these had formerly been with James Wheatley and, having been scattered abroad, now ran together, they hardly knew why. Few of them were thoroughly awakened, most, deeply ignorant, all 'bullocks unaccustomed to the yoke',[48] having never had any rule or order among them, but every man doing what was right in his own eyes. It was not therefore strange that the next year, only five hundred and seven of these were left. In 1761, they were farther reduced, namely to four hundred and twelve. I cannot tell how it was that in 1762, they were increased again to six hundred and thirty. But the moon soon changed, so that in 1763, they were shrunk to three hundred and ten. This large reduction was owing to the withdrawing the Sacrament, to which they had been accustomed from the time the Tabernacle was built. They are

[45] Orig., 'Leostoffe'. Lowestoft was a seaport, market town, and parish 44 miles north-east of Ipswich. Methodism in Lowestoft had a stormy origin, and the first person to receive the preachers was a widow converted under Baptist preaching in 1745, Mrs. Ibrooke (1720–96). The preachers who followed Wesley after this occasion were even more roughly handled than he was, but a society was soon formed, and in 1766 Mrs. Ibrooke married one of its first members, Mr. Tripp, who had interests in the fishing industry. *Methodist Magazine* 22 (1799):224-25.

[46] Orig., 'Roman', altered in *Works* (1774) to 'Romain'. Still not settled in the living of St. Anne's, Blackfriars, which he obtained after litigation in 1766, Romaine was acting as a chaplain to the Countess of Huntingdon.

[47] Cf. 2 Cor. 7:4.

[48] Cf. Jer. 31:18.

now sunk to an hundred and seventy-four. And now probably the tide will turn again.

Sun. 14. At seven, I clearly and strongly described the height and depth of Christian holiness. And (what is strange) I could not afterward find that any one person was offended. At ten, we had a congregation indeed; I trust, all of one heart. I went as usual to the cathedral in the afternoon and heard a sound, practical sermon. About five, our great congregation met, and (what has seldom been known) very quietly. We were equally quiet at the meeting of the society, which met now for the first time on a Sunday evening. So has God stilled the madness of the people.[49] Are not the hearts of all men in his hand?

Mon. 15. At the request of many, I had given notice of a watch-night. We had but an indifferent prelude: between six and seven, the mob gathered in great numbers, made an huge noise, and began to throw large stones against the outward doors. But they had put themselves out of breath before eight, so that when the service begun, they were all gone.

Tue. 16. In the evening, the whole congregation seemed not a little moved while I was enforcing those solemn words, 'He died for all, that they who live might not henceforth live unto themselves, but unto him that died for them and rose again.'[50] The same was observable, and that in an higher and higher degree, the two following evenings. If I could stay here a month, I think there would be a society little inferior to that at Bristol. But it must not be; they who will bear sound doctrine *only from me* must still believe a lie.

Sat. 20. My horses meeting me at Brentwood,[51] I rode on to Leytonstone,[52] and preached to a serious congregation on 'I will; be thou clean.'[53] The following week, I made a little tour through part of Kent and Sussex, where some of our brethren swiftly increase in goods. Do they increase in grace too? If not, let them take care that their money do not perish with them.

Sunday, November 4. I proposed to the leaders the assisting the Society for the Reformation of Manners[54] with regard to their

49 See Ps. 65:7 (BCP).
50 Cf. 2 Cor. 5:15.
51 Orig., 'Burntwood'.
52 Orig., 'Laton-Stone'.
53 Matt. 8:3.
54 On this society, a revival of the original society of this name, see Jan. 17, 1763, n. 46, and Feb. 2, 1766.

heavy debt. One of them asked, 'Ought we not to pay our own debt first?' After some consultations, it was agreed to attempt it. The general debt of the society in London, occasioned chiefly by repairing the Foundery and chapels and by building at Wapping and Snowsfields, was about nine hundred pounds. This I laid before the society in the evening and desired them all to set their shoulders to the work, either by a present contribution or by subscribing what they could pay on the first of January, February, or March.

Mon. 5. My scraps of time this week I employed in setting down my present *Thoughts upon a Single Life*,[55] which indeed are just the same they have been these thirty years. And the same they must be, unless I give up my Bible.

Thursday 8, at ten (and so every morning), I met the preachers that were in town and read over with them the *Survey of the Wisdom of God in the Creation*.[56] Many pupils I had at the university, and I took some pains with them. But to what effect? What is become of them now? How many of them think either of their tutor or their God? But, blessed be God, I have had some pupils since who well[57] reward me for my labour. Now 'I live', for 'ye stand fast in the Lord.'[58]

Mon. 12. I retired to Hoxton, to answer what was personal in the letters ascribed to Mr. Hervey.[59] How amazing is the power of

[55] These thoughts, embodied in the pamphlet *Thoughts on a Single Life* (1765; *Bibliography*, No. 263; Jackson, 11:456-63), indeed incorporated the substance of his pamphlet *Thoughts on Marriage and a Single Life* (1743) and incurred the sarcasm of Tyerman in a celebrated passage (Tyerman, *John Wesley*, 1:432-33). In these works, JW goes well beyond arguing the case that the single life may be pursued as a vocation as much as the married life, and buttresses his counsel to the 'happy few' unmarried with such exhortations as 'you are at liberty from the greatest of all entanglements, the loving one creature above all others'; 'how much easier is it . . . wholly to conquer our natural desires than to gratify them exactly so far as Christian temperance allows'; 'those who are married are necessarily taken up with the things of the world. You may give all your time to God without interruption.' When twitted with marrying after expressing such opinions and maintaining that he held them unchanged, he could only reply that he had married 'for reasons best known to himself'. To republish this farrago after marriage was even more ungracious.

[56] See *Bibliography*, No. 259; for the history of this work, see above, Dec. 11, 1758, n. 86.

[57] Orig., 'will', altered in the errata and MS notes in *Works* (1774) to 'well'.

[58] Cf. 1 Thess. 3:8.

[59] See *Bibliography*, No. 266. This phrase echoes the title of the work dated by JW, Nov. 16, 1764, and published in 1765, the *Preface to a Treatise on Justification, extracted from Mr. John Goodwin, wherein all that is personal, in letters just published, under the name of the Rev. Mr. Hervey, is answered* (Jackson, 10:316-46), a shot in the controversies between JW and James Hervey and William Cudworth (both now dead), the earlier stages of which are

prejudice! Were it not for this, everyone who knew him and me would have cried out with indignation, 'Whatever Mr. W[esley] was, none can commend or excuse Mr. H[ervey]. Such bitterness he ought not to have shown to his most cruel enemy. How much less to the guide of his youth! To one he owns to have been his "father and his friend"!'

Monday 19 and the other afternoons of this week, I took up my cross and went in person to the principal persons in our society in every part of the town. By this means, within six days near six hundred pounds were subscribed toward the public debt. And what was done was done with the utmost cheerfulness. I remember but one exception. Only one gentleman squeezed out ten shillings as so many drops of blood.

Saturday, December 1. M[ary] B[osanquet][60] gave me a farther account of their affairs at Leytonstone. It is exactly *Pietas Hallensis*[61] in miniature. What will be does not yet appear.

described above (Mar. 23, 1759, n. 12). Hervey, immediately before his death on Christmas Day 1758, had written defending his *Theron and Aspasio* (1755) against JW's attacks, but had been unwilling for his work to be posthumously published because his revision was incomplete and many of his corrections were in a private system of shorthand. The *Eleven Letters* (Edinburgh, 1765) were, however, published by Hervey's brother (who was in financial difficulties) surreptitiously, it is said, in 1764 and again in 1765 (Moore, *Wesley*, 2:248). JW's sensitiveness to the attack was doubtless increased by his open but mistaken suspicion that Cudworth (who had died in 1763 before the first edition came out) had manipulated the text; and he tended to see offence where none had been intended (Jackson, 10:34). His counter blast opened the first round in the Calvinist controversy which reached its peak in the early 1770s. John Erskine replied on the Calvinist side in a tract which made a great impression in Scotland, James Kershaw wrote against Erskine, and Walter Sellon took up the cudgels against Hervey in offensive terms.

60 Mary Bosanquet (1739–1815), one of the most celebrated women of early Methodism. Her work for orphans at Leytonstone, where she was described in the pamphlet here referred to, had prospered and continued in later years when she moved north to Cross Hall, Morley, a house which was also a haven for Methodist preachers, one of whom, John Valton, arrived in November 1781, when she married Fletcher of Madeley. 'How I was surprised when I came this morning to Cross Hall and found the Rev. Mr. John Fletcher and Miss Mary Bosanquet just returned from church with a few select friends. They had chose this day in preference as being their preaching night. Such a holy couple were scarce ever paired. Oh! what a blessed day we had! Nothing but the voice of prayer and praise was heard' (*WHS* 8 [1911]:22). Fletcher's death in 1785 cut her marriage short, but she continued in Madeley 'as a mother for his people', keeping classes of 70-100 people (*Methodist Magazine* 39 [1816]:157). Her biography, based on her journal and other papers, was written by Henry Moore, who put her above such celebrated names as Guyon, Chantel, and Bourignon, and enjoyed extensive circulation as a work of spirituality in the nineteenth century.

61 This famous tract by August Hermann Francke, *Pietas Hallensis: or, A Public Demonstration of the Footsteps of a Divine Being yet in the World: in an historical narrative of the Orphan House and other charitable institutions at Glaucha near Halle in Saxony* (London, 1705), was translated by A. W. Boehm, chaplain to Prince George of Denmark, consort to Queen Anne, and had a commendatory preface by Josiah Woodward, the advocate of

Tue. 4. I made a little excursion to Colchester. Sat. 8. I saw one who many years ago was 'a minister of God to us for good'[62] in repressing the madness of the people, Sir John Ganson,[63] who was near fifty years a magistrate and has lived more than ninety. He is majestic in decay,[64] having few wrinkles and not stooping at all, though just dropping into the grave, having no strength and little memory or understanding. Well might that good man Bishop Stratford pray, 'Lord, let me not live to be useless!'[65] And he had his desire: he was struck with a palsy in the evening, praised God all night, and died in the morning.

Monday 10 and the three following days, I visited Canterbury, Dover, and Sandwich, and returned to London on Friday 14. In the machine I read Mr. Baxter's book upon apparitions.[66] It contains several well-attested accounts. But there are some which I cannot subscribe to. How hard is it to keep the middle way! Not to believe *too little,* or *too much!*

Sun. 16. I buried Mrs. Prior, housekeeper to Mr. P——, who told me, 'On —— night, just at one, I rung, and said to my man coming in, "Mrs. Prior is dead. She just now came into my room and walked round my bed." About two the nurse came and told me she was dead. I asked at what time she died. And was answered, just at one o'clock.'

Thur. 27. I preached and administered the Sacrament at the New Chapel in Snowsfields. How well does God order all things!

religious societies. It was a notable weapon in the propaganda armoury by which Francke sought to mobilize international charitable assistance for the Orphan House and other institutions at Halle. It appeared numerous times in English as well as in most other European languages. JW first began to read it Nov. 6, 1735 (18:318-19 in this edn.). He recommended it for his Assistants' reading at the Conference of 1744, and kept a copy for his own use at London, Bristol, and Newcastle. Mary Bosanquet herself makes the comparison between the inspiration of her work and that of Francke. Moore, *Wesley*, 1:54.

62 Cf. Rom. 13:4.

63 Orig., 'Gonson'. See above, Aug. 27, 1764, n. 26.

64 See Pope, trans., Homer's *Odyssey*, xxiv.171-72:

> The ruins of himself! now worn away
> With age, yet still majestic in decay.

65 Wesley again refers to this as the prayer of Nicholas Stratford, Bishop of Chester, in a letter of June 21, 1784, and frequently uses it himself; e.g., Journal entries of Dec. 22, 1763, above; and June 28, 1783; and letters of June 24, 1771; and Jan. 6, 1791. Nicholas Stratford (1633–1707), was Dean of St. Asaph 1674–89. The link in JW's mind between Stratford and Ganson, who had extended the protection of the law to Methodists, was that Stratford had been fiercely attacked for tolerating Dissenters and was not promoted to the bench (for Chester) till the Revolution.

66 Richard Baxter, *The Certainty of the Worlds of Spirits* (London, 1691).

By losing the former chapel we have gained both a better house and a larger congregation.

Fri. 28. Between two and three in the morning, I was sent for to John Matthews.[67] For some months he had frequently said, 'I have no more doubt of being in heaven than if I was there already.' A little before we came, one asked, 'How do you do now?' He answered,

The Lord protects, for ever near.[68]

When I came in he was perfectly sensible but too weak to speak. Just at three, I began to pray. I had scarce prayed two minutes when without any struggle, or sigh, or groan, he fell asleep.

A man of so faultless a behaviour I have hardly ever been acquainted with. During twenty years, I do not remember his doing or saying anything which I would wish to have been[69] unsaid or undone.

Mon. 31. I thought it would be worth while to make an odd experiment. Remembering how surprisingly fond of music the lion at Edinburgh was, I determined to try whether this was the case with all animals of the same kind. I accordingly went to the Tower with one who plays on the German flute. He began playing near four or five lions.[70] Only one of these (the rest not seeming to regard it at all) rose up, came to the front of his den, and seemed to be all attention. Meantime, a tiger in the same den started up, leaped over the lion's back, turned and ran under his belly, leaped over him again, and so to and fro incessantly. Can we account for this by any principle of mechanism? Can we account for it at all?

Tuesday, January 1, 1765. This week I wrote an answer to a warm letter published in the *London Magazine*, the author whereof is much displeased that I presume to doubt of the modern astronomy. I cannot help it. Nay, the more I consider, the more my doubts increase. So that at present I doubt whether any man on earth knows either the distance or magnitude, I will not say of a fixed star, but[71] of Saturn or Jupiter—yea, of the sun or moon.[72]

67 See above, Aug. 27, 1764, n. 26.

68 From the Wesleys' *Hymns and Sacred Poems* (1739), p. 153; No. 264, in the *Collection of Hymns* (1780), line 4 (7:406 in this edn.).

69 'Been' is inserted only in the errata and MS notes to *Works* (1774).

70 The lions were still an attraction in the Tower in the mid-nineteenth century.

71 'But' added only in errata and MS notes to *Works* (1774).

72 This letter found various faults with JW's *Survey*; JW's reply, modestly disclaiming any professional expertise, is to be found in Telford, 4:28-57.

Sun. 6. The whole society met in the evening. The service lasted from five till near nine. And I do not remember so solemn a season since the first time we joined in renewing our covenant with God.

Wed. [i.e., Mon.] 7. In the evening, I preached at High Wycombe, and Tuesday 8 at Witney. The congregation here, though of so late standing, may be a pattern to all England. When the service was ended, no one spoke, either in the evenings or mornings. All went silently out of the house and yard. Nay, when I followed a large part of them, I did not hear any open their lips till they came to their own houses. Thur. 10. I preached again at Wycombe, and on Friday returned to London.

Sat. 12. I rode to Mr. D[owning]'s at Ovington in Essex,[73] about six and fifty miles from the Foundery. Sun. 13. Notwithstanding the rain, the church was pretty well filled. And all gave earnest heed while I opened and applied those words in the Second Lesson, 'Come unto me, all ye that labour and are heavy laden, and I will give you rest.'[74]

Titbury church[75] is considerably larger than this; accordingly the congregation was much larger than that in the morning. But I did not see one careless or inattentive person. All seemed resolved to 'seek the Lord while he may be found.'[76] At seven in the evening, I preached again, to a small company in Mr. D[owning]'s house, on fellowship with the Father and the Son. Tuesday 15, I returned to London.

Sun. 20. I looked over Mr. R[omaine]'s[77] strange book on *The Life of Faith.*[78] I thought nothing could ever exceed Mr. Ingham's,[79] but really this does, although they differ not an hair's

[73] E. Perronet MS: 'Downing, Chaplain to Lord Dartmouth'. On George Downing, one of the evangelicals of whom JW had hopes, who had just become rector of Ovington; see above, Apr. 19, 1764; and Feb. 27, 1759, n. 4. Ovington was a tiny Essex parish 6 miles west of Sudbury.

[74] Matt. 11:28.

[75] Probably 'Tilbury'. Tilbury Hall, which is a mile south of Ovington, has a church with a tower.

[76] Cf. Isa. 55:6.

[77] Orig., 'Mr. ——', *Works* (1774), 'Mr. B——', E. Perronet MS: 'Romaine'.

[78] William Romaine, *A Treatise upon the Life of Faith* (London, 1764). This was one of the innumerable eighteenth-century tracts written to help those who were already convicted of sin and broken by the law, to appropriate the full privileges of faith, faith being defined as 'the believing the word of God' (p. 28).

[79] Orig., 'Mr. I——'s', altered in *Works* (1774) to 'Mr. Ingham's'. Benjamin Ingham, *The Faith and Hope of the Gospel* (London, 1763). On Ingham's relations with the Sandemanians, see above, June 26, 1764, n. 61.

breadth from each other—any more than from Mr. Sandeman.[80]

I employed all my leisure hours this week in revising my letters and papers. Abundance of them I committed to the flames. Perhaps some of the rest may see the light when I am gone.

Fri. 31. I was considering how it was that so many who were once filled with love are now weak and faint. And the case is plain: the invariable rule of God's proceedings is, 'From him that hath not, shall be taken away even that which he hath.'[81] Hence it is impossible that any should *retain* what they receive without *improving* it. Add to this that the more we have received the more of care and labour is required, the more watchfulness and prayer, the more circumspection and earnestness in all manner of conversation. Is it any wonder, then, that they who forget this should soon lose what they had received? Nay, who were *taught* to forget it? Not to watch! Not to pray—under pretence of *praying always.*

Wednesday, [February] 13. I heard *Ruth,* an oratorio, performed at Mr. Madan's chapel.[82] The sense was admirable throughout, and much of the poetry not contemptible. This joined with exquisite music might possibly[83] make an impression, even upon rich and honourable sinners.

Mon. 18. I set out for Norwich and spent a few days there with more comfort than I had ever done before. The congregations were not only more numerous than ever, but abundantly more serious. And the society appeared to be more settled and more loving to each other. Mon. 25. In my way to Yarmouth, I read Dr. Watts on *The Improvement of the Understanding.*[84] He has many just

80 'From' added only in the errata and MS notes to *Works* (1774); the *Works* itself changes the 'Sandman' of the original to 'Sandiman', and is followed by 1789. On Robert Sandeman, see above, Apr. 14, 1756, n. 1.

81 Matt. 25:29.

82 On these annual performances at the Lock Chapel, see above, Feb. 29, 1764, n. 16. This was the first performance of *Ruth,* with music by Avison and Giordini. Charles Avison (1709–70) was organist at St. Nicholas's, Newcastle, and a fertile composer of concerti and chamber music. Felice Giordini (who had contributed hymn tunes to Madan's collection) was among the artists he employed in his Newcastle concerts, and when *Ruth* received its second performance in 1768, the music was wholly set by him. *New Grove Dictionary,* 1:750; 11:453.

83 Altered in 1789 to 'probably'.

84 Isaac Watts, *The Improvement of the Mind, or Supplement to the Art of Logic* (London, 1741). Johnson was more enthusiastic: 'Few books have been perused by me with greater pleasure than his *Improvement of the Mind* of which radical principles may indeed be found in John Locke's *Conduct of the Understanding* [London, 1762], but they are so expanded and ramified by Watts, as to confer upon him the merit of a work in the highest degree

and useful observations, mixed with some that are not just and with more that are of little use, besides that they are trite and obvious. I preached at seven in a preaching-house built for the General Baptists,[85] one of the most elegant buildings I have seen, which was well filled both this and the following evening with serious and attentive hearers. There now seems to be a general call to[86] this town; surely some will hear the voice that raises the dead. We returned to Norwich on Wednesday, and left it on Thursday morning in a wonderful day of frost and snow and sleet and wind. However, we reached Lakenheath in the afternoon. Considering the weather, there was a large congregation. Mr. I——[87] read prayers, and I preached with great liberty of spirit on 'What is a man profited, if he gain the whole world and lose his own soul?'[88]

Friday, March 1. I read prayers and preached at seven in the morning. It was noon before we could procure a post-chaise. We then pushed on, though the snow lay deep on the ground, to the great inn at Hockerill,[89] the dearest house I ever was at. So fare it well. In the morning we went on to London.

Sun. 10. I made a collection in our congregation for the poor weavers who are out of employment. It amounted to about forty pounds. In the evening our own society met and contributed fourteen pounds more to relieve a few of their own distressed members.

Mon. 11. I took horse with Mr. Penington[90] for Bristol. In two or three hours, my mare fell lame without any discernible cause, and in an hour or two after, the beast he rode was taken ill and grew worse and worse till she dropped down and died. So I was glad to go into a machine which was driving by, and the next evening I reached Bristol.

Mon. 18. I rode to Stroud, and in the evening preached in the new house.[91] But a considerable part of the congregation were

useful and pleasing. Whoever has the care of instructing others, may be charged with deficience in his duty if this book is not recommended.' Johnson, *Lives of the Poets*, 2:297.

[85] *Works* (1774), 'Anabaptists'.

[86] Orig., 'for'.

[87] As yet unidentified.

[88] Matt. 16:26.

[89] Hockerill was a village one mile north-east of Bishop's Stortford.

[90] Orig., 'Pennington', altered in *Works* (1774). William Penington (1734–67), a native of Knaresborough, as a small child had powerful convictions of sin and became a Methodist in adolescence. A schoolmaster by profession, he was recommended to JW by John Hampson and was taken into the itinerancy in 1759. He died on service in Ireland in November 1767.

[91] Built in Acre Street, Stroud, in 1763. *Methodist Recorder* (Aug. 20, 1903).

obliged to stand without. Toward the close of the sermon a young man dropped down and vehemently cried to God. This occasioned a little hurry at first, but it was soon over, and all was quiet as before.

After supper, I was speaking a little when a young gentleman cried out, 'I am damned,' and fell to the ground. A second did so quickly after and was much convulsed and yet quite sensible. We joined in prayer but had not time (it growing late) to wrestle with God for their full deliverance.

Tue. 19. We rode to Worcester and had the pleasure of spending an hour with Mr. R——, a sensible, candid man. But who is proof against prejudice? Especially when those who labour to infuse it converse with him daily, and those who strive to remove it not two hours in a year.

We came to Birmingham in the evening and had a comfortable season with the great congregation. Wednesday 20, M. Lewen[92] took me in a post-chaise to Derby,[93] where the new house was thoroughly filled; and people behaved in a quite different manner from what they did when I was here last. Thur. 21. We went on, though with much difficulty, being often ready to stick fast, to Sheffield. The house here is full twice as large as it was.[94] And so is the congregation. The little differences which had been for some time among the people were now easily adjusted. And I left them all united in love and resolved to strengthen each other's hands.

Sat. 23. We took horse in a furious wind, which was ready to bear us away. About ten, I preached in Bradwell in the High Peak, where notwithstanding the storm, abundance of people were got together. I had now an opportunity of inquiring concerning Mr. B[addele]y.[95] He did run well, till one offence after another swallowed him up. But he scarce enjoyed himself after. First his oldest daughter was snatched away, then his only son, then himself. And only two or three of that large family now remain.

Sun. 24. At seven, I preached at Manchester on 'I beseech you, suffer the word of exhortation,'[96] and observed that the

[92] Orig., 'M. L.', the fuller identification added only in *Works* (1774). On Margaret Lewen, see above, May 2, 1764, n. 5.

[93] Orig., 'Darby', an indication of the pronunciation; changed to 'Derby' in 1774 and 1789.

[94] A gallery had been added; Everett, *Sheffield*, p. 195.

[95] For John Baddeley, see above, Apr. 8, 1755, n. 18.

[96] Heb. 13:22.

exhortation which it is particularly difficult to suffer is that to accept of salvation *now*, and *now* to improve the[97] whole grace of God. The evening congregation was far larger than the house could contain, and all seemed to have the hearing ear.

Tue. 26. It rained all the way to Little Leigh, but from thence we had a pleasant ride to Chester.

As several ships were ready to sail from Parkgate, I waited here two days. But the wind continuing foul, on Friday 29, I crossed over to Liverpool. I was surprised at the evening congregations, particularly on Sunday. The house,[98] even with the addition of three new galleries, would not near contain the congregation, and I never before observed the word to take such effect upon them. So that I was not sorry the wind continued in the same point on Monday, Tuesday, and Wednesday. Only it shifted a little on Wednesday morning; on which, some impatient captains sailed immediately. But in a few hours it came full west again, so that they were glad to get well back.

Thursday, April 4. I rode to Bolton and, not being expected, was the more welcome. The house was filled in the evening, and the hearts of many filled with joy and peace in believing.[99] April 5, being Good Friday, Mr. Johnson[1] preached at five; I preached at twelve and at six. What a blessed calm has God at length given to this poor, shattered society![2] For many years the men of bitter and contentious spirits were harassing them continually. But they are now sunk into quiet, formal Presbyterians, and those they have left [now] enjoy God and one another.

Sat. 6. I returned to Liverpool, and on Wednesday 10, the wind continuing west, I set out northward and in the evening found a friend's house, James Edmondson's[3] near Garstang. Thur. 11. We rode on to F[ranci]s G[ilber]t's[4] at Kendal, where there is now

[97] Orig., 'that', altered to 'the' in the errata and MS notes to *Works* (1774).

[98] Pitt Street Chapel, opened in 1754.

[99] See Rom. 15:13.

[1] On John Johnson, see above, May 5, 1757, n. 70.

[2] For John Bennet's successful attempts to divide the society, see Mar. 31 and June 14, 1752 (20:414, 428 in this edn.).

[3] JW had written to James Edmondson about his spiritual condition as long ago as January 1749 (2:346 in this edn.). For another visit, see Apr. 8, 1770. James Edmondson was buried near the pulpit in the Independent Chapel from which JW preached in 1770. H. Fishwick, *History of the Parish of Garstang*, Chetham Society 104 (1878), p. 124.

[4] E. Perronet MS reads thus. For Francis Gilbert, see above, Jan. 17, 1758, n. 29. His niece Mary (1751–68), the daughter of Nathaniel, was present on this occasion and notes in her own journal: 'At noon we had the pleasure of Mr. Jno. Wesley's company to dinner; and in the evening he preached on Jer. viii. 22. . . . His conversation was very edifying and

a real work of God. The genuine gospel now takes root, and sinners are converted to God.

Sat. 13. We rode through much wind and rain to Barnard Castle. In the evening, I preached in the new preaching-house[5] (not opened before), and at eight in the morning. I would have preached abroad on Sunday evening, but the weather drove us into the house. And God was there, both to invite sinners and to comfort believers.

Afterwards, I spent an hour with those who once believed they were saved from sin. I found here as at London about a third part who held fast their confidence. The rest had suffered loss, more or less, and two or three were shorn of all their strength.

Mon. 15. I rode on to Newcastle, where I was quite unexpected. I found both the hearers, the society, and the believers are increased since I was here last. And several more believe they are saved from sin. Meantime, Satan has not been idle. Two were following George Bell[6] step by step as to the 'not needing self-examination', the 'not being taught by man', and most of his other unscriptural extravagancies; but as they appeared to be still of an advisable spirit, for the present at least, the snare was broken.

Thur. 18. I went to Durham with Miss Lewen[7] and spent an hour with her father. He behaved with the utmost civility, said I had done his daughter more good than all the physicians could do, and he should be exceeding glad if she would go to London again at the approach of winter. At three, I preached to the poor colliers in Gateshead Fell. How do these shame the colliers of Kingswood! Flocking from all parts on the week-days as well as Sundays, such a thirst have they after the good word!

Fri. 19. I had a little time with that venerable monument of the grace of God, Henry Jackson.[8] He is just dropping into the grave, being now quite bedrid, but praising God with every breath.

God blest it to my poor soul.' Of the next day she records: 'At five, in the morning, Mr. Wesley preached on Psalms lxxxiv.1.' *WHS* 3 (1901):19.

[5] The Methodists in Barnard Castle, multiplying in numbers but remaining mostly poor, set out to build a new chapel by direct labour. Despite opposition and the pulling down of building works by night, the chapel was ready for opening in 1765. The leading figure in the building was Matthew Justice. A. Steele, *A History of Methodism in Barnard Castle and the Principal Places in the Dales Circuit* (London, Vickers, 1857), pp. 71-74.

[6] The enthusiast and ally of Thomas Maxfield; for him, see above, Dec. 26, 1761, n. 42.

[7] See above, May 2, 1764, n. 5.

[8] See above, May 18, 1764, n. 10.

Mon. 22. Two of our friends took me in a post-chaise to Alnwick. But the road was so intolerably bad that we did not reach it till past twelve. I began preaching immediately and then hastened away. On Berwick Moor we were ready to stick fast again. And it was past seven before I reached the town, where I found notice had been given of my preaching. Hearing the congregation waited for me, I went to the town hall and began without delay. About one in the morning, we had a violent storm of thunder and lightning. The house being full of dragoons, M[iss] L[ewen] and M[iss] D[ale][9] were constrained to lodge in the same room with our landlady, who, being waked by the storm and thoroughly terrified, began praying aloud. M[iss] D[ale] laid hold on the opportunity to speak very closely to her. The words seemed to sink into her heart. Who knows but they may bring forth fruit?

Tue. 23. I preached at Dunbar about noon, and in the evening at Edinburgh. My coming was quite seasonable (though unexpected), as those bad letters, published in the name of Mr. Hervey and reprinted here by Mr. John Erskine,[10] had made a great deal of noise. Wed. 24. I preached at four in the afternoon on the ground where we have laid the foundation of our house.[11]

[9] E. Perronet MS: 'Miss Lewen and Miss D'. Margaret Dale was one of the four children, Margaret, Mary, Anne, and Edward, of Edward Dale (d. 1755) of Tunstall, near Sunderland, and his wife Eleanor, the youngest daughter of John Lawrence, rector of Bishop Wearmouth. The three girls lived near Newcastle in the care of their aunt, Margaret Lewen, who seems to have been anxious to bring them under JW's influence. Peggy Dale (1744–77) became one of JW's favourite correspondents, but it is clear that he sustained a correspondence with Molly also, and one of her letters to him was published in *Arminian Magazine* 6 (1783):327. Molly became a band-leader and was still alive and full of good works in the 1790s.

[10] John Erskine (*c.* 1721–1803), born and educated in Edinburgh, came of a distinguished legal family. Engaging in theological polemic at a very early age, he entered the ministry and, becoming minister of Kirkintilloch (1744–53), befriended George Whitefield. While never caring for JW or his theology, Erskine became one of the Scots evangelical ministers most devoted to developing the international connections of the Great Awakening, and a leader of the renewed Scots interest in missions. In 1796, he published a supplement to Gillies's *Historical Collections*. After a spell at Culross, he moved to the New Greyfriars at Edinburgh, and in 1767, he became the colleague of Principal Robertson at Old Greyfriars. Here the two, leaders of the evangelical and the moderate party in the Scots church, contrived to work in harmony. Hervey's *Eleven Letters* to JW had been printed at Edinburgh in 1765, apparently by Erskine, who followed up the controversy by an anonymous tract, *Mr. Wesley's Principles Detected: or, A Defence of the Preface to the Edinburgh Edition of Aspasio Vindicated, in an answer to Mr. Kershaw's 'Earnest Appeal'. To which is prefixed the Preface itself for the use of those who have the English Editions of Aspasio Vindicated* (Edinburgh, 1765).

[11] It is in fact not certain that JW was present when the foundations were laid, but in the following year he was able to preach in the Octagon Chapel in Low Calton, which lasted

Fri. 26. About noon, I preached at Musselburgh, where are a few living souls still. In the evening, we had another blessed opportunity at Edinburgh, and I took a solemn leave of the people. Yet how I should be able to ride I knew not. At Newcastle I had observed a small swelling, less than a pea, but in six days it was as large as a pullet's egg and exceeding hard. On Thursday it broke. I feared riding would not agree with this, especially an hard-trotting horse. However, trusting God, I set out early on Saturday morning. Before I reached Glasgow it was much decreased, and in two or three days more it was quite gone. If it was a boil, it was such an one as I never heard of, for it was never sore first or last, nor ever gave me any pain.

This evening, I preached in the hall of the hospital; the next day, morning and afternoon in the yard. So much of the form of religion is here still as is scarce to be found in any town in England. There was once the power too. And shall it not be again? Surely the time is at hand.

Mon. 29. I rode with James Kershaw[12] through a fruitful country to Kilmarnock and thence to Ayr.[13] After a short bait at Maybole[14] in the afternoon, we went on to Girvan,[15] a little town on the sea-shore. Tue. 30. We rode over high and steep mountains between Ballantrae[16] and Stranraer,[17] where we met with as good entertainment of every kind as if we had been in the heart of England.

We reached Portpatrick[18] about three o'clock and were immediately surrounded with men offering to carry us over the water. But the wind was full in our teeth. I determined to wait till morning and then go forward or backward as God should please.

till 1815, when it was demolished as part of the Regent Bridge development, and replaced. Thomas Taylor records that the congregation was 'miserably small' partly because of the controversy created by the publication of Hervey's *Letters*. A. J. Hayes, *Edinburgh Methodism 1761–1975*, p. 6; Jackson, *Early Methodist Preachers*, 5:33.

12 See above, June 11, 1764, n. 43.

13 Orig., 'Killmarnock' and 'Air'. Kilmarnock was a burgh of barony and parish 12 miles north-east of Ayr. Ayr was a seaport, burgh, and market town 34 miles south-west of Glasgow.

14 Maybole was a market town and parish 9 miles south of Ayr.

15 Orig., 'Girvane'. Girvan was a seaport, market town, and parish 12 miles south-west of Maybole.

16 Orig., 'Ballintrae'. Ballantrae was a parish 13 miles south-west from Girvan.

17 Orig., 'Strangrawer'. Stranraer was a royal burgh, seaport, and parish 50 miles south-west from Ayr.

18 Orig., 'Port Patrick'. Portpatrick was a burgh of barony, seaport, and parish 6½ miles south-west from Stranraer.

Wednesday, May 1. The wind was quite fair, so as soon as the tide served I went on board. It seemed strange to cross the sea in an open boat, especially when the waves ran high. I was a little sick till I fell asleep. In five hours and an half we reached Donaghadee.[19] But my mare could not land till five hours after. So that I did not reach Newtownards[20] till past eight.

I spent the next day here, endeavouring to lift up the hands of a poor, scattered, dejected people. In the evening, I preached on the green.[21] Though it was exceeding cold, none of the congregation seemed to regard it. And a few of them do 'remember from whence they are fallen and' resolve to 'do the first works'.[22]

Fri. 3. I rode on to Lisburn and in the evening preached in the market-house. The wind was as keen as in December, yet a large congregation attended. I then met what was left of the society, and the spirit of many that were faint revived. Sat. 4. I preached in the room at five, which had been discontinued for three years. And this alone would account for the scattering of the people and the deadness of them that remained. In the evening, I preached in the Linen Hall, so called, a large square with piazzas on three sides of it. And so deep an attention I never saw in the people of Lisburn before.

Sun. 5. For the sake of the country people I delayed the morning preaching till half an hour past nine. At eleven, the church service began, and we had an useful sermon on 'Follow peace with all men and holiness.'[23] At five, I preached in the Linen Hall again to a numerous congregation, on 'Yea, doubtless, and I count all things but loss for the excellency of the knowledge of Christ Jesus my Lord.'[24]

[19] Donaghadee was a packet-station and parish in County Down, 14 miles east from Belfast.

[20] Orig., 'Newtown'.

[21] Margaret Davidson, the blind preacher, was brought over from Comber on the occasion and records that 'Mr. Wesley preached from these words, "Truly our fellowship is with the Father, and with His Son Jesus Christ." While he was speaking my heart was inflamed with love to God and man; and as I was placed near him, I could just observe the waving of his hand between me and the light. After preaching he took me gently by the hand and said, "Faint not, go on, and you shall see in glory". . . . I was also present when he met the Society; and at parting he commended us "to God and to the word of his grace". I was melted into tears and could only say, "the will of the Lord be done"' (Crookshank, *Ireland*, 1:182-83).

[22] Rev. 2:5.

[23] Heb. 12:14.

[24] Phil. 3:8.

Mon. 6. I rode to Newry and in the evening preached in the market-house on 'Her ways are ways of pleasantness, and all her paths peace.'[25] The whole congregation seemed affected, this as well as the next evening—indeed more than I had seen them for some years. Hence, Wednesday 8, I rode to Terryhoogan and found much of the power of God among that plain, simple-hearted people. Here Mr. Ryan[26] overtook me and led me to Clonmain, where we had, as usual, a lively, earnest congregation, most of whom (except those that came from far) were present again at five in the morning. About eleven, I preached at the Grange, a small village about five miles from Clonmain. Friday 10, I took Mr. Ryan with me and set out for Londonderry. When we had rode about twelve miles, a road turned short to the left. But having no direction to turn, we went straight forward, till a woman running after us (taking one of us, I know not why, for a doctor), told us the case of her poor husband, who, she said, had kept his bed for seven weeks. After riding half an hour, we found we were out of our way and rode back again. By this means we went by the house where the man lay. When I alighted and went in, I quickly saw that he needed something more than I had prescribed before. Who knows but our losing the way may be the means of saving the poor man's life?

In the afternoon, after riding through a fruitful country (one mountain only excepted), we came to Omagh,[27] the shire town of the county of Tyrone. We found a good inn, but were not glad when we heard there was to be dancing that night in the room under us. But in a while the dancers removed to the shire hall. So we slept in peace.

Sat. 11. Having no direction to anyone in Derry, I was musing what to do and wishing someone would meet me and challenge me, though I knew not how it could be, as I never had been there before nor knew anyone in the town. When we drew near it, a gentleman on horseback stopped, asked me my name and showed me where the preacher lodged. In the afternoon, he accommodated me with a convenient lodging at his own house. So one Mr. Knox is taken away, and another given me in his stead.[28]

[25] Prov. 3:17.

[26] For Thomas Ryan, attorney, squire, itinerant, and father-in-God of the society on his estate at Clonmain, see above, Apr. 27, 1762, n. 93.

[27] Omagh was a market town 26 miles south of Londonderry.

[28] For the defaulting James Knox of Sligo, see above, June 26, 1760, n. 39. There were grounds for JW's unheralded and uninvited visit. Methodism had been introduced into

At seven, I preached in the Linen Hall (a square so called) to the largest congregation I have seen in the north of Ireland. The waters spread as *wide* here as they did at Athlone. God grant they may be as *deep!*

Sun. 12. At eight, I preached there again to an equal number of people. About eleven, Mr. Knox went with me to church and led me to a pew, where I was placed next the mayor. What is this? What have I to do with honour? Lord, let me always *fear,* not *desire* it.

The afternoon service was not over till about half-hour past six. At seven, I preached to near all the inhabitants of the city. I think there was scarce one who did not feel that God was there. So general an impression upon a congregation I have hardly seen in any place.

Monday 13 and the following days, I had leisure to go on with the *Notes* on the Old Testament.[29] But I wondered[30] at the situation I was in, in the midst of rich and honourable men! While this lasts it is well. And it will be well too when any or all of them change their countenance,

And wonder at the strange man's face,
As one they ne'er had known.[31]

Tue. 14. I wrote the following letter to a friend:[32]

Derry by Thomas Williams just before he left the connexion in 1755 (see Aug. 2, 1744, n. 73; 20:34 in this edn.). He subsequently returned and gathered a congregation and, 'as long as he conducted himself with propriety, appeared to attract both attention and respect. It is said that when he felt his unhappy propensities likely to overcome him, he wrote to Mr. Wesley, stating the promising appearance of things and begging a preacher might be sent to replace him. No preacher came . . . and Thomas Williams having made a marriage with a young woman who happened to be well known in the town, went off, leaving her behind him'; *Wesleyan Methodist Magazine* 58 (1835):123. Members of his surviving society, however, had continued to solicit the services of a Methodist preacher, and to them James Clough had just been sent. Another member, drawn to official Methodism by literary propaganda, was the wife of Alexander Knox, who here encountered JW (Crookshank, *Ireland,* 1:180). Knox, who died in 1770, continued a Methodist to the end and remained an important member of the town council, but the only member brought into the society by his influence was his brother-in-law, Fairly, who adopted Calvinist views and veered from Methodism increasingly after Knox's death. Crookshank, *Ireland,* 1:234.

29 *Explanatory Notes upon the Old Testament* (1765); see *Bibliography,* No. 294.

30 Orig., 'wondered more', the latter word omitted in the errata and MS notes to *Works* (1774).

31 For the full reference to this quotation (also used of the Knoxes of Sligo) adapted from Congreve's *Doris,* see above, May 1, 1762, n. 3.

32 The friend was John Newton, who in the previous year had been ordained to the curacy of Olney (see above, July 3, 1759, n. 4). Newton's biographer says that JW wrote

Londonderry, May 14, 1765

Dear Sir,

Your manner of writing needs no excuse. I hope you will always write in the same manner. Love is the *plainest* thing in the world. I know this dictates what you write—and then what need of ceremony?

You have admirably well expressed what I mean by an opinion, contradistinguished from an essential doctrine. Whatever is 'compatible with love to Christ and a work of grace' I term an *opinion.* And certainly the holding particular election and final perseverance is compatible with these. 'Yet what fundamental errors' (you ask) 'have you opposed with *half that fervency* as you have these opinions?' I have printed near fifty sermons, and only one of these opposes them at all. I preach about eight hundred sermons in a year, and taking one year with another for twenty years past, I have not preached eight sermons in a year upon the subject. But, 'How many of your best preachers have been *thrust out* because they dissented from you in these particulars?' Not one, best or worst, good or bad, was ever 'thrust out' on this account. There has not been a single instance of this kind. Two or three (but far from *the best* of our preachers) voluntarily left us after they had embraced those opinions. But it was of their own mere motion. And two I should have expelled for immoral behaviour—but they withdrew and *pretended* they 'did not hold our doctrine'. Set a mark therefore on him that told you that tale, and let his word for the future go for nothing.

'Is a man a believer in Jesus Christ, and is his life suitable to his profession?' are not only the *main,* but the *sole* inquiries I make in order to his admission into our society. If he is a Dissenter, he may be a Dissenter still, but if he is a churchman, I advise him to continue so, and that for many reasons, some of which are mentioned in the tract upon that subject.

I think on justification just as I have done any time these seven and twenty years, and just as Mr. Calvin does. In this respect I do not differ from him an hair's breadth.

But the main point between you and me is perfection. 'This', you say, 'has no prevalence in these parts. Otherwise I should think it my duty to oppose it with my whole strength, not as an *opinion,* but as a dangerous mistake which appears to be subversive of the very foundation of Christian experience, and which has in fact given occasion to the most grievous offences.'

two more letters 'controversial, but Christian and conciliatory'; Josiah Bull, *John Newton. An Autobiography and Narrative* (2nd edn., London, 1870), p. 148. For the text of the letter from the original to John Newton, see *Letters*, vol. 27 in this edn.

Just so my brother and I reasoned thirty years ago, 'as thinking it our duty to oppose *predestination* with our whole strength, not as an *opinion,* but as a dangerous mistake which appears to be subversive of the very foundation of Christian experience, and which has in fact given occasion to the most grievous offences.'

That it has given occasion to such offences I know—I can name time, place, and persons. But still another fact stares me in the face. Mr. H[aweis] and Mr. N[ewton] hold this, and yet I believe these have real Christian experience. But if so, this is only an *opinion*; it is not subversive (here is clear proof to the contrary) of the very foundations of Christian experience. It is 'compatible with love to Christ, and a genuine work of grace'. Yea, many hold it at whose feet I desire to be found in the day of the Lord Jesus. If then I 'oppose this with my whole strength', I am a mere bigot still. I leave *you* in your calm and retired moments to make the application.

'But how came this opinion into my mind?' I will tell you with all simplicity. In 1725, I met with Bishop Taylor's *Rule of Holy Living* and *Dying.*[33] I was struck particularly with the chapter upon *intention,* and felt a fixed intention to give myself up to God. In this I was much confirmed soon after by the *Christian's Pattern,*[34] and longed to 'give God all my heart.'[35] This is just what I mean by *perfection* now. I sought after it from that hour.

In 1727, I read Mr. Law's *Christian Perfection*[36] and *Serious Call*[37] and more explicitly resolved to be 'all devoted to God'[38] in body, soul, and spirit. In 1730, I began to be *homo unius libri,*[39] to study (comparatively) no book but the Bible. I then saw in a stronger light than ever before that only 'one thing is needful',[40] even 'faith that worketh by the love'[41] of God and man, all inward and outward holiness, and I groaned to love God with *all my heart* and to serve him with *all my strength.*[42]

January 1, 1733, I preached the sermon on 'The Circumcision of the Heart', which contains *all* that I now teach concerning salvation from *all sin* and loving God with an *undivided heart.* In the

[33] Jeremy Taylor's *Rule and Exercises of Holy Living* (London, 1650); *The Rule and Exercises of Holy Dying* (London, 1651).

[34] Thomas à Kempis, *The Christian's Pattern.* Editions appeared at Bristol in 1746 and 1761.

[35] Cf. Prov. 23:26.

[36] William Law, *A Practical Treatise on Christian Perfection* (London, 1726).

[37] William Law, *A Serious Call to a Devout and Holy Life, Adapted to the State and Condition of all Orders of Christians* (London, 1729).

[38] Cf. Lev. 27:28.

[39] 'A man of one book'. For a note on this, see Preface to *Sermons on Several Occasions* (1746), §5, n. 9 (1:105 in this edn.).

[40] Luke 10:42.

[41] Gal. 5:6.

[42] See Mark 12:30; Luke 10:27.

same year I printed (the first time I ventured to print anything) for the use of my pupils, *A Collection of Forms of Prayer*.[43] And in this I spoke explicitly of giving *the whole heart and the whole life to God*. This was then, as it is now, my idea of perfection, though I should have started at *the word*.

In 1735, I preached my farewell sermon at Epworth in Lincolnshire. In this likewise, I spoke with the utmost clearness of having *one design, one desire, one love,* and of pursuing the *one end* of our life, in all our words and actions.

In January 1738, I expressed my desire in these words:

> O grant that nothing in my soul
> May dwell, but thy *pure love alone!*
> O may thy love *possess me whole,*
> My joy, my treasure, and my crown!
> Strange flames far from my heart remove!
> My *every* act, word, thought be love.[44]

And I am still persuaded, this is what the Lord Jesus hath bought for me with his own blood.

Now whether *you* desire and expect this blessing or not, is it not an astonishing thing that you or any man living should be disgusted at *me* for expecting it? And that they should persuade one another that this hope is 'subversive of the very foundations of Christian experience'? Why then, whoever retains it cannot possibly have any Christian experience at all! Then my brother, Mr. Fletcher, and I, and twenty thousand more, who *seem* both to fear and *to* love God, are in reality children of the devil, and in the road to eternal damnation!

In God's name I entreat you, make me sensible of this. Show me by plain, strong reasons, what dishonour this hope does to Christ, wherein it opposes justification by faith, or any fundamental truth of religion. But do not wrest and wiredraw and colour my words, as Mr. Hervey (or Cudworth) has done, in such a manner that when I look in that glass I do not know my own face! 'Shall I call you' (says Mr. Hervey) 'my father or my friend? For you have been both to me.' So I was, and you have as well requited me! It is well my reward is with the Most High.

Wishing all happiness to you and yours,

I am, dear sir,
Your affectionate brother and servant,
John Wesley

[43] Wesley, *A Collection of Forms of Prayer for Every Day in the Week* (Jackson, 11:203-37; 14:270-72).

[44] *Hymns and Sacred Poems* (1739), p. 156, translated in Savannah by John Wesley from the German of Paulus Gerhardt and later incorporated in the *Collection of Hymns* (1780), No. 362, lines 7-12 (7:530 in this edn.).

On Wednesday and Thursday, I spoke severally to the members of the society. I found (just as I expected) that the work of God here is exceeding shallow. Yet while so many flock to hear, one cannot doubt but God will cut some of them to the heart.

Sun. 19. Mr. S[ampson],[45] one of the curates, preached an excellent sermon on 'Receiving the Holy Ghost'.[46] I afterwards accepted his invitation to dinner and found a well-natured, sensible man, and one well acquainted with every branch of learning which we had occasion to touch upon. At seven, I preached on 'God forbid that I should glory, save in the cross of our Lord Jesus Christ.'[47] And truly the people of this place will 'hear sound doctrine'.[48] Wednesday 22, I exhorted the little society to avoid sloth, prodigality, and sluttishness, and on the contrary to be patterns of diligence, frugality, and cleanliness.

Thur. 23. Lighting on a volume of Mr. Seed's sermons,[49] I was utterly surprised. Where did this man lie hid, that I never heard of him, all the time I was at Oxford? His language is pure in the highest degree, his apprehension clear, his judgment strong. And for true, manly wit and exquisite turns of thought, I know not if this century has produced his equal.

Sat. 25. Both in the morning and evening, I spoke as closely and sharply as I could. But yet I cannot find the way to wound the people. They are neither offended nor convinced.

Ever since I came hither, I have been amazed at the honesty which runs through this city. None scruples to leave his house open all day and the door only on the latch at night. Such a thing as *theft* is scarce heard of at Derry—no one has the least suspicion of it. No wonder therefore that the inhabitants never suspect

[45] Perhaps George V. Sampson, later curate of Inch, and in 1807 rector of Errigal, Derry. Leslie and Swanzy, *Clergy of the Diocese of Down*, p. 134.

[46] Cf. John 20:22.

[47] Gal. 6:14.

[48] Cf. 2 Tim. 4:3.

[49] Jeremiah Seed (1700–47), matriculated from Queen's College, Oxford; B.A., 1722; M.A., 1725; fellow, 1732. He was curate to Dr. Waterland, vicar of Twickenham, and preached his funeral sermon in 1741. In the same year, Seed was presented to the college rectory of Knight's Enham, Hants. Dr. Johnson remarked of his preaching that he had 'a very fine style', but 'he was not very theological.' Others thought it 'elegant but languid'. Collections of Seed's sermons appeared only posthumously; the volume now encountered by JW may have been the *Posthumous Works* which appeared in two volumes in both London and Dublin in 1750; cf. May 11, 1779. See E. Perronet MS: 'I observe amid all this profusion of compliments there is not the least notice taken of any spirituality. But what wonder, therefore, they should even admire Mr. Seed's divinity who can pass such pure eulogies on Dr. Hill's phil[osophy]! Who affirms that power in God is the same with power in us. See *Monthly Review* (March 1755), R. 171, and Mr. J.W.'s *J[ournal]* for 1765 to 68, p. 106.'

themselves to be *sinners.* O what pity that *honesty* should be a bar to salvation! Yet so it is, if a man puts it in the place of Christ.

Having a remarkable anecdote put into my hands, which some will probably be pleased to see, I may insert it here, as well as elsewhere. It is a conversation between my father's father[50] (taken down in shorthand by himself) and the then Bishop of Bristol.[51] I may be excused if it appears more remarkable to me than it will do to an unconcerned person.

Bishop. What is your name?
Wesley. John Wesley.
B. There are many great matters charged upon you.
W. May it please your lordship, Mr. Horlock was at my house on Tuesday last and acquainted me that it was your lordship's desire I should come to you; and on that account I am here to wait on you.
B. By whom were you ordained? Or are you ordained?
W. I am sent to preach the gospel.
B. By whom were you sent?
W. By a church of Jesus Christ.
B. What church is that?
W. The church of Christ at Melcombe.
B. That factious and heretical church!
W. May it please you, sir, I know no faction or heresy that church is guilty of.
B. No! Did not you preach such things as tend to faction and heresy?
W. I am not conscious to myself of any such preaching.
B. I am informed by sufficient men, gentlemen of honour of this county, viz., Sir Gerrard Napper, Mr. Freak, and Mr. Tregonnel, of your doings.[52] What say you?

[50] John Westley (1636–71), matriculated from New Inn Hall, Oxford, 1651; graduated B.A., 1658; M.A., 1657. Vicar of Winterborne Whitchurch, Dorset, 1658, he was ejected in 1662, and suffered five terms of imprisonment. JW describes this document of his grandfather as an 'anecdote', in the original sense of the word, apparently not knowing that it had been published long before in Edmund Calamy's *Account of the Ministers, etc., who were Ejected . . . and the Continuation of their History*, originally appearing in his *Abridgement of Baxter's History*, vol. 2; cf. A. G. Mathews, *Calamy Revised* (Oxford, 1934), p. 521.

[51] Gilbert Ironside the Elder (1588–1671), Bishop of Bristol, 1661–71. Ironside was rector of Winterbourne Steepleton in 1618, and in 1620 succeeded his father as rector of Winterbourne Abbas, a living he lost as a result of the act against pluralities, 1641 (Hutchins, *History of Dorset*, 1:304). He was also rector of Yeovilton, Somerset, 1662, and canon of York, 1660–62. By marriage or other means, he amassed a large fortune and was thus thought a suitable candidate for an impoverished see.

[52] Sir Gerard Napier of More Crichel, Bart., d. 1672 (Hutchins, *History of Dorset*, 2:48). His family was often known as Napper. Thomas Freke of Shroton, Dorset, d. 1698 (ibid.,

W. Those honoured gentlemen I have been with, who, being by others misinformed, proceeded with some heat against me.

B. There are oaths of several honest men, and shall we take your word for it that all is but misinformation?

W. There was no oath given or taken. Besides, if it be enough to accuse, who shall be innocent? I can appeal to the determination of the great Day of Judgment, that the large catalogue of matters laid to me are either things invented or mistaken.

B. Did not you ride with your sword in the time of The Committee of Safety and engage with them?

W. Whatever imprudences in civil matters you may be informed I am guilty of, I shall crave leave to acquaint your lordship that his Majesty having pardoned them fully, I shall waive any other answer.

B. In what manner[53] did the church you spake of send you to preach? At this rate everybody might preach.

W. Not everyone. Everybody has not preaching gifts and preaching graces. Besides, that is not all I have to offer to your lordship to justify my preaching.

B. If you preach it must be according to order, the order of the Church of England, upon ordination.

W. What does your lordship mean by ordination?

B. Do not you know what I mean?

W. If you mean that sending spoken of Rom. 10, I had it.

B. I mean that; what mission had you?

W. I had a mission from God and man.

B. You must have it according to law, and the order of the Church of England.

W. I am not satisfied in my spirit therein.

B. Not satisfied in your spirit! You have more new-coined phrases than ever were heard of! You mean your conscience, do you not?

W. 'Spirit' is no new phrase. We read of being sanctified in 'soul, body, and spirit'.[54]

B. By spirit there we are to understand the upper region of the *soul.*

W. Some think we are to take it for the *conscience;* but if your lordship like it not so, then I say, I am not satisfied in conscience, as touching the ordination you speak of.

B. Conscience argues science, science supposes judgment, and

2:318). John Tregonwell of Anderson, 1632–77 (ibid., 1:52) or John Tregonwell of Milton Abbas, 1625–80 (ibid., 2:432).

[53] Orig., 'in what a manner'.

[54] Cf. 1 Thess. 5:23.

judgment reason. What reason have you that you will not be thus ordained?

W. I came not this day to dispute with your lordship; my own inability would forbid me so to do.

B. No, no; but give me your reason.

W. I am not called to office, and therefore cannot be ordained.

B. Why have you then preached all this while?

W. I was called to the *work* of the ministry, though not the *office.* There is, as we believe, *Vocatio ad opus et ad munus.*[55]

B. Why may you not have the office of the ministry?

W. May it please your lordship, because they are not a people who are fit subjects for me to exercise office work among them.

B. You mean a *gathered church*; but we must have no gathered churches in England, and you will see it so. For there must be a unity without divisions among us, and there can be no unity without *uniformity.* . . . Well, then, we must send you to your church, that they may dispose of you, if you were ordained by them.

W. I have been informed by my cousin Pitfield[56] and others concerning your lordship, that you have a disposition inclined against morosity. However, you may be prepossessed by some bitter enemies to my person, yet there are others who can and will give you another character of me. Mr. Glisson hath done it. And Sir Francis Tulford desired me to present his service to you, and being my hearer is ready to acquaint you concerning me.

B. I asked Sir Francis Tulford[57] whether the presentation to Whitchurch was his. Whose is it? He told me it was not his.

W. There was none presented to it these sixty years. Mr. Walton[58] lived there. At his departure the people desired me to preach to them, and when there was a way of settlement appointed, I was by the trustees appointed, and by the triers approved.

B. They would approve any who would come to them and close

[55] 'A call to the work and to the office.'

[56] Mary Westley, daughter of Bartholemew Westley (d. 1671) and sister of John Westley, married Robert Pitfield.

[57] Since no Tulford appears in *Book of Knights*, this may be Sir Francis Fulford, Kt., who died in 1664 (Hutchins, *History of Dorset*, 1:528). On the other hand, a Francis Tulford of Toller is also mentioned (ibid., 1:67). He also held property in John Westley's parish of Winterborne Whitchurch, and was perhaps identical with Francis Fulford of Toller who died in 1700 (ibid., 1:67).

[58] Tobias Walton, vicar of Winterborne Whitchurch, for 56 years; d. 1658, age 89 (Hutchins, *History of Dorset*, 1:68). The patron of the living (which was generally held by sequestration) was supposed to be the Bishop of Salisbury; but the successor to the man who now displaced John Westley was presented in 1727 by the Archbishop of Canterbury *per lapsum* (ibid., 1:70).

with them. I know they approved those who could not read twelve lines of English.

W. All that they did I know not; but I was examined touching gifts and graces.

B. I question not your gifts, Mr. Wesley. I will do you any good I can; but you will not long be suffered to preach, unless you will do it[59] according to order.

W. I shall submit to any trial you shall please to make. I shall present your lordship with a confession of my faith, or take what other way you please to insist on.

B. No, we are not come to that yet.

W. I shall desire those severals laid together which I look on as justifying my preaching.

1. I was devoted to the service from mine infancy.

2. I was educated in order thereto at school, and in the University of Oxford.

B. What age are you?

W. Twenty-five.

B. No, sure, you are not.

W. 3. As a son of the prophets, after I had taken my degrees, I preached in the country, being approved of by judicious able Christians, ministers, and others.

4. It pleased God to seal my labour with success, in the apparent conversion of many souls.

B. Yea, that is [as] it may be, to your way.

W. Yea, to the power of godliness, from ignorance and profaneness. If it please your lordship to lay down any evidences of godliness, agreeing with Scripture, and that are not found in those persons intended, I am content to be discharged the ministry. I will stand or fall on the issue thereof.

B. You talk of the power of godliness, such as you fancy.

W. Yea, to the reality of religion. Let us appeal to any common-place book for evidences of graces, and they are found in and upon them.

B. How many are there of them?

W. I number not the people.

B. Where are they?

W. Wherever I have been called to preach. At Radpole, Melcombe, Turnwood, Whitchurch, and at sea. I shall add another ingredient of my mission.

5. When the church saw the presence of God going along with me, they did, by fasting and prayer, in a day set apart for that end, seek an abundant blessing on my endeavours.

[59] 'It' added only in *Works* (1774).

B. A particular church?

W. Yes, my lord, I am not ashamed to own myself a member of one.

B. Why, you may mistake the apostles' intent. They went about to convert heathens. You have no warrant for your particular churches.

W. We have a plain, full, and sufficient rule for gospel worship in the New Testament, recorded in the Acts of the Apostles, and in the Epistles.

B. We have not.

W. The practice of the apostles is a standing rule in those cases which were not extraordinary.

B. Not their practice, but their precepts.

W. Both precepts and practice. Our duty is not delivered to us in Scripture only by precepts, but precedents, by promises, by threatenings mixed. We are to follow them as they followed Christ.

B. But the Apostle said, 'This speak I, not the Lord'[60]—that is by revelation.

W. Some interpret that place, 'This speak I now by revelation from the Lord'—not the Lord in that text before instanced concerning divorces. May it please your lordship, we believe that *cultus non institutus est indebitus*.[61]

B. It is false.

W. The second commandment speaks the same: Thou shalt not make to thyself any graven image.[62]

B. That is, forms of your own invention.

W. Bishop Andrewes, taking notice of *non facies tibi,* satisfied me that we may not worship God but as commanded.

B. Well then, you will justify your preaching, will you, without ordination, according to law?

W. All these things, laid together, are satisfactory to me, for my procedure therein.

B. They are not enough.

W. There has been more written in proof of preaching of gifted persons, with such approbation, than has been answered yet by anyone.

B. Have you anything more to say to me, Mr. Wesley?

W. Nothing; your lordship sent for me.

B. I am glad to hear this from your mouth. You will stand to your principles, you say?

60 Cf. 1 Cor. 7:12.
61 'Worship not instituted is not due.'
62 Exod. 20:4.

W. I intend it through the grace of God, and to be faithful to the King's Majesty, however you deal with me.
B. I will not meddle with you.
W. Farewell to you, sir.
B. Farewell, good Mr. Wesley.

About the editors:

W. REGINALD WARD is professor emeritus of modern history at the University of Durham, England, and is vice president of the Royal Historical Society.

RICHARD P. HEITZENRATER, the decoder of John Wesley's diaries, is Albert C. Outler professor of Wesley Studies at Perkins School of Theology Southern Methodist University, Dallas, Texas.